FIGHTING PRODUCT PIRACY

FIGHTING PRODUCT PIRACY

Law & Strategies in Germany, France, the Netherlands, Spain, UK, China, USA

Claudia Milbradt (Ed.)

Isabel Carulla, Daryl Fairbairn,
Anna Gruchol, Jean-Frédéric Gaultier, Ling Ho,
Heiner Hugger, Diana Kaufmann,
Emmanuelle Levy, Mélanie Loos,
Montserrat Lopez-Bellosta, Barbara Maucher,
Claudia Milbradt, Alexandra Pygall,
Daniel Royle, Wolfgang Schönig and
Audrey Shum

GLP
German Law Publishers
www.germanlawpublishers.com

ISBN 978-3-941389-01-4

The Deutsche Nationalbibliothek lists this publication in the Deutsche Nationalbibliografie; detailed bibliographic data are available on the Internet at http://dnb.d-nb.de.

Typesetting: fidus Publikations-Service GmbH, Augsburg.
Printed on acid-free, non-ageing paper. Printed in Germany.

Short Table of Contents

Introduction
CLAUDIA MILBRADT 1

Enforcement of Intellectual Property Rights in Germany
CLAUDIA MILBRADT/HEINER HUGGER

I. Enforcement of Intellectual Property Rights in Germany 7

Trademark Piracy
DIANA KAUFMANN 25

I. Legal Requirements for Trademark Protection under the German Trademark Act 26
II. Legal Consequences of Trademark Infringement 65
III. Enforcement 75

Design Piracy
ANNA GRUCHOL

I. Introduction 83
II. Protection under the German Design Act 83
III. International Design 95
IV. Design protection and copyright law, unfair competition law and trademark law International Design 99

Patent Piracy
CLAUDIA MILBRADT

I. Definitions 107
II. Special Cases 109
III. Securing Rights from Employees, Universities and other R&D Partners 115
IV. Infringement 119
V. Legal Consequences of Infringement 125
VI. Enforcement 129

Know-How Piracy
Barbara Maucher

I.	Protection of Know-How	133
II.	Definition of Product Piracy	149
III.	Know-How Piracy as a form of unfair competition	152
IV.	Remedies in Case of Know-How Piracy	154

Music, Film and Software Piracy
Wolfgang Schönig 157

I.	Protected Works	159
II.	Scope of Copyright Protection	170
III.	Offline Digital Piracy	176
IV.	Online Digital Piracy	181
V.	Legal Consequences	206
VI.	Enforcement	208

Product Piracy in China
Ling Ho/Audrey Shum

I.	China IP Legal Framework	211
II.	Trademarks	211
III.	Patents	212
IV.	Copyright Law	213
V.	Anti-Unfair Competition Law	215
VI.	Enforcement	215
VII.	Legal Consequences	221

Product Piracy in the United States
Daryl Fairbairn

I.	Sources of Intellectual Property Law in the United States	223
II.	Substantive Intellectual Property Law	229
III.	Final Comment	249

Product Piracy in Spain
Monserrat Lopez-Bellosta/Isabel Carulla

I.	Legal Framework Overview	251
II.	Trademark Piracy	264
III.	Patent Piracy	270

IV. Know-How Piracy 279
V. Music, Film and Software Piracy 284
VI. Parallel Imports 290

Product Piracy in France
Jean-Frédéric Gaultier/Emmanuelle Levy

I. Enforcement of Intellectual Property Rights in France 295
II. Trademark Piracy 297
III. Design Rights 303
IV. Patent Piracy 307
V. Know-How Theft 313
VI. Music, Film and Software Piracy 314

Product Piracy in the Netherlands
Mélanie Loos 321

I. The Enforcement of Intellectual Property Rights in the Netherlands 322
II. Trademark Piracy 327
III. Design Rights 333
IV. Patent Piracy 339
V. Know-How Theft 347
VI. Music, Film and Software Piracy 349

Product Piracy in the United Kingdom
Alexandra Pygall/Daniel Royle

I. Overview of the Legal Framework in the United Kingdom 361
II. Enforcement of IP rights in the United Kingdom 361
III. Trademarks 368
IV. Passing Off 369
V. Unfair Competition 370
VI. Design Rights 370
VII. Patents 371
VIII. Confidential Information 374
IX. Copyright 375

Abbreviations 379

Literature 387

Table of Contents

Introduction
CLAUDIA MILBRADT 1

Enforcement of Intellectual Property Rights in Germany
CLAUDIA MILBRADT/HEINER HUGGER

I. Enforcement of Intellectual Property Rights in Germany 7
A. Civil Action 7
1. First Step – Warning letter? 7
2. Preliminary injunction vs. action on the merit 8
3. International Issues of Enforcement of Rulings 9
4. Enforcement of Intellectual Property according to the Enforcement Directive 2004/48/EC 10
B. Public Law 13
1. German Product Safety Act 13
2. Border Seizures 14
C. Criminal Action 16
1. Coercive Measures 17
2. Requirements for the Initiation of Criminal Proceedings 19
3. Criminal and regulatory sanctions 21
4. Prosecution of product piracy on the EU level 22

Trademark Piracy
DIANA KAUFMANN 25

I. Legal Requirements for Trademark Protection under the German Trademark Act 26
A. Scope of Protection 26
1. Trademarks 27
2. Company Symbols 31
3. Titles of Work 31
4. Indications of Geographic Origin 32
B. Creation of Trademark Protection 33
1. Registration 33
2. Trademark Protection through Usage/Secondary Meaning 38
3. Famous Trademarks 39
4. Company Symbols and Titles of Works 39
5. Indications of Geographic Origin 40

C. Infringing Behaviour 40
1. Trademark Infringement according to Section 14 MarkenG [Trademark Act] 40
2. Infringement of Business Designations according to Section 15 MarkenG [Trademark Act] 45
3. Special Case: Transit as an Infringing Behavior 46
4. Special Case: Internet Providers 50
5. Special case: Metatags 58
6. Special case: Context-Sensitive Advertising 59
7. Special Case: Parallel Imports 61
II. Legal Consequences of Trademark Infringement 65
A. Discontinuance 65
1. Risk of First Infringement 65
2. Risk of Recurrence 67
B. Damages 67
1. Basic Principle 67
2. Calculation of the Compensation 68
C. Information 70
D. Destruction 71
E. Recall 73
F. Presentation and Inspection 74
III. Enforcement 75
A. Civil Action 75
1. Preliminary Injunction 75
2. Action on the Merits 76
3. Choice of Courts 76
B. Border Measures 77
1. Border Seizure Request according to the EU Customs Regulation 77
2. Border Seizure Request according to National Law 78
3. Simplified Destruction Procedure 78
4. Liability of Forwarding Agents 79
C. Measures on Trade Shows 80
1. Actions at the Trade Show Itself 80
2. Actions in the Run-Up to the Trade Show 82

Design Piracy
ANNA GRUCHOL

I. Introduction 83
II. Protection under the German Design Act 83
A. Requirements for protection 84
1. Protected subject matter 84
2. Beginning of protection and entitlement 87
3. Term of protection and cancellation 88
4. Scope of protection 88
5. The spare parts issue 89

B. Acts of infringement 90
C. Legal consequences 91
1. Injunctive Relief 91
2. Information 91
3. Damages 92
4. Destruction 93
5. Recall 93
6. Sec. 44 Assertion of claims also against owners 93
7. Consequences under criminal law 93
D. Enforcement 93
1. Enforcement in court 93
2. Customs action 94
III. International Design 95
A. Community Design 95
1. Registered design 96
2. Unregistered Community design 96
B. IR designs 98
C. TRIPS and the Paris Convention 98
IV. Design protection and copyright law, unfair competition law and trademark law International Design 99
A. Design protection in copyright law 99
1. Requirements for protection 100
2. Acts of infringement 100
3. Legal consequences and enforcement 102
B. Design protection and trademark law 102
C. Design protection in competition law 103
1. Requirements for protection 104
2. Acts of infringement 105
3. Legal consequences and enforcement 106

Patent Piracy
Claudia Milbradt

I. Definitions 107
A. Patents 107
B. Utility Models 108
C. Know-how 108
II. Special Cases 109
A. Natural materials 109
B. Reach-Through-Patents 110
C. Second medicinal indication 111
D. Standard Essential Patents 111
E. Software Patents 112
F. Patentability of Nanotechnology 114

III. Securing Rights from Employees, Universities and other R&D Partners 115
A. Employees 115
B. R&D with Universities 116
1. University Claims to Employee Inventions 116
2. Impact on Contractual Structure 117
C. R&D with other Industry Partners 118
A. Determining the Scope of Protection of the Patent 119
IV. Infringement 119
B. Direct Infringement 120
C. Indirect Infringement 121
D. Transit 123
E. Objections 124
V. Legal Consequences of Infringement 125
A. Inspection 125
B. Cease-and-Desist 125
C. Damages 126
D. Information 128
E. Destruction 128
F. Recall 128
VI. Enforcement 129
A. Preliminary Injunction vs. Action on the Merit 129
B. Border Seizures 130

Know-How Piracy
Barbara Maucher

I. Protection of Know-How 133
A. Objects and Concept of Know-How Protection 133
1. The definition of 'not readily known or ascertainable' 136
2. Definition of 'linked to a business enterprise' 137
3. Definition of 'intention to keep information secret' 138
4. The definition of 'legitimate interest in keeping information secret' 139
B. Confidentiality Agreement 140
C. Practical Measures 146
1. Defining risks 146
2. Taking measures 146
II. Definition of Product Piracy 149
1. Industrial or commercial espionage 150
2. Breach of Trust 150
3. Inducement to infringe contractual obligations 151
4. Other 152
III. Know-How Piracy as a form of unfair competition 152
IV. Remedies in Case of Know-How Piracy 154

Music, Film and Software Piracy
Wolfgang Schönig

I.	Protected Works	159
	A. General Requirements and Term of Protection	159
	B. Protection of Musical Works	160
	1. Eligibility for Protection	160
	2. Copyright Owners	160
	C. Writings	161
	1. Eligibility of Protection	161
	2. Copyright Owners	162
	D. Photographic Works	162
	1. Eligibility for Protection	162
	2. Copyright Owners	162
	E. Protection of Cinematographic Works	163
	1. Eligibility for Protection	163
	2. Copyright Owners	163
	F. Television Program Formats	164
	G. Computer Programs	165
	1. Eligibility for Protection	165
	2. Copyright Owners	166
	H. Protection of Databases	167
	1. Eligibility for Protection	167
	2. Copyright Owners	168
	I. Protection of Multimedia Works, Computer and Video Games	169
	J. Websites	170
	1. Eligibility for Protection	170
	2. Copyright Owners	170
II.	Scope of Copyright Protection	170
	A. Exploitation Rights of the Author or Holder of Neighbouring Rights	170
	B. Dealing with Copyrights and Neighbouring Rights – Legal Position of Licencees	171
	C. Limitations of German Copyright Law – in particular making copies for private purposes *(Privileg der Privatkopie)*; copyright levy on recording equipment *(Geräteabgabe)* vs. DRM and individual licensing	172
	D. Comparative Legal Aspects	175
III.	Offline Digital Piracy	176
	A. Infringements	177
	B. Privilege to Make Copies for Private Purposes	178
	C. Circumvention of Protective Measures (DRM Systems)	179
	D. Liability of Manufacturers of Means to Circumvent	180
IV.	Online Digital Piracy	181
	A. Introduction	181
	B. Liability of Online Providers	181
	1. Overview of the Liability Principles and the Limits set out in the German Telemedia Act	182
	2. Liability of Content Providers	184

3. Liability of Host Providers 184
4. Usenet 189
5. Filesharing Systems 190
6. Liability of Access Providers 193
7. Conclusion 195
C. Liability of Users 196
1. Uploading Content and Making it Available for Download 196
2. Downloading Content – Difficulties of the Privilege to make Private Copies under German Law 196
3. Circumventing Protection Measures (Ripping Protected Online Streams) 197
4. Identifying Private Users in Order to Effectively Pursue Legal Measures 198
D. Other Parties Potentially Liable for Online Piracy 202
1. Liability of Search Engine Providers 202
2. Manufacturers of Online Recording Software 204
3. Responsibility for Links 205
E. International Issues in an Online Environment 205
V. Legal Consequences 206
A. Claims to Cease and Desist 206
B. Destruction, Recall and Surrender 206
C. Claims for Information 206
D. Inspection 207
E. Damages 207
VI. Enforcement 208
A. Civil Action 208
1. Plaintiff's Right of Action 208
2. Warning Letter 208
3. Preliminary Injunction versus Action on the Merit 208
B. Customs Seizures 208
1. German Custom Seizures 209
2. European Customs Seizures 209

Product Piracy in China
Ling Ho/Audrey Shum

I. China IP Legal Framework 211
II. Trademarks 211
A. Legal Requirements for Trademark Protection under the China Trademark Law 211
B. Infringing Behaviour 212
C. Parallel Imports 212
III. Patents 212
A. Legal Requirements for Patent Protection according to China Patent Law 212
B. Infringing Behaviour 213

IV. Copyright Law 213
A. Legal Requirements for Copyright Protection according to China Copyright Law 213
B. Infringing Behaviour 214
C. Internet Privacy 214
V. Anti-Unfair Competition Law 215
A. Protection of unregistered trademark, get-up or goodwill 215
B. Protection of Trade Secrets 215
VI. Enforcement 215
A. Court Actions 216
1. Which court? 216
2. What do you need to commence an infringement action if you are a foreign company? 216
3. Procedures for Intellectual Property Litigation 217
4. Evidence 217
5. Hearings 217
6. Asset Preservation/Evidence Preservation/Injunction 217
7. Common Defence Strategies 218
B. Administrative Actions 219
C. Customs Actions 219
D. Criminal Actions 220
E. Other alternatives 221
VII. Legal Consequences 221
A. Damages 221
B. Other forms of relief 221

Product Piracy in the United States
Daryl Fairbairn

I. Sources of Intellectual Property Law in the United States 223
A. The U. S. Judicial System 224
B. The U. S. Litigation Process 225
1. The Complaint 225
2. Pre-Judgment Remedies 225
3. Response to the Complaint 226
4. Discovery 226
5. Summary Judgment, Trial and Appeal 228
II. Substantive Intellectual Property Law 229
A. Trademarks 229
1. Trademark Protection 229
2. Registration versus Use in Commerce 231
3. Trademark Infringement 232
4. Trademark Remedies 234
5. Criminal Trademark Laws and Administrative Proceedings 234

B. Patents 235
1. Patentability 236
2. Novelty 236
3. Patent Infringement 238
4. Patent Law Remedies 239
5. Administrative Proceedings: Sec. 337 Actions 240
6. Design Patents 241
7. Criminal Patent Laws 242
C. Copyright 242
1. Copyright Protection 243
2. Copyright Infringement 244
3. Copyright Law Remedies 245
4. Criminal Copyright Laws and Administrative Proceedings 246
5. Digital Millennium Copyright Act 247
D. Trade Secrets 247
1. Trade Secret Protection 247
2. Trade Secret Remedies 248
3. Federal trade secret law provides criminal sanctions 248
4. Other Measures For Fighting Piracy and Counterfeiting 248
III. Final Comment 249

Product Piracy in Spain
Monserrat Lopez-Bellosta/Isabel Carulla

I. Legal Framework Overview 251
A. Protection of Intellectual Property by Substantive Law 251
1. Spanish Trademark Act, Patent Act, Utility Model Act, Copyright Act 251
2. Role of the Spanish Unfair Competition Act 252
3. Criminal Law 252
B. Enforcement of Intellectual Property Rights 253
1. Civil Action 253
2. Public Law 256
3. Criminal Action 263
II. Trademark Piracy 264
A. Legal Requirements for Trademark Protection under the Trademark Act 264
B. Infringing Behaviour 265
1. Deceit of Origin 265
2. Likelihood of Confusion 265
3. Transit as Infringing Behaviour (particularly focusing on the Decision given by the ECJ (European Court of Justice) on 9 November 2006 *(Diesel)* 266
4. Accountability for Online Auctions 266

C. Enforcement 266
1. Border Measures 266
2. Measures on Trade Fairs 267
D. Legal Consequences 268
1. Discontinuance 268
2. Information 268
3. Damages 269
4. Destruction 269
5. Recall 269
6. Criminal Sanctions 269
III. Patent Piracy 270
A. Prerequisites for Patent Protection 270
1. Service Inventions 271
2. Securing Rights in the Context of Cooperation with Third Parties 271
3. Licence Agreements 271
4. Technology Transfer Agreements 272
5. R&D Agreements 273
B. Infringing Behaviour 274
1. Direct and Indirect Patent Infringement 274
2. Doctrine of Equivalence 275
3. Transit as an Infringing Behaviour 276
C. Legal Consequences 276
1. Discontinuance 276
2. Information 277
3. Damages 277
4. Destruction 278
5. Recall 278
6. Criminal Sanctions 278
IV. Know-How Piracy 279
A. Know-How as a Trade Secret 279
1. Information must be secret 280
2. Information must entail a competitive edge 280
3. The holder of the information must take steps to keep the information secret 280
B. Measures to Protect Know-How 281
1. Contractual Measures 281
2. Practical Measures 282
C. Know-How Piracy as Unfair Competition 282
1. Disclosure or Exploitation of Trade Secrets, without the Owner's Consent 282
2. Lawful Access to Trade Secrets but under a Duty of Secrecy 283
3. Acquisition of Trade Secrets using Espionage or Similar Methods 283
4. Trade Secrets must have been violated in order to obtain personal profit or profit for a Third Party, or to cause Damage to the Owner of the Secret 283
D. Criminal Sanctions 283

V. Music, Film and Software Piracy 284
A. Substantive Requirements for Protection 284
B. Infringing Behaviour 285
1. Copy for Private Use 285
C. Enforcement 286
1. Search and Seizure – Private Persons 286
2. Duty of Disclosure of Online Providers 286
3. Border Measures 286
D. Legal Consequences 287
1. Discontinuance 287
2. Information 287
3. Damages 287
4. Destruction 288
5. Recall 288
6. Criminal Sanctions 288
VI. Parallel Imports 290
A. Exhaustion of Intellectual Property Rights and Parallel Imports 290
B. Evolution of Spanish Case Law applying to the Principle of Exhaustion of Intellectual Property Rights 291
C. Legal Action against Parallel Imports when Intellectual Property Rights are not exhausted 293

Product Piracy in France
Jean-Frédéric Gaultier/Emmanuelle Levy

I. Enforcement of Intellectual Property Rights in France 295
A. Civil Action 295
B. Public Law 296
C. Criminal Action 297
II. Trademark Piracy 297
A. Legal Requirements for Trademark Protection 297
1. The trademark must be capable of graphic representation and distinctiveness 297
2. The trademark must be lawful 298
3. The trademark must be available 298
4. Trademark protection is acquired through registration except for wellnow trademarks, within the meaning of Art. 6 bis of the Paris Convention. 299
B. Infringing Behaviours 299
1. Risk of confusion 299
2. Particular case: Transit as an infringing behaviour 300
3. Particular case: Keyword advertising 300
4. Particular case: Parallel Imports 301
C. Enforcement 301
D. Legal Consequences (discontinuance, information, damages, destruction, recall) 302

III. Design Rights 303
A. Legal Requirements for Design Protection 303
B. Infringing Behaviours 304
C. Enforcement 304
D. Legal Consequences (discontinuance, information, damages, destruction, recall) 305
E. International Designs 306
1. Community Design Rights 306
2. Design Rights under International Law and Article 25 TRIPS 306
F. Design Protection and Copyright Law, Unfair Competition Law and Trademark Law 306
1. Design Protection and Copyright Law 306
2. Design Protection and Trademark Law 306
3. Design Rights and Unfair Competition 307
IV. Patent Piracy 307
A. Legal Requirements for Patent Protection 307
1. Pre-requisite: Securing Rights to Inventions 307
2. Scope of Patent Protection 308
3. Application and Registration of Patents 309
B. Infringing Behaviours 310
1. Direct patent infringement 310
2. Indirect patent infringement 311
3. Doctrine of Equivalence 311
4. Transit 311
C. Enforcement 312
D. Legal Consequences 312
V. Know-How Theft 313
A. Protection of Know-How 313
B. Know-How Piracy as Unfair Competition 314
C. Know-How as a Trade Secret 314
VI. Music, Film and Software Piracy 314
A. Legal Requirements of Copyright Protection 314
B. Particularities of Individual Products 314
1. Music 314
2. Movies 315
3. Software 315
4. Multimedia, Computer Games 316
C. Infringement 316
1. Infringement 316
2. Liability of Users 317
D. Enforcement 318
E. Legal consequences 319

Product Piracy in the Netherlands
Mélanie Loos

I. The Enforcement of Intellectual Property Rights in the Netherlands 322
A. Civil Action 322
B. Public Law 325
C. Criminal Action 325
II. Trademark Piracy 327
A. Legal Requirements for Trademark Protection under the 327
B. Infringing Behaviour 328
1. Danger of Confusion 328
2. Particular Case: Transit as Infringing Behaviour 329
3. Particular Case: Internetprovider 330
4. Particular Case: Parallel Imports 330
C. Legal Consequences – Discontinuance, Information, Damages, Destruction, and Recall 331
D. Enforcement 332
III. Design Rights 333
A. Legal Requirements for Design Protection according to the 333
B. Infringing Behaviour 334
C. Legal Consequences – Discontinuance, Information, Damages, Destruction, Recall 335
D. Enforcement 335
E. International Design 336
1. Community Design Rights 336
2. Design Rights under International Law and 25 TRIPS 337
F. Design Protection and Copyright Law, Unfair Competition Law and Trademark Law 338
1. Design Protection and Copyright Law 338
2. Design Protection and Unfair Competition Law 338
3. Design Protection and Trademark Law 339
IV. Patent Piracy 339
A. Legal Requirements for Patent Protection under the Dutch Patent Act 339
1. Pre-requisite: Securing Rights to Inventions 340
2. Scope of Patent Protection 340
3. Application and Registration of Patents 341
B. Infringing Behaviour 341
1. Direct patent infringement 341
2. Indirect patent infringement 342
3. Doctrine of Equivalence 343
4. Transit as an infringing behaviour 343
C. Legal Consequences 344
D. Enforcement 345
V. Know-How Theft 347
A. Protection of Know-How 347
1. Confidentiality Agreement 348
2. Practical Measures 348

B. Know-How Piracy as Unfair Competition 349
C. Know-How as a Trade Secret 349
VI. Music, Film and Software Piracy 349
A. Legal Requirements of Copyright Protection According to the Dutch Copyright Act 349
B. Particularities of Individual Products 351
1. Music 351
2. Movies 351
3. Software 351
4. Multimedia, Computer Games 352
C. Infringement 352
D. Legal Consequences 358
E. Enforcement 359

Product Piracy in the United Kingdom

Alexandra Pygall/Daniel Royle

I. Overview of the Legal Framework in the United Kingdom 361
II. Enforcement of IP rights in the United Kingdom 361
A. Civil Action 361
1. Identity of Claimant 361
2. Procedural Steps 362
3. Interim Remedies 363
4. Disclosure 364
5. The Trial 366
6. Appeals 366
7. Remedies 366
B. Criminal Action 366
C. Public Law 367
III. Trademarks 368
IV. Passing Off 369
V. Unfair Competition 370
VI. Design Rights 370
A. UK Design Right 370
B. UK Registered Design 371
C. Remedies for Design Infringement 371
VII. Patents 371
A. Sources of Law 371
B. What is patentable in the United Kingdom? 372
C. Agreements regarding Patents 372
D. The Courts 372
E. Types of Proceedings 372
1. Infringement 372
2. Validity/Revocation 373
3. Amendment 373

F. Border Measures 373
G. Criminal Sanctions 373
VIII. Confidential Information 374
A. Nature of Confidential Information 374
B. Breach of Confidence 374
C. Confidential Information in Employment Relationships 374
IX. Copyright 375
A. Copyright Works 375
B. Civil Infringement and Defences 376
C. Remedies 376
D. Criminal Infringement and Defences 376

Abbreviations 379

Literature 387

Introduction

Claudia Milbradt

This handbook should be of interest to those of you whose everyday work involves safeguarding the interests of intellectual property by taking measures aimed at combating counterfeiting and product piracy. It provides both an overview of relevant intellectual property rights and the full array of measures that companies can take to enforce their intellectual property rights.

Counterfeiting and product piracy has become the catchphrase for a white collar crime, which has reached troubling dimensions. Worldwide annual losses due to counterfeit products are estimated at approximately USD 200 billion – approximately 10% of all goods traded worldwide.[1] But this figure does not show the total scope of counterfeiting and piracy, because it does not include the entirety of pirated digital products distributed via the internet or products that are produced and consumed domestically. If these items were added, the total scope of counterfeiting and piracy worldwide could well reach several hundred billion dollars more.[2] Counterfeits cost the German economy alone EUR 25 billion every year.[3] The oft-downplayed term "product piracy" constitutes an acute and serious problem for the world economy.

It affects not only large-scale industrial enterprises, but also has a particularly significant impact on medium-sized companies. Medium-sized companies in particular frequently fail to sufficiently invest in protecting know-how and in registering intellectual property rights,[4] such as trademarks and patents. This can have significant adverse effects on the company concerned. Counterfeits often result in a loss of market share and, at the same time, they can also damage a company's reputation and business through cheap copies that are technically inferior but comparatively cheaper and difficult to immediately distinguish from original products.

An effective counter-piracy strategy therefore needs to be devised. This includes taking adequate and effective steps in advance to protect the inventions, know-how and intellectual property rights of the company, as well as subsequently filing patent applica-

1 OECD, THE ECONOMIC IMPACT OF COUNTERFEITING AND PIRACY – Executive Summary, 2007, p. 15.

2 OECD, THE ECONOMIC IMPACT OF COUNTERFEITING AND PIRACY – Executive Summary, 2007, p. 15.

3 BMI/BMJ, press release of 25 May 2007.

4 A study on product/trademark piracy in China carried out by the German Chamber of Commerce and Industry (DIHK) and the German Business Action Group against Product and Trademark Counterfeiting (APM) showed that 70% of small and medium-sized business there have not registered any industrial property rights.

tions, utility model applications, trademark and design patent applications in all relevant markets. This is necessary to be able to effectively enforce intellectual property rights by way of judicial actions, customs proceedings and other proceedings before regulatory authorities. Many companies still appear to be deterred from taking such measures due to the initial investment required. But such measures are ultimately the only method to successfully counteract piracy. It should therefore be borne in mind that preventing the illegal importation and flooding of a company's own market is not enough. A registration strategy also needs to be devised and implemented so as to allow a company to expand its business and enforcement activities into other markets around the world.

Again, enforcement of intellectual property rights is required not merely through ordinary judicial proceedings, but also may be undertaken through customs proceedings and other proceedings before regulatory authorities. Cooperation and knowledge sharing is therefore essential, as the customs authorities cooperate with or actively support the public prosecutor's office for individual cases. Ultimately, the most suitable and effective anti-counterfeiting and product piracy measures are tailored to individual cases and must therefore be selected accordingly. This, however, presupposes that the relevant intellectual property rights are also registered on behalf of the holder of rights. For legal practitioners, it is thus important to understand what intellectual property rights the company has at its disposal, even on an abstract basis, and which intellectual property rights can be asserted in a specific case. This handbook therefore serves not only to demonstrate how to enforce intellectual property rights[5] but also sets out the relevant intellectual property rights in the individual chapters. In the interests of general usability, it is not practical to present detailed discussions about every aspect of patent, copyright, trademark, or registered design infringement but to provide a broad overview.

Given that approximately 60% of counterfeit goods originate in Asia,[6] it is worthwhile to pay particular attention to Asia in combating the illegal importation of counterfeit products. There are also several free-trade areas, such as those in Dubai which particularly need close monitoring.[7] Their geographical location and relaxed regulations make them particularly attractive to counterfeiters.[8]

---

5 There is already a certain amount of literature relating solely to enforcement issues. For instance, the World Trademark Review "Anti-Counterfeiting 2008" provides a very good global guide for 47 jurisdictions on how to enforce trademark rights against product piracy. *Vrius/Schneider*, Enforcement of Intellectual Property Rights through Border Measures (2006), provides comprehensive information on EU enforcement practices in 24 jurisdictions.

6 Communication from the Commission to the Council, the European Parliament and the European Economic and Social Committee on a customs response to latest trends in Counterfeiting and piracy, COM (2005) 479 final, 11 October 2005, p. 5, 24.

7 *Bogdanich*, Counterfeit Drugs' Path Eased by Free Trade Zones, The New York Times of 17 December 2007.

8 OECD, THE ECONOMIC IMPACT OF COUNTERFEITING AND PIRACY – Executive Summary, 2007, p. 14; *Bogdanich*, Counterfeit Drugs' Path Eased by Free Trade Zones, The New York Times of 17 December 2007.

In the European Union, seizures of counterfeit products have increased tenfold since 1998.[9] In contrast to the rest of Europe, IP rights suffer from a lack of consistent protection and enforcement in Eastern Europe, the gateway to the key centres for the production of counterfeit drugs in Russia and Asia. IP enforcement the member states of the European Union takes on added significance in the new Eastern European member states with borders susceptible to counterfeiters and goods entering the single market at vulnerable points.

Customs Regulation (Council Regulation (EC) No 1383/2003 of 22 July 2003 concerning customs actions against goods suspected of infringing certain intellectual property rights and the measures to be taken against goods found to have infringed such rights),[10] which embodies EU border protection laws, sets out anti-counterfeiting measures available within the enlarged European Community and has led to improved enforcement of IP rights. The regulation improves communications between rights holders and customs authorities (in conjunction with the recently amended Customs Code Regulation (Council Regulation (EC) No 648/2005 of 13 April 2005 amending Council Regulation (EEC) No 2913/92 establishing the Community Customs Code).[11] It also extends the scope of *ex officio* procedures to the benefit of genuine drug manufactures. Recent experiences with the border measures have shown them to be very efficient.

Enforcement Directive (Directive 2004/48/EC of 29 April 2004 on the Enforcement of Intellectual Property Rights)[12] on the enforcement of intellectual property rights is intended to harmonise the standards of IP enforcement among the member states of the European Union. Significantly, the level of protection afforded to IP rights holders has been strengthened in national legislation adopted across the EU. For example, there are now laws providing improved access to searches and seizures, as well as recall and destruction remedies. In Germany the Act on the improvement of the enforcement of intellectual property rights entered into force on 1 September 2008.[13]

Companies can enforce their patent rights in European Union Member States in order to combat counterfeit goods. Preliminary injunctions may be obtained from national courts in clear-cut cases. Likewise, trademark law provides a robust means to counter fake products, given that, compared to patent law, it is largely harmonised in the EU. A key factor is that expedited relief, in the form of injunctions and other remedies, is comparatively easy and inexpensive to obtain since trademark law is comparatively easy for courts and agencies to apply in practice. Companies can achieve the best results by coordinating legal actions across member states.

---

9 Communication from the Commission to the Council, the European Parliament and the European Economic and Social Committee on a customs response to latest trends in Counterfeiting and piracy, COM (2005) 479 final, 11 October 2005, p. 3, 5.

10 Official Journal of the European Union 2003 No L 196/7.

11 Official Journal of the European Union 2005 No L 117/13.

12 Official Journal of the European Union 2004 No L 157/45 and Corrigendum to Directive 2004/48/EC, Official Journal of the European Union 2004 No L 195/16.

13 German Act on the improvement of the enforcement of intellectual property rights, BT-Drucks, 16/5048.

On a broader scale, international treaties govern certain aspects of intellectual property rights concerned by product piracy, such as the Paris Convention (Paris Convention for the Protection of Industrial Property of 20 March 1883) and World Trade Organisation's law TRIPS (Agreement on Trade-Related Aspects of Intellectual Property Rights). Currently, the European Union, the United States, Japan and other states discuss to conclude an international framework Anti-Counterfeiting Trade Agreement (ACTA) leading to harmonised standards and common enforcement practices.[14]

This handbook also presents a case for a global product piracy strategy. It is important to know the specifics in the different jurisdictions in order to combat any party infringing intellectual property rights in several countries. Local specifics must always be taken into account. In China, for example, it is essential to know the laws of enforcement under local economic protection provisions, in addition to any legal loopholes enabling infringers to use delaying tactics. In order to enable readers of this handbook to envisage a possible international strategy, we have not only described the situation under German law, but also other important jurisdictions. In addition to the overview of rights and enforcement possibilities in Germany, the handbook also covers jurisdictions in Europe (UK, France, Spain, and the Netherlands), the US and China. Those chapters dealing with individual jurisdictions should serve as a basis for understanding what kind of intellectual property rights exist in that country and how they can be enforced in their respective jurisdictions.

Thank you

It is a fascinating experience to work in an international environment and to run and finalise such a book project with colleagues from all over the world.

The idea for the handbook was born out of the daily praxis fighting product piracy products and infringing goods. Once we have started with the book, new ideas came up regularly and we could further develop the book on an ongoing basis. However, we felt that, at a certain point, we have to do our – preliminary – fullstop. Comments from which side and from whereever in the world are highly appreciated.

My sincere thanks to my IP partners and colleagues who have contributed to this book – without such a wonderful global IP team such a project could never have flown.

Thanks also to Julia Steil, Anne Kessing, Beata Brochocki and Meltem Kabakci for their assistance.

---

14 Participants in the current discussion include Australia, Canada, the European Union, Japan, Jordan, Korea, Mexico, Morocco, New Zealand, Singapore, Switzerland, the United Arab Emirates, and the United States. The goal is to involve also states like China. See also homepage of the European Commission http://ec.europa.eu/trade/issues/sectoral/intell_property/pr050608_en.htm.

In particular, I am very obliged to thank my colleague Daryl Fairbairn from Clifford Chance New York for reviewing the whole book regarding English language and for his detailed and very useful comments. I also sincerely thank Inga Schirdewahn and Stefanie Schwanke. Without their help we would have never had a book with a consistent layout. Their job may have been the hardest and they did it always with a smile.

Enforcement of Intellectual Property Rights in Germany

CLAUDIA MILBRADT/HEINER HUGGER

I. Enforcement of Intellectual Property Rights in Germany

Once an infringement of a certain intellectual property right has been confirmed, the question comes up: What should be the next appropriate step? In this respect possible civil actions must be considered as well as the involvement of public authorities including the possibilities to initiate criminal proceedings.

A. Civil Action

1. First Step – Warning letter?

German law does not require a party to issue an out-of-court warning letter prior to initiating a lawsuit. Warning letters may, however, be worth considering as a way to avoid having to pay all costs in the event of an immediate acknowledgement of debt by the other party in subsequent court proceedings (sec. 93 of the Zivilprozessordnung [ZPO] [Civil procedure statute] (F. R.G.). The right holder normally requests or demands that the party infringing an intellectual property right refrain from committing any similar violations in the future. The party will be required by the right holder to issue an enforceable declaration to cease-and-desist *(strafbewehrte Unterlassungserklärung)* within an appropriate period in order to prevent court proceedings to be initiated. If an unreasonably short period is given, this will still result in a reasonable period being granted.[1] Any such warning must give a clear indication of the property rights being asserted and the specific infringement alleged (sec. 93 of the ZPO [Civil procedure statute]). If the intention is to avoid costs and to get the potential infringer to cease and desist in its actions, it may be preferable to enclose the relevant power of attorney with a warning letter. There is, however, a certain amount of dispute in the German legal literature and jurisdiction over whether this is necessary for a warning letter sent by a representative,[2] but it is still advisable to include the power of attorney. It is also useful to be able to prove that the potential infringer received the warning letter, as some German Higher Regional Courts rule, that this is a requirement for an effective warning letter.[3]

---

1 19 October 1989 BGH [Federal Supreme Court] [I ZR 63/88], GRUR 1990, 381, 382 (Antwortpflicht des Abgemahnten).

2 See *Erdmann/Rojahn/Sosnitza*, Handbuch des Fachanwalts Gewerblicher Rechtsschutz, No. 983.

3 14 June 1996 OLG [Higher Regional Court] Düsseldorf [20 W 13/96], NJWE-WettbR 1996, 256; 10 September 1997 OLG [Higher Regional Court] Dresden [14 W 854/97], WRP 1997, 1201.

There are certain instances in which this kind of warning is not necessary, such as those cases where the infringing party has made it clear that they have no intention to discontinue their actions.[4] Warnings can also be inadvisable for strategic reasons if the intention is to surprise the opposing party with another measure, such as injunctive relief.

All warnings carry the inherent risk of lacking justification. A warning based on an intellectual property right may constitute an entitlement to interfere *(eingreifendes Recht)* with the established business operations of the party receiving the warning, which may also give entitlement to damages under sec. 823 para. 1 of the Bürgerliches Gesetzbuch [BGB] [Civil Code] (F. R.G.) in the event of culpable actions *(schuldhaftes Handeln)*[5] in order to avoid culpable actions it is recommended to check with special diligence, if an intellectual property rights infringement exists.

A warning needs to be distinguished from a request to demonstrate legitimate use of the relevant product *(Berechtigungsanfrage)*. Such requests are commonly used in patent law cases to draw the potential infringing party's attention to one's own intellectual property rights and, where possible, to precipitate an open discussion between the parties. In order to avoid the risks of damages under sec. 823 para. 1 of BGB [Civil Code], one should take care of a noncommittal wording of the request. It must not include the demand that the party infringing property rights refrains from committing any similar violations in the future.[6] A request does not help to avoid having to pay all costs in the event of an immediate acknowledgement of debt by the other party in subsequent court proceedings (sec. 93 of the ZPO [Civil procedure statute]).

2. Preliminary injunction vs. action on the merit

The decision between a preliminary injunction in the meaning of sec. 938 ZPO [Civil procedure statute] and an action on the merit rests mainly on the aim of the holder of the intellectual property rights. Does it want to quickly obtain an enforceable legal instrument? Is the infringing party threatening to disappear? Are the financial resources available for the legal action limited? Or is the intention to obtain definitive clarification concerning the dispute, including the issue of the payment of damages?

Both the preliminary injunction and the ruling in the infringement proceedings only have legal effect between the parties involved.

4 8 April 1996 OLG [Higher Regional Court] Munich [29 W 616/96], WRP 1996, 930 (Entbehrliche Abmahnung).

5 19 January 2006 BGH [Federal Supreme Court] [I ZR 98/02], GRUR 2006, 432 (Verwarnung aus Kennzeichenrecht II); 19 January 2006 BGH [Federal Supreme Court] [I ZR 217/03], GRUR 2006, 433 (unbegründete Abnehmerverwarnung).

6 7 April 2006 LG [Regional Court] Mannheim [7 O 47/06], GRUR-RR 2007, 304 (Wasserinjektionsanlage).

Both the preliminary injunction and the principal proceedings may be pursued with the intention of enforcing the claim to cease-and-desist if legitimate and demonstrable reasons exist to suggest the opponent will act unlawfully in the near future.

Applications for preliminary injunctions will likely be preferable to the principal proceedings if the plaintiff's primary aim is to secure and preliminarily enforce the claim to cease-and-desist on an urgent and cost saving basis. Such injunctions are essential in the case of border seizures. Jurisdiction for the preliminary injunction lies with the court that would hear the main proceedings (sec. 937 para. 1 of the ZPO [Civil procedure statute]). All preliminary injunctions are conditional on a right to claim and on grounds for a claim. The right to claim in the case of an order to cease and desist is the claim to cease and desist arising from, for example, sec. 139 of the Patentgesetz [PatG] [Patent Act] (F. R.G.) or sec. 14 of the Markengesetz [MarkenG] [Trademark Act] (F. R.G.). This claim must be substantiated by prima facie evidence. One of the primary forms of such evidence in preliminary injunction proceedings is an affirmation in lieu of an oath *(Versicherung an Eides statt)*. The grounds for an injunction are urgency. The urgency is ruled differently by the different courts and in the different areas of intellectual property. As a general principle, an application for a preliminary injunction should be filed within four to six weeks after having gathered knowledge of all facts justifying the infringement.

However, the opponent's potential claim for damages under sec. 945 of the ZPO [Civil procedure statute] should also be taken into account when applying for preliminary injunction. If it subsequently turns out that that preliminary injunction was wrongly issued, e. g. if it was revoked, the applicant is required to reimburse the opponent for any losses suffered by it as a result of the enforcement of the injunction.

In principle proceedings, the court decides the case by judgement (sec. 300 para. 1 of the ZPO [Civil procedure statute]). The plaintiff in an infringement proceeding bears – in principle – the burden of proof for all facts on which the claim is based. The judgement provides a summary of reasons with respect to the legal and actual aspects. An appeal against the judgement is possible. In principle, only the legal aspects of the judgement can be attacked in the appeal. The appeal has to be filed within two months after the judgement has been served.

3. International Issues of Enforcement of Rulings

There can be a number of difficulties with enforcing claims internationally. If, for example, a company is based outside Germany, any ruling handed down in Germany has to be enforced in the relevant country.

As far as continental Europe and the EU are concerned, such enforcement is facilitated by the Lugano Convention of 1988 and, in particular, the Recognition Regulation (Council Regulation (EC) 44/2001 of 22 December 2000 on jurisdiction and the recognition and enforcement of judgments in civil and commercial matters).[7] The Recognition Regulation applies to all European Union Member States. Under Art. 38 para. 1 thereof, legal instruments issued in one member state are enforceable in another on request. There is no examination of the substantive basis of the foreign ruling (Art. 45 para. 2 of the Recognition Regulation). The judicial instrument simply has to be declared enforceable in the relevant Member State. Judicial remedies against a declaration of the enforceability of the ruling are only possible to a very limited degree (Art. 45 para. 1 of the Recognition Regulation). The Recognition Regulation has generally made it easier to enforce rulings within the EU.

However, it may be difficult to enforce judgements outside Europe. Germany has agreements with a number of non-European countries concerning the recognition and enforcement of foreign rulings. However, no treaty exists with the USA, which is one of Germany's most important trading partners. If a copyright holder wishes to enforce a German ruling in the USA, it basically has to bring a separate action in the USA on the basis of the German ruling. The scope of examination of the US court is, however, limited to fundamental issues such as the jurisdiction of the original court or the legal effectiveness of the German ruling. Reference can also be made in many US states to the "Uniform Foreign Money-Judgements Recognition Act".

4. Enforcement of Intellectual Property according to the Enforcement Directive 2004/48/EC

The enforcement of intellectual property rights in Europe is now much more streamlined than before.

The Enforcement Directive (Directive 2004/48/EC of 29 April 2004 on the Enforcement of Intellectual Property Rights[8]), came into force on 29 April 2004. The Enforcement Directive was meant to have been transposed into national law by 29 April 2006 (Art. 20 para. 1 of the Enforcement Directive). European Union Directives are not directly applicable in member states,[9] meaning that the legal position was far from certain at that time.[10] The member states have been required to establish substantive legal pe-

[7] Council Regulation (EC) No 44/2001 of 22 December 2000 on jurisdiction and the recognition and enforcement of judgments in civil and commercial matters, Official Journal of the European Communities 2001 No L 12/1.

[8] Official Journal of the European Union 2004 No L 157/45, Revised version: Official Journal of the European Union 2004 No L 195/16.

[9] The Federal Supreme Court's view is that the Enforcement Directive should be applied directly in the manner provided for therein once the deadline for implementation has passed, 19 April 2007 BGH [Federal Supreme Court] [I ZR 35/04], GRUR 2007, 708, 711 (Internet-Versteigerung II).

[10] *Eisenkolb*, Die Enforcement-Richtlinie und ihre Wirkung, GRUR 2007, 387 f.; *Koch*, Die „Enforcement"-Richtlinie: Vereinheitlichung der Durchsetzung der Rechte des geistigen Eigentums in der EU, ITRB 2006, 40, 42.

nalties and procedural instruments streamlining the options for intellectual property right holders to protect and pursue their own rights.[11]

In Germany, a respective draft bill to implement the Enforcement Directive into German law was just passed by the German Bundestag on 11 April 2008.[12] The Act on the Improvement of the Enforcement of Intellectual Property Rights (Gesetz zur Verbesserung der Durchsetzung von Rechten des geistigen Eigentums) entered into force on 1 September 2008.[13] As a cross section act in essence it amends identically the Urhebergesetz [UrhG] [Copyright Act] (F. R.G.), PatG [Patent Act], MarkenG [Trademark Act], Gebrauchsmustergesetz [GebrMG] [Utility Model Act] (F. R.G.), Geschmacksmustergesetz [GeschmMG] [Design Act] (F. R.G.), Halbleiterschutzgesetz [HalblSGHG] [Semiconductor Protection Act] (F. R.G.) Sortenschutzgesetz [SortSchG] [Plant Variety Protection Act] (F. R.G.).[14] The most important changes by the Act on the Improvement of the Enforcement of Intellectual Property Rights in Germany may be the right to inspection, the right to ask for recall from the distribution channels and the enlarged rights to information.

Since the exact implementation of the Enforcement Directive may differ in the different European Union Member States, we have summarised the comprehensive provisions regarding intellectual property rights and procedural law which are intended to ensure the enforcement of such rights as set out by the Enforcement Directive.

Art. 3 of the Enforcement Directive starts by setting out the general obligation of member states to establish all fair and reasonable measures, procedures, and remedies necessary for the effective enforcement of intellectual property rights. The Enforcement Directive also provides a number of individual provisions, including stricter requirements for the submission of evidence (Art. 6), preservation of evidence measures (Art. 7), extended claims for information (Art. 8), specific preliminary measures and safeguards (Art. 9), measures of relief (Art. 10) and a claim for damages and surrender of evidence (Art. 13). These radical changes are an important step towards harmonising intellectual property law and procedural provisions across Europe.[15]

Art. 2 para. 1 of the Enforcement Directive states that these provisions apply to infringement of any intellectual property rights provided for in EU law and/or under the national law of the member state concerned. The Enforcement Directive does not fur-

11 *Frey/Rudolph*, EU-Richtlinie zur Durchsetzung der Rechte des geistigen Eigentums, ZUM 2004, 522 f.; *Knaak*, Die EG-Richtlinie zur Durchsetzung der Rechte des geistigen Eigentums und ihr Umsetzungsbedarf im deutschen Recht, GRUR Int 2004, 745; *Seichter* (critical), Die Umsetzung der Richtlinie zur Durchsetzung der Rechte des geistigen Eigentums, WRP 2006, 391, 392.

12 Gesetzesentwurf der Bundesregierung [draft bill of the German government], Entwurf eines Gesetzes zur Verbesserung der Durchsetzung von Rechten des geistigen Eigentums [Draft Act on the Improvement of the Enforcement of Intellectual Property Rights], BT-Drucks. 16/5048; BMJ, Bundestag passes intellectual property protection bill, press release of 11 April 2008.

13 Bundesgesetzblatt [Federal Law Gazette], no. 28 of 11 July 2008.

14 *Kitz*, Rechtsdurchsetzung im geistigen Eigentum – die neuen Regeln, NJW 2008, 2374.

15 *Eisenkolb*, Die Enforcement-Richtlinie und ihre Wirkung, GRUR 2007, 387.

ther define what falls within the scope of an intellectual property right. The EU Commission, however, regards intellectual property rights as covering copyrights, industrial property rights associated with copyrights, sui generis industrial property rights of database producers and creators of semiconductor topographies, trademarks, registered design rights, patent rights (including those under supplementary protection certificates), details of geographical origin,[16] utility models and plant variety protection rights, as well as trade names, provided these are considered to be exclusive rights under the law of the relevant member state.[17] These examples provided by the Commission are not contained in the Enforcement Directive itself, but simply provide a guide for determining the scope defined by the EU Parliament and Council.[18]

Art. 6 para. 1 sent. 1 of the Enforcement Directive provides for courts to be able to order the submission of evidence by the opposing party. This is conditional on the holder of the right submitting all reasonably available evidence to back up its claims, that the evidence at the opposing party's disposal is specified and that the interest of the opposing party in keeping such information confidential is guaranteed.

In contrast to Art. 6, Art. 7 of the Enforcement Directive provides for pre-litigation measures for the preservation of evidence and commits member states to introduce effective preliminary measures in this regard.[19] Here too, the holder of the right is required to submit all reasonably available evidence to substantiate its claims, but this may not violate the opposing party's interest in maintaining confidentiality. Contrary to Art. 6, the evidence does not need to be specified. It is unclear from the wording whether the provisions relate solely to safeguards against the imminent loss of evidence, or whether it also covers measures to establish and safeguard new and undiscovered evidence. The legal literature supports a broad interpretation and rejects limiting the provision to safeguards against the imminent loss of evidence.[20]

Another key part of the Enforcement Directive is the right to demand information set out in Art. 8. The aim of this provision is to help establish whether other parties are infringing the intellectual property right in question.[21] The provision makes it possible to make a substantive claim against third parties and is not just limited to requiring the

16 *Seichter* (critical), Die Umsetzung der Richtlinie zur Durchsetzung der Rechte des geistigen Eigentums, WRP 2006, 391, 392.

17 Statement by the Commission on Art. 2 of Directive 2004/48/EC on the Enforcement of Intellectual Property Rights, 2005/295/EC, Official Journal of the European Union 2005 No L 94/37.

18 *Koch*, Die „Enforcement"-Richtlinie: Vereinheitlichung der Durchsetzung der Rechte des geistigen Eigentums in der EU, ITRB 2006, 40, 41.

19 See detailed description in *Tilmann*, Beweissicherung nach Art. 7 der Richtlinie zur Durchsetzung der Rechte des geistigen Eigentums, GRUR 2005, 737 f.

20 *Haedicke*, Informationsbefugnisse des Schutzrechtsinhabers im Spiegel der EG-Richtlinie zur Durchsetzung der Rechte des geistigen Eigentums, in: Ohly/Bodewig/Dreier (ed.), Festschrift für Gerhard Schricker, p. 19; *Knaak*, Die EG-Richtlinie zur Durchsetzung der Rechte des geistigen Eigentums und ihr Umsetzungsbedarf im deutschen Recht, GRUR Int 2004, 745, 748.

21 *Tilmann*, Beweissicherung nach Art. 7 der Richtlinie zur Durchsetzung der Rechte des geistigen Eigentums, GRUR 2005, 737.

persons specified in the provision to participate in litigation.[22] This allows a plaintiff to demand information on the origin and distribution channels of goods and services infringing its rights by means of a court order. This requirement applies to the infringing party itself and to any person having had infringing goods in their possession on a commercial scale, having used or provided infringing services (or services for use in infringing activities) on a commercial scale infringing the plaintiff's industrial property rights, having provided services on a commercial scale for use in activities or having been involved in the creation, production or sale of such goods or the provision of such services.[23]

This comprehensive right to demand information not only from the infringing party is also provided for in the – German – Act on the Improvement of the Enforcement of Intellectual Property Rights.

Art. 9 of the Enforcement Directive sets out a procedural requirement[24] committing member states to introduce certain preliminary measures and safeguards. Art. 9 para. 1 lit. a) of the Enforcement Directive states that there must be the possibility of taking preliminary measures to ensure that the infringing party cease-and-desist its activities in the event of the imminent infringement of an intellectual property right. Art. 9 para. 1 lit. b) of the Enforcement Directive also states that courts must be able to order the seizure or surrender of goods where there is a suspected infringement of intellectual property rights, if requested to do so during sequestration proceedings, thereby preventing such goods from reaching the market and being sold commercially. These measures are not intended to determine whether an infringement has taken place, but merely act as a means of limiting any potential losses.[25] If the infringement occurs on a commercial scale, Art. 9 para. 2 of the Enforcement Directive requires that there be a possibility to order the precautionary sequestration of movable and immovable property if the holder of the right can demonstrate that the fulfilment of its claim for damages is uncertain.

B. Public Law

1. German Product Safety Act

One of the main problems with product piracy is the fact that, aside from infringing intellectual property rights, it can give rise to products which are dangerous for consu-

---

22 *Czychowski*, Auskunftsansprüche gegenüber Internetzugangsprovidern „vor" dem 2. Korb und „nach" der Enforcement-Richtlinie der EU, MMR 2004, 514, 515; *Haedicke*, Informationsbefugnisse des Schutzrechtsinhabers im Spiegel der EG-Richtlinie zur Durchsetzung der Rechte des geistigen Eigentums, in: Ohly/Bodewig/Dreier (ed.), Festschrift für Gerhard Schricker, p. 19.

23 *Koch*, Die „Enforcement"-Richtlinie: Vereinheitlichung der Durchsetzung der Rechte des geistigen Eigentums in der EU, ITRB 2006, 40, 41.

24 *Knaak*, Die EG-Richtlinie zur Durchsetzung der Rechte des geistigen Eigentums und ihr Umsetzungsbedarf im deutschen Recht, GRUR Int 2004, 745, 749.

25 *Koch*, Die „Enforcement"-Richtlinie: Vereinheitlichung der Durchsetzung der Rechte des geistigen Eigentums in der EU, ITRB 2006, 40, 41; *Tilmann*, Beweissicherung nach Art. 7 der Richtlinie zur Durchsetzung der Rechte des geistigen Eigentums, GRUR 2005, 737.

mers. Obvious examples of this are poorly made electrical appliances which can lead to house fires or medicines which do not contain what is stated on the packet.

In a report of 11 March 2008[26] entitled "Key Ideas for better protection of patients against risk of counterfeit medicines", the European Commission highlighted the fact that there has been a sharp increase in seized counterfeit medicines, a trend towards counterfeiting life-saving drugs and active substances in medical products. The latter is caused by manufacturing active substances not in compliance with GMP standards, at sites other than registered sites, or not in accordance with declared procedures. Therefore, the European Commission supports the WHO International Medical Products Anti-Counterfeiting Task Force (IMPACT). The "Principles and Elements for National Legislation against Counterfeit Medical Products" emphasised that the activities of all operators in the distribution chain must be regulated.[27]

These safety issues for counterfeit products highlighted a principal concern of national product safety authorities, which may be called on to take action on dangerous counterfeit goods. The benefit of this is that such authorities act *ex officio* when they receive information on such safety issues. Product safety in Germany is monitored by the relevant local authorities.[28]

2. Border Seizures

Border seizure proceedings cover seizures performed in accordance with the Customs Regulation (Council Regulation (EC) No. 1383/2003 of 22 July 2003 concerning customs action against goods suspected of infringing certain intellectual property rights and the measures to be taken against goods found to have infringed such rights)[29] and in accordance with national provisions.

The key difference between the German seizure process and the EU seizure process, is the degree of probability that an infringement exists. EU law only requires the suspicion of an infringement, while German law requires the existence of an obvious infringement. Another difference is that under German law, the application may also be based on unregistered trademarks, utility models and semiconductor property rights. A third

26 European Commission, PUBLIC CONSULTATION IN PREPARATION OF A LEGAL PROPOSAL TO COMBAT COUNTERFEIT MEDICINES FOR HUMAN USE, Key Ideas for better protection of patients against risk of counterfeit medicines, 11 March 2008, available at: http://ec.europa.eu/enterprise/pharmaceuticals/pharmacos/docs/doc2008/2008_03/consult_counterfeit_20080307.pdf.

27 www.who.int/impact/events/finalprincipalsforlegislation.pdf.

28 These may have different names, such as the *Gewerbeaufsicht* (commercial inspectorate) or the *Amt für Arbeitsschutz* (occupational health and safety office).

29 Council Regulation (EC) No 1383/2003 concerning customs action against goods suspected of infringing certain intellectual property rights and the measures to be taken against goods found to have infringed such rights, Official Journal of the European Union 2003 No L 196/7.

difference is that EU seizure proceedings require an assumption of liability declaration and German proceedings require a bank guarantee.

Given that the EU provisions only require a suspicion of infringement, the proceedings are also of major practical relevance. Furthermore, in the event of the suspicion of, for example, a Community trademark having been infringed, a request may be made for all EU customs authorities to become involved. While customs authorities may in principle also act *ex officio* on the basis of the Customs Regulation (in the event of adequate legitimate suspicion, see Art. 4 para. 1 of the Customs Regulation), it is definitely advisable to generally request all customs authorities to become involved.

The application form for both – the German and the EU border seizures – is available online[30] and should be submitted to the Intellectual Property Office at Nuremberg Regional Tax Office *(Oberfinanzdirektion Nürnberg – Zentralstelle Gewerblicher Rechtsschutz* (ZGR)) in the event of infringement of a national intellectual property right. It will be valid for one year and may be extended as many times as required (a simplified procedure is applicable after the first extension).

Art. 5 para. 5 of the Customs Regulation sets out requirements for the content of the application:

- Details for the contact specified by the holder of the right
- Evidence that the applicant is the holder of the trademark rights ((certified) extracts from the German Trademark Register and/or enclosure of registration documents)
- Declaration in accordance with Art. 6 of the Customs Regulation promising to accept liability for damages relating to the border seizure and/or to bear all costs arising from the customs monitoring of the goods (see German customs form 0136[31] which is available online)

It is also highly advisable to include the following information with the application:

- A description of the potentially infringing goods which is as precise and detailed as possible (a "positive list" of the features of the original goods and a "negative list" of the features of the counterfeit products);
- Specific information on the type of forgery (if known);
- An additional application for the general delivery of prototypes and samples for analysis (see form 0133, available online at http://www.zoll.de/e0_downloads/b0_vordrucke/a0_vordruckgesamtliste/index.php);
- List of potential counterfeiters ("blacklist") and/or licencees or other authorised dealers/manufacturers ("whitelist").

The application itself is free of charge, but costs may arise for the applicant if the party involved in importing the goods cannot be made to account for its actions, or is insol-

30 http://www.zoll.de/b0_zoll_und_steuern/d0_verbote_und_beschraenkungen/f0_gew_rechtsschutz/a0_marken_piraterie/c0_antrag/index.html.

31 http://www.zoll.de/e0_downloads/b0_vordrucke/a0_vordruckgesamtliste/index.php.

vent, or if it turns out that the goods do not infringe a trademark. If an infringement of intellectual property exists, the costs arising in connection with the border seizure, including storage costs and costs for destroying the counterfeit goods, may be asserted against the infringer.

If there is a suspicion that goods infringe intellectual property rights, customs will suspend the transfer of the goods or withhold them and will inform the applicant (generally the person entitled to dispose of them) and the holder of the property rights.

Customs must be informed within a period of 10 working days (which may be extended by a period of up to 10 working days under Art. 13 of the Customs Regulation) that proceedings under Art. 10 of the Customs Regulation have been instituted, whereby such notification must specify whether an intellectual property right under the legal provisions of the member state concerned has been infringed (cf. Art. 13 of the Customs Regulation). Such proceedings in Germany are generally preliminary injunction proceedings. However, the risk of a preliminary injunction being issued and the risk of an ordinary legal action (which also constitutes proceedings within the meaning of Art. 13 of the Customs Regulation) should be weighed in each individual case. The customs authorities will be required to release the goods if no such notification is sent and the holder of the right has also failed to issue the consent of the applicant to destroy the goods under Art. 11 para. 1 of the Customs Regulation by the deadline.

According to the Act on the Improvement of the Enforcement of Intellectual Property Rights, a supplementary provision relating to the simplified procedure according to the Customs Regulation has been introduced in Germany. According to the new rules, infringing products can be destroyed by customs agents regardless of whether a court has found the products to be infringing, provided that the potential infringer agrees. The infringer is deemed to agree if he does not object to destruction within ten working days following the rights holder's application. This change yields two significant advantages for the holders of intellectual property rights. First, rights holders do not incur the costs involved in bringing court proceedings against the potential infringer. Second, it no longer represents a problem if, for example, an infringer from a foreign country "goes underground" to evade judicial proceedings. Given that the infringer is deemed to agree after the expiration of the 10-working days period, the infringing goods can be destroyed at the request of the IP rights holder without the alleged infringer saying a word. Therefore the IP rights holder can resolve the situation in a very short period of time and make sure that the infringing goods never reach the market.

C. Criminal Action

Product piracy is a criminal offence[32] and criminal law[33] provides for further possibilities to enforce intellectual property rights. There are, in particular, the following good reasons to make use of these possibilities:

---

32 The following provisions stipulate that certain infringements of intellectual property rights are criminal offences: Patentgesetz [PatG] [Patent Act], § 142 (F.R.G.); Gebrauchsmustergesetz

- Criminal prosecution authorities and courts can better investigate the facts of a case since they can use coercive measures that are not available to civil litigants and courts.[34]
- Information and evidence gathered in criminal proceedings can be obtained and used by the victims (in civil litigation, etc.).[35]
- Criminal proceedings can apply additional pressure on product pirates to stop infringements and to pay civil-law claims (for damages, etc.).
- The costs of criminal proceedings are normally borne by the State.[36]

Please see below a summary of the most relevant coercive measures in criminal proceedings (1.), the requirements for the initiation of criminal proceedings (2.), the available criminal and regulatory sanctions (3.) and the prosecution of product piracy on the EU level (4.).

1. Coercive Measures

Criminal prosecution authorities and courts can, in particular, use the following coercive measures for their investigations against product pirates:

a. Search and Seizure

The property and the premises of a (natural or legal) person may be searched in order to find evidence *(Beweismittel)* or to arrest suspects (sections 102 *et seq*. of the Strafprozessordnung [StPO] [Code of Criminal Procedure] (F. R.G.)). Items that may possibly be relevant as evidence, can be seized if they are in the custody of a person and if they are not surrendered voluntarily (sec. 94 para. 2 of the StPO [Code of Criminal Procedure]).

[GebrMG] [Utility Model Act], § 25 (F. R.G.); Geschmacksmustergesetz [GeschmMG] [Design Act], § 51 (F. R.G.); Sortenschutzgesetz [SortSchG] [Plant Variety Protection Act], § 39 (F. R.G.); Halbleiterschutzgesetz [HalblSchG] [Semiconductor Protection Act], § 10 (F. R.G.); Markengesetz [MarkenG] [Trademark Act], §§ 143 ff. (F. R.G.); Urheberrechtsgesetz [UrhG] [Copyright Act], §§ 106 ff. (F. R.G.).

33 In the German legal framework, criminal law is perceived as a special form of public law.

34 See item 1. below.

35 Victims and third parties with legitimate interests have a right to gain access to, or to obtain information from, the files of criminal proceedings. See Strafprozessordnung [StPO] [Code of Criminal Procedure], §§ 406e and 475 (F. R.G.).

36 However, they may be imposed on the infringed person if it first files, and then withdraws, a demand for prosecution *(Strafantrag)*. See StPO [Code of Criminal Procedure], § 470 sent. 1 (F. R.G.).

b. Criminal-law freezing orders

Proceeds of criminal offences may be frozen by criminal-law freezing orders (sec. 111b *et seq.* of the StPO [Code of Criminal Procedure]). With regard to the frozen assets, the victims have a prior claim to satisfy their civil-law payment claims against the product pirates (sec. 111 g of the StPO [Code of Criminal Procedure]). To the extent victims have civil-law claims resulting from product-piracy offences, proceeds cannot, in principle, be siphoned-off by a forfeiture order *(Verfallsanordnung)* to the benefit of the treasury (sec. 73 para. 1 sent. 2 of the Strafgesetzbuch [StGB] [Penal Code] (F. R.G.)).[37]

c. Confiscation Orders

Items that were generated by, or used for, an intentional criminal offence *(producta et instrumenta sceleris)*, may be confiscated (sections 74 *et seq.* of the StGB [Penal Code]). In certain cases of criminal product-piracy offences,[38] items may also be confiscated if a product-piracy offence relates to them *(Beziehungsgegenstände)*, *e. g.*, if they are the items of illegal trade. A confiscation order may ultimately result in the destruction of the confiscated items.[39]

d. Summons for Interviews

Prosecutors and judges have the right to summon suspects and witnesses for interviews (sections 48, 133, 161 a para. 1 sent. 1 and 163 a para. 3 sent. 1 of the StPO [Code of Criminal Procedure]).[40] However, suspects have the absolute right to remain silent in the criminal proceedings conducted against them (sections 163 a para. 3 sent. 2, 136 para. 1 sent. 2 of the StPO [Code of Criminal Procedure]). Witnesses have the right to remain silent only if (i) the criminal proceedings are directed against one of their close relatives (sec. 52 of the StPO [Code of Criminal Procedure]), if (ii) they are asked a question to which an answer is possible which would create the risk that criminal or regulatory proceedings may be initiated against them or one of their close relatives (sec. 55 of the StPO [Code of Criminal Procedure]), or if (iii) they are bound by a professional secrecy obligation without being released from it, *e. g.*, when being a defence counsel (sec. 53 of the StPO [Code of Criminal Procedure]).

---

37 See, however, StPO [Code of Criminal Procedure], § 111 ¶ 2 ff. (F. R.G.) stipulating a so-called subsidiary confiscation *(Auffangrechtserwerb)* by the treasury under certain conditions.

38 PatG [Patent Act], § 142 ¶ 5 sent. 1 (F. R.G.); GebrMG [Utility Model Act], § 25 ¶ 5 sent. 1 (F. R.G.); GeschmMG [Design Act], § 51 ¶ 5 sent. 1 (F. R.G.); SortenschutzG [Plant Variety Protection Act], § 39 ¶ 5 sent. 1 (F. R.G.); HalblSchG [Semiconductor Protection Act], § 10 ¶ 5 (F. R.G.); MarkenG [Trademark Act], §§ 143 ¶ 5 sent. 1 and 143a ¶ 2 (F. R.G.); UrhG [Copyright Act], § 110 sent. 1 (F. R.G.).

39 See Strafvollstreckungsordnung [Criminal Enforcement Regulation], § 63 ¶ 1 sent. 2 (F. R.G.).

40 By contrast, police officers do not have the power to summon (with binding force for the addressee) suspects or witnesses.

e. Pre-trial Detention

Pursuant to sections 112 *et seq.* of the StPO [Code of Criminal Procedure], pre-trial detention may be ordered against a suspect if there is an urgent suspicion *(dringender Tatverdacht)* and a specific ground for arrest *(Haftgrund)*. Such specific ground for arrest exists if (i) the suspect has fled or is hiding or if there is a concrete risk that the suspect will do so *(Flucht/Fluchtgefahr)*, or if (ii) the suspect illegally influenced witnesses or tampered with evidence or if there is a concrete risk that the suspect will do so *(Verdunkelung/Verdunkelungsgefahr)*.

2. Requirements for the Initiation of Criminal Proceedings

The initiation of criminal investigations requires an initial suspicion of a criminal offence (see a.) and, in certain cases, a demand for prosecution (see b.).

a. Initial suspicion of a criminal offence

German public prosecutors can initiate criminal proceedings if there is an initial suspicion *(Anfangsverdacht)* of a criminal offence (sections 152 para. 2, 160 para. 1 of the StPO [Code of Criminal Procedure]). Such initial suspicion requires that, based upon concrete facts, it appears that a criminal offence may have been committed.[41]

Generally, the German criminal provisions regarding the infringement of intellectual property rights have the following common features:

- Criminal liability requires intent *(Vorsatz)*.[42] Negligence *(Fahrlässigkeit)* will not lead to criminal liability.
- Criminal liability does not require the consummation *(Vollendung)* of an offence. An attempt *(Versuch)* is sufficient to trigger criminal liability.[43]

---

41 *Meyer-Goßner*, StPO, § 152, No. 4.

42 StGB [Penal Code], § 15 (F. R.G.) stipulates that criminal liability requires intent unless criminal provisions specifically stipulate that also negligence leads to criminal liability. Such criminal liability for negligence is not stipulated by the following criminal provisions regarding infringements of intellectual property rights: PatG [Patent Act], § 142 (F. R.G.); GebrMG [Utility Model Act], § 25 (F. R.G.); GeschmMG [Design Act], § 51 (F. R.G.); SortenschutzG [Plant Variety Protection Act], § 39 (F. R.G.); HalblSchG [Semiconductor Protection Act], § 10 (F. R.G.); MarkenG [Trademark Act], §§ 143 ff. (F. R.G.); UrhG [Copyright Act], §§ 106 ff. (F. R.G.).

43 See the following provisions: PatG [Patent Act], § 142 ¶ 3 (F. R.G.); GebrMG [Utility Model Act], § 25 ¶ 3 (F. R.G.); GeschmMG [Design Act], § 51 ¶ 3 (F. R.G.); SortenschutzG [Plant Variety Protection Act], § 39 ¶ 3 (F. R.G.); HalblSchG [Semiconductor Protection Act], § 10 ¶ 3 (F. R.G.); MarkenG [Trademark Act], §§ 143 ¶ 3, 143a ¶ 2, 144 ¶ 3 (F. R.G.); UrhG [Copyright Act], §§ 106 ¶ 2, 107 ¶ 2, 108 ¶ 2, 108a ¶ 2 (F. R.G.).

Not only main perpetrators *(Täter)*[44] may be prosecuted, but also instigators *(Anstifter)*[45] or aiders and abettors *(Gehilfen)*.[46]

Furthermore, product piracy very often accompanies other criminal offences, such as fraud (*e. g.*, by selling counterfeit products as original products),[47] falsification of documents (*e. g.*, by producing accompanying documents allegedly authorised by the holder of the infringed intellectual property rights)[48] or criminal tax and customs offences.[49]

b. Demand for prosecution

If the offender does not act on a professional basis *(gewerbsmäßig)*,[50] the German criminal provisions regarding the infringement of intellectual property rights[51] generally stipulate that the public criminal prosecution of the offence requires either (i) that the injured person *(Verletzter)*[52] files a so-called demand for prosecution *(Strafantrag)*[53] or (ii) that the prosecutor specifically confirms that the case should be prosecuted *ex officio (von Amts wegen)* because of a special public interest *(besonderes öffentliches Interesse)*.[54] If the prosecutors initiate and conduct investigations in such cases where the offender

44 See StGB [Penal Code], § 25 (F. R.G.).

45 See StGB [Penal Code], § 26 (F. R.G.).

46 See StGB [Penal Code], § 27 (F. R.G.).

47 See StGB [Penal Code], § 263 (F. R.G.) *(Betrug)*.

48 See StGB [Penal Code], § 267 (F. R.G.) *(Urkundenfälschung)*.

49 See Abgabenordnung [Tax Code], §§ 369 ff. (F. R.G.).

50 Acting on a professional basis *(gewerbsmäßig)* requires that the offender acts repeatedly in order to generate income of considerable size and duration (see *Fischer*, StGB, before § 52, No. 62).

51 See the following provisions: PatG [Patent Act], § 142 ¶ 4 (F. R.G.); GebrMG [Utility Model Act], § 25 ¶ 4 (F. R.G.); GeschmMG [Design Act], § 51 ¶ 4 (F. R.G.); SortenschutzG [Plant Variety Protection Act], § 39 ¶ 4 (F. R.G.); HalblSchG [Semiconductor Protection Act], § 10 ¶ 4 (F. R.G.); MarkenG [Trademark Act], §§ 143 ¶ 4, 143a ¶ 2 (F. R.G.); UrhG [Copyright Act], § 106 (F. R.G.).

52 See StGB [Penal Code], § 77 (F. R.G.).

53 Pursuant to StPO [Code of Criminal Procedure], § 158 ¶ 1 (F. R.G.), a demand for prosecution can be filed (in written or in oral form) with (i) public prosecutor's offices, (ii) police authorities or (ii) local courts *(Amtsgericht)*. The most efficient way will, however, normally be to file a written criminal complaint with the competent public prosecutor's office, which contains an explicit demand for prosecution and a detailed and substantiated description of the suspected offence and the available evidence. The deadline for the demand for prosecution is three months following the expiration of the day on which the entitled person acquired both knowledge of the act and the identity of the perpetrator (StGB [Penal Code], § 77b ¶ para 1 and 2 (F. R.G.)).

54 Pursuant to Richtlinien für das Straf- und Bußgeldverfahren [RiStBV] [Guidelines for Criminal and Regulatory Proceedings], No. 86 ¶ 2 sent. 1 (F. R.G.), there is normally such special public interest if the offence is not only relevant for the injured person but for the general public. In product-piracy cases, this requirement may be met, *e. g.*, if there is a risk for public safety or health, see Richtlinien für das Straf- und Bußgeldverfahren [RiStBr] [Guidelines for Criminal and Regulatory Proceedings], No. 261a (F. R.G.).

does not act on a professional basis, they can later file an indictment with a criminal court only if there is a public interest *(öffentliches Interesse)*,[55] which is a less strict test than the afore-mentioned special-public-interest test.[56] If the prosecutors do not initiate investigations or do not file an indictment, the injured person can, theoretically, file a private criminal indictment *(Privatklage)*.[57]

3. Criminal and regulatory sanctions

Under German law, criminal offences, including criminal product-piracy offences, can only be committed by natural persons, but they may lead to criminal and regulatory sanctions not only against natural persons (see a.) but also against companies (see b.).

a. Sanctions against natural persons

Generally, the German criminal provisions regarding the infringement of intellectual property rights provide that the offender may be punished (i) by imprisonment *(Freiheitsstrafe)* of up to three years or by pecuniary penalty *(Geldstrafe)* or (ii), if the offender acts on a professional basis *(gewerbsmäßig)*,[58] by imprisonment of up to five years or by pecuniary penalty.[59] Furthermore, a criminal intellectual-property offence committed by an employee of a company may lead to liability of the employee's supervising managers for a regulatory offence of violation of supervisory duties *(ordnungswidrige Aufsichtspflichtverletzung)*. Such a regulatory offence of violation of supervisory duties may be punished by a regulatory fine *(Geldbuße)* of up to EUR 1 million,[60] or even higher if necessary to siphon-off excessive additional benefits obtained by the employee because of the offence (*e. g.*, bonuses).[61]

---

55 See StPO [Code of Criminal Procedure], § 376 (F. R.G.). Pursuant to RiStBV [Guidelines for Criminal and regulatory Proceedings], Nos. 261 ff. (F. R.G), relevant aspects are, in particular, the damage to the holder of the intellectual property rights concerned and profits of the offender.

56 See *Meyer-Goßner*, StPO, § 376, No. 3.

57 See StPO [Code of Criminal Procedure], § 374 ¶ 1 No. 8 (F. R.G.). This theoretical possibility is, however, almost never used in practice (see *Meyer-Goßner*, StPO, before § 374, No. 1), since the injured persons do not have the investigation powers of public prosecutors which are needed for an efficient preparation of an indictment.

58 As mentioned above, acting on a professional basis *(gewerbsmäßig)* requires that the offender acts repeatedly in order to generate income of considerable size and duration (see *Fischer*, StGB, before § 52, No. 62).

59 See the following provisions: PatG [Patent Act], § 142 ¶ 1 and 2 (F. R.G.); GebrMG [Utility Model Act], § 25 ¶ 1 and 2 (F. R.G.); GeschmMG [Design Act], § 51 ¶ 1 and 2 (F. R.G.); SortenschutzG [Plant Variety Protection Act], § 39 ¶ 1 and 2 (F. R.G.); HalblSchG [Semiconductor Protection Act], § 10 ¶ 1 and 2 (F. R.G.); MarkenG [Trademark Act], §§ 143 ¶ 1 and 2, 143a ¶ 1 and 2 (F. R.G.); UrhG [Copyright Act], §§ 106 ¶ 1, 107 ¶ 1, 108 ¶ 1, 108a ¶ 1 (F. R.G.).

60 See Ordnungswidrigkeitengesetz [OWiG] [Regulatory Offences Act], §§ 130, 9 (F. R.G.).

61 See OWiG [Regulatory Offences Act], § 17 ¶ 4 (F. R.G.).

b. Sanctions against companies

If certain senior managers of a company are involved in a criminal or regulatory offence,[62] the company itself may, under certain circumstances, be punished by a regulatory fine of up to EUR 1 million[63] or even higher if necessary to siphon-off higher profits generated by the offence (*e. g.*, by the sale of counterfeit products).[64]

4. Prosecution of product piracy on the EU level

While harmonisation of the EU member states' criminal-law measures protecting intellectual property rights is still to be realised,[65] product-piracy is already being combated on the EU level, in particular, by means of the European arrest warrant (see a.) and by European law enforcement units (see b.).

a. European arrest warrant

The EU framework decision regarding the European arrest warrant explicitly applies, *inter alia*, to cases of product piracy.[66] The European arrest warrant stipulates that each judicial authority of a member state recognises with a minimum of formalities requests for the surrender of a person made by the judicial authority of another member state.

b. European law enforcement units

The following EU law enforcement units have competencies to combat, *inter alia*, product piracy:

- Europol (the European Law Enforcement Organisation)[67] does not have powers to investigate criminal matters on its own, but assists the EU member states' law enforcement authorities to combat serious criminal offences (*e. g.*, by facilitating the exchange of information between member states or by providing expertise and tech-

---

62 Including, in particular, a regulatory offence of violation of supervisory duties *(ordnungswidrige Aufsichtspflichtverletzung)* pursuant to OWiG [Regulatory Offences Act], §§ 130, 9 (F. R.G.).

63 See OWiG [Regulatory Offences Act], § 30 ¶ 1 and 2 (F. R.G.).

64 See OWiG [Regulatory Offences Act], § 17 ¶ 4 (F. R.G.).

65 On 26 April 2006, the EU Commission issued a proposal for an EU Directive on criminal measures aiming at ensuring the enforcement of intellectual property rights' (COM (2006) 168 final). As per July 2008, the legislative process regarding this proposal had not been completed. Regarding the status see: http://ec.europa.eu/prelex/detail_dossier_real.cfm?CL=enDosId=193131.

66 See Art. 2 No. 2 of 2002/584/JHA: Council Framework Decision of 13 June 2002 on the European arrest warrant and the surrender procedures between Member States – Statements made by certain Member States on the adoption of the Framework Decision, Official Journal of the European Communities 2002 No L 190/1.

67 See: http://www.europol.europa.eu/.

nical support for investigations and operations carried out within the EU). It is competent to deal, *inter alia*, with product-piracy cases.[68] There is the possibility to set up, for a specific purpose and a limited time period, joint investigation teams[69] consisting of law enforcement officers from different member states and including Europol officers, if a criminal investigation requires coordinated action (*e. g.*, in cross-border product piracy cases).

- Eurojust (the EU's Judicial Cooperation Unit)[70] supports the coordination and cooperation between the member states criminal courts and prosecution authorities, in particular, by facilitating the execution of international mutual legal assistance and the implementation of extradition requests. It is also competent to deal, *inter alia*, with product-piracy cases.[71]
- OLAF (the European Anti-Fraud Office [*Office Européen de Lutte Anti-Fraude*])[72] has the task to protect the EU's financial interests by fighting fraud, corruption and any other irregular activity. OLAF's activities include the coordination of member states' customs operations regarding counterfeit products.

---

68 See Art. 2 No. 1 of the consolidated Europol Convention of 26 July 1995 in connection with the Annex (OJ C 316 of 27 November 1995 and OJ C 2 of 6 January 2004).

69 See: http://www.europol.europa.eu/index.asp?page=content_jit.

70 See: http://eurojust.europa.eu/.

71 This follows from Art. 4 ¶ 1 of 2002/187/JHA: Council Decision of 28 February 2002 setting up Eurojust with a view to reinforcing the fight against serious crime, Official Journal of the European Communities 2002 No L 63/1, stipulating that Eurojust is competent for all matters for which Europol is competent.

72 See: http://ec.europa.eu/anti_fraud/index_en.html.

Trademark Piracy

Diana Kaufmann

Imitating successful distinguishing marks of others has reached unparalleled levels in the past twenty years and is threatening to increase even further given growing brand awareness and the increasing appreciation of logos by customers. Trademark protected products are gaining more and more importance as objects of prestige, but are frequently not affordable for everyone. It is therefore not surprising that the overwhelming majority of the products confiscated by customs authorities every year involve counterfeit brand-name products.[1] In 2007, the majority of articles seized by customs across Europe (92%) infringed a Community or national trademark and covered a wide variety across all product sectors.[2] The largest category of goods seized at the German border in 2007 was leisure wear (20.96%), in addition to accessories (e. g. purses) (12.81% of the total goods that were seized) as well as watches and jewelry (15.23%). In terms of value, accessories were in the lead by far in 2007 with a total value of EUR 108,745,884, no less than EUR 391,589,061 in 2006, followed by sportswear (EUR 73,380,344 in 2007 and EUR 218,238,594 in 2006), then watches and jewelry (EUR 287,850,703 in 2006) and shoes (EUR 67,057,647 in 2007).[3] In 2006, the total value of trademark-infringing products seized in Germany came up to EUR 1,175,018,615.[4]

Trademark piracy may be defined as offering cheap goods which are copies of original products using an identical label with the consumers being aware of the piracy offence or at least accepting that such products may infringe trademark rights or, in other words, trademark piracy does not dependently require consumer belief that a product labeled

1 87% of the products that were seized at external German borders overall involved trademark infringements according to the 2007 annual statistics of the customs office, available at http://www.zoll.de/e0_downloads/f0_dont_show/zgr_jahresstatistik_2007.pdf.; no less than 90% of the products seized by the customs office in 2006 involved trademark infringements.

2 Information in accordance with the Report on Community Customs Activities on Counterfeit and Piracy, available at http://ec.europa.eu/taxation_customs/resources/documents/customs/customs_controls/counterfeit_piracy/statistics2007.pdf.

3 Information in accordance with the 2007 annual statistics of the customs office, available at http://www.zoll.de/e0_downloads/f0_dont_show/zgr_jahresstatistik_2007.pdf, and the *Jahresbericht 2006 Gewerblicher Rechtsschutz des Bundesministerium der Finanzen* [2006 Annual Report on Commercial Legal Protection of the Federal Ministry of Finances], available at http://www.zoll.de/e0_downloads/d0_veroeffentlichungen/v4_gwr_jahresbericht_2006.pdf.

4 Information in accordance with the *Jahresbericht 2006 Gewerblicher Rechtsschutz des Bundesministerium der Finanzen* [2006 Annual Report on Commercial Legal Protection of the Federal Ministry of Finances], available at http://www.zoll.de/e0_downloads/d0_veroeffentlichungen/v4_gwr_jahresbericht_2006.pdf.

with a brand actually comes from the trademark owner.[5] The risk associated with trademark piracy is a damage to the brand image, combined with a loss of market share and a discreditation of the quality statements associated with the brand.[6]

Strong awareness among companies of the need to develop strategies at a very early stage to protect their trademark rights and to also actually implement these has therefore gained importance.

I. Legal Requirements for Trademark Protection under the German Trademark Act

A. Scope of Protection

In Germany, the protection of trademarks, business designations and indications of geographic origin is governed by the Markengesetz [MarkenG] [Trademark Act] (F. R.G.) which summarises them under the generic term of "marks".[7] In addition to corporate trademarks, titles of works are also considered business designations.

Section 3 MarkenG [Trademark Act] sets out the basic requirements for trademarks. It is essential for the mark to be capable of distinguishing goods or services of different companies from one another. Trademarks enable customers to distinguish products of a certain company from those of other companies. Further to the origin-related function of trademarks, a quality function is also attached to a trademark. Frequently, consumers associate certain quality expectations with a trademark. The latter constitutes a particular incentive for product pirates who attempt to exploit for themselves the good reputation of a trademark for their own purposes by deceiving consumers, i. e. they make them think the product comes from a certain – frequently prestigious – company by using identical or similar marks.

In general, any symbols, especially words including the names of persons, illustrations, letters, numbers, sound marks, three-dimensional structures including the form of a product or its packaging, as well as other presentations including colours or colour combinations, can be protected as trademarks. Only signs which consist exclusively of a shape (i) which results from the nature of the goods themselves; (ii) which is necessary to obtain a technical result; or (iii) which gives substantial value to the good are not capable of being protected as trademarks.[8]

5 *Fezer*, Markenrecht, § 14, No. 75.

6 *Fezer*, Markenrecht, § 14, No. 72.

7 MarkenG [Trademark Act] § 1 (F. R.G.).

8 MarkenG [Trademark Act] § 3 ¶ 2 (F. R.G.).

1. Trademarks

a. Words, Slogans and Letters

Words are capable of being protected as trademarks, to start with, according to the MarkenG [Trademark Act], regardless of whether German words, foreign words or purely made-up or fanciful words are involved, provided they are distinctive overall for some product or service.[9] As an example, the word "auto" may be distinctive for a product that has nothing to do with motor vehicles,[10] but it would not be capable of protection for motor vehicles.

Furthermore, entire sentences are also capable of being protected as trademarks. That is why advertising slogans are increasingly being protected as trademarks (e. g. *Partner with the Best*).[11] Whether the advertising slogan merely describes the product or whether it is distinctive (even only slightly) is decisive in determining if the slogan can be protected.[12] A lack of distinctiveness is assumed in the case of longer texts, for example.[13] The ability of so-called event marks to be protected is also largely rejected if they merely consist of a description of the event, for instance the designation "*FUSSBALL WM 2006*" [2006 SOCCER WORLD CUP], or of services associated with the event. This is owed to the need to keep purely functional information of that type available for public use.[14]

Letters are capable of serving as trademarks as a general principle, both in the form of individual letters[15] and in the form of a combination of letters,[16] regardless of whether they can be pronounced or not. However, a lower level of distinctiveness, and therefore a lesser degree of protection, may result depending on the design in individual cases.

9 *Ingerl/Rohnke*, Markengesetz, § 3, No. 26.

10 *Ingerl/Rohnke*, Markengesetz, § 3, No. 26.

11 8 December 1999 BGH [Federal Supreme Court] [I ZB 21/97], MarkenR 2000, 50 (Partner with the Best); 8 December 1999 BGH [Federal Supreme Court] [1 ZB 2/97], GRUR 2000, 321, 322 (Radio von hier); also see 10 February 2000 BGH [Federal Supreme Court] [I ZB 37/97], GRUR 2000, 720, 721 f. (Unter Uns).

12 21 October 2004 ECJ [C-64/02 P], GRUR Int 2005, 224, 226 (The Principle of Convenience); *Fuchs-Wissmann*, Neuere Entwicklungen in der markenrechtlichen Rechtsprechung des Bundespatentgerichts und des Bundesgerichtshofs, MarkenR 2008, 1, 5.

13 *Ingerl/Rohnke*, Markengesetz, § 3, No. 26.

14 27 April 2006 BGH [Federal Supreme Court] [I ZB 96/05], GRUR 2006, 850, 853 (FUSSBALL WM 2006).

15 15 June 2000 BGH [Federal Supreme Court] [1 ZB 4/98], GRUR 2001, 161 (Buchstabe K); 19 December 2002 BGH [Federal Supreme Court] [I ZB 21/00], GRUR 2003, 343, 344 (Buchstabe Z); 8 December 2006 OHIM [R 394/2006-I], GRUR 2007, 429 (Buchstabe E).

16 5 October 2000 BGH [Federal Supreme Court] [I ZR 166/98], GRUR 2001, 344, 345 (DB Immobilienfonds).

b. Numbers

Numbers and number combinations, like letters, may also be protected as a general rule.[17] The German Federal Supreme Court *(Bundesgerichtshof)* has even regarded single-digit numbers as protectable.[18]

c. Names of Persons

Names of persons may further be protected as trademarks. There is a danger when registering a name as a trademark, though, that a person with that name will require cancellation of the trademark due to his or her own name rights.[19] A final decision has not yet been rendered in German case law as to whether so-called everyday names should be rejected as marks.[20] This risk of rejection can be prevented by adding the first name to a last name, provided that the first name itself is not also very common.

d. Illustrations

Illustrations of all types may be protected as trademarks, regardless of whether they are black and white or coloured.[21] Pictures, logos and lettering of all types can be protected, especially in a combination as a word mark/picture (device) mark. Having a trademark registered in black and white also bears the advantage that it is protected against any reproduction in colour.

e. Sound Marks

Sound marks can consist of melodies or other sounds or noises.[22] As an example, protecting a jingle of a company used for advertising purposes is not only possible but also very popular.[23] The authorisation of sound and noise marks was confirmed by the ECJ (European Court of Justice)[24] and the OHIM (Office of Harmonization for the Internal

---

17 9 February 1995 BGH [Federal Supreme Court] [I ZB 21/92], GRUR 1997, 366, 367 (quattro II); 20 October 1999 BGH [Federal Supreme Court] [I ZR 110/97], GRUR 2000, 608, 610 (ARD-1); 18 April 2002 BGH [Federal Supreme Court] [I ZB 23/99], GRUR 2002, 970, 971 (Zahl „1“).

18 18 April 2002 BGH [Federal Supreme Court] [I ZB 22/99], GRUR 2002, 970, 971 (Zahl „1“); 18 April 2002 BGH [Federal Supreme Court] [I ZB 22/99], MittdPA 2002, 423, 424 (Zahl „6“).

19 MarkenG [Trademark Act], § 13 ¶ 2 No. 1 in combination with § 51 ¶ 1 (F. R.G.).

20 On this note: *Erdmann/Rohjahn/Sosnitza*, Handbuch des Fachanwalts Gewerblicher Rechtsschutz, chapter 5. B. No. 583; different view: *Ingerl/Rohnke*, Markengesetz, § 5, No. 37.

21 Cf. e. g. 5 April 2001 BGH [Federal Supreme Court] [I ZR 168/98], GRUR 2002, 171, 175 (Marlboro-Dach); *Lange*, Marken- und Kennzeichenrecht, § 3, No. 259.

22 *Lewalter*, Akustische Marken – Anmerkung zu EuGH “Shield Mark/Kist” und HABM “Roar of a Lion” und “HEXAL”, GRUR 2006, 546.

23 Cf. e. g. 10 July 1996 BPatG [Federal Patent Court] [29 W (pat) 68/96], GRUR 1997, 60 (SWF-3-Nachrichten).

Market).[25] It can be inferred from the registration practice of the OHIM that different requirements apply depending on the national background against which a registration of a sound mark is applied for.[26] There is agreement, though, that the reproduction of the sound on CD, DVD, cassette, disk or MP3 can be included when applying for the registration of the relevant mark.[27]

Sound marks must be protectable in the abstract as well as distinctive. Furthermore, they have to be capable of being graphically portrayed (sec. 8, para. 1 MarkenG [Trademark Act]). Section 11, para. 2 Markenverordnung [MarkenVO] [Trademark Regulation] (F. R.G.)[28] specifies that the graphic presentation must be provided in the customary musical notation after the ECJ found that the graphic presentation could be provided with the aid of figures, lines or characters if it was clear, unambiguous, easily accessible and understandable.[29] Since then the German Patent and Trademark Office no longer accepts that sound marks be presented by means of a sonogram. Thus, the ability to register sound marks of a non-musical nature, such as noises in particular, could be problematic (e. g. the roaring of a lion or a whooshing waterfall). The only way to obtain protection of sound marks that cannot be described by using the customary musical notation may be via acquiring secondary meaning *(Verkehrsgeltung)*. See comprehensive information on trademarks having acquired secondary meaning under I. B. 2.

f. Three-Dimensional Structures

Three-dimensional structures are likewise capable of being protected. Both the form of a product[30] or its packaging[31] and imaginary forms are capable of being protected ("Emily", for instance, Rolls Royce's famous hood ornament). An exception applies to symbols with a shape that is exclusively determined by the type of product itself (cf. sec. 3, para. 2, No. 1 MarkenG [Trademark Act]), symbols having a shape that is necessary to achieve a technical effect (cf. sec. 3, para. 2, No. 2 MarkenG) [Trademark Act] or symbols which consist exclusively of a shape which gives substantial value to the goods (cf. sec. 3, para. 2, No. 2 MarkenG) [Trademark Act]. According to sec. 9, para. 2 MarkenVO [Trademark Regulation], a two-dimensional illustration of the symbol of either pho-

---

24 27 November 2003 ECJ [C-283/01], GRUR 2004, 54 f. (Shield Mark/Kist).

25 25 August 2003 HABM [OHIM] [R 781/1999-4], GRUR 2003, 1054 (Roar of a Lion); 8 Sepember 2005 HABM, [OHIM] [R 295/05-4] GRUR 2006, 343 (Arzneimittel Ihres Vertrauens).

26 Representative *Schmitz*, Zur grafischen Darstellbarkeit von Hörmarken: EuGH contra Freiheit des markenrechtlichen Schutzes?, GRUR 2007, 290, 291 f.

27 *Becker*, Kennzeichenschutz der Hörmarke, WRP 2000, 56, 57; *Schmitz*, Zur grafischen Darstellbarkeit von Hörmarken: EuGH contra Freiheit des markenrechtlichen Schutzes?, GRUR 2007, 290, 291.

28 Regulation of May 11, 2004 to implement the German Trademark Act.

29 27 November 2003 ECJ [C-283/01], GRUR 2004, 54, 58 (Shield Mark/Kist).

30 8 April 2003 ECJ [C-53/01 to C-55/01], GRUR 2003, 514, 517 (Linde/Winward/Rado).

31 cf. 12 February 2004 ECJ [C-218/01], GRUR 2004, 428, 430 (Henkel); *Lange*, Marken- und Kennzeichenrecht, § 3, No. 263.

tographs or graphical line drawings must be included when registering three-dimensional trademarks. Considering the ECJ decision in *Philips Remington*[32] it must be stated, however, that German case law in general increasingly rejects technical forms according to sec. 3, para. 2 MarkenG [Trademark Act]. The reason for this is that it should not be possible to circumvent the maximum period of protection for technical property rights such as patents and utility models by having a three-dimensional trademark registered.

g. Colour Marks

Colour combinations without contours are not capable of trademark protection in the abstract. Protection for a colour combination requires submission of a description of the specific usage, i. e., how the colour appears in combination with the product.[33] In addition, the colour combination must be suitable for distinguishing products or services of the registrant from those of other companies. Trademark protection may also be requested for a more general colour category, provided there is no absolute block to protection, i. e., the colour category does not have to be kept available for public use.[34]

h. Other Presentations

"Presentation" *(Aufmachung)* is understood to mean any other product accessories, e. g. individual, recurring design elements in business stationary or the presentation/design of business premises (in most cases a shop).[35] So-called position marks (i. e., protection for a specific method of attaching or arranging a symbol on a product) are also covered by this category.[36]

i. Scent Marks

Scent marks may be protected, again, provided that they are distinctive.[37] Scent marks are not readily amenable to graphic presentation. Whereas the ECJ presumes that a scent mark described by the words "*odeur de fraise mure*" (scent of a ripe strawberry) is

---

32 18 June 2002 ECJ [C-299/99], GRUR Int 2002, 842 (Philips ./. Remington).

33 24 June 2004 ECJ [C-49/02], GRUR 2004, 858, 859 (Heidelberger Bauchemie GmbH); 5 October 2006 BGH [Federal Supreme Court] [I ZB 86/05], GRUR 2007, 55, 56 (Farbmarke gelb/grün II).

34 10 December 1998 BGH [Federal Supreme Court] [I ZB 20/98], GRUR 1999, 491 (Farbmarke gelb/schwarz); 19 September 2001 BGH [Federal Supreme Court] [I ZB 3/99], GRUR 2002, 427, 429 (Farbmarke gelb/grün).

35 *Ingerl/Rohnke*, Markengesetz, § 3, No. 35.

36 *Fezer*, Markenrecht, § 3, No. 294a.

37 12 December 2002 ECJ [C-273/00], GRUR 2003, 145, 147 (Sieckmann Smell Mark); 27 October 2005 ECJ [T-305/04], GRUR 2006, 327, 328 (Scent of a Ripe Strawberry); order to refer the case to another authority/court 14 April 2000 BPatG [Federal Patent Court] [33 W (pat) 193/99], GRUR 2000, 1044, 1046 (Riechmarke).

prohibited by the absolute registration block of Art. 7, para. 1 lit. a) of the Community Trademark Regulation (Council Regulation (EC) No. 40/94 of 20 December 1993 on the Community trademark) precisely because there is no graphic portrayal in the sense of Art. 4 of the Community Trademark Regulation,[38] the OHIM assumes that pure descriptions of scents may be sufficiently capable of graphical representation.[39] The practice of the OHIM will most likely be discontinued due to the ECJ ruling, however.

j. Other Forms

All other conceivable trademark forms such as touch marks,[40] taste marks and movement marks[41] are also permissible based on the non-exhaustive nature of sec. 3 MarkenG [Trademark Act].

2. Company Symbols

Company symbols are protected as business designations *(geschäftliche Bezeichnungen)* in accordance with sec. 5, para. 1 MarkenG [Trademark Act]. According to sec. 5, para. 2 MarkenG [Trademark Act], company symbols are symbols that are used as a name, company name or special designation of a business operation or enterprise in business relations. Provided that secondary meaning has been acquired, business signs and other symbols intended to distinguish a business enterprise from other business enterprises may be included.[42]

3. Titles of Work

Section 5, para. 3 MarkenG [Trademark Act] includes the names or special designations of documents, films, sound works, stage works or other comparable works among the titles of works that are likewise protected as business designations. Since the content of a creative work is frequently described by short and pithy titles that often have a descriptive character,[43] title protection may also be permissible in cases where trade-

---

38 27 October 2005 ECJ [T-305/04], GRUR 2006, 327, 328 (Scent of a Ripe Strawberry).

39 For instance according to 5 December 2001 OHIM [R 711/1999-3], GRUR 2002, 348 (The Scent of Raspberries); 11 February 2002 OHIM [R 156/1998-2], IIC 1999, 308, 309 (The Smell of Fresh Cut Grass).

40 5 October 2006 BGH [Federal Supreme Court] [I ZB 76/05], GRUR 2007, 148, 149 f. (Tastmarke).

41 With regard to the question of a movement mark, see 25 November 1999 OLG [Higher Regional Court] Frankfurt am Main [6 U 189/98], GRUR 2000, 1063, 1066 (SPEE-Fuchs) (answered in the negative there).

42 *Harte-Bavendamm*, Handbuch der Markenpiraterie in Europa, § 5, No. 26 under the reference to logos, advertising slogans or "corporate colors" of a company; for further details on secondary meaning cf. below under I. B. 2.

43 9 September 2004 OLG [Higher Regional Court] München [29 U 3870/03], MarkenR 2005, 149, 151 (Focus Money/Mon€y Spezialist).

mark registration would not be available.[44] Another example that is significant in practice – and also specifically a target of trademark pirates – involves the names of computer programs.[45]

4. Indications of Geographic Origin

In addition to classically pirated goods, food is increasingly targeted by counterfeiters, too. Whereas food with a value of around EUR 80,000 was seized by the German customs office in 2004, food confiscated by the customs office in 2006 already had a total value of EUR 305,928.[46]

According to sec. 126, para. 1 MarkenG [Trademark Act], the names of places, areas, regions, states and other information or symbols that are used in commerce to identify the geographic origin of goods or services, and food in particular, are protected within the general category of "indications of geographic origin" (*Geographische Herkunfsangaben*). Examples of indications of geographic origin are Baden wine, Thüringer grilled sausage, Spreewälder pickles, Lübeck marzipan, French cognac or champagne. Only purely generic descriptions are excluded from this protection. Names or symbols that contain indications of the geographic origin or that are derived from indications of that type, but have lost their original meaning and serve as a name for goods or services or as designations or indications regarding the type, composition, grade or other characteristics or features of goods or services, are excluded.

Section 127 MarkenG [Trademark Act] differentiates between simple and qualified origin indications. Section 127, para. 1 MarkenG [Trademark Act] protects the market's expectations regarding an origin from a certain geographic area without considering any quality associations with the area. Section 127, para. 2 MarkenG [Trademark Act], in contrast, governs qualified indications of geographic origin. Here, it is intended that indications of geographic origin with special characteristics or special quality will only be permitted if the relevant goods or services actually show such special characteristics or quality. Thus, market expectations of a special quality for products originating from a particular geographic area are protected. Finally, cases where an indication of geographic origin has a special reputation, with the consequence that the indication may not be used for goods or services of a different origin, are covered by sec. 127, para. 3 MarkenG [Trademark Act] (aspect of the exploitation of the reputation of such goods).[47]

---

[44] *Ingerl/Rohnke*, Markengesetz, § 5, No. 88 with a reference to 7 May 1997 BPatG [Federal Patent Court] [29 W (pat) 122/96], BPatGE 38, 138 (Klassentreffen).

[45] 24 April 1997 BGH [Federal Supreme Court] [I ZR 44/95], GRUR 1998, 155 ff (PowerPoint); 24 April 1997 BGH [Federal Supreme Court] [I ZR 233/94], GRUR 1997, 902 ff. (FTOS); Cf. 27 April 2006 BGH [Federal Supreme Court] [I ZR 109/03], GRUR 2006, 594, 595 (SmartKey).

[46] 2007 Annual Statistics of the Customs Office, available at http://www.zoll.de/e0_downloads/f0_dont_show/zgr_jahresstatistik_2007.pdf.

[47] 17 January 2002 BGH [Federal Supreme Court] [I ZR 290/99], GRUR 2002, 426, 427 (Champagner bekommen, Sekt bezahlen).

Details on the protection of indications of geographic origin on a European level are also set out in Regulation (EC) 510/2006 (Council Regulation (EC) No 510/2006 of 20 March 2006 on the protection of geographical indications and designations of origin for agricultural products and foodstuffs).[48] Whereas Regulation (EC) 510/2006 prevails over the national regulations in the case of qualified origin indications, protection according to national trademark law governs cases of simple indications of geographic origin.[49]

B. Creation of Trademark Protection

In addition to the registration of a trademark, trademark protection can also be created by acquiring secondary meaning *(Verkehrsgeltung)*. Furthermore, famous trademarks are protected in a quite different way.

1. Registration

There are three different systems for registering trademark rights: National trademark registrations, Community trademark (CTM) registrations (also referred to as EU trademarks) and international trademark registrations (IR trademarks). Applications for trademark registrations have to be filed with the German Patent and Trademark Office (DPMA) for German trademarks and IR trademarks (which are then registered with the WIPO (World Intellectual Property Organization) in Geneva) and with the OHIM (Office of Harmonization for the Internal Market) in Alicante (Spain) for EU trademarks.[50] An application is only rejected if absolute registration bars apply.[51] Otherwise, the trademark is registered and published in the trademark gazette of the respective trademark office. Once the trademark registration (respectively the trademark application in case of CTM) has been published, owners of earlier trademark registrations can file an opposition against the registration of the new trademark within a period of three months. Other than the mere application of a trademark (which, however, constitutes priority

---

48 ABl. EU No. L 93, p.12.

49 With regard to the preceding Council Regulation (EEC) No 2081/92 of 14 July 1992 on the protection of geographical indications and designations of origin for agricultural products and foodstuffs, Official Journal of the European Communities 1992 No L 208/1 cf. *Ingerl/Rohnke*, Markengesetz, before §§ 130-136, No. 2.

50 Whereby it has to be noted that an application for an EU trademark can also be filed with the German Patent and Trademark Office, which then forwards it to the OHIM; for details see below under I. B.1.b.

51 For further details regarding absolute registration bars and the relevant regulations contained in the MarkenG [Trademark Act] (F. R.G.), cf. below under I. B.1.a.; the regulations as to absolute registration bars on an EU or international level can be found in Art. 7 ¶ 1 Community Trademark Regulation and in Art. 6quater Paris Convention (Paris Convention for the Protection of Industrial Property of 20 March 1883), which, however, are extensively identical to the provisions as set forth in the MarkenG [Trademark Act] (F. R.G.).

of a trademark), the registration of a trademark entitles the trademark owner to enforce his trademark rights vis-à-vis infringing parties.

a. German Trademarks

In Germany, national trademark protection is granted in accordance with sec. 4, No. 1 MarkenG [Trademark Act] by registering a symbol as a trademark in the register maintained by the German Patent and Trademark Office.[52] The period of protection of a German trademark begins on the day of registration[53] and lasts for ten years.[54] The registration may be renewed for subsequent ten year periods.

A trademark cannot be registered if any absolute registration bars apply. Absolute registration bars apply to trademarks which are identical to famous trademarks[55] or which are not capable of trademark protection according to sec. 3 para. 2 MarkenG [Trademark Act].[56] Additionally, absolute bars impede trademarks from being registered if they (i) entirely lack a distinctive character;[57] (ii) consist exclusively of symbols or indications that only describe the type, composition, quantity, value of the geographic origin or other characteristics of the goods or services;[58] or (iii) have become generic for describing the goods or services that characterise them,[59] to name the most important cases of sec. 8 MarkenG [Trademark Act].

An exception from these principles only applies to trademarks that have acquired distinctiveness in the relevant fields of trade *(Verkehrsdurchsetzung)*.[60] Whether distinctiveness has been acquired in the market, and, more importantly, whether such distinctiveness is accepted by the German Patent and Trademark Office when registering a trademark, may be determined on a case-by-case basis. Considerations include the market share of products protected by the trademark, sales volumes, frequency and type of use and/or marketing measures, the geographic coverage and finally the period of time the trademark has been used etc.[61] Distinctiveness is frequently determined in practice through survey reports. Consumer opinion polls on the familiarity with a trademark as

---

52 Online database of the German Patent and Trademark Office are available at https://dpinfo.dpma.de.

53 MarkenG [Trademark Act] § 33 ¶ 1 (F. R.G.).

54 MarkenG [Trademark Act] § 47 (F. R.G.).

55 MarkenG [Trademark Act] § 4 No. 3 (F. R.G.).

56 Cf. for details in this respect above under I. A.

57 MarkenG [Trademark Act] § 8 ¶ 2 No. 1 (F. R.G.); Cf. e. g. 1 March 2001 BGH [Federal Supreme Court] [I ZB 42/98], GRUR 2001, 1151, 1152 (marktfrisch).

58 MarkenG [Trademark Act] § 8 ¶ 2 No. "(F. R.G.); Cf. e. g. 17 July 2003 BGH [Federal Supreme Court] [I ZB 10/01], GRUR 2003, 882, 883 (Lichtenstein); 9 January 2001 BpatG [Federal Patent Court] [33 W (pat) 185/00], GRUR 2001, 509 (EUROTAX).

59 MarkenG [Trademark Act] § 8 ¶ 2 No. 3 (F. R.G.).

60 MarkenG [Trademark Act] § 8 ¶ 3 (F. R.G.).

61 Cf. e. g. 4 May 1999 ECJ [C-108 and 109/97], GRUR 1999, 723 (Chiemsee); 22 June 2006 ECJ [C-25/05 P], GRUR 2006, 1022 (Wicklerform).

an indication of a company origin are also permitted.[62] There is no set minimum that defines when a mark has achieved "distinctiveness". It can reasonably be assumed, however, that distinctiveness among fewer than 50% consumers to which the product or service is offered in general is not sufficient.[63]

Finally, German law contains the principle of compulsory commercial use, similar to Community trademark law. According to this principle, a trademark owner must actually use the trademark as registered, or in a slightly modified form, provided that the descriptive character of the trademark is retained. The use must begin within a grace period of five years starting from the date of registration, or if the use of the trademark was discontinued, from the date such use discontinued. Using the trademark is necessary in order to be able to effectively enforce the trademark rights vis-à-vis third parties[64] and in order to prevent the trademark from being declared void due to forfeiture.[65] Usage can be asserted in trial, for instance, through advertising material (from print media, TV spots, radio advertising) which has been used in commercial activities prior to the expiration of the five-year period.

b. Community Trademarks

In addition to having a trademark entered in the German trademark register, a Community mark may be registered with the OHIM. Protection can be obtained in all of the Member States of the European Community simultaneously with the single registration of a Community trademark. Its procedural and substantive requirements are governed by the Community Trademark Regulation.[66] The registration of a Community trademark causes substantially lower costs than the registration of several separate national trademarks. It is not possible, however, to limit the trademark to individual Member States. If this is desired, one would instead apply for individual national trademark registrations. An inherent risk with Community trademarks is that rejection or cancellation of a Community trademark in a single Member State has a mandatory parallel effect on the entire Community. However, in such cases the applicant or proprietor of a Community trademark may request the conversion of his Community trademark into a national trademark application but should consider the additional costs. In doing so, the national trademark application may then be based – in respect of the Member State concerned – on the date of the filing or the date of priority of that application or trademark and, where appropriate, the seniority of a trademark of that State claimed under Art. 34 or 35 Community Trademark Regulation.[67]

62 4 May 1999 ECJ [C-108 and 109/97], GRUR 1999, 723 (Chiemsee).

63 Cf. as far as this is concerned 19 January 2006 BGH [Federal Supreme Court] [I ZB 11/04], WRP 2006, 1130, 1132 f. (Lotto).

64 MarkenG [Trademark Act] §§ 25, 26 (F. R.G.).

65 MarkenG [Trademark Act] § 49 ¶ 1 (F. R.G.).

66 Council Regulation (EC) No. 40/94 of 20 December 1993 on the Community trademark.

67 Art. 108 Community Trademark Regulation.

The application for the registration of a Community trademark is either submitted directly to the OHIM or to the authorities of the Member States, thus, in Germany to the German Patent and Trademark Office.[68] In the latter case, the date of submission to the German Patent and Trademark Office, who is required to forward the application to the OHIM within two weeks, is decisive.[69] Registrations that are received by the OHIM more than two months after they are submitted are deemed to have been submitted on the date the application was received by the OHIM, though.[70] To avoid such a delay, it is therefore advisable to directly submit the application to the OHIM. When applying for a Community trademark, both the priority of an earlier national trademark registration in a Member State (if the registration was within a period of six months from the date of filing of the first application)[71] (so-called priority) and the date of registration of an earlier national trademark (limited to the respective Member State)[72] (so-called seniority) can be claimed, provided that the goods and services of the national trademark and the Community trademark are identical. Thus, when there is a later registration of a Community trademark, a national trademark registration is dispensable, without simultaneously giving up the national priority date. The period of protection of a Community trademark is ten years, and may be renewed for subsequent ten year periods.[73]

A Community trademark is not subject to a challenge of failure to use if the Community trademark was actually used within five years of registration in at least one Member State.[74]

c. Internationally Registered Trademarks

International registration of trademarks (IR trademarks) is governed by the MMA (Madrid Agreement Concerning the International Registration of Marks) and the Protocol Relating to the Madrid Agreement Concerning the International Registration of Marks.[75] The register for IR trademarks is maintained by the WIPO. With an international trademark registration, protection can be claimed in the countries of the MMA[76]

---

68 Art. 25 ¶ 1 lit. b) Community Trademark Regulation; MarkenG [Trademark Act] § 125 lit. a) (F. R.G.).

69 Art. 29 Community Trademark Regulation.

70 Art. 25 ¶ 3 Community Trademark Regulation.

71 Art. 29 Community Trademark Regulation.

72 Art. 34 Community Trademark Regulation.

73 Articles 46 and 47 Community Trademark Regulation.

74 Art. 15 ¶ 1 Community Trademark Regulation.

75 In addition, regulations on IR trademarks can be found in MarkenG [Trademark Act], §§ 107-125 (F. R.G.).

76 Egypt, Albania, Algeria, Armenia, Azerbaijan, Benelux countries (Belgium, Luxemburg, Netherlands), Bhutan, Bosnia-Herzegovina, Botswana, Bulgaria, China, Germany, France, Iran, Italy, Yugoslavia (Serbia and Montenegro), Kazakhstan, Kenya, Kyrgyzstan, Korea (Democratic People's Republic), Croatia, Cuba, Lesotho, Latvia, Liberia, Liechtenstein, Morocco, Macedonia, Moldavia, Monaco, Mongolia, Mozambique, Namibia, Austria, Poland, Portugal, Rumania, Russian Federation, San Marino, Switzerland, Sierra Leone, Slovakia, Slovenia, Spain, Sudan, Swa-

or in the countries that joined the Protocol Relating to the MMA.[77] The international registration application of WIPO[78] is to be submitted to the German Patent and Trademark Office.[79] International trademark registration requires a basis trademark registration in a Member State under the MMA. Under the Protocol Relating to the MMA even a basis trademark application in a Member State is sufficient. The priority of an earlier trademark registration in a Member State can be claimed for the application, provided it is not more than six months before the international filing date.[80]

Unlike a Community trademark, an international trademark involves a "bundle of individual protective rights", i. e. the respective national government agencies decide on the registration capability and maintenance of the trademark in the respective country in which the international trademark is covered. An international trademark must not be used in a way that jeopardises the rights of the national regulations in any country where it seeks protection.

IR trademarks must further refer to the basis trademark for a period of five years. In the event the basis trademark is cancelled during such period, the international trademark registration will simultaneously be cancelled. The period of protection for an IR trademark according to the MMA is twenty years, but only ten years according to the Protocol Relating to the MMA, each with the possibility of arbitrary subsequent renewals. It is also possible to subsequently extend the geographic scope of protection to additional MMA member states.

Protection should be extended to those countries where the goods are produced, so as to effectively combat product piracy.[81] People are frequently confronted with the practical problem wanting to avoid the rejection of a Community trademark – even if only due to a rejection in one Member State. The obvious solution is to apply for international trademarks in parallel to an application for a Community trademark to obtain protection in the countries of the EU that are important to the applicant. In the event of a

---

ziland, Syria, Tadzhikistan, Czech Republic, Ukraine, Hungary, Uzbekistan, Vietnam, Belarus, Cyprus.

77 Albania, Antigua and Barbuda, Armenia, Azerbaijan, Australia, Bahrain, Benelux countries (Belgium, Luxemburg, Netherlands), Bhutan, Botswana, Bulgaria, China, Denmark, Germany, Estonia, European Community, Finland, France, Ghana, Georgia, Greece, Great Britain, Iran, Ireland, Iceland, Italy, Japan, Yugoslavia (Serbia and Montenegro), Kenya, Kyrgyzstan, Korea (Democratic People's Republic), Korea (Republic), Croatia, Cuba, Lesotho, Liechtenstein, Latvia, Lithuania, Madagascar, Morocco, Macedonia, Moldavia, Monaco, Mongolia, Mozambique, Namibia, Dutch Antilles, Norway, Austria, Oman, Poland, Portugal, Rumania, Russian Federation, San Marino, Zambia, Sweden, Switzerland, Sierra Leone, Singapore, Slovakia, Slovenia, Spain, Swaziland, Syria, Czech Republic, Turkey, Turkmenistan, Ukraine, Hungary, Uzbekistan, USA, Belarus, Cyprus, Vietnam.

78 The form is available at www.wipo.int.

79 MarkenG [Trademark Act] § 108 (F. R.G.).

80 Cf. Art. 4 of the Paris Convention for the Protection of Industrial Property of March 20, 1883.

81 *Welser/González*, Marken- und Produktpiraterie, No. 77 pointing out that China, for example, joined the MMA in 1989 and joined the Protocol Relating to the MMA in 1995.

rejection of the Community trademark application, one is at least certain to retain protection in individual countries through the international trademark application, even though it is more expensive.

2. Trademark Protection through Usage/Secondary Meaning

In addition to registering a trademark, it is also possible under German trademark law to obtain trademark protection solely through commercial use of the mark. According to sec. 4, No. 2 MarkenG [Trademark Act], a mark is protected when its use has led to secondary meaning *(Verkehrsgeltung)* within the related (domestic) fields of trade. The trademark's priority is determined by the time it has acquired secondary meaning through use. Secondary meaning is assumed if a considerable portion of the relevant adressees involved understands the trademark as indication to distinguish the goods or services of one company from the goods and services of different origin. Thus, acquiring secondary meaning is different from beginning to use the mark and the mere act of starting to use the symbol leads to neither trademark protection nor a right resulting from prior use.[82] The relevant addressees among which the secondary meaning must be achieved are, in principle, all those for the economic decision of whom the (distinctive) designation is of importance. In addition to end customers, these also include dealers and resellers.[83]

In practice, secondary meaning is verified by obtaining a market use or survey report. No set percentage defines when secondary meaning has been acquired. Instead, each case is evaluated separately, taking all of the circumstances into consideration. Consumer familiarity with the trademark or the advertising expenses for the trademark could therefore be considered, for instance. Examples from German case law indicate that a distinctiveness level of 20% was sufficient for a symbol that could be easily distinguished and for which there was no special need to keep it available for the public,[84] whereas in a different case 52.1% was held to be insufficient.[85] Secondary meaning recognition of more than 50% is generally required particularly in the case of descriptive symbols and symbols for which there is a need to keep them available for public use.

It is advisable in practice to apply for registration as early as possible, since registration can be proven much easier than secondary meaning when there is a dispute.

---

[82] 9 October 1997 BGH [Federal Supreme Court] [I ZR 95/95], GRUR 1998, 412, 414 (Analgin); 19 August 1998 OLG [Higher Regional Court] München [29 W 1532/98], NJW-WettbR 1999, 156 (Rialto-Heizkörper).

[83] cf. 12 March 1969 BGH [Federal Supreme Court] [I ZR 32/67], GRUR 1969, 681, 682 (Kochendwassergerät); *Ingerl/Rohnke*, Markengesetz, § 4, No. 18.

[84] 16 October 1959 BGH [Federal Supreme Court] [I ZR 90/58], GRUR 1960, 130, 133 (Sunpearl II); 3 May 1963 BGH [Federal Supreme Court] [Ib ZR 119/61], GRUR 1963, 622, 623 (Sunkist).

[85] 8 March 1990 BGH [Federal Supreme Court] [I ZR 65/88], GRUR 1990, 681, 683 (Schwarzer Krauser).

3. Famous Trademarks

According to sec. 4 No. 3 MarkenG [Trademark Act], the well-known nature of a trademark alone under Article 6bis of the Paris Convention (Paris Convention for the Protection of Industrial Property of 20 March 1883) establishes trademark protection. The regulation, as a practical matter, impacts only foreign trademarks that are not used domestically. This is because famous trademarks are presumed to acquire secondary meaning when used domestically according to sec. 4 No. 2 MarkenG [Trademark Act].[86] The required level of familiarity of a famous trademark is significantly greater than that usually required for secondary meaning. One of the best examples of a globally famous trademark is *Coca-Cola*. Famous trademarks in Germany include *Linux* or *Ikea*, for example.

4. Company Symbols and Titles of Works

If company symbols or titles of works as defined by sec. 5 MarkenG [Trademark Act] have original distinctiveness, i. e. the market understands the name as an individual reference of origin, they may be protected when used in commerce. Otherwise, when distinctiveness is lacking, they are only protected when they have successfully acquired secondary meaning. Such protection, however, may possibly be limited to a certain geographical territory.[87]

Typical preparatory actions such as registering the company with the commercial register, or sending out brochures to business partners, are considered to be a start of use of a company symbol. On the other hand, purely internal preparatory actions such as the development of a business concept are not sufficient.[88]

In individual cases, trademark registration may be impossible, for instance because trademark pirates have trademark names registered in Germany that were already known abroad thus, exploiting their good reputation. In those cases it may be worthwhile to investigate whether the relevant designations have been used in Germany prior to their registration in the name of those third parties eligible to constitute priority of such trademark use.[89] It might also be worthwhile to seek cancellation of the earlier registered trademark according to sec. 50, para. 1, No. 4 MarkenG [Trademark Act] due to the bad faith of the registrant.

---

86 2 April 1969 BGH [Federal Supreme Court] [I ZR 47/67], GRUR 1969, 607, 608 (Recrin); see the following for comprehensive information on this: *Kur*, Die notorisch bekannte Marke im Sinne von 6 bis PVÜ und die „bekannte Marke“ im Sinne der Markenrechtsrichtlinie, GRUR 1994, 330 ff.

87 *Ingerl/Rohnke*, Markengesetz, § 5, Nos. 33, 53, 55.

88 *Ingerl/Rohnke*, Markengesetz, § 5, No. 56.

89 Also see *Harte-Bavendamm*, Handbuch der Markenpiraterie in Europa, § 5, No. 28, which gives the general advice of maintaining ongoing internal company documentation from the first phase of the entry into the market appearance that was recognisable externally in order to prevent prior registrations of trademarks.

Also foreign companies can be the legal owner of commercial designations according to sec. 5 MarkenG [Trademark Act].[90] The commercial designation should first be used in Germany,[91] however, because foreign use is only sufficient to constitute protection for famous trademarks.[92]

Moreover, titles of works can be registered as a trademark for goods or services that are different than the designated creative work. For example, the title of the musical "*Cats*" for the goods offered in the context of the exploitation of the musical, such as clocks, calendars, etc. In addition, a title of a creative work can be registered for products that could be the subject matter of title protection as a creative work, for instance the title of a newspaper for newspapers.[93]

5. Indications of Geographic Origin

Because indications of geographic origin are not tied to a specific owner, protection of indications of geographic origin depends solely on the actual circumstances. Protection arises with use in favor of the party providing goods that actually originate from the area or the region for which the goods are named, or, in the case of qualified geographic origin indications, if they also actually have the special characteristics or the quality that the market associates with the goods or services so named. Indications of geographic origin are generally not capable of being registered as descriptive trademarks according to sec. 8, para. 2, No. 2 MarkenG [Trademark Act] if there is a current need to keep the name available for the specific goods or services. An exception is made for goods that have acquired distinctiveness according to sec. 8, para. 3 MarkenG [Trademark Act].[94] Protection of indications of geographic origin on a European level is subject to extensive registration proceedings, unlike protection according to German trademark law, which, as described, arises solely through actual use.[95]

C. Infringing Behaviour

1. Trademark Infringement according to Section 14 MarkenG [Trademark Act]

The main function of a trademark is to guarantee the origin-related identity of the marked product or service for consumers or end purchasers, thus, making it possible for

---

90 *Ingerl/Rohnke*, Markengesetz, § 5, No. 59.

91 See e.g. 12 July 1995 BGH [Federal Supreme Court] [I ZR 140/93], GRUR 1995, 825, 826 (Torres).

92 MarkenG [Trademark Act] § 4 No. 3 (F.R.G.); also see above I. B.3. with regard to famous trademarks.

93 *Fezer*, Markenrecht, § 3, Nos. 252 and 253.

94 See above under I. B.1.a. for the details on distinctiveness.

95 Individual procedural steps have been assigned to the German Patent and Trademark Office in Germany, and regulations can be found in MarkenG [Trademark Act], §§ 130-136.

them to distinguish the product or service from those with a different origin without a likelihood of confusion *(Verwechslungsgefahr)* being given.

Section 14, para. 2 MarkenG [Trademark Act] generally prohibits third parties from using an identical or similar mark for identical or similar goods or services in business dealings without the approval of the trademark owner.

Trademark piracy typically applies to the adoption of identical or nearly identical symbols (company symbols, logos, domain names) for the same or similar goods. In many cases, only single letters are replaced or individual elements of the original goods are adopted, for example, to get as close as possible to the outward appearance of the original product, so determining an infringement is usually not difficult.

a. Prohibited Usage

The concept of use is interpreted broadly, covering all of the cases in which the protected trademark is used as a distinctive mark, and thus, for instance, as a trademark, commercial designation, element of a trade name, logo, domain name or name of a computer program.

– Affixation to Goods or Packaging –
Section 14, Paragraph 3, No. 1 MarkenG [Trademark Act]

To begin with, usage occurs when a symbol is affixed to goods or their packaging.[96] Affixation of the symbol on the goods or their presentation or their packaging represents a physical connection between the goods and the trademark.[97]

– Offering, Distribution in the Market or Possession for said Purposes –
Section 14, Paragraph 3, No. 2 MarkenG [Trademark Act]

Prohibited usage also exists when goods are offered under the mark, distributed in the market or possessed for these purposes.[98] Possession of a marked product requires actual control over the pirated goods. Moreover, possession must be obtained or maintained for the purpose of offering the product or effecting its commercial distribution. If the possessor holds items in custody for a third party, the third party's purpose is also decisive, regardless of the knowledge of the actual possessor who may be acting in good faith. Consequently, shipping agents, carriers, warehouse keepers or other persons who transport pirated goods may be considered to be infringers.[99]

---

96 MarkenG [Trademark Act] § 14 ¶ 3 No. 1 (F. R.G.).

97 *Fezer*, Markenrecht, § 14, No. 463.

98 MarkenG [Trademark Act] § 14 ¶ 3 No. 2 (F. R.G.).

99 Cf. 6 April 2006 LG Düsseldorf [4a O 1/06], InstGE 6, 132, 134 ff. (Frachtführer II); *Ingerl/Rohnke*, Markengesetz, § 14, No. 194.

– Offering or Providing Services –
Section 14, Paragraph 3, No. 3 MarkenG [Trademark Act]

In addition, the offering or provision of services under the mark is prohibited.[100]

– Import and Export of Goods –
Section 14, Paragraph 3, No. 4 MarkenG [Trademark Act]

Furthermore, goods are not permitted to be either imported or exported under a protected mark.[101] Such actions constitute trademark infringement regardless of whether the product was actually placed in the domestic market.[102] The problematic cases of mere transit are specifically classified in this group. See comprehensive information on the transit problem under I. C. 3. The ECJ held that transit of counterfeit goods through a Member State where the trademark is protected cannot be prohibited as a general rule if the final destination is a different EU Member State where the trademark is not protected.[103] On the other hand, placing the counterfeit goods on the market in the transit state constitutes infringement. The mere chance that the goods will not arrive at their intended destination, but will instead enter the market in the transit state, is not sufficient to trigger infringement, as the ECJ decided for the external shipping procedure.[104] Thus, for establishing trademark infringement, actions must have been taken that necessarily entail their being put on the market within the Community.

– Use in Business Documents and Advertising
Section 14, Paragraph 3, No. 5 MarkenG [Trademark Act]

Finally, the mark may not be used in either business documents or in advertising.[105]

b. Use of the Trademark in Business Dealings

The concept of business dealings is very broadly interpreted by German case law. The only requirement is promotion of any business purpose of one's own or of others; the intention to make profit is not required.[106] The externally recognisable objective of the action is decisive in this respect.[107] Acting purely privately is usually considered to constitute an exception to this rule.[108] A sale between private parties may be considered to be a business dealing under certain circumstances, however. In particular, with Internet

100 MarkenG [Trademark Act] § 14 ¶ 3 No. 3 (F. R.G.).
101 MarkenG [Trademark Act] § 14 ¶ 3 No. 4 (F. R.G.).
102 *Fezer*, Markenrecht, § 14, No. 479.
103 9 November 2006 ECJ [C-281/05], GRUR 2007, 146, No. 23 (Diesel).
104 9 November 2006 ECJ [C-281/05], GRUR 2007, 146, No. 24 (Diesel).
105 MarkenG [Trademark Act] § 14 ¶ 3 No. 5 (F. R.G.).
106 *Ingerl/Rohnke*, Markengesetz, § 14, No. 48.
107 22 November 2001 BGH [Federal Supreme Court] [I ZR 138/99], GRUR 2002, 622, 624 (shell.de).
108 *Fezer*, Markenrecht, § 14, No. 42; *Ingerl/Rohnke*, Markengesetz, § 14, Nos. 49 ff.

auctions, the German Federal Supreme Court held that a person who only purchases items in an Internet auction in order to resell them at a profit can also be engaging in business dealings. As an example, the frequent appearance of some offerers as auctioneers (59 instances of "feedback" as purchaser reactions to earlier auctions of an offerer were sufficient for the German Federal Supreme Court) points towards business activity.[109] In addition, whether the offerers are otherwise active as entrepreneurs or business persons, and the extent and the frequency with which they place offers on the Internet do not matter. This is legitimate taking into account that an offer on the Internet is made to an indeterminate group of persons as a result of the public nature of the "World Wide Web" with the objective of obtaining as high a sales price as possible.[110] In contrast, private imports (which would only fall under this provision in exceptional cases when fairly large piece numbers are involved[111]) and items that are only intended for personal use are not covered by trademark protection.[112]

c. Occurrence of one of the Cases Specified in Section 14, Paragraph 2, Nos. 1-3 MarkenG [Trademark Act]

– Identity Protection –
Section 14, Paragraph 2, No. 1 MarkenG [Trademark Act]

So-called identity protection prohibits the use of a trademark that is identical to a protected trademark for the same goods or services. Identity protection frequently applies in piracy cases where the products are often identical, too.

– Protection against Possible Confusion –
Section 14, Paragraph 2, No. 2 MarkenG [Trademark Act]

Infringement may also occur due to the likelihood of confusion, which is given when products or services are marked with an identical or similar symbol that is also identical or similar with regard to the protected goods and services. This theory also often applies to piracy cases. The risk is that a symbol will be mentally associated with the trademark or that the market could assume that the infringing marks belong to the same company as the protected marks. The goods in this category are frequently only slightly different from the authentic goods. According to established case law of the German Federal Supreme Court in cases in which at least one mark is involved which consists of several

109 11 March 2004 BGH [Federal Supreme Court] [I ZR 304/01], MMR 2004, 668 (Internetversteigerung-ROLEX).

110 18 March 2005 OLG [Higher Regional Court] Köln [6 U 12/01], GRUR-RR 2006, 50, 51 (Rolex-Internet-Versteigerung).

111 Private usage purpose affirmed: 29 January 2002 BayObLG [Bavarian Higher Regional Court] [4 St RR 122/2001], WRP 2002, 562 (Trainingsanzüge); private usage purpose rejected: 12 February 1999 LG [District Court] Mannheim [7 O 13/99], WRP 1999, 1057 (JOOP!); *Ingerl/Rohnke*, Markengesetz, § 14, No. 49.

112 12 February 1998 BGH [Federal Supreme Court] [I ZR 241/95], GRUR 1998, 696 (Rolex-Uhr mit Diamanten).

components (word, device or form components) it is decisive for assessing the similarity of two or more trademarks that it may be possible under certain circumstances to attribute special distinctiveness "characterising" the overall mark to one single component of such trademark. The likelihood of confusion may thus be given when such characterizing components of two trademarks are identical or highly similar (so-called characterisation theory *(Prägetheorie)*).[113] In addition, according to case law from the ECJ, a risk of confusion is generally not eliminated by merely adding the corporate name of a third party to a registered trademark that has at least acquired normal distinctiveness.[114]

The trademark in its registered form is the starting point for analyzing the risk of confusion. This also applies to the goods and services with regard to which the trademark claims protection, i. e., the list of goods and services as registered for said trademarks. The scope of protection of a registered trademark, however, is not static. The scope can be broadened through a high level of public familiarity, but may also be narrowed by the use of numerous similar third-party designations.[115]

– Brand Recognition Protection –
Section 14, Paragraph 2, No. 3 MarkenG [Trademark Act]

Brand recognition protection covers unauthorised third party use of a mark that is identical or similar to a protected mark, but used for different goods or services. Protection is afforded to trademarks that are familiar domestically where the infringing use unfairly exploits or interferes with the distinctiveness or appreciation of the protected trademark without justification. Trademarks protected under this category are, however, similarly protected against the likelihood of confusion where the goods or services are identical or similar, in an analogous application of the principles as set forth in sec. 14, para. 2, No. 2 MarkenG [Trademark Act].[116]

A fixed lower limit that is to be required for verification of trademarks known domestically has not been officially set (by a court or the Patent and Trademark Office), though. Rather, courts consider the totality of the circumstances in each individual case. There exists an interdependency between the identity/similarity of the trademark and the identity/similarity of the goods and services protected. Relevant factors include the specific character, originality and uniqueness of the trademark, distinctiveness, the type of goods that are sold under the protected mark, quality and appearance, and the associated prestige. Also included is, in particular, the relationship of the unauthorised goods to those for which the reputation of the mark is exploited.[117] According to case

---

113 Cf. only 8 November 2001 BGH [Federal Supreme Court] [I ZR 139/99], GRUR 2002, 626, 628 (IMS); 10 July 1997 BGH [Federal Supreme Court] [I ZB 6/95], GRUR 1997, 897, 898 (IONOFIL); 2 July 1998 BGH [Federal Supreme Court] [I ZB 36/95], GRUR 1998, 1014 (ECCO II).

114 Cf. with regard to this 6 October 2005 ECJ [C-120/04], GRUR 2005, 1042, 1044 (Thomson Life).

115 *Ingerl/Rohnke*, Markengesetz, § 4, No. 5.

116 *Ingerl/Rohnke*, Markengesetz, § 14, Nos. 829, 830 (grounds are disputed).

117 29 November 1984 BGH [Federal Supreme Court] [I ZR 158/82], GRUR 1985, 550, 552 (Dimple); 6 December 1990 BGH [Federal Supreme Court] [I ZR 297/88], GRUR 1991, 609, 612 (SL).

law of the German Federal Supreme Court, the minimum level of recognition required in the relevant market begins at around 30%. If this benchmark is met or exceeded, trademark owners may claim the benefits of the special protection according to sec. 14, para. 2, No. 3 MarkenG [Trademark Act].[118]

Exploitation of an image (reputation exploitation) occurs when third parties imitate a trademark when designating their goods, in order to favorably benefit from the impression of luxury or prestige that the trademarks give off to consumers. The image is negatively impacted and the reputation is therefore damaged when a mark is used by a third party for low-quality products.[119] This is especially true where the mark is coupled with disparaging, incompatible or obscene additions or advertising slogans.[120]

d. Indirect Trademark Infringement

Section 14, para. 4 MarkenG [Trademark Act] governs cases of indirect trademark infringement. Third parties are prohibited from affixing an identical or similar mark on advertising or packaging or on marking means such as labels, tags, patches or the like, to offer the marked items, to distribute them in the market or to possess them for such purposes or to import or export them if there is an objective risk that they will be used in an infringing manner. Especially in trademark piracy cases, the way a trademark is used often necessarily leads to the assumption of an infringement.[121]

2. Infringement of Business Designations according to Section 15 MarkenG [Trademark Act]

According to sec. 15, para. 2 MarkenG [Trademark Act], third parties are prohibited from using identical or similar business designations in a way that can cause confusion with a protected designation. It is important here that both, an identical or similar company symbol and identical or similar trademarks of another company, can be infringed by the use of a company symbol in business dealings, provided that the infringing company and the original owner of the protected company symbol or trademark operate in similar industries *(Branchennähe)*.[122]

---

118 Cf. e. g. 29 November 1984 BGH [Federal Supreme Court] [I ZR 158/82], GRUR 1985, 550, 551 (Dimple); *Harte-Bavendamm*, Handbuch der Markenpiraterie in Europa, § 5, No. 36 with a reference to *Erdmann* in: Mostert (ed), Famous and Well-Known Marks, p. 289 f.; also cf. *Ingerl/Rohnke*, Markengesetz, § 14, No. 810: 20 % as the lowest conceivable threshold with a reference to the ECJ ruling *Chevy*, 14 September 1999 ECJ [C-375/97], GRUR Int 2000, 73 (Chevy).

119 Cf. with regard to this e. g. 4 June 1998 OLG [Higher Regional Court] Hamburg [3 U 151/97], GRUR 1999, 339, 342 (Yves Roche).

120 *Ingerl/Rohnke*, Markengesetz, § 14, No. 156.

121 *Ingerl/Rohnke*, Markengesetz, § 14, No. 212.

122 *Ingerl/Rohnke*, Markengesetz, § 15, No. 60.

If the business designation is known domestically, third parties are even prohibited from using the same or similar symbol even where there is no actual likelihood of confusion.[123] However, for this provision to apply it would be necessary that the use of the symbol unfairly and unjustifiedly exploits or interferes with the distinctiveness or the reputation of the business designation (cases of reputation exploitation, reputation damage, dilution and exploitation of attention).

3. Special Case: Transit as an Infringing Behavior

There has long since been a discussion in literature and case law as to how the Customs Regulation (Council Regulation (EC) No. 1383/2003 of 22 July 2003 concerning customs action against goods suspected of infringing certain intellectual property rights and the measures to be taken against goods found to have infringed such rights),[124] which replaced the Predecessor Customs Regulation (Council Regulation (EC) No 3295/94 of 22 December 1994 laying down measures to prohibit the release for free circulation, export, re-export or entry for a suspensive procedure of counterfeit and pirated goods),[125] should be harmonised with the Trademark Directive (First Council Directive 89/104 /EEC of 21 December 1988 to approximate the laws of the Member States relating to trademarks)[126] within the context of transit cases. This is particularly problematic for goods in transit through a Member State, assuming infringement in the transit state, but not in the destination state. For instance, one may have trademark protection concerning a certain product in Germany or for the territory of the European Community but not for Russia. The limited scope of trademark protection makes it difficult to determine what specific rights may be affected during the course of transit. The issue faced by trademark owners is whether it is possible to control the movements of goods between countries even though they only own rights in the transit state, but not in the destination state.

Procedures that do not involve the levying of duties under customs law (for example the external shipping procedure) are frequently applied to non-Community goods that are in transit, which may become subject to border seizures. Goods are transported with duty unpaid (suspended) in transit, and the customs duty payments are made at the final destination. In practice, customs authorities affix a customs seal on the means of transport to protect the goods against removal during the course of transit. But the attachment of a customs seal does not provide a guarantee that the goods will not be circulated in the transit state, via misuse for example. Thus, the question for trademark owners is whether trademark law also protects cases of pure transit where the distribution of goods in the transit market is rather a theoretical risk.

123 MarkenG [Trademark Act] § 15 ¶ 3 (F. R.G.).

124 Official Journal of the European Union 2003 No L 196/7.

125 Official Journal of the European Communities 1994 No L 341/8 (this regulation has been replaced effective 01 July 2004 by the Regulation (EC) No. 1383/2003 of 22 July 2003). Both regulations are also sometimes each referred to as the product piracy regulation.

126 Official Journal of the European Communities 1989 No L 40/1.

a. Case Law of the ECJ on Transit Cases

The decisions of the ECJ in transit cases do not provide a clear answer. The ECJ has previously ruled on several cases that were based on transit facts. In the rulings *Polo Lauren/Dwidua*,[127] *Rolex*,[128] *Rioglass*[129] and *Class International/Colgate-Palmolive*,[130] the ECJ addressed the question of infringement of industrial property rights in proceedings

127 6 April 2000 ECJ [C-383/98], GRUR Int 2000, 748 (Polo/Lauren): In this case, in 2000 the ECJ affirmed the applicability of the Predecessor Customs Regulation to the transit of imitation goods that had been manufactured in a non-Member State and that were destined for another non-Member State. The decision was justified on the grounds that the regulation governed seizure of unauthorised goods from non-Member States from entering the Common Market. The court pointed to the risk that non-Community goods could enter the Common Market in an unauthorised manner during transport in a pure transit case, as well as to the type of transport chosen. The ECJ only addressed the scope of the Customs Regulation, but not the scope of protection under trademark law. After this case, however, the provisions of the Customs Regulation (at the time of the decision still being the Predecessor Customs Regulation) became applicable to transit cases.

128 7 January 2004 ECJ [C-60/02], GRUR Int 2004, 317 (Rolex): The ECJ reinforced its legal position in this decision in 2004. It held that the Customs Regulation applies if goods are stopped in a Member State during transit between two non-Member States, regardless of whether they are transported under customs seals procedures. National regulations that do not prohibit the mere transit of imitation goods through the relevant Member State would conflict with the Customs Regulation because Community law has priority in such matters. In other words, if national law does not classify such transit as an infringement, then national law should be interpreted to be conform to Community law.

129 23 October 2003 ECJ [C-115/02], GRUR Int 2004, 39 (Administration des douanes et droits indirects v Rioglass SA and Transremar SL): In this case, the ECJ ruled in 2003 that France breached its obligations contained in Articles 28 and 30 of the EC Treaty (Treaty Establishing the European Community of 25 March 1957, consolidated version of 24 September 2002, Official Journal No C 325) (relating to the free movement of goods) by applying French design-patent law to block the transit of goods in French customs that had been legally manufactured in Spain and were on their way to the Polish market. Although Poland was not yet a Member State in 2003, the relevant goods could be legally sold there. The ECJ reasoned that intra-Community transit was not associated with the "specific subject matter" of intellectual property rights. Accordingly, transit goods legally manufactured in one Member State that are destined for another may not be confiscated by a third Member State on the basis that they infringe upon protective rights of the third Member State.

130 18 October 2005 ECJ [C-405/03], GRUR 2006, 146 (Class International/Colgate-Palmolive): In 2005, the ECJ ruled in this case that Article 5, paragraphs 1 and 3 lit. c) of the Trademark Directive must be interpreted such that the trademark owner may not oppose shipment of its original brand-name goods by another into the Community within the context of the external shipping procedure. The ECJ held that as long as the goods were not placed into free circulation under customs law, there could be no use of the trademark in business dealings. Thus, transit cases would not be covered by the trademark concept of "use" as a justification for exclusion (cf. *Leitzen*, Innergemeinschaftlicher Transit, Markenverletzung und Produktpiraterie, GRUR 2006, 89, 92).

that did not involve the levy of duties under customs law without proving one consistent approach. The ECJ finally issued a ruling in 2006 *(Diesel)* within the framework of a request of the German Federal Supreme Court for a preliminary ruling[131] that unfortunately did not provide much clarification either.

In the *Diesel* ruling, the ECJ addressed the issue of trademark infringement during transit, specifically whether the owner of a trademark registered in a Member State has the right to prohibit the mere transit of goods that are labeled with a mark identical to its protected trademark through the Member State. The ECJ found that Article 5, paragraphs 1 and 3 of the Trademark Directive must be interpreted such that the owner of a trademark can only prohibit transit through a Member State in which the trademark is protected when the external shipment procedure applies to the goods. Further, the corresponding actions of the third parties arranging for transit must also be associated with placement of the goods on the transit Member State market. The mere chance that the goods might be placed on the market in an unauthorised way in a state where the relevant trademark is protected is not sufficient to trigger trademark rights. Therefore, external shipment, and thus transit within the Community, does not constitute infringement as a general principle.

According to the ECJ, infringement requires deliberate actions of a third party that necessarily lead to the placement of goods on the market in the transit state. The mere risk that the goods might end up on the market in the transit state is thus not sufficient. On the other hand, a concrete risk of distribution in the market could establish grounds for an infringement action. Both German literature and case law agree that claims (to cease-and-desist, for instance) stemming from trademark infringement may be made not only after infringement has already occurred, but also before it actually takes place. Unfortunately, the ECJ did not provide any criteria for determining what constitutes a concrete risk in this context.

The relationship between the Customs Regulation and the regulations for the protection of intellectual property was also not clearly defined by the *Diesel* ruling. Customs officials must first suspect infringement of an intellectual property right under the Customs Regulation. In other words, customs authorities and the courts reviewing their decision must specifically analyse the relevant national trademark-law provisions in applying the Customs Regulation. Given that the scope of applicability of the Customs Regulation overlaps with national trademark law, the ECJ should have considered that taking steps under the Customs Regulation can only be justified if an infringement has taken place. On the other hand, customs authorities are specifically permitted to take action in transit cases. Thus, transit must also be regarded as usage – at least when distribution in the market of the transit Member State does not fall under an exception to usage. Otherwise, although the customs office would be permitted to block the corresponding goods, it would be required to immediately release them again since there is no basis for establishing infringement. Moreover, unjustified retention could potentially impose substantial costs (storage and court costs) on the legal owner.[132]

---

131 9 November 2006 ECJ [C-281/05], GRUR 2007, 146 (Diesel).

132 According to Art. 19 ¶ 3 of the Customs Regulation, the legal owner in the case of an unlawful

The *Diesel* ruling of the ECJ has far-reaching economic significance. Considering transit to be one of the recognised infringement actions would have improved the ability to fight international product piracy.[133] Instead, classifying transit as a generally non-infringing action endangers national trademark rights in favor of freedom of movement of goods in the Community.

b. Practice Tips

Nevertheless, trademark rights' owners must be able to obtain cease-and-desist orders against those who are likely to infringe their trademarks. Since mere transit does not constitute infringement, a reasonable question is, under what circumstances does an external transit procedure raise sufficient suspicion that the products will be marketed in the transit Member State.

Although the ECJ did not comment on the criteria proposed by the Attorney General, in practice, a "well founded suspicion" that the goods will be put on the market in the state of transit may be adequate. Evidence of such a suspicion indicates that intellectual property rights may well be infringed. This should form the starting point for practitioners to take action. The following paragraphs provide some rough guidelines to help assess the risk of marketing in a transit state.

In the *Diesel* case, the ECJ stated that it is irrelevant whether the goods have been produced legally or illegally in the state of origin for the question of whether rights are infringed in the state of transit.

The court ruling in *Class International/Colgate-Palmolive* may provide additional orientation. In that case the goods were brought into the Netherlands under the external transit procedure although there was no purchaser for the goods. The fact that the owner or the purchaser of the goods in transit was engaged in parallel trade did not sufficiently indicate the danger that the goods would be put on the market within the state of transit.

Beyond that, it remains a question of interpretation which facts provide adequate evidence of a sufficient risk that the goods will be placed on the market in the state of transit.

Applying customs seals on the means of transport reduces such risk. Furthermore, clear evidence of purchasers within the state of destination and past business practice with

---

confiscation is liable according to the law of the country in which the confiscated goods are located. As a result, pursuant to § 149 MarkenG [Trademark Act] (F. R.G.) in Germany, the party requesting confiscation, i. e., the owner of the trademark rights, must compensate the owner – regardless of the issue of culpability – for the losses incurred due to an unjustified confiscation.

133 *Sack*, Der Benutzungszwang im internationalen Markenrecht in: Erdmann/Gloy/Herber (ed.), Festschrift für Henning Piper, p. 603, 614 ff.

these purchasers support the argument that the goods will reach the state of destination instead of being marketed unlawfully in the state of transit.

Trademark owners, who bear the burden of proof, must provide evidence of an actual risk of the goods being marketed in the state of transit. Once again, the owner of the trademark cannot claim abstract risks that are inherent to the transit itself, such as the general risk of theft or the risk that the transit procedure is only used as a pretext to facilitate the fraudulent marketing of the product. Rather, other facts must be provided, such as the fact that the products cannot be put on the market legally in the country of destination or in any other country named by the person responsible for the transit procedure.

The language included on product instructions and manuals as well as other information on the product may also be relevant in some circumstances. If such information is only provided in the language of the state of transit that differs from that of the state of origin, it is more likely that marketing will take place in the state of transit. Another circumstance that can indicate unlawful marketing is where the sender or the addressee does not exist and the names are clearly given as a false pretence.

These few examples illustrate the broad scope of conceivable scenarios that can arise in transit cases. The ECJ could provide help in the fight against product piracy by defining clear criteria for determining when a transit case constitutes infringement of intellectual property rights. Without the guidance of the ECJ, it remains the thankless task of the national courts to define and apply criteria for determining the risks of infringement.

4. Special Case: Internet Providers

More than 233 million users are registered with eBay worldwide, with more than 20 million of them in Germany. eBay hosts an average of 100 million listings in more than 50,000 categories globally at any given time. The value of goods and services sold on the site was approximately USD 52.4 billion in 2006. Further, among eBay sellers, there are a growing number of businesses – more than 1.3 million people worldwide, including 170,000 in Europe and more than 64,000 in Germany – who derive a substantial portion of their income by selling on eBay. On the German eBay marketplace alone a piece of clothing is sold every second, a book every three seconds, a notebook every two minutes.[134] Not surprisingly, given the ease with which goods may be sold in a very short period of time at minimal costs and comparatively low risk, individuals engage in piracy via the Internet to offer goods that infringe protective rights.

Because the identity of users is not generally revealed, the question arises as to whether the parties conducting the Internet auctions or the Internet providers can be held liable

---

134 For comprehensive information, see *Osthaus*, Fighting Piracy and Counterfeiting in the Light of the European Principles of eCommerce – The eBay Strategy and Experience, GRUR Int 2007, 644.

for trademark infringements. The new Telemediengesetz [TMG] [Telemedia Act] (F. R.G.)[135] entered into force on March 1, 2007 and was enacted by the German legislature on the basis of the E-Commerce Directive (Directive 2000/31/EC of 8 June 2000 on certain legal aspects of information society services, in particular electronic commerce, in the Internal Market).[136] It superseded, among other laws, the former Teledienstegesetz [TDG] [Teleservices Act] (F. R.G.), which was simultaneously cancelled. The term "telemedia" is a generic term for electronic information and communication services that was created from "teleservices" and the "media services" that were formerly governed by the Mediendienstestaatsvertrag [MDStV] [Media Services Treaty] (F. R.G.). Nearly all Internet providers and consequently also online auctions such as eBay, which were formerly classified as teleservices, are deemed to be offerers of telemedia as defined by sec. 1, para. 1 TMG [Telemedia Act].[137] By contrast, live streaming or Web radio or mere Internet telephony (telecommunications) are not classified as telemedia.

a. Liability according to the Telemedia Act

Internet service providers are responsible under the general laws for their own information provided by them for use by others.[138] On the other hand, their liability is qualified under certain circumstances by the TMG [Telemedia Act].

– Qualified Liability of Service Providers

Internet service providers are subject to a qualified liability regime for information provided by a third party, thus also for an infringing use of trademarks, if certain other prerequisites are met.[139]

In principle, such qualified liability is not precluded by the trademark being a Community Trademark. Qualified liability regimes pursuant to the TMG [Telemedia Act] and to the Trademark Directive do not conflict with the Community Trademark as the latter does not contain any provisions on secondary contribution liability.[140]

– Demarcation of Third-Party/One's Own Information

---

135 Announced with Article 1 of the Elektronischer-Geschäftsverkehr-Vereinheitlichungsgesetz [Electronic Commerce Standardisation Act] (F. R.G.).

136 Official Journal of the European Communities 2000 No L 178/1.

137 Regarding an identical version as contained in the former Teleservices Act, see: *Leible/Sosnitza*, Versteigerungen im Internet, Part III, E II 1 (with further references).

138 TMG [Telemedia Act] § 7 (F. R.G.).

139 TMG [Trademark Act] §§ 8 ff. (F. R.G.); in particular TMG [Trademark Act] § 10 (F. R.G.).

140 Regarding an identical version as contained in the former Teleservices Act, see 11 March 2004 BGH [Federal Supreme Court] [I ZR 304/01], MMR 2004, 668, 669 (Internetversteigerung-ROLEX); 26 February 2004 OLG [Higher Regional Court] Düsseldorf, MMR 2004, 315, 316 – No liability of the operators of online marketplaces for trademark infringement of the sellers.

A prerequisite for the qualified liability of a service provider is that the information provided by the service provider on the Internet, e. g., an Internet auctioneer, represents third-party information for the latter.[141] The distinction between third-party information and one's own information is provided as a general principle, requiring an objective evaluation of all of the circumstances of an individual case.[142] In a series of court rulings regarding the liability of online auctioneers it was held that the contents contained in offers from users cannot be influenced by the service provider, i. e., the auctioneer and thus constitute third-party contents.[143] The German Federal Supreme Court brought about clarity in its *Internetversteigerung – ROLEX* [ROLEX Internet Auction] ruling[144] holding that there is no third-party information only in the situation in which the operator has real editorial control and structuring. If, however, the publication is done in an automated process without the use of a control mechanism, the data on the object of the purchase, including the use of a trademark, shall exclusively remain the information of the individual offerer.[145] The analysis of the German Federal Supreme Court appears to be proper, because online auctions merely specify the structure of the Web pages and the offers of the users create the core of the business model of online auctions (financing via transactions and advertising).[146]

– Knowledge of the Illegal Action or Information

A service provider can no longer invoke the qualified liability for third-party information that it stores for a user if it has actual knowledge of the illegal action or information and thus in particular of a trademark infringement.[147] No facts or circumstances that make the illegal action or information obvious are permitted to already be known by the service providers in the case of claims for compensation.

With regard to neutral information which is assumed for cases of reproduction of brand names, there is agreement that mere knowledge is not sufficient for liability. Moreover, the service provider must additionally be aware that the third-party intellectual property is being used without the consent of the legal owner.[148] This interpretation appears

---

141 TMG [Telemedia Act] § 10 (F. R.G.).

142 *Leible/Sosnitza*, "3 – 2 – 1 – meins!" und das TDG, WRP 2004, 592, 595.

143 As examples, 16 December 2003 OLG [Higher Regional Court] Brandenburg [6 U 161/02], MMR 2004, 330 – liability of an online auction (upholding the ruling of the lower court, 10 October 2002 LG [District Court] Potsdam [51 O 12/02], MMR 2002, 829); 26 February 2004 OLG [Higher Regional Court] Düsseldorf, MMR 2004, 315, 314 – no liability of the operators of online marketplaces for trademark infringement of the sellers of an auction (confirming the ruling of the lower court, 29 October 2002 LG [District Court] Düsseldorf [4a O 464/01], MMR 2003, 120, 123).

144 11 March 2004 BGH [Federal Supreme Court] [I ZR 304/01], MMR 2004, 668 (Internetversteigerung-ROLEX).

145 11 March 2004 BGH [Federal Supreme Court] [I ZR 304/01], MMR 2004, 668, 670 (Internetversteigerung-ROLEX).

146 Cf. *Mehler*, Die Verantwortlichkeit des Betreibers von Internetauktionen für Markenverletzungen in Deutschland und den USA, WRP 2006, 819, 822.

147 TMG [Telemedia Act] § 10 sent. 1 No. 1 (F. R.G.).

to be justified, because it is difficult for the service provider to recognise the illegality of neutral information and there is also no general monitoring and investigation duty incumbent upon it according to sec. 7, para. 2, sent. 1 TMG [Telemedia Act].[149]

– Prerequisites to Obtaining Knowledge

The requirements on the act of obtaining knowledge further differ depending on whether civil-law claims to compensation are asserted or the service provider is being notified of criminal offence being committed in its offerings.[150]

The act of obtaining knowledge for the purposes of criminal liability requires – when it is brought about by third parties – actual knowledge of the service provider with regard to the illegal action or the illegal information including an explanation of the illegal nature of the relevant information.[151] Knowledge of the service provider is frequently manifested in the form of a warning letter, but it may also be given in a number of other forms.[152] The service provider needs clear indications as to what content could be involved.[153] The content has to be described in concrete terms to enable one to find it with a simple search routine; the specification of the link or an exact storage location does not necessarily need to be included.[154]

148 Regarding an identical version as contained in the former Media Services Treaty: *Rossnagel*, Recht der Multimedia-Dienste, § 9 MDStV, No. 20.

149 Regarding an identical version as contained in the former Media Services Treaty: *Rossnagel*, Recht der Multimedia-Dienste, § 9 MDStV, No. 20.

150 Regarding an identical version as contained in the former Teleservices Act: *Spindler/Schmitz/Geis*, TDG, § 11, No. 49.

151 If the interpretation of § 10 TMG [Telemedia Act] (F. R.G.) that is in conformity with the Directive is followed, according to which the illegality and the knowledge of that refer to both the action and the information, the requirement of an explanation of the illegality for all types of content is relevant (cf. with regard to the identical version of the former Teleservices Act: *Spindler/Schmitz/Geis*, TDG, § 11, No. 19 with further references; *Rossnagel*, Recht der Multimedia, § 9 MDStV, No. 21, with further references; *Christiansen*, Wahrheitswidrige Tatsachenbehauptung in einem Internetportal, MMR 2004, 185, 186; *Leible/Sosnitza*, „3 – 2 – 1 – meins!“ und das TDG, WRP 2004, 592, 596). If the opinion of the German legislature is followed, this requirement only exists in the case of neutral content, whereas in the case of non-neutral content, the knowledge of the existence alone leads to a loss of the privileged liability position (see the justification for the draft of an act regarding the legal framework for electronic commerce (EEG), BT-Drucks. 14/6098, p. 25).

152 For instance, complaints of other users, notices of government agencies, reports on illegal content of the service provider in periodicals purchased by it.

153 Cf. with regard to the identical version of § 5 of the former TDG [Teleservices Act] (F. R.G.): 23 September 2003 BGH [Federal Supreme Court] [VI ZR 335/02], NJW 2003, 3764, 3765 – Liability of the Internet provider for content of Internet pages.

154 Regarding the version of § 11 of the former TDG [Teleservices Act] (F. R.G.), that is identical to § 10 TMG [Telemedia Act] (F. R.G.): *Spindler/Schmitz/Geis*, TDG, § 11, No. 20.

If, on the other hand, the service provider is notified in connection with the assertion of civil-law claims for compensation (usually by way of a warning letter), in contrast, a description of the corresponding facts and circumstances that form the basis of the illegality is sufficient.

– Requirement as regards the Blocking Duty

To retain the qualified liability for third-party content, the service provider is required to immediately take action upon obtaining knowledge and to remove the information (and thus in trademark cases the infringing trademark) or to block access to it.[155] Unlike in sec. 5, No. 2 TDG [Teleservices Act], old version, there is no longer an explicit statement that the prevention of use has to be technically possible and reasonable. However, these requirements also apply according to the new legal situation.[156] It is a principle of German law that no one may be obligated to do something impossible. Because the immediacy of the prevention of use addressed in sec. 10, sent. 1, No. 2 TMG [Telemedia Act] is to be understood in the context of culpability – (i. e., taking action without culpable hesitation) – reasonability must also be taken into consideration in the immediacy.[157] The service provider that is obligated to take immediate action is entitled to a review and consideration period. The length of the period corresponds to the importance of the protected rights that are endangered and the information to be blocked, among other things,[158] which is why rigid time periods cannot be specified.

b. Secondary Contribution Liability: No Application of the Qualified Liability Position to Cease-and-Desist Claims and Remedial Claims

According to the principles of secondary contribution liability *(Störerhaftung)*, a cease-and-desist claim can be made against a party as a secondary contributor *(Störer)*, who – without being an offender or participant – intentionally and with adequate causality contributes to the infringement of protected property based on sec. 823, para. 1 in combination with sec. 1004, para. 1 analogous to the Bürgerliches Gesetzbuch [BGB] [Civil Code] (F. R.G.).[159] The issue as to whether the qualified liability position of the TMG

155 TMG [Telemedia Act] § 10 sent. 1 No. 2 (F. R.G.).

156 See with regard to the Teleservices Act on this the justification for the draft of an act regarding the legal framework for electronic commerce (EGG), BT-Drucks. 14/6098, p. 25.

157 Regarding the version of § 11 of the former TDG [Teleservices Act] (F. R.G.), that is identical to § 10 TMG [Telemedia Act] (F. R.G.): *Spindler/Schmitz/Geis*, TDG, § 11, No. 51.

158 *Freytag*, Providerhaftung im Binnenmarkt, CR 2000, 601, 609; *Meyer*, Haftung der Internet-Auktionshäuser für Bewertungsportale, NJW 2004, 3151, 3153.

159 18 October 2001 BGH [Federal Supreme Court] [I ZR 22/99], GRUR 2002, 618, 619 (Meißner Dekor); 11 March 2004 BGH [Federal Supreme Court] [I ZR 304/01], MMR 2004, 668 (Internet-versteigerung-ROLEX) – Duldungs- und Ausgleichsansprüche für TK-Linien [Toleration and Compensation Claims for Telecommunication Lines] (with the note *Hoeren)*; 1 April 2004 BGH [Federal Supreme Court] [I ZR 317/01], MMR 2004, 529, 530 f. (Schöner Wetten) (with the note *Hoffmann)*; 19 April 2007 BGH [Federal Supreme Court] [I ZR 35/04], GRUR 2007, 708, 711 (Internetversteigerung II); *Spindler*, Hyperlinks und ausländische Glücksspiele – Karlsruhe locuta

[Telemedia Act] also applies to secondary contribution liability that only involves cease-and-desist claims and remedial claims, but not claims for compensation,[160] was in dispute for a long time until it was settled by the ruling of the German Federal Supreme Court in *Internetversteigerung – ROLEX* [ROLEX Internet Auction].[161] The German Federal Supreme Court held that the qualified liability position of sec. 10, sent. 1 TMG [Telemedia Act] does not involve the cease-and-desist claim.[162]

Liability of eBay as a secondary contributor requires, however, that the offerers of the goods infringing trademarks acted in business dealings, because only the use of a trademark in business dealings constitutes trademark infringement. The German Federal Supreme Court held that it is relatively easy to satisfy this standard.[163] Also the party who only purchases items in an Internet auction in order to resell them at a profit may be considered to be acting in business dealings in individual cases.[164] The factual characteristic of commercial activity was upheld in German case law for three[165] (in one case) respectively 14[166] (in another) similar sales actions within a short period of time. As for the rest, the frequent appearance of offerers as auctioneers (shown under the heading "seller profile" at eBay, for example) is an indication of business activity. An Internet auction house has the burden of proof that the particular facts militate against a finding of commercial activity despite these objective characteristics.[167]

A likelihood of confusion is likewise not ruled out by naming goods offered at eBay "replicas" or "imitations".[168] In the same way, the liability of the operator of an Internet

---

causa finita?, GRUR 2004, 724, 727; *Spindler/Volkmann*, Die zivilrechtliche Störerhaftung der Internet-Provider, WRP 2003, 1,5.

160 6 April 2000 BGH [Federal Supreme Court] [I ZR 67/98], GRUR 2001, 82, 83 (Neu in Bielefeld I); 18 October 2001 BGH [Federal Supreme Court] [I ZR 22/99], GRUR 2002, 618, 619 (Meißner Dekor).

161 11 March 2004 BGH [Federal Supreme Court] [I ZR 304/01], MMR 2004, 668 (Internetversteigerung-ROLEX); last confirmed by the ruling of 30 April 2008 BGH [Federal Supreme Court] [I ZR 73/05], MarkenR 2008, 235 (Internetversteigerung III).

162 Still § 11 TDG [Teleservices Act] (F. R.G.), or § 9 MDStV [Media Services Treaty] (F. R.G.) as the case may be in the ruling issued by the German Federal Supreme Court.

163 11 March 2004 BGH [Federal Supreme Court] [I ZR 304/01], MMR 2004, 668, 671 (Internetversteigerung-ROLEX); 19 April 2007 BGH [Federal Supreme Court] [I ZR 35/04], GRUR 2007, 708, 710 (Internetversteigerung II).

164 11 March 2004 BGH [Federal Supreme Court] [I ZR 304/01], MMR 2004, 668, 671 (Internetversteigerung-ROLEX); 9 November 2001 LG [District Court] Berlin [103 O 149/01], CR 2002, 371, 372 with the note *Leible/Sosnitza*; *Ingerl/Rohnke*, Markengesetz, § 14, No. 48; also see details on this below under I. C.1.b.

165 9 November 2001 LG [District Court] Berlin [103 O 149/01], CR 2002, 371, 372.

166 12 February LG [District Court] Mannheim [7 O 13/99], WRP 1999, 1057 f.

167 See 11 March 2004 BGH [Federal Supreme Court] [I ZR 304/01], MMR 2004, 668, 671 (Internetversteigerung-ROLEX).

168 11 March 2004 BGH [Federal Supreme Court] [I ZR 304/01], MMR 2004, 668, 671 (Internetversteigerung-ROLEX).

auction house should not be excluded simply because the injured party is aware of the identity of the seller in the individual case.[169]

Since infringement in this context does not require proof of intent, but instead only to the contribution towards such intent, a limitation of this otherwise unlimited liability concept in the infringement of intellectual property[170] is necessary. Secondary contribution liability is therefore only a possibility when the secondary contributor stands accused of violating its obligation to monitor.[171] The issue as to whether, and the extent to which, the secondary contributor could have reasonably been expected to review each situation is relevant for the scope of such monitoring duties.[172] The German Federal Supreme Court ruled in one case that it is not reasonable for a company like eBay to investigate every offer with regard to a possible infringement of rights before publication on the Internet. Such an onerous obligation of that type would jeopardise the entire business model. If eBay obtains knowledge of trademark infringement, however, it must block not only that specific infringing activity. To the extent that it is technically feasible and reasonable for eBay, it must also take precautions to prevent similar infringements of rights of other users from occurring in the future.[173] According to the German Federal Supreme Court, it is conceivable to expect eBay, after becoming aware of an infringement, to prevent comparable infringements by the use of appropriate resources (filter software etc.).[174] The reasonability of monitoring activity has to be strongly assumed in any case in view of the *Internetversteigerung – ROLEX* [ROLEX Internet Auction] ruling of the German Federal Supreme Court, because it can be assumed nowadays that eBay has voice-based and possibly other combined filters at its disposal[175] that can

---

169 According to the German Federal Supreme Court on the interference liability of the operator of an Internet opinion forum, 27 March 2007 BGH [Federal Supreme Court] [VI ZR 101/06], GRUR 2007, 724, 726 (Meinungsforum).

170 As an example, anyone who intentionally brings about a cause of a direct copyright infringement of third parties in any way could be responsible as a general principle according to a common formula in German case law, cf. *Dreier/Schulze*, Urheberrechtsgesetz, § 97, No. 23.

171 19 April 2007 BGH [Federal Supreme Court] [I ZR 35/04], GRUR 2007, 708, 711 (Internetversteigerung II); *Luckhaus*, Haftung einer Handelplattform für „gebrauchte Domains", GRUR-RR 2008, 113, 114.

172 30 June 1994 BGH [Federal Supreme Court] [I ZR 40/92], GRUR 1994, 841, 842 f (Suchwort); 10 October 1996 BGH [Federal Supreme Court] [I ZR 129/94], GRUR 1997, 313, 315 f. (Architektenwettbewerb); 15 October 1998 BGH [Federal Supreme Court] [I ZR 120/96], GRUR 1999, 418, 419 f. (Möbelklassiker); 17 May 2001 BGH [Federal Supreme Court] [I ZR 251/99], GRUR 2001, 1038, 1039 (ambiente.de); 11 March 2004 BGH [Federal Supreme Court] [I ZR 304/01], MMR 2004, 668, 671 (Internetversteigerung-ROLEX) with the note *Hoeren*; 19 April 2007 BGH [Federal Supreme Court] [I ZR 35/04], GRUR 2007, 708, 711 (Internetversteigerung II).

173 11 March 2004 BGH [Federal Supreme Court] [I ZR 304/01], MMR 2004, 668, 671 f. (Internetversteigerung-ROLEX).

174 11 March 2004 BGH [Federal Supreme Court] [I ZR 304/01], MMR 2004, 668, 672 (Internetversteigerung-ROLEX).

175 The question namely of the extent to which eBay is also technically in a position or would have to be in a position to not only check offers with regard to their text elements but also with regard

be used to investigate illegal offers by identifying key words in advance and filtering them out.[176]

The position that the "VeRO" (Verified Rights Owners) program used by eBay represents an actual and legally sufficient process in the fight against product piracy[177] did not hold up to scrutiny by the German Federal Supreme Court: VeRO is aimed at permitting a right owner who joins the program to continually monitor eBay pages for infringement of such rights, and then pursue and remedy violations out of court in an automated process. At the same time, there is automated offer deletion, for example, as well as a surrender of the address of the offerer given to eBay.[178] According to the German Federal Supreme Court, however, control mechanisms are to be used in the run-up to an online offer after knowledge of infringement is obtained to satisfy the duty to monitor.[179]

The German Federal Supreme Court has also recently held fast to these principles for the liability of Internet auctions for trademark infringement.[180]

c. Competition Law Liability

The German Federal Supreme Court recently accepted a cease-and-desist claim of a provider of telemedia (eBay) asserting a breach of a duty of care under competition law.[181] Such duty can be summarised in the opinion of the German Federal Supreme Court as a duty to monitor.[182] The only additional liability under competition law, i. e. the consequence of an obligation to pay compensation according to the Gesetz gegen den unlauteren Wettbewerb [UWG] [Act Against Unfair Competition] (F. R.G.), does not apply to online service providers since it can be assumed that the relevant qualified liability also refers to those cases.

---

to their picture elements is in dispute, cf. *Lubberger*, Schutzrechtsverletzungen bei eBay & Co. – Einordnung, Verantwortlichkeit, Abwehrstrategien, MarkenR 2006, 515, 520.

176 *Lubberger*, Schutzrechtsverletzungen bei eBay & Co. – Einordnung, Verantwortlichkeit, Abwehrstrategien, MarkenR 2006, 515, 520.

177 See the statement of eBay in the proceedings before the Düsseldorf Higher Regional Court, 26 February 2004 OLG [Higher Regional Court] Düsseldorf [I-20 U 204/02, 20 U 204/02], WRP 2004, 631, 633.

178 See one's own information from eBay at http://pages.ebay.de/help/community/vero-program.html.

179 11 March 2004 BGH [Federal Supreme Court] [I ZR 304/01], MMR 2004, 668, 672 (Internetversteigerung-ROLEX).

180 19 April 2007 BGH [Federal Supreme Court] [I ZR 35/04], GRUR 2007, 708, 712 (Internetversteigerung II); 30 April 2008 BGH [Federal Supreme Court] [I ZR 73/05], MarkenR 2008, 235 (Internetversteigerung III).

181 12 July 2007 BGH [Federal Supreme Court] [I ZR 18/04], GRUR 2007, 890 (Jugendgefährdende Medien bei eBay).

182 12 July 2007 BGH [Federal Supreme Court] [I ZR 18/04], GRUR 2007, 890, 894 (Jugendgefährdende Medien bei eBay).

Whether, and the extent to which, the courts will follow German literature requesting a duty to monitor to be completely eliminated from fault-independent cease-and-desist claims according to the Act Against Unfair Competition[183] is currently unclear. The most far-reaching consequence in practice would be that Internet providers who obtain financial benefits by making third-party information available – such as eBay, for instance, by receiving a commission – could be sent warning letters and charged also for the costs of the first warning letter without having to be separately notified of the infringement of rights beforehand.

d. Claim to Information

The personal identity of Internet users can frequently be determined by the operator of online auctions such as eBay, at least if the user has registered with his or her correct name. A claim for information to be provided by the Internet providers has nevertheless been lacking for a long time. Until recently, only the infringing party could be sued for a claim for information. This gap has been closed in the online area with the Act on the Improvement of the Enforcement of Intellectual Property Rights (Gesetz zur Verbesserung der Durchsetzung von Rechten des geistigen Eigentums).[184] The new version of sec. 19, para. 2 MarkenG [Trademark Act] based thereupon now provides the ability to demand information, independently of the filing of a lawsuit, not only from the infringing party, but also from certain third parties such as persons who provided services in a commercial scope used in connection with the infringing activities.[185] A breach of the duty to monitor, as case law requires for establishing secondary contribution liability,[186] is not provided in the provisions of the Enforcement Directive (Directive 2004/48/EC of 29 April 2004 on the Enforcement of Intellectual Property Rights).[187]

5. Special case: Metatags

Until the *Impuls* ruling of the German Federal Supreme Court,[188] it had long been disputed whether the use of a third-party mark as a hidden search word (metatag) in the Internet represented (infringing) trademark use. The German Federal Supreme Court has now held that trademark use in the case of metatags cannot be denied since metatags, as key words hidden in the "source text" serving in Internet page indexing, suppo-

---

183 For instance according to *Döring*, Die Haftung für eine Mitwirkung an Wettbewerbsverstößen nach der Entscheidung des BGH „Jugendgefährdende Medien bei eBay", WRP 2007, 1131, 1137.

184 A draft bill was passed by the German Bundestag on 11 April 2008 (see BT-Drucks. 16/5048); the act entered into force on 1 September 2008.

185 See details on the claim to information below under II. C.

186 See only 19 April 2007 BGH [Federal Supreme Court] [I ZR 35/04], GRUR 2007, 708, 711 (Internetversteigerung II); 11 March 2004 BGH [Federal Supreme Court] [I ZR 304/01], MMR 2004, 668, 671 (Internetversteigerung-ROLEX).

187 Official Journal of the European Union 2004 No L 157/45 and Corrigendum to Directive 2004/48/EC, Official Journal of the European Union 2004 No L 195/16; BT-Drucks. 16/5048, p. 73 f.

188 18 May 2006 BGH [Federal Supreme Court] [I ZR 183/03], WRP 2006, 1513, 1515 f. (Impuls).

sedly cannot be seen by the average Internet user. Rather, it is important that the result of the selection process is influenced with the aid of the search word and the user is led to the corresponding Internet page in this way, which is why the German Federal Supreme Court affirmed that metatags may constitute trademark infringement. While the decision *Impuls* made it clear that the actual content of the Internet page corresponding to the metatag may not be considered when determining the likelihood of confusion, the Higher Regional Court Frankfurt am Main just recently further specified this principle by stating that the short summary indicated below each hit in the hit list must be taken into account with regard to such determination.[189]

6. Special case: Context-Sensitive Advertising

Unlike the use of metatags, German case law on placing context-sensitive advertising (key word advertising) is still inconsistent. Context-sensitive advertising is given if – as in the case of AdWords from Google, for instance[190] – the advertisements of the parties who have booked the AdWord at Google appear on the right-hand side next to the hit list of the Internet search machine in a column headed by "Advertisements". Some assume that unauthorised use of a third party's trademark within context-sensitive advertising is a typical trademark use *(markenmäßige Benutzung)* and therefore constitutes trademark infringement.[191] Others, in contrast, hold the opinion that the use of a third-party trademark as a so-called AdWord does not represent trademark infringement.[192] The idea behind the latter concept is that there is no danger of infringing a trademark holder's rights where the advertisement appearing via AdWords is unambiguously recognisable as such and clearly points out the company behind it and that company's Internet site. According to the court's arguments, even an inexperienced Internet user will understand that the offerers appearing under this heading are advertising customers of the operator of the Internet search engine. The opposing point of view justifies its opinion with a comparison of AdWords to metatags and the *Impuls* ruling of the Ger-

---

189 10 January 2008 OLG [Higher Regional Court] Frankfurt am Main [6 U 177/07], GRUR-RR 2008, 292 (Sandra Escort).

190 https://adwords.google.de/select/Login?sourceid=AWOsubid=emea-de-ha-awmedium=haterm=google%20adwords.

191 5 December 2006 OLG [Higher Regional Court] Braunschweig [2 W 23/06], MMR 2007, 110; 9 August 2007 OLG [Higher Regional Court] Stuttgart [2 U 23/07], MMR 2007, 649; 6 December 2007 OLG [Higher Regional Court] München [29 U 4013/07], MMR 2008, 334.

192 23 January 2007 OLG [Higher Regional Court] Düsseldorf [I-20 U 79/06, 20 U 79/06], MMR 2007, 247, 248; 31 August 2007 OLG [Higher Regional Court] Köln [6 U 48/07], GRUR-RR 2008, 160: While the Higher Regional Courts Frankfurt/Main and Cologne based their jugdements on the argumentation that a trademark infringement is not given because of a lack of a typical trademark use being, i. a., characterised by its function to identify certain goods or services with a particular company (reference of origin), the Higher Regional Court Düsseldorf did not clearly decide on the question of a typical trademark use but denied a trademark infringement because of a lacking likelihood of confusion in the case of using AdWords; 26 February 2008 OLG [Higher Regional Court] Frankfurt/Main [6 W 17/08], WRP 2008, 830, 832.

man Federal Supreme Court.[193] Both metatagging and AdWords are similar by guiding the average Internet user towards certain hits or advertisements. In the case of AdWords, it may remain an open issue that the advertisement is marked as such and visually displayed outside of the actual hit list. With metatags, the corresponding hit notices appear in the actual hit list. Courts held that a likelihood of confusion cannot be denied in such cases. According to their view, the Internet user will not know from the Internet site that the advertiser using the AdWord and the trademark owner are not identical or at least affiliated. Instead, the user will infer, based on the advertisement's location, the advertiser had paid for having the advertisement placed in a prominent position. It remains to be seen how the issue will finally be decided by the German Federal Supreme Court. The German Federal Supreme Court has just recently requested the European Court of Justice for a preliminary ruling on the question of trademark infringement: 22 January 2009 BGH [Federal Supreme Court] [I ZR 125/07] (Bananabay), press release of the German Federal Supreme Court No. 17/2009, available at http://www.bundesgerichtshof.de.

A qualified liability of the search engine operator or the link provider according to the TMG [Telemedia Act] has been rejected until now in German case law despite resistance from the business sector.

Whether the placement of context-sensitive advertising is to be regarded as a violation of competition law from the standpoint of exploiting another's reputation and the diversion of customer flows as set forth in sections 3 para. 1 and 4, No. 10 UWG [Act against Unfair Competition] has likewise not been ruled upon with finality by the German Federal Supreme Court. Against the backdrop that the advertisement (such as the AdWords advertisement) obviously originates from a different provider from the public perspective, the argument of exploitation of another's reputation can probably be rejected.[194] It also seems fairly unlikely that the activity constitutes a diversion of customer flows. Keyword advertising might be seen as a diversion of customer flows contrary to fair competition if a party steps between the competitor and the prospective buyer in an attempt to redirect the prospective buyer's intentions and impose a buying decision.[195] A comparable situation in the real world would be someone systematically approaching and intercepting competitor's customers shortly before they enter the competitor's business. It seems more than dubious, however, whether an Internet user typing a third party's trademark into a search engine thereby establishes proximity comparable to the situation described above and expresses his or her buying decision. And rather than imposing itself upon the customer, a person placing an advertisement is offering an alternative from an advertising competitor.[196]

---

193 18 May 2006 BGH [Federal Supreme Court] [I ZR 183/03], WRP 2006, 1513, 1515 f. (Impuls).

194 23 January 2007 OLG [Higher Regional Court] Düsseldorf [I-20 U 79/06, 20 U 79/06], MMR 2007, 247, 248; 21 September 2004 LG [District Court] Hamburg [312 O 324/04], MMR 2005, 631, 633; different view: 8 June 2004 OLG [Higher Regional Court] Cologne [6 W 59/04], K&R 2006, 240, 241.

195 *Hefermehl/Köhler/Bornkamm*; Gesetz gegen den unlauteren Wettbewerb, § 4, No. 10.25.

196 Cf. also *Erdmann/Rojahn/Sosnitza*; Handbuch des Fachanwalts Gewerblicher Rechtsschutz, Chapter 5. F., No. 1278.

7. Special Case: Parallel Imports

a. Basic Principle

Parallel imports do not involve pirated goods in a narrow sense, but instead original products that enter the European market without the consent of the trademark owner. It is a basic principle that a trademark owner cannot prohibit the further sale of genuine goods marked with its trademark after the goods have been put on the market with its express or tacit consent in another Member State or in a different Treaty State of the EEC (Agreement on the European Economic Area of 3 January 1994)[197] (so-called principle of the exhaustion of rights under the trademark law[198] *(markenrechtlicher Erschöpfungsgrundsatz)*). It is the infringing party who must prove that the rights were exhausted. Thus, the dealer of the infringing goods must prove that the goods were put on the market for the first time in the EU with the consent of the trademark owner. An exception should only apply if the trademark owner puts the goods on the market via an EU-wide, exclusive sales system. In those cases, the trademark owner must prove that the goods were put on the market outside of the EU by the owner or with his or her consent.[199]

Parallel imports differ from the situation where a trademark owner has third parties manufacture the brand-name goods under a licence (in the form of an extended workbench), and the third parties misuse their position by manufacturing a greater quantity of goods than is permitted under the licence. The goods manufactured in such way, although they are likewise original goods, represent counterfeits from the beginning because they are no longer covered by the licence.[200]

Section 24, para. 2 MarkenG [Trademark Act] also provides for exceptions that are intended to entitle the trademark owner to oppose the exhaustion of his or her trademark rights. Examples are a change or deterioration of the goods after they are put on the market. Other case groups have developed which assume an exception to the exhaustion principle. The offence of repacking brand-name goods and subsequently importing them in parallel into the European Community could be especially relevant to the area of trademark piracy. The ECJ set up strict standards in this regard, the details of which are outlined below; when they are not complied with, the parallel import will be regarded as impermissible despite exhaustion.

---

197 BlPMZ 1994, 70 ff.; Official Journal No. L 001 of 3 January 1994, p. 3 ff.; Treaty States: Norway, Iceland, Liechtenstein and the EU States. Switzerland, as an EFTA Member, did not join the EEC Agreement, cf. in more detail *Baudenbacher*, Erschöpfung der Immaterialgüterrechte in der EFTA und die Rechtslage in der EU, GRUR Int 2000, 584, 585.

198 MarkenG [Trademark Act] § 24 ¶ 1 (F.R.G.).

199 Cf. 8 April 2003 ECJ [C-244/00], GRUR 2003, 512, 514 (Stüssy).

200 Cf. *Welser/González*, Marken- und Produktpiraterie, No. 10 with a reference to so-called "factory overruns".

Finally, in practice it is important to know that a border seizure of parallel imports is only possible via the national confiscation proceedings.[201]

b. Repacking Goods

The concept of repacking of goods is understood broadly, because repacking is always assumed when the importer changes the content or the appearance of the original packing.[202] Repacking consequently occurs, for instance, when new stickers cover existing labels (relabeling).[203] Another instance is where lettering is (only) put on the inner blister packs of a package of pharmaceutical products, but the outer packing corresponds to the original trademark labeling in the country where it is imported,[204] or where the package includes replacement instructions that have been translated into the relevant country's language,[205] or when original packages are topped up by adding further original goods.[206]

In the ruling *Bristol-Myers Squibb*,[207] the ECJ determined for the first time five requirements that have to be met before parallel importers of pharmaceutical products are permitted to repack or newly pack the goods and to subsequently market them whereas these principles of Community law are not limited to pharmaceutical products, but instead apply to all products for which it is necessary to effect changes in the packing:[208]

- It must be evident that assertion of trademark rights has been shown to contribute to artificial compartmentalisation of markets, which is particularly the case when the repacking is required to be able to sell the goods in the importing country.

---

201 See comprehensive information regarding the border seizer proceedings above, *Claudia Milbradt*, Enforcement of Intellectual Property Rights in Germany, I. B.2. and below under III. B.

202 For example, 14 September 1998 OLG [Higher Regional Court] Hamburg [3 W 105/98], GRUR 1999, 172 (Gonal-F); *Ingerl/Rohnke*, Markengesetz, § 24, No. 68.

203 19 October 2000 BGH [Federal Supreme Court] [I ZR 89/98], WRP 2001, 549, 550 (ZOCOR); 12 December 2002 BGH [Federal Supreme Court] [I ZR 133/00], WRP 2003, 528, 530 (Beloc); 21 September 2001 OLG [Higher Regional Court] Hamburg [3 U 41/00], GRUR 2001, 440 (PULMICORT II); now also expressly ECJ for the first time, 26 April 2007 ECJ [C-348/04], GRUR 2007, 586, 589 No. 28 f. (Boehringer/Swingward II).

204 19 October 2000 BGH [Federal Supreme Court] [I ZR 89/98], WRP 2001, 549, 550 (ZOCOR).

205 19 October 2000 BGH [Federal Supreme Court] [I ZR 89/98], WRP 2001, 549, 550 (ZOCOR); 29 March 2001 BGH [Federal Supreme Court] [I ZR 263/98], GRUR 2002, 57, 58 (Adalat).

206 29 March 2001 BGH [Federal Supreme Court] [I ZR 263/98], GRUR 2002, 57, 58 (Adalat); 25 August 1989 OLG [Higher Regional Court] Köln [6 U 22/89], GRUR 1991, 52, 53 (Bayotensin).

207 11 July 1996 ECJ [Joined Cases C-427/93, C-429/93, C-436/93], GRUR Int. 1996, 1144, 1150 (Bristol-Myers Squibb).

208 *Ingerl/Rohnke*, Markengesetz, § 24, No. 67; cf. e. g. the ruling of the ECJ in 11 November 1997 ECJ [C-349/95], GRUR Int 1998, 145, 148 Nos. 47 ff.(Loendersloot/Ballantine), in which the ECJ also applied these principles to alcohol products; cf. in addition 12 February 2004 OLG [Higher Regional Court] Hamburg [3 U 98/00], GRUR-RR 2005, 109, 110.

The requirement of the necessity of repacking was specifically addressed by the ECJ on a number of occasions. It held in the *Loendersloot./.Ballantine* ruling that the parallel importer had to choose the course of the least possible intervention as a general principle.[209] Thus, if the brand-name goods are sold in different packaging sizes, with a different presentation or under different brand-names, their repacking has to be the only possibility for being able to successfully sell the product in the importing country. In contrast to this, the trademark owner may take steps against repackaging if the parallel importer did repack the goods although it would have been just as effective to relabel the package,[210] to include an instruction leaflet in the language of the importing country or to replace any articles not approved in the importing Member State by an approved article.[211] Further, total repacking was only regarded as permissible in German case law when less severe measures, such as the application of labels, the creation of bundled packages and topping up or topping off the package content, possibly with the sale of the surplus content in a new package, are ruled out.[212] The necessity of intervention in the repacking must be affirmed in virtually all cases when there are changes in the packing size to adapt to those sold in the importing country, for instance because only certain packing sizes are approved there or accepted by the health insurance scheme.[213]

Later on, the necessity was put in more concrete terms by the ECJ. It held that the repacking must be objectively required to make it possible for the parallel importer to actually access the market of the importing country.[214] That is the case, for example, when other sales forms, for instance using different brand names or presentations of a brand-name article imported in parallel, bring about strong resistance from a considerable fraction of the market.[215] What constitutes considerable resistance by consumers requires clarification from the national courts. Factual circumstances may be proven through a demographic survey or market research institute.[216] A mere aversion of the market to pharmaceutical products pasted over with labels is not

209 11 November 1997 ECJ [C-349/95], GRUR Int 1998, 145, 148 (Loendersloot/Ballantine).

210 11 July 1996 ECJ [Joined Cases C-427/93, C-429/93, C-436/93], GRUR Int 1996, 1144, 1148 (Bristol-Myers Squibb); 23 April 2002 ECJ [C-143700], WRP 2002, 666, 671 (Boehringer/Swingward I).

211 11 July 1996 ECJ [Joined Cases C-427/93, C-429/93, C-436/93], GRUR Int. 1996, 1144, 1148 (Bristol-Myers Squibb).

212 *Wolpert*, Parallelimporte von Arzneimitteln, WRP 2008, 453, 455 with a reference to the rulings 21 Jaunary 2002 HansOLG [Hamburg Higher Regional Court], GRUR-RR 2002, 319 ff. (Überzählige Blisterstreifen); 11 July 2002 BGH [Federal Supreme Court] [I ZR 35/00], GRUR 2002, 1063, 1066 (Aspirin); 12 December 2002 BGH [Federal Supreme Court] [I ZR 141/00], GRUR 2003, 434 ff. (Pulmicort).

213 cf. e. g. 11 July 1996 ECJ [Joined Cases C-427/93, C-429/93, C-436/93], GRUR Int. 1996, 1144, 1150 No. 79 (Bristol-Myers Squibb); 23 April 2002 ECJ [C-443/99], WRP 2002, 673, 676 (Merck, Sharp & Dohme); *Ingerl/Rohnke*, Markengesetz, § 24, No. 70.

214 23 April 2002 ECJ [C-443/99], GRUR Int. 2002, 745, 747 (Merck/Paranova); 23 April 20002 ECJ [C-143700], WRP 2002, 666, 671 (Boehringer/Swingward I).

215 12 October 1999 ECJ [C-379/97], GRUR Int. 2000, 159, 162 (Upjohn/Paranova); 23 April 2002 ECJ [C-443/99], WRP 2002, 673, 676 (Merck, Sharp & Dohme).

216 *Nauta*, Ausnahmen vom Erschöpfungsgrundsatz im Markenrecht, GRUR Int 2004, 994, 997.

sufficient, though, to make repacking necessary.[217] Repacking is also not deemed necessary if it has the exclusive purpose of the parallel importer wanting to generate an economic benefit.[218]

- The original condition of the pharmaceutical product, e. g. in a blister strip, is not permitted to be impacted by the changes that the importer or its supplier makes. This may occur when a new instruction leaflet is incomplete or when it contains incorrect data.[219]

- Both, the repacking company and the manufacturer must be named on the packaging.

- Repacked pharmaceuticals are not permitted to be presented in a way that damages the reputation of the brand name. For example, the packing consequently must not be faulty, of poor quality or disorderly. Other cases of reputational damage may also occur.[220] It can also be damaging to a reputation when a parallel importer fails to place the trademark on the outer box ("de-branding") or either uses its own logo or company symbol or a presentation used for a series of different goods for the new external box ("co-branding").[221]

- The importer must finally notify the trademark owner in advance of any sales offering of the repacked pharmaceutical products and provide him with a sample of the repacked goods upon demand. That should put the trademark owner in a position to determine whether or not the requirements for exhaustion that were additionally set up by the ECJ have been met.[222]

Recent rulings where the German Federal Supreme Court faced the question of taking the ECJ practice into consideration were Aspirin II,[223] CORDARONE[224] and STILNOX.[225] The ruling was in favor of the parallel importers in all of the cases.

---

217 23 April 2002 ECJ [C-143700], WRP 2002, 666, 671 (Boehringer/Swingward I).

218 23 April 2002 ECJ [C-143700], WRP 2002, 666, 671 (Boehringer/Swingward I).

219 11 July 1996 ECJ [Joined Cases C-427/93, C-429/93, C-436/93], GRUR Int 1996, 1144, 1148 (Bristol-Myers Squibb).

220 26 April 2007 ECJ [C-348/04], GRUR 2007, 586, 590 (Boehringer/Swingward II).

221 26 April 2007 ECJ [C-348/04], GRUR 2007, 586, 590 (Boehringer/Swingward II).

222 11 July 2002 BGH [Federal Supreme Court] [I ZR 219/99], GRUR 2002, 1059, 1061 (Zantac/Zantic); 11 July 2002 BGH [Federal Supreme Court] [I ZR 35/00], GRUR 2002, 1063 (Aspirin); 12 February 2004 OLG [Higher Regional Court] Hamburg [3 U 98/00], GRUR-RR 2005, 109, 110 f.

223 12 July 2007 BGH [Federal Supreme Court] [I ZR 147/04], WRP 2008, 102 ff. (Aspirin II).

224 12 July 2007 BGH [Federal Supreme Court] [I ZR 148/04], WRP 2008, 226 ff. (CORDARONE).

225 14 June 2007 BGH [Federal Supreme Court] [I ZR 173/04], WRP 2007, 1472 ff. (STILNOX).

II. Legal Consequences of Trademark Infringement

Under the MarkenG [Trademark Act], the owner of a German national trademark or an IR trademark enjoying protection in Germany, as well as the owner of a company symbol, can seek to enjoin an infringer from committing any activities infringing upon its senior trademark rights. Moreover, the owner may claim monetary damages for infringement. In parallel, the rights owner is entitled to request the destruction of any infringing products that may still exist and to make a claim for information regarding the origin and distribution channel of such goods. Recent provisions also allow for a recall claim and a claim for presentation and inspection. Owners of Community trademarks are entitled to enforce their trademark rights directly according to the provisions of the Community Trademark Regulation.

A. Discontinuance

The cease-and-desist claim to prevent recurrence of past and imminent infringements derives from sec. 14, para. 5 MarkenG [Trademark Act] for registered trademarks or trademarks protected by virtue of a secondary meaning and sec. 15, para. 4 MarkenG [Trademark Act] for business designations (company symbols and titles of works). The claim, which assumes a risk of infringement, is not dependent on fault, which means that it is irrelevant whether the infringing party was actually aware of the infringement or could have been aware of it. In trademark piracy cases, the cease-and-desist claim is generally enforced through a preliminary injunction. The cease-and-desist claim also may be enforced by sending a warning letter upon which the infringer signs an enforceable cease-and-desist declaration *(strafbewehrte Unterlassungserklärung)* in order to prevent court proceedings to be initiated.[226]

1. Risk of First Infringement

A trademark owner can bring an action to prevent an imminent initial infringement from taking place. In other words, it is not necessary to wait until the infringement has actually occurred.[227] The risk of serious and direct likelihood of infringement is sufficient to trigger a preventive cease-and-desist claim.[228] To ensure that effective and prompt trademark protection can be guaranteed, the risk need not be excessively great. For example, making standard preparations and asserting that one is entitled to use the symbol are sufficient.

Filing a trademark application with the German Patent and Trademark Office always constitutes the risk of a first infringement regarding the commercial use of the applied

226 For details on the declaration to cease and desist see above, *Claudia Milbradt*, Enforcement of Intellectual Property Rights in Germany, I. A.1.

227 Cf. just 19 June 1951 BGH [Federal Supreme Court] [I ZR 77/50], BGHZ 2, 394, 395 (Widia/Ardia).

228 17 March 1994 BGH [Federal Supreme Court] [I ZR 304/91], GRUR 1994, 530, 532 (Beta).

designation.[229] This also applies to any application for the extension of protection of an IR trademark to Germany.[230] In contrast to this, the mere registration of an Internet domain name does not suffice to constitute the risk of a first infringement, because it cannot be derived from the domain name as such whether it will be used for private or commercial purposes and for similar goods or services as the possibly infringed trademark.[231]

With regard to incurring a risk of infringement when applying for protection of a Community trademark the following distinction should be made: If the infringement may affect an earlier Community trademark – with the applicable national law under the reference of Article 92 lit. a) Community Trademark Regulation being German law – such risk may be assumed without a special localisation being required. It does, however, not suffice to merely apply for the registration of a Community trademark in order to automatically constitute the risk of an infringement of earlier trademarks protected under the national laws in each of the Member States. Given the large number of Member States, it cannot be assumed that each applicant of a Community trademark intends to actually use the mark in all of the Member States.[232]

Contrary to the case where an infringement has already occurred, an *actus contrarius* is already generally sufficient as a rule for the elimination of the risk of first infringement.[233] A cease-and-desist declaration involving specific penalties does not have to be delivered as a general principle; the withdrawal of the trademark application or a restriction of the list of goods may instead already eliminate the risk of first infringement in individual cases.[234]

---

[229] 19 January 1989 BGH [Federal Supreme Court] [I ZR 217/86], GRUR 1990, 361, 363 (KRONENTHALER); 10 October 2002 BGH [Federal Supreme Court] [I ZR 235/00], GRUR 2003, 428, 431 (BIG BERTHA); 15 January 2004 BGH [Federal Supreme Court] [I ZR 12/01], GRUR 2004, 600, 601 (d-c-fix/CD-FIX).

[230] 19 January 1989 BGH [Federal Supreme Court] [I ZR 217/86], GRUR 1990, 361, 363 (KRONENTHALER):

[231] 21 February 2002 BGH [Federal Supreme Court] [I ZR 230/99], GRUR 2002, 898, 900 (de facto), which requires the use of the domain for the infringement (likewise *Ingerl/Rohnke*, Markengesetz, after § 15, Nos. 79, 147).

[232] *Ingerl/Rohnke*, Markengesetz, before §§ 14–19, No. 62.

[233] With regard to competition law, e. g. 16 January 1992 BGH [Federal Supreme Court] [I ZR 20/90], GRUR 1992, 404, 405 (Systemunterschiede).

[234] *Schulz*, Einstweiliger Rechtsschutz gegen Markenanmeldungen, WRP 2000, 258, 261; *Teplitzky*, Wettbewerbsrechtliche Ansprüche und Verfahren, Chapter 10, No. 21; answering in the negative with regard to the mere withdrawal of trademark applications: *Ingerl/Rohnke*, Markengesetz, before §§ 14-19, No. 69; hinting that it was trending towards this, but left open in the end: 4 February 1993 BGH [Federal Supreme Court] [I ZR 42/91], BGHZ, 121, 243, 246 (TRIANGLE); consent to a deletion request is sufficient: 12 February 2000 OLG [Higher Regional Court] Hamburg [3 U 71/99], GRUR-RR 2001, 231, 233 (planet e).

2. Risk of Recurrence

There is always a risk that an infringement may recur when past infringements suggest a possible repeat of the same or substantially similar activity.[235] The only way to eliminate the risk of recurrence is through a cease-and-desist declaration that fully covers the subject matter of the claim and that irrevocably demonstrates acceptance of an appropriate contractual penalty in the event of a future violation.[236] Even the fact that a company is bankrupt or has ceased operations does not in any case eliminate the threat.[237] The same is true with respect to the surrender of an Internet domain name.[238] The risk of recurrence is not even eliminated when the domain name is taken over by the authorised party itself, since the infringing party may attempt to use the disputed domain name again under a different top level domain. Therefore, only a corresponding enforceable cease-and-desist declaration will provide adequate protection.[239]

B. Damages

1. Basic Principle

Compensatory damages according to sec. 14, para. 6 and sec. 15, para. 5 MarkenG [Trademark Act] are unique in requiring proof of intent or negligence for infringement claims. Negligence does not require a heavy burden of proof in trademark law. Negligence is presumed when a mark is used without first performing any research on the mark or associated name in the relevant public or commercial registry.[240] The subjective capabilities or practices of the infringing party are not important here, but the standards of care of the respective industrial sector that are to be determined according to objective criteria certainly are.[241] Requirements should be placed to an increased degree on the required duties of care and the duty to review businesses with the increasing awareness of the extent of trademark piracy, especially following the enactment of the Pro-

---

235 16 November 1995 BGH [Federal Supreme Court] [I ZR 229/93], WRP 1996, 284, 285 (Wegfall der Wiederholungsgefahr II); 28 March 1996 BGH [Federal Supreme Court] [I ZR 39/94], GRUR 1996, 781, 783 (Verbrauchsmaterialien).

236 Cf. just 14 October 1999 BGH [Federal Supreme Court] [I ZR 90/97], GRUR 2000, 605, 608 (comtes/ComTel); 16 January 2002 BGH [I ZR 84/90], GRUR 1992, 318, 319 f. (Jubiläumsverkauf) with further references; 5 March 1998 OLG [Higher Regional Court] Hamburg [3 U 175/97], NJWE – WettbR 1999, 138 (Altenborger Rahm Zeege).

237 14 October 1999 BGH [Federal Supreme Court] [I ZR 90/97], GRUR 2000, 605, 608 (comtes/ComTel).

238 Cf. with regard to this 12 August 1999 OLG [Higher Regional Court] München [6 U 4484/98], GRUR 2000, 519, 520 (rollsroyce.de).

239 *Ingerl/Rohnke*, Markengesetz, before §§ 14-19, No. 55.

240 24 November 1959 BGH [Federal Supreme Court] [I ZR 88/58], GRUR 1960, 186, 188, 189 (Arctos); 8 October 1969 BGH [Federal Supreme Court] [I ZR 149/67], GRUR 1970, 87, 88 (Mushi-Blix); *Fezer*, Markenrecht, § 14, No. 515.

241 *Harte-Bavendamm*, Handbuch der Markenpiraterie in Europa, § 5, No. 86.

duct Piracy Act (Produktpirateriegesetz) in 1990.[242] The German Federal Supreme Court already addressed the duty to review businesses in its ruling *Chanel N° 5 (I)* in 1987.[243] Then, the German Federal Supreme Court stated that industrial purchasers, when purchasing widely known brand-name goods, are specifically obligated to pay attention to the authenticity of the origin of the goods where cases of trademark piracy have recently become known. If there are serious doubts as to the origin of the goods, special duties requiring investigation by the purchaser arise. It is always the question in individual cases as to when such indications might be present. Thus, the fact that goods are purchased at a very economical price or purchased outside of the distribution channels organised by the manufacturer does not necessarily mean that counterfeit goods are involved.

2. Calculation of the Compensation

The injured party may choose from three alternatives for calculating the compensation which are not mutually exclusive. The right to select one of the options only lapses when a claim asserted according to a specific manner of calculation is either fulfilled or recognised with legally binding effect. Finally, a loss that is asserted can also be based on several calculation methods in the alternative, and the awarding court is then required to use the calculation method that is most favorable for the plaintiff.[244]

a. Licence Analogy

The most common type of calculating damages in trademark cases is based on the "licence analogy" where the loss is calculated in accordance with a licence fee that would have been appropriate had a trademark licence agreement been concluded (hypothetical licence)[245] between the mark holder and the accused infringer. The usual result of such an exercise is a per-unit royalty based on net turnover.[246] Licence analogy damages are not limited to the profit of the infringing party.[247] Instead, the focus should be on the fee that reasonable contracting parties would have agreed upon taking all of the objective circumstances into consideration. Relevant factors include the level of familiarity

---

[242] Gesetz zur Stärkung des Schutzes des geistigen Eigentums und zur Bekämpfung der Produktpiraterie [Act to Strengthen Protection of Intellectual Property and to Combat Product Piracy] (F. R.G.).

[243] 18 December 1986 BGH [Federal Supreme Court] [I ZR 111/84], GRUR 1987, 520, 525 ff. (Chanel No. 5 (I)).

[244] 17 June 1992 BGH [Federal Supreme Court] [I ZR 107/90], GRUR 1993, 55, 57 f. (Tchibo/Rolex II).

[245] 12 January 1966 BGH [Federal Supreme Court] [Ib ZR 5/64], GRUR 1966, 375 (Meßmer-Tee II) for Trademarks; 16 February 1973 BGH [Federal Supreme Court] [I ZR 74/71], GRUR 1973, 375, 377 (Miss Petite) for name and company name rights; 22 March 1990 BGH [Federal Supreme Court] [I ZR 59/88], GRUR 1990, 1008, 1009 (Lizenzanalogie).

[246] 11 August 1970 BGH [Federal Supreme Court] [6 U 2/69], GRUR 1971, 221 (Pudelzeichen II).

[247] *Ingerl/Rohnke*, Markengesetz, before §§ 14-19, No. 115.

and the reputation of the infringed trademark,[248] the level of interference with the mark, the importance of the trademark for the purchaser and the duration and scope of use of the trademark.[249] The typical range in trademark cases is between 1% and 5%, where higher rates are required for famous trademarks crucial for sales.[250]

b. Actual Losses

Alternatively, in counterfeit and piracy cases damages may be based on actual losses, including lost profits.[251]

The level of sales that the trademark owner would have achieved in the absence of infringement determines the amount of damages due. It is often difficult to prove that an infringement has caused a loss of sales. The trademark holder must provide evidence that he or she would have made a sale in the absence of any infringement. The precise estimate of the lost profits is frequently difficult, especially for pirated products that are often substantially cheaper and attract different purchasers. Courts generally provide a final estimate of the loss according to sec. 287 Zivilprozessordnung [ZPO] [Civil procedure statute] (F. R.G).

Damages include not only lost sales, but also incidental expenses such as the costs of pursuing legal actions and what is referred to as "market confusion loss".[252] Market confusion occurs if identical or similar trademarks of several owners are used for identical or similar products thus impairing the customers' ability to identify the origin of the products from one particular manufacturer.[253] The costs for eliminating the market confusion may include costs for clarifying circular letters, corrective counter-advertisements or increased costs for advertising measures, for instance.

248 3 July 1974 BGH [Federal Supreme Court] [I ZR 65/73], GRUR 1975, 85, 87 (Clarissa).

249 *Ingerl/Rohnke*, Markengesetz, before §§ 14-19, No. 115.

250 *Ingerl/Rohnke*, Markengesetz, before §§ 14-19, No. 116 with a reference to 15% in the case of designer T-shirts: 7 June 2001 OLG [Higher Regional Court] München [29 U 2003/01], OLGR München, 283, 284, f.; *Ströbele/Hacker*, Markengesetz, § 14, No. 278 with a reference to 2%, for example, in the case of cheap spirits.

251 BGB [Civil Code] §§ 249, 252 (F. R.G.).

252 25 June 1954 BGH [Federal Supreme Court] [I ZR 7/53], GRUR 1954, 457 (Irus/Urus); 4 March 1982 BGH [Federal Supreme Court] [I ZR 19/80], GRUR 1982, 489, 491 (Korrekturflüssigkeit); 26 May 1988 BGH [Federal Supreme Court] [I ZR 227/86], GRUR 1988, 776 (PPC).

253 *Fezer*, Markenrecht, § 14, No. 521.

c. Disgorgement of Profits

Finally, an injured plaintiff may demand that the infringer surrender any profit obtained through infringement.[254] This method is at least theoretically attractive to the extent the infringer made "quick money" with very attractive profit margins. Such damages are generally much greater than licence analogy damages. At the same time, the owner can avoid the undesirable disclosure of its own internal cost structures, which is frequently difficult to avoid when having to calculate and substantiate one's own (differential) losses.[255] The German Federal Supreme Court has held that only the net profits need to be surrendered.[256] The infringer can therefore deduct all of the required expenses from the gross profits. In addition, the Court held that only that portion of the profit specifically linked to the trademark infringement needs to be surrendered. In contrast, the infringer is entitled to keep the portion that is linked to the quality of the goods, the type of business activity of the infringing party or the intensity of the advertising, for instance.[257]

C. Information

Until recently, only the infringing party was considered as appropriate addressee of an information claim according to sec. 19 MarkenG [Trademark Act].

The Act on the Improvement of the Enforcement of Intellectual Property Rights[258] substantially expanded actions for information in favor of the trademark owner. In the future, owners of protective rights whose trademarks are infringed will not only have a right to information from the alleged infringing party, but also from persons who, in commerce,

(i) had infringing goods in their possession,
(ii) made use of infringing services,
(iii) provided services used for infringing activities, or
(iv) participated in the production, creation or sale of goods of that type or in the provision of services of that type and have been named by one of the persons set out in (i)-(iii) (see sec. 19 para. 2 MarkenG [Trademark Act].

---

254 3 February 1909 RG [Court of the German Reich] [I 99/08], RGZ 70, 249; 13 March 1962 BGH [Federal Supreme Court] [I ZR 18/61], GRUR 1962, 401 (Kreuzbodenventilsäcke III); 29 May 1962 BGH [Federal Supreme Court] [I ZR 132/60], GRUR 1962, 509 (Dia-Rähmchen II).

255 *Harte-Bavendamm*, Handbuch der Markenpiraterie in Europa, § 5, No. 100.

256 Cf. 29 May 1962 BGH [Federal Supreme Court] [I ZR 132/60], GRUR 1962, 509, 512 (Dia-Rähmchen II).

257 24 February 1961 BGH [Federal Supreme Court] [I ZR 83/59], GRUR 1961, 354, 355 (Vitasulfal); 13 March 2003 OLG [Higher Regional Court] Frankfurt [6 U 3/02], GRUR-RR 2003, 274, 277 (Vier-Streifen-Kennzeichnung).

258 A draft bill was passed by the German Bundestag on 11 April 2008 (see BT_Drucks. 16/5048); the act entered into force on 1 September 2008.

Actions for third-party information now close a substantial gap, since such actions were previously prohibited due to the absence of an infringing party in the case. Especially in the online area, it was entities such as Internet providers, for example, who were in the possession of the required information on the infringing party but were frequently not obliged or permitted to turn this over to the aggrieved party.[259]

Also, until recently, it was not possible to claim for information as regards the origin of infringing services as it is now provided for since the claim for information is no longer limited to illegally designated goods.

Unlike before, not only must information regarding the manufacturer's suppliers be provided, but also information regarding other prior owners of the goods and commercial purchasers and the name and address of the sales offices for which the goods were destined. In addition, information is to not only be provided with regard to the goods that were manufactured, delivered, received or ordered, but also with regard to prices that were paid for the relevant goods or services. The new regulations are therefore generally welcome to owners of rights, because it makes it easier for them to identify persons who are participating in the infringement and to specify the sales channels. The Act on the Improvement of the Enforcement of Intellectual Property Rights even goes beyond the requirement that the Enforcement Directive established, because the German legislature does not necessarily presuppose court proceedings against the infringing party, but instead provides regulations on the obligation to provide information independently of such proceedings (existence of a "*case of obvious infringement of rights*" should suffice as an alternative to the filing of a suit).

D. Destruction

According to sec. 18, paras. 1 and 2 MarkenG [Trademark Act], the owner of a protected mark can demand that items that are illegally marked and which are in the possession of (or owned by) the infringing party be destroyed. This applies primarily to cases of mass trademark infringement.[260] Destruction is intended to ensure that the pirated goods disappear forever from the market.[261] The relevant regulations therefore have both preventive and sanction-related characteristics.[262] The requirement of the infringing products having to be possessed or owned by the infringer has not been changed by the Act on the Improvement of the Enforcement of Intellectual Property Rights since otherwise destruction would not be legally possible.[263]

---

259 Also see details on this above under I. C.4.d.

260 Cf. Stellungnahme der Deutschen Vereinigung für Gewerblichen Rechtsschutz und Urheberrecht, GRUR 1989, 29, 31 f.

261 BT-Drucks. 11/4792, p. 28.

262 10 April 1997 BGH [Federal Supreme Court] [I ZR 242/94], GRUR 1997, 899, 900 (Vernichtungsanspruch), cf. 23 February 2006 BGH [Federal Supreme Court] [I ZR 27/03], GRUR 2006, 504, 508 (Parfümtestkäufe); *Ensthaler*, Produktpirateriegesetz, GRUR 1992, 273, 277.

263 BT-Drucks. 16/5048, p. 79.

It is not possible to delay destruction by a payment in cash.[264] In general, an action for destruction is also still available even where removal of the mark may be possible. Only where destruction would be unreasonably disproportionate compared to less severe sanctions will the less severe method be required.[265] All individual cases must therefore be viewed in the light of proportionality.[266] Relevant factors include the degree of culpability or the losses of the trademark owner compared to the losses that may be incurred by the infringing party because of the destruction.[267] Especially if a different type of disposal is a possibility (e. g. only destruction of the packaging, not the unmarked goods as well), an action for destruction may be limited by the restraints of necessity and proportionality.[268] Also the removal of the infringing mark may possibly serve as a less severe consequence when there is trademark infringement. Merely pasting a sticker over the mark is not sufficient, though,[269] because the risk of trademark infringement is not eliminated with finality. Instead, the mark has to be permanently removed. If the mark is blacked out or if a label is pasted over it, the covering of the mark must not be removable without destroying the mark itself.[270] This is often not possible, though, for instance in cases of clothing with imprints.[271]

The enforcement of rights is further not limited to proceedings on the merits. Instead, the mark owner can also seek an order requiring surrender of the items to a sequestrator in advance of an action for destruction.[272] The destruction itself may not be ordered via a preliminary injunction, though, because it cannot be reversed.[273] The possibility of less drastic remedial measures cannot be cited in opposition to the petition for an in-

264 *Ingerl/Rohnke*, Markengesetz, § 18, No. 20; different view in *Fezer*, Markenrecht, § 18, No. 41.

265 10 April 1997 BGH [Federal Supreme Court] [I ZR 242/94], GRUR 1997, 899, 901 (Vernichtungsanspruch) *Bodewig*, Praktische Probleme bei der Abwicklung der Rechtsfolgen einer Patentverletzung – Unterlassung, Beseitigung, Auskunft, GRUR 2005, 632, 637; *Pickrahn*, Die Bekämpfung von Parallelimporten nach dem neuen Markengesetz, GRUR 1996, 383, 387.

266 10 April 1997 BGH [Federal Supreme Court] [I ZR 242/94], GRUR 1997, 899, 901 (Vernichtungsanspruch); *Bodewig*, Praktische Probleme bei der Abwicklung der Rechtsfolgen einer Patentverletzung – Unterlassung, Beseitigung, Auskunft, GRUR 2005, 632, 637.

267 BT-Drucks. 11/4792, p. 28; 10 April 1997 BGH [Federal Supreme Court] [I ZR 242/94], GRUR 1997, 899, 901 (Vernichtungsanspruch).

268 28 February 2002 OLG [Higher Regional Court] Bremen [2 U 88/01], WRP 2002, 460, 464 (lila Verpackung).

269 *Ströbele/Hacker*, Markengesetz, § 18, No. 33.

270 *Ingerl/Rohnke*, Markengesetz, § 18, No. 21.

271 Cf. *Ingerl/Rohnke*, Markengesetz, § 18, No. 22.

272 2 April 2002 OLG [Higher Regional Court] Karlsruhe [6 W 24/02], GRUR-RR 2002, 278, 279 (DVD-Player); Cf. e. g. 10 June 2003 LG [District Court] Berlin [15 O 185/03], GRUR-RR 2004, 16, 17 (Fernglas).

273 Applicable as far as this is concerned 26 September 1996 OLG [Higher Regional Court] Hamburg [3 H 83/96], WRP 1997, 106, 112 (Gucci); 13 November 1975 OLG [Higher Regional Court] Frankfurt am Main [12 U 189/75], GRUR 1976, 663 (Teppichbremse); *Ingerl/Rohnke*, Markengesetz, § 18, No. 35.

junction because security is also required in this case.[274] The need for security is only denied in injunction proceedings when the requirements for a destruction action no longer exist, because performance of the cease-and-desist obligation of the infringing party has either been ensured with a legally binding order or an enforceable cease-and-desist declaration.[275]

The action for destruction is supplemented by the possibility of also destroying certain materials and devices primarily used in illegally marking products according to sec. 18, para. 1, sent. 1 MarkenG [Trademark Act] in the new version implemented by the Act on the Improvement of the Enforcement of Intellectual Property Rights. It remains to be seen how German case law will interpret this provision. Some assume that "materials and devices" will be interpreted similarly broadly as the term "equipment" provided until recently in sec. 18, para. 2 MarkenG [Trademark Act]. There, the term "equipment" covered all resources used in reliance on the respective type of goods and production method, for example molds and special tools as well as stamping and labeling machines. In addition, photomechanical and digital reproduction devices and equipment for imitating holograms are also covered.[276]

E. Recall

Actions to recall infringing articles had not been recognised before September 2008 under the MarkenG [Trademark Act].[277] The only way to act was to try and convince the product safety authorities to take action.

German trademark law has now been supplemented for the first time with an action to recall infringing products, or have them finally removed from distribution channels (cf. the new version of sec. 18, para. 2 MarkenG [Trademark Act]) by the Act on the Improvement of the Enforcement of Intellectual Property Rights. Recall campaigns can be initiated at any time, regardless of title or possession, thus representing an effective deterrent to potential infringers. The corresponding interests of third-party owners should be looked at under the concept of proportionality.[278] In contrast to an action for destruction, which only covers goods that are still in the possession of or owned by the infringing party, a recall action permits removal from the market of infringing goods that have already been sold. This fact particularly presents a problem for the right owners in the low-price segment, since they may be exposed to warranty claims, and at the very least to reputation damage, possibly associated with substantial drops in sales volume.

---

274 24 March 2000 OLG [Higher Regional Court] Stuttgart [2 U 209/99], NJW-RR 201, 257, 258 f. (Porsche Spider 550).

275 11 February 1999 OLG [Higher Regional Court] Hamburg [3 U 184/98], NJWE-WettbR 2000, 19, 21 (Berodual).

276 *Harte-Bavendamm*, Handbuch der Markenpiraterie in Europa, § 5, No. 120.

277 Cf. 9 September 1999 OLG [Higher Regional Court] Hamburg [3 U 114/98], NJWE-WettbR 2000, 15, 16 (Spice Girls); *Ingerl/Rohnke*, Markengesetz, before §§ 14-19, No. 105.

278 Cf. The new version of § 18 ¶ 3 MarkenG [Trademark Act] (F. R.G.).

Neither the Enforcement Directive nor the revised version of the MarkenG [Trademark Act] specifies the difference between recall and final removal from distribution channels, and the difference remains unclear. One possibility is to view the final removal from distribution channels as a measure that should be taken by the party whose rights are infringed and by which the goods are removed from market circulation without destroying them.[279] The mere removal of a trademark that had been illegally applied may be an adequate measure in this respect under certain circumstances.[280]

Recall claims, however, are not very likely to be enforced vis-à-vis contractual partners of the infringing party since the infringer does not have access to the goods.[281] Thus, recalls may still fail in implementation in the future, especially where an infringing party – as in many piracy cases – lacks an orderly business operation.

F. Presentation and Inspection

Until recently, German trademark law did not contain any regulations governing actions for inspection or presentation of documents for the purpose of determining whether trademark infringement exists prior to the implementation of the Act on the Improvement of the Enforcement of Intellectual Property Rights. The revised version of sec. 19 lit. a) MarkenG [Trademark Act] should now provide for these options in the future, codifying recent German case law including the discovery procedure developed by the District Court Düsseldorf known as the "Düsseldorf inspection procedure". In conformity with the Enforcement Directive and the German Federal Supreme Court rulings *Faxkarte* (Fax Card) 2 May 2002 BGH [Federal Supreme Court] [I ZR 45/01], WRP 2002, 1173 *(Faxkarte)* and *Restschadstoffentfernung* (Residual Contaminant Removal) 1 August 2006 BGH [Federal Supreme Court] [X ZR 114/03], WRP 2006, 1377 *(Restschadstoffentfernung)*, the new MarkenG [Trademark Act] does not require a high probability, but only an adequate probability of an infringement of rights having been committed in a commercial context. In addition, the prior discussion as to whether the principles that were set up by the German Federal Supreme Court in the above-mentioned rulings do apply to protective rights other than patents or copyrights becomes superfluous because of the introduction of this provision into the MarkenG [Trademark Act].

---

279 *Dreier*, Ausgleich, Abschreckung und andere Rechtsfolgen von Urheberrechtsverletzungen, GRUR Int 2004, 706, 711 (Footnote 40); *Spindler/Weber*, Die Umsetzung der Enforcement-Richtlinie nach dem Regierungsentwurf für ein Gesetz zur Verbesserung der Durchsetzung von Rechten des geistigen Eigentums, ZUM 2007, 257, 259.

280 *Nägele/Nitsche*, Gesetzentwurf der Bundesregierung zur Verbesserung der Durchsetzung von Rechten des geistigen Eigentums, WRP 2007, 1047, 1055; *Spindler/Weber*, Die Umsetzung der Enforcement-Richtlinie nach dem Regierungsentwurf für ein Gesetz zur Verbesserung der Durchsetzung von Rechten des geistigen Eigentums, ZUM 2007, 257, 259.

281 GRUR-Stellungnahme, GRUR 2006, 393; *Nägele/Nitsche*, Gesetzentwurf der Bundesregierung zur Verbesserung der Durchsetzung von Rechten des geistigen Eigentums, WRP 2007, 1047, 1056 with further references.

III. Enforcement

A. Civil Action

1. Preliminary Injunction

A cease-and-desist claim can be specifically enforced in a number of trademark cases through preliminary injunctions[282] instead of lawsuits (which frequently extend over years). The injunction prevents trademark owners from having to passively stand by and watch as a third party continues to infringe. In addition, an accused infringer in a case of obvious infringement can be obligated to immediately provide further information.

In order to comply with the case law trends of important German Higher Regional Courts for granting injunctions, which refuse to presume urgency in trademark matters as in preliminary injunction proceedings under the UWG [Act Against Unfair Competition],[283] it is in any case recommended to explain and substantiate urgency when filing for a preliminary injunction. Urgency in trademark cases is as a rule assumed if the application for the preliminary injunction is submitted within four to six weeks from having received actual and reliable knowledge of all of the circumstances forming the basis for the trademark infringement (including knowledge of the opponent).

The precise remedy sought within the context of a request for a preliminary injunction has great practical relevance. It is mandatory to request the prohibition of possession in the form of surrender of the goods infringing upon the trademark to a sequestrator so that the main issue is not anticipated in an impermissible way.

A final arrangement that is equivalent to an enforceable judgment on the merits may be obtained via a so-called final declaration *(Abschlusserklärung)*. In a final declaration, the respondent acknowledges the arrangements provided in the preliminary injunction as a legally binding arrangement between the parties within 14 days of the receipt of the preliminary injunction as a rule. It is advisable that such undertaking is protected by a contractual penalty for each violation of the cease-and-desist order. The petitioner should usually also recognise an obligation to pay compensation to avoid litigation. The need to file a lawsuit to obtain legal protection is no longer necessary or possible for a petitioner when a final declaration has been signed by the infringing party. The respondent should therefore, in turn, undertake to waive the filing of an appeal against the preliminary injunction.[284]

---

282 Also see above, *Claudia Milbradt*, Enforcement of Intellectual Property Rights in Germany, I. A.2. with regard to preliminary injunctions.

283 See e. g. 13 November 2001 OLG [Higher Regional Court] Düsseldorf [20 U 114/01], GRUR-RR 2002, 212 (Top Ticket).

284 ZPO [Civil procedure statute] §§ 924, 926, 927 (F. R.G.).

2. Action on the Merits

An action on the merits in trademark cases is usually filed (i) when the filing for a preliminary injunction is no longer possible for lack of urgency; (ii) when the infringing party is not willing to provide a final declaration; (iii) when the expected preliminary injunction bond is too high (i. e., the obligation to pay compensation in the event the injunction was wrongly issued[285]); or (iv) when the issue of the enforcement of claims for compensation is involved, provided that an out-of-court settlement was not able to be reached. One is forced to file an action on the merits here, in order to obtain a legally binding judgment.[286] In addition, claims to destruction and claims to cancellation of recent infringing trademark registrations from the register can be enforced with the aid of actions on the merits.

3. Choice of Courts

Exclusive jurisdiction in trademark issues is assigned to the District Courts *(Landgerichte)*, regardless of the amount in dispute that is otherwise used to establish the jurisdiction of Local Courts *(Amtsgerichte)* or District Courts.[287] Aside from the aspect that one would like to choose a court that is especially experienced in trademark issues, it has to be considered that numerous German federal states have made use of the provision as set forth in sec. 140, para. 2 MarkenG [Trademark Act] to assign all trademark disputes to a specific District Court.[288]

The Community trademark courts have exclusive jurisdiction over lawsuits arising in connection with Community trademarks.[289] Each German state is required to designate an individual District Court as Community trademark court, the purpose of this being to concentrate competence.[290]

When there is trademark infringement on the Internet, such as via infringing advertising, so-called "floating jurisdiction" *(fliegender Gerichtsstand)* is also available to the injured party. That is, all responsible District Courts and Community trademark courts all over Germany are available despite the otherwise applying local competence of the courts since the trademark infringement can be called up throughout Germany over the Internet.

---

285 ZPO [Civil procedure statute] § 945 (F. R.G.).

286 Also see above, *Claudia Milbradt*, Enforcement of Intellectual Property Rights in Germany, I. A.2. with regard to the demarcation of preliminary injunction vs. action on the merits.

287 MarkenG [Trademark Act] § 140 ¶ 1 (F. R.G.).

288 In Hessen, for instance, the Frankfurt a. M. district court for the entire state of Hessen; the Leipzig district court in Saxony for the entire state of Saxony.

289 MarkenG [Trademark Act] § 125 lit. e) (F. R.G.).

290 In Hesse, for instance, the Frankfurt a. M. district court for the entire state; the Düsseldorf district court is responsible for the entire state North Rhine-Westphalia.

B. Border Measures

The border seizure process[291] at external German borders has proven to be an effective tool, especially in the case of trademark infringement. Unlike for patents, where counterfeit products in many cases only become evident through expensive testing procedures, trademark owners can facilitate the discovery of fake goods by customs officials through detailed descriptions of the brand-name goods. Such descriptions should include special identification characteristics, including any security technologies that may have been incorporated such as certification stamps, holograms or OVD (optically variable device) technologies. In 2006, customs agents in Hamburg executed what is probably the largest seizure in the world, confiscating (and subsequently destroying) goods with a value of EUR 383 million.[292] Border seizure procedures involving trademark infringements are available through EU law as well as through national regulations.

1. Border Seizure Request according to the EU Customs Regulation

a. Area of Application

According to Art. 2, para. 1 Customs Regulation, trademarks are included in the protected rights that are covered by a border seizure according to EU law. The Customs Regulation covers look-alikes as well as identical copies, according to the wording of its Art. 2, para. 1.[293] Also products protected by indications of geographic origin can be subject to the border seizure under EU law. However, only registered trademarks (but not marks protectable via secondary meaning) are subject to border seizure procedures. Parallel imports are likewise excluded from the protection granted by the Customs Regulation.[294]

To prevent the common practice of importing infringing trademark labels separately from the goods (with the labels being attached subsequently), Art. 3, para. 1 lit. a) (ii) Customs Regulation clarifies that marking means (including emblems, instructions for use and operating instructions, stickers, brochures etc. which have marking means of that type) are imitated goods as defined by the Customs Regulation and therefore also subject to seizure.

b. Application for Seizure at the Border in Trademark Matters

In any case, mandatory requirement to be included in the request for seizure at the border is evidence that the requesting party is the owner of the trademark rights (via (cer-

291 See above *Claudia Milbradt*, Enforcement of Intellectual Property Rights in Germany, I. B.2., for details on the border seizure process according to EC law and according to national law.

292 See the report at http://www.spiegel.de/wirtschaft/0,1518,druck-448326,00.html.

293 *Welser/González*, Marken- und Produktpiraterie, No. 262.

294 Art. 3 ¶ 1 Customs Regulation.

tified) excerpts from the trademark register or the inclusion of registration documents). In addition, it is strongly recommended – because it is especially promising in cases of suspected trademark infringement – to include a description of the brand-name goods that is as precise and detailed as possible. The description of features ideally contains a positive list of the original's features (i. e. characteristics including protection technologies, if any) and a negative list describing the imitation (i. e., characteristics of the counterfeit products and information on means for circumventing the protective technologies).

c. Simplified Procedure for Owners of Community Trademarks

Article 5, para. 4 of the Customs Regulation offers owners of Community trademarks simplified procedures in which the request for border seizure is extended to all of the Member States of the EU. The application must only be submitted to one Member State, and thus in Germany to the Intellectual Property Office at Nuremberg Regional Tax Office (*Oberfinanzdirektion Nürnberg – Zentralstelle Gewerblicher Rechtsschutz* (ZGR)).

2. Border Seizure Request according to National Law

According to sections 146 ff. MarkenG [Trademark Act], trademark owners can submit a request to the customs authorities to take action pursuant to national law – also in parallel with the border seizure procedure according to EU law as described above. As above, look-alikes that involve a risk of confusion are included in the scope of national law, as well as identical copies and goods protected by geographic origin indications.[295] Unlike under the EU-border seizure procedure, unregistered marks (protection acquired by use, famous trademarks or company symbols) which are protected according to sections 4, Nos. 2, 3 and 5 MarkenG [Trademark Act] also fall under the scope of the national border seizure procedure. However, the infringement must be clearly recognisable ("obvious"[296]), to qualify for seizure. As a practical matter, because pirated goods are frequently identical copies, it may become critical to include an explicit description of the brand-name goods and their identification features in the national seizure procedure.

3. Simplified Destruction Procedure

Article 11 of the Customs Regulation authorises Member States to provide for a simplified procedure for destroying infringing articles that have been seized. For this purpose, sec. 150 MarkenG [Trademark Act] has recently been revised, and the simplified destruction procedure that had been long been requested was consequently implemented into national law by means of the Act of the Improvement of the Enforcement of Intellectual Property Rights. The destruction request should be submitted in writing

---

295 *Ingerl/Rohnke*, Markengesetz, § 146, No. 3.

296 Cf. MarkenG [Trademark Act] § 146 ¶ 1 (F. R.G.).

within ten working days of the receipt of the notification of the customs authorities.[297] It must include notice that the relevant goods infringe rights protected by the MarkenG [Trademark Act] and the written consent of the applicant, holder or owner for the destruction of the goods. Alternatively, the applicant can directly deliver the written declaration as to whether he consents to destruction or not to customs authorities.

Before the simplified destruction procedure was implemented in national law, customs administration deemed it sufficient for the applicant, holder or owner to request that the customs authorities cancel the customs declaration and destroy the infringing products. So whereas destruction of infringing goods was only possible based on the practices of the customs administration until September 2008, the new law even goes a step further by creating fictitious consent to the destruction[298] if the applicant, holder or owner does not object to destruction within ten working days of the receipt of the notification by the customs authorities. Thus, destruction is possible without the infringing party having to make any statement at all.

It has consequently become considerably easier for rights owners to bring about the destruction of infringing goods. Another benefit associated with the new regulation – in particular in cases where only small amounts of seized goods are involved – is that the rights owner does not have to pay any costs that are customarily associated with the initiation of court proceedings. Moreover, since the destruction is no longer tied to a court finding, a foreign infringing party can no longer evade court proceedings by suddenly disappearing, which is what unfortunately happens in many cases in practice. Instead, it is possible for the trademark owner, specifically because of the newly added fiction of consent of the infringing party, to handle the infringement case in a very short period of time and to prevent infringing products from entering the market.

4. Liability of Forwarding Agents

A related issue is the extent of liability of forwarding agents in this fact pattern. The issue is most common where the applicant of the goods is domiciled in a foreign country or can only be reached with difficulty. Although forwarding agents are not obligated as a general principle to inspect the goods they transport for potential infringement, German case law is clear that forwarding agents are subject to a duty of review starting from the moment they receive concrete evidence of infringement.[299] As a consequence, the forwarding agent must also consent to the destruction of the goods. If it refuses to do so, it becomes a secondary contributor *(Störer)* against which a claim may be raised with respect to the costs of the destruction, which it would otherwise not have to pay.[300]

297 MarkenG [Trademark Act] § 150 ¶ 3 (F. R.G.).

298 MarkenG [Trademark Act] § 150 ¶ 4 (F. R.G.).

299 15 January 1957 BGH [Federal Supreme Court] [I ZR 59/55], GRUR 1957, 352, 354 (Taeschner (Pertusin II)); 29 November 2007 OLG [Higher Regional Court] Düsseldorf [I-2 U 51/06], No. 33.

300 6 April 2006 LG [District Court] Düsseldorf [4a O 1/06], InstGE 6, 132, 134 (Frachtführer II).

C. Measures on Trade Shows

1. Actions at the Trade Show Itself

Taking action against product pirates at trade show events is especially effective, because exhibitors from throughout the world present their goods to industry specialists. Many infringers can otherwise only be reached with difficulty or not at all.

In addition to customs officials who work as investigators for the district attorney's office, the owners of protective rights themselves (i. e., expert representatives of the individual companies) more frequently inspect individual trade show booths with their attorneys for imitations of their brand-name goods. Inspections usually take place on the first day of a trade show so that a picture of the exhibitors can be made. On the second day, it is advisable to visit the trade show accompanied by officials of the customs investigation office[301] and/or officials of the mobile inspection groups *(Mobile Kontrollgruppen)* that are part of the main customs offices and that are deployed on a nationwide basis[302] in order to call on the suspicious exhibitors in a targeted way.

If it is clear through prior examination of the exhibitor's directory that exhibitors will be present who will most likely exhibit infringing products, it is strongly advised to ensure that effective legal protection will be provided for by informing the competent court that there will be a submission of petitions for the issuance of preliminary injunctions and/or a submission of demands for prosecution. In detail, the following actions should be considered:

a. Preliminary Injunction

The cease-and-desist and removal claims against infringers must produce the desired result in view of the short amount of time available during the trade show. This goal is achieved by a petition for a preliminary injunction (including a preliminary seizure order[303]). However, merely exhibiting goods for offering purposes is not distribution in the market due to a lack of an exchange of control over the items.[304] But offering items domestically at an international trade show establishes the basis for at least a risk of first infringement, and also with regard to being put on the market",[305] forming the basis for a preventive cease-and-desist claim. In addition, offering items at a trade fair held in Germany fulfills the elements of an offering of goods (and at the very least possession for this

---

301 In Germany, eight customs investigation offices have jurisdiction (Berlin-Brandenburg, Dresden, Essen, Frankfurt am Main, Hamburg, Hanover, Munich and Stuttgart).

302 For further information see http://www.zoll.de/d0_zoll_im_einsatz/d0_mkg/a0_organisation/index.html.

303 ZPO [Civil procedure statute] § 938 (F. R.G.).

304 *Ingerl/Rohnke*, Markengesetz, § 14, No. 192.

305 19 January 1989 BGH [Federal Supreme Court] [I ZR 217/86], GRUR 1990, 361, 363 (KRONENTHALER); *Ingerl/Rohnke*, Markengesetz, before §§ 14-19, No. 65.

purpose) as defined by sec. 14, para. 3, No. 2 MarkenG [Trademark Act]. The preliminary confiscation is carried out to enforce a court order to surrender the infringing goods to the bailiff or to another person nominated by the petitioner, for instance an attorney. Although this is not mandatory, it is advisable to pursue the demand for the confiscation (seizure order) in parallel with the cease-and-desist issue.[306] Characteristics suitable for identification of the imitation should be described to the bailiff in detail via verbal paraphrases and/or illustrations or samples in the seizure order. In case of doubt, it may also be useful to arrange for an expert to become involved.[307]

b. Agreement under Civil Law

The desired goal of having the infringer remove the offending products from its booth is frequently already achieved in the run-up to a preliminary injunction and the related official confiscation. Experience has shown that many exhibitors express their willingness to enter a deal to remove the infringing goods and provide an enforceable declaration to cease and desist after receiving a request to that end and the presentation of a warning letter in order to prevent the petition for a preliminary injunction against them from being filed.

c. Border Seizure

Goods exhibited at trade shows are deemed to be in temporary use procedures under customs law, and are regarded as not having been introduced yet into the Community because they are completely or partially exempt from customs and import duties. Actions of the customs officials based on the Customs Regulation and/or based on a request under national seizure procedures are possible, even at the trade show itself, because trade-show goods are consequently regarded as non-Community goods under customs law.

The case law of the ECJ on transit cases[308] cannot be accepted without limitation for all of the non-levying procedures. A different evaluation is appropriate, at least in trade-show cases, to which the temporary use procedures under customs law apply, which likewise represent non-levying procedures: The goods are visible to every market partici-

---

306 Cf. 3 October 1980 OLG [Higher Regional Court] Nürnberg [3 W 1790/80], WRP 1981, 342 f.; *Teplitzky*, Wettbewerbsrechtliche Ansprüche und Verfahren, Chapter 22, No. 5; different view 10 July 1983 KG [Higher Regional Court] Berlin [5 W 2286/83], WRP 1984, 325 f.

307 That is usually a trademark-protection expert from the industrial sector of the petitioner, because outside experts who are only generally familiar with the relevant industrial sector usually do not have the relevant internal production specifications, material knowledge, coding systems and experience that the original manufacturer/trademark owner itself has, cf. *Harte-Bavendamm*, Handbuch der Markenpiraterie in Europa, § 5, No. 133.

308 See comprehensive information on the transit cases above under I. C.3.

pant when being exhibited at a trade show, which is why offering them or at least possessing them for the purpose of such offering must be assumed as a rule,[309] thus constituting an infringement.

2. Actions in the Run-Up to the Trade Show

Actions taken via a preliminary injunction run the risk that an injunction will be issued too late. In addition, foreign exhibitors can frequently no longer be reached after the trade show ends, so a petitioner runs the risk of being left with the costs of the litigation. It is therefore important, and more effective in most cases, to prevent the exhibition of infringing trade-show goods (to which, since being regarded as non-Community goods, the Customs Regulation applies) right from the start, for instance with a comprehensive submission of border seizure requests.

309 MarkenG [Trademark Act] § 14 ¶ 3 No. 2 (F.R.G.).

Design Piracy

Anna Gruchol

I. Introduction

Particularly original designs may provide a competitive edge that product pirates try to exploit by copying these designs without authorisation. Design piracy can be found in all business fields such as commercial art, the automobile industry or fashion. The damage caused by design piracy does not only consist in the direct loss of profit, but also in the impairment of the right holder's reputation which may arise from poor imitations.

Design law is not codified in a single law in Germany. Rather, designers or the companies who have acquired particular designs may proceed against design piracy based on different laws, with the GeschmMG [Geschmacksmustergesetz] [Design Act] (F. R.G.) being especially relevant in this context. The Community Design Regulation (Regulation 2002/06/EC of 12 December 2001 on Community Designs)[1] is also directly applicable. Additional protection for designs is provided by copyright, trademark and competition law.

II. Protection under the German Design Act

Design law aims to protect outward appearances, especially those created by industrial designs. Design protection in Germany was embodied in a law for the first time in 1876, in the GeschmMG [Design Act]. This Act remained more or less unchanged until 2004. Originally, the reason for protecting designs was to extend the protection for appearances which, due to a lack of creativity, were not eligible for copyright protection, but which nonetheless warranted investment protection as aesthetic designs.[2] Nowadays, design rights have to be seen as supplementing patent and trademark rights on the one hand, and copyrights on the other. In fact, before the change in law design law was interpreted by way of a dogmatic comparison with copyright law.[3]

In June 2004, a new GeschmMG [Design Act] came into force in Germany. The Act implements the Design Directive (Directive 98/71/EC of 13 October 1998 on the legal

---

1 Council Regulation (EC) No 6/2002 of 12 December 2001 on Community designs, Official Journal of the European Communities 2002 No L 3/1.

2 Begründung zum Gesetzentwurf der Bundesregierung, Regierungsentwurf [Reasons for the draft bill of the Federal Government, Government Draft], BT-Drucks. 15/1075, p. 29.

3 Begründung zum Gesetzentwurf der Bundesregierung, Regierungsentwurf [Reasons for the draft bill of the Federal Government, Government Draft], BT-Drucks. 15/1075, p. 29; *Wandtke/Ohst*, Zur Reform des deutschen Geschmacksmustergesetzes, GRUR Int 2005, 91 f.

protection of designs), which has approximated the national design laws in Europe. The reform made design right an independent property right, even though the amended law itself makes implicit references to the dogmatics of to copyright law, as well as to patent and trademark law.[4]

A. Requirements for protection

1. Protected subject matter

A design is eligible for protection if the design is novel and has an individual character.[5]

a. Design

The term "Design" *(Geschmacksmuster)* is legally defined in sec. 1 no. 1 GeschmMG [Design Act](F. R.G). According to this definition, a design is the two or three-dimensional appearance of the whole or a part of a product resulting from the features of, in particular, the lines, contours, colours, shape, texture or materials of the product itself or its ornamentation. The term design in German terms comprises both design in the original sense *(Muster)* as well as models *(Modelle)* whereby models designate 3-dimensional designs. A design in the form of an ornament, being a design in the original sense of "*Muster*", is e. g. a surface decoration of textiles or wallpapers.[6]

Apart from designs, products enjoy protection, too. According to the legal definition,[7] a product is any industrial or handicraft item, including packaging, get-up, graphic symbols and typographic typefaces. Computer programs are explicitly excluded from the scope of the design.

The design right therefore protects the design as such or the appearance of a design embodied in an object. Both the term design and the term product have to be construed rather broadly.[8] The prerequisite is always, however, that the design can be reflected in the product or relate to a product.[9] Therefore, contourless colours as such, as well as

---

4 Begründung zum Gesetzentwurf der Bundesregierung, Regierungsentwurf [Reasons for the draft bill of the Federal Government, Government Draft], BT-Drucks. 15/1075, p. 29; *Wandtke/Ohst*, Zur Reform des deutschen Geschmacksmustergesetze, GRUR Int 2005, 91 f.

5 GeschmMG [Design Act] § 2 ¶ 1 (F. R.G.).

6 *Eichmann/von Falckenstein*, Geschmacksmustergesetz, § 1, No. 11; Green Book of the Commission, No. 5.4.4.2.

7 GeschmMG [Design Act] § 1 no. 2 (F. R.G.).

8 *Kur*, Die Auswirkungen des neuen Geschmacksmusterrechts auf die Praxis, GRUR 2002, 661, 663; *Wandtke/Ohst*, Zur Reform des deutschen Geschmacksmustergesetzes, GRUR Int 2005, 91, 93.

9 *Eichmann/von Falckenstein*, Geschmacksmustergesetz, § 1, No. 5 and 12: Product means an object for which a design can be used (Reasons Article 3 of the proposed Regulation 1993).

fragrances and aromas are excluded from design protection.[10] Given the broad construction of the term "design", the scope of design right protection is to be limited by the prerequisites novelty and individual character.[11]

b. Novelty

Novelty is present only if no identical design has been made available to the public before the application date.[12] The relevant application date is the day the application documents were received by the German Patent and Trademark Office (Deutsches Patent- und Markenamt).[13]

Designs are considered identical if their features differ only with respect to immaterial details, i. e. if they are almost identical.[14] To determine this, the individual design to be assessed and the closest design made available to the public before the filing date are compared.[15]

Section 5 GeschmMG [Design Act] explains what is considered to have been available to the public. Such is the case if the design has been published, exhibited, used in trade or otherwise made available to the public, except where these events could not reasonably have become known in the normal course of business to the circles specialised in the sector concerned before the filing date of the design. Here, sec. 6 GeschmMG [Design Act] provides for a period of grace of twelve month after the filing date. By this, the designer can test within the grace period the effect and success of the design of the market before applying for a registered design.

The features of novelty and individual character are linked. In order to assess novelty, it is important to know whether the designs to be assessed are identical or almost identical. Yet in practice, a variation in immaterial details compared to an earlier, known design can only be assessed based on the individual character of the design in question.[16]

10 *Bulling/Langöhrig/Hellwig*, Gemeinschaftsgeschmacksmuster, No. 37; *Eichmann/von Falckenstein*, Geschmacksmustergesetz, § 1, No. 7.

11 *Bulling/Langöhrig/Hellwig*, Gemeinschaftsgeschmacksmuster, No. 37; *Eichmann/von Falckenstein*, Geschmacksmustergesetz, § 1, No. 7.

12 GeschmMG [Design Act] § 2 ¶ 2 (F. R.G.). In case priority is claimed, the date of priority is decisive.

13 GeschmMG [Design Act] § 13 ¶ 1 (F. R.G.); if however, a foreign priority is claimed, the application date is replaced with the priority date pursuant to § 14 or § 15 Design Act, see § 13 ¶ 2 Design Act (F. R.G.).

14 GeschmMG [Design Act] § 5 (F. R.G.).

15 19 January 2006 OLG [Higher Regional Court] Hamm [4 U 148/05] (Kaminöfen).

16 *Bulling/Langöhrig/Hellwig*, Gemeinschaftsgeschmacksmuster, Nos. 5 f.

c. Individual character

A design has an individual character if the overall impression it produces on an informed user differs from the overall impression produced by any other design disclosed before the filing date, see sec. 2 para. 3 GeschmMG [Design Act].

In assessing the individual character, the degree of freedom of the designer in developing the design shall be taken into consideration.[17] What is required, therefore, is a subjective evaluation of the distinctiveness between the design in question and the designs already made available to the public.[18] The necessary degree of distinctiveness is not absolute and varies depending on the number of designs already available to the public. The more designs are present in a class of products of already-known designs, the lower the requirements of individuality, and vice versa.[19]

The overall impression of the individual design is in particular determined by the elements and features of the design which are decisive for its individual character.[20] The "informed user" is neither a design expert nor the more or less superficial consumer.[21] What is relevant is that the registered design can be distinguished from individual, other designs that have already been made publicly available.[22]

d. Exclusion from protection

The GeschmMG [Design Act] in sec. 3 contains several grounds on which design protection is excluded.

According to sec. 3 para. 1 no. 1 GeschmMG [Design Act], distinctive features of products which are exclusively dictated by their technical function are not eligible for design protection. This exclusion is based on the consideration that design elements for which there is no alternative do not merit protection as designs.[23]

---

17 See GeschmMG [Design Act] § 2 ¶ 3 (F. R.G.).This provision goes back to Art. 5 of the Design Directive (Directive 98/71/EC of 13 October 1998 on the legal protection of designs).

18 20 December 2006 OLG [Higher Regional Court] Hamburg [5 U 135/05] (Handydesign); *Kur*, Die Auswirkungen des neuen Geschmacksmusterrechts auf die Praxis, GRUR 2002, 661, 665.

19 The Begründung zum Gesetzentwurf der Bundesregierung, Regierungsentwurf [Reasons for the draft bill of the Federal Government, Government Draft], BT-Drucks. 15/1075, p. 34, puts forward as an argument in favour of a possible protection of designs of little individuality that the design will be granted as an incentive for further developing the existing corpus of designs. Therefore, the design law should be able to take its effect also in areas in which there is only limited room for design variants.

20 *Bulling/Langöhrig/Hellwig*, Gemeinschaftsgeschmacksmuster, No. 62.

21 20 December 2006 OLG [Higher Regional Court] Hamburg [5 U 135/05] (Handydesign); *Jestaedt*, Der Schutzbereich des eingetragenen Geschmacksmusters nach dem neuen Geschmacksmustergesetz, GRUR 2008, 19 f.

22 GeschmMG [Design Act] § 2 ¶ 3 (F. R.G.), see also 19 January 2006 OLG [Higher Regional Court] Hamm [4 U 148/05] (Kaminöfen).

Moreover, appearances of products which must necessarily be reproduced in their exact form and dimensions in order to permit the product to be mechanically connected to another product are excluded from protection (must-fit clause).[24] These products are eligible for protection, however, if the matched elements are parts of a modular system, and the protectable aspect lies in the interchangeable nature of the elements itself (Lego clause).[25] Furthermore, designs contrary to public policy or morality are also excluded from protection.[26] Finally, computer programs as such are not protected as designs, either.[27] However, the special design of the user interface and other graphic representations which may be rendered on a computer screen may be protected as designs.[28]

2. Beginning of protection and entitlement

Protection of a German registered design arises by registration in the Design Register with the German Patent and Trademark Office.[29] Registration does not entail a substantive-law-requirements check.

It is the designer or his/her legal successor who is entitled to the substantive right to the design. If a design is created by an employee in fulfillment of his/her duties or upon instruction of his/her employer, then the right belongs to the employer, unless otherwise agreed, see sec. 7 GeschmMG [Design Act].

However, this substantive entitlement is superimposed by the formal registration which according to sec. 8 GeschmMG [Design Act] creates formal rights for the person registered in the register. If an unentitled person has registered, the entitled designer is entitled to the transfer of the rights.[30]

23 Technological innovation should not be impeded by legal protection for a design for features which are exclusively due to technical constraints, see *Eichmann/von Falckenstein*, Geschmacksmustergesetz, § 3, No. 4 and Consideration 14 of the Design Directive.

24 GeschmMG [Design Act] § 3 ¶ 1 no. 2 (F. R.G.).

25 GeschmMG [Design Act] § 3 ¶ 2 (F. R.G.).

26 GeschmMG [Design Act] § 3 ¶ 1 no. 3 (F. R.G.), Art 9 Community Design Regulation.

27 GeschmMG [Design Act] § 1 ¶ 2 (F. R.G.).

28 *Bulling/Langöhrig/Hellwig*, Gemeinschaftsgeschmacksmuster, No. 96; *Eichmann/von Falckenstein*, Geschmacksmustergesetz, § 1, No. 20.

29 GeschmMG [Design Act] § 27 (F. R.G.).

30 GeschmMG [Design Act], § 9 (F. R.G.). This claim for transfer against the bona fide applicant is valid for three years only, GeschmMG [Design Act], § 9 ¶ 2 (F. R.G.). See also *Kazemi*, Rechtswirkungen von Registereintragungen, MarkenR 2007, 149, 152 f.

3. Term of protection and cancellation

The term of German design protection is a maximum of 25 years as of the filing date. Maintenance of protection is effected by payment of a renewal fee once every five years. If protection is not maintained, it ends.[31]

The registration of a design is cancelled upon expiration of its term, when the right is waived, or consent to the cancellation is given, or on the grounds of nullity established by enforceable judgment.[32] Pursuant to sec. 33 GeschmMG [Design Act] a nullity judgment can be obtained by anyone who files an action for establishment of the nullity of the design before a regular court of law.[33] A design is null and void if the product is not a design, the design is not novel, has no individual character or is excluded from design protection pursuant to sec. 3 GeschmMG [Design Act].[34] The nullity decision has an *ex tunc* effect, so that the protective effect of the design is deemed not to have existed from the beginning.[35]

4. Scope of protection

Design protection extends against any design that does not produce on the informed user an overall impression that is different from the one produced by the protected design, see sec. 38 para. 2 sent. 2 GeschmMG [Design Act].

For the purpose of determining the scope of protection, the overall impression of a design is determined with a focus on the features which make up its individual character within the meaning of sec. 2 GeschmMG [Design Act].[36] In other words, the greater the individuality of the design, the broader the scope of protection.[37]

Next, the overall impression of the contested design is compared with the overall impression of the protected design.[38] The extent of correspondence and deviation is determined, and weighted with respect to its effect on the overall impression.[39] As explained in no. A.1.c above, the overall impression of the design is determined in particular by the elements and features of the design which are decisive for its individual character.

---

31 GeschmMG [Design Act], § 27 ¶ 2, § 28 (F. R.G.).

32 GeschmMG [Design Act], § 36 (F. R.G.).

33 GeschmMG [Design Act], § 33 ¶ 2 (F. R.G.).

34 GeschmMG [Design Act], § 33 ¶ 1 (F. R.G.).

35 GeschmMG [Design Act], § 33 ¶ 3 (F. R.G.).

36 *Eichmann/von Falckenstein*, Geschmacksmustergesetz, § 38, No. 25.

37 *Berlit*, Das neue Geschmacksmusterrecht, GRUR 2004, 635, 640; *Wandtke/Ohst*, Zur Reform des deutschen Geschmacksmustergesetzes, GRUR Int 2005, 91, 99; see also *Jestaedt*, Der Schutzbereich nach dem neuen Geschmacksmustergesetz, GRUR 2008, 19 ff.

38 20 December 2006 OLG [Higher Regional Court] Hamburg [5 U 135/05] (Handydesign).

39 20 December 2006 OLG [Higher Regional Court] Hamburg [5 U 135/05] (Handydesign); *Eichmann/von Falckenstein*, Geschmacksmustergesetz, § 38, Nos. 25 f.

In the assessment of the scope of protection, the designer's degree of freedom in developing his design is taken into account.[40] As before with respect to the individual characteristic of the design, the interaction between the number of designs already made available to the public mentioned under A.1.c and difference to the already-known designs becomes relevant. Thus, if many designs are already known, a comparably modest further development based on known designs is sufficient to obtain protection, but the scope of protection of this design will be very reduced.[41] The less individual character the design has, therefore, the smaller its scope of protection is.[42]

5. The spare parts issue

The discussion about the protectability of so-called "must-match parts" as designs is of particular importance. In the case of must-match parts, in contrast to must-fit parts, the individual parts do not have to technically match the main part exactly. Yet for aesthetic reasons, they should not look different.[43] Typical examples includes in particular automobile spare parts such as bumpers, radiator grilles and car doors.[44]

According to Sec. 4 GeschmMG [Design Act], components of complex products enjoy design protection if they stay visible when used as intended. This conforms to the original Art. 3 para. 3 of the Design Directive. A harmonisation of the spare parts market in the field of designs was not possible when the Directive was adopted on the European level. Instead, in Art. 14 of the Design Directive, the so-called "freeze plus" rule was introduced, according to which a subsequent decision of this issue should be aimed for.[45]

On December 12, 2007, the proposed amendment of the Design Directive relating to the legal protection for spare parts proposed by the European Commission was passed by the European Parliament on first reading. According to this amendment, there will be a transition period of five years after which "a spare part mounted in or applied to a product which is a component part of a complex product", i. e. a so-called must-match part, which is merely used for repairing the product in order to restore its original appearance, will no longer be eligible for design protection. This limitation does not apply if the predominant purpose for which the above-mentioned component part is marketed is

40 GeschmMG [Design Act], § 38 ¶ 2 sent. 3 (F. R.G.).

41 *Kur*, Die Auswirkungen des neuen Geschmacksmusterrechts auf die Praxis, GRUR 2002, 661, 668.

42 *Bulling/Langöhrig/Hellwig*, Gemeinschaftsgeschmacksmuster, Nos. 58 ff. and No. 101; *Eichmann/von Falckenstein*, Geschmacksmustergesetz, § 38, No. 29.

43 *Bulling/Langöhrig/Hellwig*, Gemeinschaftsgeschmacksmuster, No. 132.

44 *Bulling/Langöhrig/Hellwig*, Gemeinschaftsgeschmacksmuster, No. 132; see also 16 October 1986 BGH [Federal Supreme Court] [I ZR 6/85], GRUR 1987, 518 ff. (Kotflügel).

45 On this topic see in particular: *Drexl/Hilty/Kur*, Designschutz für Ersatzteile, GRUR Int 2005, 449 ff; *Straus*, Ende des Geschmacksmusterschutzes für Ersatzteile in Europa?, GRUR Int 2005, 965 ff.; Opinion of the European Economic and Social Committee, COM 2004, 582 fin. *Jänich*, „Automobilplagiate" – Zum Schutz des Designs von Kraftfahrzeugen vor Nachahmung, GRUR 2008, 873 ff.

one other one than the repair of the complex product. The object of this amendment is a liberalisation of the secondary market, in particular the automobile sector. Upon expiration of the transition period, the scope of the national design protection will be comparable to that of the Community Design, which pursuant to Art. 110 of the Community Design Regulation has never extended to must-match spare parts. However, currently Germany, together with few other EU member states, blocks the adoption of the amendment of the Design Directive in the European Council of Ministers. The German government is discussing wether to uphold the blockade and thus to continue design protection for spare parts in Germany.[46]

In piracy cases which are based on specifically giving the impression that the part is an original part one, if there is no design protection, legal redress might be sought through related trademark protection.[47]

B. Acts of infringement

The design right grants its holder the exclusive right to use it, and to prohibit third parties from using it without his/her consent. Acts of use in particular include the making, offering, placing on the market, importing, exporting or using of a product which incorporates or uses the design, as well as possession of such a product for the abovementioned purposes.[48]

An infringing offer here means any act which demonstrates the readiness to place the design on the market.[49] Placing it on the market means making infringing products accessible in physical form, so that the power to dispose of them is transferred; typical acts here include acts of sale, rental and leasing.[50]

A design right cannot be asserted against third parties who have acquired a right of prior use.[51] A right of prior use arises for someone who has started using in good faith a design identical to the registered design before the filing date, or who has made serious and real preparations to do so.[52] The third party is merely allowed to conduct acts of prior use, yet he/she is not permitted to grant licences.[53]

The scope of design right protection is limited by sec. 40 GeschmMG [Design Act] according to which acts performed exclusively in the private sphere for non-commercial

46 Frankfurter Allgemeine Zeitung of 19 August 2008.

47 *Drexl/Hilty/Kur*, Designschutz für Ersatzteile, GRUR Int 2005, 449, 456.

48 GeschmMG [Design Act] § 38 ¶ 1, sent. 1 and 2 (F. R.G.).

49 *Eichmann/von Falckenstein*, Geschmacksmustergesetz, § 38, No. 13.

50 *Eichmann/von Falckenstein*, Geschmacksmustergesetz, § 38, No. 14.

51 GeschmMG [Design Act] § 41 (F. R.G.).

52 It is assumed as a rule that the act of prior use was committed in good faith – this does not apply, however, in the case of a direct fraudulent abstraction, see *Brückmann/Günther/Beyerlein*, GeschmMG, § 41, No. 8.

53 GeschmMG [Design Act] § 41 ¶ 1 sent. 2 and 3 (F. R.G.).

purposes, for acts for test purposes, representations for the purpose of citation or teaching, or for facilities on foreign ships or aircrafts are no infringements of design right.

C. Legal consequences

The owner of a design is entitled to request the infringer who uses a design contrary to sec. 38 para. 1 sent. 1 GeschmMG [Design Act] to remove the infringement and, if there is a risk of a repeated commission, to cease and desist.[54] In addition to that, the right holder who has sustained the infringement may be entitled to claims for damages,[55] and for destruction and handing over of the products destined for the unlawful distribution. Further possible claims include the claim for information,[56] and the claim for publication of the judgment.[57]

1. Injunctive Relief

The claim to destruction of the infringing objects and injunctive relief pursuant to sec. 42 para. 1 GeschmMG [Design Act] is independent of the question of fault and is therefore available even if the infringer is not aware of the design right. While the claim to destruction of the infringing objects is directed at terminating an existing infringement of the right, the claim to injunctive relief is directed at the future. The only prerequisite for the claim to destruction is therefore that an act of infringement has taken place. The claim for injunctive relief, however, requires a specific and seriously imminent risk of either repetition or an initial commission of the infringement.[58] Such a risk may result in particular from an already committed infringement. The infringer has the option of removing the imminent risk of repetition or initial commission of the infringement by submitting a cease-and-desist declaration under punitive sanction. If the infringer signs such a cease-and-desist declaration, the above-mentioned claims are therefore satisfied.

2. Information

Pursuant to sec. 46 GeschmMG [Design Act], the infringed party is entitled to claim immediate information from the infringing party about the origin and sales channel of the product, unless such a claim is unreasonable in a particular case. This claim is also independent of the question of fault and serves to both enforce the damages claim and to identify the sources of the infringements by disclosing the origin and sales channels of

54 GeschmMG [Design Act] § 42 ¶ 1 (F. R.G.).

55 GeschmMG [Design Act] § 42 ¶ 2 (F. R.G.).

56 GeschmMG [Design Act] § 46 (F. R.G.).

57 GeschmMG [Design Act] § 47 (F. R.G.).

58 *Eichmann/von Falckenstein*, Geschmacksmustergesetz, § 42, No. 4; *Brückmann/Günther/Beyerlein*, GeschmMG, § 42, Nos. 6 ff.

the property right infringing products.[59] Accordingly, pursuant to sec. 46 para. 2 GeschmMG [Design Act], the infringer has to specify the name and address of the manufacturer, the supplier and other previous owners of the products, the commercial customer, and the quantities of the products manufactured, supplied, received or ordered. The enforcement of the right is facilitated by sec. 3, according to which the claim for information, in cases of obvious infringement, may also be enforced by a preliminary injunction. Under the Act Improving the Enforcement of Intellectual Property (Gesetz zur Verbesserung der Durchsetzung von Rechten des geistigen Eigentums), which came into force on 1 September 2008 the claim for information can also be asserted against third parties who e. g. possessed an infringing object or use property right infringing services. This expansion is designed to further enhance the protection against product piracy.

3. Damages

If a design has been infringed with fault, then the owner of the design right can assert damages against the infringer pursuant to sec. 42 para. 2 GeschmMG [Design Act]. Fault is generally present in the case of intentional or negligent behavior. As in trademark law design law imposes the duty of monitoring one's property rights and obligations and potential infringements resulting therefrom.[60] In case of slight negligence, instead of damages, the court may award a compensation which lies in between the infringed party's damage and the infringer's profit, sec. 42 para. 2 sent. 3 GeschmMG [Design Act].

The amount and scope of the claim for damages are determined on the basis of sec. 249 et seq. Bürgerliches Gesetzbuch [BGB] [Civil Code] (F. R.G.). There are three methods on which the infringed party may choose to calculate his damage: (i) Compensation for the damage actually incurred including lost profit (Secs. 249, 252 BGB) [Civil Code]; (ii) return of the infringer's profit; and (iii) payment of an adequate royalty calculated on the basis of a licence analogy.[61] These three methods of calculation have become established by legal custom and apply in most areas of intellectual property law, such as design law and trademark law.[62] If the infringer wishes to assert the damage actually incurred, he bears the onus of proof. This evidence is not needed to the same degree when applying the licence analogy. The German Federal Supreme Court *(Bundesgerichtshof)* has held in this respect that the representation of pirated objects in a catalog alone justifies the assertion of damages according to the licence analogy.[63]

---

59 *Eichmann/von Falckenstein*, Geschmacksmustergesetz, § 46, No. 2.

60 *Eichmann/von Frankenstein*, Geschmacksmustergesetz, § 42, No. 10.

61 27 February 1963 BGH [Federal Supreme Court] [Ib ZR 131/61], GRUR 1963, 640, 642 (Plastikkorb); *Brückmann/Günther/Beyerlein*, GeschmMG, § 42, Nos. 22 ff.; *Eichmann/von Frankenstein*, Geschmacksmustergesetz, § 42, Nos. 8 ff.; on the return of the infringer's profit see especially 2 November 2000 BGH [Federal Supreme Court] [I ZR 246/98], GRUR 2001, 329 (Gemeinkostenanteil).

62 *Brückmann/Günther/Beyerlein*, GeschmMG, § 42, No. 22.

63 23 June 2005 BGH [Federal Supreme Court] [I ZR 263/02], GRUR 2006, 143, 145 (Catwalk).

4. Destruction

According to sec. 43 GeschmMG [Design Act], the infringed party has the right to claim that all unlawfully produced or distributed products, or products destined for unlawful distribution owned or possessed by the infringer be destroyed. In the alternative, the infringed party may request that the products owned by the infringer are handed over, sec. 43 para. 2 GeschmMG [Design Act]. However, in cases in which these measures are deemed unreasonable vis-à-vis the infringer or owner, then only the infringed party has a right to the removal of the infringement of his right in a more mitigated, i. e. reasonable way.

5. Recall

Under the Act on the Improvement of the Enforcement of Intellectual Property Rights, pursuant to sec. 43 para. 2 GeschmMG [Design Act] as amended, the infringed party has a right to have unlawfully produced or distributed products, or products destined for unlawful distribution recalled or finally removed from the sales channels.

6. Sec. 44 Assertion of claims also against owners

Pursuant to sec. 44 GeschmMG [Design Act], the owner of a company is also liable for design infringements of his employees or agents, except for the damages claim.

7. Consequences under criminal law

According to sec. 51 GeschmMG [Design Act], the unlawful infringement of a design is punishable with imprisonment of up to three years or an administrative fine. In the case of EU common trade, the penalty is even up to five years of imprisonment or an administrative fine. Attempted design infringement is punishable, too.

D. Enforcement

The right holder has several options of enforcing his/her design rights. In most cases, an enforcement in court will be an option. Here, the plaintiff may have the choice between filing an action on the merits and applying for the issuance of a preliminary injunction. Furthermore, the design right holder may use the procedure of seizure of goods by the customs authorities at the border.

1. Enforcement in court

According to the German rules of procedure, the action on the merits is the standard procedure to seek remedy against design infringement. An action based on a design infringement which usually comprises the typical three requests for injunctive relief, information and damages, must be filed with a Landgericht (Regional Court). The court having jurisdiction in this matter is the court of the district in which the infringer has his place of residence, provided this is in Germany. In addition to that, an action can also be brought at the place the infringing act was committed, e. g. at the place imitations were sold.[64] The defendant may respond to the action. Further briefs may be exchanged before a day for an oral hearing is appointed. The oral hearing in the first instance usually takes place between six and twelve months after the filing of the action. In the proceedings, it is the infringed party who bears the onus of proof for the facts giving rise to its claim.[65] In particular, he needs to demonstrate, and prove, if necessary, that the infringing act was committed by the defendant.[66]

If the termination of an infringement of its right is particularly urgent for the right holder, he can also apply to the Regional Court for a preliminary injunction. The ground for an injunction of a particular urgency is present if the immediate enforcement of the right appears necessary in order to avert essential prejudice.[67] In particular, in the case of trade fairs, where immediate action is necessary in order to stop further infringing actions, a preliminary injunction is the measure of choice. The urgency has to be determined based on a weighing of interests which may e. g. take into account the extent of the claimed production damage and the market share at risk, as well as the possibilities of subsequent prosecution, and the certainty with which the property right is deemed valid.[68] This also means that the property right holder must not wait too long after having obtained knowledge of the facts establishing the property right infringement, before he takes legal steps.

2. Customs action

In addition to that, the holder of a design right may file an application for customs action. In 2007, the percentage goods detained at the border on account of designs was only 3 % of the value of all goods detained.[69] In 2006, 23 % of all applications with German customs related to actions of the customs authorities in connection with the infringement of a design.[70] Applications for customs action with respect to designs are filed for many different groups of products. The best-known examples given by German customs are Nintendo game consoles, perfume bottles and Nokia cell phone faceplates.[71]

64 Zivilprozessordnung [ZPO] [Civil procedure statute], § 12, 13 and 32 (F. R.G.).

65 *Eichmann/von Frankenstein*, Geschmacksmustergesetz, § 42, No. 30; however, for limitations of the scope of protection based on a public prior use, it is the presumed infringer who bears the onus of proof, 9 June 2004 BGH [Federal Supreme Court] [I ZR 70/02], GRUR 2004, 939, 941 (Klemmhebel).

66 *Brückmann/Günther/Beyerlein*, GeschmMG, § 42, Nos. 47 ff.

67 ZPO [Civil procedure statute], § 940 (F. R.G.).

68 *Brückmann/Günther/Beyerlein*, GeschmMG, § 42, Nos. 50 f.

69 *Bundesministerium der Finanzen*, Statistics 2007, http://www.zoll.de, dated 18 February 2009.

70 *Bundesministerium der Finanzen*, Gewerblicher Rechtsschutz Jahresbericht 2006, p. 8.

The action of the customs authorities may be based on two different grounds. As a rule, customs actions are governed by Customs Regulation (Council Regulation (EC) No. 1383/2003 concerning customs action against goods suspected of infringing certain intellectual property rights and the measures to be taken against goods found to have infringed such rights). Apart from the application, this Regulation requires that there be sufficient grounds for suspecting that the goods infringe the applicant's design.[72] In such a case, the customs authority will inform the applicant, who then has to either initiate civil law proceedings within 10 working days, or release the goods. The simplified procedure of abandoning the goods for destruction is available in Germany, since 1 September 2008. This is a possibility the right holder is now also entitled to, provided he obtains the agreement of the infringer to the simplified destruction of the infringing goods.

In addition, the detention of goods during import and export pursuant to sec. 55 GeschmMG [Design Act] may be considered as subsidiary measure – e. g. in the case of parallel imports or intra-community trade. However, the infringement must be obvious. This means that action based on the national design law requires a higher degree of likelihood that an infringement is present than a customs action based on Customs Regulation.

III. International Design

Apart from the GeschmMG [Design Act], there are also international design protection laws that govern design protection in Germany. These include in particular the Community Design Regulation and the International Registration according to the Hague Agreement. International design protection is also found in the provisions of Art. 25 TRIPS (Agreement on Trade-Related Aspects of Intellectual Property Rights).

A. Community Design

The Community Design is governed by the Community Design Regulation. This regulation is mostly identical to the Design Directive 98/71/EC, the most important difference being that – unlike in German design law – not only registered designs are protected, but unregistered Community designs may also be legally protected. The substantive requirements for protection correspond to the harmonised regulations of the German design law in most respects. Here, too, it is required that the design is new and has an individual character, see Art. 4 of the Community Design Regulation.

Concerning spare parts, i. e. the so-called "must-match" parts, the transitional provision of Art. 110 of the Community Design Regulation applies, according to which for a transitional period, protection as a Community design shall not exist for a design which

71 *Bundesministerium der Finanzen*, http://www.zoll.de, dated 07 August 2006.

72 Article 5 of the Customs Regulation. According to Article 4 of the Customs Regulation, the customs authorities may also detain goods ex officio.

constitutes a component part of a complex product used for the purpose of repair of that complex product so as to restore its original appearance. Although the Commission has committed to make a final proposal concerning protection for spare parts on the European level, a final amendment of the present Community Design Regulation is not in sight, which is certainly related to the planned amendment of spare part protection in the Design Directive, see above.

The scope of protection conferred by a Community Design – like the scope of protection according to the Design Directive – depends on the degree of freedom of the designer in the development of his/her design.

1. Registered design

The protection of the registered design takes effect as of its registration. Pursuant to Art. 12 Community Design Regulation, the protection term is five years beginning on the application date, and can be extended several times for five years each time, up to a total term of 25 years.

2. Unregistered Community design

Especially the unregistered Community design is an innovation in design law which provides a far-reaching extension of the protection for design owners and designers. Pursuant to Art. 4 Community Design Regulation, protection arises on the day the design was made available to the public in the Community for the first time. From that day, the term of protection is three years.

a. Disclosure

To obtain protection, an unregistered Community design must be disclosed in a way that it may reasonably become known in the normal course of business to the circles specialised in the sector concerned.[73] It is disputed in this context if the act of disclosure may also be performed outside the Community. According to the prevailing opinion in literature the wording suggests that only an act of disclosure within the Community is suitable to establish protection.[74] This distinction is relevant in practice, not only because an act of disclosure outside the Community is not able to establish design protection, but, above all, because a disclosure to the circles specialised in the sector concerned outside the Community, may establish public knowledge and thus foreclose the

73 For more details see *Rahlf/Gottschalk*, Neuland: Das nicht eingetragene Gemeinschaftsgeschmacksmuster, GRUR Int 2004, 821, 824 f.

74 *Eichmann/von Falkenstein*, Geschmacksmustergesetz, No. 18; *Ruhl/Schlötelburg*, Gemeinschaftsgeschmacksmuster, Article 11, Nos. 15 f.

novelty of the design and thus design protection.[75] However, German Federal Supreme Court *(Bundesgerichtshof)* ruled on 9 October 2008 that a disclosure outside the Community has to be taken into account as well.[76]

The right holder bears the burden of proving the due disclosure and the relevant disclosure date.[77]

Therefore, the right holder must disclose the design in a way that enables him to prove the disclosure and the possibility for the relevant circles of the trade to have taken notice of it. Examples include the presentation at important international exhibitions or publication in internationally relevant professional journals. The presentation of a design on a website, however, is not deemed to be sufficient.[78]

b. Protection against copies

The unregistered Community design only confers to the right holder protection against copies *(Nachahmung)* of his design, Art. 19 para. 2 sent. 2 Community Design Regulation. An act of use shall not be deemed to result from copying, if it results from an independent work of creation by a designer who may be reasonably thought not to be familiar with the disclosed Community design, see Art. 19 para. 2 sent. 2 Community Design Regulation. It may be difficult for the right holder to furnish proof of the fact that his design has been copied, because he would generally have to prove that the infringer had the possibility of taking notice of the protected design.[79] In such a case, exceptionally, it would have to be the designer of the alleged who would have to demonstrate why no copy is present.[80]

c. Legal consequences and enforcement

Art. 89 of the Community Design Regulation gives a non-comprehensive enumeration of sanctions for infringement. Among those mentioned are the order prohibiting the defendant from proceeding with the infringing acts (Art. 89 para. 1 lit. a)) and the seizure of infringing products or materials used to manufacture the infringing goods (lit. b)

---

75 *Ruhl/Schlötelburg*, Gemeinschaftsgeschmacksmuster, Article 11, No. 16; critical comments by: *Oldekop*, Das nicht eingetragene Gemeinschaftsgeschmacksmuster – Eine Chance für Designer?, WRP 2006, 801, 805.

76 9 October 2008 BGH [Federal Supreme Court] [I ZR 126/06], GRUR 2009, 79 *(Gebäckpresse)*.

77 *Ruhl/Schlötelburg*, Gemeinschaftsgeschmacksmuster, Article 11, No. 33.

78 *Oldekop*, Das nicht eingetragene Gemeinschaftsgeschmacksmuster – Eine Chance für Designer?, WRP 2006, 801, 805; *Ruhl/Schlötelburg*, Gemeinschaftsgeschmacksmuster, Article 7, Nos. 18 ff.

79 *Oldekop*, Das nicht eingetragene Gemeinschaftsgeschmacksmuster – Eine Chance für Designer?, WRP 2006, 801, 806; see also *Ruhl/Schlötelburg*, Gemeinschaftsgeschmacksmuster, Article 19, Nos. 72 f.

80 *Oldekop*, Das nicht eingetragene Gemeinschaftsgeschmacksmuster – Eine Chance für Designer?, WRP 2006, 801, 806.

and lit c)). For further sanctions, reference is made to national law, so that the German legal consequences described above apply if German law is applicable.[81]

According to sec. 63 GeschmMG [Design Act] in conjunction with Art. 80 para. 1 Community Design Regulation, the infringement of a Community design shall be prosecuted in Community design courts. The internet page of the Office of Harmonisation for the Internal Market features a list of the Community design courts. In Germany, generally the same rules of procedure apply as in national design disputes. Preliminary injunctions are possible, too. For further details we therefore refer to section D.1 above.

B. IR designs

Apart from the European laws on designs, international registration is available based on the Hague Agreement (Hague Agreement Concerning the International Registration of Industrial Designs). The Hague Agreement consists of three independent agreements the London Act of 1934, The Hague Act of 1960, and the Geneva Act of 1999. Each of these individual acts only applies to the states which have jointly acceded to the respective Act. Until 2007, Germany had only acceded to the Hague Act. However, on September 24, 2007, the EU joined the Geneva Act and has thus considerably increased the Act's importance. Apart from the states of the European Union, protection through an international registration can be obtained in a total of 14 countries, including Switzerland and Turkey. Yet, important countries such as the USA, Japan, Russia and China are not currently contracting states.

The advantage of an international registration is that a single registration with the WIPO (World Intellectual Property Organization) is able to take effect for all designated contracting states – with the application in these states having the same effect as a national design.[82] Thus, with one application one can obtain design rights in several other jurisdictions claiming the same priority date in all contradicting states. As in the case of an international trademark registration, the national office has the right pursuant to Art. 12 of the Geneva Act to refuse the registration of an international design within a period of six months on account the the grounds that national law does not allow for registration of that design.

C. TRIPS and the Paris Convention

There are further laws on the international level relating to designs. According to Art. 25 TRIPS, members shall provide for the protection of independently created industrial designs that are new or original. Members may provide that designs are not new or original if they do not significantly differ from known designs or combinations of

---

81 *Ruhl/Schlötelburg*, Gemeinschaftsgeschmacksmuster, Article 89, Nos. 1 ff.

82 Article 14 Geneva Act; *Eichmann/von Falkenstein*, Geschmacksmustergesetz, No. 26; *Bulling*, Zur Wirkung international eingetragener Muster und zur Nichtigkeit/Löschungseinwilligung bei deutschen Geschmacksmustern, MittdPA 2007, 59 ff.

known design features. Members may provide that such protection shall not extend to designs dictated essentially by technical or functional considerations. Art. 25 TRIPS establishes a minimum standard which is supplemented by the protective provision of Art. 26 TRIPS, according to which the owner of a protected industrial design may prevent third parties from making, selling or importing articles bearing or embodying a design which is a copy, or substantially a copy, of the protected design, when such acts are undertaken for commercial purposes and without the owner's consent.

In addition, the Paris Convention (Paris Convention for the Protection of Industrial Property of 20 March 1883) applies to designs. Probably the most important provision of the Paris Convention is Art. 4 which stipulates the possibility of claiming the priority of the initial application within 6 months of the application. Thus, the date of filing of the initial national application is also valid for the subsequent national application of the same design right in another contracting State. Each contracting State must protect industrial rights and may not refuse protection of design rights to nationals of any country of the Union and shall grant the same protection as granted to nationals.[83]

IV. Design protection and copyright law, unfair competition law and trademark law International Design

There have been repeated discussions as to whether design rights are copyrights or more likely other intellectual property rights, or whether they should actually form an independent category of property rights.[84] The law relating to the protection of designs overlaps with other categories of property rights, in particular with copyright law, but also with trademark law which in the case of three-dimensional designs may easily lead to delimitation problems. Ultimately, competition law may provide designers with defences against imitations and other infringements of their design.

A. Design protection in copyright law

The problem of delimitation and overlap of design law and copyright law generally arises in the context of works of applied art, because for these designs – which are usually articles of daily use – the question arises to which extent a design may claim copyright protection, seeing that historically copyright law intended more to apply to works of art rather than to articles of industrial use. This distinction between industrial property rights and copyrights is still reflected in linguistic usage today, but it is hard to determine where industrial use begins. Especially in respect of so-called designer furniture and designer clothes, an unauthorised use of copyrights is conceivable.

83 See Art. 2 Paris Covention.

84 See summary in: *Ohly*, Designschutz im Spannungsfeld von Geschmacksmuster-, Kennzeichen- und Lauterkeitsrecht, GRUR 2007, 731 ff.; *Wandtke/Ohst*, Zur Reform des deutschen Geschmacksmustergesetzes, GRUR Int 2005, 91 ff.

1. Requirements for protection

Historically, design rights used to be considered "little copyrights". This was based on the assumption that there is a gradual difference between industrial designs on the one hand, and works of art under copyright law on the other. According to this understanding, a design is initially eligible for design protection only, but if it reaches a certain degree of creativity, it is also eligible for copyright protection.[85] This historical understanding has changed, however, with the modification of the design law and in particular with its European harmonisation, because design rights are now considered independent property rights.[86] The requirements of copyright protection therefore have to be assessed independently from design protection.

Works protected by copyright law are works which constitute a personal intellectual creation.[87] In the case of a design, this will regularly be a work of applied art, such as an item of daily use or a commodity good with an artistic design.[88] Ordinarily, a low degree of creativity suffices for copyright protection (so-called "small coin"). However, in applied art field, case law requires that the work clearly exceed the average creative design.[89]

Copyright protection for a design lasts much longer than design protection and extends up to 70 years after the death of the author. In contrast to other property rights, copyrights have only partly been harmonised by the EU, so that they are governed by German law.

2. Acts of infringement

The author of a creative work has the exclusive right to exploit his work in material form (sec. 15 para. 1 UrhG [Copyright Act]. This includes the right of reproduction (sec. 16 UrhG [Copyright Act]), the distribution right (sec. 17 UrhG [Copyright Act], and the right of exhibition (sec. 18 UrhG [Copyright Act]. These rights are considered

---

85 Summary in: *Ohly*, Designschutz im Spannungsfeld von Geschmacksmuster-, Kennzeichen- und Lauterkeitsrecht, GRUR 2007, 731 f.; *Koschtial*, Zur Notwendigkeit der Absenkung der Gestaltungshöhe für Werke der angewandten Kunst im deutschen Urheberrecht, GRUR 2004, 555 ff.; *Schricker*, Urheberrecht, § 2, No. 157; *Wandtke/Ohst*, Zur Reform des deutschen Geschmacksmustergesetzes, GRUR Int 2005, 91 ff.

86 See above and: Begründung zum Gesetzentwurf der Bundesregierung, Regierungsentwurf [Reasons for the draft bill of the Federal Government, Government Draft], BT-Drucks. 15/1075, p. 29; *Wandtke/Ohst*, Zur Reform des deutschen Geschmacksmustergesetzes, GRUR Int 2005, 91 f.

87 UrhG [Copyright Act] § 2 ¶ 2 (F. R.G.).

88 UrhG [Copyright Act] § 2 ¶ 1 no. 4; (F. R.G.); see also *Schricker*, Urheberrecht, § 2, Nos. 156 ff.

89 26 January 2005 BVerfG [Federal Constitutional Court] [1 BvR 157/02], GRUR 2005, 410 (Laufendes Auge); 22 June 1995 BGH [Federal Supreme Court] [I ZR 119/93], GRUR 1995, 581 f. (Silberdistel); a. A. *Koschtial*, Zur Notwendigkeit der Absenkung der Gestaltungshöhe für Werke der angewandten Kunst im deutschen Urheberrecht, GRUR 2004, 555 ff.

personal to the author, due to the particular personal relationship of an author to his/her work. Thus, an author can only licence these exploitation rights under German law, but he/she cannot transfer them to a third party.[90]

The right of exhibition is the right to publicly exhibit an unpublished work. The distribution right includes the right to offer the work to the public or to place it on the market. Advertising, such as posting of brochures, is considered an offer to the public, and hence, distribution.[91] A distribution is also regularly present if the original, or reproductions are made available to the public by disposal or transfer of possession.[92]

Recently, the question of what constitutes distribution has often been disputed before the courts. This fact is related to the past lack of copyright protection for works of applied art in Italy, which left design classics, such as the ones from the Bauhaus era, without Italian copyright protection. The question arose as to how far German copyright protection goes in cases of furniture that was lawfully produced in Italy and then imported in Germany.

The first prominent case, regarding the distribution of the Wagenfeld lamp, was decided by the German Federal Supreme Court on February 15, 2007. According to this decision, an author's right of distribution is infringed if his work that is protected by copyright law in Germany is offered on the German market for sale abroad where the work is not protected by copyright (Italy).[93] The exclusive right of the German property right holder is impaired by the offer directed at customers in Germany although made in Italy, because customers in Germany may be attracted by the offer which has an effect on the commercial exploitation of the copyright in Germany.[94]

The second decision was taken by the ECJ (European Court of Justice) on April 17, 2008 based on a case submitted by the German Federal Supreme Court.[95] In the underlying case, Peek & Cloppenburg, a company owning fashion department stores, had displayed furniture of the designer Le Corbusier in its shop window in order to create a noble ambience. The furniture was not eligible for copyright protection in Italy and had been purchased from an Italian company that was not an official licensee of the holder of the proprietary right in Germany. The ECJ held that there was no distribution to the public, if the work was merely displayed in a shop window, without its being handed over for use or its ownership transferred. According to the ECJ it was up to the

---

90 Urheberrechtsgesetz [UrhG] [Copyright Act], § 29 (F. R.G.).

91 *Dreier/Schulze*, UrhG, § 17, No. 11.

92 5 October 2006 BGH [Federal Supreme Court] [I ZR 247/03], ZUM-RD 2007, 3 (Le-Corbusier-Möbel).

93 15 February 2007 BGH [Federal Supreme Court] [I ZR 114/04], GRUR 2007, 871 ff. (Wagenfeld-Leuchte).

94 15 February 2007 BGH [Federal Supreme Court] [I ZR 114/04], GRUR 2007, 871, 872 (Wagenfeld-Leuchte).

95 5 October 2006 BGH [Federal Supreme Court] [I ZR 247/03], ZUM-RD 2007, 3 (Le-Corbusier-Möbel).

legislator to change the provisions for the protection of the holder of an intellectual property right if an extension of these rights were intended.[96]

3. Legal consequences and enforcement

According to sec. 97 UrhG [Copyright Act] the author or licensee is entitled to injunctive relief and damages, which according to the three calculation methods may be determined on the basis of the damage actually incurred, the return of the infringer's profit, or the payment of an adequate royalty.

In addition, the author or licensee is entitled to claim the destruction or surrender of the copies,[97] as well as the destruction or surrender of the devices that are used almost exclusively for the manufacture of copies.[98] Further, the right holder may request the infringer to submit information including the name and address of the manufacturer, supplier and other previous owners of the works or copies, the commercial customer, as well as the quantities of the pieces manufactured, delivered, received or ordered.[99]

In order to enforce copyright claims, the author or licensee is again able to assert his rights in court, either by obtaining a preliminary injunction or by lodging an action on the merits. Moreover, in the case of design infringements under copyright law, a customs action may also be sought. Ultimately, the infringed party could propose prosecution under criminal law.

B. Design protection and trademark law

Special shapes may be protected not only under design law, but also under trademark law. While the aesthetic effect of a design is what warrants its design law protection, it is its distinctive character that makes it eligible for trademark protection.

Where trademarks and designs overlap, this often relates to three-dimensional designs and graphical symbols. For example, a three-dimensional design may be protected as a design because of its unique shape, but at the same time it may also be eligible for protection as a three-dimensional trademark pursuant to sec. 4 Markengesetz [MarkenG] [Trademark Act]. The prerequisite for protection of a three-dimensional trademark is that the shape is suitable to help distinguish goods or services of different companies.[100] At the same time, sec. 32 Markengesetz [Trademark Act] excludes protection for signs that exclusively consist of a shape (i) which is dictated by the type of the good itself; (ii) which is necessary to achieve a technical effect; or (iii) which confers essential value to

---

96 17 April 2008 European Court of Justice [ECJ] [C-456/06] (Peek & Cloppenburg KG v Cassina SpA).

97 UrhG [Copyright Act] § 98 (F.R.G.).

98 UrhG [Copyright Act] § 99 (F.R.G.).

99 *Dreier/Schulze*, UrhG, § 97, Nos. 78 ff.

100 *Ingerl/Rohnke*, Markengesetz, § 8, Nos. 107 ff.

the good. The third characteristic does not refer to particularly aesthetic or original designs, but to features the omission of which would negatively impact the value of the object.[101]

Just as special designs can be additionally protected as trademarks, certain signs that are protected as picture marks can be also eligible for design protection – provided the design is novel and has an individual character. Therefore, the application for a trademark may lead to an unregistered Community design in the form of a graphical symbol if it complies with all prerequisites for unregistered Community designs.[102]

Trademark rights and design rights are therefore not mutually exclusive. This does not necessarily have to lead to a conflict, because not only the prerequisites for protection under both rights differ, but also the purpose of protection. The object of trademark law is protection against the likelihood of confusion, whereas design law aims to protect the aesthetic design.[103]

C. Design protection in competition law

The discussion about the relationship between protection by special design laws and competition law has gained new impetus through the Unfair Competition Practices Directive (Directive 2005/29/EC of the European Parliament and of the Council of 11 May 2005 concerning unfair business-to-consumer commercial practices in the internal market and amending Council Directive 84/450/EEC, Directives 97/7/EC, 98/27/EC and 2002/65/EC of the European Parliament and of the Council and Regulation (EC) No 2006/2004 of the European Parliament and of the Council) relating to unfair trade practices.[104]

Past, the practice used to be that special protection by industrial property rights, as the more specific form of regulation, excluded protection against anti-competitive imitations under the Gesetz gegen den unlauteren Wettbewerb [UWG][Act Against Unfair Competition] (F. R.G.).[105] Now, however, supplementary protection under competition law may be considered if further anticompetitive circumstances are present which are outside the scope of the special laws and make the conduct appear unfair.[106]

101 *Ingerl/Rohnke*, Markengesetz, § 3, No. 58; diverging opinion in *von Schultz*, Markenrecht, § 3, Nos. 19 f.

102 See in greater detail *Schlötelburg*, Musterschutz an Zeichen, GRUR 2005, 123 ff.

103 *Ohly*, Designschutz im Spannungsfeld von Geschmacksmuster-, Kennzeichen- und Lauterkeitsrecht, GRUR 2007, 731; *the same:* Die Europäisierung des Designrechts, ZEuP 2004, 296, 308 f.; *Schlötelburg*, Musterschutz an Zeichen, GRUR 2005, 123 ff.

104 See *Köhler*, Das Verhältnis des Wettbewerbsrechts zum Recht des geistigen Eigentums, GRUR 2007, 548 ff.; *Lubberger*, Alter Wein in neuen Schläuchen, WRP 2007, 873 ff.

105 24 March 2005 BGH [Federal Supreme Court] [I ZR 131/02], GRUR 2005, 600, 601 (Handtuchklemmen); *Hefermehl/Köhler/Bornkamm*, Gesetz gegen den unlauteren Wettbewerb, § 4, No. 9.6; *Lubberger*, Alter Wein in neuen Schläuchen, WRP 2007, 873 ff.

106 *Hefermehl/Köhler/Bornkamm*, Gesetz gegen den unlauteren Wettbewerb, § 4, No. 9.6.

The offer of goods or services which imitate the goods or services of a competitor is an unfair trade practice according to secs. 3, 4 no. 9 UWG [Act Against Unfair Competition], particularly if it involves an avoidable deception about the true origin of the goods or services (lit. a), if it constitutes an exploitation or diminution of the appreciation of the imitated goods or services (lit. b), or if the imitation was based on knowledge and documents obtained in bad faith (lit. c).

With respect to the Community design, the German Federal Supreme Court held in 2006 that actions based on supplementary protection under competition law on grounds of an avoidable deception about the origin of goods or services. The fact that does not exclude protection existed or exists for an unregistered Community design.[107] The court held that the laws in the Member States relating to unfair competition remained unaffected by the Community Design Regulation, as the objective of design law to protect the result of a certain creative achievement, is a different one than the objective of the UWG [Act Against Unfair Competition] which is merely to protect the competitive advantage.[108]

1. Requirements for protection

Supplementary protection under competition law pursuant to secs. 3, 4 no. 9 lit a UWG [Act Against Unfair Competition] applies when imitations of a distinctive product are sold and there is a risk of deception about the origin of the products, and the imitator has failed to take reasonable and suitable measures to avoid the deception.[109]

It must be taken into account in this context that the term distinctive character does not have the same meaning as the term individual characteristics used in design law. A product has a distinctive character if its specific design or certain features are suitable to indicate to the interested trade parties the product's origin with a certain company or its particular features.[110] The distinctive character of a product may also result from features which are dictated by the intended use, but which can be chosen at will and are exchangeable.[111] There is an interdependency among the degree of distinctiveness of the product, the intensity of the imitation and the particular competitive circumstances – e. g. of the deception of origin. The higher the degree of distinctiveness, and the high-

---

107 15 September 2005 BGH [Federal Supreme Court] [I ZR 151/02], GRUR Int 2006, 334, 336 (Jeans).

108 15 September 2005 BGH [Federal Supreme Court] [I ZR 151/02], GRUR 2006, 334, 336 (Jeans).

109 24 March 2005 BGH [Federal Supreme Court] [I ZR 131/02], GRUR 2005, 600, 601(Handtuchklemmen).

110 8 November 2001 BGH [Federal Supreme Court] [I ZR 199/99], GRUR 2002, 275, 276 (Noppenbahnen); 24 March 2005 BGH [Federal Supreme Court] [I ZR 131/02], GRUR 2005, 600, 601 (Handtuchklemmen); 11 January 2007 BGH [Federal Supreme Court] [I ZR 198/04], GRUR 2007, 795, 797 (Handtaschen); see also *Köhler/Hefermehl/Bornkamm*, Gesetz gegen den unlauteren Wettbewerb, § 4, Nos. 9. 24 ff; *Fezer*, Lauterkeitsrecht, § 4-9, Nos. 25 ff.

111 24 March 2005 BGH [Federal Supreme Court] [I ZR 131/02], GRUR 2005, 600, 601 (Handtuchklemmen).

er the degree of imitation, the lower are the requirements with respect to the particular circumstances that have to be met in order for the product to be considered anticompetitive.[112]

In practice, the particular circumstance of an "avoidable deception of origin" is the most relevant element of the offence stipulated in sec. 4 no. 9 UWG [Act Against Unfair Competition]. This element usually requires that the imitated product is known to a certain degree, because otherwise there is no risk of a deception about its origin – however, a particular public knowledge is not necessary.[113]

2. Acts of infringement

In the field of product piracy the relevant act of infringement consists of the offer of imitated products within the meaning of sec. 4 no. 9 UWG [Act Against Unfair Competition]. Offering here means any act directed at sales, including advertising and keeping for sale.[114] Manufacture is not considered an act of infringement.[115] One particular feature of protection against imitations under competition law is the prohibition to slip into, produce and market products that fit into a competitor's series in order to shift the competitor's market success to oneself.[116] The imitation of short-lived products like fashion articles can also be anticompetitive according to the case law of the German Federal Supreme Court, because such an imitation may prejudice the particular achievement of the couturier.[117] Here, the relationship between unfair competition law and design right law is of a particular interest, because the purpose of an unregistered community design right is also to protect short-lived designs such as fashion rights where the registration often is not appropriate.[118]

---

112 7 February 2002 BGH [Federal Supreme Court] [I ZR 289/99], GRUR 2002, 820 (Bremszangen).

113 15 September 2005 BGH [Federal Supreme Court] [I ZR 151/02], GRUR Int 2006, 334, 337 (Jeans); 24 March 2005 BGH [Federal Supreme Court] [I ZR 131/02], GRUR 2005, 600, 602 (Handtuchklemmen).

114 *Hefermehl/Köhler/Bornkamm*, Gesetz gegen den unlauteren Wettbewerb, § 4, No. 9.39.

115 *Hefermehl/Köhler/Bornkamm*, Gesetz gegen den unlauteren Wettbewerb, § 4, No. 9.39, this differs from the GeschmMG [Design Act] under which the manufacture is an act of infringement; see GeschmMG [Design Act] § 38.

116 6 November 1963 BGH [Federal Supreme Court] [Ib ZR 37/62], GRUR 1964, 621 (Klemmbausteine) which held that it is not allowed for competitor of Lego to produce and market bricks that fit into the *Legostein*; *Fezer*, Lauterkeitsrecht, § 4-9, No. 69.

117 19 January 1973 BGH [Federal Supreme Court] [I ZR 39/71], GRUR 1973, 478 (Modeneuheit); *Fezer*, Lauterkeitsrecht, § 4-9, No. 72.

118 See *Oldekop*, Das nicht eingetragene Gemeinschaftsgeschmacksmuster – Eine Chance für Designer?, WRP 2006, 801; *Rahlf/Gottschalk*, Neuland: Das nicht eingetragene Gemeinschaftsgeschmacksmuster, GRUR Int 2004, 821 ff.

3. Legal consequences and enforcement

In case of anticompetitive imitations, the infringed party may initiate an action for removal and injunctive relief,[119] and damages,[120] where the damage can be calculated using one of the three methods: as (i) compensation for the damage actually incurred; (ii) return of the infringer's profit; or (iii) payment of an adequate royalty. In addition, the infringed party has the right to request information.[121]

In order to enforce its claim for injunctive relief, the infringed party may apply for the issuance of a preliminary injunction in case of a particular urgency. Moreover, the infringed party can assert its claims by filing an action on the merits. Unlike the case of industrial property rights, the infringed party does not have the option of applying for a customs action.

---

119 UWG [Act against Unfair Competition] § 8 (F. R.G.).

120 UWG [Act against Unfair Competition] § 9 (F. R.G.).

121 *Hefermehl/Köhler/Bornkamm*, Gesetz gegen den unlauteren Wettbewerb, § 9, No. 4.1.

Patent Piracy

Claudia Milbradt

Product piracy involving patents is a particularly challenging area. Patent infringement is considerably more difficult to identify than trademark infringement, and should be taken into account when deciding on which enforcement measures to apply. While it is true that the losses associated with patent infringements may reach or surpass losses from trademark infringement, they tend not to have the same level of media impact. The significance of patent piracy should not be underestimated, given that patents offer exclusivity as a reward for the holders' investment in research and development.

I. Definitions

A. Patents

In accordance with sec. 1 Patentgesetz [PatG] [Patent Act] (F. R.G.), patents may protect technical inventions, chemical substances, processes and applications provided that the claimed invention is new, innovative and amenable to industrial application. Section 1 para. 3 PatG [Patent Act] in accordance with sec. 52 para. 2 EPC. For European Patent sec. 52-57 EPC (European Patent Convention) applies which reflect sec. 1-5 PatG [Patent Act]. Excludes several categories from patentable subject matter, including discoveries, academic/scientific theories and mathematical methods, as well as designs, plans, rules and methods for performing mental acts, for language and programs for data processing equipment and information reproduction. Thus, mere discoveries, such as X-rays are not eligible for patent protection. However, a discoverer may become an inventor if the knowledge gained leads to a certain action in connection with the discovery, such as the application of X-rays in medical science or isolation of a substance to be found in nature. Thus, this means that an invention must contain some technical teaching that may be implemented in practice on a recurring basis and which solves a particular problem.[1] Aesthetic creations do not comprise any "technical teaching" and are therefore not patentable.

A general distinction is made between product patents *(Erzeugnispatente)* as defined in sec. 9 para. 2 no. 1, PatG [Patent Act] and process patents *(Verfahrenspatente)* as defined in sec. 9 para. 2 no. 2. PatG [Patent Act] Product patents cover all products made by applying the "technical teaching". Process patents, in contrast, provide protection for the application of specific technical processes.

1 3 November 1987 BGH [Federal Supreme Court] [X ZR 27/86], GRUR 1988, 290, 293 (Kehlrinne).

An invention must be new and demonstrates an inventive step in order to qualify for patent protection. This process filters out those inventions that are mere embodiments of the existing art. Analysis of the inventive step includes an assessment of whether the invention is taken directly from the state of the art or whether some innovative advance is involved. Section 4 sent. 1 PatG [Patent Act] and Art. 56 sent. 1 EPC state that a product or process is considered as involving an inventive step if, with regard to the state of the art, it is not obvious to a person skilled in the art. The final requirement is that an invention must be suitable for industrial application (sec. 5 para. 1 PatG [Patent Act] and Art. 57 EPC).

B. Utility Models

Utility models may also benefit from protection of a technical invention. However, unlike patents, there is no process protection for utility models. Utility model protection also requires both "inventive step" and "novelty". However, the degree of novelty required is lower than for patent protection. According to sec. 3 para. 2 Gebrauchsmustergesetz [GebrMG] [Utility Model Act] (F. R.G.), the invention must be used commercially, meaning that the invention can be used in any way for economic purposes. The protection of the utility model is the same as for patents. However, the requirements of a utility model are only examined in a judicial infringement proceeding or in a utility action. The term of a utility model is limited to ten years (see sec. 23 para. 1 GebrMG [Utility Model Act]. An advantage of utility models is that they are cheaper to obtain. Further, the grant of the utility model is easier to achieve through non-material examination by the relevant authorities. However, there are also certain disadvantages with respect to term of protection and scope of protection. Additionally, further to current court decisions it might be difficult to claim for discontinuance on the basis of a utility model which has so far not been proved in an opposition proceeding. Some district and some higher regional courts seem to tend to suspend an infringement action until a decision on the validity of the utility model has been rendered in pending opposition proceedings.

C. Know-how

Know-how is a defined concept in intellectual property law. Know-how refers to the protection of special functional applicatory knowledge based upon experience and tests but which is not capable of patent protection. Furthermore, such knowledge must be secret and not accessible to the public. Otherwise, it is simple common knowledge. In the Regulation (EC) No 772/2004 of 27 April 2004 on the application of Art. 81 (3) of the treaty to categories of technology transfer agreements[2] know-how is defined as:

Know-how means a package of non-patented practical information, resulting from experience and testing, which is: (i) secret, that is to say, not generally known or easily accessible; (ii) substantial, that is to say, significant and useful for the production of the

2 Official Journal of the European Union 2004 No L 123/11.

contract products; and (iii) identified, that is to say, described in a sufficiently comprehensive manner so as to make it possible to verify that it fulfils the criteria of secrecy and substantiality.[3]

Know-how can be a very valuable asset of a firm. The problem of know-how infringement is that once the information is made publicly available, the know-how can lose its value. It is also difficult, as an evidentiary matter, to prove that the know-how has been used in an unauthorised manner. In contrast to a patent infringement where the patent retains value even in the face of infringement, the know-how infringement must instead be regarded as know-how theft. Particular attendance should be given to the protection of know-how in the context of R&D cooperations, joint ventures and presentations to cooperation partners. However, also the protection of know-how within a company should not be underestimated.

II. Special Cases

As already mentioned, sec. 1 para. 3 PatG [Patent Act] specifies a number of discoveries and scientific theories which may not be patented in principle. There are other areas where the situation is disputed, particularly as regards new areas of research and technology.

A. Natural materials

Generally speaking, it is not possible to obtain patent protection to natural materials, since they are considered the "common heritage of mankind". It has even been raised that any form of patent protection for natural materials has to be considered to be a form of bio-piracy.[4] However, there are notable exceptions to this general rule. The BioTech Directive (Directive (EC) No. 98/44 of 6 July 1998 on the legal protection of biotechnological inventions)[5] addresses the problem regarding natural materials. Further to the Bio Tech Directive synthetically produced substances that may exist in natural are also subject to patent protection, provided that the substance does not yet exist in pure form. Even if the substance would exist in pure form, one could still seek patent protection for the process to produce synthetic substances. The respective in cooperation in German law is laid down in sec. 9a PatG [Patent Act]. However, no protection is granted under the BioTech Directive for human bodies during the individual development and synthesis phases for the mere discovery of one of its ingredients including the sequence or part of a sequence of a gene. Additionally, protection is also not available in for instances of breach of law or violation of public morals.

---

3 For details, please refer to chapter Know-How-Piracy by *Barbara Maucher*.

4 *Gollin*, Biopiracy: The Legal Perspective, 2001, American Institute of Biological Science.

5 Official Journal of the European Communities 1998 No L 213/13.

B. Reach-Through-Patents

A recent phenomenon in the field of bio-technology has been the filing by applicants of so-called "reach-through-claims". Reach-through-patents are claims to future inventions based on currently disclosed inventions. For example, such claims may be directed to any compounds or inventions resulting from utilising an already identified basic screening method. Reach-through-patents were in particular a problem in the past ten years, and led to an increasing number of applications claiming all possible pharmaceutical compounds identified by an identified research screening tool or claiming to methods of using such compounds. Many consider such claims beyond the scope of the subject matter contributed by the inventor.[6]

Generally, "reach-through-claims" in bio-technology and pharmaceutical cases have been attacked on three grounds, namely (i) written description; (ii) enablement; and (iii) inherent anticipation. "Reach-through" claims are argued to provide no teaching that shows a person skilled in the art how to produce structurally undefined agents. In some cases it also remains unclear precisely what inventions might actually be patented. At the forefront was the issue of whether protection may be claimed for a reach-through-patent and, in particular, whether licence fees may also be demanded in this regard. The permissibility of such licence fees is an essential requirement for being able to assess any loss in the event of the infringement of a reach-through-patent. According to the licence analogy, the parties would be required to be put in the same position as if they had entered into a standard licence agreement.[7]

It is now generally agreed that turnover generated from agents or medications is not considered relevant when assessing losses in the event of infringement of reach-through-patent claims. There are also certain exceptional cases where a reach-through patent may be considered to overlap with a medicine to some extent, but these will remain the exceptions.[8] The reason why demands for licence fees for drugs based on research tool claims are not generally permissible is that such fees are not allowed under German antitrust legislation. Section 17 para. 1 Gesetz gegen Wettbewerbsbeschränkungen [GWB] [Act against Restraint on Competition] (F. R.G.) (old version) states that requiring the payment of a licence fee for such a derivative product would be contrary to antitrust provisions.[9]

---

6 Mutual understanding of the European Patent Office, Japanese Patent Office and United States Patent and Trademark Office 5 November to 9 November 2001 "Report on Comparative Study and Bio-Technology Patent Practices".

7 22 March.1990 BGH [Federal Supreme Court] [I ZR 59/88], GRUR 1990, 1008 f. (Lizenzanalogie).

8 Also *Badenbach/Söder*, Lizenzvertragsrecht nach neuem GWB: Lizenzgebührenpflicht über den Inhalt des Schutz-rechts hinaus und nach Schutzrechtsende, MittdPA 2007, 353, 358 and *Meibom*, Durchlassansprüche – Reach-Through-Ansprüche bei Patenten für Research Tools, MittdPA 2006, 1, 5.

9 *Badenbach/Söder*, Lizenzvertragsrecht nach neuem GWB: Lizenzgebührenpflicht über den Inhalt des Schutzrechts hinaus und nach Schutzrechtsende, MittdPA 2007, 353, 358; *Wolfram*, "Reach-

C. Second medicinal indication

It is possible under Article 54 para. 4 and para. 5 of the EPC,[10] to protect an earmarked substance claim and its novelty. Such substances are only regarded as novel if either the substance itself, the pharmaceutical application of the substance or at least one specific therapeutic application of the substance is new. There is no problem with novelty if the relevant substance is being used as a medicinal treatment for the first time (first indication). Nor is there a problem if a substance is being used to treat an illness for which it has not previously been used (classic "second indication"). It is now recognised as an additional second indication if a substance is used to treat a previously treated illness, but is used on a different group of people, is administered differently, in a different dosage, using a different technical method, or with a different intention.[11] It is therefore generally not necessary to seek protection for the entire area of medicines concerned. Instead it is much more important that the indication is the subject of protection by the patent claim.[12]

D. Standard Essential Patents

The issue of standard essential patents has recently garnered considerable discussion, and have already become a relevant topic for courts. They are particularly important in the area of mobile communications. Some market operators believe that certain technologies, such as GSM and UMTS, require specific patents in order to be sold in specific markets. The ETSI (European Communication Standard Institute) analyses claims for relevancy, and may recognise a patent as a standard essential patent.[13] If a patent is deemed to be a standard essential, the patent owner cannot obtain a cease and desist order against the relevant a user for using the patent in the relevant technology. Instead, a corresponding licence to use the patent must be obtained from the patent holder and the corresponding licence fee paid.

Requirement for making a successful objection to the existence of a standard essential patent in infringement proceedings is that the defendant has already made a concrete offer of a licence to the patent holder. However, any such licence offered must (only) meet the FRAND standard which stands for fair, reasonable and non-discriminatory terms and is required by the SSOs (standard setting organisations).

The term "fair" relates to the various licensing conditions under which a specific technology can be licensed. Licence agreements are subject to certain limitations under

Through Claims" und "Reach-Through Licensing" – Wie weit kann Patentschutz auf biotechnologische Research Tools reichen?, MittdPA 2003, 57, 62.

10 This has been in force since 13 December 2007 and replaces the European Patent Convention of 5 October 1973.

11 19 December 2006 BGH [Federal Supreme Court] [X ZR 236/01], GRUR 2007, 404 (Carvedilol II).

12 16 June 1987 BGH [Federal Supreme Court] [X ZR 51/86], GRUR 1987, 794 (Antivirusmittel).

13 23 October 2007 LG [District Court] Mannheim [2 O 72/07], No. 53.

German antitrust law. On the other hand, such provisions would be unfair if the licencee was required to licence technologies which do not actually relate to the technologies (bundling), which make technologies freely available to the licensor (free grantback) and/or which tell the licencee how to act towards competitors (mandatory exclusivity).

"Reasonable" refers to the appropriateness of the licence fees. The licence fees may not be so expensive that they prevent genuine competition in the relevant sector.

"Non-discriminatory" does not mean that all licencees be identically treated. There may still be differences based on the volumes and creditworthiness of the various licencees, but market access must still be available to other parties.

The licence conditions under the FRAND standard may also be upheld by a court. ETSI suggests a particular dispute resolution process. ETSI states that the selective enforcement of patent rights should be prevented in the case of standard essential patents.

It should also be noted that the burden of proof for the defendant having been treated in a discriminatory manner lies with the party claiming the breach of the non-discrimination requirement. This might in practice be the reason why the so called antitrust objection in patent infringement cases in Germany has only been successful in one case so far.[14]

E. Software Patents

The protectability of software patents is still under discussion. In the United States it is already common practice that software may receive patent protection. The Court of Appeals for the Federal Court explicitly recognise that software qualifies as patentable subject matter in its 1994 decision *In re Alapatt*, 33 F.3d 1526.[15] In the EU, there had been several discussions regarding the patentability of computer programs.[16] There are some indications that at least computer implemented inventions are protectable by patents provided there is some specific technical effect. The general principle that patent software could be patented was explicitly confirmed in the precedent ruling on IBM/ computer program product handed down by the European Court of Appeal on 1 July 1998.[17]

---

14 13 February 2007 LG [Regional Court] Düsseldorf [4a O 124/05] (Kartellrechtseinwand im Mobilfunkbereich).

15 See also *Arriola*, Aktuelle Entwicklungen im Patentschutz von Computerprogrammen und mathematischen Algorithmen in den USA, GRUR Int 1996, 9 f.

16 See also *Milbradt*, Schutzfähigkeit von Software, K&R 2002, 522 ff.

17 1 July 1998 Technische Beschwerdekammer des Europäischen Patentamts [Boards of Appeal of the European Patent Office] [T 1173/97- 3.5.1], CR 2000, 91 (Patentierungsverbot für Computerprogrammprodukte).

In Europe, the European Patent Office, established in 1973 under the EPC, is currently the only institution that issues software patents, especially following the aforementioned ruling of 1 July 1998.[18] The European Patent Office is not, however, an organ of the EU, but is actually an independent institution. This means that European Patents are not automatically valid across the EU because they are national patents. However, even under the EPC the limits of patentability in the field of software are not clear. In October 2003 the President of the European Patent Office referred to the Enlarged Board of Appeal four questions concerning the limits of patentability of programs for computers.

Already on 20 February 2002, the European Commission proposed a new Software Directive (Proposal for a Directive on the patentability of computer-implemented inventions).[19] This Software Directive provides that an invention implemented by the execution of software on a computer or similar apparatus, if it is intended to be patented, must contribute to the area of technology which stands out from the state of the art and which is not obvious to a person skilled in the art.[20] However, following controversial discussions, the majority of members of the Commission rejected the Software Directive in July 2005.[21] The main obstacle to agreement are the different opinions on the scope of patent protection to be offered and its economic benefit, as well as the resulting risks and benefits.[22] This is also why the European Commission's goal of harmonising patent granting practice in the EU failed. But talks, which had apparently failed, are now moving to the next stage. Germany has announced its intention to push ahead with the creation of a Community Patent.[23] Charlie McCreevy, the European Commissionar for the Internal Market and Services, submitted a notice on 3 April 2007 entitled "Strengthening Europe's Patent System" proposing the creation of an integrated patent jurisdiction consisting of elements from the EPLA and the Community jurisdiction for patent disputes.[24] The opponents of software patents view this as the danger that the Community Patent will be used to open a back door for software patents.[25]

---

18 1 July 1998 Technische Beschwerdekammer des Europäischen Patentamts [Boards of Appeal of the European Patent Office] [T 1173/97 – 3.5.1], CR 2000, 91 (Patentierungsverbot für Computerprogramme).

19 Proposal for a Directive on the patentability of computer-implemented invention, presented by the Commission of the European Communities, COM (2002) 92 final – 2002/0047 (COD), 20 February 2002.

20 Article 4 of the proposal for a Directive on the patentability of computer-implemented invention, presented by the Commission of the European Communities, COM (2002) 92 final – 2002/0047 (COD), 20 February 2002.

21 *Wimmer-Leonhardt*, Softwarepatente – eine "Never-Ending-Story", WRP 2007, 273, 275.

22 *Basinski/de Beaumont/Betten/Faria Correa/Freischem/Laurie/Miyaska/Visscher*, Patentschutz für computer-softwarebezogene Erfindungen, GRUR Int 2007, 44, 45, 51.

23 German justice minister, Brigitte Zypries, budget speech in the Bundestag on 21 November 2006, available at http://www.bmj.bund.de/enid/0,0/Reden/Brigitte_Zypries_zc.html?druck=1pmc_id =3306.

24 Communication from the Commission to the European Parliament and the Council, enhancing the patent system in Europe, COM (2007) 165 final, 3 April 2007.

25 *Wimmer-Leonhardt*, Softwarepatente – eine "Never-Ending-Story", WRP 2007, 273, 275.

The normative starting point for the issue of the patentability of computer related inventions under German patent law is sec. 1 para. 2 no. 3 of the PatG [Patent Act], according to which programs for data processing systems cannot be viewed as patentable inventions. Parallel to Art. 52 of the EPC, these restrictions also apply to computer programs *per se*, sec. 1 para. 3 of the PatG [Patent Act]. The German Federal Patent Court and the German Federal Supreme Court have both attempted to assess the impact of this in their rulings.

The dispute over the patentability of software was characterised for some time by the "core theory" of the German Federal Supreme Court.[26] The key criterion for the issue of whether software inventions display the necessary technical character should be assessed according to whether the core of the new and innovative aspects of the invention are technical in nature. The necessary technicality is only given if the technical methods used are a component of the solution itself.[27] The new and innovative technical features must contain a complete solution to the relevant problem.

The German Federal Supreme Court has since held that computer-implemented inventions must always constitute a solution to a specific technical problem.[28] Such inventions can therefore be patented. Software may also be protected as a copyright under sec. 2 para. 1 no. 1 Urheberrechtsgesetz [UrhG] [Copyright Act] (F. R.G.) as a literary work and under sec. 69 a UrhG [Copyright Act] as software as such.[29]

F. Patentability of Nanotechnology

Over the next few years, the issue of how to provide adequate patent protection to nanomachinery is likely to come under closer scrutiny. Nanomachinery refers to structures which are at least with respect to two dimensions below 100 nm. Within the family of product patents one must distinguish between protecting substances *(Stoffschutz)* and protecting devices *(Vorrichtungsschutz)*. Processes and devices incorporating nanotechnology may be regarded as falling within both classes of substance and device inventions. The consequences of the allocation may result in a difference in defining the precise contours of the scope of the patents as well as legal consequences of such scope. No jurisprudence exists so far in this respect.[30] However, German practice in terms of

---

26 14 February 1978 BGH [Federal Supreme Court] [X ZB 3/76], GRUR 1978, 420, 421 (Fehlerortung); 22 June 1976 BGH [Federal Supreme Court] [X ZB 23/74], NJW 1976, 1936, 1937 ff. (Dispositionsprogramm).

27 22 June 1976 BGH [Federal Supreme Court] [X ZB 23/74], NJW 1976, 1936, 1937 ff. (Dispositionsprogramm); 17 Oktober 2001 BGH [Federal Supreme Court] [X ZB 16/00], GRUR 2002, 143, 144 (Suche fehlerhafter Zeichenketten).

28 17 Oktober 2001 BGH [Federal Supreme Court] [X ZB 16/00], GRUR 2002, 143, 144 (Suche fehlerhafter Zeichenketten).

29 See below, *Wolfgang Schönig*, Music Film and Software Piracy.

30 For further illustration see: *Uhrich/Zech*, Patentierung von Nanomaschinen versus Vorrichtungsschutz, GRUR 2008, 768.

patentability of nano-technology appears to be reversed at present stage.[31] It remains to be seen whether this practice will adapt to the apparently more generous approach in Europe.[32]

III. Securing Rights from Employees, Universities and other R&D Partners

Before a company can file for patent protection of its inventions, or decide to keep its innovations secret as company know-how, it is crucial that the company holds the relevant rights to the relevant inventions in question. Inventions are generally made by employees of the company or its R&D partners.

A. Employees

Employers have a claim to inventions made by their employees as part of their work for the company, a so-called service invention that can be claimed in full or in part by the employer. Service inventions are either (i) the result of a specific set task *(Aufgabenerfindungen)* (sec. 4 para. 2 no. 1 Arbeitnehmererfindungsgesetz [ArberfG] [Employee Inventions Act] (F. R.G.)); or (ii) based on existing experience or knowledge *(Erfahrungserfindungen)* (sec. 4 para. 2 no. 2 ArberfG [Employee Inventions Act]).[33] Any claims by the employer must be made within four months of being duly informed of the invention. Notice requires a description of the relevant task, the solution and of how the invention was made. Once notice is given, the employer must assert its claims to the invention to the employee in writing within the relevant deadline.

Many companies fail to comply with this very formal procedure provided for in sec. 6 of the ArberfG [Employee Inventions Act], with disastrous consequences. If an invention becomes freely available, the employee will have an unconditional claim for its use. The worst case scenario is that employees are able to sell their un-claimed inventions to their employers' competitors, provided this does not breach any employment contract requirement to act in good faith. Alternatively, the employer may register the patent without actually holding rights to the invention. In such case, the inventor may demand the transfer of the patent from its holder as part of a "patent vindication claim".

It is therefore crucial for companies to implement an effective and practical system for making claims to employee inventions. Importantly, provisions in employment agreements stating that employee inventions will be transferred to the employer are invalid. Sec. 22 ArberfG [Employee Inventions Act] states that statutory provisions may not be contracted away from the outset to the disadvantage of the employee. Contractual arrangements that adversely affecting the statutory rights of an employee are only permis-

31 *Hübner*, Zur Neuheit von Erfindungen aus der Nanotechnologie, GRUR 2007, 839 (839).

32 EPA GRUR Int. 1985, 827 – Thiochlortormiate.

33 For further details see B, R&D with Universities.

sible once the relevant invention has been registered. The practical problems experienced with the existing system have led to calls for a revision of the ArberfG [Employee Inventions Act] in this regard.

Discussions are currently ongoing regarding a fundamental principal of the ArberfG [Employee Inventions Act]. A first draft bill of the Federal Ministry of Justice was published on 25 October 2001, but this was withdrawn due to major differences of opinion between employers and employees. This draft still forms the basis for the current discussions, however.

The current period within which employers are required to claim an invention is four months under sec. 6 para. 2 sent. 2 second half-sentence ArberfG [Employee Inventions Act]. However, given that claiming within this period often results in practical difficulties, a further draft bill provides for a fictional claiming of the rights in the invention after the notification if the employer does not object to the claim within four months (sec. 6 para. 2 sent. 3 of the draft). This provision would remove a significant burden from employers, but it is still uncertain as to if and how this proposal might be implemented. This proposed change is part of the current pending proposal to modernize the German Patent law (the Patentrechtsmodernisierungsgesetz) which should come into force in the course of 2009.

B. R&D with Universities

The abolition of the "professor's privilege" in 2002 has made it more difficult to decide on the legal content of R&D agreements. The revised version of sec. 42 of the ArbErfG [Employee Inventions Act] allows universities to claim inventions in return for payment of 30% of the proceeds from the application of the invention (cf. sec. 42 no. 4 ArberfG [Employee Inventions Act]). This is also conditional on the invention having been made in the context of performing a service on behalf of another party (i. e. a task-related invention or an invention based on knowledge or experience as referred to above).

1. University Claims to Employee Inventions

An invention is generally defined as task-related in sec. 4 para. 2 no. 1 ArberfG [Employee Inventions Act] if the employee receives a specific research or development instruction from the employer, and the invention results from work on the task.[34] The assumption that all inventions made by a professor should be regarded as "task-related" inventions has been repeatedly called into question on the grounds that the definition

34 *Bartenbach/Volz*, Arbeitnehmererfindergesetz, § 4, No. 22 with reference *inter alia* to 23 May 1952 BGH [Federal Supreme Court] [I ZR 149/51], GRUR 1952, 573 (Zuckerdiffuseur) and 4 December 1973 LG [District Court] Düsseldorf [4 O 165/69], GRUR 1974, 275 (Mischröhre).

of the scope of a professor's work is somewhat vague.[35] It is generally agreed that an invention made by a professor should only be regarded as a task-related invention if it is attributable to a specific research or development order,[36] whereby it is insufficient to simply refer to "research work". However, this requirement of specificity is usually met where externally financed university projects are concerned. This means that most inventions are "task-related" and may therefore be claimed as "employee inventions" by the university.

There have been various suggestions to circumvent universities' rights in this regard by concluding externally financed projects directly with the professor concerned, which was common practice in the past. Thus, any work on the project by the professor is regarded as a sideline activity *(Nebentätigkeit)*, and is sometimes called the "sideline activity" approach.[37] It has led to considerable uncertainty on the part of universities as to how they should structure their own agreements with professors. It is argued that there can be no task-related invention in such a case, and that the university has no claims to such inventions.[38]

The relevant parties still need to be particularly cautious when entering into such agreements. A major concern is the strict limitations placed on professor's secondary activities under German employment law in recent years.[39] It is also conceivable that the university may seek claims to the invention as one based on existing knowledge and experience within the meaning of sec. 4 para. 2 no. 2 ArberfG [Employee Inventions Act].

2. Impact on Contractual Structure

The abolition of the "professor's privilege" has had a substantial impact on the content and structure of contracts between universities and professors. There is a major risk that a university might make a lawful and legitimate claim to a professor's invention as a task-related or knowledge-based invention (see above), thereby preventing the smooth transfer of the invention to the principal. It is therefore necessary to make the university

35 *Bartenbach/Volz*, Erfindungen an Hochschulen – Zur Neufassung des § 42 ArbEG, GRUR 2002, 743, 748; *Peter*, Die „Flucht in die Nebentätigkeit" – ein Schlupfloch aus der Neuregelung des § 42 ArbnErfG bei Erfindungen von Hochschullehrern?, MittdPA 2004, 396, 397.

36 4 December 1973 LG [District Court] Düsseldorf [4 O 165/69], GRUR 1974, 275 (Mischröhre); *Bartenbach/Volz*, Erfindungen an Hochschulen – Zur Neufassung des § 42 ArbEG, GRUR 2002, 743, 748.

37 *Peter*, Die „Flucht in die Nebentätigkeit" – ein Schlupfloch aus der Neuregelung des § 42 ArbnErfG bei Erfindungen von Hochschullehrern?, MittdPA 2004, 396, 401.

38 See also Gesetzesentwurf der Bundesregierung, Entwurf eines Gesetzes zur Änderung des Gesetzes über Arbeitnehmererfindungen [German draft Act of the Federal Government], BT-Drucks. 14/5975, p. 6.

39 On general public services law and university law relating to medical professors see *Dieners*, Zusammenarbeit der Pharmaindustrie mit Ärzten, p. 27 ff.

itself a party to the underlying agreement. There are essentially two recommended contractual models – the "Berlin"[40] model and the "Hamburg" model.[41]

The "Berlin" model secures the subsequent transfer of technology by requiring both the university and the professor to assign any rights to future research findings to the industry partner in advance. This has the disadvantage that the principal may receive rights to inventions which are not relevant to its business, while it must nevertheless bear the cost of the patents that may be registered in this regard.

The "Hamburg" model secures the aforementioned transfer by requiring the university to waive its right to make claims to inventions made by the professor and requiring the professor to assign all future findings from the project in advance. Both models achieve the goal of securing future rights for the industry partner.

A third potential and maybe preferable solution is to include both the university and the professor as parties to the agreement. Each of them would then be required to immediately inform the other parties to the agreement of any resulting inventions and the industry partner can decide whether or not the university should claim the rights to such inventions. If the industry partner decides in favour of claiming by the university, the statutory mechanism will be triggered and the rights will be transferred to the industry partner once the appropriate claims to the rights have been made. Provision may be made in the R&D agreement for the transfer of these future rights of the university. The main advantage of this third approach is that it (i) complies with the statutory provisions (claims asserted by the university within four months of registration of the invention) and (ii) the industry partner only receives the rights it really needs. The latter has the consequence that any dispute which may come up with respect to the compensation of such invention will only relate to at least relevant inventions.

C. R&D with other Industry Partners

Steps should also be taken in R&D projects with other industry partners to ensure that one's own company has sufficient rights to any inventions. A distinction should also be made here between research assignments and R&D assignments.

With R&D assignments, it should be ensured that the party paying for the research also receives all rights to potential inventions to other results, to the extent permissible under antitrust legislation.

Collaboration in any R&D project works best when the parties minimise the possibility of disputes by integrating carefully circumscribed IP clauses into their agreement that

---

40 See *Winzer*, Forschungs- und Entwicklungsverträge, p. 223 ff.; a specimen contract is available online from Berlin Humboldt University at http://forschung.hu-berlin.de/administration/0000bvfa2.pdf (available at 12 June 2008).

41 See *Klawitter/Zintler*, Neuer Mustervertrag für F & E-Kooperationen zwischen Wirtschaft (industriellen Auftraggebern) und Hochschulen, MittdPA 2006, 116, 118.

reflect their business and strategic needs. Typically, any background IP owned, developed or otherwise control-led by one of the parties before starting the R&D project remains the sole property of the original owner. The other party, however, may require a non-exclusive licence under market conditions to use such background IP after the successful termination of the R&D project, if necessary for use of the results of the R&D project.

The parties also need to account for the right to use any foreground IP rights. A practical patent/know-how protection strategy is necessary for the protection of such new IP rights. Should the inventions just be kept confidential as trade secrets or do the parties wish to file patent applications? If so, where should any patent application(s) be filed? If not, how can know-how be kept secret and is the scope of protection adequate to protect the business needs of the parties? Additio-nally, both parties need to ensure that they adequately protect their employees' inventions, such as by using appropriate invention assignment provisions in their employment agreements. Also, they should properly claim the rights to their employees' inventions in accordance with the applicable law in those jurisdictions where they are required to do so in order to perfect their rights.

Furthermore, foreground IP rights should be allocated to the parties according to their intellectual, financial and actual contribution, as well as under consideration of their core business objectives and future inventions. The field of use must also be determined, while at the same time managing potential anti-trust issues must be managed. Other significant problems may arise in con-nection with the principle of exhaustion if both parties are free to use the new IP without restriction and if they are entitled to grant licences to third parties. The potential insolvency of one of the collaboration partners must also be addressed in the R&D agreement.

IV. Infringement

Firstly, it must be established whether the alledgedly infringing product or process objected to actually makes use of the technical teaching of the patent-in-suit. This requires a proper determination of the scope of protection of the patent. Further, a distinction should be made between direct and indirect infringements. The infringement may also relate to actions not taking place directly in Germany. Particular emphasis should also be placed on the problem of infringements in transit.

A. Determining the Scope of Protection of the Patent

The patent must be interpreted within the context of the whole claim and in light of the description and the figures. The patent description is the basis for its own dictionary, which prevails over any general dictionary.[42]

42 7 June 2005 BGH [Federal Supreme Court] [X ZR 198/01], GRUR 2005, 754 (Knickschutz).

According to German case law every feature included in a patent claim is indispensable for the description of the invention and is never non-essential *per se*.[43]

Thus, the interpretation of a patent claim is less complex if the terminology is clear and all features are clearly met by the infringing product or process. The analysis differs when the product or process comprises only some of the features contained in the patent.

In addition to the literal fulfilment of patent features, the mere equivalence of patent features may be sufficient to justify an infringement in accordance with sec. 14 PatG [Patent Act] and Art. 69 EPC. In the absence of literal infringement, whether there is still infringement should be analysed by interpreting the content of the patent claims, again taking into account the patent description and drawings. The purpose here is not, however, to determine whether an abstract scope of equivalence exists,[44] but to determine whether the accused embodiment solves the underlying problem of the invention using equivalent means. It is also crucial whether a person skilled in the art would be aware of these equivalent means as of the priority date. If a person skilled in the art easily recognises an equivalent means, consideration needs to be given to whether the corresponding solution is also equivalent in the opinion of a person skilled in the art. If the invention is not equivalent, there may be an equivalence outside the scope of protection of the patent. A distinction again must be made between dependent inventions which fall within the scope of a previous patent but which also contain their own, new inventive step.[45]

An assertion of infringement by equivalence may be challenged on the basis that the accused embodiment is not a patentable invention as of the priority date of the asserted patent.[46] Thus, the extent of protection conferred by a patent ends at the point where non-inventive further development of prior art begins.[47]

B. Direct Infringement

Direct patent infringement under sec. 9 sent. 2 PatG [Patent Act] occurs when the product covered by the patent claims is manufactured, offered for sale, put on the market or used or is imported or possessed for such purposes. Process patents are directly infringed if the process covered by the claims is used or if the third party is aware, or if it is obvious, that the use of the process is not permitted without the consent of the patent holder, or if the product manufactured directly from the process is offered for sale, put on the mar-

---

43 15 June 2000 [Higher Regional Court] Düsseldorf [2 U 47/99], GRUR-RR 2001, 145 (Abflussrohre).

44 *Busse*, Patentgesetz, § 14, No. 99.

45 12 July 1990 BGH [Federal Supreme Court] [X ZR 121/88], GRUR 1991, 436, 439 (Befestigungsvorrichtung II).

46 "Formstein" objection in 29 April 1986 BGH [Federal Supreme Court] [X ZR 28/85], GRUR 1986, 803, 805 (Formstein).

47 *Falck*, Überlegungen zum „Formstein"-Einwand, GRUR 1998, 218.

ket or used or is imported or possessed for such purposes. As regards manufacture, it should be noted that it is sufficient for the product to be manufactured such that it displays all the essential features of the protected invention, while it may still be necessary to add secondary non-essential features for completion of the product.[48] Offering does not require that all features of the protected teaching be disclosed in the accused product like in an advertising brochure, provided other aspects allow for the conclusion that specific features of a patent are being infringed.[49] Offering a product online is sufficient for a finding of infringement provided it is also possible for a German resident to order the product.

C. Indirect Infringement

Sec. 10 PatG [Patent Act] states that the indirect use of a patented invention can also constitute a patent infringement. An indirect patent infringement prevents third parties from using key features of the invention without the consent of the patent holder in Germany, or other persons entitled to use the patented invention, to offer the inventions in Germany or to supply them there if the third party is aware, or if it is obvious to it, that such items are suitable or intended to be used for the use of the invention. From an objective standpoint, indirect patent infringement therefore requires a third party in Germany to offer and supply means which are based on a key element of a patented invention. In subjective terms, this requires that the third party is aware of the fact, or it is obvious that, such items are suitable and intended for the use of the invention. Sec. 10 para. 2 PatG [Patent Act] states that offering generally available goods only constitutes an indirect infringement if the third party wilfully causes the party receiving the goods to act in an impermissible manner.

The subjective criteria of knowledge or obviousness means that there is at least a sufficiently definite expectation that a customer will use the offered or supplied key elements in a manner which infringes a patent. Evidence of such an expectation arises if such use is referred to in instruction leaflets or advertising, for example. Even if a product has a potential infringement warning, it may still be obvious that the product is intended for infringing a patent. On the other hand, it cannot be automatically assumed that the relevant customers have infringed the patent.

In addition to the subjective intention on the part of the customer, there is also the issue of the objective suitability and purpose of the means to use the invention. Strict requirements need to be applied in this regard.[50] The question should be asked whether the relevant item may be used without infringing a patent (so-called non-infringing uses). In this case, it may suffice to take precautions to ensure that an item is used in a manner which does not infringe patent rights.

---

48 *Erdmann/Rojahn/Sosnitza*, Handbuch des Fachanwalts Gewerblicher Rechtsschutz, No. 308.

49 16 September 2003 BGH [Federal Supreme Court] [X ZR 179/02], GRUR 2003, 1031.

50 20 February 2002 OLG [Higher Regional Court] Düsseldorf [2 U 81/99], MittdPA 2003, 252 (Haubenstretchautomat).

It may be difficult to distinguish between generally available goods and key features of the invention. An item relates to a key element of the invention if it is suitable for acting together with one or more features of a patent claim by realising the idea behind the protected invention.[51] Only non-essential elements of the invention may be excluded from consideration.[52] This distinction may be particularly difficult for consumables. It may be argued here that the elements of patent claims also often represent a crucial element of the invention.[53] Consumables often relate to the actual technical and economic benefit of the invention. In such case, consumables may also form a key element of the invention.

The patent holder is entitled to a claim to cease and desist under sec. 139 PatG [Patent Act] against any party indirectly infringing its patent. A total ban on offering and supplying an item is only possible if the item can only be used in a manner which infringes patent rights (i. e., it has no non-infringing uses).[54] The operative provisions may therefore be limited, e. g. to "precautions" or "warnings". Such warnings generally refer to potential patent infringements in the event a party makes use of the subject matter covered by the patent's scope. It is therefore assumed that the recipient will act in a lawful manner.[55] The specific precautions to be taken depend on the individual circumstances of the case. However, under very recent German Federal Supreme Court legislation, it is no longer permissible in the case of an indirect patent infringement to take the view that the warning must be displayed "explicitly and prominently".[56] It will presumably however also not be enough to argue "that reference should be made to …" in attempting to justify otherwise infringing actions. When offering and delivering goods the existing patent protection must be pointed out clearly and unambiguously. Whether this will have to be done in the future by using a specific form (in order to comply with certain layout requirements) or can simply be done by attaching an explicit and prominent warning is still open.[57]

---

51 27 February 2007 BGH [Federal Supreme Court] [X ZR 38/06], GRUR 2007, 769 (Pipettensystem).

52 4 May 2004 BGH [Federal Supreme Court] [X ZR 48/03], GRUR 2004, 758 (Flügelradzähler); 7 June 2005 BGH [Federal Supreme Court] [X ZR 247/02], GRUR 2005, 848 (Antriebsscheibenaufzug).

53 21 November 2007 LG [Regional Court] Düsseldorf [4 a O 333/06] (Bremsbeläge für Scheibenbremsen II).

54 13 June 2006 BGH [Federal Supreme Court] [X ZR 153/03], GRUR 2006, 839, 841 (Deckenheizung).

55 *Kühnen*, Die Tenorierung des Warnhinweises in Fällen mittelbarer Patentverletzung, GRUR 2008, 218.

56 9 January 2007 BGH [Federal Supreme Court] [X ZR 173/03], GRUR 2007, 679 (Haubenstretchautomat).

57 *Kühnen*, Die Tenorierung des Warnhinweises in Fällen mittelbarer Patentverletzung, GRUR 2008, 218, 219.

D. Transit

The transit of goods through another country can be of particular interest to patent owners. A patent grants exclusive rights to its owner only in the territory of the State in which the patent is registered. For instance, one may have patent protection concerning a certain product in Germany but not in Russia. The limited scope of patent protection makes it difficult to determine which rights may be affected during the course of transit. Is it possible to control the movements of goods to other countries even though one does not own an intellectual property right in the State of destination, but only in the State of transit?

In some cases, the movements of non-Community goods are carried out under the so-called "external transit procedures" where the goods are not subject to import duties and other charges or to commercial policy measures until they reach the customs office in the destination country. In practice, the customs authorities affix a customs seal on the means of transport to protect the goods against removal during the course of transit.

Still, there is at least an abstract risk that those goods could be put on the market in the state of transit rather than being transported to the country of destination. Such marketing may not only breach customs procedures, but may also infringe patents within the State of transit.

The question is whether a patent grants its proprietor the right to prohibit the transit of goods which are covered by the claims of the patent.

A patent confers on its proprietor the exclusive right to place its product on the market as well as to offer such products to the market – this right is laid down in the patent law of the relevant jurisdictions, e. g. sec. 9 of the PatG [Patent Act].

In order to examine whether external transit of goods constitutes the marketing of a product, one must also consider Customs Regulation (Council Regulation (EC) No 1383/2003 of 22 July 2003 concerning customs action against goods suspected of infringing certain intellectual property rights and the measures to be taken against goods found to have infringed such rights),[58] which replaced the Predecessor Customs Regulation (Council Regulation (EC) No 3295/94 of 22 December 1994 laying down measures to prohibit the release for free circulation, export, re-export or entry for a suspensive procedure of counterfeit and pirated goods).[59] The Customs Regulation concerns customs seizure of goods suspected of infringing certain intellectual property rights and the measures to be taken against goods found to have infringed such rights.

The interpretation of the Customs Regulation has been subject to several judgements of the ECJ in trademark cases.[60] The ECJ has not yet had the opportunity to rule on the interpretation of patent law in relation to the Customs Regulation. However, it has

58 Official Journal of the European Union 2003 No L 196/7.

59 Official Journal of the European Communities 1994 No L 341/8.

60 For details of those ECJ judgements please see above, *Diana Kaufmann*, Trademark Piracy, I C 11.

issued several judgements on the law of trademarks and the question when a good is "put on the market" or "used in the course of trade" based on the Trademark Directive (Directive 89/104/EC of 21 December 1988 to approximate the laws of the Member States relating to trademarks).[61] The arguments brought forward in these judgements can be considered in relation to patent law, too, since the same questions and interests arise.[62] At first glance the recent European case law is not always coherent and might result in potentially contradictory arguments. Even the recent *Diesel* judgement given by the ECJ on 4 July 2006 did not clarify the question.

The *Diesel* case holds that transit alone without any further indications of unlawful marketing, does not constitute a marketing of products in the state of transit as required for a patent or trademark infringement action. The court explained that otherwise, every external transit of goods would need to be regarded as marketing of the product in question.

Thus it has become more difficult for patent owners of a patent to obtain an injunction when referring to goods that are placed under an external transit procedure. The mere transit of goods as such does not constitute an act of marketing in the state of transit. Instead it is likely that the courts will require further evidence before issuing an injunction against the owner of goods in transit. Such evidence could be manuals in the language of the state of transit or other evidence that proves that the goods will be put on the market in the state of transit.

E. Objections

The infringer may assert objections to the supposed patent infringement.

A material objection is that with equivalent embodiments this is known from the state of the art and therefore falls outside the scope of the patent. In the case of the so-called *Formstein* objection, the infringer is asserting that the equivalent embodiment being attacked is not a patentable invention with regard to the state of the art at the time of priority of the patent-in-suit.[63]

Other permissible objections are for example the existence of a prior right of use or the exhaustion of the patent right due to a lawful put on the market by the patent holder or a respective licensee.

Good faith is also always a permissible objection. Good faith constitutes a principle which is part of the whole legal system. According to the principle of good faith, a claim cannot be enforced if it is in contrast to an earlier position. Under German law, the principle of estoppel is not as strong as in the USA. However, once a certain declaration,

61 Official Journal of the European Communities 1989 No L 40/1.

62 See the comparative presentation in *Rübel*, Patent Infringement by Transit of Goods through Germany, Patent World, November 2006.

63 29 April 1986 BGH [Federal Supreme Court] [X ZR 28/85], GRUR 1986, 803, 805 (Formstein).

position or behaviour has created confidence, the enforcement of a claim must be seen as being made in bad faith.

Under German patent law, the lack of protection of the patent cannot be used as an objection in the infringement proceedings, but only in the nullity proceedings. However, the judge can suspend the infringement proceedings at its discretion because of a pending nullity proceeding.

A currently frequently discussed objection is the antitrust object, discussed as the FRAND[64] objection. Further to this antitrust objection an infringement will not lead to a cease-and-desist order nor to damage claims if the respective patent protects a standard essential technology and the user of that technology has offered the owner of the patent a licence agreement under FRAND standard. So far, this objection has only been accepted by a court in German in one case.[65]

V. Legal Consequences of Infringement

A. Inspection

As introduced by the Act on the Improvement of the Enforcement of Intellectual Property Rights in sec. 140 c PatG [Patent Act] and in accordance with the *Faxkarte*[66] and *Restschadenstoffentfernung*[67] rulings made the German Federal Supreme Court *(Bundesgerichtshof)*, the right to inspection does not require a "high" degree, but only a "certain" degree of probability of infringement. Rights holders will continue to be able to resort to the relatively new tool known as the "Düsseldorf inspection procedure" by simultaneously applying for a preliminary injunction as well as pre-trial measures for the collection and preservation of evidence. Thus, the infringer can be ordered by an injunction granted by the court to allow access to, for example, a potentially infringing machine and to allow its inspection by a court-appointed expert. Because the inspection is conducted by a court-appointed expert in proceedings for the collection and preservation of evidence, there is no need to have another taking of evidence in the infringement proceeding.

B. Cease-and-Desist

Sec. 139 PatG [Patent Act] states that the patent holder may demand that an infringer cease-and-desist, regardless of fault, if the patented invention has been used in an unlawful manner. Such a cease and desist order may only be requested if a further legal

64 FRAND stands for fair, reasonable, non-discriminatory terms of a licence agreement.

65 13 February 2007 LG [Regional Court] Düsseldorf [4a O 124/05] (Kartellrechtseinwand im Mobilfunkbereich).

66 2 May 2002 BGH [Federal Supreme Court] [I ZR 45/01], GRUR 2002, 146 (Faxkarte).

67 1 August 2006 BGH [Federal Supreme Court] [X ZR 114/03], GRUR 2006, 962 (Restschadenstoffentfernung).

infringement has taken place (risk of repetition) or if there is an imminent specific risk of a first-time infringement taking place (risk of initial infringement). The object in the infringement dispute is the accused infringing embodiment. The legal action can only be worded according to the patent claim if the infringement is literal. If the accused infringement is based on equivalence, the form of infringement should be described in detail in the legal action, describing the conduct to be prohibited with precision.

C. Damages

Furthermore, an infringing party culpably infringing a patent may also be held liable for damages. If a patented invention has been used unlawfully, it is assumed that such use occurred through the fault of the infringer. Otherwise the infringer prove its lack of culpability.[68]

Damages for infringing intellectual property rights in Germany may be calculated using three different methods.

Further to Sec. 139 para. 2 PatG [Patent Act] which has been amended by the Implementation of the Enforcement Directive the patent owner can choose between three different methods to calculate the damages: (i) Actual damages including lost profit of the patent owner[69]; (ii) profit made by the infringer[70] **or** (iii) royalty payments under a licence analogy[71].

The patent owner cannot mix those three methods of calculation but has to choose one of them. However, the patent owner is not bound by his first choice but can switch between the dif-ferent methods until a final or legally binding judgment has been rendered or the payment has been made.

First, the patent owner may claim damages in the amount of its own losses, including any lost profits[72]. This requires the party whose rights have been infringed to provide evidence that it has received the relevant orders for the covered products. As an evidentiary matter, it is difficult to prove that the loss of profits was caused by the patent infringement.

The patent holder may also claim damages in the amount of the profit made by the infringer from the infringement of the patent[73]. The grounds for the claim for surrender of the infringer's profit are not, however, completely clear and may also be difficult to prove[74]. It is assumed that the patent holder would have made the profit instead of the

68 3 June 1976 BGH [Federal Supreme Court] [X ZR 57/73], GRUR 1976, 579 (Tylosin).
69 Sec. 139 para. 2 sent. 1 PatG [Patent Act].
70 Sec. 139 para. 2 sent. 2 PatG [Patent Act].
71 Sec. 139 para. 2 sent. 3 PatG [Patent Act].
72 Sec. 139 para. 2 sent. 1 PatG [Patent Act].
73 Sec. 139 para. 2 sent. 2 PatG [Patent Act].
74 See *Busse*, Patentgesetz, § 139, No. 164.

infringer if he would have commercialised his patent. Judge *Klaus Grabinski* of the District Court of Düsseldorf estimates in a recent article that in the last year the claimants chose in approximately 3/4 of the trials on damage claims this calculation method[75].

In the past, it was not easy to claim the infringer's profit, as according to prior judgements, the infringer could deduct his overall fixed costs from its total revenues. The situation changed in 2000 where the German Federal Supreme Court (*Bundesgerichtshof*, BGH) held that fixed costs can only be deducted from the revenues made directly by the infringing product if and only to the extent that such fixed costs can be allocated directly to the production of the infringing product[76].

A further common method is based on the "licence analogy"[77], where damages are based on a reasonable licensing fee as would have been due under standard market conditions (analogous to a "reasonable royalty")[78]. The argument for this method is that at a minimum, the infringer should be in no better position than if he had obtained a licence. However, the infringer does not have to pay any kind of punitive damages but "only" the standard market price. It is discussed in legal literature whether Art. 13 of the Enforcement Directive instead asks also for such kind of compensation, but the German legislator refused to implement such additional damages[79].

It is discussed whether the above-mentioned rules also apply accordingly in case the patent owner has issued licences. The German Federal Supreme Court held in 2008 that even in case of an exclusive licence, the exclusive licensee as well as the patent owner (and licensor) may calculate their damages according to all three methods of calculation[80]. The damages occurred to the licensor and the licensee are seen as one unitary damage caused by the patent infringement calculated by one of the three methods of calculation. For example, the right holders cannot claim compensation of the infringer's profit twice, but only once. The right holders have to show which part of the unitary damage is allocated to the licensor and which part is allocated to the licensee. The right holders may choose to sue together or one on behalf of the other or they may also sue independently.

The non-exclusive licensee has no rights to damages under Section 139 PatG. He may only conduct the case if the licensor assigns his claims for damages (which also include the damages which occur to the licensee).

75 *Grabinski*, Gewinnherausgabe nach Patentverletzung, GRUR 2009, 260, 262.

76 BGH [Federal Supreme Court], [1 ZR 246/98], GRUR 2001, 329 – *(Gemeinkostenanteil)*.

77 See *Reimann*, Bericht Q 136 für die Deutsche AIPPI-Landesgruppe Nr. 43 [Report Q 136 for the German AIPPI country group No. 43] in approximately 95% of cases.

78 Sec. 139 para. 2 sent. 3 PatG [Patent Act].

79 See *Tetzner*, GRUR 2009, 6 ff.

80 20 May 2008 BGH [Federal Supreme Court], GRUR 2008, 896 *(Tintenpatrone)*.

D. Information

It is often necessary to get the infringer to provide details on the origin, distribution and quantity of the items infringing the patent in order to assess which of these calculation methods should be used. Such a claim for information exists under sec. 140 b PatG [Patent Act]. The injured party or its legal successor is entitled to make a claim, as is the case with claims to cease and desist under sec. 139 of the PatG [Patent Act]. A culpable violation is not a requirement for the claim for information, but the use of the patent must be unlawful. There is no unlawful use if one of the exceptional circumstances is satisfied under sec. 11 to sec. 13 of the PatG [Patent Act] exist,[81] or if exhaustion has occurred.[82] The information extends to the origin of the infringing product according to the marketing of the products in accordance with sec. 140 b para. 2 of the PatG [Patent Act]. The information duty is only not given in the event that the information duty is disproportional. The claim for information may also be asserted in proceedings for a preliminary injunction. Under the Act on the Improvement of the Enforcement of Intellectual Property Rights, the right to information can also be asserted against third parties such, for example, persons having had infringing goods in their posession or having been involved in the production or sale of such goods.

E. Destruction

The patent holder may also request the destruction of the infringing products in the possession or ownership of the infringer in accordance with sec. 140 a para. 1 of the PatG [Patent Act]. However, destruction may only be asked in cases of direct infringement or in other word; only if the respective product cannot be used in a non-infringing manner.

F. Recall

The improvements provided by the Enforcement Act do not only relate to the pre-trial phase of collecting facts and evidence. The legal position of rights holders is further improved by the introduction of additional remedies that go beyond the claim for destruction available so far. In the past, the infringer could not be required to remove all the products from the market that had already been sold. According to sec. 140 a PatG [Patent Act] – introduced by the Act on the Improvement of the Enforcement of Intellectual Property – for the first time, right holders will have a claim for recall or the removal from the distribution channels against infringers. Whether the claim for removal from distribution channels can be enforced even if the products are no longer in the infringer's posession has yet to be clarified by case law. However, recall campaigns can be initiated at any time, regardless of title or posession.

---

81 E. g. § 11 of the German Patent Act provides for allowed acts. This allows, for example, usage for private purposes and for testing purposes.

82 The effect of industrial property rights is limited by the exhaustion principle. That states that a protected object used or marketed by the holder of such rights or another authorised party with its permission may be freely used by third parties. This does not require any special consent.

VI. Enforcement

A. Preliminary Injunction vs. Action on the Merit

Particularly in the case of the patent infringement, the issue arises of how the corresponding claims are enforced.

Claims can be made to courts either by applying for a preliminary injunction or by alledging infringement in principal proceedings. For all actions whereby a claim arising out of one of the legal relationships regulated in the PatG [Patent Act] is asserted, the civil chambers of the first instance courts shall have exclusive jurisdiction (sec. 143 para 1 PatG [Patent Act]). By statutory order, patent litigation cases are allocated to specific patent litigation courts. In Germany, Düsseldorf and Mannheim are the most famous patent litigation courts. Other courts such as Hamburg have an increasingly importance due to the fact of having one of the largest harbours and therewith facing increasing border seizures in product piracy cases.

The plaintiff and the applicant of a preliminary injunction are both required to bear the burden of proof for all facts supporting the claims in patent infringement proceedings. However, only in the principal proceedings all facts have to be proven, while in preliminary injunction proceedings facts of the infringement have to be made credible *(prime facie evidence)*. The assessment of the scope and the classification of the alleged infringement is the responsibility of the court handling the matter. The burden of proof may shift only for process patents to the extent a new product is manufactured with the same features.

As part of the preliminary injunction proceedings, a claim for information may also be asserted. Damages may only be pursued in principal proceedings, however.

The advantage of obtaining a preliminary injunction from the court is that the claim to cease-and-desist can be obtained and, therefore, enforced more quickly than in principal proceedings. Unlike in preliminary injunction proceedings under the UWG [Gesetz gegen den unlauteren Wettbewerb] [Act Against Unfair Competition], the urgency in patent infringement proceedings only exists if the applicant submits the application for a preliminary injunction within four weeks from becoming aware of all facts justifying the infringement and the opponent. Such a preliminary injunction is obtained very quickly, generally within one to two days. It only takes longer if the court requests an oral hearing.

Principal proceedings on the other hand take 6 to 18 months in the first instance. German patent infringement proceedings differ from other jurisdictions such as the US, in that there is no jury, no actual disclosure and no enhanced damages.

Preliminary injunction proceedings are particularly common in cases involving products exhibited at trade fairs, where prompt action is often required. The aim then is to use the injunction to get the bailiff to seize the infringing goods. In preparation for preliminary injunction proceedings at a trade fair, a copy of the patent certificate and all other relevant property rights should be collected beforehand. Furthermore, a current printout from the roll of deeds/register is required. One of the disadvantages of the preliminary injunction may be that the validity of the patent must be likely while in principal proceedings the court judges on the basis of the registered patent and does only suspend the proceeding if it is likely that the patent will be held invalid in a pending nullity action.

Finally, one further change by the current draft Patentrechtsmodernisierungsgesetz should be mentioned: The principle as laid down in sec. 145 PatG [Patent Act] that an action has to be based on all relevant patents likely to be infringed *(Konzentrationsmaxime)* will most likely be abolished under the Patentrechtsmodernisierungsgesetz which shall enter into force in the course of 2009.

B. Border Seizures

Border seizure proceedings under Customs Regulation are possible in the case of a patent infringement. However, it can be difficult to identify the relevant patent infringement from the product, especially for customs officers who are not familiar with the product(s). In addition, a patent is only effective in those countries for which it has been issued. Thus a German patent cannot prevent products it covers from being produced in China, for example. A German patent may, however, block the importation from China.

Border seizures in patent cases are rarely compared to border seizures relating to trademarks, even though they are an effective measure to combat increasing levels of product piracy leading to patent infringement.

In Germany, border seizures in patent matters were introduced under sec. 142a of the PatG [Patent Act]. The EU introduced such seizures in patent matters under Council Regulation (EC) No. 241/1999 of 25 January 1999,[83] which amended the Predecessor Customs Regulation. By this amendment, the coverage of the Predecessor Customs Regulation was extended to patents. With effect of 1 July 2004 the Predecessor Customs Regulation was replaced by the Customs Regulation.

EU border seizure proceedings are generally instituted by a request from the holder of the infringed right under Art. 5 of the Customs Regulation.[84] However, Art. 4 of the Customs Regulation states that customs authorities may also institute proceedings *ex*

[83] Council Regulation (EC) No 241/1999 of 25 January 1999 amending Regulation (EC) No 3295/94 laying down measures to prohibit the release for free circulation, export, re-export or entry for a suspensive procedure of counterfeit and pirated goods, Official Journal of the European Communities 1999 No L 27/1.

[84] For details of the general procedure regarding border seizures, please see *Claudia Milbradt*, Enforcement of Intellectual Property Rights in Germany, B 2.

officio if there is sufficient evidence for suspicion,[85] where the patent holder and the licensee are able to submit an application for a border seizure within three days.[86]

An application in accordance with Art. 5 para 5 of the Customs Regulation must include details of the patent infringed, a detailed description of the goods concerned, details of the type of counterfeiting to identify for the existence of a patent infringement. The customs authorities must be able to assess with sufficient accuracy whether there are grounds to suspect that a patent infringement has been committed.

The proceedings under sec. 142 a of the PatG [Patent Act] are essentially similar to EU border seizure proceedings, but differ crucially as regards the degree of probability required for an infringement to exist.[87] The Customs Regulation merely requires that the suspicion of an infringement exists, but sec. 142 a of the PatG [Patent Act] requires an obvious infringement. For an infringement to be considered obvious, the details provided by the applicant must be coherent and credible and the other facts and circumstances apparent to the customs officers must not lead to any reasonable doubt that an infringement has been committed.[88] On the other hand, a patent infringement only has to be highly likely for the existence of a suspicion of an infringement.[89]

Since 1 September 2008 the Act on the improvement of the enforcement of intellectual property rights offers another opportunity with the establishment of sec. 142b of the PatG [Patent Act] . This clause gives, in accordance with Art. 11 of the Customs Regulation, the possibility to have destroyed seized goods without a court ruling having been obtained. The substantial simplification compared to the standard proceedings is a result of the consent fiction. Consent to destruction of the goods is regarded as having been given if the applicant, holder or owner of the goods fails to make an explicit objection to the destruction of the goods within 10 working days of being informed of such.

85 *Welser/González*, Marken- und Produktpiraterie, No. 267; *Cordes*, Die Grenzbeschlagnahme in Patentsachen, GRUR 2007, 483; *Heermann/Hirsch*, Lauterkeitsrecht, Band I, EG P Produktpiraterie, No. 24.

86 *Cordes*, Die Grenzbeschlagnahme in Patentsachen, GRUR 2007, 483, 484.

87 *Benkard*, Patentgesetz, § 142a, Nos. 18 f.

88 *Cordes*, Die Grenzbeschlagnahme in Patentsachen, GRUR 2007, 483, 485.

89 *Benkard*, Patentgesetz, § 142a, No. 20.

Know-How Piracy

Barbara Maucher

I. Protection of Know-How

Know-how protection covers the wide spectrum of business-related and technical information that is not afforded registered protection under intellectual property law. Any information relating to inventions, aesthetic information, distinguishing marks, and plant genetic information are generally know-how protected before and independently of any protection afforded under industrial property law.

Protecting a company's know-how is akin to protecting the company. Know-how is an intangible asset that mostly is very valuable for a company. It is protected under an independent protection scheme, which is distinguishable from technical protective rights, intellectual property rights or trademark rights. Know-how protection is not pre-eminent or subordinate to these other forms of protection, but rather, it is a real *aliud*. This is due to the fact that the prerequisites for know-how protection differ fundamentally from those applying to any other kind of technical property rights, which in turn is due to the fact that an infringement of know-how also greatly differs from an infringement of a registered intellectual property right.

Despite its immense practical importance, know-how protection has, for the most part, tended to be neglected in Germany. This is already evident by the fact that German know-how protection is predominantly based on a multitude of older provisions which appear in various laws: To date, there is no law that is specific to the protection of know-how, such as the Markengesetz [MarkenG] [Trademark Act] (F. R.G.), which protects marks and labels. Rather provisions on know-how protection are chiefly scattered in the Gesetz gegen den unlauteren Wettbewerb [UWG] [Act Against Unfair Competition] (F. R.G.), the Bürgerliches Gesetzbuch [BGB] [Civil Code] (F. R.G.), provisions of individual and collective labour law, the Arbeitnehmererfindungsgesetz [ArberfG] [Employee Inventions Act] (F. R.G.),[1] commercial and business law, and procedural law.

A. Objects and Concept of Know-How Protection

German law does not contain a statutory definition of know-how. On the contrary, some international legal instruments provide for a definition.

1 Sec. 24 ArberfG [Employee Inventions Act] obliges both, employer and employee, to keep any invention made by the employees confidential for a certain time.

In the Technology Transfer Regulation (Commission Regulation (EC) No 772/2004 of 27 April 2004 on the application of Article 81(3) of the Treaty to categories of technology transfer agreements), know-how is defined as *(a package of non-patented practical information, resulting from experience and testing, which is: (i) secret, that is to say, not generally known or easily accessible; (ii) substantial, that is to say, significant and useful for the production of the contract products; and (iii) identified, that is to say, described in a sufficiently comprehensive manner so as to make it possible to verify that it fulfils the criteria of secrecy and substantiality)*.[2] As it results from the text, this definition only comprises technical information, but not business and economic know-how.

Art. 39 TRIPS (Agreement on Trade-Related Aspects of Intellectual Property Rights) requires all WTO (World Trade Organization) members to provide protection (solely) for information which is 'not generally known or readily ascertainable' and which has commercial value for this reason, can be regarded as know-how capable of protection,[3] provided that those who lawfully hold such information take reasonable measures to keep it secret. Art. 39 TRIPS does, however, not contain any definition of items capable of protection comparable to the definition in sec. 1 para. 2 Patentgesetz [PatG] [Patent Act] (F. R.G.).

Under German law, due to the lack of a statutory definition, the term 'know-how' and the scope of its protection are determined by jurisprudence and legal literature, inspired by practical experience. This has led to a rather broad approach: with the aim of protecting innovation and business in general, know-how protection is frequently available for any information, which would otherwise not be obviously eligible for protection, and this further underscores the value and importance of know-how protection for industrial property law in Germany.[4]

In general, there is agreement on the possible objects of know-how protection, even though these – as said before – differ greatly. *Inter alia*, the possible objects of know-how protection include models, formulae, technical details such as dimensions and compositions, schematic diagrams, customer lists, certain operational procedures and computer programs. In addition, the specific know-how of a firm always consists of the accumulated skills and experience of its employees. The list could be extended further. The broadest definition of know-how is simply knowledge, which goes beyond what is generally available.[5]

---

2 Article 1, 1 (i) of the Technology Transfer Regulation.

3 "not generally known or readily ascertainable", Article 39 ¶ 2 c) TRIPS.

4 *Ann*, Know-how: Stiefkind des Geistigen Eigentums?, GRUR 2007, 39, 41.

5 *Erdmann/Rojahn/Sosnitza*, Handbuch des Fachanwalts Gewerblicher Rechtsschutz, No. 1313.

German court rulings have time and again upheld a broad definition of know-how, most recently in the German Federal Supreme Court's *(Bundesgerichtshof)* "*Präzisionsmessgeräte*" ruling[6, 7], which contains references to the older German Federal Supreme Court rulings "*Möbelpaste*"[8] and "*Wurftaubenpresse*".[9]

Within the scope of know-how protection, it is not the use of information *per se* that is prohibited, but rather the overcoming of factual (non-disclosure) barriers set up by the owner of the information. Know-how protection consists of protection against unauthorised disclosure of and unauthorised access to know-how.[10] Unauthorised access may take the form of plain and simple theft. The unauthorised disclosure of information may take the form of betrayal of information by in-house staff or espionage perpetrated by third parties. In the event that know-how merely is, however, disclosed as a simple result of a negligent failure to maintain secrecy, it loses its protection – and, also quite often, its value. In that respect, the protection of know-how differs from the protection of technical protective rights, given that the protection afforded by technical protective rights consists of prohibiting any unauthorised use of the protected information (although there are a few, rather specific exceptions to this).[11] While the broadness of the scope covered by know-how protection is an advantage, know-how law thus has the disadvantage that it affords no protection if third parties lawfully come into possession of protected information, like for instance, by way of own R&D work.[12]

Keeping both the aim of protecting innovation and business in general as well as the concept of know-how protection in mind, German jurisprudence and legal literature have developed the following criteria for eligibility of information for know-how protection:

– the information must not be readily known or ascertainable,
– the information must be linked to a business enterprise,

6 7 November 2002 BGH [Federal Supreme Court] [I ZR 64/00], GRUR 2003, 356 ff. (Präzisionsmessgeräte).

7 14 March 2006 BVerfG [Federal Constitutional Court] [1 BvR 2087/03 und 1 BvR 2111/03], MMR 2006, 375.

8 15 March 1955 BGH [Federal Supreme Court] [1 ZR 111/53], GRUR 1955, 424 (Möbelpaste).

9 1 July 1960 BGH [Federal Supreme Court] [I ZR 72/59], GRUR 1961, 40 (Wurftaubenpresse).

10 Ann, Know-how: Stiefkind des Geistigen Eigentums?, GRUR 2007, 39 f. (Journal published by the German Association for Intellectual Property Rights and Copyright Law *(Deutsche Vereinigung für gewerblichen Rechtsschutz und Urheberrecht e.V.)*.

11 *Beckerman-Rodau*, The Choice Between Patent Protection and Trade Secret Protection: A Legal and Business Decision, 84.J. P. T. O.S. 371 (2002). The wording of Article 1, 1 (i) of the Technology Transfer Regulation also underlines the difference between the two protection concepts by delimiting negatively the term 'know-how' as being a 'package of non-patented practical information'.

12 Ann, Know-how: Stiefkind des Geistigen Eigentums?, GRUR 2007, 39, 41; *Beckerman-Rodau*, The Choice Between Patent Protection and Trade Secret Protection: A Legal and Business Decision, 84.J. P. T. O.S. 371 (2002).

– the party having the information intends to keep it secret, and
– the party having the information has a legitimate interest in keeping it secret.

Further eligibility criteria for protection comparable to 'technicality', 'innovativeness', 'inventiveness' or 'commercial usability', as they exist under the Patentgesetz [PatG] [Patent Act], are alien to know-how protection law, which, again, underlines the difference of the protection concepts.

1. The definition of 'not readily known or ascertainable'

The term 'not readily known or ascertainable' is not legally defined, but legal commentators agree that it is to be interpreted broadly under German law.[13]

In order to provide some guidance, the terms 'trade secret' and 'industrial secret' are often used when referring to information that is 'not readily known or ascertainable'.[14] The term 'trade secret' is generally understood to relate to internal operational and business matters, whereas an 'industrial secret' tends to relate to technical procedures and proceedings.[15] Examples of potential trade and industrial secrets include such various things as design plans, chemical and pharmaceutical formulae and production methods, software, specifications, price estimates and customer lists. Given that the terms 'trade secret' and 'industrial secret', however, are not legally defined either, they are only of little to no assistance for clarifying the meaning of 'not readily known or ascertainable'.[16] They provide no indication as to what eligibility criteria information must fulfil in order for it to be conferred the status of protected know-how.[17] On the other hand, they make it clear, that the information in question in general is not commonly publicly available.

It, therefore, all comes back to the basic concept that know-how protection means the protection of the access to information.[18] As said before, this approach is due to the fact that know-how protection is not based on any relationship by virtue of which the state first grants the owner of the information monopolistic rights to the information for a certain period, as it is the case for patents, for instance.[19]

13 Prevailing opinion; cf. *Hefermehl/Köhler/Bornkamm*, Gesetz gegen den unlauteren Wettbewerb, § 17, No. 4; *Harte-Bavendamm/Henning-Bodewig*, UWG, § 17, No. 1.

14 *Ann*, Know-how: Stiefkind des Geistigen Eigentums?, GRUR 2007, 39, 41.

15 *Hasselblatt*, Münchner Anwaltshandbuch Gewerblicher Rechtsschutz, § 26, No. 2 with reference to *Kraßer*, Der Schutz des Know-how nach deutschem Recht, GRUR 1970, 587, 589.

16 See 7 November 2002 BGH [Federal Supreme Court] [I ZR 64/00], GRUR 2003, 356 (Präzisionsmessgeräte): A trade or industrial secret means any information concerning a business that is not generally known, but rather, is known only to a limited group of persons and which shall be kept secret in accordance with the express wishes of the proprietor of the business, who has a reasonable economic interest in maintaining secrecy in this regard.

17 See also *Ann*, Know-how: Stiefkind des Geistigen Eigentums?, GRUR 2007, 39, 41.

18 *Westermann*, Handbuch Know-How-Schutz, Chapter 4, No. 5.

19 *Ann*, Know-how: Stiefkind des Geistigen Eigentums?, GRUR 2007, 39, 41.

Information is not readily known or ascertainable if only a narrowly restricted group of persons obtains knowledge of those certain facts that are regarded as a trade secret.[20] Such a restricted group of persons most likely consists of individuals who are subject to contractual and/or statutory duties to observe secrecy and who are in some way controlled by the owner of the relevant information.[21] Even external parties, possibly including persons employed by a competitor, may rightfully gain access to such company secrets, provided that this occurs in a manner which safeguards the secrecy of the information, e. g. under a licence agreement.[22] Likewise, the term 'not readily known or ascertainable' also refers to cases where a company uses known information in a way it was not previously known that such information could be used.[23]

Information, on the contrary, known or available to others cannot be referred to as 'not readily known or 'not readily accessible for anyone'. Protection ceases to be available when information becomes generally known to and/or readily available to other persons by proper means. Information thus becomes readily known or readily ascertainable if it is in the public domain or is readily available: in other words, if the interested public actually has the possibility of obtaining knowledge of the relevant information by normal means, i. e. legally and without major difficulties or particular financial or technical effort.[24]

The accessibility of the information, therefore, is key in the qualification of specific information as know-how eligible for protection. In order to ensure that certain information does not become 'readily known or readily ascertainable', and thus public, it is incumbent upon each enterprise to take measures or precautions, which prevent its trade secrets from being accessed by third parties.

2. Definition of 'linked to a business enterprise'

The definition of 'linked to a business enterprise' can also be delimited negatively.

Information is not deemed to be linked to a business enterprise, if the information, while it is secret, relates solely to the private sphere of the business enterprise itself or to business activities of third parties.[25]

---

20 *Harte-Bavendamm/Henning-Bodewig*, UWG, § 44 No. 10.

21 21 December 1962 BGH [Federal Supreme Court] [I ZR 47/61], GRUR 1963, 367, 371 (Industrieböden); 10 July 1963 BGH [Federal Supreme Court] [Ib ZR 21/62], GRUR 1964, 31 (Petromax II).

22 *Doepner*, Anmerkungen zum wettbewerbsrechtlichen Geheimnisschutz im Zivilprozess, in: Keller/Plassmann/Falck (ed.), Festschrift für Winfried Tilmann, p. 105, 109.

23 1 September 1992 OLG [Higher Regional Court] Hamm [4 U 107/92], WRP 1993, 36, 38 (Tierohrmarken).

24 *Harte-Bavendamm/Henning-Bodewig*, UWG, § 44 No. 9; *Doepner*, Anmerkungen zum wettbewerbsrechtlichen Geheimnisschutz im Zivilprozess, in: Keller/Plassmann/Falck (ed.), Festschrift für Winfried Tilmann, p. 105, 109.

25 *Hefermehl/Köhler/Bornkamm*, Gesetz gegen den unlauteren Wettbewerb, § 17, No. 5.

Even if there once was a link, information is not deemed to be linked to a business enterprise, either, if such link has become so loose that the information is attributable more to the market in general, or to third parties, rather than to the business enterprise which claims protection.

For instance, the OLG (Higher Regional Court) of Stuttgart ruled that the link between a manufacturer of copiers and written information on the susceptibility of such copiers to break down was insufficient for such information to be regarded as an operating secret for which the manufacturer of the copiers could claim protection.[26] The Higher Regional Court justified this decision arguing that this information was also attributable to others, at least those who used the copiers, and not only to the manufacturer.

The issue of any links existing between a business enterprise and the information for which protection is sought is of special importance in cases where generally known information is used in a way it was not previously known that such information could be used.[27] According to jurisprudence and legal literature, such use of information constitutes a secret, which is linked to the business enterprise, too.[28]

Anyways, when analysing the different cases dealing with the issue of 'linked to a business enterprise', the term may simpy be defined as follows: a link to a business enterprise always exists if the company's turnover is affected.

3. Definition of 'intention to keep information secret'

Again, the term 'intention to keep information secret' is delimited negatively. An 'intention to keep information secret' always exists if and to the extent no intention to disclose is recognisable.[29]

---

26 30 October 1981 OLG [Higher Regional Court] Stuttgart [2 U 43/81], GRUR 1982, 315 (Gerätewartung). The court held as follows in its decision: "The susceptibility of the individual devices to breakdown does not constitute an industrial secret of the Plaintiff. There is not a sufficiently close connection to the Plaintiff's business. The susceptibility of a device to breakdown depends on the average quality of the fungible products concerned. The breakdown rate experienced by an individual user of a device and the sustained adverse effect such user experiences are facts which he can easily ascertain without requiring particular resources of any kind for this purpose. The breakdown rate and the type of fault should not be equated with facts such as the details of the construction which even specialists can only ascertain by way of a through technical inspection".

27 15 March 1955 BGH [Federal Supreme Court] [1 ZR 111/53], GRUR 1955, 424 (Möbelpaste), 1 September 1992 OLG [Higher Regional Court] Hamm [4 U 107/92], WRP 1993, 36, 38 (Tierohrmarken).

28 *Piper/Ohly*, Gesetz gegen den unlauteren Wettbewerb, § 17 No. 6; *Hefermehl/Köhler/Bornkamm*, Gesetz gegen den unlauteren Wettbewerb, § 17, No. 5; *Ann*, Know-how: Stiefkind des Geistigen Eigentums?, GRUR 2007, 39, 42.

29 10 May 1995 BGH [Federal Supreme Court] [I StR 764/94], NJW 1995, 2301.

Thus, all should be done that no 'intention to disclose' is 'recognisable', which may be achieved by the conclusion of an explicit (confidentiality) agreement: An intention to keep the information secret always exists if non-disclosure is specifically agreed to. Furthermore, in order to document an intention to keep information secret vis-à-vis third parties, documentation containing specific know-how should be marked as secret or confidential[30] in order to be able to invoke protection under sec. 18 UWG [Unfair Competition Act].

However, according to the German Federal Supreme Court, no excessive demands are to be made regarding a manifestation of the intention to maintain secrecy.[31] In its '*Petromax II*' ruling the German Federal Supreme Court held that it is sufficient if the 'intention to keep information secret' ensues from the nature of the information to be kept secret.[32]

The relevant facts of the '*Petromax II*' ruling of the German Federal Supreme Court concerned a party, which, upon the failure of contractual negotiations on intended future co-operation, used construction drawings obtained in the course of those negotiations to manufacture a certain product itself. It was not clear from the drawings themselves that any non-authorised use thereof was actually prohibited. The German Federal Supreme Court, therefore, did not address the issue of whether the requisite intention to maintain secrecy existed and was adequately documented in order for sec. 18 (old version) UWG [Unfair Competition Act] to apply. Instead, the German Federal Supreme Court ruled that because the technical drawings had been handed over in the course of negotiations regarding an agreement on the manufacture of tools, i. e. within the framework of a relationship based on trust, and because using the drawings meant saving considerable development and design engineering expenses, an intention to keep information secret on the part of the disclosing company was recognisable. The unauthorized use made of the drawings by the other party, therefore, breached sec. 1 (old version) UWG [Unfair Competition Act], although the parties had never entered into an express undertaking to maintain secrecy.

4. The definition of 'legitimate interest in keeping information secret'

The requirement of having a legitimate interest in keeping information secret in order to be afforded know-how protection ensues from the general legal prohibition of arbitrarily exercising legal rights.[33] The requirement of having an interest in maintaining secrecy on the one hand helps verify whether a purported intention to maintain secrecy is justified.[34] This prevents the owner of a secret from being able to claim protection if there is no recognisable need for such protection. On the other hand, there are no particular legal requirements that need to be fulfilled in order to be able to claim an interest

30 "confidential", "unauthorised use expressly prohibited".

31 10 May 1995 BGH [Federal Supreme Court] [I StR 764/94], NJW 1995, 2301.

32 10 July 1963 BGH [Federal Supreme Court] [Ib ZR 21/62], GRUR 1964, 31 (Petromax II).

33 *Ann*, Know-how: Stiefkind des Geistigen Eigentums?, GRUR 2007, 39, 42.

34 *Westermann*, Handbuch des Know-How-Schutzes, Chapter 1, No. 51.

in maintaining secrecy – thus it will be very difficult to allege that there is no such 'legitimate interest in keeping information secret' in a particular case. In general, such interest is always deemed to exist if disclosure of information regarded as confidential can have a tangible negative impact on the competitive situation of a business enterprise, i. e. if and to the extent potential competitors obtain knowledge of the information.[35]

B. Confidentiality Agreement

In accordance with the above and, in particular, with the concept of know-how protection consisting of protection against unauthorised access and disclosure, confidentiality agreements play a decisive role and may be a perfect means to protect a certain information and/or knowledge.

The first step to be taken in each specific case, therefore, is to carefully examine precisely what the relevant know-how consists of. If it transpires that the know-how pertains more to a specific product which embodies the know-how and does not so much consist of any specialist knowledge, one must examine whether special proprietary rights can be invoked, for instance in accordance with the Patentgesetz [PatG] [German Patent Act] or, in the case of computer programs, under sec. 69 lit a) *et seq*. Urhebergesetz [UrhG] [German Copyright Act] (F. R.G.). If such proprietary rights are not available, or if such protection is not wanted, e. g. to avoid disclosure of know-how within a patent registration process, the only other option is to protect the relevant know-how by making it subject to a duty to observe secrecy. Therefore, secrecy clauses in service and employment agreements as well as in contractual agreements entered into with other business enterprises regarding the joint commercial exploitation of know-how are of particular importance.

– Secrecy clauses in service and employment agreements

During the existence of a service or employment relationship, protection of company know-how is ensured either by way of express confidentiality agreements, or through the ancillary duty under sec. 241, para. 2 of the BGB [Civil Code] to be considerate of the rights, interests and other objects of legal protection of the other party to a contract.

This contractual ancillary duty (previously called a fiduciary duty) is of particular importance in respect of certain duties of care under employment law, in particular a special duty to maintain confidentiality and, above all, to protect business secrets.[36] In general, an employee must maintain secrecy in relation to business or personal internal matters of the employer if otherwise the legitimate interests of the employer might be adversely affected. The duty to maintain confidentiality commences once the employ-

---

35 *Reimann*, Einige Überlegungen zur Offenkundigkeit im Rahmen von §§ 17 ff. UWG und von § 3 PatG, GRUR 1998, 298, 300; *Hefermehl/Köhler/Bornkamm*, Gesetz gegen den unlauteren Wettbewerb, § 17 No. 9.

36 *Hasselblatt*, Münchner Anwaltshandbuch Gewerblicher Rechtsschutz, § 26, No. 24.

ment relationship has been constituted and in principle exists (at least) until the employment ends, irrespective of whether it is terminated by regular termination or for cause.

Breaches of this obligation may, for example, be committed by memorising know-how, customer details, and details relating to technical devices, or by systematically collecting documentation.[37] It is therefore not permissible for an employee to use mailing lists of his employer for sending farewell letters aimed at enticing away clients of his employer, in order to set up his own business.[38]

Such duties to maintain confidentiality also exist for any individual employed as company officer under a service contract, e. g. as board member or managing director. Special statutory duties to observe secrecy are, for example, contained in the Gesetz betreffend die Gesellschaften mit beschränkter Haftung [GmbHG] [Limited Liability Companies Act] (F. R.G.) or in the Aktiengesetz [AktG] [Stock Corporation Act] (F. R.G.). Pursuant to sec. 85 GmbHG [Limited Liability Companies Act], for instance, managing directors, supervisory board members or liquidators make themselves liable to criminal prosecution if, without prior authorisation, they disclose company secrets, namely, trade or industrial secrets, which they gained knowledge of by virtue of their capacity as managing director, member of the supervisory board or liquidator. In accordance with sec. 404 AktG [Stock Corporation Act] this applies *mutatis mutandis* to members of the managing board, the supervisory board or liquidators of a stock corporation. In accordance with sec. 79 Betriebsverfassungsgesetz [BetrVG] [Works Council Constitution Act] (F. R.G.), members and substitute members of the works council are also obligated not to disclose or to use any explicitly classified trade or industrial secrets, which come to their knowledge by virtue of their membership in the works council.

In general: The closer a relationship based on mutual trust, the stricter the obligation and ancillary duty under sec. 241, para. 2 of the BGB [Civil Code] to maintain secrecy. This is particularly applicable to employees in whom the employer places particular confidence such as holders of registered powers of representation *(Prokurist)* or authorised agents *(Handlungsbevollmächtigter)*.[39]

By virtue of this general legal duty to maintain confidentiality, confidentiality agreements usually have a purely declaratory value only, but may be nonetheless useful.[40] A confidentiality agreement may well be tailored to the specific position, functions and tasks of the different employees and officers. The conclusion of a confidentiality agreement may specify the protected rights and interests further and shape the legal ancillary duty under sec. 241, para. 2 of the BGB [Civil Code]. In addition, a confidentiality agree-

37 *Hasselblatt*, Münchner Anwaltshandbuch Gewerblicher Rechtsschutz, § 26, No. 24.

38 22 April 2004 BGH [Federal Supreme Court] [I ZR 303/01], GRUR 2002, 91 (Verabschiedungsschreiben).

39 *Hasselblatt*, Münchner Anwaltshandbuch Gewerblicher Rechtsschutz, § 26, No. 25.

40 *Berscheid/Kunz/Brand*, Praxis des Arbeitsrechts, No. 2269; *Hümmerich/Boecken/Düwell*, Arbeitsrecht, § 611, No. 1080.

ment may also serve as a warning sign and raise awareness with regard to the interests at stake. This is particularly true in case the relationship comes to an end.

– Former employees or officers

In the event that an employment agreement or the service agreement of a company officer is terminated, this poses the question of whether or not the former employee or officer is permitted to use legitimately acquired knowledge about internal company procedures.

Sec. 17 UWG [Unfair Competition Act], which imposes penalties on any parties betraying trade or industrial secrets[41], and which can lead to the imposition of civil liability via sec. 823 para. 2 BGB [Civil Code], ceases to apply at the end of an employment or service relationship. In principle, the former employee/officer may then use legitimately acquired knowledge as he may see fit. Of course, this does not apply when special statutory or contractual duties to observe secrecy are applicable even after termination of the engagement, such as aforementioned sec. 85 GmbHG [Limited Liability Companies Act], sec. 404 AktG [Stock Corporation Act] and sec. 79 BetrVG [Works Council Constitution Act].

Aside from these provisions, the German Federal Supreme Court has consistently ruled that an employee or officer whose employment relationship has ended is, in principle, free to disclose and use any industrial secrets legitimately acquired in the course of the employment relationship.[42] However, in its *Industrieböden* ruling the German Federal Supreme Court held that there can be an ongoing duty to maintain secrecy incumbent upon an employee towards his employer under employment law in exceptional circumstances and any use or disclosure then constitutes a breach of a prohibition to compete.[43] In the *Spritzwerkzeuge* ruling, the German Federal Supreme Court affirmed this decision. In order to determine whether such an ongoing duty to maintain secrecy exists, the interests of all parties involved in the individual case must be considered, whereby certain provisions of constitutional law, such as Art. 12 of the Grundgesetz [GG] [Basic Law] (F. R.G.) (career advancement) and Articles 2 and, 14 of the GG [Basic Law] (interest in maintaining secrecy of know-how used in the course of carrying out commercial activities) must also be taken into account in any such weighing of interests.

41 See below in more detail.

42 16 November 1954 BGH [Federal Supreme Court] [I ZR 180/53], GRUR 1955, 402 f. (Anreißgerät); 21 December 1962 BGH [Federal Supreme Court] [I ZR 47/61], GRUR 1963, 367 (Industrieböden); 6 November 1963 BGH [Federal Supreme Court] [Ib ZR 41/62 und 40/63], GRUR 1964, 215 f. (Milchfahrer); 19 November 1982 BGH [Federal Supreme Court] [I ZR 99/80], GRUR 1983, 179, 181 (Stapel-Automat); 3 May 2001 BGH [Federal Supreme Court] [I ZR 153/99], GRUR 2002, 91 f. (Spritzgießwerkzeuge).

43 21 December 1962 BGH [Federal Supreme Court] [I ZR 47/61], GRUR 1963, 367 (Industrieböden).

In this regard, it should be taken into consideration on the one hand whether the former employee contributed to the development of the relevant know-how, whether he needs the knowledge in question to advance his career, and whether his employment lasted for a lengthy period of time. A long length of service with the company may mean that the knowledge and skills acquired by a withdrawing employee in the course of his employment are such that any prohibition on the use of such knowledge might jeopardise or seriously impair his professional existence.[44]

On the other hand, it should be taken into consideration whether the company has an interest in maintaining secrecy in respect to the relevant know-how, whether the withdrawing employee or officer was holding a position that required placing particular trust in him, whether a prohibition of competition was contractually agreed to and whether the former employee or officer may in fact intend to sell the know-how instead of using it for his own professional purposes.[45] Even though the mere enticing away of a staff member entrusted with confidential information is permissible and in general does not constitute a breach of competition law,[46] the specific circumstances of the staff member's departure may nonetheless weigh to its former company's benefit: In a case where a former employee had enticed away all of his former employer's customers in one fell swoop, the German Federal Supreme Court ruled that a breach of the prohibition of competition had been committed due to the fact that the employer's commercial existence had been ruined.[47] The German Federal Supreme Court also held that a breach of competition law is committed if a material industrial secret is exploited;[48] or if an employee uses the know-how of a company to develop competing products shortly before his employment ends;[49] or if an employee provokes the termination of his employment to enable him to subsequently use the employer's know-how.[50]

The highest German court for employment law matters, namely the German Federal Labour Court *(Bundesarbeitsgericht)*, takes a slightly different approach with regard to the issue of employees' post-contractual duties of confidentiality: According to the precedents of the German Federal Labour Court, former employees are under a duty to maintain confidentiality in relation to trade or industrial secrets, even without a confidentiality agreement, simply by virtue of their ongoing duties of good faith towards their former employer under employment law. Former employees are merely entitled to

44 21 December 1962 BGH [Federal Supreme Court] [I ZR 47/61], GRUR 1963, 367 (Industrieböden).

45 3 May 2001 BGH [Federal Supreme Court] [I ZR 153/99], GRUR 2002, 91 f. (Spritzgießwerkzeuge).

46 *Berscheid/Kunz/Brand*, Praxis des Arbeitsrechts, No. 2273.

47 6 November 1963 BGH [Federal Supreme Court] [Ib ZR 41/62 und 40/63], GRUR 1964, 215 f. (Milchfahrer).

48 21 December 1962 BGH [Federal Supreme Court] [I ZR 47/61], GRUR 1963, 367 (Industrieböden).

49 19 November 1982 BGH [Federal Supreme Court] [I ZR 99/80], GRUR 1983, 179, 181 (Stapel-Automat).

50 16 November 1954 BGH [Federal Supreme Court] [I ZR 180/53], GRUR 1955, 402 f. (Anreißgerät).

use knowledge they gained through experience during the course of their employment.[51]

Given the diverging judgments pronounced by the German Federal Supreme Court and the German Federal Labour Court on post-contractual duties of confidentiality, it is advisable to include a confidentiality clause in employment or service contracts which survives termination of the employment or service relationship. This is especially advisable if an employee or officer acquires knowledge of know-how that is essential to business operations.

In the view of the German Federal Labour Court, such confidentiality agreements are also valid and effective even without payment of compensation, provided they are restricted to specific secrets.[52] However, to the extent that post-contractual duties to maintain confidentiality result in a situation in which the employee is effectively no longer able to continue to be active in his chosen field of work, such confidentiality agreements must provide for (adequate) compensation in order to be in compliance with competition law. In addition, such post-contractual duties must be limited in terms of time.[53] Limiting a duty to maintain secrecy to two years after the termination of an employment or service relationship is considered reasonable in all cases.

As an additional safeguard to ensure compliance with confidentiality agreements, it is advisable to provide for the payment of liquidated damages in the event of any breach of such confidentiality duties.

– Commercial agents

In order to protect its business, especially its customer lists, a company might want to consider entering into confidentiality agreements with those mainly dealing with the customers, i. e. its commercial agents. According to German jurisprudence, a commercial agent does not act unfairly if he utilises his customer contacts that are still etched in his memory after leaving the company. He does not act unfairly, either, if he uses contacts to parties who have not been or are not regular customers of his previous employer for his own benefit.[54]

Thus, in view of this liberal jurisprudence, it is particularly conceivable and advisable to agree with commercial agents on a clause prohibiting the post-contractual use of know-how. Here again, it further is advisable to provide for the payment of liquidated damages in the event of any breach of such confidentiality duties.

---

51 16 March 1982 BAG [Federal Labour Court] [3 AZR 83/79], NJW 1983, 134 f.; 15 December 1987 BAG [Federal Labour Court] [3 AZR 47/86], NJW 1988, 1686-1687.

52 16 March 1982 BAG [Federal Labour Court] [3 AZR 83/79], NJW 1983, 134.

53 15 December 1987 BAG [Federal Labour Court] [3 AZR 474/86], DB 1988, 1020.

54 28 January 1993 BGH [Federal Supreme Court] [I ZR 294/90], NJW 1993, 1786 f.; 14 January 1999 BGH [Federal Supreme Court] [I ZR 2/97], GRUR 1999, 934 f. (Weinberater); 19 December 2002 BGH [Federal Supreme Court] [I ZR 119/00], GRUR 2003, 453 (Verwertung von Kundenlisten).

– Other contractual relationships

Even between companies, the need to exchange know-how may arise – for instance, within the framework of joint ventures or other forms of co-operation, or even a technical due diligence.[55] In that respect, a company in possession of pertinent know-how must make various decisions.[56] In particular, it needs to decide how much know-how it is willing to disclose to its contractual partner, the extent to which it wishes to monitor the use of such know-how, and how it hopes to prevent any use that might be contrary to the terms of the agreement, i. e. its own interests. The contractual arrangements to be made in this regard are freely negotiable, but it is advisable to let oneself be guided in this regard by provisions that are typically contained in licence agreements on (registered) industrial property rights.

In this type of relationship between companies, it really is common practice to enter into pre-contractual non-disclosure agreements and thus, to agree upon a duty to observe secrecy at the outset of any contractual negotiations. A standard non-disclosure agreement is generally a good idea for long-term business relationships. These also generally involve the obligation to pay liquidated damages in the event of any infringement of the contractual provisions.

However, it should always be borne in mind that any such agreement does not guarantee that confidential information will not be disclosed. Once know-how has been disclosed to third parties, there is no way of undoing the damage. The threat of liquidated damages alone certainly often is enough to deter parties from disclosing information, but is generally only of limited consolation when privileged know-how is disclosed. It is often difficult to bring successful claims for damages, given the difficulty of proving that the relevant information was confidential or that actual losses have been incurred. One potential approach would be to demand advance payment for the provision of information which could then be offset against a corresponding performance following conclusion of any contractual agreement.

From an antitrust perspective, non-disclosure agreements with contracting parties should not cover information which is generally available, the recipient's own know-how and know-how received from third parties authorised to disclose it.

55 A technical due diligence may precede a joint venture concluded for research and development reasons. Each party discloses its (technical, research …) abilities and facilities in order to allow the other party to judge whether the conclusion of a joint venture seems reasonable, and to estimate the chance of success.

56 For instance, any holder of know-how must first clarify whether the relevant know-how is freely transferable and may be used by others. Any legal restrictions holders of know-how are themselves subject to, such as the provisions of the Datenschutzgesetz [DSG] [Data Protection Act] (F. R.G.), need to be observed and may hinder such transfer of know-how.

C. Practical Measures

Apart from the conclusion of confidentiality agreements, there are other means available for protecting a company's know-how.

1. Defining risks

Before taking any measure, however, the first important step for any company is to commission experts to carry out an analysis of weak points of the company's know-how protection.[57] This includes identifying and analysing any existing risks for a loss of know-how. Such analysis can then serve as basis for determining which precautions and preventive measures should be taken. The analysis should include a review and documentation of the existing know-how as well as an analysis of the market in which the company operates.

The key to effective know-how protection is to clearly identify the information that needs protecting. Effective measures can then be taken to safeguard the most important information and knowledge. This includes an analysis of the relevant employees which embody know-how, as well as of all documents crucial for the success of the firm and its undertaking, too.

The likelihood of an unwanted loss of know-how also depends in particular on the number of competitors in the same sector. Therefore, the market in which the respective company operates should be carefully analysed, too. The more competitors there are, the more likely it is that one of them has the same know-how.[58] Other critical factors include the number of employees and the costs required for entering the market. In addition, there is an increased risk of industrial espionage for companies working in areas where R&D is highly cost-intensive and where the prospective returns are very high. On the contrary, it is more likely that the same know-how will be developed by two independent sources in cases where there are several different technological methods for creating the same result or product and it is very difficult for companies to take measures to combat this.[59]

2. Taking measures

For businesses whose most important asset is know-how, preventive measures are particularly important because in many cases there may be no way to compensate for lost know-how. This includes legal and practical measures within and outside the firm.

---

57 See also http://www.sicherheitsforum-bw.de/downloads/Sicherheitsforum2.pdf

58 *Beckerman-Rodau*, The Choice between Patent Protection and Trade Secret Protection: A Legal and Business Decision, 84 J. P. T. O.S. 371 (2002).

59 *Beckerman-Rodau*, The Choice between Patent Protection and Trade Secret Protection: A Legal and Business Decision, 84 J. P. T. O.S. 371 (2002).

– IT Safeguards

It is crucial, for example, to introduce effective IT safeguards within the firm. Firewalls and virus scans are the first step towards preventing industrial espionage and additional security can be achieved by saving confidential information on a number of standalone computers. Another potential safeguard would be for a company to keep its intranet site separate from the internet and to ensure a secure internet connection by selecting a suitable internet service provider and obtaining suitable network components. Individual divisions and departments may then also introduce additional safeguards allowing access to authorised individuals only, such as passwords and access barriers. When using passwords, it is recommendable to install a real password management system setting out rules for the creation of the password (form, length, quality) and ensuring that these passwords are changed regularly. It is also advisable to create a data back up plan and back up the data consistently.

– Employees

Diligent employee guidelines are also key to prevent an unwanted loss of know-how. It is advisable to educate the company's own employees with regard to the importance of the know-how and the possible measures that will protect it.[60] It might be a good idea to establish a specific code of conduct, a "know-how code", as well as general company policies.

The provision of detailed organisational guidelines and recommended working practices can help with the implementation of strategic security requirements.

The "know-how code" established by the company in question to be observed by its employees should set out general rules for handling new and existing information on know-how protection, e. g., what type of information should or should not go into a newsletter or website, how information is to be transferred from one physical location to another, etc.[61] It would contain items, types and the value of know-how, the rights and obligations of an owner of know-how as well as the role of employees and business partners.

A "know-how code" should also provide for designated contact points for employees who want to sound the alarm about wrongdoing. In the event that such wrongdoing is actually reported, a system must be in place, too, that clearly specifies which employees and external experts are in charge and who is or is not to be informed of any matters.[62] Such an action plan is essential to avoid irreparable mistakes from being made in relation to the preservation of evidence and asset protection. It also helps ensure the observance of time limits for taking appropriate action under employment law and/or the raising of claims. Making a company "know-how code" an integral component of employment contracts can serve as basis for sanctioning breaches thereof.

---

60 See also http://www.sicherheitsforum-bw.de/downloads/Sicherheitsforum2.pdf.

61 See also *Lang*, The Protection of Commercial Trade Secrets [2003] E. I. P. R. Issue 10, p. 462, 471.

62 See also http://www.sicherheitsforum-bw.de/downloads/Sicherheitsforum2.pdf.

In addition, any employee training should also foster an awareness of security issues. Only if employees are made aware of the applicable company policies and "know-how code", they may be reasonably expected to comply with company procedures and company policies. The employer should also make them aware that security is crucial for the company as a whole and therefore also for individual jobs: A loss of know-how often results in serious economic loss and thus may indeed affect the entire workforce.

Disgruntled employees who move to a competitor pose a particular risk.[63] Disgruntled employees who remain with their employer may also fail to take their confidentiality obligations seriously enough. This is why it is particularly important for companies to aim for the long-term retention of employees working in areas involving the use of know-how. Employee migration should be kept to an absolute minimum, particularly in R&D departments.[64] This long-term retention is best achieved by implementing a transparent staffing policy. In the event that such an employee's contract is terminated or otherwise ends, they should be immediately released from their duty to work (on full pay) to prevent the potential loss of any further know-how. As said before, it further is recommendable to conclude confidentiality agreements with certain (key) employees.

In general, it also is a good idea to diversify know-how among the employees instead of concentrating all know-how with a few employees.[65] If and to the extent some of the employees leave the firm, not all of the know-how is lost and the profit for another competitor that employs the former employee is kept small.

– Outsourcing of production

In the event of outsourcing production to third parties, for example as an "extended workbench", good communications between the parties involved are essential. With regard to know-how that shall be disclosed in the course of such outsourcing production, it should be considered that the know-how disclosed is not described and/or specified in detail to the other party. If and to the extent a detailed description and/or specification of the know-how to be disclosed cannot be avoided, it might be advisable to write the know-how down and deposit it with a neutral person, such as a notary public. This alleviates the burden of proof in case a dispute about the origin of certain know-how arises. In any case, a company also might want to ensure that all goods and packaging, as well as any manuals, samples, templates and other documents, are returned to the principal at the end of the contract. Claims for the return of these materials are easier to enforce if a precise record is kept of the documents handed over.

– Third parties

---

63 See also *Welser/González*, Marken- und Produktpiraterie, No. 697.

64 *Beckerman-Rodau*, The Choice between Patent Protection and Trade Secret Protection: A Legal and Business Decision, 84 J. P. T. O.S. 371 (2002).

65 *Beckerman-Rodau*, The Choice between Patent Protection and Trade Secret Protection: A Legal and Business Decision, 84 J. P. T. O.S. 371 (2002).

Generally, the amount of the know-how to be made available to a contracting party for use depends on the commercial objectives of the contract. When determining the amount of know-how to be made available, one should endeavour, in the interests of both contracting parties – and especially to protect the rights of the holder of the relevant know-how – to limit the know-how to be disclosed to the minimum amount that is imperative to realise the economic objectives of the contract. The commercial value of know-how may be adversely affected if too much of it is disclosed.

In any case, it is advisable to define the know-how to be disclosed in as much detail as possible, either during the contractual negotiations or as part of a technical due diligence. It might also be useful to deposit the relevant information with a neutral party, such as a notary public, for safekeeping prior to starting contractual negotiations. This makes it easier to prove the origin of any know-how in the event of any subsequent infringement of the non-disclosure agreement or any use of the know-how acquired during the negotiations and thus, to enhance chances to successfully claim damages. It is also advisable to keep a precise record of any contractual negotiations, setting out the know-how disclosed by each of the parties. Any description should generally consist of a definition in the agreement, supplemented by annexes containing, for example, drawings, processing instructions and technical details. At the start of negotiations the other party should be required to indicate which of the disclosed information it is already aware of.

– Communication

The most frequent form of non-material damage is damage to reputation. Good communications in crisis situations can avert damage to the reputation of a company and canny Public Relations skills in crisis situations can even enhance the image of a company.

II. Definition of Product Piracy

Know-how usually constitutes new knowledge put to use in the manufacture of products, which – due to the immaterial nature of knowledge – means that the precise nature of the know-how often may not be immediately obvious from the product. But this does not mean that it is not important for the production or design of the product: it actually may be the crucial difference between two similar products.

The hidden nature of know-how means that know-how pirates need to research and investigate know-how before it becomes any use to them. This may be achieved, for example, by industrial espionage, bribery of the relevant employees or by fraudulent activities.

"Reverse engineering" is one possible method, which may be used. This involves reversing the development process and analysing products with the intention of determining their composition and construction and coming up with a new design plan. This is generally done with the objective of producing imitation products.[66] The problem is that purchasers of products are in general allowed to do whatever pleases them with the product purchased, thus, in principle, also to undertake this kind of analysis.

As it results from the aforementioned examples and in accordance with the basic concept that know-how protection protects the access to information, product piracy occurs if access is forced, protection measures are being violated and thus the know-how is snatched from its proprietor.

1. Industrial or commercial espionage

Industrial or commercial espionage *(Betriebsspionage)* consists of infiltrating third parties into the business of a competitor.[67] Such practices are illegal except in very rare cases where, according to the German Federal Supreme Court, a legitimate interest may be invoked to justify such conduct.

In the case in which the German Federal Supreme Court handed down its *Betriebsspionage* judgment, the plaintiff asserted that the detective caught engaging in such spying, was hired to obtain certain information on manufacturing processes. The defendant, on the other hand, maintained that the detective had been hired to find out whether certain contracts had been obtained through bribery. The German Federal Supreme Court ruled that it was illegal for the defendant to commission somebody to infiltrate a company by taking up employment with it for the purpose of spying on it in order to surreptitiously obtain trade or industrial secrets. According to the German Federal Supreme Court, the plaintiff satisfies his burden of proof within a claim for damages due to industrial spying, if the plaintiff submits (and proves, if necessary) that a third party infiltrated its company. The onus of proof then is on the party who commissioned the agent, i. e., the defendant, to adduce evidence of it having had a legitimate interest to do so. The German Federal Supreme Court, however, has not specified what interest could be qualified as 'legitimate' in order to justify espionage. It may be assumed that in fact there is no such interest, at all, and a justification never is possible.

2. Breach of Trust

A "breach of trust" occurs if the imitator exploits a trade or business secret that has been confided to him by the proprietor of the know-how.[68] Trade or business secrets may be

---

66 If the protected technology can be easily reverse engineered by competitors of the company in question, trade secret law should not be the choice of protection. In such case, the company should rather resort to protection under patent law. Therefore, in any case it is important to assess the likelihood of third parties to successfully reverse engineering the technology in question, see also *Beckerman-Rodau*, The Choice between Patent Protection and Trade Secret Protection: A Legal and Business Decision, 84 J. P. T. O.S. 371 (2002).

67 16 March 1973 BGH [Federal Supreme Court] [I ZR 154/71], GRUR 1973, 484, 485 (Betriebsspionage); *Hasselblatt*, Münchner Anwaltshandbuch Gewerblicher Rechtsschutz, § 26, No. 12.

confided during contract negotiations. A breach of trust then occurs where know-how disclosed in the course of contractual negotiations is used by the potential contracting party after the breaking off of contract negotiations, even though the disclosing party only disclosed the know-how in reliance on the continuation of the contractual relationship.[69]

In general, unauthorised use of know-how constituting a breach of trust can only occur in cases where a special relationship of trust exists between the contracting parties. Another requirement is that the know-how acquired during the contract negotiations was in fact the know-how that was subsequently used without proper authority.

Therefore, a party which, following the breaking off of contractual negotiations, then decides to compete with the party with which it formerly negotiated, is not acting unfairly *per se*. It always depends on the circumstances of the individual case whether a use of specialist know-how acquired in the course of contract negotiations is considered to amount to unauthorised exploitation of such knowledge, i. e. a breach of trust.[70]

In order to determine whether there has been a breach of trust, it is necessary to establish the precise nature of the know-how that was obtained. In the event that such a determination proves to be fruitless because, for instance, the know-how was or could have been obtained from generally accessible sources without great effort or expense, the party that obtained such know-how cannot be charged with having obtained it fraudulently.[71] It is therefore advisable to document, even as early as the negotiations stage, what information is being made available to the respective other party. In addition, as said before, it is sensible for any party disclosing know-how to obtain a formal commitment from the other party prior to the commencement of negotiations that it will advise the disclosing party immediately if any of the disclosed information is already known to it.

3. Inducement to infringe contractual obligations

An "inducement to infringe contractual obligations" exists if a competitor or another external person obtains know-how through a third party acting in breach of the contractual duty of secrecy incumbent upon it.[72] For the purpose of the foregoing sentence, a "third party" can be a current or former employee or officer of the company possessing the know-how, who discloses know-how in violation of a duty to maintain confidenti-

68 1 July 1960 BGH [Federal Supreme Court] [I ZR 72/59], GRUR 1961, 40 (Wurftaubenpresse).

69 21 March 1991 BGH [Federal Supreme Court] [I ZR 158/89], GRUR 1992, 523, 524 (Betonsteinelemente).

70 See 17 May 1960 BGH [Federal Supreme Court] [I ZR 34/59], GRUR 1960, 554, 555 (Handstrickverfahren).

71 21 March 1991 BGH [Federal Supreme Court] [I ZR 158/89], GRUR 1992, 523, 524 (Betonsteinelemente).

72 9 November 1967 BGH [Federal Supreme Court] [I ZR 158/89], GRUR 1968, 272, 274f (Trockenrasierer III).

ality, or who uses such confidential know-how for his own purposes, or who possibly is induced by a competitor to commit such breach of contract. Unfortunately, in practice, it is very difficult to prove such behaviour since it often is virtually impossible to differentiate between trade secrets of the current or former employer that are worthy of protection from freely exploitable know-how that employees gained by experience.[73]

4. Other

In addition, legal commentators and practitioners agree that the following groups of cases of misappropriation and/or illegal exploitation of another party's trade secrets may also constitute know-how-piracy:[74]

- A company is systematically enticing away the qualified staff of a competitor in order to obtain and exploit trade and industrial secrets of this competitor;
- A company is enticing away a competitor's customers by using trade secrets procured by unfair means;
- A company is exploiting the achievements of third parties by way of unfairly obtained knowledge, including, but not limited to, obtaining documents by deception, abuse of trust, unauthorised use after breaking off of licensing negotiations, enticing away of employees, breach of secrecy;
- Employees are preparing to set up a competing enterprise utilising trade and industrial secrets of the company by which they are still employed.[75]

III. Know-How Piracy as a form of unfair competition

The UWG [Unfair Competition Act] does not define the term "know-how", nor does it contain a provision that explicitly affords comprehensive protection to a company's know-how. The only know-how-related provisions contained in the UWG [Unfair Competition Act] are contained in the legal definition of criminal offences in sec. 17 *et seq*. UWG [Unfair Competition Act], namely relating to the disclosure of trade and industrial secrets; improper use of templates; and offering to betray secrets or induce others to betray secrets, which under sec. 17 UWG [Unfair Competition Act] all are punishable by a fine or, in severe cases, by imprisonment. However, the other provisons of the UWG [Unfair Competition Act] also might provide a remedy against know-how-piracy.

- Protection under secs. 17, 18 UWG [Unfair Competition Act]

---

73 *Doepner*, Anmerkungen zum wettbewerbsrechtlichen Geheimnisschutz im Zivilprozess, in: Keller/Plassmann/Falck (ed.), Festschrift für Winfried Tilmann, p. 105, 107.

74 *Doepner*, Anmerkungen zum wettbewerbsrechtlichen Geheimnisschutz im Zivilprozess, in: Keller/Plassmann/Falck (ed.), Festschrift für Winfried Tilmann, p. 105, 107.

75 3 May 2001 BGH [Federal Supreme Court] [I ZR 153/99], WRP 2001, 1174 (Spritzgießwerkzeuge).

In the event that protected know-how is infringed in any manner referred to in secs. 17, 18 UWG [Unfair Competition Act], this may justify claims for damages under sec. 823 para. 2 BGB [Civil Code] because secs. 17, 18 UWG [Unfair Competition Act] are remedial statutes intended to provide protection *(Schutzgesetz)*, as stipulated in sec. 823 para. 2 BGB [Civil Code].

In addition, a breach of secs.17 or 18 UWG [Unfair Competition Act] may trigger claims for damages in accordance with sec. 826 BGB [Civil Code].[76]

– Protection in accordance with sec. 4 UWG [Unfair Competition Act]

Sec. 4 no. 9 c) UWG [Unfair Competition Act] contains a special provision which applies when the necessary knowledge or required documents for the production of imitations are obtained by dishonest means.[77] The terms "knowledge" and "documents" are not defined in the UWG [Unfair Competition Act].

The term "obtained by dishonest means" should be interpreted broadly. It covers every impermissible procurement or exploitation of know-how,[78] irrespective of whether such know-how is to be used to imitate or replicate a competitor's goods or services. Anyways, the term presupposes a certain level of activity on the part of the imitator. A party that obtains knowledge of a secret purely by coincidence may, in principle, use the relevant information, without running the risk of being held liable.[79]

From the official explanatory statement to the UWG [Unfair Competition Act] it is also clear that the UWG [Unfair Competition Act] covers cases in which an imitator surreptitiously acquires know-how by spying on industrial secrets or through disloyal conduct, such as a breach of trust.[80] The term "obtaining something surreptitiously" covers those cases of spying as addressed in sec. 17 para. 2 no. 1 UWG [Unfair Competition Act], i. e. cases where information that constitutes a trade or industrial secret is obtained through the use of technical means.

Know-how is further protected under sec. 4 no. 10 UWG [Unfair Competition Act] which renders it illegal to systematically obstruct a competitor in its activities.

– Protection under sec. 3 UWG [Unfair Competition Act]

---

76 18 February 1977 BGH [Federal Supreme Court] [I ZR 112/75], GRUR 1977, 539, 541 (Prozeßrechner).

77 The elements of an act of unfair competition listed in sec. 4 no. 9 c) UWG [Unfair Competition Act] are non-cumulative and cited by way of example only. They merely describe the three most important groups of cases where "supplementary protection" is afforded against improper exploitation of achievements of another party *(ergänzender Leistungsschutz)*.

78 13 October 1965 BGH [Federal Supreme Court] [Ib ZR 93/63], GRUR 1966, 152, 154 (Nitrolingual).

79 *Hasselblatt*, Münchner Anwaltshandbuch Gewerblicher Rechtsschutz, § 26, No. 10.

80 Official reasoning published in relation to § 4 No. 9 UWG [Unfair Competition Act], Draft Act of the Federal Government, Federal Parliament Document No. 15/1487 of 22 August 2003, p. 18.

Finally, the general clause sec. 3 UWG [Unfair Competition Act] covers all other cases in which interference with know-how of another party is deemed to be unfair.[81] This might lead to an overlapping of different sections. A breach of secs. 17 or 18 UWG [Unfair Competition Act], for instance, also constitutes a breach of sec. 3 UWG [Unfair Competition Act].

Industrial or commercial espionage, breach of trust and inducement to infringe contractual obligations are the three groups of cases where it is generally accepted that protection of the law may be claimed under sec. 3 UWG [Unfair Competition Act].

Liability under competition law may result in claims to cease and desist, claims for remedy, claims for damages and claims for the provision of information.[82]

IV. Remedies in Case of Know-How Piracy

In cases of know-how infringements, the party to which the know-how belongs will also be entitled to assert general tort claims and claims for unjust enrichment.[83] These claims generally result in a requirement to cease and desist, to provide legal remedy, to pay damages or to provide information.

Tort protection is generally granted under sec. 823 para. 2 BGB [Civil Code] in conjunction with a protective law, such as sec. 202 et seq. Strafgesetzbuch [StGB] [Penal Code] (F. R.G.), which imposes criminal penalties in the event of the infringement of confidential information, the provisions of sec. 85 GmbHG [Limited Liability Companies Act], sec. 404 AktG [Stock Corporation Act] and sec. 333 Handelsgesetzbuch [HGB] [Commercial Code] (F. R.G.), which make it a criminal offence to infringe a duty of non-disclosure. In addition, know-how infringements also are infringements against 'miscellaneous protected rights' within the meaning of sec. 823 para. 1 BGB [Civil Code].[84] Infringements contrary to the *ordre public* with the intention of causing damage and/or under tacit acceptance of damage are grounds for claims under sec. 826 BGB [Civil Code].

The legal consequences of tort liability are generally claims to cease and desist, claims for remedy, claims for damages and claims for the provision of information. The holder of know-how can use claims to cease and desist as a means of preventing future know-how infringements by prohibiting any impending or further procurement, backup, dis-

---

81 The *de minimis* threshold stipulated in sec. 3 UWG [Unfair Competition Act] also applies in this respect, even if an infringement of protected know-how is normally likely to have a greater impact on competitors anyway.

82 *Hefermehl/Köhler/Bornkamm*, Gesetz gegen den unlauteren Wettbewerb, § 9 No. 4.1.

83 9 March 1989 BGH [Federal Supreme Court] [I ZR 189/86], GRUR 1990, 221 (Forschungskosten).

84 25 January 1955 BGH [Federal Supreme Court] [I ZR 15/53], GRUR 1955, 388 (Dücko-Geheimverfahren); 18 March 1955 BGH [Federal Supreme Court] [I ZR 144/53], GRUR 1955, 468 (Schwermetall-Kokillenguss).

semination or use of protected know-how.[85] The holder can also arrange for the prohibition of the manufacture, use, processing, sale and distribution of products whose manufacture is based substantially on protected know-how.[86] Holders may use claims for legal remedy to end an ongoing infringement by demanding the surrender or destruction of secured or procured records and any products manufactured via the illegal use of protected know-how, whereby the principle of proportionality should be ensured. If the infringing party has acted culpably, the know-how holder is also entitled to receive damages. Such damages may be calculated (i) on the basis of compensating for the damage incurred; (ii) on the basis of the profits made by the infringing party; or (iii) on the basis of the payment of an appropriate licence fee.[87] The know-how holder may also demand surrender of any records and other items used in the infringement. The holder may assert any liquidated damages agreed as minimum damages in the event of an infringement in order to secure the relevant contractual obligations. There is no need to demonstrate specific damage in such case.[88]

In any case it is advisable during any legal proceedings not to give any details of the infringed know-how in the statement of claim or the operative provisions of the ruling beyond what is essential for immediate enforcement, in order to prevent any further loss or publication of know-how.[89] The presumed infringing party is required to demonstrate and prove any actual independent making available of other coincidentally identical information. In trade secrets actions, it, therefore, often is very helpful if it can be proven that there was some form of protection strategy.[90] Not only does it underline the confidential nature of the lost information, but it also makes it more difficult for the defendant to prove an independent provision of other – coincidentally identical – information. The defendant must give specific evidence for such information being made available. It is not sufficient for such provision to only have been theoretically possible.

---

85 *Kraßer*, Grundlagen des zivilrechtlichen Schutzes von Geschäfts- und Betriebsgeheimnissen sowie Know-how, GRUR 1977, 177.

86 19 December 1984 BGH [Federal Supreme Court] [I ZR 133/82], GRUR 1985, 294 (Füllanlage); 3 May 2001 BGH [Federal Supreme Court] [I ZR 153/99], WRP 2001, 1174 (Spritzgießwerkzeuge).

87 18 February 1977 BGH [Federal Supreme Court] [I ZR 112/75], GRUR 1977, 539 (Prozessrechner); 17 June 1992 BGH [Federal Supreme Court] [I ZR 107/90], GRUR 1993, 55 (Tchibo/Rolex II).

88 In the case of several know-how infringements liquidated damages may be warranted on several occasions due to their generally high economic weighting, 25 January 2001 BGH [Federal Supreme Court] [I ZR 323/98], NJW 2001, 2622.

89 1 July 1960 BGH [Federal Supreme Court] [I ZR 72/59], GRUR 1961, 40 (Wurftaubenpresse); 19 May 1998 BAG [Federal Labour Court] [9 AZR 394/97], NZA 1999, 200 (Kantenbaender).

90 *Lang*, The Protection of Commercial Trade Secrets [2003] E. I. P. R. Issue 10, p. 462, 471.

Music, Film and Software Piracy

WOLFGANG SCHÖNIG

Digitalisation is both a blessing and a curse. On the one hand, it provides a multitude of new business models and distribution channels for exploiting digital content such as films or music. The software industry owes its very existence to digitalisation. Digital media is, however, particularly prone to piracy. Virtually anyone can make illegal high-quality copies of copyrighted content relatively inexpensively. The holders of intellectual property rights receive nothing in return. The Internet holds the greatest dangers. An illegal copy accessed on the Web can be duplicated countless times in a split second which can then in turn be used as a master copy for even further copies.

Product piracy results in grave economic losses for the companies affected. According to IFPI (International Federation of Phonographic Industry), the widespread availability of copyright infringing music online has led to a situation where there are 20 illegal downloads for every legal digital music track sold. This has led to a reduction in income for record companies – that typically invest up to 20 per cent of their revenues in discovering and nurturing new musical talent – of about USD 35 billion annually.[1] The MPAA (Motion Picture Association of America) estimates that the US motion picture industry loses approximately USD 10 billion annually as a result of piracy.[2] The BSA (Business Software Alliance), the international association of the world's leading software manufacturers, puts its losses at USD 48 billion.[3] These figures are, of course, only estimates and vary amongst sources.

Given these figures, further profitable innovation and creation, particularly in relation to digital products, hinges to a large degree on effective legal protection of copyrights and other intellectual property rights. The European Union recognised this at an early stage and significantly strengthened the rights of holders of intellectual property rights through the Copyright Directive (Directive 2001/29/EC of 22 May 2001 on the harmonisation of certain aspects of copyright and related rights in the information society).[4] Pursuant thereto, for example, making protected content publicly available on the Internet constitutes a clear copyright infringement. Also efforts to establish a functional DRM (Digital Rights Management) system are supported by providing for sanctions for circumventing technological protective measures. The position of intellectual property rights holders was further enhanced by the Enforcement Directive (Directive 2004/48/

1 www.ifpi.org.

2 www.mpaa.org.

3 www.bsa.org.

4 Official Journal of the European Communities 2001 No L 167/10.

EC of 29 April 2004 on the enforcement of intellectual property rights).[5] The Enforcement Directive aims, for example, to facilitate the identification of offenders by enabling injured parties to assert far-reaching claims to the disclosure of information e. g. vis-à-vis access providers regarding the identity of Internet users. Both directives have, in the meantime, been transposed into German law by modifications made to the Gesetz über Urheberrecht und verwandte Schutzrechte [UrhG] [Copyright Act] (F. R.G.).[6] Furthermore, copyright infringements represent also a criminal offence under German law. This enables the rights holders to rely on the assistants of the public prosecution authorities when fighting infringers who are, in some cases, linked to all organised crime.[7]

However, some aspects of German law also weaken the position of the rights holders. One problemat is that in Germany it is permitted to make copies of copyrighted content for private purposes *(Privileg der Privatkopie)*. This applies especially to physically making a copy offline. It, however, also makes it difficult to analyze the legality of online downloading activities. Further, the E-Commerce Directive (Directive 2000/31/EC of June 2000 on certain legal aspects of information society services, in particular electronic commerce in the Internal Market),[8] which has been implemented in the Telemediengesetz [TMG] [Telemedia Act] (F. R. G.), provides for a special regime of limited liability for online service providers. Access and cache providers, but also host providers, assume only a limited liability for infringements of third parties. As is ultimately the case with all Internet–related matters, serious problems can arise with law enforcement if the provider is not based in Germany.

The following is a description of the tools within the UrhG [Copyright Act] available to owners of intellectual property rights to prevent their rights from being infringed. To begin with, the works eligible for protection under German law will be identified and the concept of legal ownership of rights will be addressed (I.). This is followed by a summary of the scope and limits of the UrhG [Copyright Act] (II.). A detailed description is then provided of the various parties against whom claims may potentially be asserted (III. and IV.). In conclusion, the possibilities available to holders of intellectual property rights in enforcing their intellectual property rights against infringers will be outlined (V. and VI.).

---

5 Official Journal of the European Union 2004 No L 157/45 and Corrigendum to Directive 2004/48/EC, Official Journal of the European Union 2004 No L 195/16.

6 Gesetz zur Regelung des Urheberrechts in der Informationsgesellschaft [Act on the Regulation of Copyright Law in the Information Society], Bundesgesetzblatt [Federal Law Gazette] No. 46 of 12 September 2003 (1. Korb); Zweites Gesetz zur Regelung des Urheberrechts in der Informationsgesellschaft [Second Amendment of he Act on the Regulation of Copyright Law in the Information Society], Bundesgesetzblatt [Federal Law Gazette] No. 54 of 31 October 2007 [2. Korb]; Gesetz zur Verbesserung der Durchsetzung von Rechten des geistigen Eigentums [Act on the Improvement of the Enforcement of Intellectual Property Rights], Bundesgesetzblatt [Federal Law Gazette], no. 28 of 11 July 2008.

7 Cf. *Heiner Hugger*, Enforcement of Intellectual Property Rights in Germany, C.

8 Official Journal of the European Union 2000 No L 178/1.

I. Protected Works

A. General Requirements and Term of Protection

German copyright law is a 'droit d'auteur' style copyright law. Section 1 UrhG [Copyright Act] stipulates that authors of literary, scientific and artistic works shall enjoy protection of their works. In accordance with sec. 2 para. 1 UrhG [Copyright Act], protected literary, scientific and artistic works include, in particular[9] works of language, such as writings and computer programs, musical works, cinematographic works, and photographic works. Collections and database works enjoy protection in Germany under sec. 4 UrhG [Copyright Act]. In Germany copyright protection is afforded with the creation of the work for the benefit of the author *(Schöpferprinzip)*. Fixation in a tangible medium, or filing for copyright registration, or going through similar formalities is not necessary.

However, pursuant to sec. 2 para. 2 UrhG [Copyright Act], personal intellectual creations alone constitute works within the meaning of this Act. That is, any copyright protected work must exhibit a certain amount of creativity and originality. It must have some intellectual content and a certain degree of individuality. It must reflect some intention or expression of its author and be distinguishable from other works. The work must possess a unique character that distinguishes it from previous works.[10] It is, of course, not possible to define any general criteria in this regard. In addition, courts have handed down diverging rulings depending on the type of work involved.[11] Mere ideas or facts, however, are not copyrightable.

Following the principles of authorship, it is clear that only natural persons can be authors of works within the meaning of the Act. Legal entities, such as publishing houses, database manufacturers, film producers, phonogram producers, broadcasting organisations, or concert promoters are not afforded copyright protection. They must always ensure that they derive the requisite rights for commercial exploitation of the works by entering into licensing agreements with authors of the works. The foregoing may not be necessary if the author has created the work in execution of his duties under a contract of employment or service (sec. 43 UrhG [Copyright Act]). In this case the UrhG [Copyright Act] provides for a statutory licence in favour of the employer. The scope of the licence is, however, not clearly defined and can hence be subject to dispute. Therefore, clear stipulations in employment contracts are recommendable.

The aforementioned legal entities may, however, be vested with own proprietary rights to a work. Such related rights are referred to as neighbouring rights *(Leistungsschutz-*

---

9 Other works protected under UrhG [Copyright Act]: speeches, works of pantomime, including choreographic works; works of fine art, including works of architecture and of applied art and plans for such works; illustrations of a scientific or technical nature, such as drawings, plans, maps, sketches, tables and three-dimensional representations.

10 most recently, 8 July 2004 BGH [Federal Supreme Court] [I ZR 25/02], GRUR 2004, 855 ff. (Hundefigur); *Schricker*, Urheberrecht, § 2, No. 41.

11 Cf. *Schricker*, Urheberrecht, § 2, Nos. 26 ff.

rechte). Whereas copyrights protect creative authorship, neighbouring rights protect the economic investment made in producing and disseminating works.[12] These rights are primarily provided for in sections 85 to 94 UrhG [Copyright Act].

Also performers, who are not the author of a work, but who recite or perform a work are afforded protection as neighbouring right under German law (sec. 73 *et seq.* UrhG [Copyright Act]). Furthermore, neighbouring right protection subsists in certain works which do not possess the degree of creativity required for copyright protection, but should, according to the Act, nevertheless be protected. Such cases include simple photographs (sec. 72 UrhG [Copyright Act]), moving pictures (sec. 95 UrhG [Copyright Act]) and non-original databases [Copyright Act] (sec. 87 lit. a) UrhG [Copyright Act]).

Copyrights expire 70 years after the author's death (sec. 64 UrhG [Copyright Act]) and may be transferred by inheritance (sec. 28 UrhG [Copyright Act]). Neighbouring rights expire 50 years after performance/publication of the relevant work took place and can likewise by transferred by inheritance if they are held by a natural person.

B. Protection of Musical Works

1. Eligibility for Protection

Pursuant to sec. 2 para. 1 no. 2 UrhG [Copyright Act], musical works are copyright protected works. In order to qualify for protection, musical works must be original and exhibit a certain degree of creativity (sec. 2 para. 2 UrhG [Copyright Act]). As a rule, however, the requisite degree of creativity is low.[13] Practical problems rarely arise in this respect. Components of musical works are also copyright protected if they have a unique sound that is specific to them.[14] This must, of course, be determined on a case-by-case basis.

2. Copyright Owners

Musical works are generally works of multiple ownership. Copyrights are afforded to the composer of the melody and the author of the lyrics. Both can also be qualified as joint authors. Moreover, performing artists often perform musicals works of others with their own interpretation (either live or for a recording). Such performance is protected as

---

12 Cf. *Schricker*, Urheberrecht, Introduction, Nos. 27 f.

13 *Schricker*, Urheberrecht, § 2, Nos. 38 f. – „Kleine Münze"; 26 September 1980 BGH [Federal Supreme Court] [I ZR 17/78], GRUR 1981, 267, 268 (Dirlada); 3 February 1988 BGH [Federal Supreme Court] [I ZR 143/86], GRUR 1988, 810, 811 (Fantasy); in general *Schricker*, Urheberrecht, § 2, Nos. 118 ff.

14 18 April 1991 OLG [Higher Regional Court] Hamburg [3 W 38/91], GRUR Int 1992, 390 (Tonträgersampling); *Schricker*, Urheberrecht, § 2, No. 122.

neighbouring right by sec. 73 *et seq.* UrhG [Copyright Act]. Apart from authors of musical works and performers, phonogram producers *(Tonträgerhersteller)* are also afforded own proprietary rights under German law pursuant to sections 85 and 86 UrhG [Copyright Act] based on the fact that they bear the financial risk the first technical sound fixation and in the production and commercial exploitation.

Phonogram producers play a dual role of simultaneously holding their own neighbouring rights and of commercially exploiting and distributing copyright protected works or performances of others. As a rule, the phonogram producers must acquire licences from both the authors of musical works (composers und lyrics writers) and obtain permission from the performers before they can use the sound recording by, for example, the production and distribution of CDs. In general, there is an individually negotiated contract between these parties which serves the purpose of comprehensively exploiting the relevant recordings. Licences to copyrights on musical work can be obtained from so-called collecting societies such as GEMA,[15] which is the German royalty collection society for musical works and which charges fixed royalties for such licences.

The above similarly applies to concert promoters *(Veranstalter)*, who are granted original proprietary rights (sec. 81 UrhG [Copyright Act]) which are comparable to those of phonogram producers and which cannot be separated from the rights of performers and authors of musical works performed.

C. Writings

1. Eligibility of Protection

Section 2 para. 1, no. 1 UrhG [Copyright Act] affords copyright protection to writings. In order to qualify for protection, a text must possess a certain degree of creativity and originality (sec. 2 para. 2 UrhG [Copyright Act]). This originality requirement is, however, not particularly strict. A "moderate degree of intellectual creation" should suffice.[16] Stricter requirements may apply regarding the eligibility for protection of texts that are of a practical nature, e. g., scientific papers or operating instructions.[17] However, mere facts, as well as the underlying idea of a novel, or so-called scènes à faire are not protected.

15 Gesellschaft für Aufführungs- und mechanische Vervielfältigungrechte, GEMA; www.gema.de.

16 27 February 1981 BGH [Federal Supreme Court] [I ZR 29/79], GRUR 1981, 520 (Fragensammlung); 21 November 1980 BGH [Federal Supreme Court] [I ZR 106/78], GRUR 1981, 352 (Staatsexamensarbeit); *Schricker*, Urheberrecht, § 2 No. 81.

17 For scientific works 11 April 2002 BGH [Federal Supreme Court] [I ZR 231/99], GRUR 2002, 958 (Technische Lieferbedingungen); for operating instructions 10 October 1991 BGH [Federal Supreme Court] [I ZR 147/89], GRUR 1993, 34 (Bedienungsanweisung).

2. Copyright Owners

Generally, the author of the writing is the sole holder of all rights relating to his work. This also includes the right to turn a novel into a film *(Verfilmungsrecht)* according to sec. 88 UrhG [Copyright Act]. Yet, if the writing has been created in execution of duties under a contract of employment, sec. 43 UrhG [Copyright Act] provides for a statutory licence for the benefit of the employer . The scope of such licence is, however, not very clear and often subject to dispute. Hence, in case of employees having a job that includes the creation of texts or novels, it is recommendable to provide for detailed regulations in the employment contract in this regard.

Writings are often marketed by publishing houses. The author concludes a contract of publication with a publishing house for that purpose (sec. 1 of the Gesetz über das Verlagsrecht [VerlG] [Publishing Act] (F. R.G.)). In accordance with the contract of publication, the publishing house is authorised and obligated to reproduce and distribute the work in the appropriate and usual way (sec. 14 VerlG [German Publishing Act]).

D. Photographic Works

1. Eligibility for Protection

Photos qualify for protection as photographic works within the meaning of sec. 2 para. 1 no. 5 UrhG [Copyright Act] if they are original. The test applied often requires that the photograph must show an "artistic expression" of the author.[18] Even if this requirement is not met, neighbouring right protection subsists in virtually any photograph according to sec. 72 UrhG [Copyright Act]. The term of protection of such 'simple' photographs *(Lichtbild)* is, however, limited.

2. Copyright Owners

The copyright owner in relation to both photographic works and 'simple' photographs is its author, i. e., the person who took the photograph.[19] Therefore, only natural persons can qualify as the author and original holder of copyrights to a photograph. As mentioned above, this can be different in case of photographic works or 'simple' photographs made in execution of duties under an employment contract.

---

18 *Dreier/Schulze*, UrhG, § 2, No. 192.

19 *Dreier/Schulze*, UrhG, § 72, No. 32.

E. Protection of Cinematographic Works

1. Eligibility for Protection

Cinematographic works, such as films, are copyright protected works under sec. 2 para. 1, no. 6 UrhG [Copyright Act]. In order to qualify for protection the film must be original and possess the requisite degree of creativity. The originality threshold requirements are not particularly high, however, but recordings based on purely mechanical or electronic processes do not qualify for copyright protection. Recordings made by permanently installed surveillance cameras, for example, are not capable of being protected by copyright. Borderline cases include, for instance, holiday camcorder recordings. Recordings of live events are also problematic. If not protected as a cinematographic work a film, however, can still enjoy neighbouring rights protection as 'simple' moving pictures *(Laufbilder)* under sec. 95 UrhG [Copyright Act].

The film genre and classification in terms of content (documentary film or music video clip) carry no relevance for the legal definition of what is a cinematographic work. Individual or excerpts or single scenes and even still images if these constitute an intellectual creation in their own right are included.[20] Should a still image not be considered to constitute a piece of cinematographic work, it can be nevertheless copyrightable as a piece of photographic work. Also uncut film material and advertising trailers are copyright protected.

Section 2 para. 1, no. 6 UrhG [Copyright Act] also expressly includes works produced by processes similar to cinematography. For example, this includes cartoons and computer-animated films. Provided they have film elements, multimedia productions, computer and video games are also copyrightable, even if they include other interactive components.[21] According to the prevailing view, gameshow and talkshow formats, in principle, do not qualify for protection as cinematographic works.[22] In exceptional circumstances, however, the opposite view may prevail.[23]

2. Copyright Owners

Authors of cinematographic works are all those who have made a personal creative or intellectual contribution to its production going beyond purely practical or technical

20 For excerpts most recently the ruling 20 February 2007 BGH [Federal Supreme Court] [I ZR 42/05], WRP 2008, 1121 (TV-Total); for scenes compare 15 May 1997 OLG [Higher Regional Court] Hamburg [3 U 153/95], GRUR 1997, 822, 825 (Edgar Wallace Filme); for still images compare 21 April 1953 BGH [Federal Supreme Court] [I ZR 110/52], BGHZ 9, 262, 267 f. (Schwanenbilder).

21 Detailed information provided under I. I.

22 26 June 2003 BGH [Federal Supreme Court] [I ZR 176/01], GRUR 2003, 876 (Sendeformat).

23 Most notably *Schricker*, Werbekonzeptionen und Fernsehformate – Eine Herausforderung für den urheberrechtlichen Werkbegriff?, GRUR Int 2004, 923; also under I. D.

skills.[24] The term 'author of a film' covers e. g. the film director, film camera crew, film cutters, film sound editors, and film makeup artists. Therefore, films usually have many joint authors. Authors of preexisting works used to make a film, such as authors of novels, screenplays or music, are not deemed to be authors of the film. The right to these existing works have to be acquired separately when used in a film. Actors are classified as joint authors of a film neither, but rather as performers who hold rights that are protected as neighbouring rights under sec. 73 *et seq*. UrhG [Copyright Act].

As under German law copyright protection is only conferred to natural persons, legal persons assuming the role of a film producer *(Filmhersteller)* enjoy legal protection only as holders of neighbouring rights under sec. 94 UrhG [Copyright Act]. These neighbouring rights do not protect the cinematographic work as such, but rather the entrepreneurial contribution of the film producer that is behind the cinematographic work. In order to be able to fully exploit a cinematographic work, the producer of a film generally needs to acquire all requisite rights of the authors of a film as well as the actors. However, sec. 89 UrhG [Copyright Act] provides for the statutory presumption that any person who undertakes to participate in the production of a film grants the producer of the film an exclusive right to exploit the film. The same applies for actors (see sec. 92 UrhG [Copyright Act]).

As regards preexisting works such as underlying novels, screenplays or music, the film producer must arrange for its rights in such to be assigned to him separately. This is particulary important with regard to film rights vested in the author of an underlying novel. This can be difficult with regard to music if composers have already transferred their rights to collecting societies such as GEMA. In such cases, the film producer can obtain all requisite rights from these collecting societies. Once the production of the film has begun, the film producer can freely dispose of the aquired rights and transfer them without the consent of the the author (sec. 90 UrhG [Copyright Act]). Before, the transferability is subject to the stipulations of the relevant licence agreement.

F. Television Program Formats

As mentioned above, according to the prevailing opinion, the program format of TV shows such as talk shows, game shows and voting shows are not protectable copyright subject matter. In the view of the German Federal Supreme Court *(Bundesgerichtshof)*, unlike conventional films or fictitious series, a show concept does not constitute an intellectual creation on a given subject, but merely provides a platform for creativeness. As with rules for a game, such platforms shall not be eligible for copyright protection.[25] The ruling was, however, linked to a very specific case. Hence, in exceptional circumstances the opposite view may prevail. Currently, it is also being discussed whether such program

24 In Spain, Portugal, Italy and France, there is a statutory presumption that the screen writer, the composer of the film music as well as the director are the film's authors. In the United States, on the other hand, the film production companies are considered to be the original owners of the cinematographic work if the film authors rendered their services as 'work made for hire'.

25 26 June 2003 BGH [Federal Supreme Court] [I ZR 176/01], GRUR 2003, 876 (Sendeformat).

formats may be afforded protection under the legislation on protection against misappropriation *(unmittelbare Leistungsübernahme)*, as provided for in sec. 4 no. 9 of the Gesetz gegen den unlauteren Wettbewerb [UWG] [Unfair Competition Act] (F. R.G.) This can be the case when a format is being imitated that has gained a certain level of distinctiveness which makes such imitation appear unfair.[26] As regards the title of a series and any company logo, these are likely to be protected under sec. 5 para. 1 Markengesetz [MarkenG] [Trademark Act] (F. R.G.). The title music, background images and a distinctive layout of stage design may also enjoy protection. Finally, protection may be available for unpublished formats as trade secret under sec. 18 UWG [Unfair Competition Act] for example for concepts presented to a television production firm.[27]

G. Computer Programs

Although they are not cultural creations, computer progams also fall within the scope of protection of the UrhG [Copyright Act]. As early as 1985, they were included in the list of works eligible for protection in sec. 2 para. 1 UrhG [Copyright Act]. In addition, special provisions regarding rights for computer programs were included in sections 69 lit. a) to lit. g) UrhG [Copyright Act] in 1993 in implementation of the Software Directive (Directive 91/250/EC of 14 May 1991 on the legal protection of computer programs).[28] Patent protection for computer programs is also available under German law. However, comparatively stringent conditions apply given the technical requirement for patentability of software under sec. 1 para. 1 Patentgesetz [PatG] [Patent Act] (F. R.G.).[29]

1. Eligibility for Protection

The UrhG [Copryright Act] nor the Software Directive contain a reliable definition of the term 'computer program'. In practice, however, a definitive definition of the term 'computer program' can easily be dispensed. Having initially imposed very high requirements as regards the eligibility threshold for protection of computer programs in its earlier judgments, the Federal Supreme Court has adopted a considerably more liberal attitude following the implementation of the Software Directive. Like other works, computer programs are eligible for protection if they embody a personal intellectual creation of certain originality. As regards originality, protection is granted even for minimal creativity.[30] There is, however, no general statutory presumption that computer programs

26 *Hefermehl/Köhler/Bornkamm*, Wettbewerbsrecht, § 4 No. 9.7.; Overall cf. *Fezer*, Lauterkeitsrecht, § 4-S 6 Nos. 41 ff.

27 Cf. the reference to advertising concepts *Wüterich/Breucker*, Wettbewerbsrecthlicher Schutz von Werbe- und Kommunikationskonzepten, GRUR 2004, 389 ff. and generally in relation to protection of presentation *Zentek*, Präsentationsschutz, WRP 2007, 507 ff.

28 Official Journal of the European Communities 1991 No L 122/42.

29 Cf. see *Claudia Milbradt*, Patent Piracy, II. E.

30 14 July 1993 BGH [Federal Supreme Court] [I ZR 47/91], GRUR 1994, 39 (Buchhaltungsprogramm); 29 November 2001 OLG [Higher Regional Court] Hamburg [3 U 288/00], GRUR-RR 2002, 217, 218 (CT – Klassenbibliothek); *Schricker*, Urheberrecht, § 69 a), Nos. 14 ff.

are eligible for copyright protection.[31] The existence of the requirements for copyright protection must be ascertained and, as the case may be, proven on a case-by-case basis. However, generally, no copyright protection is afforded to ideas or principles which underlie a computer program.

Computer programs qualify for protection in any form or appearance they may take. In other words, full protection is afforded to computer programs whether in object or source code. It extends to software, as well as to operating systems.[32] Parts of computer programs are also capable of protection, provided that they meet the originality requirements. The term also includes draft materials prepared for the development of such a computer program. Mere accompanying materials such as manuals, operating instructions and maintenance manuals are not capable of protection.[33] Also the user interface is considered no more a program than a text or graphic which is displayed on the screen.[34] Manuals and user interfaces may, however, enjoy protection in their own right as writings or scientific/technical works in accordance with sec. 2 para. 1 UrhG [Copyright Act].

2. Copyright Owners

According to the authorship principle, copyright protection and all rights of exploitation are afforded solely to the person who brought about the personal intellectual creation. Under German law, however, this principle does not fully apply to computer programs created in execution of duties under a contract of employment. Pursuant to sec. 69 lit. b) para. 1 UrhG [Copyright Act][35] a computer program created by an employee in the execution of his duties or following the instructions given by his employer, only the employer shall be entitled to exercise all the economic rights in the program and receive a right of use which is unlimited in terms of subject matter, territory and time.[36] This concept is gradually broader than the statutery license under sec. 43 UrhG [Copyright Act]. An employee is a person in an employment relationship who is obligated to carry out his/her activities in line with instructions issued by the employer. Freelancers are, in principle, therefore not classified as employees.[37] Another exception applies to professors working in tertiary education institutions (e.g. universities).[38] Rights to computer programs made by such freelancers or professors must be transferred and remunerated before exploitation.

---

31 Gesetzentwurf der Bundesregierung, Entwurf eines Zweiten Gesetzes zur Änderung des Urheberrechtsgesetzes [Draft bill of the Federal Government on the Second Amendment of the UrhG [Copyright Act]], BT-Drucks. 12/4022, p. 9.

32 11 January 2001 OLG [Higher Regional Court] Hamburg [3 U 120/00], CR 2001, 434, 435.

33 12 July 1999 OLG [Higher Regional Court] Düsseldorf [20 U 40/99], MMR 1999, 602.

34 *Schricker*, Urheberrecht, § 69 a), No. 7; *Wandtke/Bullinger*, Urheberrecht, § 69a, No. 14.

35 This provision stems from Art. 2 ¶ 3 of the Software Directive.

36 24 October 2000 BGH [Federal Supreme Court] [X ZR 72/98], GRUR 2001, 155, 157 (Wetterführungspläne I); 23 October 2001 BGH [Federal Supreme Court] [X ZR 72/98], GRUR 2002, 149, 151 (Wetterführungspläne II).

37 *Schricker*, Urheberrecht, § 69 b), No. 3.

38 For further details, see *Schricker*, Urheberrecht, § 69 b), No. 6.

Opinion is divided as to whether sec. 69 lit. b) UrhG [Copyright Act] is applicable if the employee did not create the computer program in the execution of his duties or following the instructions given by his employer, but rather, by using work equipment and know-how acquired from the employer's business. Some are of the view that the employer has the right to claim ownership of such computer programs and must compensate the employee accordingly.[39] Others are of the opinion that the programmer alone is entitled to the copyrights to a computer program created by him. Hence, this is currently an open question under German law and must be decided on a case-by-case basis.[40]

H. Protection of Databases

Databases do not constitute computer programs within the meaning of sec. 69 lit. a) UrhG [Copyright Act].[41] Pursuant to the Database Directive (Directive 96/9/EC of 16 February 1996 on the legal protection of databases),[42] the Copyright Act draws a distinction between database works described in sec. 4 para. 2 UrhG [Copyright Act] and 'simple' databases as per sec. 87 a *et seq*. UrhG [Copyright Act]. Broadly speaking, this distinction is based on the following classification scheme: A database work is a collection of data which is original in selection or arrangement of the elements. 'Simple' databases lack this element of intellectual achievement. Under certain circumstances, 'simple' databases may, however, be afforded protection with regard to investments made in the making of the database as a neighbouring right in accordance with sec. 87 a *et seq*. UrhG [Copyright Act].[43]

1. Eligibility for Protection

a. Database Works

A database work is a collection of data arranged in a systematic or methodical way, the elements of which are individually accessible either by electronic or by other means (sec. 4 para. 2 UrhG [Copyright Act]). The decisive factor is that selection or arrangement of the elements are original and, hence, constitute a personal intellectual achievement.[44] Arrangement in mere alphabetical or chronological order is insufficient to qua-

39 16 January 1997 LG (District Court) München [7 O 15354/91], CR 1997, 351, 354; upheld by 25 November 1999 OLG [Higher Regional Court] München [29 U 2437/97], CR 2000, 429; not addressed by 24 October 2000 BGH [Federal Supreme Court] [X ZR 72/98], GRUR 2001, 155, 157 (Wetterführungspläne I).

40 *Dreier/Schulze*, UrhG, § 69 b), No. 8; *Schricker*, Urheberrecht, § 69 b), No. 9.

41 *Wandtke/Bullinger*, Urheberrecht, § 69 a), No. 16.

42 Official Journal of the European Communities 1996 No L 77/20.

43 *Milbradt*, Urheberrechtsschutz von Datenbanken, CR 2002, 710 ff.; *Schricker*, Urheberrecht, before § 87a ff., Nos. 2 ff.

44 *Schricker*, Urheberrecht, § 4, Nos. 32 ff.; 9 November 2004 ECJ [C-203/02], GRUR 2005, 244 (BHB-Pferdewetten); 29 May 2001 OLG [Higher Regional Court] Nürnberg [3 U 337/01], GRUR 2002, 607 (Stufenaufklärung nach Weissauer).

lify for protection. The subject of protection is the structure or arrangement of the database and not its contents (Art. 1 para. 2 of the Database Directive). Only collections containing a minimum amount of data are eligible for protection. There are, however, no fixed limits. Database works which enjoy protection include not only collections of literary or musical works, but can also be collections of medical data, for example.[45]

b. Databases

If there is no personal intellectual creation involved, a database may be eligible for protection if it consists of data or other independent elements arranged in a systematic or methodical way the elements of which are individually accessible either by electronic or by other means, and the obtaining, verification or presentation of which requires a qualitatively or quantitatively substantial investment (sec. 87 lit. a) UrhG [Copyright Act]). This is clearly in keeping with the notion of neighbouring right protection of the economic investment.[46] The requirements for protection are undefined and must be determined on a case-by-case basis. Databases representing insignificant economic investment are not eligible for protection[47] which means that databases containing relatively few elements do not qualify for protection for lack of size.[48] Telephone directories for instance can represent a database.

2. Copyright Owners

a. Authors of Database Works

The author of a database work is the natural person or group of natural persons who created the database. Generally, if the author created the work in execution of his duties under a contract of employment or service the UrhG provides for a statutory licence for the benefit of the employer (sec. 43 UrhG [Copyright Act]). The scope of the statutory licence is, however, not clearly defined and often subject to dispute. Hence, as in any other intellectual property driven industry, also with regard to databases it is advisable to draft employment contracts in as much detail as possible.

---

45 In relation to case material: 9 November 2004 ECJ [C-203/02], GRUR 2005, 244 (BHB-Pferdewetten); 9 November 2004 ECJ [C-338/02], GRUR 2005, 252 (Fixtures-Fußballspielpläne I); 29 May 2001 OLG [Higher Regional Court] Nürnberg [3 U 337/01], GRUR 2002, 607; 17 September 2002 OLG [Higher Regional Court] Frankfurt [11 U 67/00], CR 2003, 50; 12 July 2000 LG [District Court] Hamburg [308 O 205/00], ZUM-RD 2001, 33.

46 09.11.2004 ECJ [C-203/02], GRUR 2005, 244 (BHB-Pferdewetten); *Schricker*, Urheberrecht, § 87a, Nos. 3 ff.

47 *Milbradt*, Urheberrechtsschutz von Datenbanken, CR 2002, 710 ff.; *Schricker*, Urheberrecht, § 87a, No. 24.

48 *Schricker*, Urheberrecht, § 87a, No. 5.

b. Makers of 'Simple' Databases

The person vested with original ownership rights to a 'simple' database as per sec. 87 lit. a) *et seq*. UrhG [Copyright Act] is the maker of the database as prescribed by sec. 87 lit. a) para. 2 UrhG [Copyright Act] *(Datenbankhersteller)*. The maker is the one who made the principal investment and who bears the organisational and financial risk involved in setting-up the database.[49]

I. Protection of Multimedia Works, Computer and Video Games

Multimedia works such as interactive DVDs combing texts, images, films and music are generally considered combinations of different individual types of works. In this case, all elements of the multimedia work must be reviewed separately to ascertain whether they are eligible for protection and on whom the relevant rights are conferred. In addition, multimedia works can also enjoy protection as database works if they are original in arrangement or selection. Moreover, they can constitute an own type of work if the various elements merge into one inseperable entity.[50] It is, however, generally accepted that multimedia works are not afforded protection as a computer program within the meaning of sec. 69 lit. a) UrhG [Copyright Act]. The creative effort that goes into making multimedia works is expressed in the form of language, picture and sound and does not consist of the computer program required for their operation. Only in very exceptional cases is protection afforded (indirectly) to multimedia products under sec. 69 lit. a) UrhG [Copyright Act], namely if a computer program is integrated into a multimedia product.[51] Multimedia products in the form of EXE-files are an example for this.

In relation to the protection of computer games (video games), a distinction must be made between the protection of audio-visual display on the screen and the computer program creating it. The computer program can be protected under sec. 69 lit. a) UrhG [Copyright Act]. Due to its moving images (action of the game), the audio-visual display is eligible for protection as a cinematographic work as defined in sec. 2 para. 1, no. 6 UrhG [Copyright Act]. Protection as moving pictures *(Laufbildschutz)* can be claimed in accordance with sections 94 and 95 UrhG [Copyright Act] if the audio-visual display lacks originality. Individual images can enjoy protection as photographic works in accordance with sec. 2 para. 1, no. 5 UrhG [Copyright Act] or, as the case may be, as 'simple' photographs in accordance with sec. 72 UrhG [Copyright Act]. The individual figures and characters in a computer game can also be protectable by copyright.[52]

The rights of producers of multimedia works or computer games are conditional on the rights in the constituent elements having been transferred to the producer in full. No

---

49 *Milbradt*, Urheberrechtsschutz von Datenbanken, CR 2002, 710 ff.; *Schricker*, Urheberrecht, § 87a, No. 45.

50 Compare *Schricker*, Urheberrecht, § 87a, No. 6.

51 29 June 1999 OLG [Higher Regional Court] Düsseldorf [20 U 85/98], CR 2000, 184 (Framing); *Wandtke/Bullinger*, Urheberrecht, § 69 a) No. 21.

52 Compare *Schricker*, Urheberrecht, § 69 a), No. 26.

explicit provision conferring own proprietary rights to the producer such as for phonogram producers, database or film makers exist. The respective provisions in the UrhG [Copyright Act] may apply analogously. This is, however, an open question under German law.

J. Websites

1. Eligibility for Protection

Like multimedia works, websites also do not form a separate category of works protected under German copyright law either. If of sufficient originality and creativity it is conceivable to seek protection of a website as literary work,[53] as a representation of a scientific or technical nature, or as a database work. Of course, the individual features, such as images or movie sequences, can enjoy separate protection.

One problem that often arises in relation to websites is a situation where an infringer only copies a portion of the website and not the entire website. Such partial copying of a website constitutes copyright infringement if the portion copied is capable of copyright protection as such.

2. Copyright Owners

The principle that the person who creates the work is deemed the author also applies to websites. Websites are often designed by specialist firms. In that respect, from the customer's perspective, it is important that it secures by contractual means an exclusive right to use the website. This is of importance with respect to certain rights that might otherwise be asserted by the author of the website as well as in order to be able to deal with any unauthorised use of the website.

II. Scope of Copyright Protection

A. Exploitation Rights of the Author or Holder of Neighbouring Rights

In accordance with sec. 15 UrhG [Copyright Act], the author has the exclusive right to exploit his work. These exploitation rights comprise the right of reproduction *(Vervielfältigungsrecht)* (sec. 16 UrhG [Copyright Act]), the right of distribution *(Verbreitungsrecht)* (sec. 17 UrhG [Copyright Act]), the right of exhibition *(Ausstellungsrecht)* (sec. 18 UrhG [Copyright Act]), the right of recitation, performance and presentation *(Vortrags-, Aufführungs- und Vorführungsrecht)* (sec. 19 UrhG [Copyright Act]), the right to make copyrighted work publicly available, e. g. via Internet *(Recht der öffentlichen Zugänglichmachung)* (sec. 19 lit. a) UrhG [Copyright Act]), the right of broadcasting *(Senderecht)* (sec. 20 UrhG [Copyright Act]), the right of cable re-transmission *(Kabelweiter-*

53 27 June 2007 OLG [Higher Regional Court] Rostock [2 W 25/07], MMR 2008, 116.

senderecht) (sec. 20 lit. b) UrhG [Copyright Act]), the right of communication by video or audio recording *(Recht der Wiedergabe durch Bild- oder Tonträger)* (sec. 21 UrhG [Copyright Act]) as well as the right of communication of broadcasts *(Recht der Wiedergabe von Funksendungen und von öffentlicher Zugänglichmachung)* (sec. 22 UrhG [Copyright Act]). Also the right to make derivative works is conferred exclusively to the author *(Recht zur Bearbeitung)* (sec. 23 UrhG [Copyright Act]).

Additionally, the UrhG [Copyright Act] provides for certain moral rights which vest in the author of a work. Such moral rights are, e. g., the right of recognition of authorship *(Anerkennung der Urheberschaft)* (sec. 13 UrhG [Copyright Act]), the right concerning the distortion of the work *(Entstellung des Werkes)* (sec. 14 UrhG [Copyright Act]), or the right of acces to the work *(Zugang zum Werk)* (sec. 25 UrhG [Copyright Act]).

The scope of the neighbouring rights is specially regulated. Performing artists have, in essence, the exclusive right to make an audio or visual recording of their performances, to reproduce and distribute the video or audio recording and to make their performances publicly available (sections 77, 78 UrhG [Copyright Act]). Also some limited rights regarding distortion and recognition of performership vest in the performer (sections 74 and 75 UrhG [Copyright Act]). The organiser of a performance, e.g, a concert promoter, has the same rights as the performing artist except the moral rights (sec. 81 UrhG [Copyright Act]). The phonogram producer has the exclusive right to reproduce, distribute and broadcast the recording (sec. 85 para. 1 UrhG [Copyright Act]). The producer of a film has the exclusive right to reproduce, distribute and use for public presentation or broadcasting the picture carrier or picture and sound carrier on which the cinematographic work is recorded (sec. 94 para. 1, sent. 1 UrhG [Copyright Act]). The rights of the database maker includes the right to reproduce, to distribute and to communicate to the public the database (sec. 87 lit. b) UrhG [Copyright Act]).

B. Dealing with Copyrights and Neighbouring Rights – Legal Position of Licencees

Following the authorship principle, under German law copyrights are regarded to be linked with the personality of the author. Therefore, the author may not assign the copyright itself to a third party. However, he may grant rights to use his work to third parties by way of licence agreements (sec. 31 para. 1 UrhG [Copyright Act]) and collect royalties for the exploitation of their work in turn. The moral rights linked with the work are not transferable and remain with the author. Only in limited cases a waiver of such moral rights is possible.

In contrast, most of the neighbouring rights can be freely transferred in whole. This applies in particular to the rights vested in the film or phonogram producers, organisers of performances, and the makers of databases as these rights have no moral right component.

When drafting copyright licence agreements, one should take into account the fact that under sec. 31 para. 5 UrhG [Copyright Act], the following rule applies (the so-called purpose-specific transfer doctrine *(Zweckübertragungslehre)*): If the types of use granted have not been specifically designated in the contract, the licensee will only be entitled to such rights necessary for the contractually agreed purposes. This should be assessed from an economic and a technical perspective.[54] In case of doubt, however, it will be deemed that the author wanted to retain the maximum rights possible.[55] For example, if the author of a television film grants a film producer the "rights for all broadcasting and film purposes" then this does not include any exploitation by way of VHS video cassettes, given that video exploitation is a different type of use that does not fall within the scope of "broadcasting and film purposes".[56] If, however, the right to exploit using VHS video cassettes is granted, this also covers exploitation by using DVDs.[57] The right to transmit via terrestrial broadcasting also includes the right to transmit via cable or satellite.[58] It is, however, highly doubtful if such language would include exploitation via mobile devices. The so-called purpose-specific transfer doctrine also applies in relation to the issue of whether the right of use is being granted, whether it is a non-exclusive or an exclusive right of use, and as regards the scope of the right of use in terms of territory and other the restrictions to which the right of use may be subject.

In principle, in addition to the author, licencees who hold exclusive use rights are authorised to enforce their rights against infringers.[59] This also applies where licencees have sub-licensed such rights to third parties and thus continue to derive material benefits from the rights.[60] An exclusive license also includes the right to raise claims for damages without the need for a separate stipulation under German law.[61] Accordingly, even holders of indirect exclusive rights of use, such as classical film distribution, video on-demand services or online music download portals, can fully enforce their rights.

C. Limitations of German Copyright Law – in particular making copies for private purposes *(Privileg der Privatkopie)*; copyright levy on recording equipment *(Geräteabgabe)* vs. DRM and individual licensing

The scope of application of German copyright law is not unlimited. To begin with, copyright protection ceases to apply where entire works or parts thereof are worked on in a manner that leads to the creation of a new piece of work existing in its own right

54 *Schricker*, Urheberrecht, § 31, No. 38.

55 *Schricker*, Urheberrecht, § 31, No. 34.

56 26 April 1974 BGH [Federal Supreme Court] [I ZR 137/72], GRUR 1974, 786 (Kassettenfilm); likewise for cinema rights and VHS, 11 October 1990 BGH [Federal Supreme Court] [I ZR 59/89], GRUR 1991, 133 (Videozweitauswertung).

57 19 May 2005 BGH [Federal Supreme Court] [I ZR 285/02], GRUR 2005, 937 (Der Zauberberg). For further examples, see *Schricker*, Urheberrecht, § 31, Nos. 42 ff.

58 04 July 1996 BGH [Federal Supreme Court] [I ZR 101/94], GRUR 1997, 215 (Klimbim).

59 29 April 1965 BGH [Federal Supreme Court] [Ia ZR 260/63], GRUR 1965, 591 (Wellplatten); 17 June 1992 BGH [Federal Supreme Court] [I ZR 182/90], GRUR 1992, 697 (ALF).

60 17 June 1992 BGH [Federal Supreme Court] [I ZR 182/90], GRUR 1992, 697 (ALF).

61 cf. 17 June 1992 BGH [Federal Supreme Court] [I ZR 182/90], GRUR 1992, 697 (ALF); 24 April 2006 OLG [Higher Regional Court] Hamburg [5 U 103/04], ZUM-RD 2007, 13.

(freie Bearbeitung) in the meaning of sec. 24 UrhG [Copyright Act]. This is the case if the individual features taken from a copyright protected older work pale in comparison to the distinctive nature of the newly created work.[62]

Furthermore, in the interest of the general public, an author or a holder of a neighbouring right may not prohibit the use of the protected work in the cases described in sections 44 lit. a) – 63 lit. a) UrhG [Copyright Act]. This includes, for example, to the right quote passages from a work (sec. 51 UrhG [Copyright Act]) or to make copies of such a work for teaching purposes (sec. 53 para. 3 UrhG [Copyright Act]). Also, purely technical and temporary acts of reproduction, such as so-called caching, which merely serves to speed up access to web pages, or other purely technical acts of this kind undertaken in the context of authorised use of protected work, are explicitly exempted from copyright restrictions, provided they have no independent economic significance (sec. 44 lit. a) UrhG [Copyright Act]).

In the present context, the most important provision limiting the scope of German copyright law is sec. 53 para. 1 UrhG [Copyright Act] which provides for the right to make reproductions for private purposes *(Privileg der Privatkopie)*. Section 53 para. 1, sent. 1 UrhG [Copyright Act] stipulates that it is permissible to make single copies of a work for private use, and for reasons that are neither directly nor indirectly commercial, provided, however, that no obviously unlawfully made master copy is used. It is important to note that this privilege explicitly does not apply to computer programs, which may solely be copied for back-up purposes (sections 69 lit. d) and 69 lit. e) UrhG [Copyright Act]). Nor does the private copy privilege apply to digital databases or database works (sec. 53 para. 5 UrhG [Copyright Act]). Especially in this digital age, the ability to make copies e. g. of music or films for private purposes causes numerous problems with regard to the safeguarding the interests of rights holders.[63]

In 1965 the legislature permitted the making of copies for private purposes because, in light of the rapid development of copying media it was clear that any prohibition of making copies for private purposes would not be enforceable as a practical matter. The legislature instead opted to permit the making of copies for private purposes under certain circumstances. In turn, a copyright levy on copying or recording equipment *(Geräteabgabe)* was introduced to finance certain lump-sum royalty payments to authors as a compensation. The copyright levy is often referred to as a 'statutory license'. Authorizing the making of private copies therefore is ultimately to protect intellectual property and not chiefly a right granted to users.

---

62 11 March 1993 BGH [Federal Supreme Court] [I ZR 264/91], GRUR 1994, 191 (Asterix-Persiflagen); 20 March 2003 BGH [Federal Supreme Court] [I ZR 117/00], GRUR 2003, 956 (Gies Adler). Pursuant to sec. 23 UrhG [Copyright Act], the copy constitutes an adaptation without consent. Although the person making such adaptation acquires its own copyrights in the adaptation, it is nonetheless not permitted to exercise these rights without the prior consent of the creator of the creator of the work.

63 Compare under III.B for the field of offline uses and IV. C.2 for the field of online uses.

The copyright levy is charged on copying or recording equipment in accordance with sections 54–54 lit. c) UrhG [Copyright Act]. It is charged on all sales of equipment intended for copying or recording purposes (photocopiers, tape recorders and CD burners) as well as video and audio carriers, video cassettes, audiotapes and blank rewritable CDs. The levy is collected by the collecting societies which then distribute the funds raised to copyright owners.[64] The legislature has failed to regulate precisely what devices and media are subject to the copyright levy. This must, in principle, be determined according to whether and the extent to which any specific copying or recording equipment or storage media are generally used for reproduction purposes. The collecting societies are to fix appropriate rates or to conclude master agreements with the relevant industry associations. In the event of a dispute, a court must rule on the appropriateness of the rates.[65]

Encouraged by the Copyright Directive, parallel to the lump sum remuneration scheme, the German legislature has been calling for increased efforts to establish an alternative remunerative scheme of individual licensing in mass media as well. The aim is to achieve this by providing for specific standards for the protection of DRM systems. DRM systems enable copyright owners to determine the potential number of copies which may be made and the types of media on which content can be stored. In addition, DRM systems are paving the way for content to be exploited on a pay-per-use basis which totally prohibits storing content on any medium. If authors or holders of a right of use

---

64 A collecting society is an organisation which undertakes the collective management of copyrights or neighbouring rights for the account of a large number of authors or holders of neighbouring rights. The statutory basis therefor is the Urheberrechtswahrnehmungsgesetz [UrhWG] [Copyright Administration Act] (F. R.G.). The supervisory authority is the German Patent Office *(Patentamt)* in Munich. Collecting societies are required to grant exploitation rights or authorisations to any person so requesting on equitable terms in respect of the rights that they administer (sec. 11 UrhWG [Copyright Administration Act]). Collecting Societies are required to fix rates and, in so doing, they must have due regard to the religious, cultural and social interests of the persons liable to pay the remuneration, including the interests of youth welfare (sec. 13 UrhWG [Copyright Administration Act]). Finally, the collecting societies are required to set up welfare and assistance schemes for the holders of the rights and claims that they administer (sec. 8 UrhWG [Copyright Administration Act]). The most important collecting societies in Germany are the following: Gesellschaft für musikalische Aufführungs- und mechanische Vervielfältigungsrechte (GEMA), which is the society which represents the worldwide repertoire of copyrighted music, Gesellschaft zur Verwertung von Leistungsschutzrechten (GVL), which is responsible for the exploitation in Germany of performers' rights, producers of of sound storage mediums and of music video clips; Verwertungsgesellschaft Wort (VG Wort), administers many different rights in literary works on behalf of authors and publishers; Verwertungsgesellschaft für Nutzungsrechte an Filmwerken mbH (VGF), is responsible for the exploitation of rights of German and foreign film producers, and the rights of producers of other cinematographic works such as television producers; Verwertungsgesellschaft Bild-Kunst (VG Bild-Kunst), administers the exploitation and re-exploitation righs on behalf of fine artists.

65 E. g. printers and plotters without any additional features are not subject to a levy according to 21 January 2007 OLG [Higher Regional Court] Düsseldorf [20 U 38/06], GRUR 2007, 416 (Druckerabgabe).

opt for the individual licence, they will have the law on their side. For example, sections 95 lit. a) *et seq.* UrhG [Copyright Act] protect copyrights or other exploitation rights against the circumvention of technological measures implemented by the copyright owner to prevent the unlawful use of its content. This also applies if the measures are circumvented for the purpose of creating digital copies for private purposes (sec. 95 lit. b) para. 1, sent. 1 no. 6 UrhG [Copyright Act]). This demonstrates that the private copy privilege has always been considered the second-best solution and that rights holders shall be encouraged to establish individual licence schemes instead of relying on statutory licences. Furthermore, the prohibition is not restricted to the circumvention of measures, but also covers the manufacture, import, distribution and sale of devices for the circumvention of protective measures (sec. 95 lit. a) para. 2 UrhG [Copyright Act]).

D. Comparative Legal Aspects

Unlike material property, the nature of intellectual property means that it transcends national borders. This, however, is also true with respect to product piracy. Under the Copyright Act, it is not only German nationals and companies with registered seats in Germany who enjoy copyright protection with respect to content or exploitation rights which have been first published in Germany. Under sec. 120 UrhG [Copyright Act], nationals of another Member State of the European Union or of another Contracting State of the Convention Concerning the European Economic Area are deemed equal to German nationals and enjoy protection if their works have been published in at least one such Member State. Furthermore, the Federal Republic of Germany is a signatory to numerous conventions and treaties which afford protection to copyrights and neighbouring rights. The most important of these have been the Berne Convention for the Protection of Literary and Artistic Works, TRIPS (the Agreement on Trade-Related Aspects of Intellectual Property Rights), the WCT (World Copyright Treaty), the Rome Convention, the Geneva Phonograms Convention, as well as WPPT (the WIPO Performances and Phonograms Treaty). Each of these conventions and treaties regulate certain aspects of the protection of copyright and neighbouring rights, but together afford virtually 100% protection for the owners of rights. Their provisions have been adopted and transposed into German law and are provided for under sec. 121 para. 4 UrhG [Copyright Act] and sec. 126 para. 3 UrhG [Copyright Act]. In short,[66] rights holders who are nationals of another contracting state[67] may enforce their rights for copyright infringements committed in the territory of the Federal Republic of Germany as if copyright protection had been afforded to them in Germany, provided that the relevant work was first published in a contracting state (the "principal of national treatment" *(Inländerbehandlungsgrundsatz)*).

In the event that the owner of a right seeks protection in Germany under these conventions and treaties, the subject and scope of protection and the issue of whether an

66 Detailed information in *Schricker*, Urheberrecht, before §§ 120 ff., Nos. 13 ff.

67 i. e., a natural or legal person residing / based outside the EU or the European Economic Area but whose country is a signatory to one of the said treaties/conventions.

infringement of the right has actually been committed, the questions relating to the legal ownership, as well as the legal consequences and must be determined in accordance with German law, irrespective of the legal provisions in the country in which the work was first published (the "country of protection" principle *(Schutzlandprinzip)*).[68] Given the high level of protection provided in Germany, this can put the owner of the right in a more advantageous legal position than it would have in its country of origin. However, it also means that, for example, an American film producer who brings an action before a German court for unlawful exploitation of a film in Germany cannot claim that he is the author of the cinematographic work in accordance with the American "work made for hire" doctrine.[69] On the contrary, he must be treated as a film producer within the meaning of sec. 85 UrhG [Copyright Act] or prove that he is the legal owner by furnishing relevant licence agreements.

The "country of protection" principle also ultimately applies to the issue of whether a licencee has sufficient standing to bring suit in a German court even if, according the choice of law provision, the contract is subject to a foreign jurisdiction.[70] This can also prove to be a considerable advantage.

Lastly, TRIPS, the Bern Convention and the WCT provide for an exception to the country of protection principle in respect of terms of protection. They set out a "comparison of terms" rule *(Schutzfristenvergleich)*. Comparison of terms means that a country where protection is sought should be obligated to grant a term of protection exceeding the term granted by the country of origin of the work.[71] Given the numerous exceptions and special constellations it could well be that the German terms of protection are deemed to apply even if the work had already been in the public domain in the country of origin.[72]

III. Offline Digital Piracy

Music, films, video games or software are frequently subject to illegal copying. This is primarily facilitated by the fact that such content is now predominantly distributed in

---

68 *Schricker*, Urheberrecht, before § 120, No. 129.

69 2 October 1997 BGH [Federal Supreme Court] [I ZR 88/95], GRUR 1999, 152 (Spielbankaffaire).

70 17 June 1992 BGH [Federal Supreme Court] [I ZR 182/90], GRUR 1992, 697 (ALF).

71 *Schricker*, Urheberrecht, before § 120 ff., No. 129.

72 Examples: 27 January 1978 BGH [Federal Supreme Court] [I ZR 4/77], GRUR 1978, 302 (Wolfblut); 11 July 1985 BGH [Federal Supreme Court] [I ZR 50/83], GRUR 1986, 69 (Puccini); 7 October 2003 OLG [Higher Regional Court] Frankfurt [11 U 53/99], GRUR-RR 2004, 99 (Anonyme Alkoholiker). The German-American Convention of 1892, for example, excluded a comparison of terms. The German terms of protection apply at all times to American works, irrespective of any expiry of protection granted in the United States. This applies even if the work was not protected at any point in time due to any non-fulfilment of requirements of form. Compare 27 January 1978 BGH [Federal Supreme Court] [I ZR 97/76], GRUR 1978, 300 (Buster-Keaton) and 7 October 2003 OLG [Higher Regional Court] Frankfurt [11 U 53/99], GRUR-RR 2004, 99 (Anonyme Alkoholiker).

digital form, making it easier to copy. Even if rightholders seek to protect their content by using DRM systems, infringers invariably find a way to get round these mechanisms. Some copies are made for private purposes, but the bulk of the losses incurred by the relevant industry stem from large-scale commercial copying.

A. Infringements

Physically copying a work onto storage media constitutes an infringement of the rightholder's reproduction right in accordance with sec. 16 UrhG [Copyright Act]. In the view of the Federal Supreme Court it is not necessary that an illegal copy already exists. Offering to make pirate copies to order is sufficient to violate the reproduction right.[73] Finally, an infringement of the reproduction right does not require intent to sell the copies on the German market. Infringement would, for example, also be deemed to occur if the copyrighted work was reproduced domestically with the intention of exporting the replicas abroad.[74]

Furthermore, the owner of the copyright holds the exclusive distribution right in the meaning of sec. 17 UrhG [Copyright Act], e. g. the right to place his work on the market in Germany. This only does not apply, however, where the rights in the work is exhausted, i. e. having been legitimately put into circulation within the European Union or in the territory of a state with which an appropriate treaty has been concluded. Exhaustion does not apply, however, to counterfeit products. Hence, importing and exporting pirate copies can constitute an infringement of the distribution right and give a seperate course of action regardless of who has made the actual illegal copy. Importation is, however, solely attributable to the foreign exporter. The domestic importer is only liable for the re-distribution domestically.[75] Exporting is deemed to constitute placing on the market as early as the dispatch of the copy.

Importation must be distinguished from the case of "transit" of pirate copies infringing copyright.[76] The mere carriage over German territory does not entail placing the product on the market. This is true regardless of whether the transiting was carried out on the basis of a uniform contract for the carriage of goods or whether a new contract for the carriage of goods is concluded on the re-forwarding conducted from German terri-

73 13 December 1990 BGH [Federal Supreme Court] [I ZR 21/89], GRUR 1991, 316 (Einzelangebot); 25 February 1999 BGH [Federal Supreme Court] [I ZR 118/96] GRUR 1999, 707 (Kopienversanddienst); 18 October 1991 OLG [Higher Regional Court] Köln [6 U 58/91], GRUR 1992, 312 (Amiga Club).

74 15 January 1957 BGH [Federal Supreme Court] [I ZR 39/55], BGHZ 23, 100 (Taeschner I) (in relation to the patent right); 3 March 2004 BGH [Federal Supreme Court] [2 StR 109/03], GRUR 2004, 421 (Tonträgerpiraterie durch CD-Export); 8 July 2004 BGH [Federal Supreme Court] [I ZR 25/02], GRUR 2004, 855 (Hundefigur).

75 27 February 1981 BGH [Federal Supreme Court] [I ZR 186/78], BGHZ 80, 101 (Schallplattenimport); 17 June 1992 BGH [Federal Supreme Court] [I ZR 182/90], GRUR 1992, 697 (ALF); 18 February 1993 BGH [Federal Supreme Court] [I ZR 71/91], GRUR 1993, 550 (The Doors).

76 As regards transiting, cf. in detail above *Diana Kaufmann*, Trademark Piracy, I. C.3.

tory.[77] Actual placing on the market – and not mere transit – occurs, however, when work samples are imported for the purpose of re-export and are thereby the subject matter of a domestic commercial or sales transaction.[78] Even if in cases in which the mere transiting of goods is not deemed to constitute a domestic infringement of copyright, this does not, however, preclude the assumption of copyright infringement in the country of export and/or the country of destination and legal proceedings being brought there. Such proceedings would, however, have to be judged in accordance with the principle of territoriality as regards eligibility for copyright protection, infringements and legal ramifications in accordance with the relevant laws of the foreign jurisdiction in question.

B. Privilege to Make Copies for Private Purposes

Not every reproduction without consent of the rightholder is a copyright violation under German law. Section 53 para. 1, sent. 1 UrhG [Copyright Act] stipulates that it is permissible to make single copies of a work for private use and for purposes that are neither directly nor indirectly commercial. It is still not entirely clear how many such copies may be made. The only definite rule is that it is illegal to make more than seven copies.[79] The reproduction may also be made by a third party provided that no payment is received for it (sec. 53 para. 1, sent. 2 UrhG [Copyright Act]). In any case, the privilege cannot be invoked for commercial use.

Furthermore, a copy cannot be made from an obviously unlawful master copy. This might be difficult to determine when it comes to offline use. It is completely irrelevant whether the master copy is an original or not. For example, further copies of lawful private copies, e. g. from a familiy member, are legal, too. Even a copy of an illegal master copy is legal, provided that the unlawfulness of the master copy is not obvious. This is meant to protect the end user who acted in good faith. The obligation imposed on the end user to conduct an examination of the master copy should not be particularly strict.[80] Ultimately, this can only be decided on a case-by-case basis. If, however, a DVD is used as a master copy, for example, which was clearly manufactured by copyright pirates (e. g. although packaged similar to the genuine article it is nonetheless an obvious fake or the circumstances surrounding its acquisition necessarily lead to that conclusion), one can assume that such a master copy is obviously unlawful.[81]

It is important to note that the privilege of making copies for private purposes does, however, not extend to computer programs. Only the making of back-up copies of software is permissible in this regard (sections 69 lit. d) and 69 lit. e) UrhG [Copyright Act]). The privilege does not apply to digital database or database creations either

77 9 November 1996 ECJ [C-281/05], GRUR 2007, 146 (Diesel).

78 15 January 1957 BGH [Federal Supreme Court] [I ZR 39/55], BGHZ 23, 100 (Taeschner I).

79 14 April 1978 BGH [Federal Supreme Court] [I ZR 111/76], GRUR 1978, 474 (Vervielfältigungsstücke).

80 *Schricker*, Urheberrecht, § 53, Nos. 14b f.

81 *Schricker*, Urheberrecht, § 53, No. 14c.

(sec. 53 para. 5 UrhG [Copyright Act]). For these, the legitimate use is specially regulated in sections 87 lit. c) and 55 lit. a) UrhG [Copyright Act].

C. Circumvention of Protective Measures (DRM Systems)

The Copyright Act does not just afford protection to the work itself. Technological protection measures *(technische Schutzmaßnahmen)* also fall within the scope of the Act. This technological protection is provided by means of any technology designed to protect copyrighted works or to prevent their unauthorised use (also called DRM-Systems). The legal definition provided in sec. 95 lit. a) para. 2. no. 1 UrhG [Copyright Act] mirrors the definition set out in Art. 6 of the Copyright Directive. Such technological protection measures include, for example, blocking access and preventing copying. Other technological solutions designed to facilitate the prosecution of copyright infringements, such as "watermarking", are not deemed to constitute technological protection measures within the meaning of sec. 95 lit. a) UrhG [Copyright Act]. They are nonetheless afforded protection under sec. 95 lit. c) UrhG [Copyright Act], where it is stipulated in para. 1 that electronic rights management information may not be altered or removed. Section 95 lit. c) para. 3 UrhG [Copyright Act] provides for a blanket ban on the exploitation of works and other copyrighted items in which electronic rights management information was altered or removed.

Under the statutory requirements, technological protection measures are only protected if they are "effective". Such measures do not have to be able to completely prevent every circumvention to be deemed "effective" within the meaning of the Act. This is obvious, since otherwise there would be no need to protect this type of copyrighted work in accordance with sec. 95 lit. a) UrhG [Copyright Act]. What is required is an appreciable effective protection.[82] Provided the conditions of sec. 95 lit. a) UrhG [Copyright Act] are met, any circumvention is prohibited. It is also prohibited to engage in any circumvention-related preparatory work such as manufacturing, importing, distributing, advertising or marketing, or possessing for commercial purposes such devices for the purpose of circumvention.

When circumventing a DRM system one cannot invoke the privilege of making copies for private purposes within the meaning of sec. 53 UrhG [Copyright Act]. The privileg of making copies for private purposes is drafted in a way that severely curtails its practical enforceability. This shows that the privilege of making private copies, accompanied by a copyright levy system, has always been regarded as second-best solution. Hence, the exploiter of a copyrighted DVD film is not obligated to provide consumers with the means to make copies of the DVD. Only in cases where CDs and DVDs can no longer be played on conventional players, claims relating to material defects under civil law, such as rescission in accordance with sec. 434 *et seq.* of the Bürgerliches Gesetzbuch [BGB] [Civil Code] (F. R.G.), can be taken into consideration.

---

82 *Wandtke/Bullinger*, Urheberrecht, § 95a, No. 47.

As for computer programs sec. 69 lit. f) para. 2 UrhG [Copyright Act] provides for a parallel rule stemming from the Software Directive. This provision specifically covers programs used for the circumvention of any technical device that may have been applied for protecting thr software against copying. It also covers programs designed to circumvent dongles which shut down programs[83] which use a dongle query.[84]

D. Liability of Manufacturers of Means to Circumvent Protection Measures

Under sec. 95 lit. a) para. 3 UrhG [Copyright Act], it is illegal to manufacture, import into the territory UrhG [Copyright Act], distribute in tangible and intangible forms, sell or advertise for sale devices which are primarily designed and intended almost exclusively for enabling or facilitating the circumvention of technological protective measures, or to acquire such devices for the purpose of circumventing technological measures. It is also illegal to be in possession of such devices for commercial purposes.[85] A classic example of this kind of device is the AnyDVD software, the sale of which is banned in Germany.[86] The Regional Court *(Landgericht)* of Cologne ruled that such copying software offered by eBay constituted advertising for sale within the meaning of the rule.[87] According to the prevailing opinion in legal literature, the sale of "modchips" for game consoles is also prohibited.[88] There are, however, no court precedents confirming this view. Section 95 lit. a) para. 3 UrhG [Copyright Act] aims to combat actual circumvention activities prior to their being perpetrated. The wording "almost exclusively" or "primarily" nevertheless demonstrates that the software in dispute must be thoroughly examined in each individual case. At any rate, rather lenient standards should be applied since, according to the explanatory statement to the Act, the intent is to exclude chiefly all-purpose devices which likewise facilitate the circumvention of protective mechanisms.[89] The use by the vendor viewed objectively is deemed to be the decisive factor. In the case of devices subject to a charge such as modchips, it can be important for example, whether only illegal use would be economical after pricing.[90]

---

83 The software is, for example, supplied with a dongle which is plugged into one of the ports of the computer (parallel ports, USB port etc). The "dongled" software controls use on a regular basis by detecting whether or not the dongle is plugged in and when the dongle is not present, the software runs in a restricted mode or refuses to run.

84 E. g. 27 March 1997 OLG [Higher Regional Court] Düsseldorf [20 U 51/96], CR 1997, 337; cf. also in relation to competition law claims in 9 November 1995 BGH [Federal Supreme Court] [I ZR 220/95], CR 1996, 79 (Dongle-Umgehung).

85 *Schricker*, Urheberrecht, § 95a, Nos. 23 ff.

86 28 July 2005 OLG [Higher Regional Court] München [29 U 2887/05], GRUR-RR 2005, 372.

87 23 November 2005 LG [District Court] Köln [28 S 6/05], MMR 2006, 412.

88 *Arnold*, Rechtmäßige Anwendungsmöglichkeiten zur Umgehung von technischen Kopierschutzmaßnahmen?, MMR 2008, 144.

89 Cf. *Schricker*, Urheberrecht, § 95a, No. 35.

90 Cf. *Arnold*, Rechtmäßige Anwendungsmöglichkeiten zur Umgehung von technischen Kopierschutzmaßnahmen?, MMR 2008, 144.

Section 95 lit. a) para. 3 UrhG [Copyright Act] does not provide for any legal consequences under civil law. The prevailing view amongst legal commentators is that claims for cease and desit or damages are derived by applying *mutatis mutandis* the provision of sec. 97 UrhG [Copyright Act]. The injured party may demand the destruction or the surrender of the device under analogous application of sections 98 and 99 UrhG [Copyright Act]. The injured party may demand information as to the origin and distribution channels of such copies under analogous application of sec. 101 lit. a) UrhG [Copyright Act].[91] The consequences under criminal law are, however, specially regulated in sections 108 lit. b), 110 and 111 lit. a) para. 1 UrhG [Copyright Act].

IV. Online Digital Piracy

A. Introduction

There are numerous potential sources of copyright infringement on the Internet. These include popular file-sharing systems such as Gnutella, Edonkey or Kazaa, which allow users to upload and download copyrighted content, mostly film and music files. Also Usenet, an Internet discussion system mainly used by experienced users gives users the opportunity to share illegal copies of films and music. Another common source of potential infringements includes online radio stations where it is possible to record tracks with appropriate software. A number of online video recording systems are also available for users wishing to record video files. The legality of such systems can be doubtful. Furthermore, "Web 2.0" and user-generated content platforms are opening up whole new horizons for potential copyright infringements. Sites such as MySpace allow users to set up detailed personal profiles and communicate with friends. These profiles often provides access to copyrighted material such as music, music videos or photos without requiring consent. Platforms like YouTube give private users the opportunity to post video clips for everyone to see, but it also happens quite often that copyrighted materials are shown without the required permission.

The Internet is a minefield when it comes to the protection and enforcement of legal rights. Questions range from whether a copyright infringement actually exists to the issue of who copyright claims can be made against. The following will first cover the potential liability of online providers (B.). Further, the liability of Internet users, as well as the issue of identifying them will be addressed (C.). Lastly, the liability of further parties in the context of online copyright infringement will be assessed (D.).

B. Liability of Online Providers

Making copyrighted content available on the Internet without consent of the rightholder constitutes a clear infringement of the right of making available to the public

---

91 Regarding the legal consequences, see *Arnold/Timmann*, Ist die Verletzung des § 95a Abs. 3 UrgG durch den Vertrieb von Umgehungsmitteln keine Urheberrechtsverletzung?, MMR 2008, 286.

afforded by sec. 19a UrhG [Copyright Act]. It is usually in the copyright holder's interest to take legal action against the provider of the online service through which such content can be up- or downloaded rather than bringing proceedings against each individual user of illegal online services. However, whether and to what extent the different online providers may be held liable depends on the specific nature of the online system and on the actions and obligations of the parties involved. Distinctions need to be made between content providers, which make their own content available, and host providers like Usenet providers, providers of user-generated content platforms and share hosters. Different rules also apply with respect to providers of peer-to-peer systems. Ultimately, it may be in the interest of copyright holders to assert claims against access providers to prevent online copyright infringements. In contrast to liability for online trademark infringements,[92] the issue of liability for online copyright infringements has not yet been clarified in any precedents of the Federal Supreme Court. The legal situation in this area is far from clear.

1. Overview of the Liability Principles and the Limits set out in the German Telemedia Act

Section 97 para. 1 UrhG [Copyright Act] states that an injured party may bring claims against any party unlawfully infringing its copyright or other protected rights. Such claims include for remedying an infringement, claims to cease and desist (in cases where there is a risk of repeated infringements) and claims for damages in the event that the infringing party has acted in a wilful or negligent manner. Infringer *(Verletzer)* is the party committing, aiding or abetting in the infringement. The legal definition of the term infringer is quite narrow, both as regards the actual acts of the party as well as its subjective attitude, which often makes it difficult to bring proceedings against online providers.

In order to ensure full legal protection of copyrights and neighbouring rights, sections 823 and 1004 para. 1 of the BGB [Civil Code] may be applied analogously to bring forward claims for secondary contribution to a copyright infringement *(Störerhaftung)*. The liability of secondary contributors is initially limited to remedying the infringement and/or agreeing to cease and desist any infringing activities. Secondary contributors are any parties which, without being infringer, deliberately contribute to an unlawful infringement of the rights of another party and which do not prevent an infringement from happening or continuing, although it would be in their power to do so. The key factor is the extent to which reasonable obligations to check and monitor the availability of infringing content were violated. The scope of these obligations depends on the role of the party against which claims are brought in the specific case and its possibilities to avoid the infringement, on the one hand, as well as on the degree of personal responsibility of the acting individuals, on the other hand.

The degree of responsibility of online providers either for direct infringement or secondary contribution must be assessed in the light of section 7/10 of the Telemedienge-

---

92 See above, *Diana Kaufmann*, Trademark Piracy, I. C.4.

setz [TMG] [Telemedia Act] (F. R.G.).[93] The Act is based on the E-Commerce Directive and provides for a tiered system of liability privileges for online content and services, similar to the US Digital Millennium Copyright Act.[94] The term telemedia includes all electronic information and communication services that are not limited to the transfer of signals via telecommunications networks and that are not value-added or broadcast services. According to the explanatory statement published with regard to the TMG [Telemedia Act], this includes content providers, host providers and providers of user-generated content platforms or share hosters, as well as Usenet providers or standard access providers.[95] It should be noted, however, that the term telemedia does not include search engines or services provided via peer-to-peer systems.

The TMG [Telemedia Act] makes a basic distinction between liability for a provider's *own* content and liability for the content of third *parties*, which the provider only passes on, or stores on behalf of its users.

As stipulated in sec. 7 para. 1 TMG [Telemedia Act], content providers, who make their own content available, have full legal responsibility for such content.[96] Own content can include information of third parties which the provider uses for its own purposes.[97] This is sometimes difficult to assess, in particular in cases where providers require the user to assign all rights in the uploaded content to the provider. Where third parties' content is, however, merely stored by host providers or passed on by cache or access providers, sec. 7 para. 2 sent. 1 TMG [Telemedia Act] states that service providers are intitially not required to monitor or check such third-party content.

The TMG [Telemedia Act] does not, however, release providers from liability as secondary contributors.[98] Once being alerted of infringing content, the provider is required to remedy any legal infringements immediately ("notice and take down"). The extent to which precautions must be taken by a provider to prevent similar future infringements depends on the extent to which taking such precautions is technically feasible and reasonable, and must therefore be determined on a case-by-case basis.

---

93 See also above, *Diana Kaufmann*, Trademark Piracy, I. C.4.

94 Cf. below, *Daryl Fairbairn*, Product Piracy in the United States, II. C.5.

95 Gesetzentwurf der Bundesregierung [Draft bill of the Federal Government], Entwurf eines Gesetzes zur Vereinheitlichung von Vorschriften über bestimmte elektronische Informations- und Kommunikationsdienste [Draft Act on the Harmonisation of Rules on Certain Electronic Information and Communication Services], BT-Drucks. 16/3078, p. 17.

96 *Schmitz/Laun*, Die Haftung kommerzieller Meinungsportale im Internet, MMR 2005, 208, 210.

97 Gesetzentwurf der Bundesregierung [Draft bill of the Federal Government], Entwurf eines Gesetzes über rechtliche Rahmenbedingungen für den elektronischen Geschäftsverkehr [Draft Act on the Harmonisation of Rules on Certain Electronic Information and Communication Services], BT-Drucks. 14/6098, p. 23. For precise distinction see *Schmitz/Laun*, Die Haftung kommerzieller Meinungsportale im Internet, MMR 2005, 208, 210.

98 11 March 2004 BGH [Federal Supreme Court] [I ZR 304/01], GRUR 2004, 860 (Internetversteigerung-ROLEX); 19 April 2007 BGH [Federal Supreme Court] [I ZR 35/04], GRUR 2007, 708 (Internetversteigerung II); 30 April 2008 BGH [Federal Supreme Court] [I ZR 73/05], MarkenR 2008, 235 (Internetversteigerung III).

Neither does the TMG [Telemedia Act] completely exclude providers' liability for damages. Host providers are liable for damages if they continue with an infringement despite becoming aware of it, i. e., if the infringement is obvious to them (sec. 10 no. 1 TMG [Telemedia Act]). Access and cache providers are liable for damages if it can be demonstrated that they deliberately collaborated with the infringing party in committing the infringement (sec. 8 para. 1 sent. 1 TMG [Telemedia Act]).

In particular, for access providers which only provide access to third-party content, it is significant that sec. 7 para. 2 sent. 2 TMG [Telemedia Act] can require them to remove or block access to certain content even if they are *not responsible for it*, i. e., even if they are not even secondary contributors. The explanatory statement on the Act makes it clear, however, that providers are only subject to this obligation if it is technically possible and reasonable to require them to remove or block the relevant content, and the kind of infringing content at play justifies such obligation.[99] This can be difficult to prove when it comes to copyright infringements.

2. Liability of Content Providers

Content providers may be held liable as infringer. Section 7 TMG [Telemedia Act] states that content providers may not rely on the privileges afforded by the Telemedia Act. They are therefore liable to remedy infringements or to cease and desist in accordance with sec. 97 para. 1 UrhG [Copyright Act]. They are also required under sec. 101 lit. a) UrhG [Copyright Act] to notify copyright holders of the duration the relevant works were available to users and the number of times the copyrighted work was accessed. Claims for damages under sec. 97 para. 1 UrhG [Copyright Act] are conditional on the party held liable being at fault. But given that such fault may consist also of mere negligence content providers may be liable for damages in many cases.

3. Liability of Host Providers

Host providers are not generally regarded as infringing parties due to the fact that they only make third party content available. But they may be held liable as secondary contributors. In principle, it is agreed that the "notice and take-down rule" applies in such cases, according to which providers are required to block content as soon as they are made aware of such content constituting an obvious copyright infringement. Host providers may be liable for damages if despite such a notice they fail to block content constituting a clear copyright infringement.

It is debatable whether having been put on notice of a copyright infringement results in an obligation to prevent copyright infringements of the relevant kind in future. The legal situation in this regard in Germany is still developing. The rulings issued by var-

99 Gesetzentwurf der Bundesregierung [Draft bill of the Federal Government], Entwurf eines Gesetzes über rechtliche Rahmenbedingungen für den elektronischen Geschäftsverkehr [Draft Act on Legal Framework for the Electronic Commerce], BT-Drucks. 14/6098, p. 23, 25.

ious lower courts have been very different in certain respects. The key factor is to examine in detail what the services provided by a specific host provider consist of and then to assess the degree of the reasonable checking and control obligations of the host provider.[100] The following sets out a number of examples:

a. Share Hosters

Share hosters offer users the opportunity to pay to use the providers server as external storage space. One of the main German share hosters is the site rapidshare.de. The site allows any user to upload files of up to 300 MB. The user is then supplied with a unique download URL referring to this file. The user can thereupon enable anyone to download the file by providing the URL. No external user is allowed to search the server for content and all files have to be downloaded by following the given URL. It is therefore completely up to the uploader whether and how easily content on the server is available to third parties. The provider is not aware of the nature of the content which is uploaded. In addition, there are usually link lists published by third parties known as link hosters. These link lists allow interested parties to browse the available content. It is then free to download any content, which is often copyrighted.

The extent to which share hosters are liable for such copyright infringements is the subject of some dispute. It is generally the case that share hosters can only be considered secondary contributors. What they give access to is not their own content. They are generally unaware of the nature of the content and therefore of whether any infringement exists. Hence, share hosters are required to take down any infringing content once they have been alerted by the copyright holder in accordance with the notice and takedown principle.

Currently, there is a legal debate on whether providers should also be required to prevent further infringements that are similar to an infringement brought to their notice, i. e., whether they should at least be required to prevent repeated uploads of the same content. In the event of trademark infringements which take place on Internet portals such as eBay, the Federal Supreme Court ruled that any provider which directly benefits from prohibited content (e. g. by earning commission) is required not only to block such content but also to take measures to prevent similar future infringements. However, the Federal Supreme Court also stated that the obligation to check on the permissibility of content only exists if the cost and effort involved is reasonable and is sufficiently likely to be well-invested.[101]

---

100 Cf. *Schmitz/Laun*, Die Haftung kommerzieller Meinungsportale im Internet, MMR 2005, 208, 212, on the liablility of portal providers in particular.

101 11 March 2004 BGH [Federal Supreme Court] [I ZR 304/01], GRUR 2004, 860 (Internetversteigerung-ROLEX); 19 April 2007 BGH [Federal Supreme Court] [I ZR 35/04], GRUR 2007, 708 (Internetversteigerung II); 30 April 2008 BGH [Federal Supreme Court] [I ZR 73/05], MarkenR 2008, 235 (Internetversteigerung III). See also above *Diana Kaufmann*, Trademark Piracy, I. C.4.

The German collecting society GEMA recently won a legal battle against Rapidshare at Higher Regional Court *(Oberlandesgericht)* of Cologne in September 2007[102] and subsequently at the Düsseldorf District Court in January 2008.[103] Both courts found that Rapidshare should be held responsible for the uploading of infringing material to its site. Cologne Higher Regional Court stated that Rapidshare is required to regularly monitor, manually where necessary, the link lists referred to in a warning notice issued to it. The Court also stated that it was irrelevant that the provider did not profit directly from individual copyrighted content being accessed. The Court held that the frequency of the infringements committed via the share hoster and the fact that uploaders are required to pay for the service Rapidshare provides were sufficient to impose such an obligation. The Court added that a share hoster could only avoid liability for any further infringements if it can demonstrate that it has implemented an effective monitoring procedures to prevent copyright violations.

Rapidshare has therefore set up an "abuse department" with the aim of uncovering copyright infringements and deleting the relevant content. Members of the department regularly visit sites which are known to publish links to such files. Rapidshare also implemented a word filter to identify suspicious filenames and such files are immediately removed if the suspicion proves to be correct. An MD5 filter was also introduced to prevent deleted files from being uploaded again. Nevertheless, infringing content continued to be discovered.[104]

Despite the above-described measures having been taken the Regional Court in Düsseldorf ruled against Rapidshare again. It held that, given the frequency of infringements ocurring on its site, Rapidshare should also have made all users complete a registration process. Experience had shown that registered users are far less likely to commit copyright and other infringements online than unregistered users. The Court stated that although it could be argued that users can give false information when registering, there were a number of checks which could be made to determine whether the information provided is accurate. These possibilities included data comparisons with Schufa

---

102 21 September 2007 OLG [Higher Regional Court] Köln [6 U 86/07], GRUR-RR 2008, 35 (Sharehoster-Haftung).

103 15 January 2008 OLG [Higher Regional Court] Düsseldorf [I-20 U 95/07, 20 U 95/07], ZUM 2008, 332.

104 The use of an MD5 filter is not sufficient to prevent such infringements. It can only prevent identical files from being uploaded again, but cannot identify a particular copyrighted work. Given that the defendant based its claim to cease and desist on the works saved in the relevant files and not on the specific files themselves, the use of such a filter was not sufficient. This is due to the fact that different recordings of, for example, the same song would only have to contain minor differences (in the volume, for instance) in order for the MD5 filter to not recognise that it is the same song, despite the song already being in the search list. The use of a word filter would also be insufficient since such a filter does not work if the user selects a file name that is not the same as the title of the song. Pirates are able to take advantage of this in that by making the download link published by them the only link necessary for accessing their files containing a song or film etc. Pirates can use any filename for such files and these file names can then be changed by users following the download.

(Schutzgemeinschaft für allgemeine Kreditsicherung) [German Credit Reference Agency] (as used by eBay) and even the use of the so called German PostIdent procedure, an individualised legitmation procedure offered by Deutsche Post AG. Should these measure not prove effective either, the court suggested that Rapidshare might be required to shut down its service.[105]

Both of the rulings were issued in preliminary injunction proceedings. It remains to be seen whether the Federal Supreme Court will reach a different conclusion in any action on the merits proceedings.

b. Link Hosters

As mentioned, link hosters provide link lists for files held by host providers (generally share hosters). They thereby provide third parties with access to third-party file storage systems, such as those of share hosters, via their own search platform. This assumes that the share hoster's customers have correctly indicated and linked the file links with the link hosters.

There is not currently any published ruling on the liability of link hosters. Under German law, one cannot be held liable as a secondary contributor for storing infringing third-party content. However, if a search platform is specifically made available to find, for example, music files stored on a third-party system, this may give rise to liability as a secondary contributor. Compared to traditional search engines such as Google or Yahoo, which cannot generally be held liable as secondary contributors due to the fact that they merely provide links to third-party content,[106] illegal usage is much more likely using link hosters which do not simply provide a systematic list of freely available links, which are already available to all Internet users anyway.[107] Furthermore, the business model of listers is to get customers of share hosters to spread content stored by the share hosters. Should link hosters explicitly advertise the possibility of illegal downloads, this would possibly be the strongest argument for liability.[108]

c. User-Generated Platforms

User-generated content generally refers to content which is created by users rather than providers of websites. The providers of this kind of service do not generally check this content before it is uploaded. Well-known examples are video portals such as YouTube or Clipfish or other portals such as Flickr or MySpace. The amount of user-generated content has risen dramatically over the past few years with technical advances in the

105 15 January 2008 OLG [Higher Regional Court] Düsseldorf [I-20 U 95/07, 20 U 95/07], ZUM 2008, 332.

106 17 July 2003 BGH [Federal Supreme Court] [I ZR 259/00], GRUR 2003, 958 (Paperboy). See also below on liability for links and liability for search engine providers (IV. D.1 and IV. D.4).

107 As is the case with traditional search engines.

108 *Wilmer*, Überspannte Prüfpflichten für Host-Provider?, NJW 2008, 1845.

Internet. The main driving factors have been the falling cost of storage space, computer equipment and the increase in the number of broadband connections. However, the freely accessible content of these sites often infringes copyrights.

The liability of providers for such infringements is limited.[109] They may only be held liable as secondary contributors since the content they make publicly available is not their own and they are generally unaware of the nature of the content and of whether it infringes any copyrights. Providers are initially required to follow the notice and take-down principal and remove any content on being alerted by the copyright holder.

There is some uncertainty, however, as to how far providers are liable for further infringements of the same type. There is little meaningful case law in this area in Germany, such as, for example, the action brought by Viacom against YouTube in the USA. According to the Federal Supreme Court ruling on trademark infringements on Internet sites such as eBay, providers of such sites that may profit directly from trademark infringing content (e. g. by earning commission) are required not only to immediately remove such content, but also to take measures to ensure that to the greatest possible extent that there is no repetition of such infringements. Providers may be required to install filter software for this purpose.[110] However, unlike eBay, sites such as YouTube do not profit directly from infringing content as they do not charge a download fee and do not have a pay-per-view system in place. Such sites are freely accessible without charge but financed by advertising. Whether the latter is sufficient to assume liability in an open question under German law. There is also the issue that the use of filter software (word filters or MD5 filters) is not yet very effective for media files (unlike for trademark infringements).[111]

However, if the view taken by Cologne Higher Regional Court and Düsseldorf Regional Court[112] in the Rapidshare case becomes generally accepted, providers of user-generated content sites could face serious copyright claims. Another issue which potentially increases provider liability is that providers of such sites generally require uploaders to assign extensive rights of use to the content to them. This could be construed to mean that providers of user-generated content sites make such content their own, thereby making themselves liable in the same way as content providers. It will be interesting to see how the legal situation develops in this area.

---

[109] Cf. *Ott*, Haftung für Embedded Videos von YouToube und anderen Videoplattformen im Internet, ZUM 2008, 556.

[110] 11 March 2004 BGH [Federal Supreme Court] [I ZR 304/01], GRUR 2004, 860 (Internetversteigerung-ROLEX); 19 April 2007 BGH [Federal Supreme Court] [I ZR 35/04], GRUR 2007, 708 (Internetversteigerung II); 30 April 2008 BGH [Federal Supreme Court] [I ZR 73/05], MarkenR 2008, 235 (Internetversteigerung III). see also *Diana Kaufmann*, Trademark Piracy, I. C.4.

[111] Cf. 11 March 2004 BGH [Federal Supreme Court] [I ZR 304/01], GRUR 2004, 860 (Internetversteigerung-ROLEX); 19 April 2007 BGH [Federal Supreme Court] [I ZR 35/04], GRUR 2007, 708 (Internetversteigerung II); 30 April 2008 BGH [Federal Supreme Court] [I ZR 73/05], MarkenR 2008, 235 (Internetversteigerung III).

[112] Cf. above IV. B.3.a.

4. Usenet

Usenet is a global electronic network which was originally intended to be a discussion forum. It is spread across a number of independent news servers and divided into newsgroups, many of which are subdivided further. Today, however, all kind of files, including media files (binaries) may be uploaded to the newsgroups in addition to text entries. These often contain copyrighted material and are the key issue of the controversial legal discussion.

Users generally have to pay to use the service. Access to Usenet generally takes place via Usenet providers and in most cases users use a newsreader to access newsgroups that are of interest to them. Usenet providers call up the requested information from the news server and generally save it within the system for a certain period. All users may upload content to groups on individual news servers. There is no editing staff making any pre-selection of the content to be published.

a. Liability of Usenet Providers

The liability of Usenet providers based in Germany is disputed. There is however no question that, if at all, they may only be regarded as secondary contributors, given that the content is not their own and they are often unaware of the content. Usenet providers are initially required to follow the notice and take-down principle, i. e., to remove any copyrighted content on being given notice by the copyright holder, unless the content has already been deleted following the limited storage period which is often in place.

However, the extent to which Usenet providers are also liable for any further infringements is open to question. Hamburg Regional Court[113] ruled that Usenet providers are liable for any subsequent similar infringements if they explicitly advertise the possibility of illegal downloads since they are deliberately inciting users to break the law. Munich Regional Court[114] and Düsseldorf Higher Regional Court[115] have both ruled that no liability exists if there is no explicit reference to the possibility of making illegal downloads. Düsseldorf Higher Regional Court views Usenet providers as mere cache providers. Under sec. 9 TMG [Telemedia Act], cache providers are significantly less likely to be viewed as secondary contributors than host providers. The Court pointed out that pointed out that unlike host providers Usenet providers, which cache Usenet data on the basis of individual requests, cannot permanently remove data from Usenet. They can only delete data which is cached on their own servers. Any new requests made by users for the same data means that it is reloaded onto the server. This can continue for as long as the relevant data may be requested on Usenet. The court ruled that it is not reasonable to expect Usenet providers to distinguish between all copyrighted material and

113 19 February 2007 LG [District Court] Hamburg [308 O 32/07], ZUM 2007, 492.

114 19 April 2007 LG [District Court] München [7 O 3950/07], ZUM 2007, 496.

115 15 January 2008 OLG [Higher Regional Court] Düsseldorf [I-20 U 95/07, 20 U 95/07], ZUM 2008, 332.

legal content and to prevent access to such, given the huge volume of data, the text coding of binary content and the fact that Usenet providers have no control over the posting and dissemination of content within Usenet. It is not financially possible or otherwise reasonable for a cache provider to perform sufficiently detailed manual checks of all data and to filter it in view of the potentially large number of infringements.

It remains to be seen whether this situation will be interpreted differently in future rulings. The strict rulings handed down by Düsseldorf Higher Regional Court and Cologne Higher Regional Court as regards share hosters, and particularly the requirement to only allow identified users, mean that a different result is conceivable. Furthermore, if rightholders were able to prove that effective filter methods are in fact available, a liability would be more likely.

b. Liability of News Server Providers

Just like conventional host providers, providers of news serves on which contents which infringes copyrights is stored for any length of time should be made subject to extensive monitoring and checking obligations. Claims to cease and desist, as well as claims for damages, are possible if content which clearly infringes a copyright is held on servers despite the provider having been informed of this (sec. 10 no. 1 TMG [Telemedia Act]). However, there is no published ruling on this particular situation from a German court so far.

5. Filesharing Systems

Popular filesharing systems such as Gnutella, Edonkey, eMule or Kazaa are often a source of copyright infringements. When analyzing a potential liability, however, centralised and decentralised filesharing systems must be distinguished.

a. Centralised Filesharing Systems

With centralised filesharing systems, users are directed to a server after their initial log-in. Here they can download the free software and install it on their own computers. Examples of this were Napster[116] and Audiogalaxy,[117] which were closed down following numerous lawsuits brought by the music industry. These systems inform users, via the provider's central server, of which other users are currently online and what content they are offering. No content is available directly from the server. The files are available only on users' hard drives. When a user starts a search, the server searches the available

[116] In 2001 Napster was shut down in the US according to judgement, 12 February 2001 Court of Appeals for the Ninth Circuit San Francisco [C 00-16401], Medien und Recht 2001, 6 (A&M Records v Napster).

[117] Also Audiogalaxy wents offline after a complaint brought forward by RIAA (Recording Industry Association of America) in 2002.

user files for any matches. These files are then displayed in a list (directory). If the user who initiated the search selects one of the files from the list, the server forwards this request to the provider of the content. All users with the relevant file are then connected and the download can begin.

b. Liability

There is no published case law on the liability of centralised filesharing systems under German law. It is likely that systems must be regarded solely as access providers sec. 8 TMG [Telemedia Act]. They merely provide access to a virtual network and do not make any content available themselves. It is important to note that unlike host providers, they have no way of deleting content from users' computers.[118]

As mentioned, the privileged treatment provided for in the TMG [Telemedia Act] does not exclude liability for secendary contribution. In this regard the directories, giving such providers actual knowledge of the shared content, should consitute a solid cause of action under German Law. Furthermore, centralised filesharing systems may be held liable if it can be established that they actively encourage the filesharing.[119] They are required under the resulting checking obligation to install filter systems and use these to prevent copyright infringements. The ruling issued by Düsseldorf Regional Court regarding share hosters[120] shows that it is possible that case law may develop requiring filesharing systems to be restricted to identifiable users, if these filter systems did not prove to be effective, or to shut down entirely.

Providers of centralised filesharing systems may be required to pay damages in certain cases. The liability privileges set out in sec. 8 TMG [Telemedia Act] do not apply for access providers if they have collaborated with the perpetrator of the actual infringement (sec. 8 para. 1 sent. 2 TMG [Telemedia Act]). This is particularly likely to have been the case if a filesharing system increases the possibility of copyright infringements and if its directories contain a significant amount of copyrighted content.[121] There is not yet any German case law in this area.

c. Decentralised Filesharing Systems

Unlike centralised filesharing systems, decentralised systems involve users communicating with each other without a central server. Communication is therefore achieved solely via software. Examples of this kind of site include eMule, LimeWire or Kazaa Lite++. The software alone processes the search requests and is therefore the core ele-

118 *Köster/Jürgen*, Haftung professioneller Informationsvermittler im Internet – Eine Bestandsaufnahme nach der Novellierung der Haftungsregelungen, MMR 2002, 420; *Wenzl*, Musiktauschbörsen im Internet, p. 122 ff.

119 *Wenzl*, Musiktauschbörsen im Internet, p. 126.

120 23 January 2008 LG [District Court] Düsseldorf [12 O 246/07], ZUM 2008, 338 (Rapidshare).

121 *Wenzl*, Musiktauschbörsen im Internet, p. 170.

ment of decentralised systems. The transfer of data and the actual filesharing take place in the same way as with centralised systems.

d. Liability

No suit has been brought against decentralised systems in Germany, yet. It is, however, generally agreed that the manufacturers of such software are not subject to the provisions of the TMG [Telemedia Act] as they do not use communication networks or provide access to them. It is the users themselves who search for and establish the connection, much like a search engine, using the software. Privileged liability treatment therefore does not come into consideration and the general liability provisions of copyright law and the law of torts apply.[122]

It is unlikely that manufacturers of filesharing software would be considered infringer under German law, as they do not actively participate in the filesharing process. Yet, they could be considered to be secondary contributors since their software enables illegal filesharing. However, it seems to be difficult to construe any checking or monitoring obligations since they do not have directories which could be accessed. The general view is that manufacturers of this type of software can avoid any liability by advising users that the software should not be used to commit copyright infringements.[123] Against this background it is advisable for copyright holders to engage in finding way and means to actively and effectively prevent copyright infringements via decentralised systems e. g. by developing or proving that effective filter software exists. This would ease to impose checking and monitoring obligations to manufacturers of decentralised filesharing software.

e. Cybersky Case

The *Cybersky* case is currently the only one case in Germany concerning filesharing systems. However, other than systems as eMule or Kazaa Lite++, *Cybersky* software creates a virtual network between all users of the software and makes it possible for a pay TV subscriber to stream pay TV programmes on the Internet so that other users of the software can view them without being subscribers, rather than enabling them to share single files. The information fed into the peer-to-peer network is broadcast almost in realtime and gives network members free access to various programmes. Hamburg High-

---

122 *Spindler/Leistner*, Die Verantwortlichkeit für Urheberrechtsverletzungen im Internet – Neue Entwicklungen in Deutschland und in den USA, GRUR Int 2005, 773; *Wenzl*, Musiktauschbörsen im Internet, p. 124 ff.

123 *Wenzl*, Musiktauschbörsen im Internet, p. 129; Kazaa was also declared legal in the Netherlands in the ruling 28 March 2002 Court of Appeal Amsterdam in preliminary proceedings (1370/01 SKG), AMI 2004/4, 134 (BUMA/Kazaa); the Dutch Supreme Court upheld this decision but was not in a position to give an answer if offering such type of software was legal or not. 19 December 2003, Supreme Court of the Netherlands in cassotion proceedings [CO2/186HR] (BUMA-SIEMRA/Kazaa), see also Mélanie Loos, VI. C.Internet.

er Regional Court correctly held in the *Cybersky* ruling that this was an infringement of the right of the broadcasting company to re-broadcast their programmes (sec. 87 UrhG [Copyright Act]).[124] But in this case, the provider of the software was held to be liable, especially because in its advertising it had explicitly mentioned the possibility of infringing copyrights.[125] Today *Cybersky* is online again, after having incorporated software that filters and blocks broadcasts that are secured by DRM-Systems, in particular pay TV channels. Futhermore, the advertisment has been changed. To date no further attempt to challenge the legality of *Cybersky* has been undertaken in Germany.

6. Liability of Access Providers

It is of particular importance to find ways to impose obligations on access providers to avoid any legal infringements. As gatekeepers of the Internet, this would represent a particularly effective means of fighting copyright piracy on the Internet since access providers can in theory block sites containing infringing material from a large number of users (lowest cost avoider approach). However, the legal situation in Germany in this regard is highly problematic.

a. Liability as a Secondary Contributor

Access providers enjoy special privileges, especially under sec. 8 TMG [Telemedia Act]. Providing only the infrastructure to access to third-party information they are not liable for damages if their users break the law (sec. 8 para. 1 TMG [Telemedia Act]). However, also an access provider can generally be liable as secondary contributors, but only to the extent it violates its checking and monitoring obligations after having been informed about an infringement.

There is, however, currently considerable dispute over the extent to which access providers liable for third-party infringements.[126] The majority of the courts denied any liability so far. It was held that by making Internet connections available, access providers do not actually create any new risks of any proprietary rights being infringed. They simply provide the necessary infrastructure allowing users to access third-party content.[127] Furthermore, it should also be taken into account that no obligations may be imposed on access providers unless these obligations have been shown to be sufficiently effective.

---

124 8 February 2006 OLG [Higher Regional Court] Hamburg [5 U 78/05], GRUR-RR 2006, 148; continuation of this ruling by 14 February 2007 OLG [Higher Regional Court] Hamburg [5 U 134/06], ZUM-RD 2007, 569 (Cybersky II); cf. also discussion of Cybersky I in *Brinkel*, Haftung für Peer-to-Peer-Software, CR 2006, 306.

125 8 February 2006 OLG [Higher Regional Court] Hamburg [5 U 78/05], GRUR-RR 2006, 148.

126 Restrictive, 22 January 2008 OLG [Higher Regional Court] Frankfurt [6 W 10/08], MMR 2008, 166 f.; 23 November 2007 LG [District Court] Kiel [14 O 125/07], ZUM 2008, 246; 13 December 2007 LG [District Court] Düsseldorf [12 O 550/07], ZUM-RD 2008, 151; more favourable, 12 September 2007 LG [District Court] Köln [28 O 339/07], ZUM 2007, 873 ff.

127 22 January 2008 OLG [Higher Regional Court] Frankfurt [6 W 10/08], MMR 2008, 166 f.

Blocking individual domains on a domain name server (DNS block) may be quite ineffective just because as providers can simply switch to alternative domains. The alternative to blocking a site's IP address has the disadvantage that a number of legal sites which may be accessed via the same address are also blocked. Most experienced Internet users are able to circumvent most blocks with the help of tricks such as anonymisers like AO.ON.[128] Another option would be to require access providers to install filter software to check the legality of transferred data. However, this poses significant concerns as regards the secrecy of telecommunications *(Fernmeldegeheimnis)* which is a fundamental right under Art. 10 Grundgesetz [GG] [German Constitution] (F. R.G.) and sec. 88 Telekommunikationsgesetz [TKG] [Telecommunication Act] (F. R.G).[129]

On the other hand, it also appears inappropriate to completely release access providers from any liability as secondary contributors to copyright infringements. There are cases, for example, where content or host providers are based in countries where foreign legal rulings cannot or only very difficult be enforced. It has to be taken into account that Art. 8 para. 3 of the Copyright Directive explicitely requires Member States to provide right holders means to effectively prevent their rights being infringed. Legal rules on the liability of access providers are also gradually being developed in other EU states.[130] Hence, it is not excluded that further changes to the obligations of access providers will be established, either by German courts or the lawmaker. Also voluntuary cooperations between access provider and right holders seem to be an option.

As regards damages, due to the liability privileges enjoyed by access providers under the TMG [Telemedia Act], access providers can only be held liable if it can be demonstrated that they collaborated with the party committing the actual infringement (sec. 8 para. 1 sent. 2 TMG [Telemedia Act]). Other than in rare instances, this is unlikely.

b. Administrative Blocking Order

However, it is important to note that pursuant to sec. 7 para. 2 sent. 2 TMG [Telemedia Act] access providers may also be required by the competent authorities to remove or block the use of information even if they are not in any way liable for it, i. e., they are not even liable as secondary contributors, by way of a so called administrative blocking order *(Sperrverfügung)*. Such administrative blocking orders have already been issued in Germany. For example, the Regional Government Authority *(Bezirksregierung)* in Düsseldorf has issued a number of blocking orders against Internet providers. These orders

---

128 *Schöttle*, Sperrungsverfügungen im Internet: Machbar und verhältnismäßig?, K&R 2007, 366.

129 *Schnabel*, Porn not found – Die Arcor-Sperre, K&R 2008, 26 ff.

130 In Belgium, the Tribunal de Première Instance ordered the access provider Scarlet on 29 June 2007 to install filter software. In Denmark in 2006 a provider was required to cut the Internet connection of two users who were using it to operate illegal FTP servers. The Danish provider Tele 2 was ordered in February 2008 to block access to the Swedish site www.piratebay.org. In France and England they rely on voluntary cooperation between access providers and content providers. The European Commission also rgued for this in its strategic paper "Creative Online Content in the Single Market" of 3 January 2008.

involved access to websites with content suitable to stirring up hatred against national, ethnic, racial or religious groups, a serious criminal act under German law. The courts do not appear to have been particularly critical of these regional government orders[131] and none of them appears to have been revoked by a judicial ruling. However, there is still some doubt as to whether such orders are lawful and particularly as regards whether such measures are suitable and proportionate.[132] It is doubtful whether blocking a website is a suitable measure if it is very easy to circumvent the block. It is also possible to view the blocking of an entire website as being disproportionate if only a certain part of the content it offers is of unlawful origin or may not be published.

Given that these blocking orders were based on German public law provisions and issued by German public authorities, it is difficult to apply them by analogy to private interests such as copyrights. However, as illegal copying is a criminal offence in Germany, especially if done for commercial purposes (sections 106 and 108 UrhG [Copyright Act]), it is conceivable that some legal concept may be found to achieve this by means of a "detour" via criminal and administrative law (*Gefahrenabwehr*). It could be argued that extensive copyright violations pose a threat to the legal system which is to be averted by the public authorities.

Also on European level measures to involve access providers more in the prevention of copyright infringements have been increasingly discussed in the past few years, which holds true for both private and public law.[133] It is not unlikely that this will develop into a legal concept or legal rules making it possible to bring blocking claims against access providers in Germany as well.

7. Conclusion

With the exception of content providers, the crucial problem with liability for other online service providers is the issue of what checking and cooperation obligations may be imposed to prevent copyright infringements. Technical issues are of particular importance. When it comes to enforcing their rights, it is essential for copyright holders to be able to identify the technical options and possibilities to be applied by online service providers to prevent copyright infringements. Possibly it is even in the interest of right holders to help develop new options and possibilities in this regard for their own sake. German lawmakers will most likely have to address this problem again at some point in the future. It is also likely that there will be moves towards some sort of voluntary cooperation, primarily between access providers and copyright holders, in Germany. This

131 19 March 2003 OVG [Higher Administrative Court] Münster [8 B 2567/02], NJW 2003, 2183; 10 May 2005 VG [Administrative Court] Düsseldorf [27 K 5968/02], MMR 2005, 794, 800.

132 Cf. for example *Schöttle*, Sperrungsverfügungen im Internet: Machbar und verhältnismäßig?, K&R 2007, 366, 369 f.

133 *Schnabel*, Böse Zensur, guter Filter? – Urheberrechtliche Filterpflichten für Access-Provider, MMR 2008, 281 f.

is the recommendation made by the European Commission in its paper "Creative Online Content in the Single Market" of 3 January 2008.

C. Liability of Users

There is no copyright infringement in the Internet without individuals actually committing them. When it comes to the issue of the liability of users of online content, a distinction needs to be made between uploading content and making it available for download by third parties, on the one hand, and actually downloading copyrighted material illegally, on the other hand. Another problem is that user often act anonymously in the Internet. The combat of copyright piracy is therefore dependent on effective means to identify infringers.

1. Uploading Content and Making it Available for Download

Any party offering copyrighted content for download using a filesharing system or as part of another online service is generally committing a number of copyright infringements which are considered legal offences under the German copyright law. Any user converting content only available to it in analogue format into a digital format is making reproduction in the meaning of sec. 16 UrhG [Copyright Act]. The same applies to the conversion of digital content, e. g. into mp3 format. Finally, saving such files on an internal or external storage medium constitutes a further reproduction.

Such reproduction is only covered by the private copying privilege under sec. 53 para. 1 UrhG [Copyright Act][134] to the extent that there is no intention of subsequently making the copies publicly available within the meaning of sec. 19 lit. a) UrhG [Copyright Act], whether by copying them into a folder on one's own PC which can be accessed by third parties (e. g. a shared folder for a filesharing system) or by uploading them onto a publicly accessible external server (e. g. at a host provider). Firstly, the privilege of private copying only covers passing them on to friends and family, but not making them available to a global public. Secondly, sec. 53 para. 1 UrhG [Copyright Act] only affects the right of reproduction, but does not allow infringements of the right to public reproduction by making such content publicly available under sec. 19 lit. a) UrhG [Copyright Act], which is the sole right of the copyright holder.

2. Downloading Content – Difficulties of the Privilege to make Private Copies under German Law

Downloading copyrighted material from music sharing or other websites constitutes reproduction of the original and is therefore, in principal, an infringement of the copyright holder's right of reproduction under sec. 16 UrhG [Copyright Act]. The problematic issue is how far the privilege to make private copies set out in sec. 53 para. 1 UrhG

---

134 Cf. III. B. above on this issue for offline piracy.

[Copyright Act] releases the downloading party from liability. In the offline world, making a copy of the original or even of a copy made by a third party would be permissible provided this copy is not obviously unlawful.[135]

However, when it comes to the online world, a private copy is not only illegal if it was copied from an obviously unlawful file, but also, since 1 August 2008, if it is produced from file which has obviously unlawfully been made publicly available. Protected content made available for download on the Internet is, in principle, an unlawful source within the meaning of sec. 53 UrhG [Copyright Act]. The only exception is for music which is made available by the copyright holder expressly for distribution via music filesharing systems, e. g. because the copyright holder wishes to make his music known.

The problem is however that users are only prohibited from making a private copy if the source file is *obviously* unlawful. This additional criterion of obviousness is intended to protect persons making private copies they believe to be legal and to prevent consumers being unnecessarily criminalised. The crucial aspect when making any kind of legal assessment is the user's level of awareness and of knowledge of the Internet.[136] Whether a source file with copyrighted content on the Internet should be regarded as being obviously illegal is often a matter of opinion and may only be decided on the circumstances of the individual case. One difficulty in this respect is that there is a lot of creative content freely available on the Internet, primarily from unknown artists looking to raise their profile.

A recognised sign of obvious illegality is, for example, when a film is made available for download prior to its official release or when a film has obviously been copied using a video camera.[137] It is also generally accepted as being quite clear that any content that is known to be supplied with copy protection may not be available for filesharing. Another indication is the name or title of any content made available for download.[138] No one can expect current music or film chart titles to be freely available on the Internet. Apart from that, it must be determined in the light of the facts and circumstances of the individual case whether available downloads are based on source files which are clearly illegal. The design of the website may also be important in this regard, whether it be a filesharing site or another download option. In some cases, the illegal nature of a download is explicitly mentioned or is otherwise obvious.[139]

3. Circumventing Protection Measures (Ripping Protected Online Streams)

It is illegal under German law for users to circumvent copy protection measures for online streams such as Internet radio (ripping). It is, however, legal to record a legally

135 Cf. III. B. above on offline piracy.

136 *Schricker*, Urheberrecht, § 53, No. 14c.

137 *Schricker*, Urheberrecht, § 53, No. 14c; *Wandtke/Bullinger*, Urheberrecht, § 53, No. 15.

138 *Schricker*, Urheberrecht, § 53, No. 14c; *Wandtke/Bullinger*, Urheberrecht, § 53, No. 15.

139 *Schricker*, Urheberrecht, § 53, No. 14c; *Wandtke/Bullinger*, Urheberrecht, § 53, No. 15.

transmitted radio or television programme for private purposes. This is also covered by sec. 53 para. 1 UrhG [Copyright Act]. However, under sec. 95 lit. a) UrhG [Copyright Act] the exception does not apply if technical protection measures have to be bypassed,[140] as is the case when ripping an online stream. Any such copying is illegal and results in obligations to cease and desist and to pay damages.

4. Identifying Private Users in Order to Effectively Pursue Legal Measures

A major problem arising with regard to the taking of legal action against private users who infringe copyrights online is that they generally act anonymously. The effectiveness of measures to combat such infringements is therefore dependent on the effectiveness and reliability with which infringers' identities can be established, be it uploaders or downloaders. There is software available which makes it relatively easy to identify the IP address of any computer used to commit a copyright infringement. However, the assistance of access providers is required to identify the person behind the IP address since only access providers have this information. Access providers are not liable in principle for any legal infringements committed with third-party information to which they only provide access and over the content of which they have no influence (see the liability privileges set out in sections 8-11 of the Telemedia Act).[141] Access providers cannot therefore simply be required based on alleged secondary contribution to provide information on who is behind an IP address.[142] Nevertheless, there are two alternatives for identifying parties committing infringements, both of which, however, involve certain obstacles.

a. Involving Public Prosecution Authorities

A common method has been to call on the services of public prosecution authorities *(Staatsanwaltschaft)*. The first step is for the copyright holder to file charges against an unknown party for the unlawful exploitation of copyrighted material in accordance with sec. 106 UrhG [Copyright Act]. By virtue of the obligation to provide information in criminal proceedings, as set out in sections 100 lit. g) and 100 lit. h) Strafprozessordnung [StPO] [Code of Criminal Procedure] (F. R.G.), access provider are required to provide the public prosecutor's office with details of the registered owner of an Internet connection. The copyright holder can then ask to inspect the file of the public prosecutor's office in order to establish the identity of the infringing parties and may use this information for enforcing its civil claims, while the criminal proceedings are often discontinued on the grounds of insignificance under sec. 153 lit. a) StPO [Code of Criminal Procedure]. In practice, this way of identifying users has become more difficult, however, as some prosecution authorities are more and more reluctant to act at all unless a significant number of illegal files are at play.

---

140 Cf. II. C. above on the relationship of the private copy to the technical safeguards.

141 Cf. see above IV. B.6.

142 Cf. *Schmitz/Laun*, Die Haftung kommerzieller Meinungsportale im Internet, MMR 2005, 212, concerning claims for information against portal providers and data protection.

b. Direct Request for Information from Access Providers

Section 101 UrhG [Copyright Act] sets out the civil claim for information in the case of copyright infringements. Section 101 para. 1 UrhG [Copyright Act] provides for the obligation of parties committing copyright infringements as part of any business activities to provide information on these activities. However, enforcing a direct demand for information against an access provider under this provision is only possible if the access provider is at least a secondary contributor to the relevant copyright infringement. As mentioned, for the time being this is not the case under German law.[143]

In order to provide a way round these problems, a claim for information against third parties, which may be enforced irrespective of fault, was introduced in sec. 101 para. 2 UrhG [Copyright Act] as part of the implementation of the Enforcement Directive. This gives copyright holders a direct claim for information against access providers regardless their own liability. Under sec. 101 para. 2 UrhG [Copyright Act], a request may be made for information on third parties, such as the name and address of a copyright infringer, provided such infringer used the services of an access provider for engaging in *obvious* copyright infringements. The official explanatory statement on this rule explicitly states that this only applies in cases where the infringement was committed as part of *commercial activities*.[144] Further, especially with regard to online infringements, sec. 101 para. 9 UrhG [Copyright Act] provides that information on communication data (*Verkehrsdaten*, as defined in sec. 3 no. 30 TKG [Telecommunications Act] may only be provided if a *judicial order* is obtained in advance. A judicial order is necessary since the provision of such information constitutes an infringement of the fundamental right of secrecy of telecommunications guaranteed by Art. 10 para. 1 GG [German Consitution] and may only be set aside if such order is obtained (Art. 10 para. 2 GG [German Constitution]). The practical application of these provisions involves considerable difficulties, as set forth below.

(1) Obviousness of the infringement

The first problem is that the copyright infringement has to be obvious. The official explanatory statement of the legislator makes it clear that this requirement is necessary to protect access providers. The risk of such an interference being unjustified could only be ruled out if there is no *de facto* or legal doubt regarding the obviousness of the infringement.[145] This may be controversial in borderline cases, for instance when works of not so well known artists are involved.

---

143 See IV. B.6. above.

144 Gesetzentwurf der Bundesregierung [Draft bill of the Federal Government], Entwurf eines Gesetzes zur Verbesserung der Durchsetzung von Rechten des geistigen Eigentums [Draft Act on the Improvement of the Enforcement of Intellectual Property Rights], BT-Drucks. 16/5048, p. 49.

145 Cf. *Schwarz/Brauneck*, Verbesserung des Rechtsschutzes gegen Raubkopierer auf der Grundlage der EU-Enforcement-Richtlinie und deren Umsetzung in deutsches Recht, ZUM 2006, 701.

(2) Requirement of commercial nature of the infringement

According to the official explanatory statement a claim for information against the access provider requires that both the access provider as well as the user infringing copyrights are acting on a commercial basis. Showing that this requirement is fulfilled may often be difficult with regard to the user, given that most online infringements are not of a commercial nature and take place without any consideration being charged. This condition was the subject of considerable criticism,[146] since the Enforcement Directive states in Recital 14 that Member States may choose not to include this requirement in national law. Official explanatory statement is however watering down that requirement by stating that a commercial transaction is generally assumed if its scope extends beyond that associated with private use.[147]

But nevertheless there are significant practical considerations that go against this. The requirement that the infringing party has acted on a commercial basis generally requires evidence that there have been repeated copyright infringements. Copyright holders can only attribute infringements via IP addresses. However, given the limited number of addresses available, users are often allocated dynamic IP addresses. This means that each time a user logs on to the Internet he is allocated a different IP address. It is therefore virtually impossible to meet this requirement of showing that copyrighted material is repeatedly being offered from the same IP address. There is also a problem e. g. arising from the technical infrastructure of filesharing systems. Users offering illegal downloads via a filesharing system generally offer many different music titles, but it is generally impossible to identify all of them. Often items are only displayed individually and on specific request so that the actual scope of the copyright infringements remains unknown. Although copyright holders can request other titles hoping that they are offered from the same IP address, this is hardly a viable method for identifying users offering illegal downloads in a commercial scale.[148]

The first rulings handed down by German courts regarding the commercial nature of up- or downloading activities are, however, quite lenient. Even in cases where only the exchange of a few files could be proven, the courts granted an order to disclose the identity

---

146 Vor allem *Schwarz/Brauneck*, Verbesserung des Rechtsschutzes gegen Raubkopierer auf der Grundlage der EU-Enforcement-Richtlinie und deren Umsetzung in deutsches Recht, ZUM 2006, 701; cf. Stellungnahme des Bundesrates [Comments of Federal Council] in: Gesetzentwurf der Bundesregierung [Draft bill of the Federal Government], Entwurf eines Gesetzes zur Verbesserung der Durchsetzung von Rechten des geistigen Eigentums [Draft Act on the Improvement of the Enforcement of Intellectual Property Rights], BT-Drucks. 16/5048, p. 53 ff.

147 Gesetzentwurf der Bundesregierung [Draft bill of the Federal Government], Entwurf eines Gesetzes zur Verbesserung der Durchsetzung von Rechten des geistigen Eigentums [Draft Act on the Improvement of the Enforcement of Intellectual Property Rights], BT-Drucks. 16/5048, p. 49.

148 Cf. *Schwarz/Brauneck*, Verbesserung des Rechtsschutzes gegen Raubkopierer auf der Grundlage der EU-Enforcement-Richtlinie und deren Umsetzung in deutsches Recht, ZUM 2006, 701, 704 ff. on these considerations.

of the user, if newly released or very famous songs were at issue.[149] It remains to be seen whether the German Supreme Court will also rule in favor of the rightholders.

(3) Judicial approval

There is also criticism of the fact that any claims for information made under sec. 101 para. 9 UrhG [Copyright Act] regarding communication data, e. g. the time and duration of Internet connections, require judicial approval. Some claim the approval requirement unnecessarily delays enforcement of legal claims. However, a judicial order may not be dispensed with due to considerations of German constitutional law. In order to identify IP addresses, data is required which relates to the actual communication procedure, but such data is protected under the secrecy of telecommunications set out in Art. 10 GG [German Constitution].

(4) Data storage period

A further problem when it comes to identifying infringers is that under the law as it stands access providers may not store telecommunication data any longer than necessary. There is dispute as to precisely how long is appropriate, but it is almost unanimously agreed that it is certainly not permissible to store telecommunication data for more than two months.[150] This means that the timescale for bringing claim for online infringements is severely limited. The Data Retention Directive (Directive 2006/24/EC of 15 March 2006 on the retention of data generated or processed in connection with the provision of publicly acailable electronic communications services or of public communications networks and amending Directive 2002/58/EC),[151] which provides for a required storage period of 6 to 24 months, will not be of any assistance for the time being. In Germany, it currently only applies to combating terrorism and cannot be used in cases of copyright infringement.[152] It remains to be seen how things will develop in this area. The European Court of Justice ruled in spring 2008 that data protection and the secrecy of telecommunications should be made compatible with the rights of the holders of intellectual property rights.[153] There will definitely be a move towards protection of

---

149 5 September 2008 LG [District Court] Köln [28 AR 6/08]; 26 September 2008 LG [District Court] Köln [28 OH 8/08]; 15 September 2008 LG [District Court] Oldenburg [5 O 2421/08]; more strict 26 September 2008 LG [District Court] Frankenthal [6 O 340/08] in the case of software released three months before download.

150 only 7 days 5 July 2007 AG [Local Court] Bonn [9 C 177/07], MMR 2008, 203; *Beck/Kreissig*, Tauschbörsen-Nutzer im Fadenkreuz der Strafverfolgungsbehörden, NStZ 2007, 304.

151 Official Journal of the European Union 2006 L 105/54.

152 The Federal Constitutional Court imposed this restriction during expedited proceedings on 19 March 2008 BVerfG [Federal Constituional Court] [I BvR 256/08] (Vorratsdatenspeicherung). A final decision is not expected before the end of 2008.

153 29 January 2008 ECJ [C-275/06], ZUM 2008, 288 (Productores de Música de Espana (Promusicae) ./. Telefónica de Espana (KaZaA)).

the rights of copyright holders, but it remains to be seen whether courts alone will be able to provide relief or if new legislation will be required.

D. Other Parties Potentially Liable for Online Piracy

1. Liability of Search Engine Providers

Providers of search engines such as Google or Yahoo are not entitled to privileges under the TMG [Telecommunications Act]. An analogous application of the privilege provisions to search engines is almost unanimously rejected.[154] The liability of these parties is therefore determined according to general liability principles. Most of the case law and literature relates to Google.

a. Google Results List

The Google results list in response to a query gives a list of hyperlinks to pages with the requested content, meaning that Google provides access to the relevant content. The Federal Supreme Court ruled in the *Paperboy* case that providing a link does not constitute a copyright infringement under sec. 16 UrhG [Copyright Act].[155] However, the decision did not exclude liability as a secondary contributor for providing access to unlawful content. There is as yet no reliable case law on the subject. One argument in Google's favour is that the search function is entirely automated. In addition, Google cannot be expected to monitor and check the vast number of external websites it lists. Still, Google has certain responsibilities. It is required to remove obviously illegal content from its index at the request of the copyright holder. Yet it cannot be expected to ensure that such content does not appear in the results list via an alternative route. Like with the liability of online service providers the crucial aspect here will also be whether it can be shown that effective filter solutions do exist in this regard.[156]

b. Google Image Search

There is currently significant debate over the legal position with regard to Google's image search. The search function reproduces reduced "thumbnail" images that match the search term on a Google page.[157] The images are reduced in size by using special software and posted as a link to a certain webpage. According to prevailing opinion in Germany,

---

154 *Köster/Jürgen*, Die Haftung von Suchmaschinen für Suchergebnislisten, K&R 2006, 108 ff.; Ott, Die Entwicklung des Suchmaschinen- und Hyperlink-Rechts im Jahr 2007, WRP 2008, 393.

155 17 July 2003 BGH [Federal Supreme Court] [I ZR 259/00], GRUR 2003, 958 (Paperboy).

156 Cf. above IV. B.6.

157 5 September 2003 LG [District Court] Hamburg [308 O 449/03], K&R 2004, 404; 27 February 2008 OLG [Higher Regional Court] Thüringen [2 U 319/07], ZUM 2008, 522; 27 February 2008 OLG [Higher Regional Court] Jena [2 U 319/07], GRUR-RR 2008, 223; overall, *Meyer*, Aktuelle Rechtsentwicklung bei Suchmaschinen 2007, K&R 2008, 201.

the creation of thumbnails constitutes a copyright infringement.[158] In particular, the creation of thumbnails does not constitute a permissible adaptation of a picture within the meaning of sec. 24 UrhG [Copyright Act]. The issue is, however, whether the display of such thumbnails in the Google's image search list constitutes an infringement. Just recently, the District Court Hamburg handed down a decision holding that such infringement exists. It held that no consent of the copyright owner can be assumed. Google cannot invoke the right of quotation pursuant to sec. 51 UrhG [Copyright Act] or any other limitation of copyright set out in the Act. Finally, it pointed out that there is no "fair use doctrine" in Germany like there is in the USA, which is based on the notion of the benefit of such reproduction for the public.[159] An appeal is currently pending in this matter. In an earlier decision, however, it was decided that copyright holders may not make claims based on their copyrights if they simultaneously use methods to optimise the Google search result for their own content. Such claim would be abusive.[160]

c. Google Book Search

Google's continually expanding book search also raises certain legal issues. The prevailing opinion in legal literature in Germany is that it is unlawful under German law to scan copyrighted material without the consent of the copyright holder.[161] In additional to the Google book search, there are now also other projects for digitalising books, but in these cases the content of the books is being compiled with the consent of the copyright holders.[162] In the USA, however, it is still considered permissible to compile copyrighted material without the express consent of the copyright holder, namely by virtue of the fair use doctrine, although this still lacks any stable and reliable case law.[163] This significant difference between the legal position in Germany and the USA means that determining the applicable law is crucial.[164] German law is only applicable to scanning in material if the actual scanning takes place within Germany. The situation is different for the distribution of the scanned content. It is arguable that this might infringe the right holders rights granted under the UrhG [Copyright Act] although the work might be first published e. g. in the US. However, it should be noted that generally only extracts, but not entire texts, are available, meaning that not all of the scanned material is freely available at Google Book Search, which would certainly be a clear copyright infringement.[165]

---

158 5 September 2003 LG [District Court] Hamburg [308 O 449/03], GRUR-RR 2004, 313 (thumbnails); *Wandtke/Bullinger*, Urheberrecht, § 72, No. 23.

159 29 September 2008 LG [District Court] Hamburg [308 O 42/06], MMR 2009, 55.

160 27 February 2008 OLG [Higher Regional Court] Thüringen [2 U 319/07], ZUM 2008, 522.

161 Ott, Die Google Buchsuche – Eine massive Urheberrechtsverletzung?, GRUR Int 2007, 562; cf. also *Heckmann*, Zum Erfordernis der Einwilligung in eine retrospektive Digitalisierung von Printwerken zu Werbezwecken, AfP 2007, 314.

162 Ott, Die Google Buchsuche – Eine massive Urheberrechtsverletzung?, GRUR Int 2007, 562, 563.

163 Ott, Die Google Buchsuche – Eine massive Urheberrechtsverletzung?, GRUR Int 2007, 562

164 Ott, Die Google Buchsuche – Eine massive Urheberrechtsverletzung?, GRUR Int 2007, 562, cf. Above III. D. for comparative aspects.

165 Cf. *Meyer*, Aktuelle Rechtsentwicklung bei Suchmaschinen 2007, K&R 2008, 201.

2. Manufacturers of Online Recording Software

One potentially infringing onlice services are virtual video recorders. Such recorders allow users to record individual programmes from Internet TV stations which they then receive via a streaming service. These services are illegal under German law, at least if offered on a commercial basis (i. e., on the basis of one-off fees or a flat-rate), since they infringe the broadcasting rights of broadcasting companies under sec. 87 UrhG [Copyright Act]. The holders of copyrights to the actual programmes may also have claims stemming from their right of reproduction under sec. 16 UrhG [Copyright Act] is being infringed.

Dresden Higher Regional Court correctly ruled that the provider of such a virtual video recorder had unlawfully reproduced the right holders programmes within the meaning of sec. 16 UrhG [Copyright Act] by storing them on its server. These reproductions would then be viewed by the user on some display following the download. This cannot be viewed as a temporary reproduction within the meaning of sec. 44 lit. a) UrhG [Copyright Act]. The storage of the material is not temporary or incidental in nature (as is the case with caching, for example, which is used to save time for each new access), but has independent economic significance.[166] Nor does the right to make private copies under sec. 53 para. 1 sent. 1 UrhG [Copyright Act] apply here. In contrast to the means available to private end users to receive and record programmes, the service exceeds accepted private use since it involves third parties working for a commercial profit.[167]

Another source of potential infringement is so called "intelligent recording software". However, users can use this software to access numerous Internet radio or TV stations, simultaneously in certain cases, and to record music or film content of their choice. This software generally works by identifying the various types of metadata, such as title, artist or album, which generally come with these programmes. The recorded title is then stored as a separate file in a specified file on the user's computer. There is hardly any loss of quality of the kind experienced with analogue recordings.[168] The sale and use of such software has so far been considered legal under German law as such recording is covered by the privilege of private copies as long as the source, hence the respective station, is not obviously unlawful. This might be the case for so called pirate stations. The fact whether a station has the required licences from the rights holders is, however, hardly to determine by the individual user. The only option currently open to copyright holders wishing to use of the new media of Internet TV and radio is to negotiate their licensing agreements so that their titles do not contain such metadata or even so that additional protection measures are applied when their titles are broadcasted. In the latter case, any circumvention of these measures would constitute an infringement of sec. 95 UrhG [Copyright Act] and claims could be brought either against makers of software to circumvent such measures or against the user applying them.[169]

---

166 28 November 2006 OLG [Higher Regional Court] Dresden [14 U 1071/06], K&R 2007, 278, 279; cf. II. C. above on privileges under UrhG [Copyright Act], § 44a (F. R.G.).

167 28 November 2006 OLG [Higher Regional Court] Dresden [14 U 1071/06], K&R 2007, 278; the copy may also be made by third parties for private use (see III. B. above).

168 *Langhoff/Oberndörfer/Jani*, Der Zweite Korb der Urheberrechtsreform, ZUM 2007, 593, 601.

3. Responsibility for Links

The *Paperboy* ruling held that the provision of links to copyrighted content does not constitute unlawful reproduction of such content.[170] The manual provision of links to unlawful content can, however, be prohibited, for example in the case of links to sources of software for breaking copy protection measures (e. g. AnyDVD) on the website of a computer magazine. The provider of an online magazine is required under the principles on the liability of secondary contributors not to provide such links, since would amount to advertising for designed to circumvent safeguards against unauthorised copying and would cause and objectively support the commission of copyright infringements under sec. 95 lit. a) para. 3 no. 1 UrhG [Copyright Act].[171]

E. International Issues in an Online Environment

The territoriality principle must be considered when it comes to copyright infringements in the Internet. Copyrights and neighbouring rights are granted by individual countries. Each country may only issue binding provisions for its own territory. Provisions on copyright infringements can therefore only be applied to infringements committed in the relevant country. The Internet is characterised by the ubiquity of content unlike any other medium. Content can be accessed from virtually anywhere in the world. The challenge for copyright law is determining whether an infringement is subject to any national legal provisions at all.

The correct starting point is the place of primary infringement of copyright.[172] This is fairly easy to determine for users of online content. As soon as content is accessed by users, the place of infringement is the location where the reproduction takes place, i. e., the location of the user at the time. This is more difficult to determine for providers. When copyrighted material is made publicly available on the Internet, the place of infringement may be considered to be the place where the material is being offered (i. e., the location of the server or the upload) or all of the locations where downloads take place. This is a moot point. The prevailing tendency is towards the latter alternative (in line with the so-called Bogsch theory)[173] so that the place of jurisdiction is essentially anywhere the material can be accessed and downloaded. Despite this broad approach,

---

169 Cf. IV. C.3. above on the circumvention of protection measures.

170 17 July 2003 BGH [Federal Supreme Court] [I ZR 259/00], GRUR 2003, 958 (Paperboy).

171 28 July 2005 OLG [Higher Regional Court] München [29 U 2887/05], ZUM 2005, 896 (Heise online); 14 November 2007 LG [District Court] München I [21 O 6742/07]. Juris; in conjunction with the relevant legal provisions for the protection of minors, the same applies to links to content jeopardising the protection of minors. 18 October 2007 BGH [Federal Supreme Court] [I ZR 102/05], MMR 2008, 400 (ueber18.de).

172 *Hoeren/Sieber*, Handbuch Multimedia Recht, § 25, No. 196.

173 *Berger*, Die internationale Zuständigkeit bei Urheberrechtsverletzungen in Internet-Websites aufgrund des Gerichtsstands der unerlaubten Handlung nach Art. 5 Nr. 3 EuGVO, GRUR Int. 2005, 465, 468; *Schack*, Urheber- und Urhebervertragsrecht, [No. 932 f.].

there have been attempts to limit the jurisdiction of the courts.[174] Accordingly, making copyrighted material available on a website only constitutes a copyright infringement in those places for which the website is intended.[175] This comes down to the individual case. A website may be regarded as intended for Germany if, for example, the top-level domain is ".de" or the site is in German. This is then clearly intended for German users and is therefore subject to German copyright law. In other cases the site must be carefully analyzed on a case basis in order to determine whether an intention for Germany can be assumed.

V. Legal Consequences

A. Claims to Cease and Desist

Claims to cease and desist under sec. 97 para. 1 UrhG [Copyright Act] are intended to prevent future unlawful use of copyrighted material and are of crucial importance in practice. Cease and desist claims may be asserted irrespective of whether the party held liable is at fault, Activities constituting secondary contribution to an infringement are sufficient to justify a claim to cease and desist, provided there is a risk of an infringement being repeated. This is indicated by the initial infringement and may only be remedied by the infringing party by means of an enforceable order to cease and desist. Claims to cease and desist may also be asserted as a preventative measure in cases where no infringement has been committed, but where there is a demonstrable risk of this happening (risk of initial infringement).

B. Destruction, Recall and Surrender

Under sec. 98 UrhG [Copyright Act], copyright holders are entitled to assert claims against the infringing party to destroy any copies of material in its possession which has been unlawfully produced, disseminated or is intended for unlawful dissemination. Alternatively, copyright holders may demand that any copies in the infringing party's possession be surrendered in return for suitable remuneration, which may not exceed the manufacturing costs. Claims for destruction apply *mutatis mutandis* to any equipment in the infringing party's possession that was primarily used to make the illegal copies. Copyright holders also have the option of demanding the recall or permanent deletion of any unlawful copies available through any distribution channels.

C. Claims for Information

If an infringement takes place in the context of business activities, i. e., where the illegal copies are not simply distributed for free or made freely available on the Internet, copy-

---

[174] See e. g. *Hoeren/Sieber*, Handbuch Multimedia Recht, § 25, No. 281.

[175] 15 February 2007 BGH [Federal Supreme Court] [I ZR 114/04], GRUR 2007, 871 (Wagenfeld-Leuchte); *Hoeren/Sieber*, Handbuch Multimedia Recht, § 25, No. 281.

right holders are entitled to demand that the infringing party provide information on the origin, distribution and prices of the illegal copies in accordance with sec. 101 para. 1 UrhG [Copyright Act]. In Germany, claims to cease and desist and claims for information are generally made against the infringing party initially so that claims for damages and claims against other parties can be subsequently made.

In the event of an obvious infringement, or in cases where the copyright holder has brought a legal action against the infringing party, claims for information may also be asserted under sec. 101 para. 2 UrhG [Copyright Act] against third parties who are not directly involved in the commission of an infringement. For example, claims may be made if the third party had enough illegal copies in their possession to suggest a commercial operation, or if they availed themselves of services infringing rights of third parties, or if they provided services used for this purpose, or if they were involved in the production or distribution of copyright-infringing copies or other products or services.

Such claims for information against parties not directly involved in the commission of an infringement may principally be asserted against forwarding agents which import illegal copies on a large scale. They are also the legal basis for claims for information against access providers asserted in order to identify the individual behind an IP address, albeit that a court order is required in these cases.[176]

D. Inspection

Section 101 lit. a) UrhG [Copyright Act] also entitles copyright holders to make an inspection claim if there is sufficient likelihood of an infringement. This claim may also be enforced by means of a preliminary injunction. Such claims give copyright holders an opportunity under civil law to document material held by the alleged infringing party and which may later be used as evidence. The competent court must ensure that the alleged infringer's legitimate confidentiality interests are met.

E. Damages

Damages may be payable under sec. 97 para. 1 UrhG [Copyright Act] where the infringing party is deemed to be at fault, even through negligence. This is almost always the case where intellectual property rights have been infringed. It should be taken into account with Internet providers that they have extensive privileges under the Telemedia Act with regard to damages (with the exception of content providers). It is virtually inconceivable that claims for damages could be brought against access and cache providers.[177] In line with standard German legal practice, claims may only be asserted for the actual damages incurred, possibly in the form of compensation for lost licence royalties.[178]

---

176 Cf. IV. C.4.b above.

177 Cf. IV. B.1 above.

178 Cf. see *Diana Kaufmann*, Trademark Piracy, II. B.2., on assessing damages.

VI. Enforcement

A. Civil Action

1. Plaintiff's Right of Action

Both copyright holders and exclusive licencees are entitled to assert claims as plaintiffs. Collecting societies also have this right under sec. 13 UrhWG [German Copyright Administration Act].

2. Warning Letter

In cases where an amicable solution seems possible, e. g. vis-à-vis individual infringing only on a low scale or vis-à-vis reputable online providers in the business of which an infringement occurred it is recommendable to approach the other side by a warning letter first. Generally the right holders can recoup the incurred attorney fees for such warning letter to the extent provided by Rechtsanwaltsvergütungsgesetz [RVG] [Attorney Fee Act] (F. R.G.). With respect to consumers, however, attorney fees are limited to EUR 100.

3. Preliminary Injunction versus Action on the Merit

Preliminary injunctions under sec. 940 Zivilprozessordnung [ZPO] [Civil procedure statute] (F. R.G.) have the benefit that they provide a relatively quick way to safeguard the relevant rights. They also require less evidence of an infringement than is the case with principal proceedings. The claim only has to be credibly demonstrated, although there must also be a certain degree of urgency involved.

The infringing party may demand the institution of action on the merits, in which all claims must be properly proven (sec. 926 ZPO [Civil procedure statute]). If a preliminary injunction turns out to be unjustified in either legal or *de facto* terms, the copyright holder is required to pay the alleged infringer damages in this regard (sec. 945 ZPO [Civil procedure statute]).[179]

B. Customs Seizures

Customs authorities can also be called on the combat copyright infringements. This is because pirate copies of films, CDs, software and computer games are also produced abroad on a large scale and imported into Germany or the EU. There are two options available under German law:

---

179 Cf. *Claudia Milbradt*, Enforcement of Intellectual Property Rights in Germany, I. A.2., on preliminary injunctions and principal proceedings.

1. German Custom Seizures

German customs seizures are governed by sec. 111 lit. b) UrhG [Copyright Act], which relates to Germany's external borders. Customs authorities may only act if specifically requested to do so. Any such request is valid for one year which must then be renewed. Any suspect items discovered by the customs authorities will be seized if they clearly infringe the rights that form the subject of the request. The alleged infringing party and the copyright holder are then notified and the alleged infringer has 2 weeks within which to submit an objection to the destruction of the items. The goods are destroyed in the event that no such objection is received. If an objection is made, the copyright holder must apply for a preliminary injunction from a civil court. The goods can then be destroyed once the injunction has been obtained.[180] The destruction of the items takes place at the applicant's risk.

2. European Customs Seizures

Section 111 lit. c) UrhG [Copyright Act] also provides for customs seizures under EU law as part of the implementation of the Customs Regulation (Council Regulation (EC) 1383/2003 of 22 July 2003 concerning customs action against goods suspected of infringing certain intellectual property rights and the measures to be taken against goods found to have infringed such rights).[181] The key difference to German customs seizures is that the customs authorities can take action on the basis of a probable infringement (i. e. the infringement does not have to be obvious). The alleged infringing party only has 10 days in which to submit a complaint.[182]

---

180 Cf. *Claudia Milbradt*, Enforcement of Intellectual Property in Germany.

181 Cf. *Claudia Milbradt*, Enforcement of Intellectual Property in Germany.

182 Cf. *Diana Kaufmann*, Trademark Piracy, III. B., for details of European customs seizures relating to intellectual property rights.

Product Piracy in China

LING HO/AUDREY SHUM

I. China IP Legal Framework

The PRC Trademark Law, Patent Law, Copyright Law and Anti-Unfair Competition Law together with the relevant subsidiary legislation and judicial interpretations form the backbone of the IP legal framework in China. Except for the Anti-Unfair Competition Law, all IP laws and regulations went through major reforms in early 2000 as part of China's effort to bring its IP laws in line with international standards as well as to comply with its obligations under TRIPS (Agreement on Trade-Related Aspects of Intellectual Property Rights). The new China Patent Law has been promolugated and will come into effect on 1 October 2009.

China is a party to several important International Conventions relating to IP, including the Paris Convention (Paris Convention for the Protection of Industrial Property of 20 March 1883); the Madrid Agreement for the International Registration of Trademarks, the Protocol Relating to the Madrid Agreement, the Berne Convention for the Protection of Literary and Artistic Works, the Universal Copyright Convention, the Geneva Phonograms Convention, the PCT (Patent Cooperation Treaty) and the Trademark Law Treaty.

Infringements of IP in China expose an infringer not only to civil and criminal liabilities, but also to administrative penalties, which are quite peculiar to China.

II. Trademarks

A. Legal Requirements for Trademark Protection under the China Trademark Law

Trademark registrations are valid for 10 years and may be renewed every 10 years. China has adopted a "first to file" trademark filing system i. e. in the event of a conflict between competing applications for registration for similar or identical marks, the person who filed the first application will generally be entitled to register the mark. A registered mark may be cancelled on various grounds, including that the mark has not been used for 3 consecutive years or that registration was obtained through deceptive or improper means or that the mark is non-distinctive. The Trademark Law also gives additional protection to well known trademarks.

B. Infringing Behaviour

The trademark owner's exclusive right to use the mark is infringed by anyone who (i) uses a mark identical or confusingly similar mark to the registered mark without the owner's permission on the same or similar goods (or services) for which the infringed mark is registered; (ii) sells goods (or services) bearing an infringing mark; or (iii) actually replaces the original trademark on a product with his own. Any person who sells without knowledge of the infringement, who can prove that his goods were acquired legally, and reveals the source of the infringing goods may be exempted from liability to pay damages.

C. Parallel Imports

The issue of parallel imports is not expressly addressed in Chinese laws relating to protection of IP. There is, however, one well known case in this area; the highly controversial *Lux* soap case. In the *Lux* soap case, the Chinese exclusive licencee of Unilever managed to obtain a judgment against the defendant who claimed to be selling parallel imported *Lux* soap. However, the judgment does not seem to have created a floodgate of court actions against or involving parallel imported products. One of the reasons may be that in the *Lux* soap case, the Court was never totally convinced by the defendant's claim that the soaps it sold originated from Unilever or were licensed by Unilever.

III. Patents

A. Legal Requirements for Patent Protection according to China Patent Law

The Patent Law and its Implementing Regulation (2001) govern the protection of inventions, utility models and designs. An invention or utility model must be novel, inventive and of practical applicability to be registrable as a patent. In this context, novelty means that no identical invention or utility model has been disclosed in China or anywhere in the world or publicly used or made known to the public in China before the filing date. The novelty requirement has been changed by the new Patent Law. The new Patent Law requires "absolute novelty" for patentability. As a result, the law will no longer distinguish publication or use of a technology subject to a patent or patent application in China from publication or use of a technology outside of China. For registrability of designs, only the novelty requirement applies. China has a "first-to-file" rather than a "first-to-use" system of entitlement to patent protection.

Patent protection for inventions lasts for a period of 20 years, whereas the term of protection for utility models and designs is 10 years. The patentee must pay an annual fee beginning with the year in which the patent right was granted; a failure to do so will terminate the patent right before the expiration of its protection period.

Since China is a signatory to the PCT and the Paris Convention, a patent applicant can designate China as one of the countries in its PCT application or file a national patent application in China claiming priority of an earlier patent filed in one of the signatory territories under the Paris Convention (for example: Germany) in respect of the same invention, utility model or design.

B. Infringing Behaviour

Following the grant of a patent for an invention or a utility patent, generally, and except in the case of compulsory licensing, no one may make, use, sell or offer to sell the patented product or use the patented process or use or sell a product manufactured using the patented process, without the patentee's permission. The patentee also has the right to prevent unauthorised imports of infringing products and to prohibit an unauthorised offer for sale. However, a person who uses or sells without knowledge that the product is patented and who can prove that the product comes from a lawful source will not be liable to pay damages.

Similarly, without the design patentee's authority, no one may make or sell a product incorporating the patented design, for production or business operation purposes. However, under the current PRC Patent Law, using or offering for sale of a design patent without authorisation is not considered an act of infringement. As a result, when preparing for a design patent infringement action, a complainant would have to obtain an actual sample of the infringing product, either by purchasing it directly from the infringer or through an evidence preservation order, as evidence of the design infringement. Evidence such as marketing brochures, cost quotations, price lists, etc. are generally considered evidence of "offer for sale" only, which is not an act of infringement for design patents. However, this is about to be changed.

Under the new Patent Law "offer for sale" will be considered an act of infringement for design patents.

IV. Copyright Law

A. Legal Requirements for Copyright Protection according to China Copyright Law

The Copyright Law protects literary works, oral works, musical, operatic, dramatic and acrobatic works, fine art, architectural works, photographic works, cinematographic works (and other works created by a similar method), engineering drawings, design drawings, graphic works such as maps, sketches and models, computer software and other works as provided by law. The term of protection of most copyrights is generally 50 years beginning from the first production or publication of the work.

Registration is not a pre-requisite for copyright protection in China. However, the China Copyright Registration Office offers a registration service to copyright owners. The registration process is mainly an administrative process. There is no substantive examination on originality, artistic quality or other legal criteria for copyright subsistence as required under the Copyright Law.

While registration is not a pre-requisite, registration for important copyright works or works subject to a potential infringement litigation is generally recommended. Despite the lack of substantive examination in the copyright registration process, the copyright registration would serve as *prima facie* evidence of copyright ownership.

B. Infringing Behaviour

Copyright may be infringed by various restricted acts including copying, publishing, exploiting or broadcasting a work without the permission of the copyright owner. However, despite the law reform in early 2001, the issue of three-dimensional copying remains a controversial and uncertain area.

C. Internet Privacy

The Judicial Interpretation issued by the Supreme People's Court on "The Explanation on Certain Questions on the Applicable Law relating to copyright dispute cases involving the Internet" provides some guidance to the Court in determining some difficult issues when handling Internet related copyright infringement cases including: the determination of the jurisdiction of the Court and the liability and responsibility of the Internet service provider. Under this Judicial Interpretation, an Internet service provider will be held jointly liable for the copyright infringement committed by its cusomter or user if it has been notified of the infringing activities but has failed to take any action to take down the infringing materials. The Judicial Interpretation also obliges an Internet service provider to provide the registration details of its customer or user upon receiving from the copyright owner a demand which is supported by proof of copyright ownership and evidence of infringement. This Judicial Interpretation has helped many copyright owners in resolving Internet piracy cases swiftly by working with the more reputable Internet service provider which hosts the infringing contents thereby eliminating the need to locate and negotiate with the content provider.

The movie and music industries have been very active in pursuing and enforcing their rights against infringers in PRC. The MPAA (Motion Picture Association of America) as well as the IFPI have been very active in pursuing the rights of its members and have brought numerous actions against Internet service providers and website operators for "sharing" of illegal copy of its members' movies and has received over RMB 2,000,000 compensation since it started its vigorous enforcement strategies in 2006. Companies like Universal Music, Sony BMG Music Entertainment and Warner Music have brought legal actions in China against leading search engine websites operated by local companies as well as international companies. The recent high profile cases brought by these music companies include their joint actions against Baidu and Yahoo. They were successful in their action against Yahoo, but failed in their action against Baidu. The music companies have since filed a new action against Baidu, which is still on-going.

V. Anti-Unfair Competition Law

A. Protection of unregistered trademark, get-up or goodwill

The Anti-Unfair Competition Law filled a significant gap in China's intellectual property protection regime. Previously there had been no specific protection for unregistered trademarks or the get-up or trade dress of well-known products. The unauthorised use of "... the characteristic name, packaging or get-up of a well-known commodity" is now prohibited. In corroboration with this, the Trademark Law now specifically extends protection to unregistered well-known trademarks by prohibiting application for registration or use of another confusingly similar mark in relation to identical or similar commodities when confusion is likely to result. The *Starbuck* and the *Ferrero Rocher* cases are two recent cases which demonstrate the application of the PRC Anti-Unfair Competition Law. In both cases, the defendants adopted the get-up or trade dress of the IP owners' products/services as well as their names in Chinese characters or "pin-yin" (i. e. the spelling of the sound of the Chinese name of the product).

B. Protection of Trade Secrets

The Anti-Unfair Competition Law also protects trade secrets. "Trade secrets" are defined as "*... technological information and business information not in the public domain, which brings economic benefits to the party entitled thereto, which is of practical use, and which is kept confidential by the party entitled thereto*".

The Anti-Unfair Competition Law prohibits general business operators or any person from obtaining commercial secrets by unfair means disclosing, using or permitting others to use commercial secrets belonging to others, and breaching confidentiality agreements. It also provides some basic guidelines to trade secrets owners on the types of protective measures they could apply to safeguard their trade secrets.

VI. Enforcement

In most cases, IP owners have the option of suing the infringer in a Chinese Court or bringing administrative actions through administrative authorities. In blatant infringement cases, particularly trademark counterfeiting, the more popular avenue by far is the administrative route. It is also possible for an IP owner to enlist the help of customs if it is aware of an export or import of infringing products. If the seriousness of the infringement justifies, the infringers may be subject to criminal prosecution.

A. Court Actions

1. Which court?

Generally, the PRC court system is divided into 4 levels: Basic People's Court, Intermediate People's Court, Higher People's Court and the Supreme People's Court. Most IP disputes have to be commenced at the Intermediate People's Court level. However, a number of Basic People's Courts in relatively more developed commercial or industrial areas have now been granted the jurisdiction to hear certain intellectual property related disputes.

In IP infringement cases, the jurisdiction of the court is determined by (i) the place where a defendant is based or (ii) the place where the infringing activities took place. In respect of contractual disputes, depending on the existence of any agreement of the parties with regard to the jurisdiction of the court, the court located in the place where (i) the defendant or the complainant locates, (ii) the contract is performed or executed, or (iii) the subject matter is located, may have jurisdiction over the dispute. Where there is more than one defendant in a case, there may be more than one court which may have jurisdiction over the case.

Where choices are available to a complainant, it is important to select a court which is the most appropriate to hear the case. The complainant should consider issues including the experience of the court in conducting a particular type of intellectual property right disputes, the reputation and experience of the court, the impartiality of the court, the appellant court of that court, etc. For example, a complainant may wish to avoid litigating a dispute in the hometown of a defendant, particularly when it is not a very developed jurisdiction.

2. What do you need to commence an infringement action if you are a foreign company?

- A complaint
- A legalised and notarised power of attorney in favour of your local legal representatives
- A legalised and notarised certificate of incorporation
- Copy documents in support of the complaint. For example, infringing samples, marketing brochures, invoices, etc.
- Payment of court fees. The amount of court fees payable is proportionate to the claimed amount.
- For utility patent cases the courts would also require the provision of a search report issued by the PRC State Intellectual Property Office to show that the novelty to the utility patent in suit has not been destroyed at the time of filing. Under the new Patent Law, the requirement has been extended to design patent infringement cases.

3. Procedures for Intellectual Property Litigation

Once a complaint has been filed, the court would consider whether the complaint has included all the basic facts for establishing a *prima facie* case and whether it has jurisdiction over the case. According to the China Civil Procedure Law, the Court shall decide within 7 days whether to accept a complaint. Once the complaint has been accepted, the Court shall serve the complaint on the defendant within 5 days. The defendant will have 15 days to file its defence from the date it receives the complaint.

One thing which may be peculiar to litigation in China is the lack of importance attached to the filing of a defence by a defendant. Under Chinese laws, a defendant's right to defend a complaint will not be lost simply because it fails to file its defence by the deadline imposed by the court. There is also no procedure similar to that of many common law jurisdictions which allows a complainant to apply for a judgment for default of filing a defence. The defendant can still file evidence and appear in hearings to be held at a later stage despite its failure to file a defence.

4. Evidence

There is no discovery process similar to that of many common law jurisdictions. Generally, the burden of proof is on the party who asserts a particular fact or allegation, except for the case of an infringement of a process patent. In theory, the Court has the power to investigate into the matter and ask the parties to provide for information. However, in practice, a complainant will have to ensure that it has sufficient evidence to prove its claims.

5. Hearings

At an early stage of the litigation, the Court will hold an evidence exchange hearing. At the hearing, the parties will be asked to exchange their respective evidence and produce the originals for inspection. The parties will also be given an opportunity to challenge any evidence produced in respect of its admissibility, relevancy or authenticity, etc. The Court would also use this opportunity to understand the key points of the dispute. Where the facts are very simple, this could be the only hearing held for a case. However, in practice, there will be more than one hearing for most foreign related intellectual property cases.

6. Asset Preservation/Evidence Preservation/Injunction

If there is *prima facie* evidence that a party is conducting infringing acts or will soon do so resulting in damages to a trademark, copyright or patent that are difficult to remedy, the IP owner may apply to the Court for injunction, asset preservation and/or evidence preservation measures prior to the commencement of or in the course of a court action. An interested party may apply to the Court for preservation of evidence before institut-ing proceedings if the evidence is likely to be destroyed or will be difficult to be obtained later. The applicant will be required to give a sufficient bond or undertaking to the Court to compensate the defendant if it turns out at the end of the trial that the relief should not have been granted.

7. Common Defence Strategies

General

In the course of the evidence exchange hearing, any deficiency in any formality that should have been complied with by the complainant would normally be vigorously challenged. So, it is important that the complainant takes care of all formalities (such as legalisation and notarisation) properly.

For documents originated from China, the complainant should be in the position to produce the original evidence. Copy documents may be vigorously challenged and would most likely be rejected.

Patents

It is a common strategy in patent infringement cases that a defendant would seek to stay an infringement action by filing an invalidation action with the China State IP Office. Such an action is particularly common in design and utility patent infringement cases. The Chinese Courts would usually grant an order to stay a utility or design patent infringement case if a defendant files an invalidation action against the patent in suit before the deadline for the filing of the defence expires unless (i) the search report produced by the complainant shows that novelty of the utility patent in suit has not been destroyed; (ii) the defendant can produce sufficient proof that the patent in suit has already been made public; (iii) the grounds of the invalidation application are obviously deficient; or (iv) any other reasons. The Chinese Courts would be less inclined to stay an invention patent infringement action because an invention patent would have been substantially examined by the China State IP Office.

Trademarks

Recent developments in the law show that an infringer may also be able to utilise the strategy of challenging the validity of a trademark for the purpose of delaying or staying a trademark infringement action. If this practice is allowed or not properly regulated, trademark owners may be unfairly prejudiced and it may become more difficult to enforce trademarks in China. Unfortunately, there are currently insufficient rules and regulations to facilitate a uniform handling of this type of issue and to prevent abuses of the process. Further, the Supreme People's Court is actually seeking to introduce a new judicial interpretation which may facilitate the use of such a delaying strategy. The Supreme People's Court is currently consulting the public on this new judicial interpretation. If the judicial interpretation is passed in its current form, infringement actions may be stayed pending the final determination of simultaneous opposition or cancellation actions, which would be a major set-back to the progress made to the trademark enforcement system. Unless the Trademark Office and the Review Board are able to expedite cancellation and opposition proceedings, which, at a first instance, currently take at least 3–5 years on average, this would allow an infringer to delay a trademark infringement action easily for 3-5 years. Moreover, unless the clarity and the availability of interim injunction improve, the IP owner may be left with no interim relief pending the long stay of the action.

Copyright

If a copyright owner does not have any copyright registration over its copyright work before it commences an action, the infringer would often challenge the ownership and subsistence of the copyright work in question. Unless the copyright owner keeps a good record of the creation of its copyright work, the owner would have the onerous burden to rebut the infringer's challenges particularly when the copyright work in question was created a long time ago and it might be difficult to trace records.

B. Administrative Actions

For cases relating to trademark infringement, counterfeiting of names, packaging, get-up or other misrepresentation on the quality or origin of goods, a complaint can be filed with the AIC (Administrative for Industry and Commerce) and/or the TSB (Technical Services Bureau). The local offices of the State Intellectual Property Offices and the Copyright Bureau also have power under the relevant laws to handle patent and copyright related complaints administratively. However, due to the nature of patent and copyright complaints, which often requires a good understanding of the interpretation and application of the law, the limited resources of these authorities means the administrative route for patent and copyright infringement cases is often less effective.

The benefits of using the administrative route, especially an action brought with the AIC or TSB, are its relatively low costs and speediness. Authorities like the AIC or TSB have power to conduct raids, seize the infringing products and destroy them if the seizure was not challenged, order a fine and enjoin future infringement. However, an administrative authority generally has no power to order an infringer to pay damages to a complainant. Having said that, the complainant who has successfully brought an AIC action could also file a court action for damages based on the AIC decision.

C. Customs Actions

In addition to the administrative actions discussed above, an intellectual property right owner can also enlist the assistance of Customs. The Implementing Methods of the Regulations of the Protection of Intellectual Property by Customs of the People's Republic of China allows an IP owner to record his/her rights with the Customs office headquarters in Beijing. The recordal process is fairly simple and once completed, the recordal is valid for 10 years.

If an IP owner receives intelligence that certain infringing products are about to be exported from or imported into China, the IP owner can file an application to Customs requesting Customs to detain the suspected infringing products. Alternatively, if Customs discover suspected infringing products when conducting spot checks of export and import cargos, they will notify the IP owner who has recorded its rights with the Customs. Upon receipt of the request and the relevant intelligence from the IP owner, Customs will also inspect and detain the suspected shipments. In both cases, the IP owner will have to provide a bond and also pay for any expenses incurred by Customs for detaining the infringing goods.

After the infringing goods have been detained, the IP owner may bring a court action based on the infringing goods detained. Alternatively, the owner could rely on Customs to make a decision regarding the detained goods. If Customs determines that the detained goods are infringing products, and such a determination is not challenged by any party, Customs has the power to confiscate and dispose of the goods by donating them to charity, transferring them to the IP right owner for consideration, auctioning them after the infringing features have been removed, or destroying the goods. Again, Customs do not have authority to order any damages against the owner or shipper of the infringing goods. The IP owner has to commence a court action if it intends to seek damages based on the amount of the infringing goods seized.

D. Criminal Actions

For a more serious infringement, an infringer could be prosecuted and held criminally liable. If convicted, the infringer could be liable for a fine as well as imprisonment. The China Criminal Law requires a certain threshold to be met before a riminal action can be brought against an infringer of certain intellectual property rights.

In order to increase the deterrent effect, the Supreme People's Court and the Supreme Procuratorate issued a joint judicial interpretation towards the end of 2004 to lower the threshold for criminal punishment for crimes of counterfeiting trademarks, selling goods using counterfeit registered trademarks or producing or selling fake registered trademarks. The general threshold for criminal punishment has now been reduced to activities resulting in illegal revenues exceeding RMB 50,000 or illegal profits exceeding RMB 30,000 for individuals, and RMB 150,000 or RMB 90,000 respectively for legal entities. The value of illegal revenues is calculated based on the value of the infringing goods, rather than the value of the genuine goods.

According to the Xinhua News Agency report in April 2008, an individual in Beijing was sent to jail for a year and fined RMB 10,000 (USD 1,430) for selling fake DVDs. He is the first man to be imprisoned in Beijing for criminal piracy. This case involves over 10,000 fake DVDs.

E. Other alternatives

As well as the common channels above, an IP owner may also have other alternatives to stop infringing activities, directly or indirectly, if it is operating in a regulated industry such as the pharmaceutical, food, telecommunication, software industry, etc. So, it is always worthwhile to check regulations governing the manufacturing and distribution of a specific product to explore other options available, particularly in more complex infringement cases.

VII. Legal Consequences

A. Damages

The amount of compensation is calculated based on the illegal profits made by the infringer or the losses suffered and incurred by the IP right owners including reasonable expenses incurred for stopping the infringing acts. If the amount of damages cannot be ascertained, the Court may order discretionary damages not exceeding RMB 500,000. Nevertheless, unless a plaintiff provides very strong evidence to establish its damages, the damages ordered by the Court tend to be very low.

However, a number of recent decisions show that the Courts have become more willing to grant more substantive damages awards when the defendant involved is a foreign or a foreign related company. In a case brought by a PRC company against a Hong Kong based fashion chain called "G2000", the People's Court ordered G2000 to pay USD 2.6 million to the PRC company for infringement of its trademark "2000". In another case, the Court ordered Schneider Electric to pay USD 45 million as damages for infringement of the patent of the PRC company. Both of these cases are now being appealed.

B. Other forms of relief

Besides ordering damages, the Court has the discretionary power to order a permanent injunction stopping the infringement, a publication of an apology, a recall and/or destruction of the infringing products, and/or remedial steps to be taken by the infringer to minimise the effects of the infringement.

Product Piracy in the United States

Daryl Fairbairn

Strong intellectual property rights and enforcement mechanisms are crucial in the fight against counterfeit and pirated products.[1] In developing and implementing a total anti-counterfeiting strategy, it is important to coordinate closely with customs and border control authorities, regulatory agencies and law enforcement. This is particularly true for companies whose value and goodwill depend heavily on their intellectual property [IP] rights, which deserve special attention for vigorous protection and defence.

This chapter focuses primarily on strategies relating to the ownership and enforcement of IP rights in the battle against counterfeit goods.[2] It begins with a brief overview of the U. S. judicial and procedural framework, including its unique application of discovery tools in civil litigation to describe the background within which the battle is fought. It then examines the main substantive forms of IP rights, including trademarks, patents, copyrights, and related IP rights. Each section provides a description of the relevant right, and examines infringement and enforcement opportunities, including criminal sanctions, where available.

I. Sources of Intellectual Property Law in the United States

U. S. laws are made at the federal and state levels. Intellectual property laws relevant to the fight against counterfeits derive from federal legislation, regulations issued by federal executives, and case law developed by the courts.

Significant federal legislation governing IP enacted by Congress includes patent laws set forth in Title 35 of the U. S. C. [United States Code], and federal trademark law and copyright laws contained in Titles 22 and 17 U. S. C. respectively. Executive officers, generally acting through administrative agencies, also issue legally binding regulations that impact IP laws.

In addition to the statutory law from the legislature and binding regulations from executive officers, as a "common law" country, the United States recognises law developed

1 *Fairbairn/Shum/Schönig/Milbradt*, Intellectual property and the fight against counterfeit drugs, IAM supplement, February 2007, 19.

2 The term "counterfeit" describes products that are not genuine (i. e., fakes). The term "piracy" generally refers to the act of reproducing copyrighted works without permission from the copyright owner. In this chapter, the term "counterfeit" is generally used for convenience, and in some instances where the context implies both trademark and copyright laws, it includes pirated goods as well.

by and deriving from court decisions. Common law relies upon the doctrine of *stare decisis*, meaning that where a court has previously laid down a principle of law as applicable to a specific set of facts, it will apply the same principle to future cases where the facts are substantially the same. As a result, court opinions must be followed by subsequent courts hearing similar cases. *Stare decisis* does not, however, mean that court decisions stand forever. Earlier precedents may be modified or overturned by later court decisions, and duly enacted statutes and regulations take precedence over and can "strike down" common law.

A. The U. S. Judicial System

Judicial authority in the United States is divided between federal and state courts. With a few notable exceptions, intellectual property cases are heard in federal courts[3] since the federal district courts have exclusive subject matter jurisdiction over cases relating to federal IP laws.[4] United States district courts serve as the trial courts of the federal court system, with jurisdiction to hear federal IP cases, in addition to other federal cases. Federal district court decisions may be appealed to a relevant circuit court of appeals. In addition to the appellate circuit courts, the Federal Circuit [United States Court of Appeals for the Federal Circuit] has nationwide jurisdiction to hear certain types of appeals, including exclusive jurisdiction over issues of patent law.[5]

The losing party in a civil district court case is, in most instances, entitled to appeal to the relevant court of appeals as a matter of right. In addition, a party that received an adverse ruling by certain federal administrative agencies may also appeal to a court of appeals. For example, a patent applicant may ask the Federal Circuit to review a denial of a patent application by the U. S. Patent and Trademark Office.

A court of appeals decision will usually be the final decision in a case. In some cases, the appeals court remands the decision back to the trial court for further proceedings in light of its findings. On occasion, a party may petition the U. S. Supreme Court for a writ of certiorari to review the appeals court decision. Almost all petitions are denied, since the Supreme Court reserves its limited resources for only cases raising important questions of federal or constitutional law. In practice, the Supreme Court entertains only a few IP cases in any given year.

The various state court systems resemble the federal system in that they are generally comprised of trial courts with broad original jurisdiction, intermediate appellate courts and a final state court of appeals. Unlike the federal system, state trial courts generally divide jurisdiction over criminal and civil actions between separate courts.

3 As is discussed below, trademark law is governed by both federal and state law; thus trademark cases may be brought in state courts in some circumstances, in addition to the federal courts.

4 28 U. S. C. [United States Code] § 1338.

5 28 U. S. C. § 1295.

B. The U. S. Litigation Process

The procedural rules for litigation before the district courts are set forth in the F. R. C. P. [Federal Rules of Civil Procedure]. Presented below is the basic structure for U. S. civil procedure that is common to the various actions that an IP right holder may pursue, regardless of the form of right or legal claim. To a very large extent, procedures in the various states courts mirror the federal rules set forth below.

1. The Complaint

To initiate a lawsuit, a claimant (plaintiff) whose rights have been infringed by another party (defendant) files a complaint with the relevant court, which must include "a short plain statement" of the plaintiff's claim. The complaint also sets forth the basis for the court's jurisdiction as well as a demand for relief.[6]

The complaint is not required to set forth the claims in extensive detail. Rather, it need only provide sufficient notice of the claims to permit the defendant to begin preparing a defence. Nor is the complaint required to include any evidence in support of its claims. Facts may be alleged in a conclusory manner (with a few exceptions that are not common between the various IP cases), so long as they (1) provide proper notice of the claims being made; and (2) would, if proven, entitle the plaintiff to the requested remedies.

The relief requested may consist of money damages and/or equitable relief such as an injunction forbidding the defendant from continuing its infringing activities. Plaintiffs may also seek pre-judgment relief, as set forth below. In counterfeiting cases, an important procedural tool available to IP right holders is the availability of injunctive relief.

2. Pre-Judgment Remedies

U. S. courts may grant preliminary injunctions to provide immediately relief from harm, and to maintain the status quo while an action is pending. To obtain a preliminary injunction, an applicant must show the likelihood that it will suffer irreparable harm if the injunction is not granted and, either, (1) the probability of success on the merits of the underlying action or (2) sufficiently serious questions going to the merits to make them a fair ground for litigation and the harm to the applicant (if the injunction is denied) outweighs the injury to others (if the injunction is granted). Harm that can be adequately compensated by monetary damages is not considered irreparable injury.

Applicants for preliminary remedies may seek to initiate such an action in secret, to keep from alerting the counterfeiter, by filing the complaint and related documents under seal.

---

6 F. R. C. P. [Federal Rules of Civil Procedure] Rule 8(a).

Under certain circumstances, a court will issue an *ex parte* TRO (temporary restraining order).[7] A TRO is an emergency remedy that can be issued without notice to the defendant. A TRO will be issued only if: (1) specific facts clearly show that immediate and irreparable injury, loss or damage will result to the applicant before the adverse party can be heard in opposition; and (2) the applicant's attorney certifies any efforts taken to give notice, and the reasons that notice should not be required. Absent an extension by the court, a TRO normally expires after a maximum of 10 days.[8]

3. Response to the Complaint

After receiving the complaint,[9] the defendant basically has two choices: (1) to file an "answer" either admitting or denying each of the allegations in the complaint, including any affirmative defences and counterclaims the defendant may have against the plaintiff; or (2) to file a motion to dismiss, requesting that the court dismiss the complaint and terminate the lawsuit.

4. Discovery

The process of discovery draws the most attention and negative publicity of all aspects of litigation, given its potential expense and comparatively onerous obligations. Discovery is the process that allows the parties to demand from one another the evidence that is required to prove their respective cases at trial. Such evidence includes documents and sworn testimony that "appears reasonably calculated to lead to the discovery of admissible evidence.[10]"

Nearly all information, unless protected for example by the attorney client privilege, is subject to discovery. Even confidential information may be required to be produced, although the court usually imposes a "protective order" forbidding its improper use or disclosure. In addition, discovery is not limited to the named parties in the litigation, but may be taken from third parties who have potentially relevant information. Failure to comply with the rules of discovery can have severe consequences, including dismissal of the underlying case.[11]

Soon after the complaint is served, the plaintiff and defendant are required to meet to develop a proposed plan for the discovery process provided for under the F. R. C. P.

---

7 F. R. C. P. Rule 65(b).

8 F. R. C. P. Rule 65(b)(2).

9 The discussion here, for the sake of simplicity, ignores that the complaint must be "served" on the Defendant within specific time limits and satisfying certain requirements. "Receiving the complaint" as used above assumes that Defendant has been properly served.

10 F. R. C. P. Rule 26.

11 A patent case was very recently dismissed for discovery violations in the U. S. District Court for the Eastern District of Texas: ClearValue v. Pearl River Polymers, Inc., 242 F. R.D. 362 (E. D.Tex. 2007).

Around the same time, they are required to make certain mandatory disclosures to one another.[12] They also generally exchange detailed discovery requests setting forth a description of the material and information that they wish the other party to produce. Although parties commonly object to the scope of the requests by the other party, U. S. courts generally allow broad discovery.

In counterfeiting cases, courts may grant expedited discovery orders, allowing the IP rights owner to seek and obtain discovery while the information is still available and before it becomes stale. Further, if the remedy sought is to identify additional members of an illegal distribution scheme, then it will not normally be necessary to seek extensive discovery.

The three primary methods of discovery permitted under the F. R. C. P. and in most states include: (1) requests for the production of documents and other physical evidence; (2) written questions (interrogatories); and (3) questions asked live, under oath, known as depositions.

Documents that are produced to the other side encompass any documents relevant to the subject of the litigation, computer records and e-mail messages. As a result, parties often exchange enormous amounts of information in an effort to ensure all relevant subjects are adequately considered. In IP cases, a plaintiff will commonly ask for documents that provide evidence of infringement and damages, while a defendant will ask for documents tending to show that the asserted IP rights are invalid and/or not infringed. Given the broad scope of discovery, in complex patent cases it is not uncommon for parties to exchange hundreds of boxes of documents.

Interrogatories consist of written questions submitted to the other party that must be answered under oath in writing. Common interrogatories include questions relating to revenues and other information useful for calculating appropriate damages, for example. The parties also generally ask for the other side to describe its case theories. The number of interrogatories is generally limited.

Depositions provide a means for parties to obtain live testimony under oath from a witness prior to trial. Questions are asked of the witness by an attorney, usually in a conference room. Deposition witnesses are typically those with actual knowledge of the facts relevant to a claim or defence in the case. The attorney for the witness can object to improper questions. Questions, answers and objections are recorded by a court reporter, and are often filmed.

Many counterfeit cases include accused activities that occur across several jurisdictions. IP rights holders have several procedural tools at their disposal to seek obtaining information in such cases. For example, U. S. courts may assist parties to obtain discovery in the U. S. for use in proceedings outside of the U. S., or conversely, U. S. courts may seek

12 F. R. C. P. Rule 26.

the assistance of foreign tribunals in order to assist in the discovery process in a U. S. action.[13]

5. Summary Judgment, Trial and Appeal

The purpose of a trial in the U. S. legal system is to decide disputed issues of fact. Cases where there is no serious dispute concerning the relevant facts can be resolved without a trial. This is done by means of a motion for summary judgment. A district court may dismiss a case on summary judgment if, after reviewing the evidence obtained through discovery, there is no genuine dispute of any material fact. Defendants very commonly file motions for summary judgment when discovery closes. Common summary judgment filings in IP cases include motions for a finding of no infringement, or that a trademark or patent is invalid or unenforceable, for example.

Very few of the civil lawsuits filed every year in the United States actually proceed to trial. Some cases are disposed of through motions for dismissal or summary judgment, while the majority of cases are settled by agreement between the parties. The federal court system guarantees both parties the right to a trial before a jury on nearly all civil claims involving money damages, including in IP cases. A jury is not mandatory if both parties choose to waive their right. Juries are composed of people living in the geographic area served by the court.

At trial, the parties present witness testimony and any documentary evidence in support of their respective cases. The plaintiff's case is presented first, followed by the defendant's case. The party calling a witness begins with direct examination, and the other party follows with cross examination of the same witness. Once all of the evidence has been presented and summarised by the attorneys in closing statements, the court instructs the jury regarding the applicable law.

The jury is responsible for resolving all questions of fact and for determining damages, while the judge determines issues of law. Judges have the power to set aside unreasonable jury verdicts or to order a new trial, but rarely exercise that power. Trials are generally open to the public and the press. Trials in IP cases commonly last a few weeks or more, but can be shorter if the case is simple. They can also last considerably longer, on the other hand, for very complex cases.

As previously mentioned, the federal court system, and most state systems, guarantee a party to a civil action one appeal as a matter of right. Appeals from the federal district court go to the U. S. court of appeals for the geographic circuit in which the district court is located, while patent cases go to the Federal Circuit.

13 28 U. S. C. § 1782; see also F. R. C. P. Rule 28 (b).

II. Substantive Intellectual Property Law

United States intellectual property law is comprised of patent, trademark, copyright, trade secret, and unfair competition law. Although there may be some resemblance in the rights of these different types of IP, they are different and serve different purposes. From the perspective of combating counterfeit and pirated goods, trademark law provides useful and powerful tools for IP right holders, since it can be easily and quickly applied by the courts to stop illegal behaviors. In addition, U. S. law provides a wide range of remedies that can be used in the fight against fake products.

A. Trademarks

A trademark is a word, symbol, or phrase, used in commerce to identify and distinguish a manufacturer or its products from those of another.[14] For example, shoes made by the company Nike are identifiable by the trademark "Nike", along with the Nike "swoosh", and thus distinguishable from the products of its competitors. Marks used to identify services instead of products are called service marks, and are generally treated the same as trademarks.

Trademark protection may, in some cases, extend beyond words, symbols, and phrases. They might, for example, include other aspects of a product, such as its colour or its packaging. Common examples include the pink colour fiberglass insulation or the unique shape and colour of a pharmaceutical product. These characteristics are often referred to as "trade dress", and are protectable if consumers associate that characteristic with a specific manufacturer. Such features cannot be protected, however, if they are merely functional.[15] The U. S. Supreme Court held that trade dress law will not protect an unregistered product's design unless there is a showing of secondary meaning.[16]

Trademarks are governed by both state and federal law in the United States. The primary source of law is the federal statute known as the Lanham Act,[17] which provides the most extensive protection for trademarks. However, state common law actions are still available in some instances, and may be heard in the various state courts.

1. Trademark Protection

In order to qualify as a trademark, a mark must be distinctive. In other words, it must be able to identify the source of a particular good. In determining whether a mark is distinctive, U. S. courts categorise marks based on their relationship to the underlying pro-

14 15 U. S. C. § 1127.

15 Inwood Laboratories, Inc. v. Ives Laboratories, Inc., 456 U. S. 844, 850 n.10 (1982) ("[i]n general terms, a product feature is functional and cannot serve as a trademark, if it is essential to the use or purpose of the article or if it affects the cost or quality of the article.").

16 Wal-Mart Stores, Inc. v. Samara Brothers, Inc., 529 U. S. 205 (2000).

17 15 U. S. C. §§ 1051, et seq.

duct as follows: (1) arbitrary or fanciful; (2) suggestive; (3) descriptive; or (4) generic. Each separate category indicates a different level of distinctiveness. As such, the degree of protection afforded to a trademark depends on the category within which it falls.

An arbitrary or fanciful mark is one that has no inherent relationship to the underlying product. For example, the words "Yahoo!" and "Apple" have no logical relationship to internet sites or computers. Arbitrary or fanciful marks are inherently distinctive, and are therefore given a high degree of protection by the courts.

A suggestive mark is one that suggests or evokes a particular feature of the underlying good. For example, "Mustang" is suggestive of a fast car, but does not by itself describe the underlying product. Although in some respects the mark is associated with the underlying product, it may require a little creative thinking to make the association. As with arbitrary or fanciful marks, suggestive marks are inherently distinctive, and are given a high degree of protection in the United States.

A descriptive mark directly describes (rather than suggests) some feature or quality of the underlying product. For example, "Computer Land" is descriptive of a computer store, "Vision Center" is descriptive of optical services, and "Roach Hotel" is descriptive of an insect trap. Each example describes some characteristic of the underlying product or service, thereby giving consumers some information about the product. Unlike arbitrary or suggestive marks, descriptive marks are not inherently distinctive. They are protected only if they have acquired "secondary meaning."

A descriptive mark acquires secondary meaning when consumers associate that mark with a particular source company, instead of with the underlying product. The public does not need to be able to identify the identity of specific producer. It only needs to be able to recognise that the product or service comes from a single producer. Courts generally look at several factors to determine whether a mark has acquired secondary meaning, including (1) the amount and manner of advertising; (2) the volume of sales and number of customers; (3) exclusivity, manner, and length of use of a mark; (4) survey evidence and direct consumer testimony; (5) established place in the market; and (6) proof of intentional copying by the defendant.[18]

Finally, a generic mark generally describes the category within which the underlying product falls. For example, use of the term "Car" as a trademark would be a generic use. Generic marks are entitled to no protection under U. S. trademark law. Thus, a company that markets "Car" brand cars would not be able to exclude any other person or entity from using the term "Car" to sell a competing car. Under some circumstances, terms that began as protected brand names can become generic and thus lose their protection.

18 Grupo Gigante SA De CV v. Dallo & Co., Inc., 391 F.3d 1088 (2004).

2. Registration versus Use in Commerce

Trademark rights can be acquired in the U. S. in two ways. They can be the first mark registered with the P. T. O. (U. S. Patent and Trademark Office) for a specific purpose, with a bona fide intention to use the mark in commerce.[19] Alternatively, they may become protected by being used first in commerce. Since descriptive marks must have achieved secondary meaning before they can be protected, there may be a period of time after which the descriptive mark was first used in commerce before it acquires secondary meaning sufficient to warrant protection. Fanciful and suggestive marks, on the other hand, qualify for protection without having to acquire secondary meaning.

Although registration is not required for a trademark to be protected, the trademark holder obtains a number of benefits by registration.[20] An important distinction between registration and use rights is that the registration confers rights throughout the U. S. by giving constructive notice of ownership to others,[21] while use rights are limited in geographic scope to that area of actual use. Thus, the holder of a use right in California as a general rule would not be able to prohibit use of the identical mark in New York (or any other state), for example. Registration allows infringement suits to be brought in federal court,[22] and after five years the mark can become "incontestable", conclusively establishing the exclusive right to use the mark.[23]

Applications for registration are subject to approval by the P. T. O. The P. T. O. may reject a registration on any number of grounds, including if the mark is generic or if a descriptive mark has not acquired secondary meaning. The P. T. O. can also reject marks that are likely to cause confusion with existing marks and "immoral or scandalous" marks. Even if the P. T. O. rejects a mark, it may still be entitled to trademark protection through "use" rights. However, the mark may not be entitled to the statutory benefits of registration.[24]

A trademark owner can give up its rights if the mark is abandoned, improperly licensed, or if it becomes generic. A trademark is abandoned through discontinued use with intent not to resume such use. Non-use for three consecutive years is prima facie evidence of abandonment.[25]

Trademark rights can also be lost through improper licensing or assignment. Where a trademark is licensed without adequate quality control or supervision by the trademark owner (a so-called "naked licence"), that trademark may be found to be abandoned, since the ceases to function as a symbol of quality and controlled source.[26]

---

19 15 U. S. C. § 1051.

20 15 U. S. C. § 1051.

21 15 U. S. C. § 1072.

22 15 U. S. C. § 1121.

23 15 U. S. C. § 1065.

24 15 U. S. C. § 1125.

25 15 U. S. C. § 1127.

26 Barcamerica Intern. USA Trust v. Tyfield Importers, Inc., 289 F.3d 589, 595–596 (9th Cir. 2002).

Trademark rights can also be lost when the mark becomes generic over time, even when the mark was originally distinctive. A word becomes generic when a substantial majority of the public uses the word to describe the general category within which a product falls, rather than as an indicator of a specific source or manufacturer. Once famous trademarks, such as "aspirin"[27] and "shredded wheat",[28] lost their trademark protection through extensive public use. This is because the use was uncontrolled with respect to the mark's source identification function. Thus generic terms become synonymous with the general category of product.

3. Trademark Infringement

In the U. S., a party that owns the rights to a particular trademark can sue other parties that use the mark without authorization for infringement.[29] In order to prevail on a trademark infringement claim, a plaintiff must establish that it has a valid mark that is entitled to protection under the Lanham Act and that defendant used the mark in commerce, without the plaintiff's consent.[30] The plaintiff must also show a "likelihood of confusion". In other words, use of a trademark in connection with the sale of a product constitutes infringement if there is a likelihood that such use will cause consumers to become confused with respect to the source of those goods. Courts consider a number of factors in analyzing likelihood of confusion, including: (1) the strength of the mark; (2) the degree of similarity between the two marks; (3) the proximity of the products; (4) the likelihood that the prior owner will "bridge the gap"; (5) actual confusion; (6) the defendant's good faith in adopting its mark; (7) the quality of the defendant's product; and (8) the sophistication of the buyers.[31]

U. S. trademark law also recognises indirect infringement, such as contributory infringement.[32] Such theories are useful for mark owners, allowing them to pursue those who specifically enable infringement.[33] For example, internet service providers that know-

---

27 Bayer Co. v. United Drug Co., 272 F.505 (S. D. N. Y. 1921).

28 Kellogg Co. v. National Biscuit Co., 305 U. S. 111 (1938).

29 15 U. S. C. §§ 1114, 1125.

30 See e. g., Time, Inc. v. Petersen Publ'g Co., 173 F.3d 113, 117 (2d Cir. 1999).

31 Arrow Fastener Co. v. Stanley Works, 59 F.3d 384, 391 (2d Cir. 1995) citing Polaroid Corp. v. Polarad Elecs. Corp., 287 F.2d 492, 495 (2d Cir. 1961).

32 Inwood Laboratories, Inc. v. Ives Laboratories, Inc., 546 U. S. 844, 854 (1982) ("[I]f a manufacturer or distributor intentionally induces another to infringe a trademark, or if it continues to supply its product to one whom it knows or has reason to know is engaging in trademark infringement, the manufacturer or distributor is contributorally responsible for any harm done as a result of the deceit.").

33 Grant Airmass Corp. v. Gaymar Indus., Inc., 645 F.Supp. 1507, 1511 (S. D. N. Y. 1986) ("[L]iability under the Lanham Act has been construed to extend beyond those who actually misrepresent goods or directly place such goods in commerce."); Power Test Petroleum Distributors, Inc. v. Manhattan & Queens Fuel Corp., 556 F. Supp. 392, 395 (E. D. N. Y. 1982) ("one may be held liable as a contributory infringer, notwithstanding the fact that one does nothing to assist an infringing party.").

ingly host websites that sell counterfeit products have been found liable for contributory infringement.[34]

In a closely watched recent case, the U. S. District Court for the Southern District of New York ruled that the online retailer eBay had no legal responsibility to prevent its users from selling counterfeit "Tiffany" items on its electronic marketplace.[35] Instead, the court found that brand owners are ultimately responsible for protecting their own trademarks.[36]

In addition to an infringement action, trademark owners can also bring an action for trademark dilution under either federal or state law. Under federal law, the owner may only bring a dilution claim if the mark is "famous." In deciding whether a mark is famous, the courts consider: (1) the degree of inherent or acquired distinctiveness; (2) the duration and extent of use; (3) the amount of advertising and publicity; (4) the geographic extent of the market; (5) the channels of trade; (6) the degree of recognition in trading areas; (7) any use of similar marks by third parties; and (8) whether the mark is registered.[37]

Provided the elements for a dilution claim are met, the owner of a mark can bring an action for dilution either through "blurring" or "tarnishment" of the mark. Blurring occurs when the power of the mark is weakened through its identification with dissimilar goods, such "Apple" brand cars, or "Yahoo!" brand clothing. Consumers are not likely to be confused by such hypothetical products, but they "dilute" the distinctiveness of the original brand.

Tarnishment involves an unauthorised use of the mark in association with products that are of inferior quality, or use that portrays the mark in an unwholesome or unsavory context that may reflect poorly on the owner's product. Since counterfeit and pirated goods are frequently of inferior quality to the genuine goods, this theory is particularly well suited to protecting brand owners.

Trademark owners may also bring a federal claim for unfair competition pursuant to the "catch-all" provision of the Lanham Act.[38] In addition to the various federal claims, other state-law causes of action can arise under relevant state unfair competition law, such as misappropriation and passing off. Passing off occurs when the defendant attempts to "pass off" its product as the plaintiff's product, the typical counterfeit case.

---

34 Gucci America, Inc. v. Hall & Associates, 135 F Supp. 2d 409 (S. D. N. Y. 2001)

35 Tiffany (NJ) Inc. v. eBay, Inc., – F.Supp.2d –, 2008 WL 2755787 (S. D. N. Y. July 14, 2008).

36 Note that this decision is in stark contrast to the recent French recent decision holding eBay liable for the sale of fake Louis Vuitton and Dior brand products.

37 See e. g., 15 U. S. C. § 1125(c).

38 15 U. S.C § 1125(a) regarding false advertising and unfair competition.

4. Trademark Remedies

Successful plaintiffs in trademark cases are entitled to many remedies under the federal Lanham Act, providing them a wide range of benefits against counterfeiters. Plaintiffs are commonly awarded injunctions to prevent further infringing or diluting use of the trademark by the defendants.[39] Money damages are also available in trademark infringement suits, including actual damages to the plaintiff, defendant's profits, and the costs of litigation.[40] Plaintiff may also seek statutory damages in lieu of actual damages,[41] which can be difficult to prove in many cases. In addition, damages may be enhanced up to triple the amount of actual damages upon showing of bad faith or in counterfeit cases.

Trademark owner may obtain a court order directing law enforcement to accompany its attorneys on raids, permitting searches and seizure.[42] The items seized may include not only the counterfeit products, but also anything used to manufacture or package the counterfeit products.[43] The owner may also seek an order from the court directing banks to seize the financial assets of the counterfeiters, which can be used to satisfy any judgment.

As previously mentioned, trademark owners may also seek injunctive relief, through temporary restraining orders, or through preliminary (before final judgment) and permanent (after final judgment) injunctions against the activities of the counterfeiters.

5. Criminal Trademark Laws and Administrative Proceedings

U. S. law also provides criminal penalties for infringing IP rights including trademarks. Criminal sanctions apply to "[w]hoever intentionally traffics or attempts to traffic in goods or services and knowingly uses a counterfeit mark on or in connection with such goods or services." The availability of criminal actions significantly increases the stakes for trademark counterfeiters when they are caught. The federal criminal TCA [Trademark Counterfeiting Act] was amended by the SCMGA [Stop Counterfeiting in Manufactured Goods Act of 2006], which significantly strengthened the ability of prosecutors to disable counterfeiters.[44]

Prior to the 2006 Act it was already illegal to manufacture, ship, or sell counterfeit products. However, some counterfeiters were able to evade prosecution by separately shipping and selling the fake goods from the fake labels. The 2006 Act amended the legislation by (1) making it illegal to traffic in counterfeit labels, even if the labels are not attached to any product; (2) making it illegal to import, export or possess counterfeit goods or labels with the intent to transport, transfer or dispose of them; (3) provid-

39 15 U. S. C. § 1116(a).

40 15 U. S. C. § 1117(a).

41 15 U. S. C. § 1117 (c) and (d).

42 15 U. S. C. § 1116 (d).

43 See e. g., 15 U. S. C. § 1116(d)(1)(A).

44 18 U. S. C. § 2320.

ing for destruction of all counterfeits goods and labels seized from a counterfeiter; (4) requiring forfeiture of any property used in, or derived from the proceeds of, counterfeiting; and (5) providing for court orders that require counterfeiters to pay restitution to trademark owners.

On July 24, 2008, a bill[45] was introduced in the United States Senate to further strengthen these criminal sanctions, in addition to tightening other IP laws relating to criminal copyright infringement. The new bill, if enacted as law, would provide for enhanced monetary penalties for counterfeiting, and for stronger forfeiture provisions.

U. S. law further authorises customs agents to take certain actions with respect to imported products bearing infringing marks. Federal trademark legislation prohibits the importation in the U. S. of goods that "copy or simulate" registered trademarks.[46] U. S. Customs is authorised to seize or exclude such infringing products from the U. S. on this basis.

The Tariff Act likewise prohibits the importation into the U. S. of goods bearing a registered trademark owned by a U. S. citizen, U. S. corporation or other association in the U. S., without the consent of the trademark owner.[47] The Tariff Act also provides that any imported articles that are found to bear a "counterfeit" mark as defined in the Lanham Act[48] may be subject to seizure and forfeiture for violating customs law.[49] In order to obtain customs enforcement of a registered trademark the mark owner must apply for recordation of its registered trademarks with U. S. Customs, providing owners with another form of relief from counterfeit products as such products first enter the country.[50]

B. Patents

The United States Constitution creates federal patent rights. It provides that "Congress shall have the power … [t]o promote the progress of science and the useful arts, by securing for limited times to authors and inventors the exclusive right to their respective writings and discoveries".[51] A patent grants the inventor the right to exclude all others from making, using, selling and offering for sale the invention claimed by the patent for a period of twenty years from the earliest date of filing of the patent application.[52] Patent applications, like trademark applications, are filed in the P. T. O.

45 Enforcement of Intellectual Property Rights Act of 2008, S. 3325.

46 15 U. S. C. § 1124.

47 19 U. S. C. § 1526.

48 15 U. S. C. § 1127.

49 19 U. S. C. § 1526 (e).

50 Title 19 of the Code of Federal Regulations [C. F. R.] Part 133.

51 United States Constitution [U. S. Constitution], Article I, Section 8.

52 Previously, the patent term in the United States was seventeen years from the date the patent issued. The rules for calculating patent life changed when the U. S. implemented the policies set forth by the Agreement on Trade Related Aspects of Intellectual Property Rights [TRIPS]. For

To qualify for patent protection, an invention must fall within the scope of patentable subject matter. The Patent Act provides that "Whoever invents or discovers any new and useful process, machine, manufacture, or composition of matter, or any new and useful improvement thereof, may obtain a patent therefor" subject to certain conditions.[53]

Precluded from patent coverage are laws of nature, natural phenomena, and abstract ideas.[54] U. S. patent law takes a more inclusive approach to patentable subject matter than many jurisdictions, allowing patents for business method claims, methods for treating illnesses, computer software, and other inventions that are precluded from patent coverage in some other jurisdictions.

The Federal Circuit has recently addressed whether certain business methods and mental methods are patentable as "processes" within the meaning of the Patent Act. In the Comiskey case,[55] some patent claims covered an arbitration method without recitation of a computer or other means for implementing the method, and were found invalid. Other claims, however, recited the use of computers or other machines were deemed to satisfy sec. 101. More recently, the Federal Circuit affirmed denial of claims directed to a method of hedging the risk of bad weather through commodities trading. It applied a "machine-transformation test" as the test to be used for assessing patentable subject matter. That is, a claimed process must either be (1) tied to a particular machine or apparatus, or (2) transform a particular article into a different state or thing.[56]

1. Patentability

Aside from whether an invention qualifies as patentable subject matter under sec. 101, there are additional elements which an invention must possess in order to qualify for patent coverage. It must be novel, useful and nonobvious. U. S. patent law also contains certain statutory bars to patentability.

2. Novelty

An invention must be novel in order to qualify for a U. S. patent. That is to say, it must not have been know prior to the filing date. A patent application will fail for lack of novelty if there is enough information in the prior art (e. g., instances of public knowledge) to enable someone skilled in the relevant field of the invention to perform the

---

example, patents filed prior to June 8, 1995, have a term of the longer of either 17 years from issuance or 20 years from filing.

53 35 U. S. C. § 101.

54 Laboratory Corp. of America Holdings v. Metabolite Laboratories, Inc., 548 U. S. 124 (2006) (dismissing certiorari as improvidently granted) (Justice Breyer dissenting from dismissal).

55 In re Comiskey, 499 F.3d 1365, 1376-77 (Fed. Cir. 2007).

56 In re Bilski, 545 F.3d 943 (Fed. Cir. 2008).

process or produce the product covered by the claims of the patent.[57] Since the U. S. is based on a "first to invent" system rather than a "first to file" system like most other jurisdictions, there are a number of technical rules governing the novelty. The technical rules governing whether a particular piece of prior art is sufficient to destroy novelty depends on its nature and where the invention was made.

A statutory bar under U. S. law focuses on anticipation events that may occur more than twelve months prior to the filing in the P. T. O. of the inventor's patent specification, such as the commercial sale of the invention. An inventor is, thus, given a grace period of twelve months from the event within which he may still apply for a patent.

a. Utility

The utility requirement originates from language in the United States Constitution, which indicates that the purpose of empowering Congress to authorise the granting of patents is "to promote the progress of … useful arts." To meet the utility requirement, a new product or process must be shown to be "operable," that is, it must be capable of accomplishing the purpose proposed in the patent. Utility is demonstrated when an invention meets at least one of its stated objectives, and is easily accomplished.

b. Nonobviousness

To be patentable, an invention cannot be obvious to those skilled in the relevant field.[58] An invention may satisfy the technical requirements of novelty, yet is so obvious that it is not patentable. For example, an invention is obvious if someone familiar with the subject matter *could have* invented it with comparative ease, notwithstanding the fact that no one has actually described or made the invention before.

Whether an invention is obvious is decided in context of the teachings of the prior art. However, there is no requirement that an invention have actually been previously described in order for it to be deemed obvious. The U. S. Supreme Court recently held that the obviousness inquiry is somewhat flexible, and that certain specific requirements that some courts had been demanding to invalidate patents on grounds of obviousness were not so rigid. In particular, the court stated that "[t]he combination of familiar elements according to known methods is likely to be obvious when it does no more than yield predictable results".[59] By easing the requirements to prove obviousness, the court made it easier for U. S. courts to find patent claims to be invalid.

---

57 35 U. S. C. § 102. There are several technical requirements, depending on the type of art, which must be examined.

58 35 U. S. C. § 103.

59 KSR Int'l Co. v. Teleflex Inc., 127 S. Ct. 1727, 1739 (2007).

c. Written Description and Enablement

U. S. patent law further requires that "[t]he specification shall contain a written description … of the manner and process of making and using [the invention] in such full, clear, concise and exact terms as to enable any person skilled in the art to which it pertains, or with which it is most nearly connected, to make and use the same".[60] This statutory provision contains two critical requirements referred to as "enablement" and "written description." These two requirements form the basis of the agreement between the inventors and the general public. In exchange for being excluded from practicing an invention for a limited time, the public demands a meaningful disclosure of the invention in return, so that it can make use of the invention once the patent term expires.

Although the applicant need not exactly describe the claimed subject matter, the description must clearly allow those of ordinary skill in the art to recognise that the applicant invented what is claimed. Whether claims are sufficiently enabled by a disclosure in a specification is determined as of the date that the patent application was first filed.

There must be some reasonable relationship between the scope of an enabling description and the scope of the claims. On the other hand, it is permissible that the specification may require some experimentation to make and use the claimed invention, provided that it does not require *undue experimentation*. Whether a disclosure requires undue experimentation is analyzed by considering the following factors: (1) the quantity of experimentation necessary; (2) the amount of direction or guidance necessary; (3) the presence or absence of working examples; (4) the nature of the invention; (5) the state of the prior art; (6) the relative skill of those in the art; (7) the predictability or unpredictability of the art; and (8) the breadth of the claims.[61]

3. Patent Infringement

Infringement analysis in the United States is a two step process. First, a court must construe the relevant claims of the patent to determine their scope.[62] Then the court must compare the claims to the accused product, and determine whether *each* limitation of the claims is also present in the accused product. The interpretation of patent claims is a question of law exclusively within the jurisdiction of the court. The court first looks to intrinsic evidence, which is the patent itself, including the claims, the specification and the prosecution history.[63] In construing the scope of a patent claim, the actual words of the patent claim are controlling. Additionally, extrinsic evidence such as expert and inventor testimony, and learned treatises may be relevant if there is ambiguity in any of the terms of the claim.[64] Courts frequently conduct a special "Markman" hearing in connection with construing the terms in patent claims.

60 35 U. S. C. § 112.

61 In re Wands, 858 F.2d 731, 737 (Fed. Cir. 1988).

62 Markman v. Westview Instruments, Inc., 517 U. S. 370 (1996).

63 Phillips v. AWH Corp., 415 F.3d 1303 (Fed. Cir. 2005).

A patent can be directly or indirectly infringed. Anyone who makes, uses, sells or offers for sale a patented invention without permission is a direct infringer of that patent.[65] U. S. law also recognises indirect infringement through inducement or by contributory infringement.[66]

United States patent law also recognises patent infringement under the doctrine of equivalents. The doctrine of equivalents holds that each element of a patent claim need not be identically present in the accused product or process. Instead, all that is required is a substantial equivalent. U. S. courts may apply different articulations of the test for equivalence.[67] Under the "insubstantial differences" test, an element in the accused device is equivalent to a claim limitation if the "only differences between the two are insubstantial".[68] Alternatively, under the "function-way-result "test, an element in the accused device is equivalent to a claim limitation if it "performs substantially the same function in substantially the same way to obtain substantially the same result".[69]

Applicability of the doctrine of equivalents may be limited by statements by the patent applicants during prosecution before the P. T. O. Any claim element that had been amended for reasons related to patentability may receive no range of equivalents, thus limiting the availability of the doctrine of equivalents.

4. Patent Law Remedies

There are several remedies available to a successful patent owner in the U. S. A patent owner can obtain a temporary restraining order, a preliminary injunction, a permanent injunction, damages that are adequate to compensate it for the infringement (but in no event less than a reasonable royalty for the use made of the invention by the infringing defendant) together with prejudgment interest and costs as fixed by the court. The successful patent owner can also seek enhanced damages to be assessed by the court (limited to up to triple the amount of actual damages). In exceptional cases the successful patent owner can also seek reasonable attorneys' fees.

Actual damages can include lost profits due to lost sales, price erosion, as well as any other injury resulting from the infringement that was or should have been reasonably foreseeable by the infringing party, including lost sales of un-patented articles that competed with the infringing product.

---

64 Vitronics Corp. v. Conceptronic, Inc., 90 F.3d 1576 (Fed.Cir.1996).

65 35 U. S. C. § 271.

66 35 U. S. C. § 271(b) and (c).

67 Warner-Jenkinson Co., Inc. v. Hilton Davis Chem. Co., 520 U. S. 17, 20 (1997) (explaining that different tests for equivalence may be "more suitable to different cases, depending on their particular facts").

68 Honeywell Int'l Inc. v. Hamilton Sundstrand Corp., 370 F.3d 1131, 1139 (Fed. Cir 2004).

69 Voda v. Cordis Corp., 536 F.3d 1311 (Fed. Cir. 2008).

A recent U. S. Supreme Court altered the ability of patent owners to obtain injunctions after a finding of infringement by a defendant.[70] Before the decision, the Federal Circuit affirmed the grant of an injunction in virtually every case following a judgment of infringement by the defendant. However, the Supreme Court held that district courts must apply the traditional four-factor test analyzing whether to award permanent injunctive relief. As with non-patent cases, a successful plaintiff in a patent case must demonstrate: (1) that it has suffered an irreparable injury; (2) that remedies available at law, such as monetary damages, are inadequate to compensate for that injury; (3) that, considering the balance of hardships between the plaintiff and defendant, a remedy in equity is warranted; and (4) that the public interest would not be disserved by a permanent injunction.

5. Administrative Proceedings: Sec. 337 Actions

Patent owners can attempt to block counterfeit products at the border from entering the United States. The procedural method is to bring an action under sec. 337 of the Tariff Act of 1930 before the ITC [International Trade Commission] alleging infringement by an importer [a so-called "337 Action"]. Some patent rights holders seek to bring actions in the federal courts and before the ITC simultaneously. 337 Actions prohibit any importation into the United States, the sale for importation, or the sale within the United States after importation, of articles that infringe a valid and enforceable patent, or articles made by a process covered by the claims of a valid and enforceable patent.[71] Whereas patent infringement litigation in the federal courts may take years to complete, 337 Actions are usually complete within only 12 to 18 months.

To prove a sec. 337 violation, a rights holder must prove that the imported article infringes a U. S. patent. The basic elements of a 337 action also require proof that the infringed patent is being used in an existing domestic industry, or an industry in the process of being established.[72] The domestic industry test is considered to be satisfied if the right holder can show at least one of the following: (1) significant investment in U. S. plant and equipment; (2) significant employment of labor or capital in the U. S.; or (3) substantial investment in the industry's exploitation, including U. S.-based engineering, research and development, or licensing.[73] The domestic industry requirement can be relatively easy to satisfy.

a. Sec. 337 Procedure

The patent holder initiates a 337 Action by filing a complaint. The complaint includes presentation of the facts that constitute the illegal activity, such as specific instances of

---

70 eBay Inc v. MercExchange, L. L. C., 547 U. S. 388 (2006).

71 19 U. S. C. § 1337(a)(1)(B).

72 19 U. S. C. § 1337(a)(2).

73 19 U. S. C. § 1337(a)(3).

the allegedly unlawful importation or sales. The complaint is usually directed at specific companies, and may include a large number of allegedly infringing entities.

The ITC is required to decide whether to initiate an investigation within 30 days of receiving the complaint. Assuming the ITC initiates the investigation, the case is referred to an ALJ [administrative law judge] at the ITC. The ALJ conducts the case in a manner similar to cases before a U. S. district court, with comparable discovery procedures and similar hearings. Upon reaching a decision on the facts and the law, the ALJ issues an "initial determination" on whether a sec. 337 violation has occured. The ITC automatically adopts the initial determination unless a Commissioner votes for its review within a specified period of time.[74] Any determination that a violation has taken place is subject to review by the U. S. President.[75] A party that is adversely affected by the final determination of the Commission may appeal the decision to the U. S. Court of Appeals for the Federal Circuit,[76] the same court that hears appeals of patent cases from the U. S. district courts.

b. Sec. 337 Remedies

If the ITC finds a violation of sec. 337, it is authorised to issue an "exclusion order" against the allegedly infringing articles. The order may be limited (e. g., issued against specific parties), or general in nature (e. g., issued against all persons, even non-parties to the action, to combat a pattern of violations where it is difficult to identify the source of infringing goods). The ITC may also issue a "cease and desist order" to prohibit the infringing party from engaging in certain activities. Exclusion and cease-and-desist orders are generally effective until the expiration of the asserted patents. The ITC may also, under certain circumstances, issue an order for the seizure and forfeiture of infringing imports.[77]

6. Design Patents

U. S. law provides for protection of design patents.[78] A design consists of the visual ornamental characteristics embodied in, or applied to, a manufactured article. The subject matter of a design patent application may relate to the configuration or shape of an article, to the surface ornamentation applied to an article, or to the combination of configuration and surface ornamentation.[79] On the other hand, where a design is primarily dictated by the function of the article, it is not proper statutory subject matter for a design patent because it lacks "ornamentality".[80]

74 19 C. F. R. § 210.42.

75 19 U. S. C. § 1337(j).

76 19 U. S. C. § 1337(c).

77 19 U. S. C. § 1337(i).

78 35 U. S. C. § 171.

79 MPEP (Manual of Patent Examining Procedure), Chapter 1502.

80 MPEP (Manual of Patent Examining Procedure), Chapter 1504.01 (c).

Applications for design patents may only have a single claim.[81] Independent and distinct designs must therefore be filed in separate design patent applications since they cannot be supported by a single claim. Designs may be considered distinct if they have different shapes or appearances, even though they are related articles. However, modified embodiments of a single design may be filed in a single application.

Many of the same rules that apply for patents also generally apply for design patents. Notably, since a design must be original to qualify as patentable, one that merely mimics naturally occurring or well known objects is not protectable with a design patent. Design patents are protected for a period of fourteen years from the date of issuance.[82]

7. Criminal Patent Laws

No criminal penalties are recognised under U. S. law for patent infringement.

C. Copyright

Under U. S. federal legislation, copyright protection is given to "original works of authorship fixed in a tangible medium of expression." A work must be "original" in order to qualify for protection by copyright law. However, since the degree of originality required is extremely low, copyright rights are easily secured under this definition.

Works exhibiting no originality are not protectable. Telephone directories, which are merely compilations of names of people living in a defined area, and sorted alphabetically, have been found to warrant no protection.[83] Compilations are defined as a works that are formed by the "collection and assembling of preexisting materials or of data that are selected, coordinated and arranged in such a way that the resulting work as a whole constitutes an original work of authorship".[84] Thus, mere compilations of information, such as databases, may contain a minimum level of creativity to warrant at least some protection.

Although a database may qualify as a protected compilation, the underlying data itself is not automatically granted protection. The copyright in a compilation only extends to the compilation, and not to the underlying materials or data.[85] Since the underlying data cannot be protected, U. S. copyright law does not usually serve as a basis to prevent someone from copying portions of the unprotected data from the database.

---

81 37 CFR § 1.153.

82 35 U. S. C. § 171.

83 Feist Publications, Inc. v. Rural Tel. Serv. Co., Inc., 499 U. S. 340 (1991).

84 17 U. S. C. § 101.

85 17 U. S. C. § 103(b).

Ideas, procedures, principles, or discoveries are all specifically excluded from copyright protection.[86] Articles that have utilitarian function may not receive the benefits of a copyright.

1. Copyright Protection

A work must be "fixed" in a tangible medium of expression in order to be protected. A work is considered fixed when it is stored or embodies in a sufficiently stable form in which it can be perceived, reproduced, or otherwise communicated.[87] Copyrights are protected from the moment an original work becomes fixed.[88] No other specific act, such as filing an application with the Copyright Office, is required for copyright protection. Nor is there any requirement to place a copyright notice on the work. However, these formalities do impact the remedies and expand the protection available to copyrights.

Congress categorised several "works of authorship" that are protected by U. S. copyright law. The eight categories, interpreted broadly in practice to encompass most protected works, include (1) literary works; (2) musical works, including any accompanying words; (3) dramatic works, including any accompanying music; (4) pantomimes and choreographic works; (5) pictorial, graphic, and sculptural works; (6) motion pictures and other audiovisual works; (7) sound recordings; and (8) architectural works.[89]

The Copyright Act grants certain exclusive rights to the owners of most copyrighted works, including (1) the right to reproduce the copyrighted work; (2) the right to prepare derivative works based upon the work; (3) the right to distribute copies of the work to the public; (4) the right to perform the copyrighted work publicly; and (5) the right to display the copyrighted work publicly.[90]

In some situations, the person who conceives of the idea for a work does not actually produce the work directly, but instead hires someone else to make the work. For example, some works are created in the course of employment by employees, while other works are commissioned to be made by non-employee third parties. In determining which party is the legal author of the work, U. S. courts assess the facts in light of the "work-made-for-hire" doctrine. According to the Copyright Act, a work-made-for-hire doctrine is (1) a work prepared by an employee within the scope of his or her employment; or (2) a work specially ordered or commissioned for use under certain conditions enumerated by the statute.[91]

---

86 17 U. S. C. § 102(b).

87 17 U. S. C. § 101.

88 For example, a song is fixed when it is written down on paper, and a computer program is fixed when stored on a computer hard drive.

89 17 U. S. C. § 102(a).

90 17 U. S. C. § 106.

91 17 U. S. C. § 101.

Whether an individual is an "employee" for the purposes of the work-made-for-hire doctrine is determined by analyzing certain factors that characterise an "employer/employee" relationship as defined by common law rules of agency.[92] Courts thus look at facts such as (1) the degree of control exerted by the employer over the employee; (2) the control exerted by the employer over how and where the work is done; (3) whether equipment is supplied for the employee's use; and (4) the payment of benefits and the withholding of taxes.

2. Copyright Infringement

Anyone who exercises any of the exclusive rights of a copyright granted by Congress, without the authorization of the copyright owner, infringes the copyright.[93] Thus, any activity within the scope of the specifically defined exclusive rights – not just the reproduction right – of the copyright owner constitutes infringement. U. S. courts generally use the term "copying" as shorthand to refer to a violation of any of the owner's exclusive rights. To prevail in a claim of copyright infringement, a plaintiff must prove (1) ownership of a valid copyright and (2) unauthorised copying or a violation of one of the other exclusive rights afforded copyright owners pursuant to the Copyright Act.[94] Copyright infringement is determined without considering the intent of the infringing party.

As evidence of infringement, the accused work need not be an identical copy of the original work. Even if none of the copied words, images, software code, etc. are identical to the original, for example, the similarity may be substantial enough to justify a finding of infringement.[95] U. S. courts have applied a variety of tests to determine whether there has been sufficient copying to constitute a substantial similarity between a copyrighted work and an accused work. A highly regarded U. S. judge developed a well-known test referred to as the "abstractions test." The test proposes a hierarchy of levels of abstraction in any copyrighted work, ranging from potentially protectable expression to unprotectable ideas.[96] The analytically similar "subtractive" test dissects the copyrighted work, ignores the nonprotected elements of the work, and compares only those elements of the original work that are protected to the allegedly infringing work.[97]

Another commonly applied example is the three-part "abstraction-filtration-comparison" test.[98] The first step is to apply an "abstractions" test to separate the non-copyrightable idea of a work such as a computer program from the protectable elements. The second step entails "filtering" the infringed original work at each level of abstraction

---

92 Community For Creative Non-Violence v. Reid, 490 U. S. 730 (1989).

93 17 U. S. C. § 501(a).

94 Hasbro Bradley, Inc. v. Sparkle Toys, Inc., 780 F.2d 189 (2d Cir. 1985).

95 See, e. g., Three Boys Music Corp. v. Bolton, 212 F.3d 477, 481 (9th Cir. 2000).

96 Nichols v. Universal Pictures, Corp., 45 F.2d 119 (2d Cir. 1930).

97 Universal Athletic Sales Co. v. Salkeld, 511 F.2d 904 (3d Cir. 1975).

98 Computer Associates International, Inc. v. Altai, Inc., 982 F.2d 693 (2d Cir. 1992).

through various copyright doctrines to deny protection to certain types of materials. The various filters include (1) a test for originality, (2) whether there has been a merger of the idea and the expression or the related scenes a faire doctrine applies and (3) whether a public domain exception applies. The final step is to "compare" the remaining core to the accused infringing work, to determine whether the defendant impermissibly copied any aspect of the remaining protected expression of the original work.

One test applied to assess infringement of computer software works was the "iterative approach".[99] To establish infringement, plaintiff must show that (1) the defendant "used" the copyrighted work in preparing the alleged copy; and (2) that the defendant's work is an iterative reproduction, i. e., it was produced by iterative or exact duplication of substantial portions of the copyrighted work. Another widely used test is to examine the "totality," comparing works through a "total concept and feel" standard to determine whether they are substantially similar.[100]

U. S. law recognises causes of action for indirect, as well as direct infringement. The Copyright Act grants to copyright owners not only the right to exercise their exclusive rights, but also the right "to authorise" use of those rights. The right "to authorise" is intended to impose liability for indirect infringement in addition to direct infringement. However, the Copyright Act does not provide explicit definitions for "contributory infringement" or "vicarious liability," which have instead been developed through case law.[101] The most famous cases are the "dance hall" cases, where vicarious liability was found when dance hall owners allowed the unauthorised public performance of musical works by the bands they hired.[102] They were found vicariously liable even though they had warned the bands not to perform copyrighted works without authorization. Today, these theories are asserted in attempts to prevent, for example, certain forms of file sharing technologies.

3. Copyright Law Remedies

Like the other forms of IP rights reviewed above, copyright owners have several remedies available in infringement actions. A copyright owner may seek a preliminary or permanent injunction to prevent infringement.[103] Permanent injunctions are generally granted by courts against adjudicated infringers where there is a threat of continuing infringement.[104] Courts may also grant a seizure order to impound of all infringing copies.[105] As part of a final judgment, a court may also order the destruction all copies of

---

99 E. F. Johnson Co., v. Uniden Corp. of America, 623 F.Supp 1485 (D. Minn. 1985).

100 Roth Greeting Cards v. United Card Co., 429 F.2d 1106 (9th Cir. 1970).

101 Indirect infringement of intellectual property rights is explicitly provided in patent legislation for inducing infringement and contributory infringement. See 35 U. S. C. § 271(b) and (c).

102 See, e. g., Dreamland Ball Room, Inc. v. Shapiro, Bernstein & Co., 36 F.2d 354 (7th Cir. 1929).

103 17 U. S. C. § 502 (1988).

104 Superhype Publishing, Inc. v. Vasiliou, 838 F. Supp. 1220, 1226 (S. D. Ohio 1993).

105 17 U. S. C. § 503(a).

the works that were made or used in violation of the copyright owner's exclusive rights.[106]

Copyright owners are also entitled to actual or statutory damages.[107] Actual damages may be awarded in the amount of the copyright owner's losses plus any profits of the infringer due to the infringement. Statutory damages, which the owner may elect at any time before final judgment is rendered, may also be awarded on a per work infringement basis. If an infringer was not aware and had no reason to believe that his or her acts constituted copyright infringement, the court may find there was an innocent infringement. Such a finding does not remove liability entirely, but the court may, in its discretion, reduce the award of statutory damages.[108] Courts may also award reasonable attorney's fees to the prevailing party, and may also increase statutory damages if the infringement was found to be willful.

4. Criminal Copyright Laws and Administrative Proceedings

U. S. copyright law provides criminal sanctions against infringers if the infringement was willful and for purposes of commercial advantage or private financial gain.[109] If an infringer is found guilty of a criminal violation, the court is required to order the forfeiture and destruction of all infringing copies, including the "all implements, devices, or equipment" used in the manufacture of the infringing copies.[110] Criminal infringers are subjected to fines and imprisonment.[111]

The Copyright Act also criminalises certain other non-infringing acts. For example, similar to how the Stop Counterfeiting in Manufactured Goods Act of 2006 criminalises trade in counterfeit labels as violations of trademark law, U. S. law also prohibits and criminalises the use of labels on copyrighted works.[112]

As with trademarks, U. S. law provides mechanisms for subjecting counterfeit versions of copyright-protected goods to seizure and forfeiture by Customs authorities.[113] Copyright owners may record their interests with customs in order to facilitate enforcement of such remedies.[114]

---

106 17 U. S. C. § 503(b).
107 17 U. S. C. § 504.
108 17 U. S. C. § 504(c).
109 17 U. S. C. § 506(a).
110 17 U. S. C. § 506(b).
111 18 U. S. C. § 2319.
112 18 U. S. C. § 2318.
113 19 U. S. C. § 1595.
114 19 C. F. R. Part 133.31.

5. Digital Millennium Copyright Act

The DMCA [Digital Millennium Copyright Act] prohibits the circumvention of anti-piracy measures built into commercial software. Signed into law on October 28, 1998, it implements the 1996 WIPO [World Intellectual Property Organization] Copyright Treaty, and the 1996 WIPO Performances and Phonograms Treaty. The DMCA also addresses a number of other significant copyright-related issues.

In addition to prohibiting circumvention of copyright protective measures, the DMCA also prohibited tampering with copyright management information, creating civil remedies and criminal penalties for violating the prohibitions.

The prohibitions of the DMCA are subject to several notable exceptions, including permission to reverse engineer a technological measure "for the sole purpose of identifying and analyzing elements of the program necessary to achieve interoperability with other programs," or in order to identify "flaws and vulnerabilities of encryption technologies," or for the purposes of testing computer security systems.

Any person injured by a violation the law can bring a civil action in Federal court. The courts are also granted the power to grant a broad range of equitable and monetary remedies similar to those available under the Copyright Act.[115]

In addition, willful violations of the law for purposes of commercial advantage or private financial gain constitute a criminal offence. Violations are punishable by penalties including fines and imprisonment.[116]

D. Trade Secrets

Trade secrets have been historically protected in the United States through state law. Trade secret principles developed in the United States primarily through common law and have been modified in the UTSA [Uniform Trade Secrets Act], model legislation drafted by the National Conference of Commissioners on Uniform State Laws. The UTSA has been adopted by a majority of the states.

1. Trade Secret Protection

A trade secret, is generally defined as information, including a formula, pattern, compilation, program, device method, technique, or process that derives independent economic value from not being generally known, and is the subject of reasonable efforts to maintain its secrecy. Many businesses choose to protect commercially valuable informa-

---

115 17 U.S.C. § 1203.

116 17 U.S.C. § 1204.

tion through reliance on state law trade secret protection, rather than federal patent law.[117] The classic example of a trade secret is the recipe for Coca Cola.

2. Trade Secret Remedies

The owner of a trade secret may obtain injunctive relief and compensatory damages for improper use and/or disclosure of the trade secret by another. The test for obtaining an injunction relating to improper use of trade secrets by an employee generally requires: (1) the information is a trade secret; (2) the information was of value to the employer and important to the conduct of the business; (3) the employer had the right to the use and enjoyment of the secret by reason of discovery or ownership; and (4) the secret was communicated to the defendant while employed in a position of trust and confidence.

In a case testing the strength of trade secret law against the right of free speech (i. e., the right to disclose), the California Supreme Court unanimously ruled that a preliminary injunction prohibiting a web site operator from disclosing on its web site the source code for a DVD decrypting program containing another party's trade secrets does not violate free speech rights in the First Amendment or the California Constitution.[118]

3. Federal trade secret law provides criminal sanctions

The EEA [Economic Espionage Act of 1996] federally criminalises misappropriation or theft of trade secrets.[119] The EEA makes it illegal to steal trade secrets for the benefit of foreign powers (foreign economic espionage).[120] It also makes it illegal to steal trade secrets for commercial or economic purposes regardless of the beneficiary (commercial economic espionage).[121] Both provisions require a prosecutor to prove that: (1) the defendant misappropriated information (or attempted or conspired to do so); (2) the defendant knew or believed that this information was a trade secret; and (3) the information was in fact a trade secret. The EEA provides different penalties for the two offences, including penalties of fines and imprisonment.

4. Other Measures For Fighting Piracy and Counterfeiting

In addition to forms of IP protection described above, other laws and regulatory initiatives play an important role in the fight against counterfeit products. Among government and agency initiatives, such as the STOP! [Strategy Targeting Organised Piracy

[117] Kewanee Oil Co. v. Bicron Corp., 416 U. S. 470 (1974).

[118] DVD Copy Control Assn., Inc. v. Bunner (2003) 31 Cal.4th 864, 889.

[119] 18 U. S. C. §§ 1831-1839.

[120] 18 U. S. C. § 1831.

[121] 18 U. S. C. § 1832.

initiative],[122] are examples brought by specific agencies for application in certain industries. For example, the FDA [United States Food and Drug Administration] has implemented several initiatives to combat counterfeit drugs.[123] Among its activities, the FDA established a Counterfeit Drug Task Force that focuses on the issues relating to fake drugs. It created a "Counterfeit Alert Network," a coalition of professional industry associations and consumer groups that coordinate in disseminating information and furthering the coalition's goal to safeguard the county's drug supply.

The FDA's law enforcement arm, the OCI [Office of Criminal Investigations],[124] has been given the primary responsibility for conducting all of its criminal investigations, including suspected counterfeit products. Through the OCI, the FDA works closely with state and federal enforcement officers to identify and prosecute drug counterfeiters. FDA initiates and conducts drug investigations leading to criminal sanctions including fines and imprisonment.

III. Final Comment

As this chapter explains, U. S. intellectual property laws provide a wide range of opportunities to combat counterfeit products. The best approach, however, will depend on the facts, and will undoubtedly be flexible, using the range of rights and remedies available, while at the same time coordinating private and governmental efforts. Ideally, the approach reaches across borders, reducing the incentives and significantly raising the risks, for those who would participate in the crimes of counterfeiting and piracy.

---

122 See http://www.stopfakes.gov/pdf/Memo_STOP_Sheet_September_2007.pdf: STOP! coordinates the efforts of the U. S. Departments of Commerce, Justice, Homeland Security, and the FDA, the State Department, and the Office of the U. S. Trade Representative to "fight global piracy by systematically dismantling piracy networks, blocking counterfeits at our borders, helping American businesses secure and enforce their rights around the world, and collaborating with our trading partners to ensure the fight against fakes is global."

123 Information available at http://www.fda.gov/oc/initiatives/counterfeit/.

124 Information available at http://www.fda.gov/ora/inspect_ref/iom/ChapterText/8_9.html.

Product Piracy in Spain

MONSERRAT LOPEZ-BELLOSTA/ISABEL CARULLA*

I. Legal Framework Overview

A. Protection of Intellectual Property by Substantive Law

1. Spanish Trademark Act, Patent Act, Utility Model Act, Copyright Act

The term "intellectual property" includes a wide range of subject-matter (trademarks, patents, utility models, industrial designs, integrated circuits, geographical indications, copyright and rights related to copyright), protected by various laws.

With regard to trademarks, sec. 2 and sec. 4 of the Trademark Act (Ley 17/2001, de 7 de diciembre, de Marcas [Law 17/2001 of 7 December on Trademarks] (ES)) define and protect as a trademark any mark duly registered at the Spanish Patent and Trademark Office. A trademark may be represented graphically, provided that such mark is capable of distinguishing one company's goods or services from those offered by another. Unregistered but well-known trademarks are also protected, pursuant to the provisions of sec. 6 of the Paris Convention (Paris Convention for the Protection of Industrial Property of 20 March 1883).

With regard to patents, sec. 4 of the Patent Act (Ley 11/1986 de 20 de Marzo, de Patentes de Invención y Modelos de utilidad [Law 11/1986 of 20 March on Patents and Utility Models] (ES)) protects as a patent any new invention involving inventive step and capable of industrial application. Subject matter may be protected by patents even if it is a composite, contains biological matter or consists of a process through which biological matter can be obtained, transformed or used. With regard to utility models, sec. 143 of the Patent Act protects as a utility model any new invention involving inventive step consisting of giving an object a configuration, structure or form that results in a material practical advantage for the use or manufacture thereof.

With regard to copyright, sec. 1 and sec. 10 of the Copyright Act[1] grant ownership and confers protection upon the author, when he/she produces an original creation, expressed in any media, tangible or intangible, known or to be invented.

---

* The co-authors of the Product Piracy in Spain chapter are: Mireia Aguila, Rais Amils, Marta Baylina, Ana Bayó, Ana Benetó, Xisca Borrás, Isabel Carulla, Juan Cuerva, Pablo Ferrándiz, Julia Hernández, Montserrat López-Bellosta, Josep Montefusco, Carlos Rivadulla and Sonia Sebé.

1 Real Decreto Legislativo 1/1996, de 12 de abril, por el que se aprueba el Texto Refundido de la Ley de Propiedad Intelectual, regularizando, aclarando y armonizando las disposiciones legales vigentes sobre la materia [Legislative Royal Decree 1/1996, of 12 April, approving the Codifying

2. Role of the Spanish Unfair Competition Act

The Unfair Competition Act (Ley 3/1991, de 10 de enero, de Competencia Desleal [Law 3/1991 of 10 January on Unfair Competition] (ES)) is the first regulation in Spain that systematically addresses the issue of unfair competition. Acting as a general law, it applies in cases where no special regulations apply, thus also serving as a closure mechanism. However, that does not mean that the Unfair Competition Act can be invoked when special regulations, such as the Trademark Act or the Patent Act, apply to a specific case; it is not a valid legal framework for acts that are expressly provided for in special regulations.

The Unfair Competition Act is targeted at the market as a whole. Apart from protecting competitors' private interests on the market, it also protects the public interests of consumers as a group, since it is deemed that unfair competition not only harms competitors, but also occasionally consumers. One example of the protection of public interests is that consumer associations can file some of the actions provided for in the Unfair Competition Act.

In addition, individuals engaging in acts of unfair competition do not necessarily have to be business owners: the Unfair Competition Act also applies to acts committed by any individual or legal entity participating in the market. Lastly, an act or practice may in some cases be considered as unfair under the Unfair Competition Act, even if there is no direct competition between the persons involved in the act.

Three conditions must be met by a potentially unfair competition act for the Unfair Competition Act to apply: (i) the act must be projected externally, i. e. it must have an impact on the market; (ii) it must be performed for competitive purposes;[2] and (iii) it must have significant effects on the Spanish market.

3. Criminal Law

The development of new technologies has resulted in the commission of new and more complex forms of intellectual property crimes. The great ease of perpetrating an offence against intellectual property, the low cost of the infringing behaviour and the substantial benefits so rapidly obtained, have attracted the interest of many individuals and international criminal organisations hoping to earn "easy money".

In Spanish law, the protection of intellectual property is established in chapter XI of the Spanish Criminal Code (Ley Orgánica 10/1995, de 23 de noviembre, del Código Penal [Organic Law 10/1995 of 23 November on the Criminal Code] (ES)) (Articles 270-277), Title XIII, which is dedicated to crimes against property and socio-economic or-

Legislation of the Law on Intellectual Property, regularizing, clarifying and harmonizing the legal provisions in force on the subject] (ES).

2 An act is presumed to be performed for competitive purposes if, objectively speaking, it is capable of promoting or ensuring the dissemination of one's own services or a third party's services.

der. The first section of chapter XI refers to copyright offences and the second section, to offences against patents, utility models, trademarks, plant variety names and geographical indications for classifying food and beverage products of a certain quality.

Organic law 15/2003 (Ley Orgánica 15/2003, de 25 noviembre, por la que se modifica la Ley Orgánica 10/1995, de 23 de noviembre, del Código Penal [Organic Law 15/2003 of 25 November by which Organic Law 10/1995 of 23 November on the Criminal Code was amended] (ES)), amending the Criminal Code, introduced a major change to the configuration of offences against intellectual property rights, in an attempt to provide a solution to this new social reality, by reinforcing protection against crimes. Offences against intellectual property became public crimes pursued *ex officio*. Thus, it is not necessary for the party sustaining damage to file a formal complaint in order to initiate criminal proceedings. Penalties were increased and it became possible for intellectual property right-collecting societies to take criminal action as the damaged parties. Moreover, the law allows for special fast-track legal proceedings, provided for in the Law on Criminal Procedure Real Decreto de 14 de septiembre de 1882, Ley de Enjuiciamiento Criminal (Royal Decree of 14 September 1882 on the Spanish Law on Criminal Procedure] (ES)), to be brought in the case of very serious intellectual property offences.

In May 2006 the Public Prosecution Office published a Circular[3] establishing the guidelines to be followed by Public Prosecutors in Spain when prosecuting intellectual property offences.

B. Enforcement of Intellectual Property Rights

1. Civil Action

a. Interim Injunctions vs. Action on the Merits of the Case

Under Spanish law, the holder of an intellectual property right (trademark, patent, utility model, industrial design, integrated circuit, geographical indication, copyright or rights related to copyright) may file a claim for infringement (or, where appropriate, for unfair competition) in ordinary proceedings before the Civil Courts. The claim must be filed before the Mercantile Courts and can be brought against any third party who allegedly exploits the subject-matter of the intellectual property right, without the consent of the holder or its exclusive licencee. In the writ or complaint the holder, as the plaintiff, must state the defendant's details, provide a clear statement of facts, and detail the nature of the alleged infringement. The holder must also raise the legal grounds upon which the petition is based and specify the request sought from the Court, including the remedies and asking the Court to award the Court costs against the defendant.

3 Circular 1/2006, de 5 de mayo, de la Fiscalía General del Estado sobre los delitos contra la propiedad industrial e intelectual tras la reforma de la LO 15/2003 [Circular 1/2006, of 5 May, on the Public Prosecution Office against intellectual property offences after the reform of Organic Law 15/2003].

In order to ascertain the infringement (or the unfair competition, as the case may be) the holder must prove all of the following facts: (i) that a prohibited act has been performed; (ii) that the prohibited act has been performed in Spain; and (iii) that the prohibited act falls within the scope of protection of the exclusive right to be enforced in Spain. The defendant has 20 days in which to file a writ of reply or a counterclaim. In the writ of reply the defendant can deny and/or challenge the facts and the legal grounds raised in the claim (including any procedural matters preventing the proceedings from continuing) and ask the Court to set it aside and award the Court costs against the plaintiff. Furthermore, the defendant can file a counterclaim. For example, in patent cases the counterclaim may be for the patent to be declared null and void. Any counterclaim must meet exactly the same prerequisites as the claim and the plaintiff has 20 days in which to file its writ of reply against the defendant's counterclaim. Thereafter, the Court calls the parties to an oral hearing. At the oral hearing the Court first invites the parties to reach a settlement agreement to avoid litigation, although they rarely do so. If no settlement agreement is reached between the parties, the oral hearing continues based on any procedural matters raised by the parties in their respective writs of reply to the claim or counterclaim. In the event no procedural matters were raised, the parties can present complementary allegations to their petitions and propose evidence. The Court subsequently fixes the date for the trial and, once heard, delivers its Judgment.

Judgments delivered at first instance by the Mercantile Courts can be appealed before the Provincial Court in the same Province. This appeal must be announced within five days of the Judgment. Once admitted by the Court, the appeal must be lodged within a period of twenty days. In some very specific cases, an appeal may be lodged before the Supreme Court in Madrid against the decisions handed down by the Provincial Court.

Obviously, in order to avoid delay in the main proceedings and minimise damage, it may be appropriate to take swift action in an attempt to prevent the infringement, via interim injunctions. The application for interim injunctions must be made in writing. In this written application, the plaintiff is required to specify the measures it seeks in relation to the acts in question, and file the evidence it deems necessary, accompanied by the relevant documents. This process requires establishing *prima facie* evidence of the infringement: *fumus boni iuris*, which means that the judge must have a certain positive opinion that the outcome of the main proceedings will be in favour of the claimant, with regard to the facts alleged and the rights claimed; and *periculum in mora* whereby it must be proven that a delay in obtaining relief could thwart the purpose of the claim. In other words, the holder must show the Court that irreparable damage will be caused unless relief is granted. To that end, the party applying for an interim injunction should furnish a bond, sufficient to cover any loss and damage that the interim injunctions might cause *(bail)*.

In patent litigation, evidence proving that the patent is in commercial use in a WTO (World Trade Organization) Member State, or that serious and effective preparations have been made to that end, is required for the patentee to be entitled to apply for interim injunctions.

Interim injunctions may be sought prior to, simultaneously with, or subsequent to the main action, and is heard separately. When the application is made prior to the main action, the latter must be filed within twenty days of the decision granting the interim injunction.

The general principle is for the Court to rule on the application for interim injunctions in accordance with the principle of contradiction, which means that, after the interim injunctions' application has been filed, notice thereof should be served upon the defendant and the parties should be summoned to a hearing so that the Court can decide on the interim injunctions. However, in exceptional cases (i. e. if a delay in granting the interim injunctions would cause the plaintiff irreparable and irreversible damage) the judge may allow the application for interim injunctions *ex parte*.

An appeal may be lodged against the decision granting or setting aside the interim injunctions, within five days of the day after the date on which notice thereof is served.

b. Implementation of Enforcement Directive

The Enforcement Directive (Directive 2004/48/EC of 29 April 2004 on the Enforcement of Intellectual Property Rights)[4] was implemented in Spain through Law 19/2006 (Ley 19/2006, de 5 de junio, por la que se amplían los medios de tutela de los derechos de propiedad intelectual e industrial y se establecen normas procesales para facilitar la aplicación de diversos reglamentos comunitarios [Law 19/2006 of 5 June on the extension of the means protecting Industrial and Intellectual Property Rights] (ES)).[5] Law 19/2006, on the one hand, amended and extended the "*diligencias*" regime provided in the Law on Civil Procedure (Ley 1/2000, de 7 de enero, de Enjuiciamiento Civil [Law 1/2000, of 7 January, on Civil Procedure] (ES)) and, on the other hand, expanded the scope of the interim injunctions and the actions that can be brought by holders of rights contained in the corresponding material laws, i. e. Intellectual Property Law (Copyright Act); Trademark Act; Patent Act and the Law on Industrial Design (Ley 20/2003, de 7 Julio, de Protección Jurídica de Diseño Industrial [Law 20/2003 of 7 July on Industrial Design] (ES)).

Firstly, the reform introduced in the Law on Civil Procedure through Law 19/2006, focused on the measures for collecting evidence of the alleged infringement, the so-called "*diligencias preliminares*", a preliminary procedure prior to the main proceedings in which the plaintiff simply requests that the defendant provide certain information ("*diligen-*

4 Official Journal of the European Union 2004 No L 157/45 and Corrigendum to Directive 2004/48/EC, Official Journal of the European Union 2004 No L 195/16.

5 Law 19/2006 came into force on 7 June 2006 and introduces amendments and new means of protection on two (2) levels: on the one hand, it amends and extends the "*diligencias*" regime provided for in the Law on Civil Procedure (ES) and, on the other hand, it expands the scope of the interim injunctions and the actions that can be brought by the holders of rights contained in the corresponding material laws, i. e. the Copyright Act (ES); the Trademark Act (ES); the Patent Act (ES) and the Law on Industrial Design (ES).

cias"). Law 19/2006 introduced a new "*diligencia*" consisting of allowing access to financial, commercial, banking and customs-related documents, controlled by the alleged offender of the IP Rights on a commercial scale.

Secondly, the reform of the sectorial laws (Patent Act, Trademark Act, Copyright Act and the Law on Industrial Design) brought about by Law 19/2006 focused on:

(1) extending the interlocutory injunctions available;[6]
(2) subjectively extending the interlocutory injunctions to the third parties whose services may use the alleged offender of the IP rights, even when the acts of these third parties are not themselves an act of infringement;[7] and
(3) substituting the three former alternative criteria for calculating compensation for damages by a new twofold alternative criterion,[8] consisting of: (a) combining lost profits (i. e. the profits that the claimant would have made had the infringement not existed) and the gains obtained by the offender as a result of infringing the Intellectual Property Rights, and moral damages (Art. 66 of the Patent Act); or (b) the royalties the offender ought to have paid the patent holder for a licence to exploit the invention lawfully.

In addition, Art. 139.1 of the Patent Act, implementing Art. 9.5 of the Enforcement Directive, fixes a time limit of 20 working days for the claimant to file the complaint as of the date from which the interlocutory injunction is adopted, as opposed to the 2-month period previously granted.

2. Public Law

a. Spanish Product Safety Act

The Product Safety Directive (Directive 2001/95/EC of 3 December 2001 on general product safety),[9] was implemented in Spain through Royal Decree 1801/2003 (Real Decreto 1801/2003, de 26 de diciembre, sobre seguridad general de los productos [Royal Decree 1801/2003 on general product safety] (ES)). The purpose of this Royal Decree 1801/2003 is to ensure that products introduced to the market are safe.

This Royal Decree 1801/2003 applies to any product -including in the context of providing a service- which is intended for consumers or likely, under reasonably foreseeable conditions, to be used by consumers even if not intended for them, and is supplied or

---

6 §§ 63 ¶ 1 and 134 ¶ 1 Patent Act (ES); § 41.1 Trademark Act (ES); § 139 Copyright Act and § 53 ¶ 1 Law on Industrial Design.

7 §§ 63 ¶ 3 and 135 Patent Act (ES);§ 41 ¶ 3 Trademark Act (ES); § 138 Copyright Act (ES) and § 53 ¶ 3 Law on Industrial Design (ES).

8 § 66 ¶ 2 Patent Act (ES); § 43 Trademark Act (ES), § 140 ¶ 2 Copyright Act (ES) and § 55 ¶ 2 Law on Industrial Design (ES).

9 Official Journal of the European Communities 2002 No L 11/4.

made available, whether at a price or free of charge, in the course of a commercial activity, and whether new, used or reconditioned.

Notwithstanding the foregoing, this Royal Decree 1801/2003 does not apply to used products supplied as antiques or as products to be repaired or reconditioned prior to being used, provided that the supplier clearly informs the person to whom he supplies the product to that effect.

Where products are subject to specific safety requirements, the Royal Decree 1801/2003 only applies as a supplementary regulation to those risks or categories of risks not governed by the specific regulation.

The Royal Decree 1801/2003 applies notwithstanding the provisions related to liability for damages caused by defective products and other obligations which, according to civil and commercial law, may arise for businesspeople in the event of a product's withdrawal and recall from consumers.

In that respect, according to this Royal Decree 1801/2003 a "safe product" means any product which under normal or reasonably foreseeable conditions of use, including duration and, where applicable, putting into service, installation and maintenance requirements, does not present any risk or only the minimum risks (i) compatible with the product's use and (ii) considered to be acceptable and consistent with a high level of protection for the health and safety of persons, taking into account: a) the characteristics of the product, including its composition and packaging; b) the effect on other products, where it is reasonably foreseeable that it will be used with other products; c) the labelling, any warnings and instructions and any other indication or information regarding the product; d) product marketing and presentation; and e) the categories of consumers at risk when using the product, in particular children and the elderly.

According to the Royal Decree 1801/2003 a, any product to be marketed in Spain will be safe insofar as it complies with compulsory Spanish regulations establishing health and safety requirements or with the national technical standards transposing relevant European harmonised standards, which regulate some aspects of the aforementioned compulsory Spanish regulations. Therefore, the provisions contained in the Royal Decree 1801/2003 are to be applied with other specific regulations. If no specific and compulsory product safety regulations exist or do not cover all risks or categories of risks, a product's compliance with the general safety requirements will be assessed by particularly taking into account the following elements, where appropriate: (i) national technical standards transposing relevant non-harmonised European standards; (ii) UNE standards; (iii) Commission recommendations establishing guidelines on product safety assessment; (iv) product safety codes of good practice, in force in the sector in question; or (v) the state of the art.

The product's compliance with any of these regulations or standards, including having passed the relevant compulsory administrative controls does not, however, constitute an obstacle for the Administrative Authorities to adopt any measures if the product is considered dangerous.

In order to adopt the corresponding administrative measures referred to in this regulation, a product is assumed to be dangerous when: (i) the product or the facilities where it is manufactured have not been granted the relevant authorisations or passed the preventive administrative controls to protect the health and safety of consumers and users. In particular, when the product does not bear the CE mark or any other compulsory safety mark that it should; (ii) the product does not contain the minimum information in order to identify its manufacturer; (iii) the product belongs to a batch of products of the same class or description in which a dangerous product has previously been detected.

In order to ensure product safety, the Royal Decree 1801/2003 on product safety establishes several obligations for product manufacturers and importers. With regard to manufacturers, the Royal Decree 1801/2003 establishes several obligations, including the following: launch **only safe products on the market**; inform consumers of any potential risks inherent in a product's normal use and which cannot be detected immediately due to the nature thereof, and the conditions for the duration of the product and the market to which it is targeted; be informed of any potential risk inherent in the product and inform distributors thereof; adopt the necessary measures to avoid any risk when aware that a product placed on the market may pose such a risk; state its company name and other information on the product, etc. With regard to distributors, it establishes the **obligation to distribute only safe products**; the obligation to contribute to the compliance with safety regulations when storing, delivering and presenting a product; and the obligation to participate in the monitoring of the safety of the products placed on the market, etc.

Finally, the Royal Decree 1801/2003 on product safety also contains the administrative measures, which the Administrative Authorities may apply when the provisions established in this regulation are breached.

Therefore, **if a product does not comply with the safety regulations established in this Royal Decree 1801/2003 and is consequently considered dangerous**, under the aforementioned regulation, the corresponding Administrative Authorities, on their own initiative or as a result of a consumer's complaint, may issue a warning to the manufacturers or distributors of such dangerous product to force them to comply with the safety obligations established in such regulation. Whether or not a warning is effective, the corresponding Administrative Authorities are entitled to adopt measures, including the following: (i) temporarily prohibit the delivery or proposed delivery of the product, if there is circumstantial evidence that the product is dangerous; (ii) prohibit the product's launch on the market and other complementary measures, when the product is dangerous; and (iii) withdraw and destroy the product, if already introduced to the market and is dangerous.

In order to adopt the above measures, an administrative procedure should be processed, during which it would be possible to adopt provisional measures such as freezing and recalling the product, suspension of activities, etc.

The measures established in this regulation can affect manufacturers; distributors, in particular, the party responsible for the initial distribution in Spain; service providers and any other person contributing to the risk or on whom the outcome of the risk and the fulfilment of the measures depend.

These measures are not punitive, and the adoption thereof is without prejudice to any possible criminal or administrative liability.

b. Examples from the Healthcare, Electronics and Automotive Industries

(1) Healthcare

With regard to healthcare safety regulations, Law 29/2006 (Ley 29/2006, de 26 de julio, de garantías y uso racional de los medicamentos y productos sanitarios [Law 29/2006 on the Guarantees and Rational Use of Medicines and Medical devices] (ES)) establishes, as a safety guarantee, that medicines, basic active ingredients and raw materials comprising the former, are subject to clinical and toxicological studies to ensure that they are safe in normal conditions of use and for the duration of the treatment.

In addition to these studies, this Law also establishes that any person applying for marketing authorisation must prove that he or she can adequately monitor the safety of the medicines subsequent to marketing, submit the necessary specific plans on pharmacovigilance and risk management, and undertake to implement and fulfil the same. Safety guarantees on medicines also include any risk inherent in their use.

Under this Law, and without prejudice to personal liability, all authorities and healthcare professionals as well as pharmaceutical companies and wholesale traders are obliged to collaborate diligently on product safety knowledge. Furthermore, healthcare professionals, pharmaceutical companies and wholesale traders are under the obligation to notify healthcare authorities of any irregularities of which they are aware, pursuant to the provisions of this Law.

In addition, this Law also establishes the pharmacovigilance of medicinal products for human use, as a public health activity aimed at identifying, quantifying, assessing and preventing the risks associated with the use of these medicinal products, once marketed. The provisions of this Law on the pharmacovigilance of medicinal products are implemented by Royal Decree 1344/2007 (Real Decreto 1344/2007, de 11 de octubre, por el que se regula la farmacovigilancia de medicamentos de uso humano [Royal Decree 1344/2007, regulating pharmacovigilance of medicinal products for human use] (ES)). In accordance with the Royal Decree 1344/2007, and based on the assessment of pharmacovigilance data, the Spanish Drug and Health Product Agency may, for example temporarily suspend or permanently revoke an authorisation for a health product for any reason when it poses a foreseeable risk for the health or safety of individuals.

Lastly, any breach of a safety provision established in Law 29/2006, can be sanctioned. In that respect, this Law classifies breaches as minor, serious and very serious. Examples of what the Law construes as a very serious breach include counterfeiting a medicine, marketing a medicine without the corresponding authorisation, not filing safety reports or failing to notify the health authorities of the adverse results obtained in a clinical trial.

With regard to medical devices, Royal Decree 414/1996 (Real Decreto 414/1996, de 1 de marzo, por el que se regulan los productos sanitarios [Royal Decree 414/1996 regulating medical devices] (ES))[10] also contains provisions on the safety of such products. In that respect, this Royal Decree 414/1996 establishes several essential requirements, such as the obligation that medical devices be manufactured and designed in such a way so as not to affect patients' clinical status, health and safety when using such products in accordance with the conditions and for the purpose for which they are intended. Such medical devices must not pose a risk either to the people who use them or to third parties. According to this Royal Decree 414/1996, medical devices can only be marketed when they contain the CE mark (although there are exceptions to this obligation for certain medical devices). The CE mark indicates that such medical devices comply with the essential requirements established in this Royal Decree 414/1996 and have passed the evaluation procedures.

With regard to healthcare protection measures, to ensure health and safety, this Royal Decree 414/1996 establishes that the competent healthcare authorities may adopt certain measures (such as seizing or freezing the products, suspending the activities, etc.) if a medicinal device product affects the health or safety of patients, users or third parties, according to the purpose for which it is intended. Finally, with regard to breaches, Royal Decree 414/1996 also contains a list of breaches classified as minor, serious and very serious. Examples of what this Royal Decree 414/1996 construes as very serious breaches include placing on the market medical devices which have not satisfied the evaluation procedures for such products, marketing medical devices which affect/undermine patients', users' or third parties' health or safety, and the inadequate installation or maintenance of medical devices in such a way that they could undermine patients', users' or third parties' health or safety.

(2) Electronics

Electronics in Spain are protected as patents, pursuant to the provisions of the Patent Act. Particularly, with regard to telecommunication patents, the Spanish regulations follow the regulations and standardisation process approved by the ETSI (European Telecommunication Standard Institute) regarding the declaration of essentiality of patents for a particular technology standard.

10 This Royal Decree does not apply to medical devices for in vitro diagnosis and active implantable medical devices, which are governed by specific Regulations, although these are strikingly similar.

(3) Automotive Industry

IP rights may be enforced, albeit indirectly, in accordance with Public Law regulations on product safety, by filing actions before the competent Administrative Authorities in relation to pirated products not complying with safety standards. Set out hereunder is a brief description of the applicable regulations establishing safety standards in the automotive industry.

Royal Decree 2028/1986 (Real Decreto 2028/1986 de 6 de Junio [Royal Decree of 6 June] (ES)), implements the Council Directive 70/156/EEC (Council Directive 70/156/EEC of 6 February 1970 on the approximation of the laws of Member States relating to the type-approval of motor vehicles and their trailers).[11] Its Annexes, listing the vehicles and their components and parts, have been successively updated by Ministerial Orders, the latest of which is dated 5 June 2008. Please note that this Ministerial Order updates the Annexes contained in Royal Decree 2028/1986 (Real Decreto 2028/1986, de 6 de junio, por el que se dictan normas para la aplicación de determinadas directivas de la CEE, relativas a la homologación de tipos de vehículos automóviles, remolques y semirremolques, así como de partes y piezas de dichos vehículos [Royal Decree 2028/1986 of 6 June, which sets out rules for the application of certain EEC directives regarding the type-approval of certain kinds of automobiles, trailers and semitrailers, as well as for parts and components of such vehicles] (E. S.)) in view of the Framework Directive (Directive 2007/46/EEC of the European Parliament and of the Council of 5 September 2007 establishing a framework for the approval of motor vehicles and their trailers, and of systems, components and separate technical units intended for such vehicles),[12] which substituted Council Directive 70/156/EEC.

Furthermore, the General Vehicle Regulation (Real Decreto 2822/1998, de 23 de diciembre, Reglamento General de Vehículos [Royal Decree 2822/1998, of 23 December, on General Vehicle Regulation] (ES)) sets out the technical conditions that must be met by different types of vehicles to be registered or issued road clearance.

Finally, specific regulations exist for two or three-wheel motor vehicles: Directive 2002/24/EEC, of 18 March 2002, on type-approval of these vehicles.

c. Border Measures; Customs Regulation (Council Regulation (EC) No. 1383/2003 of 22 July 2003 concerning the customs action against goods suspected of infringing certain intellectual property rights and measures to be taken against goods found to have infringed such rights)

The rules governing the procedure followed by the Spanish customs authorities are set out in Customs Regulation and in European Community Commission Regulation.[13]

---

11 Official Journal of the European Communities 1970 No L 42/1.

12 Official Journal of the European Union 2007 No L 263/1.

13 Commission Regulation (EC) No 1891/2004 of 21 October 2004 laying down provisions for the implementation of Council Regulation (EC) No 1383/2003 concerning customs action against

Both Regulations provide a framework for the Spanish customs authorities to detain and seize pirated products.

The customs authorities' seizure of goods suspected of infringing intellectual property rights may be initiated: (a) *ex officio* by the customs authorities; or (b) as a result of admitting an "application for action" previously submitted by the patent holder or its legal representative before the Sub-department of Customs Administration at the Department of Customs and Special Taxes ("*Subdirección General de Gestión Aduanera en el Departamento de Aduanas e Impuestos Especiales*").

If the customs authorities detain the goods *ex officio* as a result of any of the surveillance functions established in the relevant customs Regulations, such seizure will only last for a period of three (3) working days, during which time the patent holder must submit its "application for action" to the Subdepartment of Customs Administration. However, this type of *ex officio* seizure of goods suspected of infringing intellectual property rights is not normal or usual, especially if it is difficult for the customs authorities to identify pirated goods.

Should the requirements set out in the Regulations be fulfilled and the "application for action" be granted, the Subdepartment of Customs Administration will order the seizure of the infringing products, and such order will be forwarded to the Spanish customs offices handling the import/export of the allegedly infringing goods.

Given that Art. 4 of the Customs Regulation does not require conclusive evidence of infringement, but only "sufficient grounds to suspect that goods infringe an intellectual property right", the Spanish customs authorities may seize a particular pirated product, provided that there are "sufficient grounds to suspect" that the product falls within the scope of an intellectual property right. Therefore, this is a useful tool to combat product piracy.

If the Spanish customs office is satisfied that certain goods correspond to the description of the allegedly pirated products provided by the Subdepartment of Customs Administration, it will suspend the release of the goods or detain them.

The customs office will immediately inform the Subdepartment of Customs Administration thereof, which will, in turn, inform the patent holder and the party declaring at customs or the owner of the goods seized.

goods suspected of infringing certain intellectual property rights and the measures to be taken against goods found to have infringed such rights, Official Journal of the European Union 2004 L 328/16.

3. Criminal Action

a. Public Prosecution vs. Private Prosecution

According to the Criminal Code, criminal offences against intellectual property rights are public crimes and, therefore, should be prosecuted *ex officio* by the Public Prosecutor even when no previous complaint has been filed by the offended party. The offended party is obviously also allowed to intervene in the criminal proceedings, since the Public Prosecutor does not have exclusive liability for these actions. In that respect, the prosecution of criminal offences against intellectual property rights is a duty for the Public Prosecutor, whereas it is a right for citizens.

From amongst the different Spanish criminal proceedings, criminal offences against intellectual property rights are judged in so-called "summary proceedings", in which prison sentences of less than 9 years may be imposed. During the summary proceedings, both the Public Prosecutor and the private prosecutor are active parties, gathering information to prepare the oral hearing and file the accusation against the accused (a sentence cannot be delivered if an accusation has not been filed).

b. Search and Seizure (including at Trade Fairs)

The exhibition of products infringing intellectual property rights at trade fairs frequently constitutes sufficient grounds for the right holder to file a complaint with the Spanish police. The damaged party provides information regarding the location where its products are displayed so that they can be seized. In many instances of exhibition of products clearly infringing intellectual property rights at trade fairs, the Spanish Police acts *ex officio*.

No specific regulations on trade fairs are established in Spanish criminal law. Hence, the consideration of which acts regarding trade fairs should be considered as criminal offences against intellectual property rights is made on a case-by-case basis.[14]

The penalty imposed for an intellectual property offence entails the loss and destruction of the seized goods. The Law on Criminal Procedure (Art. 338) establishes the possibility of destroying the seized goods, but retaining sufficient samples, when they have been examined by experts, when necessary or appropriate due to the nature of the seized pro-

14 In a Judgment delivered by the Provincial Court of Barcelona, the Court acquitted the accused, who had exhibited protected products at trade fairs, on the grounds that it was not proven that the accused was aware of the unlawfulness of the exhibited products, because the accused was not professionally dedicated to the type of products displayed, 25 September 2001 Provincial Court of Barcelona, WL JUR 2001 \ 327724.
In another case, the Court found that attending trade fairs in a certain commercial sector for years was evidence of being a trader and, therefore, proved the awareness of a certain well-known brand which had been infringed, 28 June 2005 Provincial Court of Barcelona [Judgment nº 533/ 2005], WL JUR 2006 \ 214542.

ducts or due to the real or potential danger of storing or holding them, after hearing the Public Prosecutor and the owner, if known, or the person in whose possession the products to be destroyed were found.

c. Criminal Liability and Sanctions

The Criminal Code (Articles 270-277) classifies conduct that may constitute a criminal offence against intellectual property. In criminal copyright offences, both the profit of the offender and damages inflicted on a third party must be proven in order to demonstrate the existence of criminal liability.

With regard to patents, utility models, trademarks, plant variety names and geographical indications, two prerequisites must be met in order to determine criminal liability: (i) the rights must be registered; and (ii) the party found guilty must have knowledge of such registration.

Under the Criminal Code, criminal sanctions for intellectual property offences include prison sentences and monetary fines, which are cumulative. For these criminal offences, the penalty is six months to two years in prison and fines between twelve and twenty-four months (ranging from EUR 2 to EUR 400 per day).

The penalty is one to four years in prison and fines between twelve and twenty-four months when some of the following specific circumstances apply: (i) when the profit obtained is particularly significant from a financial point of view; (ii) when the facts are particularly serious, taking into account the value of the objects unlawfully produced, or the special importance of the damages caused; (iii) when the guilty party belongs to an organisation or association, including of a transitory nature, the purpose of which is to perform activities that infringe intellectual property rights; and (iv) when minors are used to commit such offences. The Court can suspend the enforcement of prison sentences of less than two years.

The Court can also determine public liability derived from the offence, and sentence the accused to pay compensation for the loss and damage caused to the aggrieved party.

II. Trademark Piracy

A. Legal Requirements for Trademark Protection under the Trademark Act

Pursuant to the provisions of sec. 2 and sec. 4 of the Trademark Act, trademarks in Spain are protected once they have been duly registered at the Spanish Patent and Trademark Office. Unregistered but well-known trademarks are also protected under sec. 6 of the Paris Convention. Trademark protection is only granted for marks that can be represented graphically, provided that such marks are capable of distinguishing one company's goods or services from those offered by another.

B. Infringing Behaviour

Pursuant to the provisions of sec. 34 of the Trademark Act, infringing behaviour is defined as any use in trade, without the trademark holder's consent, of:

- any mark identical to the trademark in relation to goods or services, which are identical to those for which the trademark is registered;
- any mark which, as a result of being similar to the trademark and the goods or services covered by the trademark and the mark being similar, gives rise to the likelihood of confusion on the part of the public, including the likelihood of association between the mark and the trademark; and
- any mark identical or similar to goods or services which are not similar to the goods or services covered by the trademark, when the trademark is well-known or famous in Spain and by using the mark, without just cause, a connection might be created between the goods or services and the trademark holder or, in general, when the use amounts to undue profit or the dilution of the distinctiveness of the trademark or of the well-known and famous nature thereof.

1. Deceit of Origin

Deceit of origin, or likelihood of association, is a sub-category of likelihood of confusion, under sec. 34 of the Trademark Act. In accordance with the Supreme Court case law,[15] the Spanish Courts usually apply a restrictive concept of deceit of origin, construed as the confusion that may be caused amongst consumers with regard to the origin of the goods or services, by deceiving them into thinking that such goods or services are produced by the same company, or legally or commercially connected companies.

2. Likelihood of Confusion

As a general criterion, in its case law the Spanish Supreme Court has laid down that the marks in question must be examined and compared from a general or global perspective in order to ascertain the likelihood of confusion. Other criteria refer to taking into account the class of goods and services of the trademarks to be compared, the first-impression analysis, and the predominance of word marks v. graphic marks, as the most relevant elements of comparison to be taken into account.

---

15 22 October 1992 Supreme Court (GAL/GALMIX).

3. Transit as Infringing Behaviour (particularly focusing on the Decision given by the ECJ (European Court of Justice) on 9 November 2006 *(Diesel)*[16]

The Trademark Act does not specify whether customs transit may amount to infringing behaviour.[17] However, contrary to the decision given by the ECJ on 9 November 2006 in *(Diesel)*, one of the few Spanish Court decisions on the subject[18] held that, although in a patent case, such custom transit and deposit in Spain of goods to be exported could in fact amount to infringing behaviour. In view of recent decisions given by the ECJ, however, the Spanish Courts may review this doctrine.

4. Accountability for Online Auctions

The Information Society and Electronic Commerce Act (Ley 34/2002, de 11 de julio, de servicios de la sociedad de la información y de comercio electrónico [Law 34/2002, of 11 July, on Information Society and Electronic Commerce] (ES)) regulates the liability of Internet Service Providers in Spain with regard to the intermediary services they provide on the Internet. Particularly, sec. 16 of the Information Society and Electronic Commerce Act establishes that, unless the service provider has actual knowledge, or in the case that it had actual knowledge and acted promptly to remove the illegal content, they will not be held liable for the information stored, at the request of a recipient of the service. However, neither legal doctrine nor case law is clear as to whether Internet Service Providers operating online auction services may be included in this category of liability exclusion or if they should be held liable directly with the direct infringer.

C. Enforcement

1. Border Measures

Given that trademark piracy can be detected easily, the border measures provided for in the Customs Regulation and European Community Commission Regulation are effective mechanisms to seize pirated products that infringe trademarks.

Therefore, the Sub-department of Customs Administration at the Department of Customs and Special Taxes *(Subdirección General de Gestión Aduanera en el Departamento de Aduanas e Impuestos Especiales)* has extensive experience in detaining and seizing copies of trademarked products created without the trademark holders' consent.

---

16 9 November 2006 ECJ [C-281/05], GRUR 2007, 146 (Diesel).

17 As opposed to the Ley 32/1988, de 10 de diciembre de marcas [Law 32/1988, of 10 December, on Trademarks; also Trademark Act, old version] (ES) which specifies that the mere transit amounted to infringing behaviour.

18 12 June 2001 Provincial Court of Barcelona (section 15) [Appeal 844/1998], WL AC 2002/235.

2. Measures on Trade Fairs

There are no specific trade fair-related provisions regarding measures that right holders can adopt during trade fairs to protect their IP rights. Therefore, the general mechanisms to be followed are those established in the Law on Civil Procedure and other relevant laws, such as the Trademark Act or the Patent Act, bearing in mind the relevant modifications introduced by Law 19/2006. These regulations state that interventions may be requested and will be granted if certain conditions are met. Essentially, the right holder has the following judicial mechanisms available to protect IP rights during trade fairs:

1. **Interim injunctions** ("*medidas cautelares*"). Generally, the purpose of these interim injunctions is to obtain a Court order prohibiting the exhibition or offer for sale of specific products potentially infringing IP rights. In the case of trade fairs, the right holder may ask the Court in advance to prohibit a specific product from being exhibited. If the interim injunctions are granted, the plaintiff must file a complaint within 20 days. Failing that, the injunctions will be rendered null and void, the plaintiff will bear the Court costs and the Court will hold it liable for the damages caused to the defendant.

2. **Preliminary proceedings** ("*diligencias preliminares*"). These proceedings offer the plaintiff the possibility of asking the defendant to provide certain information prior to the main proceedings. Law 19/2006 introduces the possibility of requesting access to financial, commercial, banking and customs-related documents, provided that the right holder files circumstantial evidence of the infringement of its IP rights with the court. Obviously, such circumstantial evidence must be assessed on a case-by-case basis.

Preliminary proceedings could be useful to the right holder if it wishes to obtain certain information on the products that a defendant is to exhibit at a trade fair. However, if the Court accepts the preliminary proceedings, the plaintiff must file a complaint within one month from the date the defendant provides the information. Failure to do so without just cause will result in the right holder losing the bond, which it had previously deposited at Court and which is required by law for the Court to process these proceedings.

3. **Proceedings to verify facts** ("*diligencias para la comprobación de hechos*"). These proceedings are established in the Patent Act, but also apply to trademark rights. The prerequisites to qualify for these proceedings are stricter than for preliminary proceedings, because: (i) they require a higher levels of evidence of the alleged infringement; and (ii) they can only be applied for when the right holder has no other means of ascertaining the infringement and obtaining evidence thereof.

Proceedings to verify facts consist of a judge physically visiting previously-identified premises (in this case, the trade fair) to determine whether the samples, products, etc. inspected could, in fact, infringe the IP rights. As of the date on which the judge provides the applicant with the information and documentation gathered during the inspection (this will only happen when the judge finds that the information and documentation prove the infringement), the right holder has two months to file the complaint. Failing that, the outcome of the inspection cannot be used in subsequent proceedings.

Apart from these judicial mechanisms, right holders may also request the presence of a Notary Public at a trade fair, so that the **Notary Public** can certify, for example, that a specific product is exhibited at the fair. This Certificate may be used later as evidence in legal action.

In any case, right holders do not frequently have recourse to this type of action for trade fairs, mainly due to timing. For example, in the case of the application for interim injunctions, a right holder would need two or three weeks at the very least to obtain a decision from the Court to prohibit an exhibitor from promoting an allegedly infringing product at a trade fair in Spain. Therefore, it would need to know at least three weeks in advance that a potentially infringing product will be exhibited at a certain trade fair; however, in practice this does not always occur.

That did in fact occur in a case where Honda Motor Co., Ltd. (right holder) applied for interim injunctions against a defendant which, most presumably, planned to exhibit a scooter that infringed a design right (also applicable to a trademark) held by the applicant during a trade fair in Barcelona in May 2006. In one of the very few cases in which the Courts have been able to hear this kind of application for interim injunctions, in a Ruling given on 11 May 2006[19] Mercantile Court number 1 of Barcelona ordered the defendant to refrain from exhibiting the scooter at the trade fair.

D. Legal Consequences

1. Discontinuance

Pursuant to the provisions of sec. 34 and sec. 41 of the Trademark Act, the trademark holder may ask the Court to give a decision (interim injunction or judgment) ordering the discontinuance of the use of the infringing mark on the market. It may also ask the Court to adopt any specific measures to put an end to the infringing acts, such as the use on the market of any products, labels, packaging, advertising material or any other media displaying the infringing mark.

2. Information

As a result of the implementation of the Enforcement Directive and of the Council, sec. 256 of the Law on Civil Procedure was amended to introduce the possibility for an intellectual property right holder to ask the Court, prior to filing an action for infringement, to grant preliminary proceedings to gather certain information. Such information includes the names and addresses of the producers, distributors and suppliers of the potentially infringing goods, and their wholesalers and retailers, as well as any information

[19] 11 May 2006 Mercantile Court nº 1 of Barcelona [302/2006], WL AC 2002/235.

on the number of goods produced or distributed and the amount of money paid for such products.

3. Damages

The trademark holder may seek compensation for damages, under sec. 43 of the Trademark Act, by opting for either of following two compensation criteria:

- the negative economic consequences sustained, including, lost profits and the unfair profit made by the infringer. Moral damages may also be sought, even if no negative economic consequences are proven; or
- the amount of royalties that would have been due, had the infringer requested authorisation to exploit the trademark.

In any case, the trademark holder, without furnishing any proof, may request as damages a sum representing 1% of the infringer's total revenue derived from exploiting the trademark without authorisation. A higher amount may even be sought, if the holder proves that the damages exceeded 1%.

4. Destruction

Pursuant to the provisions of sec. 41 of the Trademark Act, the trademark holder may also request that the Court order the destruction of the infringing products or give them to charity, if appropriate. The Court may not, at its discretion, order the destruction of the infringing products if the infringing mark can be removed from the products or if the destruction of the products may cause disproportionate damage to the infringer.

5. Recall

Pursuant to the provisions of sec. 34 and sec. 41 of the Trademark Act, the trademark holder may ask the Court to issue a decision (interim injunction or judgment) ordering the recall of the infringing products.

6. Criminal Sanctions

Art. 274 of the Criminal Code protects the distinctive marks of a company and its products and services, which means that trademarks and commercial names are protected in Spain, provided that: (i) they are previously recorded at the corresponding Registry (due to the fact that the rights over a trademark arise as of the date of registration); and (ii) the holder of the distinctive mark has not granted its consent for the exploitation thereof.

This Art. 274 imposes a prison sentence of six months to two years, as well as a fine between twelve and twenty-four months (ranging from EUR 2 to EUR 400 per day), upon anyone who, for industrial or commercial purposes, without the consent of the holder of an intellectual property right registered in accordance with the Spanish law on trademarks, and aware of such registration, reproduces, imitates, modifies or in any other way exploits a distinctive mark which is identical to or may easily be confused with the intellectual property right, to distinguish the same or similar products, services, activities or establishments for which the intellectual property right is registered.

Likewise, the same penalties will be imposed on those who intentionally import such products without consent, whether they are of lawful or unlawful origin in their country of origin; nevertheless, importing the products from an EU Member State will not be sanctioned when such products have been acquired directly from the holder of the rights in the State, or with its consent.

Finally, the same penalties referred to above will be imposed upon anyone who knowingly possesses for marketing purposes, or puts on the market, products or services bearing distinctive marks which, as previously stated, infringe the holder's exclusive rights, even if these products are imported from abroad.

III. Patent Piracy

A. Prerequisites for Patent Protection

Reproducing the wording of Art. 52 of the EPC (European Patent Convention), the Patent Act establishes that inventions, including biological material, may be patentable, provided that they are novel, involve inventive step and are capable of industrial application. Discoveries, scientific theories, mathematical methods, literary, scientific and any other aesthetic creations, rules and methods for performing intellectual activities, playing games or doing business, computer programmes or the manner in which information is presented are not patentable. Inventions whose publication or use would be contrary to public order or good practice cannot be patented either.

It is not possible to obtain a patent for an invention if it is a new animal or plant variety, a method for treating the human or animal body by surgery or therapy, or a method of diagnosis.

Some of the following processes cannot be patented: processes for cloning human beings or for modifying the germ line genetic identity of human beings and uses of human embryos for industrial or commercial purposes, amongst others.

1. Service Inventions

Under the Patent Act, service inventions are those inventions arising as a result of research, which explicitly or implicitly constitute the subject-matter of a contract between an employer and an employee.

In those cases, the employer will be the owner of the invention discovered by the employee. The employee, who will be regarded as the inventor, will not be entitled to earn additional remuneration for his/her achievement, except where his/her personal contribution to the invention and its importance to the company exceed the explicit or implicit terms of the employee's contract, work or service.

All other inventions will belong to the inventor employee, provided that: (i) the invention is not related to his/her professional activity; (ii) knowledge gained within the company has not had a decisive influence on the invention; and (iii) the employee has not used means provided by the company in the invention. If so, the employer will be entitled to claim ownership of the invention or reserve the right to use it, and the employee will receive equitable financial remuneration.

Similar provisions, albeit containing special features, apply to: (i) civil servants, and State employees and workers; and (ii) University professors. The latter, who should be considered as the authors of the inventions, will be entitled to a share in the profits obtained by the University as a result of the achievement.

2. Securing Rights in the Context of Cooperation with Third Parties

If various parties discover an invention, Art. 10 Patent Act establishes that such parties are jointly entitled to obtain patent protection. However, if different parties discover the same invention separately, the party who first files the invention with the Spanish Trademark and Patent Office is entitled to patent the invention.

In order to secure rights where the patent applicant is not the sole inventor, Art. 23 Patent Act requires that a declaration stating how the applicant acquired the right to the patent must accompany the patent application.

3. Licence Agreements

The Patent Act contains several provisions regulating the contents and effects of licence agreements, including licences of right and compulsory licences.

Depending on the nature of the licence agreement, in Spain, such agreement has adopted the form of a services agreement (as opposed to the supply of goods) pursuant to the provisions of the Civil Code.

Another relevant point to be considered in this area, is the subject-matter of the agreement itself, which can either be a patent or a patent application and, in the latter case, the difficulties that might arise must be expressly foreseen by the parties.

The general rule is that, unless otherwise agreed by the parties: (i) licencees are not free to assign or sub-licence the invention to third parties; and (ii) the licence will be non-exclusive, leaving the licensor free to licence the same invention to other parties.

The parties' obligations are also stipulated in the Law, especially those regarding the licensor, including the licensor's: (i) liability for eviction (or its responsibility for the lack of the necessary ownership over the patent or patent application, which is the subject-matter of the licence); (ii) liability for any defects inherent in the patented invention, distinguishing the conditions and scope thereof; and (iii) its controversial obligation to communicate the necessary teachings and knowledge for the adequate exploitation of the invention.[20]

Furthermore, the licencee's obligations mainly focus on: (i) the payment of the royalties or price established; (ii) the obligation to exploit the invention; (iii) a series of obligations relating to how to exploit the invention; and (iv) other obligations, such as the obligation to comply with certain rules on quality or on acquiring certain products or services from certain suppliers.

Furthermore, one of the most relevant subjects to be covered in licence agreements, which is also regulated in the Patent Act, is the definition of the territorial area of the licence, which is also regulated in Art. 85.3 of the EU Treaty on technology transfer agreements.[21]

In addition, within the context of intellectual property rights, depending on the registration at the relevant Registry, licences for patents and patent applications do not take effect *vis-à-vis bona fide* third parties, unless filed at the Spanish Patent and Trademark Office.

4. Technology Transfer Agreements

When analysing this type of agreement, three different aspects should be taken into account: (a) contractual; (b) intellectual property rights-related issues; and (c) competition law-related matters.

Firstly, from a contractual point of view, this type of agreement is defined as an agreement whereby a company transfers or licences the use of technical know-how and/or intellectual property rights to another company. In Spain no specific law regulates this

20 § 76 Patent Act (ES).

21 Commission Regulation (EC) No 772/2004 of 27 April 2004 on the application of Art. 81(3) of the Treaty to categories of technology transfer agreements, Official Journal of the European Union 2004 No L 123/11.

type of agreement, other than competition law-related matters. And, in general, these agreements also include an assignment or licence for use, either exclusive or non-exclusive, over: (i) patents; and/or (ii) know-how; and/or (iii) copyright over software. It is also common for the subject-matter of the agreement to include complementary services such as staff training and technical assistance after the assignment has been executed, as well as the assignment of technical equipment.

Secondly, the characteristic mutual obligations incumbent on the licensor of technology, know-how and/or intellectual property rights and on the licencee, albeit not expressly established by law, are generally imported from the specific regulation governing patent licence agreements (Chapter II of the Patent Act), as stated in the previous subsection, save the provisions on non-exclusivity and the prohibition to sub-licence, unless expressly established by the parties, and other specific patent-related provisions.

From the point of view of intellectual property rights, we must also refer here to the previous sub-section on licence agreements. In cases where the technology transfer agreement involves the licence of patent(s) and/or patent application(s), the specific provisions laid down in Chapter II of the Patent Law apply.

Finally, technology transfer agreements are also governed by certain EU competition rules[22] and by Spanish Law 15/2007, of 3 July, on the Defence of Competition, which is equivalent to Art. 81 of the EU Treaty (exemptions per category).

5. R&D Agreements

The most common R&D Agreements in Spain are those entered into between Universities and companies, whereby the latter commission the former (one or several of its lecturers or teachers) to carry out research on a certain subject. This type of agreement is not specifically regulated in Spanish law.

Depending on the nature of the agreement, most scholars agree that it is an agreement involving an obligation of means and not of results, according to the classification established in the Civil Code. That means that the professors in charge of carrying out the

---

22 Treaty Establishing the European Community of 25 March 1957, consolidated version of 24 September 2002, Official Journal No C 325; Commission Regulation (EC) No 772/2004 of 27 April 2004 on the application of Article 81(3) of the Treaty to categories of technology transfer agreements, Official Journal of the European Union 2004 No L 123/11; Commission Regulation (EC) No 2790/1999 of 22 December 1999 on the application of Article 81(3) of the Treaty to categories of vertical agreements and concerted practices, Official Journal of the European Communities 1999 No L 336/21; Commission Regulation (EC) No 2658/2000 of 29 November 2000 on the application of Article 81(3) of the Treaty to categories of specialisation agreements, Official Journal of the European Communities 2000 No L 304/3; Council Regulation (EC) No 1/2003 of 16 December 2002 on the implementation of the rules on competition laid down in Articles 81 and 82 of the Treaty, Official Journal of the European Communities 2003 No L 1/1.

research are under the obligation to observe certain standards of diligence when engaging in their activities, but will not be liable for the outcome of such research, and will be under no obligation to obtain specific results from their work.

Furthermore, with regard to termination of contract, both parties are usually free to terminate the contract by mutual agreement and, also, the company may unilaterally terminate it at any time during the term of the agreement without justification. In addition, a company unilaterally terminating an R&D Agreement will be under no obligation to compensate the University for early termination of the contract, unless the termination was inconvenient, e. g. if the University had refused to enter into another R&D Agreement with one of its competitors.

R&D Agreements do not necessarily always contain IP-related clauses, assigning the ownership of the IP rights inherent in the research. In such cases, where no express IP-related clause exists, the ownership thereof would depend on the parties' intentions, derived from the other clauses in the agreement. For instance, if the outcome of the research requested by companies was patentable, the company would have both the priority and the option to file the corresponding patent applications, and the University researchers would appear as the inventors.

The most common clauses in R&D Agreements are those regarding: (i) the execution of the work (submission of interim reports and a final report, all of which are confidential); (ii) financial contribution and payment conditions; (iii) mutual liability; (iv) knowledge and IP Rights, prior and subsequent; (v) confidentiality, publicity and information on the result, exploitation and marketing; (vi) entry into force and term of the agreement; (vii) termination; and (viii) governing law (in the case of international agreements) and competent Courts in the event of a dispute.

B. Infringing Behaviour

1. Direct and Indirect Patent Infringement

A patent confers upon its holder the right to prevent any third party, without its consent, from:

- manufacturing, offering, putting on the market or using a product, which is the subject-matter of the patent, and from importing or possessing the same for any of the aforementioned purposes;
- using a process, which is the subject-matter of the patent, or offering the use when the third party knows, or it is obvious from the circumstances, that the use of the process is prohibited without the patent holder's consent; and/or
- offering, putting on the market or using the product directly obtained following the process, which is the subject-matter of the patent, or from importing or possessing the product for any of the aforementioned purposes.

The patent also confers upon its holder the right to prevent any third party, without the holder's consent, from supplying or offering to supply to a person not entitled to work the invention, any means, relating to an essential element of the invention, for putting the invention into effect, where such third party knows, or it is obvious from the circumstances, that such means are suitable and intended for putting the invention into effect.

The following prerequisites must be met for indirect patent infringement to exist:

- the third party must know, or it must be obvious from the circumstances, that the elements are capable of putting the invention into effect and are intended for that purpose; and
- the elements must not be products commonly found on the market.

2. Doctrine of Equivalence

Spanish Courts have clarified that a patent's scope of protection is not limited to the literal wording of its claims, supported by the description and the drawings. On the contrary, the scope includes secondary, unessential and insubstantial elements, and alternative processes for its invention, which would have been foreseen by a person skilled in the art. Spanish courts and accept the "Doctrine of Equivalence", the purpose of which is to avoid circumventing the patent's scope of protection merely by varying unessential secondary elements of the patented invention.

The Doctrine of Equivalence was first applied by the Supreme Court in the late 1960's.[23] Thereafter, the criterion of "unsubstantiability" of differences has applied, consisting of assessing the infringement with regard to the existence or non-existence of "essential differences" between the patented invention and the alleged infringement. The difference between them will be essential when the variation affects an essential element of the patent and not a secondary or complementary element.

Since 2000, sec. 15 of the Provincial Court of Barcelona, which specialises in patent cases, has defined the scope of the Doctrine of Equivalence in different judgments.

With regard to mechanical patents, in a Judgment delivered on 18 September 2006,[24] Section 15 of the Provincial Court of Barcelona abandoned the "insubstantial differences" criterion due to the practical difficulties inherent therein, to apply the "substantial triple identity test", concluding that a characteristic falls within the scope of protection of an earlier patent if it substantially performs the same function, substantially in the same way and substantially produces the same result as the invention claimed in the earlier patent.

---

23 10 June 1968 Supreme Court (Contentious-Administrative Chamber), Arcanzadi, JUR 1968/3155.

24 18 September 2006 Provincial Court of Barcelona (Section 15) [415/2006], WL JUR 2008/19163.

With regard to pharmaceutical process patents, in its recent Judgment delivered on 17 January 2008,[25] Section 15 of the Provincial Court of Barcelona confirmed that the "3-questions test", traditionally applied by the English Courts (the so-called "Catnic" questions), apply to ascertain whether or not a process is "equivalent" to a patented process:

(1) "Does the variant alter the functioning of the invention?" If the answer is affirmative, equivalence does not exist. However, if the answer is negative, and the functioning is not altered, it is necessary to answer the next question.
(2) "Would the variant have been obvious to a person skilled in the art who read the patent on the date on which it was published?" If the variant were not obvious, then equivalence would not exist. However, if the answer is affirmative, the next question needs to be asked.
(3) "Would the person skilled in the art who read the patent have understood, given the terms used in the claim, that the patent holder intended, as an essential prerequisite of the invention, that it be subject to the strict wording thereof?" If so, equivalence would not exist. However, if following the literal wording were not essential, the variant could be equivalent.

3. Transit as an Infringing Behaviour

The Patent Act does not expressly state whether a patent confers upon its holder the right to prevent third parties from putting a product "in transit" on Spanish territory.

In its Judgment delivered on 12 June 2001,[26] Section 15 of the Provincial Court of Barcelona declared that the transit of patented goods constitutes patent infringement.

In order to draw this conclusion, the Provincial Court made a contextual interpretation of the Patent Act in view of the former Trademark Act, which entitled the trademark holder to prohibit, in particular, the "import and export of the products, or subjecting them to any customs regime such as, for example, transit or deposit", invoking "identity reasons in the protection of intellectual property" to construe Art. 50 Patent Act as the patent holder's right to prohibit the transit of a patented product.

C. Legal Consequences

1. Discontinuance

If an act of infringement were deemed to have been committed in Spain, the company that performed the same would be ordered to cease and desist from engaging in the infringing activity whilst the patent is in force.

---

25 17 January 2008 Provincial Court of Barcelona (Section 15) [8/2008].

26 12 June 2001 Provincial Court of Barcelona (Section 15) [Appeal 844/1998], WL AC 2002/235.

2. Information

The patent holder is entitled to request: (i) the publication of the Judgment finding the infringer guilty of patent infringement in different media, at the infringer's expense (i. e. specialised journals and press, or even in the mass media); and (ii) that notice of the Judgment finding the infringer guilty of patent infringement be served upon any interested persons or authorities, also at the infringer's expense.

3. Damages

The patent holder is entitled to obtain compensation for any damages sustained as a result of the infringement of its patent, including: (i) the loss and damage sustained by the patent holder as a result of the infringement (i. e. damage to its good name and its relationship with clients, and damage to the good reputation of the patented invention, for example, as a result of defects in the infringer's product or inadequate marketing); and (ii) income not earned because of the infringement.

Under the Patent Act, the patent holder is entitled to opt for one of the following criteria to evaluate the unearned income:

- the income the patent holder could foreseeably have earned from manufacturing and selling the patented invention had no competition existed from the company infringing its rights; and the profits made by the infringing party from manufacturing and selling the patented invention; or
- the amount the infringing party ought to have paid the patent holder for a licence in order to exploit the patent lawfully, i. e. a royalty.

In fixing this amount, special attention will be paid to certain factors, for example, the economic importance of the patented invention and the remaining term of the patent when the infringement commenced.

The patent holder's right to compensation, and the amount to be paid by the party engaging in the acts of infringement prior to the patent's expiry date, will, of course, depend on the specific acts performed by the infringer.

The party manufacturing or importing pirated products or using patented processes without the patent holder's consent, will be held liable for the damages caused.

In addition, persons who, while not manufacturing or importing the product, otherwise use the subject-matter protected by the patent, will only be held liable for compensation for the loss and damage caused if the patent holder has provided advance notice of the existence of the patent in question and their infringement thereof, and has asked them to cease such infringement, or if their actions were wilful or negligent.

The statute of limitations for bringing a civil action for patent infringement is five years from the date on which that right could have been exercised. The patent holder can only claim for loss and damage for acts performed during the five years immediately prior to the date on which the action is brought.[27]

4. Destruction

If possible, the infringing product can be seized, at the patent holder's request, in which case the value of the product would be deducted from the amount of damages awarded. If the value exceeds the amount of damages awarded, the patent holder will pay the excess amount to the infringer.

The infringing products may also be destroyed, when that is essential to prevent the patent infringement.

In the context of border seizures, once it has been confirmed that the products seized by the customs authorities infringe third parties' patent rights, the customs authorities will be entitled to destroy the goods or dispose of them outside commercial channels in order to preclude injury to the right holder. In such cases, the infringer will not be entitled to compensation. The exchequer will not meet the cost of the destruction of the goods.[28] When a Judgment orders the destruction of goods found to be pirated products, the infringer must destroy the goods during the enforcement of Judgment. Failing that, the executor (i. e. the patent holder) will be entitled to: (i) request that a third party destroy the goods on its behalf; or (ii) seek compensation for damages. In that case, the infringer will meet the cost of destroying the infringing goods.[29]

5. Recall

Spanish Courts find that an order to cease and desist from engaging in infringing activity implicitly includes the order to withdraw the infringing product from the market within a reasonable period of time. Otherwise, it would be easy to circumvent a cease and desist order by putting the infringing product on the market before a Judgment is enforced. Furthermore, the Spanish Law on Civil Procedure establishes that the offender should undo those acts that were unlawfully performed.

6. Criminal Sanctions

The rights over inventions and technological innovations and, in particular, the rights arising from patents, utility models, industrial or artistic models, drawings and topogra-

27 § 64 Patent Act (ES).

28 Art. 17 of Council Regulation (EC) No 1383/2003 concerning customs action against goods suspected of infringing certain intellectual property rights and the measures to be taken against goods found to have infringed such rights, Official Journal of the European Union 2003 No L 196/7.

29 § 706 Law on Civil Procedure (ES).

phies of semiconductor products are protected under Art. 273 of the Criminal Code. Secret patents have separate criminal protection under Art. 277 of the same Code. According to Art. 119.1 of the Patent Act, the content of all patent applications shall be kept secret for the two months following their date of filing, unless the Intellectual Property Registry authorises their prior disclosure.

For patent and utility model rights to be protected under Art. 273 of the Criminal Code, the invention or innovation must be recorded at the corresponding Registry (since patents and utility models generate exclusive rights only as of the date of registration), and the holder of the patent or utility model must not have granted its consent to the exploitation thereof.

Art. 273 Criminal Code, referring to patents and utility models protecting an object, establishes that anyone who manufactures, imports, possesses, uses or offers a protected article or puts it on the market, for industrial or commercial purposes, without the right holder's consent and in the knowledge of the registration thereof, is committing a criminal offence against patent rights or utility model rights and is, therefore, liable to be sentenced to six months' to two years' in prison and a daily fine payable over twelve and twenty-four months (ranging from EUR 2 to EUR 400 per day).

The same penalties will be imposed upon anyone who, also for those purposes, uses or offers the use of a process, which is the subject-matter of a patent, or possesses, offers, puts on the market or exploits the product directly obtained using the patented process. Under the Spanish Patent Act, the holder of an intellectual property right may prohibit third parties from engaging in these punishable acts.

Secret patents are separately protected under Art. 277, which establishes prison sentences of six months to two years and a fine between six and twenty-four months (ranging from EUR 2 to EUR 400 per day) imposed upon anyone who intentionally discloses the invention, which is the subject-matter of a secret patent application, in breach of the provisions of patent law, provided that that is to the detriment of national defence.

IV. Know-How Piracy

A. Know-How as a Trade Secret

Know-how comprises any knowledge or information which is not common knowledge, and which is required: (i) to manufacture or market a product; (ii) render a service; or (iii) organise a business unit or office, since know-how provides its holder with an advantage over its competitors.[30] Know-how is, therefore, information that can be used to solve certain technical and business problems.

---

30 24 October 1979 Supreme Court, Civil Chamber [WL RJ 19793\459]; 21 October 2005 Supreme Court, Civil Chamber [Judgment nº 754/2005], WL RJ 2005\8274.

The term "*trade secret*" is not legally defined. However, Spanish case law establishes the following prerequisites to be able to consider know-how as a "*trade secret*":[31]

1. Information must be secret

Information is secret when a third party is interested in, but has no knowledge of, the information, either in whole or in part. The fact that few people know this information, when such people are: (i) related to the company (thus explaining how they know the secret); and (ii) subject to a general undertaking to keep the information confidential or to a contractual obligation of secrecy, does not undermine the secrecy of the information.

Information comprising an individual's ability, capacity and professional experience, or knowledge and relations with clients is not considered secret,[32] even when such ability, capacity and experience have been acquired as a result of performing certain duties.

2. Information must entail a competitive edge

Competitive edge is the advantage that the owner of the information has when using such information *vis-à-vis* companies which do not know the same.[33] The status of information as a trade secret does not depend on the high or low economic value of the trade secret *per se*, but on the competitor's knowledge and the possibility of it obtaining a profit by exploiting such information.

3. The holder of the information must take steps to keep the information secret

Whether the information is obtained as a result of a contractual relationship or obtained unlawfully, the use of the same will not be considered unfair competition, unless the owner of the business information has taken the appropriate steps to keep it secret: (i) both externally (preventing third parties from accessing the information); and (ii) internally (whereby only employees may access the information they need to know to perform their duties).

---

[31] 21 December 2001 Provincial Court of Barcelona, Civil Chamber, WL AC 2003/1868 inter alia; 26 November 2004 Provincial Court of Barcelona, Civil Chamber [Judgment nº 506/2004], WL AC 2004/2199; 26 October 2005 Provincial Court of Barcelona, Civil Chamber [Judgment nº 443/2005], WL AC 2006/365.

[32] 26 October 2005 Provincial Court of Barcelona, Civil Chamber [Judgment nº 443/2005], WL AC 2006/365; 8 October 2007 Supreme Court, Civil Chamber [Judgment nº 1032/2007], WL RJ 2007/6805.

[33] 10 June 1998 Provincial Court of Navarra (Civil Chamber) [Judgment nº 133/1998], WL AC 1998/1455; 14 January 2003 Provincial Court of Barcelona (Civil Chamber), WL AC 2004/202.

B. Measures to Protect Know-How

Under Spanish law, the owners of know-how may protect it by implementing various measures, which can be classified as either: (i) contractual; or (ii) practical, designed to control the access to and the use of such know-how.

1. Contractual Measures

a. Confidentiality Clause

Although some individuals have a legal duty of secrecy[34] inherent in their duties, an effective measure for protecting know-how is to include a confidentiality clause in contracts entered into with employees, collaborators, suppliers and any other individuals who may have access to the know-how. The contents of such clause are not legally defined. Hence, the clause must be freely agreed by the parties. In any case, it is clear that such clause should guarantee that the individual who will have access to the know-how keeps the information secret and does not misuse it for his/her own profit, during the term of the contract and upon termination thereof.[35]

b. Confidentiality Agreement

Parties usually sign a confidentiality agreement when negotiating the acquisition of a company, or in the framework of the joint development of new software, technology, etc. The contents of such agreement are not legally defined. Hence, it must be freely agreed by the parties.[36] However, due to the complexity of such transactions, confidentiality agreements usually contain rather specific obligations, such as: (i) using the information provided exclusively for the purposes intended; (ii) returning all documentation and media containing confidential information after the transaction has been closed; (iii) refraining from confirming or refuting information from third parties, which is consistent with or contrary to the information exchanged; (iv) taking the necessary steps to ensure that the parties' representatives and employees fulfil any obligation imposed upon them, etc.

---

34 This is the case for employees (Real Decreto Legislativo 1/1995, de 24 de marzo, por el que se aprueba el texto refundido de la Ley del Estatuto de los Trabajadores [Workers' Statute], § 5 ¶ a) (ES)), top executives and company directors (Real Decreto Legislativo 1564/1989, de 22 de diciembre, por el que se aprueba el texto refundido de la Ley de Sociedades Anónimas [Companies' Act], § 127 quater (ES), and Ley 2/1995, de 23 de marzo, de Sociedades de Responsabilidad Limitada [Limited Liability Companies' Act], § 61 ¶ 2) (ES).

35 10 June 1998 Provincial Court of Navarra, Civil Chamber [Judgment nº 133/1998], WL AC 1998/1455.

36 According to the general principles and rules of the Civil Code and the Real Decreto de 22 de agosto de 1885 por el que se publica el Código de Comercio [Commercial Code] (ES).

In addition, confidentiality agreements are more advantageous from a litigation point of view than pursuing an unfair competition action. The statute of limitations for bringing civil actions for the breach of a confidentiality agreement expires after 15 years, compared to 1 or 3 years for unfair competition actions.[37] Furthermore, it is only necessary to prove a breach of contract and not the subjective element of the unfair competition acts (i. e. to obtain a profit personally or for a third party, or to cause damage to the owner of the confidential information).

2. Practical Measures

In order to preserve the secrecy of know-how, an owner can implement appropriate practical measures, not only to prevent third parties from gaining access, but also to restrict access to and use of such know-how to ensure that only employees and collaborators who need it to perform their duties, do so.

Some of the many practical measures that an owner may adopt to protect its know-how include: (i) security access controls for certain premises; (ii) use of passwords required to access certain confidential information; (iii) conservation of relevant materials in restricted-access areas; (iv) appropriate warnings placed on documents or materials; (vi) advisories stating that certain information or documents are confidential and must be returned if the user is not the intended recipient; (v) preventing copies of information from being made using USB or similar devices, etc.

C. Know-How Piracy as Unfair Competition

Article 13 of the Unfair Competition Act establishes that the disclosure or exploitation of trade secrets which have been obtained lawfully but under a duty of secrecy without the owner's consent is considered an unfair act. The acquisition of trade secrets using espionage or similar methods is also considered an unfair act. In addition, trade secrets must have been violated in order to obtain personal profit or profit on behalf of a third party, or to cause damage to the owner of the secret.

1. Disclosure or Exploitation of Trade Secrets, without the Owner's Consent

"Disclosure" includes the communication of the information through any media, which allows for such information to be re-used at a later date. The party obtaining the trade secret will perhaps disclose such information to: (1) the general public; or (2) a specific individual who is not authorised to know the business information. "Disclosure" exists even if the recipient of the secret does not earn a profit from exploiting it. "Exploitation" is the use of the secret information to obtain an advantage for any purpose or in any manner.

---

37 § 1,964 Civil Code (ES) and § 21 Unfair Competition Act (ES).

2. Lawful Access to Trade Secrets but under a Duty of Secrecy

Access to information is considered lawful when such access is permitted and agreed by the parties. The duty of secrecy should be construed as the obligation incumbent on the parties to keep the information confidential, without permitting third parties to gain access thereto.

3. Acquisition of Trade Secrets using Espionage or Similar Methods

Industrial espionage or similar methods include all acts of misappropriation of trade secrets, both the media containing the confidential information and the information itself, obtained using any means (photograph, photocopy, scanner, etc.), by individuals not authorised by the owner of the trade secrets.

4. Trade Secrets must have been violated in order to obtain personal profit or profit for a Third Party, or to cause Damage to the Owner of the Secret

The Unfair Competition Act requires a subjective element to consider conduct as unfair, i. e. that trade secrets must have been breached in order to obtain a profit personally or for a third party, or to cause damage to the owner of the secret. Therefore, the acquisition, disclosure or exploitation of trade secrets does not *per se* constitute an act of unfair competition, unless that is the underlying purpose thereof.

An individual's acts, which cumulatively meet such legal requirements, may be considered as acts of unfair competition as a result of a breach of trade secrets.[38] In that case, the Unfair Competition Act provides various legal actions for the benefit of the owner of the trade secret: (i) declaratory action, stating the unfairness of the act; (ii) actions for the cessation of the unfair act or for the prohibition thereof, if not yet implemented; (iii) actions to remove the effects produced by the act; (iv) actions seeking compensation for the loss and damage caused; and (vi) actions for unfair enrichment.

D. Criminal Sanctions

The Criminal Code protects trade secrets under Articles 278 and 279, which establish the sanctions for criminal offences against such trade secrets.

Indeed, Art. 278 Criminal Code, referring to obtaining data or articles to discover a trade secret, establishes a prison sentence of two to four years and a fine payable over

38 However, in some cases in which not all of these prerequisites are met, some Judgments have considered the acts as unfair on the grounds that they breach the general principle of good faith (§ 5 Unfair Competition Act). In that respect, 24 November 2006 Supreme Court, Civil Chamber [Judgment nº 1169/2006], WL RJ 2007/262; 8 October 2007 Supreme Court, Civil Chamber [Judgment nº 1032/2007], WL RJ 2007/6805.

twelve to twenty-four months (ranging from EUR 2 to EUR 400 per day) for anyone who obtains, and through any means, data, written or electronic documents, computer programmes or other objects for the purpose of discovering a trade secret. A conviction will be higher -in particular, a prison sentence of three to five years and a daily fine payable over twelve to twenty-four months- when the person found guilty spreads, discloses or passes on the discovered secrets to third parties. In addition, these penalties will apply, without prejudice to any other sanctions that may be imposed for obtaining or destroying the computer programmes.

For its part, Art. 279 Criminal Code, on the spreading, disclosure or passing on of trade secrets establishes that anyone legally or contractually bound to maintain the confidentiality of a trade secret who is found guilty of spreading, disclosing or passing on the trade secret, will be sentenced to two to four years in prison and a daily fine payable over twelve to twenty-four months. In that respect, it should be noted that the sanctions would be applied at a rate of 50% when the guilty person uses the secret for personal profit.

V. Music, Film and Software Piracy

A. Substantive Requirements for Protection

Art. 10.1 of Legislative Royal Decree No. 1/1996 (Real Decreto Legislativo 1/1996 de Propiedad Intelectual [Legislative Royal Decree No. 1/1996 on Intellectual Property] (ES)) establishes that copyright protection covers all original literary, artistic or scientific creations, expressed through any means or in any medium, tangible or intangible, known at present or invented in the future.[39] This article stipulates the two substantives requirements for a work to enjoy copyright protection: (i) a form of expression; and (ii) the originality of that form of expression.

There are no formal requirements for the protection of copyright works. Therefore, the recording of a work at the Intellectual Property Registry is always declarative (voluntary) and does not constitute a requirement for protection (Art. 145 of Legislative Royal Decree No. 1/1996).[40]

In addition to copyright, reference must also be made to rights related to copyright ("*Droits Voisins*" or Neighbouring Rights). This term refers to several rights, including the Rights of Artists (Interpreters or Performers), Producers of Sound Recordings, Producers of Audiovisual Recordings and Broadcasters. Each one gives rise to a production

---

39 Real Decreto Legislativo 1/1996 de Propiedad Intelectual [RLD No. 1/1996] [Legislative Royal Decree No. 1/1996 on Intellectual Property] Art. 10.1 (ES) contains a non-limitative (illustrative and non-exhaustive) list of such works ("*musical works, with or without words*", "*motion pictures and any audiovisual works*" and "*computer programs*" are types of works specifically mentioned).

40 Nevertheless, works created prior to 7 December 1987 must be recorded at the Intellectual Property Registry.

warranting protection, without having to meet the prerequisite of originality or registration.

B. Infringing Behaviour

A copyright holder's rights are infringed when, without the holder's consent, a third party performs an act requiring such consent. Thus, the use of a work protected by copyright falling within the scope of the rights granted under Art. 17 Legislative Royal Decree No. 1/1996[41] constitutes an act of copyright infringement. With regard to rights related to copyright, any third party performing an act of reproduction, distribution or communication to the public of the subject-matter of a Related Right, without the holder's consent, also commits an act of infringement.[42]

Finally, specific provisions are established in the Organic Law on the Criminal Code with regard to piracy. In particular, Art. 270 Organic Law on the Criminal Code states that: "*1. Any person shall be punished with a prison term of six months to two years or a fine of six to 24 monthly units* [ranging from EUR 2 to EUR 400 per day] *who, with gainful intent and to the detriment of third parties, reproduces, plagiarises, distributes or communicates to the public all or part of a literary, artistic or scientific work or transformation or artistic performance thereof fixed in any kind of material or communicated by any medium, acting without the authorisation of the holders of the corresponding intellectual property rights or their licencees.*"

1. Copy for Private Use

Pursuant to the provisions of Art. 31.2 Legislative Royal Decree No. 1/1996, the reproduction in any medium of a disclosed work (excluding computer programmes and databases) does not require the author's consent, if performed by a natural person for his/her private use, and provided that the copy is not used for either collective or gainful purposes, without prejudice to the fair compensation provided for in Art. 25 Legislative Royal Decree No. 1/1996.

---

41 According to Legislative Royal Decree No. 1/1996 Art. 17 "*The author is invested with the exclusive exercise of the rights pertaining to the exploitation of his work in whatever form and especially the rights of reproduction, distribution, communication to the public and transformation, which may not be exercised without his authorisation, except where this Law so provides*".

42 See Legislative Royal Decree No. 1/1996 Art. 107 to 109 with regard to the rights of artists; Legislative Royal Decree No. 1/1996 Art. 115 to 117 (ES) with regard to the rights of the producers of sound recordings; Legislative Royal Decree No. 1/1996 Art. 121 to 125 (ES) with regard to the rights of the producers of audiovisual recordings; and Legislative Royal Decree No. 1/1996 Art. 126 (ES) with regard to the rights of broadcasters.

C. Enforcement

1. Search and Seizure – Private Persons

Without prejudice to criminal sanctions, the holder whose copyright or rights related to copyright have been infringed may file civil proceedings or apply for interim injunctions to restrain the unlawful activity committed by the infringing party, either a natural or private person. In particular, the holder may seek the adoption of the necessary measures to prevent the continued infringement of its rights, including the search for and seizure of the copies produced or used infringing its rights, as well as any means (equipment, devices and materials) used for such production. The holder can also seek the destruction of the objects or means seized, in order to prevent such infringement.

2. Duty of Disclosure of Online Providers

According to the Judgment delivered by the ECJ on 29 January 2008 (C- 275/06; *Promusicae* v. *Telefónica*) European law "*does not require member states to lay down an obligation to disclose personal data in the context of civil proceedings*". In that case, that was referring to the duty of disclosure of the Internet Service Provider *Telefónica*. Under Spanish law, *Promusicae* had asked that company to disclose the names and addresses of the users who allegedly infringed copyright songs via the p2p software "KaZaA". Mercantile Court No. 5 of Madrid asked the ECJ for the interpretation of the E-Commerce Directive (Directive 2000/31/EC of 8 June 2000 on certain legal aspects of information society services, in particular electronic commerce, in the Internal Market) on this matter. In its Judgment, the ECJ found that although "*community rights do not oblige Member States to disclose personal data in order to ensure the effective protection of copyright, in the context of civil proceedings*", when adapting their national legislation to EU law, countries must "*base their adaptations on an interpretation of these laws that guarantees the fair balance between the fundamental rights protected*", which includes respecting the right of privacy and copyright.

3. Border Measures

The border measures established in Customs Regulation and European Community Commission Regulation, which constitute the framework for the Spanish customs authorities to detain and seize pirated products, are a useful tool to combat music, film and software piracy.

The Sub-department of Customs Administration at the Department of Customs and Special Taxes *(Subdirección General de Gestión Aduanera en el Departamento de Aduanas e Impuestos Especiales)* is fully aware of the turnover generated by the music, film or computer games industries devoted to leisure activities and the harm that piracy products cause to copyright and related right holders.

D. Legal Consequences

1. Discontinuance

Pursuant to the provisions of Articles 138 and 139.1 Legislative Royal Decree No. 1/1996, the holder whose copyright or rights related to copyright have been infringed may, without prejudice to any other action, apply for an injunction restraining the unlawful activity.

In particular, the Court may issue a restraining order to suspend the infringing exploitation, prohibit the infringer from resuming it and withdraw from the market and destroy the copies and means used for the infringement.

Specific restraining orders are established in Art. 139.1 lit. e) to lit. h) Legislative Royal Decree No. 1/1996 with regard to the means used for the unlawful activities of public communication of works (including the suspension of the activity of internet service providers) and for the circumvention of technological measures designed to protect software or prevent or restrict unlawful acts.

2. Information

Under Law 19/2006, of 5 June 2006, implementing in Law Enforcement Directive, the holder of copyright or related rights may require, prior to the commencement of the main proceedings on the merits of the case, that the financial or commercial documentation belonging to the person responsible be submitted in order to prove the alleged infringement on a commercial scale. Additional information may also be required: (i) the names and addresses of the producers, manufacturers, distributors, suppliers and other previous holders of the goods or services, as well as the intended wholesalers and retailers; (ii) the origin and distribution networks of the goods or services infringing copyright or rights related to copyright; and (iii) the quantities produced, manufactured, delivered, received or ordered, as well as the price obtained for the goods or services in question.

3. Damages

The holder of copyright or rights related to copyright may seek compensation for the damages it sustains as a result of the infringement thereof.

Art. 140.2 Legislative Royal Decree No. 1/1996 establishes that compensation for damages can be calculated in accordance with one of the following criteria, at the damaged party's choice: (a) the negative economic consequences for the holder, including the profits the holder could foreseeably have made and the profits earned by the infringing party from exploiting the copyright or rights related to copyright; and (b) the amount the infringing party ought to have paid the holder for a licence which would have enabled it to exploit the rights lawfully.

Lastly, the holder can also claim for moral damages (on his reputation), in addition to lost profits.

4. Destruction

Pursuant to the provisions of Art. 139.1 Legislative Royal Decree No. 1/1996, the holder of copyright or rights related to copyright may seek the destruction of the copies produced or used infringing its rights –including copies circumventing technological measures designed to prevent or restrict acts– and any means (equipment, devices and materials) used for producing such copies or for circumventing technological measures designed to prevent or restrict acts. The cost of destruction will be borne by the infringing party.

5. Recall

Pursuant to the provisions of Art. 139.1 Legislative Royal Decree No. 1/1996, the holder whose copyright or rights related to copyright have been infringed may seek the withdrawal of the copies and means used for the infringement.

6. Criminal Sanctions

Art. 270 Criminal Code provides for penalties of a prison sentence of six months to two years and a daily fine payable over twelve to twenty four months (ranging from EUR 2 to EUR 400 per day). Penalised acts include the reproduction, plagiarism, distribution or public communication, in whole or in part, of any literary, artistic or scientific work, or its transformation, interpretation or artistic execution recorded in any format or communicated through any means, for profit-making purposes and to the detriment of a third party, without the consent of the holders of the corresponding intellectual property rights or their assignees.

The same penalties apply with regard to: (i) exporting or storing copies of the works, productions or executions without consent; and (ii) intentionally importing these products without consent, whether they are of lawful or unlawful origin in their country of origin. Nevertheless, importing the products from an EU Member State will not be penalised when they have been acquired directly from the holder of the rights in the State or with its consent. Copies of the works that have been exported, imported or stored could be produced either legally or illegally, as in both cases the acts that may be sanctioned affect the distribution right.

The protection established in this article would cover music, film and software because, according to the Copyright Act, the subject-matter of intellectual property is all original literary, artistic or scientific creations expressed in any manner or medium, whether tangible or intangible, that is known at present or may be invented in the future, including musical compositions with or without words, cinematographic works and any other audiovisual works and computer programmes.

It is not necessary to register the work in order to obtain criminal protection because, according to the Copyright Act, the intellectual property in a literary, artistic or scientific work belongs to the author merely by virtue of its creation.

In order to consider certain conduct as punishable under this article, wilful misconduct must be proven. In that respect, anyone performing the prohibited acts (reproduction, plagiarism, distribution or public communication) must have known that the work belongs to a third party and that such acts are committed without the right holder's consent.

Reproduction and distribution

Marketing pirated copies of DVDs and renting CDs or DVDs without authorisation are clear acts of distribution, which are criminally punishable. Legal doctrine and case law are divided regarding whether or not effective damage to a third party is an essential prerequisite, in order to determine the existence of a criminal offence. One view considers that if the damage to a third party is not proven, the infringement would not fall under the category of a criminal offence.[43] However, case law is inclined to consider that the mere offer and distribution of CDs and DVDs is sufficient to find that the offence has been committed, since the aim to make a profit is clearly proven.[44]

Plagiarism

Plagiarism is construed as a copy or an appropriation of the essential contents of the work belonging to a third party. Although it is easy to detect plagiarism in clear copies, this it more difficult in the case of imitations. It is especially difficult to detect plagiarism in computer programmes where, in order to determine what is essential or not, that can only be resolved by taking expert reports into account.

The Criminal Chamber of the Supreme Court has considered as plagiarism tape recordings of songs performed by a third party imitating the original performer's manner of singing, as this was sufficient evidence that a real attempt existed to replace the original performance.[45] However, legal doctrine has interpreted that "cover versions", in which it is clearly shown that the singer is imitating a famous singer, would not be considered as plagiarism punishable under criminal law.[46]

---

43 7 February 2001 Provincial Court of Las Palmas, Criminal Chamber [Judgment 25/2001], WL ARP 2001\24 states that the holders of the rights over video tapes do not sustain any damage due to the sale on street markets of certain video tapes bearing characteristics that prove that they are crude copies of the original.

44 23 May 1994 Supreme Court, Criminal Chamber [Judgment 1015/1994], WL RJ 1994\3946; 20 April 2005 Provincial Court of Alicante [Judgment nº 282/2005], WL JUR 2005\164656.

45 9 June 1990 Supreme Court, Criminal Chamber, WL RJ 1990\5251.

46 30 May 2002 Provincial Court of the Balearic Islands [Judgment 87/2002], WL JUR 2002\204360.

Means for neutralising copyright protection (copyright circumvention technology)

The protection of software is specifically regulated in Art. 270.3, which establishes the same punishment for anyone who manufactures, imports, puts on the market or possesses any means specifically aimed at facilitating the unauthorised suppression or neutralisation of any technical device used to protect computer programmes or any other works, interpretations or executions. This regulation protects computer programme security systems, and sanctions the preparatory work carried out for those acts, which constitute the effective infringement of intellectual property rights.

Considering that the possession of any means for neutralising copyright protection must be for profit-*making* purposes, part of legal doctrine states that the possession of any means for neutralising a technical device to make a private copy (for example, of a CD), cannot be considered as a criminal offence.

Civil liability derived from criminal offences is governed by the provisions of the Spanish Property Law relating to ceasing to engage in the unlawful activity and compensating the loss and damage. The Criminal Code also states that, in the event of a Judgment allowing the plaintiff's claims, the Court or Tribunal may order the publication of the Judgment in an official newspaper, at the infringing party's expense.

VI. Parallel Imports

Parallel imports are non-counterfeit products imported from another country without the consent of the holder of the Intellectual Property Right protecting such products. The debate that revolves around parallel imports focuses on the boundary between the principle of free movement of goods, on the one hand, and Intellectual Property Rights, on the other hand. In particular, the extent to which the holder of the Intellectual Property Right (albeit a trademark, patent or copyright) is entitled to exercise its rights to restrict the importation by a third party of products, which are subject to the Intellectual Property Right, after the products in question have been placed on the market somewhere else by its holder or with its consent.

A. Exhaustion of Intellectual Property Rights and Parallel Imports

Intellectual Property Rights grant their holders an exclusive right to use their subject-matter on the market, conferring upon them the right to prohibit unauthorised third parties from using the Intellectual Property Right at hand without their consent. However, Intellectual Property Rights do not confer an absolute right upon their holders, as they can be exhausted. In fact, according to the Spanish law regulating trademarks,[47]

[47] § 36 ¶ 1 Trademark Act (ES): "*The rights conferred by a registered trademark shall not entitle its proprietor to prohibit third parties from exploiting it for products bearing such a trademark marketed in the European Economic Area by the proprietor or with its consent.*"

patents[48] and copyright,[49] the so-called principle of exhaustion applies to each of these Intellectual Property Rights.

According to the principle of exhaustion, the right conferred by the Intellectual Property Right does not entitle its holder to prohibit third parties from exploiting its subject-matter regarding products marketed in the European Economic Area by the holder or with its consent.

The conditions for the exhaustion of Intellectual Property Rights to apply can be summarised as follows: (i) it refers to the original products, and not to counterfeits; (ii) the products have been placed on the market in the European Economic Area by their holder or with its consent; and (iii) the goods have been placed on the market under a transfer of ownership agreement. If any of these three conditions is not met, the exhaustion of rights does not apply and, consequently, the Intellectual Property Right holder will be entitled to defend its Intellectual Property Right against the parallel import.

B. Evolution of Spanish Case Law applying to the Principle of Exhaustion of Intellectual Property Rights

When analysing Spanish case law on the principle of the exhaustion of Intellectual Property Rights, it is worth mentioning the unfortunate line that was followed by the first set of Judgments delivered by Spanish Courts on the principle of exhaustion, which were incompatible with the ECJ's case law, as they initially defended its international scope. This international principle of exhaustion of Intellectual Property Rights was first established by the Supreme Court in its Judgment delivered in the *Scotsman* case[50] and followed by its Judgment in the *Bacardi* case.[51]

Notwithstanding the foregoing, this tendency has finally been overridden by several Judgments delivered by the Spanish Courts, which have applied the principle of exhaustion of rights in view of the ECJ's case law, therefore, limiting its scope to the European Economic Area.

---

48 § 52 ¶ 2 Patent Act (ES): "*The rights conferred by the patent shall not cover the acts regarding a product protected under the said patent after it has been put on the market in the territory of a European Union Member State by the patent holder or with its consent.*"

49 Real Decreto Legislativo 1/1996 de Propiedad Intelectual [Legislative Royal Decree 1/1996 on Intellectual Property], § 19 ¶ 2 (ES): "*When the distribution is implemented through the sale or through any other property transfer title, within the European Union, by the right holder or with its consent, these rights will be exhausted with the former, but only regarding the subsequent sales and property transfers that take place within this territory.*"

50 15 May 1985 Supreme Court, Civil Chamber [Judgment bearing no docket number], WL RJ 1985\2393 (Scotsman).

51 28 September 2001 Supreme Court, Civil Chamber [Judgment nº 2/2001], WL RJ 2001\8718 (Bacardi).

With regard to the recent line of argument adopted by Spanish case law, we refer to Judgments on trademarks and, in particular, the Judgment handed down by the Spanish Supreme Court[52] in the *Reebok* case, in which the Supreme Court found that the claimant's right was not exhausted by the first marketing of the goods bearing its trademarks, since it occurred outside the European Economic Area. As a result, it concluded that the claimant was entitled to control the first marketing in the area by means of exercising *ius prohibiendi* with regard to the importation carried out by the defendant.[53] This train of thought was confirmed by the recent Judgment delivered by the Spanish Supreme Court in the *Philip Morris* case[54] and by lower Spanish Courts.[55]

This case law established and followed by the Spanish Courts regarding the Community's exhaustion of trademarks *vis-à-vis* products which were parallel imported bearing the trademark, has also been followed when the Intellectual Property Right affected is copyright. In that respect, we refer to the Supreme Court Judgment in the *Dienc* case.[56]

With regard to parallel imported products falling under the scope of protection of a patent, there is no Spanish case law implementing the exhaustion principle regarding patent rights. However, taking into account the wording of Art. 52.2 Patent Act, the case law developed by Spanish Courts regarding trademarks and copyright and the ECJ's case law regarding patent rights,[57] it is likely that the Spanish Courts will also apply the Community exhaustion principle as described above.

---

52 20 December 2006 Supreme Court, Civil Chamber [Judgment nº 99/2005], WL RJ 2006\288 (Reebok).

53 Third Point of Law of 20 December 2006 Supreme Court, Civil Chamber [Judgment nº 999/2005], WL RJ 2006\288 (Reebok).

54 23 March 2007 Supreme Court, Civil Chamber [Judgment nº 311/2007], WL RJ 2007\2317 (Philip Morris).

55 We refer to the following Judgments: 26 May 2003 Provincial Court of Asturias (Section 6), Civil Chamber [Judgment nº 247/2003], WL AC 2003\1574; 30 January 2004 Provincial Court of Barcelona (Section 15) [Judgment bearing no docket number], WL AC 2004\506; 10 February 2004 Provincial Court of Madrid (Section 14), Civil Chamber [Judgment nº 86/2004], WL JUR 2004\250554; 21 June 2004 Provincial Court of Madrid (Section 10), Civil Chamber [Judgment nº 765/2004], WL JUR 2004\235551; 2 February 2005 Provincial Court of Madrid (Section 20), Civil Chamber [Judgment nº 90/2005], WL AC 2005\880; 5 October 2007 Provincial Court of Valencia (Section 9), Civil Chamber [Judgment nº 52/2007], WL AC 2007\2063.

56 29 November 2006 Supreme Court, Civil Chamber [Judgment nº 1190/2006], WL RJ 2007\372 (Dienc).

57 31 October 1974 ECJ [Case 15/74], [1974] ECR 1147 (Centrafarm v Sterling); 9 July 1985 ECJ [Case 19/84], [1985] ECR 2281 (Pharmon v Hoechst); 14 July 1981 ECJ [Case 187/80], [1981] ECR 2062 (Merck v Sephar).

C. Legal Action against Parallel Imports when Intellectual Property Rights are not exhausted

If parallel imports are made without the consent of the Intellectual Property Right holder and the principle of exhaustion does not apply (because the products were placed on the market by the holder or with its consent outside the European Economic Area), the holder would be entitled to file against it the corresponding civil action for Intellectual Property Right infringement before the corresponding Mercantile Court in the city where the defendant has its registered address or where the infringement has taken effect.

In the case of trademarks and copyright, the holder may also take criminal action against the parallel importer. Under the Criminal Code,[58] the importation of products bearing a registered trademark wilfully carried out without the holder's consent is a criminal offence against trademark rights, provided that the importation of these products from a Member State of the European Union had not been directly acquired from the holder of the rights in that State or with its consent. No similar provision is established in the Criminal Code for patents because, when implementing the criminal offence against patent rights, it does not expressly classify parallel imports as a means of committing such an offence.

---

58 § 270 Criminal Code (ES) as amended by Organic law 15/2003 regarding the criminal offence against copyright and § 274 Criminal Code (ES) as amended by Organic law 15/2003 regarding the criminal offence against trademarks (ES).

Product Piracy in France

Jean-Frédéric Gaultier/Emmanuelle Levy

I. Enforcement of Intellectual Property Rights in France

Intellectual property rights infringement is a civil tort and a criminal offence punishable by a fine of up to EUR 300,000 and imprisonment of up to three years.[1] Both fine and imprisonment sentences may be increased when infringers are members of a criminal organization (sentences of a fine of up to EUR 500,000 and imprisonment of up to five years). Intellectual property rights infringement is also a customs offence. Legal proceedings may be initiated before either criminal or civil courts, at the discretion of the rights-holder.

Before initiating proceedings, the rights holder may have to carry out preliminary acts with a view to collect evidence. Infringement can be proven by any means. The most common way to collect evidence of intellectual property infringement is known as "saisie-contrefaçon" (infringement seizure). The claimant applies *ex parte* to the judge to be authorised to have investigation carried out at the premises where the alleged infringing goods are likely to be found. Claimant must only prove he owns an intellectual property right. The judge may authorise a mere description of the goods, by taking samples and relevant documents or, more rarely, a seizure *in rem*. Evidence so collected may be used in civil or criminal proceedings and, in some circumstances, in proceedings initiated abroad.

A. Civil Action

Two main types of proceedings may be contemplated.

Claimant may apply for a **preliminary injunction** in an *inter partes* procedure, or on an *ex parte* basis if circumstances justify it (e. g. delay would cause the plaintiff irreparable damage). The injunction will be granted subject to the production of evidence, reasonably accessible to the claimant, that are likely to establish that the infringement is plausible. A decision is usually rendered within a month or two, though when a specific urgency is demonstrated it could be dealt with in a matter of days. Proceedings on the

1 Trademarks: Code de la propriété industrielle [CPI] [Intellectual Property Code], art. L.716-10 (F. R.); Designs: Code de la propriété industrielle [CPI] [Intellectual Property Code], art. L.521-9 (F. R.); Patents: Code de la propriété industrielle [CPI] [Intellectual Property Code], art. L.615-14 (F. R.); Author Rights Code de la propriété industrielle [CPI] [Intellectual Property Code], art. L.335-4 (F. R.)

merits must then be initiated. The decision may be appealed and is likely to be reviewed by the court of appeal through fast track proceedings within two to three months.

Proceedings on the merits are initiated by a writ of summons notified by the claimant to the defendant, which details the grounds for the action. The list of documents in support of the claim is attached thereto (but not the documents themselves). The notified claim is then filed with the court. The court will regularly set dates by which the parties file submissions replying to the other's arguments. Standard proceedings on the merits usually last around twelve months until a first instance decision is rendered. In specific circumstances, fast track proceedings on the merits can be initiated, with a view to try to obtain a decision within a matter of days or, more generally, three to four months. Once the lower court has rendered its decision, it is possible to lodge an appeal before the court of appeal. The proceedings before the court of appeal may last between eighteen and twenty-four months. Enforcement is stayed pending appeal, unless immediate enforcement is ordered, which is often the case in intellectual property matters.

B. Public Law

In addition to an infringment of intellectual property right, importation of infringing goods is also a customs offence.

French customs agents may seize imported infringing goods, usually at the request of intellectual property right owners or, more rarely, on their own initiative. Intellectual property right owners need to file either a French or a European customs application designating, *inter alia*, France. The purpose of such application is to seek the involvement of customs agents in looking out for and impounding potential counterfeit goods.

If French customs agents find goods suspected of being counterfeits, they retain them and inform the intellectual property rights holder. The goods can be retained for up to ten working days from notification of the information to the right holder. During this time period, customs agents are authorised to disclose limited information such that the intellectual property rights holder can determine whether the goods are counterfeits.

If the goods are counterfeits, the intellectual property rights holder has ten days, beginning when the seizure is notified to him, to initiate proceedings before French courts. Since intellectual property rights infringement is also a customs offence, customs agents are empowered to seize and destroy the goods when such goods are obvious counterfeits, without any legal action being required from the intellectual property rights holder. This solution is generally chosen when the number and/or value of the counterfeited products is limited. Otherwise, failing a court action initiated by the intellectual property right owner, products will be released.

C. Criminal Action

Intellectual property rights holders may also elect the criminal route; they usually do so with a view to set a precedent and serve as a deterrent. The action may be initiated by filing a direct criminal claim *(citation directe)* or a criminal complaint. Filing a complaint that will lead to a criminal investigation carried out by a judge is rarely the route chosen. Right holders prefer to file a direct claim as it is likely to be dealt with more quickly by the court. The direct claim is the equivalent of a writ of summons before civil courts. The public prosecutor is compelled to join the proceedings. He does not have discretion to close the matter without the parties consent. Conversely, the plaintiff may decide to withdraw his/her claims, but the public prosecutor may decide to continue the action on his/her own.

After the filing of the claim, a first procedural hearing takes place in order to set the schedule of the trial. The plaintiff is required to make a deposit *(consignation)*, the purpose of which is to guarantee payment of a potential fine in case of dismissal of the claim. The amount of this deposit rarely exceeds EUR 5,000, and will be fully reimbursed if the claim succeeds. Criminal proceedings usually last eight to ten months. Once the lower criminal court has rendered its decision, it is possible to lodge an appeal before the court of appeal. Appeal proceedings may last between eighteen and twenty-four months. Enforcement will be stayed pending appeal.

II. Trademark Piracy

A. Legal Requirements for Trademark Protection

Various signs may constitute a trademark such as words, letters, numbers, logos, shapes, colours, sounds, musical phrases, etc. These signs must comply with the following requirements:

1. The trademark must be capable of graphic representation and distinctiveness[2]

The requirement of graphic representation does not raise specific issues, safe for olfactory and gustatory signs. In a decision of 3 October 2003,[3] the Paris Court of Appeal confirmed the dismissal of a trademark application for "artificial taste of strawberries" since this representation was neither objective nor precise.

Distinctiveness means that the chosen sign is arbitrary with respect to the goods and/or services it designates and, consequently, not generic nor descriptive. That is, the sign must not be necessary or commonly used to designate the object. The sign does not need to be new. A sign already existing may be arbitrary, and therefore distinctive in respect of specific goods and/or services.

2 Code de la propriété industrielle [CPI] [Intellectual Property Code], art. L.711-1 (F. R.).

3 3 October 2003 Paris Court of Appeal, PIBD III 2004, 2433.

Distinctiveness may be acquired through use of the mark amongst the public. The acquisition of the distinctive character of the mark through use is appreciated on a case-by-case basis by the courts. For instance, it has been judged that the use for more than ten years of the packaging of the Smarties's candies (made of a cylindrical tube, in cardboard, with a specific end shape) contributed to make the figurative trademark attractive and distinctive.[4]

2. The trademark must be lawful[5]

French laws prohibit the adoption of the following as trademarks:

(a) sign prohibited by Art. 6 ter of the Paris Convention (Paris Convention for the Protection of Industrial Property of 20 March 1883), namely armorial bearings, flags and other state emblems, official signs and marks for warranty and control purposes, and initials or denominations of international organisations;
(b) sign contrary to public policy or morality, or whose use is prohibited by the law;[6]
(c) deceptive sign, i. e. when it evokes in the mind of the public features that the good or service bearing the mark does not actually own. Such features may consist in the nature, quality or geographic origin of the product or service.

3. The trademark must be available[7]

One cannot adopt as a trademark a sign that harms prior rights. In particular, availability is not satisfied if it harms prior rights on a trademark, a corporate name when there is a risk of confusion in the public mind, a trade name known throughout the French territory where there exists a risk of confusion in the public mind, a protected appellation of origin, authors' rights, designs rights, personality rights (e. g. name, surname, pseudonym, image), name, or image and reputation of a public body.

The French trademark office does not carry out availability searches prior to registration of a trademark and can, therefore, register a trademark that violates prior rights. It will be upon the owner of the prior rights to claim for cancellation of the trademark.

---

4 4 October 1990 Paris Court of Appeal, PIBD 1991, III, 196.

5 Code de la propriété industrielle [CPI] [Intellectual Property Code], art. L.711-3 (F. R.).

6 This is the case for signs that consist in slogans or labels inciting to racial discrimination, as well as those advocating religious intolerance. One may also mention the law concerning fight against tobacco, which prohibits the use as a trademark of signs already used for tobacco products, for products or services other than tobacco products.

7 Code de la propriété industrielle [CPI] [Intellectual Property Code], art. L.711-4 (F. R.).

4. Trademark protection is acquired through registration[8] except for well-know trademarks, within the meaning of Art. 6 bis of the Paris Convention

B. Infringing Behaviours

Trademark rights confer a monopoly of use, which allows its holder to preclude a number of acts by third parties. According to Articles L.713-2 and L.713-3 Code de la propriété industrielle [CPI] [Intellectual Property Code] (F. R.), there are two main types of infringement:

- identical reproduction of the trademark for identical goods and/or services.[9]
- imitation of the trademark for goods and/or services identical or similar to those designated in the prior registration. In such a case, the claimant needs to evidence a risk of confusion in the mind of the public.[10]

Articles L.713-2 and L.713-3 CPI [Intellectual Property Code] list the acts that fall within trademark infringement:

- reproduction, imitation or affixing of a trademark; the mere filing of an infringing trademark regardless of any use constitutes an act of infringement.[11]
- use of a trademark, meaning any use of the trademark in the business life for the purposes of designating the origin of goods and/or services, e. g. use of a mark as a corporate name, detention of goods bearing an infringed trademark, the commercialisation and/or offer for sale of goods/services under an infringed trademark, etc.
- importation or exportation of goods bearing an infringed trademark, removal or alteration of a trademark

1. Risk of confusion

The trademark owner must prove a risk of confusion in case of infringement by imitation. Risk of confusion is defined as the risk that the public could believe that the products or services in question originate from the same person.

The risk of confusion must be assessed between the signs taken in their entirety. It may result from visual, phonetical or conceptual similarities between the signs at issue. With regard to conceptual similarities, French courts ruled that the trademark EAU DYNA-

---

8 Code de la propriété industrielle [CPI] [Intellectual Property Code], art. L.712-1 (F. R.). Anyone (individual, company, non-profit organisation) can file a trademark in France. The applicants not domiciled or established in France must elect domicile with a representative domiciled in France.

9 Code de la propriété industrielle [CPI] [Intellectual Property Code], art. L.713-2 (F. R.).

10 Code de la propriété industrielle [CPI] [Intellectual Property Code], art. L.713-3 (F. R.).

11 31 January 1968 Paris Court of Appeal, RTD Com. 1968/707.

MISANTE had been illegally imitated by the trademark EAU STIMULANTE,[12] and the trademark LE REVERBERE by the trademark LE LAMPADAIRE.[13]

2. Particular case: Transit as an infringing behaviour

The transit of infringing products that are intended for a country other than France does not constitute an act of infringement, as there is no release of products on the market.[14]

3. Particular case: Keyword advertising

Since 2003, there have been more than 30 decisions of French courts on the liability of providers of sponsored-links in cases of position squatting.[15] Providers of sponsored-links are almost always held liable. Case law, however, remains uncertain as to the legal grounds of such liability, i. e. civil liability, misleading advertising or trademark infringement, and the status of providers of sponsored-links – as in, if they qualify as internet-service provider or advertising agency.

The scenario at issue is the following: a provider of sponsored-links (e. g. Google AdWords) offers his customer a sponsored link to his website which is displayed as soon as a key word, previously chosen by the advertiser, is entered by a user in connection with an internet search. This sponsored link is displayed to the right or on top of the search results, under the heading "*commercial links*". The key word is the cornerstone of the success of the sponsored link in that it triggers website display. However, even though a key word may be free of any rights, it may also be identical or similar to the trademark of a third party that has not authorised such use. The resulting referencing is what the internet professionals call "*position squatting*".

As far as trademark infringement is concerned, French judges are fluctuant on whether the suggestion and the commercialisation of a key word that is identical/similar to the

---

12 28 June 2000 Paris Court of Appeal (4th Moot Hall), PIBD 2000, 708, III, 549.

13 19 June 1996 Paris Court of First Instance, PIBD 1996 III, 573.

14 For instance: 7 June 2006 Commercial Chamber of the Supreme Court for Civil and Commercial Matters, Legifrance Decision n°04-12274.

15 See, especially: 10 March 2005 Versailles Court of Appeal, Juriscom.net: http://www.juriscom.net/jpt/visu.php?ID=670 (Google France vs. Viaticum and Luteciel) and the first-instance judgment given in this case: 13 October 2003 Nanterre Court of First Instance, Juriscom.net: http://www.juriscom.net/jpt/visu.php?ID=367 (Google France vs. Viaticum and Luteciel); 16 December 2004 Nanterre Court of First Instance, Juriscom.net: http://www.juriscom.net/jpt/visu.php?ID=622 (Hôtels Méridien vs. Google France); 4 February 2005, Paris Court of First Instance (TGI), Juriscom.net: http://www.juriscom.net/jpt/visu.php?ID=641, (Louis Vuitton Malletier vs. Google); 17 January 2005 Nanterre Court of First Instance, Juriscom.net: http://www.juriscom.net/jpt/visu.php?ID=628 (Accor vs. Overture and Overture Inc.).

trademark of a third party qualify as trademark business use and, as a result, whether sponsored-link providers are liable on the basis of trademark infringement.

This issue is likely to be clarified in the coming years. Indeed, in a decision of 20 May 2008,[16] in a case of position squatting opposing Google to Louis Vuitton Malletier, the Cour de Cassation (Supreme Court) decided to refer two prejudicial questions to the ECJ (European Court of Justice): (i) does the use made by a provider of sponsored-links of the trademark of a third party constitute a use that the trademark owner is entitled to prohibit on the basis of Art. 9 of the Community Trademark Regulation (Council Regulation (EC) No. 40/94 of 20 December 1993 on the Community trademark)[17] and, (ii) if the trademark owner is not entitled to prohibit such use, under which conditions the provider of sponsored-links may be liable.

4. Particular case: Parallel Imports

The question of parallel importation is related to exhaustion of intellectual property rights.

The owner of a French trademark cannot oppose the entry or the resale in France of products bearing his trademark when such products have been put on the market within the EU by the owner or with his consent. However, the owner is entitled to oppose any further act of commercialisation if he can demonstrate a legitimate reason, e. g. when the goods have been substantially modified or altered. For example, in the *Levi Strauss* case, the Cour de Cassation held that the modification of the colour of the clothes by the distributor without the consent of the owner of the trademark constitutes an illicit use of the trademark.[18]

C. Enforcement

The owner of a trademark, or its exclusive licencee,[19] may initiate civil proceedings for up to three years after trademark infringement.

Before initiating proceedings, the rights holder may have to carry out preliminary acts with a view to collect evidence of infringement. Evidence of infringement may normally be submitted by any means. The most common and efficient way to collect evidence

16 20 May 2008 Commercial Court of the Supreme Court for Civil and Commercial Matters, Legalis.net: http://www.legalis.net/jurisprudence-decisi-on.php3?id_article=2313 (Google France, Google Inc c/Louis Vuitton Malletier).

17 Council Regulation (EC) No 40/94 of 20 December 1993 on the Community trademark, Official Journal of the European Communities 1993 No L 11/1.

18 28 January 1992, Commercial Court of the Supreme Court for Civil and Commercial Matters, RD propr. intell. 1994, No. 53, p. 58, RTD com. 1992. 370, obs. A. Chavanne.

19 Unless stipulated otherwise in the licence agreement and after a cease and desist letter addressed to the owner remained unanswered.

of intellectual property infringement is known as "saisie-contrefaçon" (infringement seizure). The claimant applies *ex parte* to the judge to be authorised to carry out an investigation at the premises where the alleged infringing goods are likely to be found. Claimant must only evidence that he owns an intellectual property right.

The judge may authorise a mere description of the goods, by taking samples and relevant documents or, more rarely a seizure *in rem*. Evidence so collected may be used in civil or criminal proceedings.

Depending on the circumstances of the case, the claimant may apply for a preliminary injunction or initiate proceedings on the merits.

In case of preliminary injunction, a decision is usually rendered within a month or two, though when a specific urgency is demonstrated, it could be dealt with in a matter of days. Preliminary injunction proceedings may result in the infringer being ordered to pay an account on damages. Standard proceedings on the merits would normally take ten to twelve months until a first instance decision is rendered. In specific circumstances, fast track proceedings on the merits can be initiated, with a view to try to obtain a decision within a matter of days or, more generally, three to four months.

Any person having standing to sue on the grounds of infringement has the right to initiate summary proceedings to ask the court to order the alleged counterfeiter any measures intended to (i) prevent an imminent infringement; or (ii) prevent the continuation of alleged infringing acts. A court may also order on an *ex parte* basis any urgent measures when circumstances require that such measures be taken *ex parte*.

D. Legal Consequences (discontinuance, information, damages, destruction, recall)

If the trademark holder succeeds, the measures ordered by civil courts are usually the following:

- permanent injunction to cease the infringing acts;
- confiscation or destruction of the infringing goods and the equipments used for the manufacturing or distribution of the infringing goods;
- recall of the infringing goods from commercial networks at the expenses of the infringer;
- payment of damages: courts must take into account (i) the negative economic consequences, suffered by the injured party, including loss of profits; (ii) the profits made by the infringer; and (iii) the moral damage caused to the trademark owner. Courts may, alternatively and at the request of the claimant, grant as damages a fixed sum that cannot be lesser than the amount of royalties that would have been paid by the infringer had he asked the authorisation to use the infringed trademark.
- publication of the court decision, in whole or in part, in a number of newspapers determined by the court, at the expenses of the infringer;

- reimbursement in whole or in part by the infringer of the legal costs exposed by the trademark holder. Courts costs are fully reimbursed to the winning party, and are usually not substantial. Attorneys fees are reimbursed to the winning party at the discretion of the court. A lump sum is awarded that rarely covers the total amount spent, though amounts awarded by French courts over the last ten years have drastically increased.

The court may also order the defendant or any person found in possession of counterfeiting products, or any person who acted in the production, manufacturing, or distribution process, to communicate information (such as names, addresses, etc.) which may help to determine the origin and the distribution networks of the litigious items.

As infringement also constitutes a criminal offence, criminal courts can, in addition to the above, order an imprisonment sentence of up to three years and a fine of up to EUR 300,000.

III. Design Rights

French law on design rights protects the appearance of a product or a part of a product, which is particularly characterised by its lines, outlines, colours, shape, texture or materials. These features can be those of the product itself or its ornamentation.

French law expressly excludes protection of computer programs. Mere ideas are also excluded from protection.

A product protected by design right is also eligible to protection by copyright law, both regime benefits are likely to be applied concurrently. The following paragraphs will be devoted to the protection by registered designs only.

A. Legal Requirements for Design Protection

A design is protected provided that two types of conditions are met:

(1) Formal conditions: the design must be registered before the French Intellectual Property office. The registrant must provide the French Intellectual Property office with a description of the design and a graphic description such as pictures, drawings, samples. The French Intellectual Property office will only reject demands which are contrary to public policy or accepted principles of morality.

(2) Substantial conditions: a design shall only be protected if:

   (a) It is new, which will be the case if, on the date of filing of the application or on the date of priority claimed, no identical design has been disclosed. Designs shall be deemed to be identical if their essential features are reproduced, i. e. they differ in minor details only.

(b) It has an individual character, which will be the case if the overall visual impression it produces on the well-informed observer differs from the impression produced by any design disclosed before the date of the filing of the application for registration or before the date of priority claimed. In assessing individual character, the degree of freedom of the creator in developing the design is taken into consideration, e. g. the technical nature of the product may dictate some specific designs which are thus unlikely to be protected by design rights.

A registered design is protected for a period of five years and renewable for up to twenty-five years.

B. Infringing Behaviours

French law prohibits the manufacturing, offering for sale, sale, importing, exporting, using or retaining, of a product comprising the design, when it is made without of the consent of the owner of the design.[20]

C. Enforcement

The owner of a design, or its exclusive licencee,[21] may initiate civil proceedings in case of infringement of design rights, in a three years time period starting from the date the infringement took place.

Before initiating proceedings, the rights holder may have to carry out preliminary acts with a view to collect evidence of infringement. Evidence of infringement may normally be submitted by any means. The most common and efficient way to collect evidence of intellectual property infringement is known as "saisie-contrefaçon" (infringement seizure). The claimant applies *ex parte* to the judge to be authorised to carry out an investigation at the premises where the alleged infringing goods are likely to be found. Claimant must only evidence that he owns an intellectual property right.

The judge may authorise a mere description of the goods, by taking samples and relevant documents or, more rarely, a seizure *in rem*. Evidence so collected may be used in civil or criminal proceedings.

Depending on the circumstances of the case, the claimant may apply for a preliminary injunction or initiate proceedings on the merits.

In case of preliminary injunction, a decision is usually rendered within a month or two, though when a specific urgency is demonstrated, it could be dealt with in a matter of days. Preliminary injunction proceedings may result in the infringer being ordered to

20 Provided that the theory of exhaustion of rights does not apply.

21 Unless stipulated otherwise in the licence agreement and after a cease and desist letter addressed to the owner remained unanswered.

pay an account on damages. Standard proceedings on the merits would normally take ten to twelve months until a first instance decision is rendered. In specific circumstances, fast track proceedings on the merits can be initiated, with a view to try to obtain a decision within a matter of days or, more generally, three to four months.

Any person having standing to sue on the grounds of infringement has the right to initiate summary proceedings to ask the court to order the alleged counterfeiter any measures intended to (i) prevent an imminent infringement, or (ii) prevent the continuation of alleged infringing acts. A court may also order on an *ex parte* basis any urgent measures when circumstances require that such measures be taken *ex parte*.

D. Legal Consequences (discontinuance, information, damages, destruction, recall)

If the design-holder succeeds, the measures ordered by civil courts are usually the following:

- permanent injunction to cease the infringing acts;
- confiscation or destruction of the infringing goods and the equipments used for the manufacturing or distribution of the infringing goods;
- recall of the infringing goods from commercial networks at the expenses of the infringer;
- payment of damages: courts must take into account (i) the negative economic consequences suffered by the injured party, including loss of profits; (ii) the profits made by the infringer; and (iii) the moral damage caused to the design-owner. Courts may, alternatively and at the request of the claimant, grant as damages a fixed sum that cannot be lesser than the amount of royalties that would have been paid by the infringer had he asked the authorisation to use the infringed design.
- publication of the court decision, in whole or in part, in a number of newspapers determined by the court, at the expenses of the infringer;
- reimbursement in whole or in part by the infringer of the legal costs exposed by the design-holder. Courts costs are fully reimbursed to the winning party, and are usually not substantial. Attorneys fees are reimbursed to the winning party at the discretion of the court. A lump sum is awarded that rarely covers the total amount spent, though amounts awarded by French courts over the last ten years have drastically increased.

The court may also order the defendant or any person found in possession of counterfeiting products or any person who acted in the production, manufacturing, or distribution process, to communicate information (such as names, addresses, etc.), which may help to determine the origin and the distribution networks of the litigious items.

As infringement also constitutes a criminal offence, criminal courts can, in addition to the above, order an imprisonment sentence of up to three years and a fine up to EUR 300,000.

E. International Designs

1. Community Design Rights

All legal consequences described in paragraph D above for French designs apply to Community designs. In addition, one can invoke a non-registered design pursuant to Community Design Regulation (Council Regulation (EC) No 6/2002 of 12 December 2001 on Community designs).[22]

2. Design Rights under International Law and Article 25 TRIPS

France, as a member of the WTO (World Trade Organization), has ratified the TRIPS (Agreement on Trade-Related Aspects of Intellectual Property Rights). The provisions of TRIPS have been implemented in French law.

France is also party to the Bern Convention (Bern Convention for Protection of Literary and Artistic Works of 9 September 1886), the Paris Convention, and the Hague Agreement concerning the International Deposit of Industrial Designs of 6 November 1925.

F. Design Protection and Copyright Law, Unfair Competition Law and Trademark Law

1. Design Protection and Copyright Law

Designs can also be protected under Copyright Law, which expressly provides that "works of applied art" shall be considered works of the mind. Both grounds can therefore be claimed by the owner of a creation. Protection granted to copyrights lasts longer than the one granted to registered design. Therefore, when protection under design law has elapsed, the creator may still be able to claim copyrights on its work.

2. Design Protection and Trademark Law

French laws allow registration as trademark of designs, such as drawings or shapes – particularly those of a product or its packaging. Therefore, a design registered as a trademark may be protected with no time limit, provided that the trademark is duly renewed.

---

22 Council Regulation (EC) No 6/2002 of 12 December 2001 on Community designs, Official Journal of the European Communities 2002 No L 3/1.

3. Design Rights and Unfair Competition

The use of a work that is not protected by a right is licit. If a work is in the public domain, any competitor is entitled to copy it.[23] Such copy is, however, likely to be illicit if it creates a risk of confusion in the mind of the public (unfair competition) or if it unduly trails on someone's notoriety (parasitic behaviour). A company that has no intellectual property right on its product is entitled to initiate an action on the grounds of unfair competition and/or parasitism.[24] Such action should, however, not be a way to extend the duration of protection afforded by intellectual property. Thus, courts usually sanction facts that go beyond the mere copying of a product. The following must generally be proven: (i) the copied product is distinctive, (ii) some essential characteristics are reproduced,[25] (iii) the copy is commercialised on French territory, (iv) the parties are in competition (save for parasitism), and (v) the public is likely to be confused as to the origin of the product.

IV. Patent Piracy

A. Legal Requirements for Patent Protection

1. Pre-requisite: Securing Rights to Inventions

a. Claming rights to service inventions

There are two kinds of inventions performed by an employee that may belong to the employer:

- the "invention under mission", defined as the invention performed either pursuant to an employment contract comprising an inventive mission or in the framework of studies or research expressly entrusted to the employee by the employer. Such invention belongs to the employer *ab initio*.
- the "inventions beyond mission that may be attributed to the employer", defined as inventions performed during the execution of the employee functions and/or in the

---

23 For instance: 9 June 2004, Commercial Chamber of the Supreme Court for Civil and Commercial Matters, http://www.legifrance.gouv.fr/WAspad/UnDocument?base=INCA&nod=IXCXCX2004X06X04X00101X036; 17 September 2004, Paris Commercial Court of First Instance, JCP E 2005, 1004; 9 March 2005, Paris Court of Appeal, JCP E 2006, 1017; 24 June 2004, Amiens Court of Appeal, JCP E 2005, 1004.

24 For example: 30 January 1996, Commercial Chamber of the Supreme Court for Civil and Commercial Matters, Bulletin 1996 IV n°32 p.24; 22 October 2002, Commercial Chamber of the Supreme Court for Civil and Commercial Matters, Bulletin 2002 IV N° 152 p. 174 (Métro v/Cartier); 22 October 2002, Commercial Chamber of the Supreme Court for Civil and Commercial Matters, Bulletin 2002 IV N° 149 p. 171 (Go sport v/Décathlon); 26 May 2004, Commercial Chamber of the Supreme Court for Civil and Commercial Matters, http://www.legifrance.gouv.fr/WAspad/UnDocument?base=INCA&nod=IXCXCX2004X05X04X00103X099 (Neressis).

25 Most matters, but not all, require that the copy be slavish.

field of activity of the company and/or by reason of knowledge or use of the means of the company. They belong to the employee. The employer must claim ownership, by means of a letter sent to the employee specifying the nature – ownership or use – and scope of the rights claimed.

Whatever the type of invention, an employee who makes an invention must give his employer a declaration describing the invention and the circumstances in which it was made, together with a statement of the category of invention concerned. The employer may object the classification within two months and will otherwise be deemed to have accepted the classification. In case of "inventions beyond mission that may be attributed to the employer", the employer must exercise its right of attribution within four months after having received the report from the employee.

b. Securing rights in the context of cooperations with third parties

Before filing a patent application, one must secure for the confidentiality of the information communicated to third parties. If disclosures are necessary, a confidentiality agreement is advisable.

Between co-owners of a patent, it is advisable to draft a co-ownership agreement in order to organise the relationship between the parties, e. g. who files patent applications, what happens if one party wants to sell its share in the patent, who may use the patent in what business sector, etc.

Between a patent owner and its licencees, rights of each party must also be clearly defined, e. g. (i) rights of the licencee to patent improvements, (ii) right to patent the invention in countries where the patent is not yet protected (iii) cooperation against infringers, etc.

2. Scope of Patent Protection

To be patentable, the invention must be new, involve an inventive step, and be susceptible of industrial application (i. e. not to be confined to an abstract principle). The two main conditions are novelty and inventiveness:

- An invention is new if it does not form part of the state of the art. An invention is not new if all its essential characteristics are found in a single prior art reference (as opposed to being found in a combination of several references). The state of the art is defined by "everything made available to the public before the date of filing of the patent application, especially by means of a written or oral description or by use". The novelty of a patent application can be destroyed by a disclosure made by the inventor himself. The novelty must also be absolute in space. Thus, a foreign publication, or a use that took place abroad is likely to destroy the novelty of the invention. Also, a French patent application or a European or international patent appli-

cation designating France, as filed but not yet published, constitutes prior art which has to be taken into account in order to consider the novelty.
- The inventive step: a patent cannot be granted to protect what can be deduced in an obvious manner from the state of the art by one skilled in the art. The inventive step is judged on the basis of an obvious combination of several elements of the state of the art. This comprises a two step test: first, documents must be part of prior art, and, secondly, combining these documents must be obvious. For example, if the invention consists of a juxtaposition of means described in prior art references, and is thus considered an obvious combination, then there is no inventive step.

Pursuant to Art. L. 611-10 CPI [Intellectual Property Code], the following are expressly excluded from patentability:

- discoveries and scientific theories (though their applications can be patentable) ;
- aesthetic creations (which can be protected by copyright and the design and model right) ;
- schemes, rules and methods ;
- software (which can be protected by copyright) ; and
- presentation of information.

These can be included in an invention, but they cannot constitute the invention itself.

3. Application and Registration of Patents

The invention must be described in a manner sufficiently clear and complete for it to be carried out by a man skilled in the art (Art. L. 612-5 CPI [Intellectual Property Code]). Consequently, the patent application must have a sufficient description. The description and the drawings shall be used to interpret the claims.

If a patent application has been filed in a country that is party to the Paris Convention, or of the WTO, the applicant benefits from a priority right and may, in a twelve months time period, ask for an extension of the protection to France and benefit from the original date of filing.

The European Patent Office, on behalf of the French Patent Office, will draft a preliminary search report (citing prior art references related to the prospected patent on an international scale) and give its opinion on the patentability. The applicant will have three months (renewable for an additional three months time period) to make observations and modify the claims if necessary. The French Patent Office will publish the application eighteen months after its filing. Anyone may file observations and cite additional prior art references within a three months time period. Again, the applicant will have three months (renewable for an additional three months time period) to make observations and, if necessary, modify the claims. Then the French Patent Office will issue a final report. If the invention is considered new, then the French Patent Office will grant the patent, and it will be published at the Bulletin Officiel de la Propriété Industrielle.

The courts of appeal adjudicate on recourses against decisions of the Director of the French Patent Office.

B. Infringing Behaviours

Patent protection is effective from the date of filing of the application, but infringement may be asserted only as of the date of publication of the application, or the date on which a certified copy of the application was notified to the infringer. If action is taken on the basis of a patent application, the court stays proceedings until the patent is granted.

There are circumstances justifying infringement, namely:

- Acts accomplished for private and non-commercial purposes, i. e. without any direct or indirect connection with a professional activity;
- Acts accomplished for pure experimental purposes;
- Preparation of medicines in demand in pharmaceutical offices.

Personal possession: Art. L613-7 CPI [Intellectual Property Code] provides that any person who, in good faith, at the date of filing or the date of priority of the patent was in possession of the invention in France, has the right to personally exploit the invention despite the existence of the patent. Such right can be assigned only concurrently with the business undertaking, the enterprise, or the part of the enterprise of which it is a constituent element.

1. Direct patent infringement

Articles L613-3 and L613-4 CPI [Intellectual Property Code] define acts of infringement as follows:

(a) Product patents:
- manufacturing of the products subject matter of the patent;
- importing of the infringing products into France, subject to the "exhaustion of rights" doctrine;
- exhibition and offer for sale;
- marketing of the product (under any form), including offer for sale for export purposes;
- possession of patented product for anyone of the above purposes; and
- use of an infringing product.

(b) Process patents:
- working of the process or offer to work the process;
- importing, marketing, and use of a product obtained through the patented process.

2. Indirect patent infringement

Art. L613-4 CPI [Intellectual Property Code] also precludes the delivery or offer of delivery on French territory to a person other than those allowed to work the invention, of the means to work in France such invention in relation to one of its essential elements, when the party is aware, or when the circumstances make it obvious that such means are meant to work the invention. Infringement may thus be constituted even if the means delivered are not sufficient on their own to work the invention, as long as these means relate to an essential element of the invention. Said essential element is determined on a case-by-case basis by the judge.

3. Doctrine of Equivalence

The doctrine of equivalence is applied by the courts. Two means are said to be technically equivalent if they fulfil the same function in order to obtain the same result or a result of similar nature, while having a different form or structure.

Courts' reasoning consists of two inquiries:

(a) Is the mean used in the supposedly infringing product a "technical equivalent"? The Court assess if the function of a mean corresponds to its primary technical effect. The function is different from the global result of the invention. Unlike a result, a technical mean is patentable.

(b) Does the patent cover not only the form of the means, but also its functions? The Court assess if the claim covers the function or if it is strictly limited to the specific definition of the said infringed element. If a claim is directed to a specific means, the scope of this claim depends on the novelty of the function of this means:
- if the function of this means was known in the prior art on the day the patent was filed, the scope of the claim shall be limited to the claimed structure of the means.
- on the contrary, if the function of the means was not known in the prior art, and is therefore novel, the scope of the means shall be extended to any structure having the same function and leading to the same result.

4. Transit

As with trademarks, the transit of infringing products that are intended for a country other than France does not constitute an act of infringement, as there is no release of products on the market.

C. Enforcement

The owner of a patent, or its exclusive licencee,[26] may initiate civil proceedings for up to three years after trademark infringement occurs.

Before initiating proceedings, the rights holder may have to carry out preliminary acts with a view to collect evidence of infringement. Evidence of infringement may normally be submitted by any means. The most common and efficient way to collect evidence of intellectual property infringement is known as "saisie-contrefaçon" (infringement seizure). The claimant applies *ex parte* to the judge to be authorised to carry out an investigation at the premises where the alleged infringing goods are likely to be found. Claimant must only evidence that he owns an intellectual property right.

The judge may authorise a mere description of said goods, by taking samples and relevant documents or, more rarely, a seizure *in rem*. Evidence so collected may be used in civil or criminal proceedings.

Depending on the circumstances of the case, the claimant may apply for a preliminary injunction or initiate proceedings on the merits.

In case of preliminary injunction, a decision is usually rendered within a month or two, though when a specific urgency is demonstrated, it could be dealt with in a matter of days. Preliminary injunction proceedings may result in the infringer being ordered to pay an account on damages. Standard proceedings on the merits would normally take ten to twelve months until a first instance decision is rendered. In specific circumstances, fast track proceedings on the merits can be initiated, with a view to try to obtain a decision within a matter of days or, more generally, three to four months.

Any person having standing to sue on the grounds of infringement has the right to initiate summary proceedings to ask the Court to order the alleged counterfeiter any measures intended to (i) prevent an imminent infringement, or (ii) prevent the continuation of alleged infringing acts. A Court may also order on an *ex parte* basis any urgent measures when circumstances require that such measures be taken *ex parte*.

D. Legal Consequences

If the patent holder succeeds, the measures ordered by civil courts are usually the following:

- permanent injunction to cease the infringing acts;
- confiscation or destruction of the infringing goods and the equipments used for the manufacturing or distribution of the infringing goods;

[26] Unless stipulated otherwise in the licence agreement and after a cease and desist letter addressed to the owner remained unanswered.

- recall of the infringing goods from commercial networks at the expenses of the infringer;
- payment of damages: courts must take into account (i) the negative economic consequences suffered by the injured party, including loss of profits; (ii) the profits made by the infringer; and (iii) the moral damage caused to the patent owner. Courts may, alternatively and at the request of the claimant, grant as damages a fixed sum that cannot be lesser than the amount of royalties that would have been paid by the infringer had he asked the authorisation to use the infringed patent.
- publication of the court decision, in whole or in part, in a number of newspapers determined by the court, at the expenses of the infringer;
- reimbursement in whole or in part by the infringer of the legal costs exposed by the patent holder. Courts costs are fully reimbursed to the winning party, and are usually not substantial. Attorneys fees are reimbursed to the winning party at the discretion of the court. A lump sum is awarded that rarely covers the total amount spent, though amounts awarded by French courts over the last ten years have drastically increased.

The Court may also order the defendant or any person found in possession of counterfeiting products or any person who acted in the production, manufacturing or distribution processto communicate information (such as names, addresses, etc.), which may help to determine the origin and the distribution networks of the litigious items.

As infringement also constitutes a criminal offence, criminal courts can, in addition to the above, order an imprisonment sentence of up to three years and a fine of up to EUR 300,000.

V. Know-How Theft

Know-How is not defined by French law and is not an intellectual property right. It is usually defined as a technical knowledge which can be assigned, but which is not directly accessible to the public.

A. Protection of Know-How

Companies can protect their know how by drafting confidentiality agreements.

(1) Within the company, in order to protect the company's know how from a disclosure or a non-authorised use by a employee, employment agreements usually provide confidentiallity clauses as well as non-compete clauses. (In order to be valid, non-compete clauses must be limited in time and geographical scope and must offer a financial compensation to the employee.)
(2) Confidentiality agreements will provide, as an incentive, a high lump sum of damages in case of a breach of the agreement.
(3) Confidentiality agreement also provide that contractors of the company commit to maintain strictly confidential any information disclosed and to impose the same obligation for their employees and sub-contractors.

B. Know-How Piracy as Unfair Competition

The owner of know-how can seek protection on the grounds of unfair competition or parasitism. The liability of the author of the damage is engaged if the following three conditions are met: (1) the author of the damage must have committed a fault, (2) the victim must have suffered a damage, and (3) the causality relation between the fault and the damage is established. The victim of unfair competition or parasitism may obtain compensation for the loss suffered.

C. Know-How as a Trade Secret

Violation of a trade secret by an employee constitutes a criminal offence punishable by a fine of up to EUR 30,000 and imprisonment of up to two years (Art. L.621-1 CPI [Intellectual Property Code] and L.1227-1 Code du Travail [CT] [Labour Law Code]). As a criminal offence, the bad faith of the defendant must be proven.

VI. Music, Film and Software Piracy

A. Legal Requirements of Copyright Protection

The protection afforded by the Intellectual Property Code on copyrights extends to all "*works of the mind, irrespective of their gender, form of expression, merit or purpose*". The protection concerns any work provided it is:

(1) fixed in tangible form. This condition excludes the protection of mere ideas; and
(2) original. That is, the work reflects the personality of its author. Originality is appreciated on a case by case basis by the courts. Although some decisions are sometimes unpredictable, standards for originality are not very high. Even if the creation is utilitarian, it is likely to be protected by copyrights. The only limitation is purely functional work, which cannot be protected by copyrights.

B. Particularities of Individual Products

The neighbouring rights apply to performers, phonogram and video-recording producers and broadcasting organisations. Holders of neighbouring rights have an exclusive right of authorising the use or exploitation of their performance or production. Such rights are independent from the author's rights.

1. Music

Authors benefit from copyrights on their musical compositions during their life and 70 years after.

Performers benefit from neighbouring rights on their interpretation for a period of 50 years starting from 1 January of the year following their first interpretation to the public.

Phonogram producers, defined as the person who takes the initiative and responsibility of the first recording of a sequence of sounds, benefit from neighbouring rights on their phonogram for a period of fifty years starting from 1 January of the year following the recording or the disclosure of the phonogram to the public.

The authorization of the phonogram producer is required prior to any reproduction, making available to the public by way of sale, exchange or rental, or communication to the public of his phonogram.

2. Movies

Authors (film director, scriptwriters, etc.) and actors benefit respectively from copyrights and neighbouring rights on their work. French law provides that these rights are deemed to be assigned to the movie producer. The movie producer is "*the person who takes the initiative and responsibility for making the movie*",[27] i. e. the one who actively participates in the initiative of the production and is responsible for it.[28]

The videogram producer, defined as the person who takes the initiative and the responsibility for the initial recording of a sequence of images whether accompanied by sounds or not, is also vested in neighbouring rights. Therefore, the authorization of the videogram producer is required prior to any reproduction, any making available to the public by means of sale, exchange or rental, or any communication to the public of his videogram.

3. Software

A software is eligible for copyrights protection provided it is original. It is governed by specific rules which depart from other authors' works. The most important ones are the following:

Regarding ownership, in the case of creation of software within the scope of an employee's tasks or according to the employer's instructions, the employer is originally vested in the author rights in the software. Therefore, the employer will be entitled to commercialise the software, make further adaptations and developments, etc. The moral right of the employee(s) who actually created the software is limited. He only benefits from a paternity right, and can thus ask to have his name mentioned.

Regarding the remuneration due to the employee who created a software, a lump sum can be granted, whereas normally a remuneration proportional to the exploitation of the work is due to an author of a copyrighted work.

27 Article L.132-23 of the Intellectual Property Code.

28 31 January 1995 Court of Appeal of Paris, RIDA, July 1995, 339.

4. Multimedia, Computer Games

Multimedia and Computer Games are eligible to the copyrights protection. There are, however, uncertainties regarding their legal qualification. Particularly, case law is fluctuant as to whether (i) they should be considered as software or audiovisual work, and (ii) they should be considered as collective work or as work of collaboration. The qualification will lead to different rules of ownership and rights of the co-owners.

A court decision[29] ruled that a video game using a software is a mixed work. Therefore, the author of its musical composition could benefit from a remuneration proportional to the sales of the video game, instead of a lump sum as would have been the case if the computer game were qualified as a software only. The same decision considered that the video game is a "*work of collaboration*", so that it is the property of the different creators.

C. Infringement

(Right to make copies for private use; Protective measures (Digital Rights Management); Liability of Users; Liability of online provider; Liability of makers of software facilitating copyright infringements; Liability for links)

1. Infringement

Copyright is made up of a moral part and a patrimonial part. The author of a work protected by copyright is granted a monopoly on the representation, the reproduction and the communication to the public of the work – which includes the right to prevent others from making, selling, or offering for sale infringing products, and more generally any use of the protected work. Similar rules exist regarding neighbouring rights.

The reproduction, representation or communication of a work to the public without the authorisation of the copyright holder is an act of infringement.

– The exception to the reproduction right: the right to make copies for private use

Once a work has been disclosed, the author may not prohibit copies or reproductions reserved strictly for the private use of the copier and not intended for collective use. In certain cases, however, (such as video on demand), the right to make copies for private use is precluded.

As authors, performers, producers, etc., do not have absolute control of their reproduction rights, holders of both copyrights and neighbouring rights receive a private remuneration to compensate for the loss of control of their work. This copyright levy can be

---

[29] 20 September 2007 Paris Court of Appeal, Lexisnexis: http://www.lexisnexis.com/fr/droit/search/casessubmitForm.do.

defined as the amount paid by the manufacturers when purchasing blank recordable/ audiovisual materials.

A Committee appointed by the government is deciding on potential extensions of the copyright levies to different media, and on the applicable tariffs. The Committee's most recent decision, rendered on 27 February 2008, extended the basis of the copyright levy to smartphones (such as the iPhone).

A decision of the Paris Court of Appeal dated 22 March 2007 (*"Société CD Folie E. G. et autres c/SA Rue du Commerce et autres"*) ruled that foreign companies operating commercial internet websites that sell goods to French consumers are not subject (i) to French private copy remuneration and (ii) to the obligation to inform the internet users of the existence of such levies.

– Protective measures (Digital Rights Management)

Technical measures of protection, defined as any mean of control of copying products, notably by access code or encryption, have been implemented in order to prevent or limit non-authorised use of copyrighted products.

Unlocking such technical measures of protection is an act of infringement, punished by a fine of EUR 3,750, increased up to EUR 30,000 for the person who provided the means to unlock the protection.

The law provides that technical measures of protection should not prevent a final user from making copies for his private use. The Regulation Authority of Technological Measures is responsible for the settlement of conflicts that may arise between right holders and users, when said users pretend that technological measures prevent them from benefiting from making copies for their private use.

In any case, the consumer will have to be duly informed, notably by a note on the cover of any material medium, of the access conditions to such medium.

2. Liability of Users

Case law considers that downloading protected works from an illicit source constitutes an act of infringement.

In a decision dated 5 September 2007, the Court of Appeal of Aix-en-Provence held an internet user liable for using peer-to-peer software to download movies onto hardware and then provide copies to his friends. The Court ruled that by doing so, he was not making a copy for private use.

– Liability of online providers

Online providers have the obligation to send internet users messages in order to raise their awareness of downloading issues and illicit communication of copyrighted works.

Two sets of rules govern the responsibility of online providers:

(a) Online providers have no obligation to keep watch on information stored or transferred on the web, nor to search for illicit content or activities. Online providers who store works of writing, images, sounds, etc., transmitted by internet users, cannot be held responsible if they did not have any knowledge of the unlawful character of such information or activities.
(b) Once the online provider has been notified of the infringing contents, he must act swiftly to remove such content or to render impossible any access to it.
   – Liability of editors of software facilitating copyright infringements

Art. L.335-2-1 CPI [Intellectual Property Code] provides that is punishable by a fine of up to EUR 300,000 and three years of imprisonment:

– to publish, provide the public with or communicate to the public, intentionaly, a software obviously intented to make availbale to the public protected works;
– to encourage the use of such software.

In addition, Art. L.336-1 CPI [Intellectual Property Code] provides that when a software is mainly used to make available to the public works protected by copyrights, the President of the Court, may order as a preliminary injunction any measures required to protect copyrights.

– Liability for links

French courts have considered that a person who creates hyperlinks redirecting internet users to a site offering infringing contents, e. g. sites offering to download pirated software games,[30] commits an act of infringement by providing such facilities. The Court considered that through the hyperlink, the person is "making available to the public" protected works without the authorisation of their authors. Some authors share the same point of view.[31]

D. Enforcement

Authors or their stake-holders can ask the police or the judge to seize copies of infringing work, as well as any product or device violating technical measures of protection. If

---

[30] 10 March 2004, Aix-en-Provence Court of Appeal (5e ch. corr.), Juris-Data n° 2004-240851; Comm. com. électr. sept. 2004, comm. 103; Lamy, RD immatériel, janv. 2005, p. 21, obs. L. Costes.

[31] *Rojinsky*, Sens interdit: la responsabilité du créateur de lien hypertexte du fait du contenu illicite du site cible: Lamy, Cah. dr. informatique et réseaux (J) févr. 2003, n° 155, p. 7; *Sardain*, Liens hypertextes: J.-Cl. Communication, Fasc. 4730, p. 7, n° 23 ; *Sardain*, La contrefaçon du fait des liens hypertextes, Com. Com. Elct. 2005, n° 6, Etude 21.

such seizure would postpone or cancel a scheduled performance, a specific authorization must be obtained.

The judge may also order on an *ex parte* basis, *inter alia*: to suspend the manufacturing of the alleged infringing goods, the seizure of the alleged infringing goods, and the seizure *in rem* of the equipements and instruments used to manufacture or distribute the alledged counterfeiting products, seizure of the proceeds related to the infringing reproduction or representation of the protected work. The enforcement of the measures may be subject to a guarantee on the part of the petitioner.

E. Legal consequences

If the author right holder or neighbour of author right holder succeeds, the measures ordered by civil courts are usually the following:

- permanent injunction to cease the infringing acts;
- confiscation or destruction of the infringing goods and the equipments used for the manufacturing or distribution of the infringing goods;
- recall of the infringing goods from commercial networks at the expenses of the infringer;
- payment of damages: courts must take into account (i) the negative economic consequences suffered by the injured party, including loss of profits; (ii) the profits made by the infringer; and (iii) the moral damage caused to the author right holder or neighbour of author right holder. Courts may, alternatively and at the request of the claimant, grant as damages a fixed sum which cannot be lesser than the amount of royalties that would have been paid by the infringer had he asked for the authorisation to use the infringed work.
- publication of the court decision, in whole or in part, in a number of newspapers determined by the court, at the expenses of the infringer;
- reimbursement in whole or in part by the infringer of the legal costs exposed by the author right holder or neighbour of author right holder. Courts costs are fully reimbursed to the winning party, and are usually not substantial. Attorneys fees are reimbursed to the winning party at the discretion of the court. A lump sum is awarded that rarely covers the total amount spent, though amounts awarded by French courts over the last ten years have drastically increased.

The Court may also order the defendant or any person found in possession of counterfeiting products or any person who acted in the production, manufacturing or distribution process, to commnicate information (such as names, addresses, etc.), which may help to determine the origin and the distribution networks of the litigious items.

As infringement also constitutes a criminal offence, criminal courts can, in addition to the above, order an imprisonment sentence of up to three years and a fine up to EUR 300,000.

Product Piracy in the Netherlands

MÉLANIE LOOS

Author: M. P. M. Loos, senior associate at Clifford Chance LLP in Amsterdam, the Netherlands.

Mélanie Loos is a senior associate in the Intellectual Property group of the Amsterdam office of Clifford Chance LLP. She specialises in litigation and counselling clients in the fields of advertising, trademark, copyright, and unfair competition, as well as internet and e-commerce issues. Melanie often deals with transactions and commercial contracts with a focus on intellectual property and shares management responsibility for the Intellectual Property group.

Ever since the Dutch East India Company ruled the seas in the Golden Age (about 1580-1740), the Netherlands has been a trading nation. Today, two major international hubs located in the Netherlands, Schiphol airport near Amsterdam and Europe's busiest seaport at Rotterdam, see a huge amount of traffic every day. As a result, the number of counterfeit products intercepted in the Netherlands increases every year. According to the Ministry of Finance, Dutch customs officials have intercepted more than 4 million counterfeit products in 2006,[1] ranging from bath foam to batteries, and representing an estimated value of more than EUR 128 million. Approximately 85% of the products originate from Asia (mainly China, Hong Kong, Singapore, and Taiwan). In recent years, customs officials have detected a notable rise in counterfeit toys, athletic wear, accessories (such as handbags and sunglasses), and electronics.

Product piracy in the Netherlands can be combated through civil actions, public law, and criminal actions. In addition, both the Customs Regulation (Council Regulation (EC) No. 1383/2003 concerning customs action against goods suspected of infringing certain intellectual property rights and the measures to be taken against goods found to have infringed such rights)[2] and the Enforcement Directive (Directive 2004/48/EC of 29 April 2004 on the Enforcement of Intellectual Property Rights)[3] have impacted the Dutch legal environment.

1 See article on the Ministry of Finance's website at http://www.minfin.nl/nl/actueel/nieuwsberichten,2007/03/Van-laminaat-tot-batterijen-Douane-pakt-veel-nam.html.

2 Official Journal of the European Union 2003 No L 196/7.

3 Official Journal of the European Union 2004 No L 157/45 and Corrigendum to Directive 2004/48/EC, Official Journal 2004 No L 195/16.

I. The Enforcement of Intellectual Property Rights in the Netherlands

A. Civil Action

Civil action can be based on specific Dutch and/or Benelux intellectual property (IP) laws, which will be discussed in more detail below. Once the IP right holder is aware of a possible infringement of its IP rights, several courses may be pursued, including seizure of the goods.

All proceedings are before professional judges, as jury trials do not exist in the Netherlands. In the context of IP litigation, three types of proceedings are available: (i) preliminary proceedings (*"kort geding"*), (ii) ex-parte injunction proceedings, and (iii) regular proceedings on the merits (*"bodemprocedure"*).

Preliminary proceedings

Intellectual property cases in the Netherlands are largely litigated through preliminary proceedings. In order for a matter to be admissible as a preliminary proceeding, the plaintiff needs to demonstrate an urgent need for preliminary relief. Generally however, the factual circumstances surrounding IP infringements typically set out an urgent interest on the part of the right holder. The plaintiff first sends a draft of the writ of summons to the District Court. Serving the writ of summons upon the defendant starts the proceedings. The court will then set a date for oral argument, taking into consideration the court's schedule and, to an extent, the schedules of counsel. Usually, a hearing will be scheduled within two to eight weeks after the writ has been submitted. At the hearing, both parties may present their arguments and only then is the defendant required to present the true scope and nature of its defence. Preliminary proceedings take place before only one judge, and only allow for preliminary measures to be awarded. Preliminary proceedings are informal by nature and the judge has broad discretionary powers, particularly in evidentiary matters. Evidence is primarily in the form of documents that are submitted to the court before the oral hearing. As a general rule, live testimony by witnesses is not available in preliminary proceedings. Judgements can usually be obtained within within approximately 2 to 3 months from the date of the writ of summons.

However, it is important to note that TRIPS (Agreement on Trade-Related Aspects of Intellectual Property Rights) and the Wetboek van Burgerlijke Rechtsvordering [Code of Civil Procedure] (NL) provide that if the plaintiff obtained an injunction in preliminary proceedings, he or she must start additional proceedings on the merits of the case within a reasonable period of time thereafter. The Court will determine the length of the reasonable period, but failure to begin such proceedings will lead to lapse of the injunction. In practice, parties in many cases reach settlement after preliminary proceedings in order to avoid additional lengthy and costly litigation.

Ex-parte injunction proceedings

The Enforcement Directive was implemented in the Wetboek van Burgerlijke Rechtsvordering [Code of Civil Procedure] on 1 May 2007, more than one year later than prescribed by the European Commission. The Enforcement Directive improved the ability of IP right holders to take adequate and timely action by introducing ex-parte injunctions. The ex-parte injunction is similar to the *Einstweilige Verfügung*, which existed in Germany even before the Enforcement Directive. Ex-parte injunctions allow IP right holders to take action in urgent matters if a delay would cause irreparable damage. For instance, ex-parte injunctions can prevent the exhibition of infringing products at a fair or convention. Courts tend to be fairly lenient in accepting a plaintiff's claim of irreparable damage. If the right holder has made the infringement appear plausible in its request, the court will render an interim injunction without first hearing from the defendant. After obtaining an interim injunction, the right holder needs to file full-fledged proceedings since the ex-parte injunction is only a preliminary measure. If the injunction is not upheld in a proceeding on the merits, the court can order the right holder to compensate the defendant for any damages resulting from enforcement of the ex-parte injunction. If a defendant does not wish to await the outcome of proceedings on the merits, he or she may also initiate preliminary injunction proceedings and request the court to lift the ex-parte injunction.

Regular proceedings on the merits

In regular proceedings on the merits each party has the opportunity to file procedural documents. The plaintiff files a writ of summons and the defendant a statement of defence. At the judge's discretion the parties will have to appear in court in order to provide more information, to try and reach a settlement, and/or to file further briefs. Once all briefs have been filed, the court can schedule oral pleadings at the request of either party. If the court believes that the parties have had sufficient opportunity to discuss the case in a prior personal appearance, it may decide not to schedule oral pleadings. Oral pleadings are usually held 10 to 12 months after the start of the proceedings. Judgement may be expected 6 to 12 weeks from the date of oral pleadings.

Relief

In both preliminary and regular proceedings on the merits, a court may impose an injunction ordering the defendant to refrain from any further infringing actions. The court may also mandate other actions, such as: (i) order the recall or destruction of the infringing products, (ii) order the publication of a rectification, (iii) require the defendant to supply information regarding the infringement (i. e. the identity of customers or suppliers of infringing products and the details of such transactions). Such court orders are issued under threat of fine for non-compliance.

Damages

In proceedings on the merits, the court may, in addition to the relief set out above, order the infringing party to pay damages or surrender its profits. Case law regarding the calculation of damages is not well developed in The Netherlands. If damages are awarded, a party is entitled to compensation for actual damages. However, determining such damages is in most cases not an exact science. In this regard, it is important that Dutch courts tend to take a conservative approach towards the calculation of damages. Punitive damages, or the awarding of double or triple damages, is not possible under Dutch law. Alternatively, one can ask for the surrender of profits resulting from the infringement, or for a determination of damages based on a fixed amount.[4] However, determining such profits can be a cumbersome exercise as well. Against this background, most IP cases are about obtaining injunctive relief and hardly ever about substantial sums of money.

The Enforcement Directive allows right holders to claim reimbursement for the costs of the proceedings including attorney fees.

Civil law seizures

Under relevant Dutch IP laws, the right holder has the right to seize infringing materials. In order for such seizure to take place, a court order must first be obtained in ex-parte proceedings. Once the goods have been seized, the right holder has to start court proceedings[5] within a time period specified by the court that granted permission for the seizure. This period can vary from one week to several months, depending on the urgency of the matter. If the right holder fails to start proceedings within this period, the seizure is lifted. Furthermore, the opposing party can object to the seizure through preliminary proceedings and, if it can show that the right holder's position is weak, may not only obtain an order to lift the seizure, but also to enjoin the right holder from further exercising such measures.

The Enforcement Directive has expanded the possibilities for the seizure of evidence and for measures relating to the collection and preservation of evidence.

Organisations combating counterfeiting

In general, the IP right holder will need to initiate civil action to combat counterfeiting. In addition, we note that there is a growing number of organisations, coalitions, and alliances focusing on the prevention and combating of counterfeiting, such as Foundation Brein (*Stichting Brein*, which acts to protect the rights of the entertainment industry), SNB-REACT (which acts mainly against trademark piracy), and Business Software Alliance (BSA, which acts against software piracy).

For example, SNB-REACT (formerly *Stichting Namaakbestrijding)*,[6] is a non-profit coalition created in 1991 at the initiative of the Amsterdam Chamber of Commerce to actively fight counterfeit trade. SNB-REACT offers legal and practical services to its members that are in line with the member companies' own anti counterfeiting strategies.

4 This option was introduced by implementation of the Enforcement Directive.

5 These proceedings can be preliminary proceedings or regular proceedings on the merits.

6 http://www.snbreact.org/snb-react/EN/UnitsNLNL.htm.

Companies (right holders, licencees and/or exclusive distributors) suffering, or likely to suffer, from counterfeiting can apply for membership. Membership in SNB-REACT requires enforceable rights. This means that the prospective member's IP rights must be well protected. To maintain its position as a neutral and objective body mandated to act fiercely against counterfeiting, SNB-REACT has certain discretionary powers, which allow it to take certain actions in accordance with its governing statutes.

For example, SNB-REACT can act when Dutch customs intercept containers that are loaded with counterfeit sportswear, even if the containers are originating from an unknown exporter in China and destined for an unknown trader in Russia. SNB-REACT can initiate confiscation and destruction procedures on behalf of its members and can file a criminal complaint in order to trace the actual source and destination of the goods. If there is not enough information for criminal action, SNB-REACT will revert to civil action as a follow up measure. In addition, SNB-REACT carries out an Internet Monitoring Program on trade in counterfeit goods in the Netherlands, concentrating on the national auction sites as well as commercial sites by periodical checks.

B. Public Law

The Customs Regulation gives national customs authorities several important tools with which to combat product piracy.[7] Custom authorities can postpone, release, or retain products, either *ex officio* or at the request of the right holder, in order to monitor for infringing goods. Customs can retain the allegedly infringing products for up to 20 working days ("customs seizure"), after which the customs authorities have to release the goods unless the right holder has obtained a court order for civil law seizure or other protective measures through preliminary proceedings.

Furthermore, the Customs Regulation provide for a simplified destruction procedure in which customs authorities play an important role. If the owner of the counterfeit products agrees to the destruction of the products or does not explicitly object to the destruction, customs will destroy the products. Customs will keep a sample of the products in case it is required later in legal proceedings.

Other than involvement by customs authorities through the Customs Regulation, public law does not play a role in combating piracy in the Netherlands.

C. Criminal Action

Both specific IP laws and the Wetboek van Strafrecht [Criminal Act] (NL) include provisions that penalise the infringement of IP rights. We will discuss these provisions in the context of the respective IP right in more detail below.

7 *Gielen*, Kort begrip van het intellectuele eigendomsrecht, § 782.

In practice, criminal enforcement hardly ever occurs for a number of reasons.[8] The main reason is that criminal action against product piracy does not seem to be a high priority on the agenda of investigative authorities in the Netherlands. The investigative authorities feel that civil action by the right holder is the starting point and criminal prosecution is the "ultimum remedium" in such situations.[9] Moreover, criminal prosecution requires that intent must be proven on the part of the infringing party, which is often difficult in practice. Finally, although the Wetboek van Strafrecht [Criminal Act] allows for the confiscation of profits made illegally through infringing actions, it is difficult to quantify profits because proper administration is often lacking.[10] As a result, the Public Prosecution Service *(Openbaar Ministerie)* has little incentive to bring criminal actions since the chances of success are relatively slim.

Criminal prosecution in practice is limited to cases that have a certain general interest (i. e. in the event of a health or safety risk, large-scale counterfeiting that affects the market, the involvement of criminal organisations, and cases of repeat offence). Alternatively, criminal action may also be brought if the right holder reports the matter to the police.

In the Netherlands, criminal investigation of IP infringement and counterfeiting is one of the tasks of the FIOD-ECD (Fiscal Information and Investigation Service and Economic Investigation Service). The FIOD-ECD, which is a department of the Tax and Customs Administration *(Belastingdienst)*, is responsible for law enforcement with respect to (i) fiscal, financial and economic fraud, (ii) securing business integrity, (iii) consumer protection, and (iv) fighting organised crime.[11] The FIOD-ECD includes a special team, the Piracy Investigation Team *(Team Opsporing Piraterij)*. This team mainly focuses on the investigation of copyright infringement in music, film, and interactive software. The FIOD-ECD cooperates internationally with Europol and OLAF (Organisation de la Lutte anti Fraude) the European organisation for the prevention of fraud.

On 1 June 2007, the Wet op de bijzondere opsporingsdiensten [Special Investigation Service Act] (NL) entered into force, setting out the special competences and supervision of investigative authorities such as FIOD-ECD. For instance, the Special Investigation Service Act stipulates that FIOD-ECD officials have the same investigative authority as policemen. In addition, customs and investigative authorities such as the FIOD-ECD and the police also cooperate with organisations such as Foundation Brein and SNB-REACT. When these authorities detect counterfeit products, they will notify Foundation Brein, SNB-REACT, and any potential right holders.

---

8 *Gielen*, Kort begrip van het intellectuele eigendomsrecht, § 78 and 298.

9 Note from the Board of Procurators General *(College van Procureurs-generaal) Aanwijzing intellectuele-eigendomsfraude*, Staatscourant 9 januari 2006, nr. 6, p. 10.

10 *Brohm*, Namaakbestrijding: onvoldoende rechtsmiddelen?, March 2001.

11 http://www.minfin.nl/nl/onderwerpen,belastingen/uitvoering/fiod_ecd/index.html.

II. Trademark Piracy

A. Legal Requirements for Trademark Protection under the Benelux Treaty on Intellectual Property

The Netherlands does not have a national law to protect trademark holders. The governments of Belgium, The Netherlands, and Luxembourg decided to cooperate and create one collective legal framework for the Benelux, which resulted in the Eenvormige Benelux Merkenwet [Benelux Trademark Act]. The Benelux Trademark Act has since been replaced by the Benelux-Verdrag inzake de intellectuele eigendom [BTIP] [Benelux Treaty on Intellectual Property], which governs both Benelux trademark law and Benelux design right law.[12]

Art. 2.2 of the BTIP provides that a trademark right must be obtained through registration in the Benelux with the Benelux-Bureau voor de Intellectuele Eigendom [BOIP] [Benelux Office for Intellectual Property]. Art. 2.10 provides that the right to use a trademark in the Benelux can also be obtained by filing an international application with WIPO in Geneva pursuant to the Madrid Agreement or the Protocol to this Agreement, dated 27 June 1989. Furthermore, a community trademark (CTM) valid in the EU can be obtained through application with OHIM in Alicante based upon the Community Trademark Regulation (Regulation 40/94/EC of 20 December 1993 on the Community trademark).[13]

The BOIP will refuse a trademark if the sign (i) is not fit to be a trademark pursuant to Art. 2.1 and 2.2 of the BTIP,[14] (ii) if the sign lacks any distinguishing characteristics, (iii) if the sign is a generic name for the goods or services it is applied for, or (iv) if the sign consists of words that have become common in normal language. Furthermore, a third party can oppose the registration of a Benelux trademark if the application will infringe upon the older trademark rights of the opposing party. Although registration of colours, shapes, and the like is technically possible, in practice registration is often refused.

A trademark is initially granted for a period of 10 years as of the application date and can be renewed for 10 year terms without a maximum duration of protection.[15] Even

---

12 The Benelux Treaty on Intellectual Property (Beneluxverdrag inzake de intellectuele eigendom) of 25 February 2005, The Hague, as amended on 1 February 2007. This Convention came into operation on 1 September 2006. The text of the Convention is only available in French and Dutch and can be found at the official website of the Benelux Office for Intellectual Property http://www.boip.int/en/generalLegalRegulations.html.

13 Council Regulation (EC) No 40/94 of 20 December 1993 on the Community trademark, Official Journal of the European Communities 1993 No L 11/1.

14 Art. 2.1 of the BTIP requires that a trademark be a sign that is capable of being represented graphically. Art. 2.2 of the BTIP provides that a sign that (i) solely consists of a form determined by the nature of the good, (ii) gives essential value to the good, or (iii) is necessary in order to achieve a technical result, cannot be a trademark.

15 Art. 2.9, ¶ 1 of the BTIP.

though the registration may be renewed without limitation, a trademark may become invalid if it is not used in the Benelux in the normal course of trade, for the goods or services that it was registered for, for more than five consecutive years.[16]

Pursuant to Art. 2.20 of the BTIP, the holder of a registered trademark has the exclusive right to use its trademark and can prohibit others from using the same or a similar sign under certain circumstances. However, the mere application of a trademark does not give the trademark holder the right to invoke its application against a third party.[17] The Benelux trademark application process allows for an "urgent registration" *(spoedinschrijving)*, under of which a trademark can be registered immediately. Such a trademark can still be cancelled at a later stage as a result of formal BOIP requirements[18] or due to opposition proceedings. A Benelux trademark registered through such urgent procedures can be invoked against third parties immediately.

B. Infringing Behaviour

1. Danger of Confusion

Art. 2.20 (1) (a) and (b) of the BTIP form the basis of the actions that a trademark holder can bring against counterfeit producers who use a sign that is either identical to the registered mark or is confusingly similar. Benelux trademark law is meant to act in harmony with the Trademark Directive (Directive 89/104 /EEC of 21 December 1988 to approximate the laws of the Member States relating to trademarks, Official Journal of the European Communities 1989 No L 40/1). Therefore, Art. 2.20 of the BTIP is interpreted by taking into account the Trademark Directive and decisions of the ECJ (European Court of Justice).

Art. 2.20 (1) (a) of the BTIP provides that the holder of a registered trademark shall be entitled to prevent third parties from using any sign in the course of trade that is identical to the trademark, in relation to goods or services that are identical with those for which the trademark is registered. This article is the most common basis for an action by the trademark holder when a copy of the trademark has been used by a third party on counterfeit products. If use is made of a sign that is identical to the registered trademark, danger of confusion or dilution is presumed. According to the ECJ, a sign is identical to the trademark if it depicts, without change or addition, all elements of the trademark, or if the sign shows differences that are so minor that the average consumer will not notice.[19]

Often in clear counterfeit cases, the defendant does not argue non-infringement of the trademark, but rather that the infringement was trivial and that the requested claims

---

16 Art. 2.26, paragraph 2 of the BTIP.

17 Art. 2.19 of the BTIP.

18 Art. 2.11 of the BTIP.

19 20 March 2003 ECJ [C-291/00], BIE 2003, 203 (Arthur & Felicie).

should not be awarded.[20] However, even if a limited number of counterfeit products were sold, the fact that there was extensive advertising for a counterfeit product could be sufficient to award broad claims even in preliminary proceedings.[21] On the other hand, in preliminary proceedings, the plaintiff will have to demonstrate why broad claims, such as the destruction of the infringing goods, are required and why the outcome of a full proceeding on the merits cannot be awaited.[22]

If the sign used on the counterfeit product is not identical to the registered trademark, the trademark holder can still invoke Art. 2.20 (1) (b) of the BTIP. This article provides that the holder of a registered trademark shall be entitled to prevent third parties from using any sign in the course of trade that is identical or similar to the trademark, where there is a likelihood of consumer confusion (taking into account the likelihood of association between the sign and the trademark). In order to determine whether the sign and the trademark are confusingly similar, the sign and the trademark must be assessed broadly as to their overall impression for both *direct confusion* (the two show an aural/visual likeness or likeness in its meaning, such that the relevant public could be confused between the sign and the trademark) and *indirect confusion* (the sign could create the impression that there is connection between the trademark owner and the sign).[23] When evaluating the likelihood of consumer confusion, all relevant facts and circumstances need to be taken into account (i. e. the degree of similarity between the goods or services, the distinguishing characteristics of the trademark, and whether or not the trademark is widely known).

2. Particular Case: Transit as Infringing Behaviour

Goods in transit are goods that are physically kept on or transported through the territory of the EU under the supervision of customs authorities, but without clearing the goods into the EU.[24] The third consideration of the preamble of the Customs Regulation clarifies that the entering of counterfeit goods into the EU even under a suspension of customs procedure, should be prohibited.[25] Based upon the Customs Regulation, Dutch courts have traditionally applied the "fiction of manufacture". Counterfeit goods found in transit on Dutch territory were considered infringing to the extent that the manufacture of such goods in the Netherlands would have constituted an infringement. The

20 As noted earlier, these claims may include recall, destruction of infringing products, publication of a rectification, and supplying information regarding the infringement (including the identity of customers or suppliers of infringing products and the details of such transactions).

21 18 October 2005 District Court, The Hague (in preliminary proceedings) [KG 05/1216], NJF 2006/32.

22 8 July 2005 District Court, The Hague (in preliminary proceedings) [KG 05/536].

23 See amongst others 11 November 1997 ECJ [C-251/95], NJ 1998, 523 (Puma/Sabel).

24 This is a so called suspensive procedure as provided for in Council Regulation (EEC) No 2913/92 of 12 October 1992 establishing the Community Customs Code, Official Journal of the European Communities 1992 No L 302/1.

25 *Schmutzer*, Montex: is transitohandel ongrijpbaar geworden, IER 2007/5, 287.

final destination of the counterfeit goods was considered irrelevant. This legal fiction was confirmed by the Dutch Supreme Court in *Philips/Postech.*[26]

The fiction of manufacturing was eventually superseded by the decision of the ECJ in *Diesel/Montex.*[27] This decision is the most recent in a series of cases concerning transit issues.[28] *Diesel/Montex* dealt specifically with counterfeit goods in transit. Counterfeit *Diesel* jeans were manufactured in Poland (before Poland became an EU Member State). While in transit through Germany (with a final destination in Ireland, where Diesel did not have any trademark rights), German customs authorities seized the goods based on product piracy. The ECJ ruled that regarding goods being transported under a suspension of customs procedure, there is only infringement to the extent that a third party committed an act regarding the counterfeit goods, which implied that the goods were to be traded in the Member State. It is not relevant where the goods originated from or whether the goods were manufactured legally.

Courts in the Netherlands will likely follow the ruling of the ECJ in *Diesel/Montex.* This will make it more difficult for authorities to seize goods in transit in the future.

3. Particular Case: Internetprovider

See paragraph VI C, where the position of internet providers is set out.

4. Particular Case: Parallel Imports

Parallel imports are not counterfeit goods. They are genuine goods originating from the right holder (or a licencee of such right holder), which were first put into the market in one European Economic Area (EEA) country and are later imported into another EEA country. Can IP rights in one country be used to prevent the importation or sale of the product in another country? The answer depends on the Doctrine of Exhaustion. Once a product has been placed on the market in one EEA Member State by the right holder or its licencee, his IP rights are deemed to have been exhausted. The right holder can no longer prevent the circulation and sale of the product in the EEA by invoking parallel IP rights in other Member States. The purpose of EEA exhaustion is to screen off the EEA from the rest of the world.

The ECJ has decided that the parallel importer has the burden of proof to show that the product has been put onto the market in the EEA by, or with the consent of, the right holder and that the IP rights have therefore been exhausted (unless the burden of proof allows the trademark owner to partition the markets within the EEA).[29] If goods are first

26 19 March 2004, Dutch Supreme Court [C-02/110 HR], IER 2004, 50 (Philips/Postech).

27 9 November 2006, ECJ [C-281/05], IER 2007, 30 (Diesel/Montex).

28 6 April 2000, ECJ [C-383/98] (Polo/Lauren); 23 October 2003 ECJ [C-115/02] (Rioglass); 18 October 2005 ECJ [C-405/03] (Class/SKB).

29 8 March 2003 ECJ [C-244/00] (Van Doren/Lifestyle Sports).

put on the market outside the EEA and then imported into the EEA, the parallel importer has the burden of proof to show that the trademark owner consented to such importation.[30] The burden of proof applies to the entire route of each specific batch of goods.

In the *Class* case, the ECJ held that goods that have entered the EEA in transit have not been imported or put onto the market in the EEA. Such goods in transit can be traded to countries outside the EEA, unless this necessarily implies that the goods are put unto the market in the EEA.[31]

What happens if genuine parallel imported goods are seized by customs as counterfeit goods? In order to claim destruction, the right holder will need to prove that the goods are counterfeit based on the Customs Regulation. If the goods are in fact genuine, the question arises whether the rights of the trademark holder have been exhausted. If not, the trademark holder could still act on the basis of trademark infringement.

Courts in The Netherlands follow the rulings of the ECJ. In 2006, the Court of Appeal in The Hague decided a case between Nike International Ltd. and Marimina B. V. Customs authorities seized Nike shoes in the port of Rotterdam and Nike petitioned the court for destruction of the shoes. The court in preliminary proceedings denied the requested destruction. The Court of Appeals decided that Nike had not sufficiently proved that the shoes were in fact counterfeit. As a result, the Customs Regulation did not apply. With reference to the *Class* Judgement of the ECJ as mentioned before, the Court of Appeals denied Nike's claims. According to the Court of Appeals it was up to Nike to prove that the shoes originating from the United Arabic Emirates were cleared by customs and put onto the EEA market in the Netherlands (which Nike did not succeed in proving).[32] Whereas, it is the parallel importer who has the burden to show that it had the consent of the right holder to put the goods onto the EEA market. This case clarifies that the right holder in fact needs to prove whether or not the goods were imported into the EEA.

C. Legal Consequences – Discontinuance, Information, Damages, Destruction, and Recall

Without prejudice to the plaintiff's right to damages, a trademark holder can request that the court in civil proceedings grant an injunction prohibiting the use of the infringing sign.[33]

In addition, the trademark holder has a number of ancillary claims. The court can order a recall of the infringing goods, the permanent removal of the goods from the stream of commerce, destruction of the infringing goods, and in certain cases, destruction of the

30 20 November 2001 ECJ [C-414/99, C-415/99 C-416/99] (Davidoff & Levi Strauss).

31 18 October 2005 ECJ [C-405/03] (Class International/Colgate c. s.).

32 13 April 2006, Court of Appeals The Hague [05/1100] (Nike International Ltd/Marimina B. V.).

33 Art. 2.20 of the BTIP.

materials and machines used for the production of the goods. The cost of recalling, removing, and destroying the goods or equipment are borne by the infringer unless there are special circumstances. The court will take into account the seriousness of the infringement and any third party interests when deciding upon any order.[34] The court can also order the infringer to provide information about the origin and distribution of the infringing goods and/or publicise the court's decision at its own cost.[35] These rights stem from Part III of the TRIPS Agreement which deals with the protection of IP rights in general.[36]

Last, but not least, the trademark holder can claim compensation for damages.[37] Following from Art. 45 of the TRIPS Agreement, liability for compensation only exists if the infringer knew, or had reasonable grounds to know, that he was infringing upon a trademark.[38] In such cases, the trademark holder can claim the higher of either: (i) compensation for damages it incurred as a result of the infringement, or (ii) payment by the infringer of the amount of profits it made as a result of the infringement. In order to establish the profits made, the infringer will generally be ordered to report its profits after verification by a registered accountant.[39] As held by the Benelux Court of Justice, profit refers to net profit, which is calculated by deducting the purchase price of the products, taxes, and costs from the sales price.[40] As an alternative to calculating the actual damages incurred by the trademark holder, the court can determine damages as a fixed amount based on elements such as the amount of royalties that the trademark holder would have received if the infringer had permission to use the trademark.[41]

D. Enforcement

Once a right holder is aware of a possible infringement of its IP rights, several civil actions are possible. The trademark holder can request that the court grants an injunction. Such requests can be made (i) as an ex-parte request to the court if a delay would cause irreparable damage, (ii) in preliminary proceedings (where the plaintiff still needs to establish an urgent interest to obtain preliminary relief), or (iii) in proceedings on the merits. For more details please refer to paragraph I A above.

---

34 Art. 2.22 ¶ 1 of the BTIP.

35 Art. 2.22 ¶ 4 and 7 of the BTIP and *Gielen*, Kort begrip van het intellectuele eigendomsrecht, § 350-351.

36 Agreement on trade-related aspects of intellectual property rights, in force as of 1 January 1996.

37 A licensee may independently claim damages to the extent that licencee explicitly agreed such competence with the trademark holder. Art. 2.21 ¶ 5 jo art. 2.32 ¶ 4 and 5 of the BTIP.

38 Art. 2.21 ¶ 1 of the BTIP.

39 Art. 2.21 ¶ 1 and 3 of the BTIP.

40 24 October 2005, Benelux Court of Justice [2004/5], BIE 2006, 172 (Dior/Delhaize).

41 Art. 2.21 ¶ 2 of the BTIP. This paragraph was added as result of implementation of the Enforcement Directive.

The trademark holder could seize the infringing goods before initiating court proceedings. A seizure can be made either by requesting permission from the court to seize the goods as provided for in the Wetboek van Burgerlijke Rechtsvordering [Code of Civil Procedure] or by customs as provided for in the Customs Regulation. After the allegedly infringing goods are seized, the trademark holder will have to initiate either preliminary proceedings or proceedings on the merits.[42] Furthermore, the trademark holder could request that the court permits the seizure of evidence or take measures related to the collection and preservation of evidence.

Pursuant to art. 3:305 (a) and 3:305 (b) of the Burgerlijk Wetboek [Civil Code], a foundation or association that represents the interests of trademark holders may enforce trademark rights as well. However, the foundation or association cannot claim damages.

In addition to civil proceedings, criminal action against trademark infringement is also possible. Art. 337 of the Wetboek van Strafrecht [Criminal Code] provides that trademark fraud *(merkvervalsing)* is a crime. This article applies to the intentional import, export, transport, sale, offering for sale, delivery, distribution, and storing of imitation, counterfeit, or illegally manufactured trademarks and goods (including packaging with the trademark, or goods with an imitation of the trademark, even if there is a slight deviation). For an infringer to be convicted on the basis of trademark fraud, intent is required. The maximum penalty is one year imprisonment (or four years if there is a fear of danger to persons or goods or if the trademark fraud is the infringer's business) and/or a penalty of EUR 74,000. The requirement of intent makes the crime difficult to prove, so that in practice, criminal action with respect to trademark counterfeiting is an exception.[43]

III. Design Rights

A. Legal Requirements for Design Protection according to the Benelux Treaty on Intellectual Property

As is the case for trademarks, there is no national law in the Netherlands to protect the proprietors of a design right. Protection of design rights falls under the province of the BTIP, which offers Benelux-wide protection. The Design Directive (Directive 98/71/EC on the legal protection of designs)[44] was implemented as a part of the Eenvormige Benelux Wet inzake tekeningen of modellen [BTMW] [Uniform Benelux Act on Designs and Models]. Today, this Act has been replaced by the BTIP. As Benelux design right laws are harmonised with the Design Rights Directive, the BTIP is therefore interpreted taking into account the Design Rights Directive and the decisions of the ECJ.

42 Preliminary proceedings or proceedings on the merits are not required if the goods have been destroyed in accordance with the simplified destruction procedure provided in the Customs Regulation (EC) No 1383/2003.

43 *Gielen*, Kort begrip van het intellectuele eigendomsrecht, § 345.

44 Directive 98/71/EC of the European Parliament and of the Council of 13 October 1998 on the legal protection of designs, Official Journal of the European Communities 1998 No L 289/28.

A design can be protected by a design right to the extent that it is new and has individual characteristics.[45] The requirements of novelty and individual character are further detailed in the BTIP. A design consists of the appearance of a product or parts thereof.[46] A design right shall not rest upon features or appearances of a product that are solely dictated by its technical function.

Art. 3.5 of the BTIP provides that a design right is obtained through registration in the Benelux with the BOIP. The BOIP will refuse a design right if certain formal requirements are not met. If the requirements are met, the BOIP publishes the application (pursuant to BTIP Art. 3.11 (2). Opposition against a design right application is not possible. Design protection is initially granted for a period of five years from the application date and can be renewed for four five-year terms, with a maximum duration of 25 years.

In addition to Benelux design rights, international design rights that are recognised in the Benelux and Community Designs can also be invoked for protection (see paragraph III E).

B. Infringing Behaviour

Pursuant to Art. 3.16 (1) of the BTIP, the holder of a registered design right may oppose the use of a product that has a similar appearance, or an appearance that produces the same overall impression on an informed user. This article forms the basis for actions where a copy of a right holder's design is used by a third party in or on counterfeit products. The court will compare the registered design with the allegedly infringing product as it is used to assess whether the items have a similar appearance, focusing on the user's overall impression of both the design and the product. The assessment of infringement is very factual and should be made through the eyes of the informed user. The informed user is not a specialist, but does have knowledge of the relevant market and sector. An informed user would therefore notice certain differences between the design and the product that would escape the eye of an average consumer.

The scope of protection offered to a design right depends upon the designer's level of freedom when developing the design. If the designer's freedom is limited, small differences could lead to a different overall impression of the design and the product, therefore resulting in a non-infringement decision.

In addition to opposing common activities such as the trading, sale, and delivery of a design, a right holder may also oppose the import/exporting, renting, stocking, or displaying of the design. However, a right holder can only oppose the use of a design with an industrial or commercial purpose. Private uses of a design cannot be opposed by a right holder.

---

45 Art. 3.1 (1) of the BTIP.

46 Art. 3.1 (2) of the BTIP.

C. Legal Consequences – Discontinuance, Information, Damages, Destruction, Recall

Injunctions prohibiting the use of an infringing product and damages claims are the most important enforcement measures in the Benelux. In addition, the design right holder has a number of ancillary claims, which are similar to the ancillary claims under Benelux trademark law.

Art. 3.18 of the BTIP provides that the court can order a recall of the infringing goods, a permanent removal of the infringing goods from the stream of commerce, destruction of the infringing goods, and in certain cases, destruction of the materials and machines used for the production of the goods. The costs of the recall, removal, and destruction are payable by the infringer unless there are special circumstances. The court will take into account the seriousness of the infringement and any third party interests when deciding upon any order. The court can also order the infringer to provide information about the origin and distribution of the infringing goods and/or publicise the court's decision at its own cost.[47]

According to Art. 3.17 (1) of the BTIP, the design right holder can claim compensation for damages in the event of infringement.[48] Damages can only be claimed for activities that occured after publication of the design right application and only to the extent that the application sufficiently illustrated the distinguishing characteristics of the design. Following from Article 45 of the TRIPS Agreement, liability for compensation only exists if the infringer knew, or had reasonable grounds to know, that he was infringing upon the design of the rights holder. The holder of a design right can claim the higher of either: (i) compensation for damages it incurred as a result of the infringement, or (ii) payment by the infringer of the profits it made as a result of the infringement. In order to establish the amount of profits, the infringer will generally be ordered to report on its profits after verification by a registered accountant. As an alternative to actually calculating the damages incurred by the rights holder, the court can determine a fixed amount for damages based on factual elements such as the amount of royaltyies that the holder of the design right would have received had the infringer actually obtained permission to use the design right. The court can also order the surrender of the infringing products to the right holder as a means of compensation.[49]

D. Enforcement

Pursuant to Art. 3.16 of the BTIP, the holder of a design right has the exclusive right to use its design and to prohibit others from using the same or similar design in the Benelux. Once the holder of a design right is aware of a possible infringement of its rights, several civil actions are possible. The right holder can request that the court grant an

47 Art. 3.18 ¶ 4 and 7 of the BTIP.

48 A licencee may independently claim damages to the extent the licencee explicitly agreed such competence with the design right holder. Art. 3.17 ¶ 2 jo 3.26 ¶ 4 of the BTIP.

49 Art. 3.17 ¶ 3 of the BTIP.

injunction. Such a request can be made either (i) as an ex-parte request to the court if a delay would cause irreparable damage, (ii) in preliminary proceedings (where the plaintiff still needs to establish an urgent interest to obtain preliminary relief), or (iii) in proceedings on the merits. For more details please refer to paragraph I A.

If the right holder takes civil action to prevent the infringement of its design right, the right holder will need to detail the infringement in the writ of summons as much as possible. If a non-registered Community Design is enforced, the right holder must file sufficient materials and photographs of the design as exhibits. The right holder will have to submit these exhibits before the oral hearing, as the court holds that it is not sufficient for the right holder to await the oral hearing to present the un-registered design to the court.[50]

The holder of a design right could also seize the infringing goods before initiating court proceedings.[51] A seizure can be made either by requesting permission from the court to seize the goods as provided for in the Wetboek van Burgerlijke Rechtsvordering [Code of Civil Procedure], or by customs as provided for in the Customs Regulation. After the allegedly infringing goods are seized, the rights holder will have to initiate either preliminary proceedings or proceedings on the merits.[52] Furthermore, the rights holder could request that the court permit the seizure of evidence, or take measures related to the collection and preservation of evidence.

Pursuant to Art. 3:305 (a) and Art. 3:305 (b) of the Burgerlijk Wetboek [Civil Code], a foundation or association that represents the interests of design right holders may enforce design rights as well. However, a claim for damages is not an option.

There are no specific criminal provisions related to design rights.

E. International Design

1. Community Design Rights

Based upon the Community Design Regulation (Regulation 2002/06/EC of 12 December 2001 on Community designs,[53] as amended by regulation (2007/876/EC of 24 July 2007),[54] a community design right valid in the EU can be obtained through application

---

50 24 May 2005 District court The Hague in preliminary proceedings [KG 05/379] (Reckitt/Action). See also *Gielen*, Kort begrip van het intellectuele eigendomsrecht, § 207.

51 Art. 3.18 ¶ 2 of the BTIP.

52 Preliminary proceedings or proceedings on the merits are not required if the goods have been destroyed in accordance with the simplified destruction procedure as provided for in the Customs Regulation (EC) 1883/2003.

53 Council Regulation (EC) No 6/2002 of 12 December 2001 on Community designs, Official Journal of the European Communities 2002 No L 3/1.

54 Commission Regulation (EC) No 876/2007 of 24 July 2007 amending Regulation (EC) No 2245/2002 implementing Council Regulation (EC) No 6/2002 on Community designs following the

with OHIM (Office for the Harmonisation in the Internal Market). The Community Design Regulation is largely based upon the Design Rights Directive, and contains largely similar provisions as a result. This means that the enforcement of Community Design Rights in the Benelux largely follows the same system described above for Benelux design rights.

An important tool introduced by the Community Design Regulation was the non-registered community design right. This design right does not require an application or registration process and is free from charge. This type of protection is developed specifically for industries where large numbers of designs are produced with a limited life cycle in a short period of time (such as fashion and textile). For such manufacturers, registration requirements are unnecessarily onerous. However, the duration of protection for such non-registered designs is only three years and the design right holder can only act against the deliberate copying of its designs.[55] The alleged infringer has the burden of proof to substantiate that he or she was not aware of the right holder's design right. The same material requirements apply to unregistered design rights, namely that the design should be novel and have an individual character.

2. Design Rights under International Law and 25 TRIPS

A design right valid in the Benelux can be obtained not only by registering a Benelux design right but also by applying for an international design right where the Benelux is one of the designated jurisdictions.[56] An international application takes place according to the provisions of the 6 November 1925 Convention of the Hague regarding the international application of design rights[57] (Art. 3.15 of the BTIP). Other than for international trademarks, an international design right does not require a prior basis registration of a design right from a local country. An international design right can be applied for directly with the WIPO. The EU has recently acceded the Convention, making it possible to file for an international design right that is valid for the entire EU, as well as for other designated countries.[58] An international design right with validity in the Benelux is considered a Benelux design right. As a result, the enforcement of these design rights is governed by provisions of the BTIP as described above.

accession of the European Community to the Geneva Act of the Hague Agreement concerning the international registration of industrial designs (Text with EEA relevance), Official Journal of the European Union 2007 No L 193/13.

55 Community Design Regulation; Art. 19 (2).

56 Art. 3.5 ¶ 1 of the BTIP.

57 As amended in London on 2 June 1934 and in The Hague on 28 November 1960.

58 Council Regulation (EC) No 1891/2006 of 18 December 2006 amending Regulations (EC) No 6/2002 and (EC) No 40/94 to give effect to the accession of the European Community to the Geneva Act of the Hague Agreement concerning the international registration of industrial designs, Official Journal of the European Union 2006 No L 386/14.

In addition to Art. 4.7 of the BTIP, Benelux nationals can directly invoke TRIPS, particularly Articles 25, and 26 which relate to design rights. The BTIP is in conformity with Articles 25 and 26 of TRIPS.[59]

F. Design Protection and Copyright Law, Unfair Competition Law and Trademark Law

1. Design Protection and Copyright Law

The concurrence of a design right and a copyright is possible under Dutch law.[60] This follows from Art. 3.28 of the BTIP and Arts. 10 (1) and 11 of the Auteurswet [AW] [Copyright Act] (NL). In order to qualify for copyright protection, Dutch law only requires that the design has an individual and original character, which bears the personal stamp of the originator.[61]

Designs that are either not protected by a design right, or are no longer protected by such right, can still be protected by copyright if the aforementioned requirements are met.

2. Design Protection and Unfair Competition Law

In addition to claiming design right infringement a design right holder can also invoke the protection against needless copying, which is also referred to as the Doctrine of Slavish Imitation. A slavish imitation claim is based on the general prohibition to act unlawfully pursuant to Art. 6:162 of the Burgerlijk Wetboek [Civil Code].

The protection against slavish imitation is based on various decisions by the Dutch Supreme Court. The Dutch Supreme Court ruled that imitation is a permitted starting point as long as no IP rights are infringed upon, since fair competition is an essential part of trading. This is allowed even if there is a risk of confusing the relevant public. However, imitating a competitor's product is prohibited if it was possible to take the design in a different direction without negatively affecting the stability and usability of the product. The failure to implement these differences increases the likelihood of product confusion. The imitator is therefore obliged to do everything reasonably possible to avoid the risk of confusion caused by the similarity between the products.[62] The party invoking protection under the Doctrine of Slavish Imitation has the burden to show that the imitator could have chosen a different design route.[63]

---

59 *Gielen*, Kort begrip van het intellectuele eigendomsrecht, § 241.

60 22 May 1987 Benelux Court of Justice [A 85/3], NJ 1987, 881 (Screenoprints).

61 The Uniform Benelux Act on Designs and Models provided in art. 21 and 24 that design rights and copyrights could concur but that after expiration of a design right, the copyright on that design also expired unless the copyright holder filed a so called 'declaration to maintain'. This provision has been deleted and no longer exists under the BTIP.

62 26 June 1953 Dutch Supreme Court, NJ 1954, 90 (Hyster/Karry Krane).

Until 2003, the BTMW [Uniform Benelux Act on Designs and Models] prohibited concurrent claims of design right infringement and slavish imitation. A design feature that could have been protected by a design right could only rely on design rights and could not invoke the doctrine of slavish imitation, even if the owner had not registered a design right. However, para 14,8 of the BTMW [Uniform Benelux Act on Designs and Models] was deleted in 2003. This means that the creator of an original design who failed to register such design before 1 December 2003 can now rely on the doctrine of slavish imitation for protection.

3. Design Protection and Trademark Law

A product design can be registered as a design right, a trademark, or both. Pursuant to Art. 2.1 BTIP and Art. 4 of the Trademark Regulation (Regulation 94/40/EC on the community trademark), physical shapes can be registered as trademarks if the formal qualifications requirements are met. This means that the shape of the product being registered as a trademark must have a distinguishing characteristic. Furthermore, the shape should not be determined by the nature of the product, nor should it influence the value of the product or form the basis for any industry findings. The BOIP and OHIM review these formal requirements strictly and applications for shape trademarks are often refused.

While designs must be new when registering for design rights, Benelux trademark law does not have the same requirement for trademarks. Therefore, it is possible to register a shape as a trademark, even if it is no longer new at the time of registration and thus no longer qualifies for design right protection.

IV. Patent Piracy

A. Legal Requirements for Patent Protection under the Dutch Patent Act

The Netherlands only introduced patent protection in 1910 after severe international pressure. The Rijksoctrooiwet [ROW 1910] [Patent Act 1910] (NL) was revised several times to comply with standards such as the EPC (European Patent Convention) and the PCT (Patent Cooperation Treaty). The ROW 1910 [Patent Act 1910] was replaced by the ROW [Patent Act] of 1995 which is currently still in place. Most recently, the ROW [Patent Act] was amended to implement the Enforcement Directive.

In the Netherlands there are two types of national patents, giving protection for either six years or twenty years. Registering and obtaining a six-year patent is relatively simple but the scope of protection is restricted. For instance, before legal injunction proceedings can be initiated, an investigation regarding the validity of the particular patent must be conducted. Obtaining a twenty-year patent requires a novelty report, which is issued after extensive investigation to establish whether the invention is part of the

63 28 February 1969 Dutch Supreme Court, NJ 1969, 366 (Trekkerhoes).

prior art (latest technical knowledge, *stand van de techniek*) before registration. However, the applicant is not obliged to take account of the results of the novelty report since these results do not prohibit the patent grant. This chapter will focus on the twenty-year patent since the large companies that are usually confronted with piracy usually have such patents.

In addition, European patents that list the Netherlands as one of the designated countries are valid in the Netherlands (this is discussed in more detail below).

1. Pre-requisite: Securing Rights to Inventions

a. Securing Rights in the Context of Cooperations with Third Parties

Art. 13 of the ROW [Patent Act] addresses to the situations where an invention was made in the context of cooperation between various parties or persons. To the extent that the cooperating parties agreed that any invention following from their cooperation will become their joint right, the cooperating persons indeed have a joint right regarding the invention. This is true even if some of the cooperating persons did not in fact provide an inventive contribution to the invention. Art. 59 of the EPC, which provides that a patent application can be made on behalf of more than one applicant, follows from the concept of such joint invention rights.

In practice, other arrangements are also often made. It is not uncommon for parties to agree that the results of a joint development program or research will belong to a third party.[64]

2. Scope of Patent Protection

Art. 2.1 of the ROW [Patent Act][65] states that a patent can be obtained for an invention that is (i) new, also known as the "novelty" requirement; (ii) the result of an inventive step, also known as the "obviousness" requirement; and (iii) can be applied in the field of industry.

Furthermore, inventions must be of a technical nature pursuant to Art 52 of the EPC. Patent applications must disclose information about the invention in a sufficiently clear and complete manner, such that a person skilled in the industry could replicate the invention.[66] The need for sufficient disclosure ("obviousness") derives from the fundamental nature of the patent system – in return for the limited monopoly provided by the protection, the patentee must teach the public what his or her invention is.

---

64 *Huydecoper/Van Nispen*, Industriele eigendom, bescherming van technische innovatie, § III.7.2.14.

65 See also Art. 52 of the EPC.

66 Art. 25 of the ROW [Patent Act] (see also Art. 83 of the EPC).

3. Application and Registration of Patents

According to Art. 24 of the ROW [Patent Act], a patent application has to be filed with the Netherlands Patent Office *(Octrooicentrum Nederland)*. A detailed description of the patent has to be filed along with the patent claim. A specialised patent attorney *(octrooigemachtigde)* will usually draft the patent description. However, the Netherlands Patent Office does not check whether the application for the twenty-year patent meets the material requirements set out above. The Patent Office only checks whether the formal filing requirements (i. e. the inclusion of a novelty report) have been met. This means that even if a twenty-year patent is granted, the validity of the patent is not guaranteed.

In addition to local patent offices, the EPC provides a central application procedure for a European patent. After registration, the European patent is divided into a bundle of national patent registrations. The European patent shall, in each of the contracting states for which it is granted, have the effect and be subject to the same conditions as a national patent granted by that state (unless otherwise provided in the EPC) Unlike the Netherlands Patent Office, the European Patent Office does check the validity of patent applications before granting a European patent. In the case of European patent applications, opposition proceedings can be initiated before the European Patent Office within nine months of the publication of the grant of a European Patent. Opposition proceedings can result in the revocation of the patent, a rejection of the opposition, or an amendment to the granted European Patent.

Dutch patents issued by the Netherlands Patent Office and European patents can both be invalidated, either entirely or only partially, by a Dutch Court. This is accomplished through a full proceeding based on the merits of the case. Often, defendants will file a counterclaim of invalidity as part of an infringement proceeding. Such a partial invalidity of the patent may result in an amendment of the relevant patent claims provided that the remaining claims as amended stay within the limits of the original patent claims.[67]

B. Infringing Behaviour

1. Direct patent infringement

The scope of a patent's protection is dependent on the patent's subject matter as well as the specific activities that are reserved for the patent holder.[68] Art. 53 of the ROW [Patent Act], 1(a) gives the patent holder the exclusive right to: (i) manufacture the product for or on behalf of the company; (ii) make use of the product; (iii) commercialise

67 9 February 1996 Dutch Supreme Court, BIE 1996/94 (Spiro Research/Flamco); 16 February 2001 Dutch Supreme Court [C99/195 HR], BIE 2002/26 (Van Egmond Mechanisch Transport B. V./Wiva Verpakkingen B. V.).

68 *Huydecoper/Van Nispen*, Industriele eigendom, bescherming van technische innovatie, § III.5.4.3.

the product or placing it into sales circulation; (iv) rent out the product; (v) deliver or otherwise trade the product, as well as offer the product in someone else's name; (vi) import the product; and finally (vii) keep the product in stock. Art. 53, 1(b) of the ROW [Patent Act]provides that the patent holder of a patented process has the exclusive right to apply the process for or on behalf of the company, or to use a product directly resulting from the application of the process, for or on behalf of the company and to: (i) commercialise the product place it into sales circulation; (ii) rent out the product; (iii) deliver or otherwise trade the product, as well as offer the product in someone else's name; (iv) import the product; and finally (v) keep the product in stock.

The rights reserved for the patent holder are broad but not unlimited. As a result, not each unauthorised use of the patent constitutes an act of infringement. Performing of any of the activities described in Art. 53 of the ROW [Patent Act] by a third party without the permission of the patent holder, assuming that such rights have not been exhausted, constitutes patent infringement according to Art. 70(1) Art. 53(4) of the ROW [Patent Act] provides that the rights of the patent holder are exhausted to the extent that the patent holder has put the product on the market in the Netherlands or the EEA for the first time or has allowed a third party to do so.

The scope of protection for Dutch national patents, as well as European patents, are determined by Dutch national law.[69]

2. Indirect patent infringement

Pursuant to Art. 73 of the ROW [Patent Act], the patent holder can also enforce its patent vis-à-vis a third party that does not infringe upon the patent directly, but produces or offers resources as part of its business that overlaps with a substantial part of the patent. If this third party subsequently offers these resources to other third parties the patent holder can enforce its patent versus the resource providing party. This kind of patent infringement is called "indirect patent infringement". Art. 73 of the ROW [Patent Act] requires that the party offering the resources knew, or had reasonable grounds to know, that it was infringing upon a patent.

Art. 73 of the ROW [Patent Act], which defines the scope of indirect patent infringement is rather vague and leaves it up to the court to interpret the language of the provision.[70]

---

69 See Art. 64 of the EPC.

70 *Huydecoper/Van Nispen*, Industriele eigendom, bescherming van technische innovatie, § III. 5.5.13.

3. Doctrine of Equivalence

On the question of infringement, the Dutch Court apply a doctrine of equivalence. This is done within the framework as provided by Art. 69 of the EPC and the Protocol on its interpretation:

Art. 69 (1) of the EPC:

The extent of the protection conferred by a European patent or a European patent application shall be determined by the terms of the claims. Nevertheless, the description and drawings shall be used to interpret the claims.

Protocol on the Interpretation of Art. 69 of the EPC:
Art. 69 should not be interpreted in the sense that the extent of the protection conferred by a European patent is to be understood as that defined by the strict, literal meaning of the wording used in the claims, the description and drawings being employed only for the purpose of resolving an ambiguity found in the claims. Neither should it be interpreted in the sense that the claims serve only as a guideline and that the actual protection conferred may extend to what, from a consideration of the description and drawings by a person skilled in the art, the patentee has contemplated. On the contrary, it is to be interpreted as defining a position between these extremes, which combines fair protection for the patentee with a reasonable degree of certainty for third parties.

There is no specific test used for determining equivalence under Dutch law. Historically, Dutch law applied a very broad scope of protection to patents. The claims were primarily seen as a guideline to determine the *essence of the patented invention*.[71] This approach however, seems to be one of the "extremes" that the Protocol on Art. 69 wants to steer away from. Dutch courts realised this, but have not yet developed a clear set of rules to be used when applying the Protocol. However, one can see a trend in recent years that the courts have tended to be more restrictive in finding equivalence by giving more weight to the language of the claims.[72]

4. Transit as an infringing behaviour

We refer to paragraph II B.2 where transit as an infringing behaviour is discussed.

71 For example 27 January 1989 Dutch Supreme Court [Rolnummer 13318], NJ 1989/56 (Meyn/Stork).

72 13 January 1995 Dutch Supreme Court [Rolnummer 15564], NJ 1995/391 (Ciba Geigy/Oté Optics); 29 March 2002 Dutch Supreme Court [Rolnummer C00/201HR], NJ 2002/530 (Van Bentum/Kool).

C. Legal Consequences

Without prejudice to the plaintiff's right to damages, a patent holder can request that the court in civil proceedings grant an injunction prohibiting the infringement of the patent.[73] A patent infringement claim is only admissible if the holder of a Dutch national patent submits a copy of the novelty report together with the claim.[74]

In addition, the patent holder has a number of ancillary claims. The court can order a recall of the infringing goods, the permanent removal of the goods from the stream of commerce, destruction of the infringing goods, and in certain cases, destruction of the materials and machines used for the production of the goods. The cost of recalling, removing, and destroying the goods or equipment are borne by the infringer unless there are special circumstances. The court will take into account the seriousness of the infringement and any third party interests when deciding upon any order.[75] The court can also order the infringer to provide information about the origin and distribution of the infringing goods and/or publicise the court's decision at its own cost.[76]

A patent holder may request that the court order intermediaries, whose services are used for the infringement, to immediately cease their services.[77] If the defendant is allowed to temporarily continue the alleged infringement, the patent holder may also request that the defendant, or an intermediary of the defendant, provide security for any damages that the patent holder may suffer as a result of the defendant's continued activities.[78]

Last but not least, the patent holder can claim compensation for damages.[79] According to Art. 70.3 of the ROW [Patent Act], liability for compensation only exists if the defendant is knowingly infringing upon the patent. This paragraph also provides a legal fiction of awareness. An infringer is deemed to have acted knowingly if such infringement took place (or continues to take place) 30 days after the infringer was notified of the infringement by bailiff's notification. However, in 1993, the Dutch Supreme Court held that this notification requirement of the ROW [Patent Act] is a breach of Art. 45 of the TRIPS agreement, as TRIPS only requires that the infringer knew, or had reasonable

---

73 Art. 70 of the ROW [Patent Act].

74 Art. 70 ¶ 2 of the ROW [Patent Act]. To the extent a patent holder wishes to invoke a 6 year patent, a novelty report is not yet available and the patent holder will need to arrange for such novelty report before filing a claim. The requirement of filing a novelty report only applies to Dutch national patents and not to European patents as the EPO has reviewed the novelty of the invention as part of the application process whereas such review is not performed when a Dutch national patent is granted.

75 Art. 70 ¶ 6 of the ROW [Patent Act].

76 Art. 70 ¶ 9 and 11 of the ROW [Patent Act].

77 Art. 70 ¶ 8 of the ROW [Patent Act].

78 Art. 70 paragraph 10 of the ROW [Patent Act].

79 Art. 70 paragraph 5 of the ROW [Patent Act] provides that a patent holder can also seek damages on behalf of the licencee(s) or pledgee(s). The licencee and pledgee can also start individual proceedings, but only if they are granted permission by the patent holder to do so.

grounds to know, that he was infringing.[80] Following this decision, a bailiff notification is no longer required. Nevertheless, "awareness" can also arise through other means, for example by sending a cease and desist letter per registered mail.

The patent holder can claim the higher of either: (i) compensation for damages it incurred as a result of the infringement, or (ii) payment by the infringer of profits it made as a result of the infringement. In order to establish the amount of profits made, the infringer will generally be ordered to report its profits after verification by a registered accountant.[81] As held by the Benelux Court of Justice, profit refers to net profit, which is calculated by deducting the purchase price of the products, taxes and costs from the sales price.[82] As an alternative to calculating the actual damages incurred by the trademark holder, the court can determine damages as a fixed amount based on elements such as the amount of royalties that the patent holder would have received if the infringer had permission to use the patent.[83]

D. Enforcement

Once the right holder is aware of a possible infringement of its IP rights, several civil actions are possible. The patent holder can request that the court grant an injunction. Such request can be made (i) as an ex-parte request to the court if a delay would cause irreparable damage, (ii) in preliminary proceedings (where the plaintiff still needs to establish an urgent interest to obtain preliminary relief), or (iii) in proceedings on the merits. For more details please refer to paragraph I A.

In addition to the three standard proceedings set out above, a fourth type exists in patent cases. Accelerated proceedings on the merits are a special type of proceedings on the merits that the District Court at The Hague introduced for patent cases in 1996.[84] In recent years, these accelerated proceedings have become the proceedings of choice for relatively complex patent litigation in the Netherlands. Usually, these proceedings are held before a panel of three judges. They differ from regular proceedings on the merits in that a date for a hearing is scheduled immediately at the start of the litigation. Due to such expedited scheduling, these proceedings are much faster than regular proceedings on the merits. The hearing must be scheduled on a date 5 to 6 months after the start of litigation. Due to the success of these proceedings, the court sometimes has to schedule a hearing date 6 to 9 months after the start of litigation. Since preliminary measures can also be granted within the framework of these accelerated proceedings, they are a good alternative to preliminary proceedings, particularly if there are substantial issues with regard to infringement or validity. Based on a draft writ of summons, the court may grant

80 19 December 2003 Dutch Supreme Court [Rolnummer C02/228HR], IER 2004, 32 (Roche/Immunomedics).

81 Art. 70 ¶ 4 of the ROW [Patent Act].

82 24 October 2005 Benelux Court of Justice, BIE 2006/28, 172 (Dior/Delhaize).

83 Art. 70 ¶ 4 of the ROW [Patent Act]. This option was added as result of implementation of the Enforcement Directive.

84 The District Court in The Hague is the competent court in patent cases.

permission for such accelerated proceedings on the merits. The writ of summons must specify in detail the manner in which the patent is infringed. A copy of the patent also needs to be submitted to the court at the same time, along with dates when counsel will be available for a hearing. The court will then schedule a date for the hearing and an earlier date on which a Statement of Defence needs to be filed by the defendant. Any counter-claims by the defendant, such as challenges to the invalidity of the patent, should be filed together with its Statement of Defence. The plaintiff will then be allowed to file a Statement of Defence on any counterclaims. Any motions by the defendant dealing with jurisdictional issues should also be made together with the Statement of Defence. All the dates set by the court are "carved in stone". Any and all written evidence that a party wishes to rely upon and is available to that party needs to be filed together with the respective Statements. The parties may submit additional documents up to ten days prior to the hearing, but the court may refuse these additional documents if they were already available to the party on an earlier date and the court believes that they should have been submitted at that earlier occasion. The time frame is rigid up to the date of the hearing. The court will usually render a judgement within 6–12 weeks from the date of the hearing.

The patent holder can seize the infringing goods before initiating court proceedings. A seizure can be made either by requesting permission from the court to seize the goods as provided for in the Wetboek van Burgerlijke Rechtsvordering [Code of Civil Procedure] or by customs as provided for in the Customs Regulation. After the allegedly infringing goods are seized, the patent holder will have to initiate either preliminary proceedings or proceedings on the merits.[85] Furthermore, the patent holder can request that the court permit the seizure of evidence or take measures related to the collection and preservation of evidence.

Pursuant to Arts. 3:305 (a) and 3:305 (b) of the Burgerlijk Wetboek [Civil Code], a foundation or association that represents the interests of patent holders may enforce patent rights as well. However,the foundation or assocation cannot claim damages.

In addition to civil proceedings, criminal action against patent infringement is also possible. Art. 79 of the ROW [Patent Act] provides that an intentional infringement of the rights reserved for a patent holder, as provided for in Art. 53 of the ROW [Patent Act], constitutes a crime. Intent is required for convictions. The maximum penalty is 6 months imprisonment (or four years if there is a fear of danger to persons or goods, or if patent infringement is the infringer's business) and/or a maximum penalty of EUR 740,000. The requirement of intent makes the crime difficult to prove, so that in practice, criminal action with respect to patent counterfeiting is an exception.[86]

---

85 Preliminary proceedings or proceedings on the merits are not required if the goods have been destroyed in accordance with the simplified destruction procedure as provided for in the Product-piracy Regulation.

86 *Gielen*, Kort begrip van het intellectuele eigendomsrecht, § 78.

V. Know-How Theft

A. Protection of Know-How

The Netherlands is a party to the TRIPS Agreement, which addresses the topic of know-how protection and sets out rules that should be implemented in the national laws of its signatories. Section 7 of the TRIPS agreement deals with the protection of undisclosed and/or secret information. Art. 39 of TRIPS provides that in the course of ensuring effective protection against unfair competition, Members shall protect undisclosed information. According to Art. 39 paragraph 2 of TRIPS, natural and legal persons shall be able to prevent information lawfully within their control from being disclosed to, acquired by, or used by others without their consent in a manner contrary to honest commercial practices.[87] However, the information (i) must be secret in the sense that it is not, as a body or in the precise configuration and assembly of its components, generally known among or readily accessible to persons within the industry (ii) must have commercial value due to its secrecy, and (iii) under the circumstances, the person lawfully in control of the information must have taken reasonable steps to keep it a secret.[88]

The TRIPS Agreement is addressed to the Member States. In the Netherlands, there is no specific law regarding the protection of undisclosed information as prescribed by Art. 39 of TRIPS. As a result, there is no definition of Know-How in the Netherlands.

The question is whether natural and legal persons can invoke Art. 39 of TRIPS directly. The ECJ in *Dior/Tuk*[89] ruled that regarding aspects left unregulated by the EU, it is a matter for the national courts to decide whether TRIPS has direct effect or not. Dutch courts so far have not held that the TRIPs agreement has direct effect. However, a party could ask the court to decide that TRIPS has direct effect regarding Art. 39 and to apply the article to the case at hand.

Dutch law does prohibit unfair competition which is considered a tort pursuant to Art. 6:162 of the Burgerlijk Wetboek [Civil Code]. To invoke a tort claim under Dutch law, five elements need to be proven: (i) an unlawful act, (ii) accountability of this act to the principal, (iii) damages, (iv) a causal relationship between the unlawful act and the damages and (v) relativity (the breached provision should protect against damages suffered as a result of the breach of this particular provision). An unlawful act can be: (i) an infringement of a right, (ii) an act or omission in violation of a statutory duty, or (iii) behaviour that is a violation of generally accepted standards according to unwritten law.

---

87 For the purpose of this provision, "a manner contrary to honest commercial practices" shall mean at least practices such as breach of contract, breach of confidence and inducement to breach, and includes the acquisition of undisclosed information by third parties, who knew, or grossly negligent in failing to know, that such practices were involved in the acquisition.

88 *Gielen*, Kort begrip van het intellectuele eigendomsrecht, § 749.

89 14 December 2000 ECJ [C-300/98 and C-392/98], § 49 (Dior/Tuk).

Profiting from Know-How owned by another party does not constitute unfair competition *per se* but could constitute unfair competition, depending on the surrounding facts and circumstances. For instance if the Know-How was discovered through spying or theft, such acts would in principle constitute an unlawful act.

Protection of Know-How does not fall under the Customs Regulation.[90]

Arts. 272 and 273 of the Wetboek van Strafrecht [Criminal Code] extend the protection of criminal law over secret information. Art. 272 of the Wetboek van Strafrecht [Criminal Code] provides that it is a crime to deliberately violate a secret by a person who knows, or should reasonably suspect, that he or she is required to keep the secret due to employment, professional, or legal obligations. The maximum penalty is one year imprisonment and/or a fine of up to EUR 18,500 for natural persons and EUR 74,000 for legal entities.[91] Art. 273 of the Wetboek van Strafrecht [Criminal Code] provides that it is a crime to intentionally make public information regarding a company that was made available on a confidential basis. Maximum penalty is 6 months imprisonment and/or a fine of up to EUR 18,500 for natural persons and EUR 74,000 for legal entities.[92]

1. Confidentiality Agreement

In practice, it is possible to protect undisclosed information through Dutch contract law. Art. 6:74 of the Burgerlijk Wetboek [Civil Code][93] sets out the general cause of action in case of breach of contract. If for some reason there is no contractual liability for the disclosure of information, it is still possible to invoke Art. 6:162 of the Burgerlijk Wetboek [Civil Code], the general tort article.

2. Practical Measures

Since the law does not explicitly protect Know-How, the owners of valuable secrets should take precautionary measures to avoid Know-How from becoming public. Such arrangements are of a practical nature. For instance, it is important to have internal policies in place to safeguard the secret nature of Know-How. For instance, by limiting the number of persons with access to the Know-How or by storing the Know-How in a safe environment. Furthermore, contractual arrangements with both employees and third parties who have access to Know-How should be designed so that the Know-How is kept secret, shielded from abuse, and remains the property of the owner.

Art. 7:611 of the Burgerlijk Wetboek [Civil Code] provides that an employee is obliged to keep confidential the company secrets of his employer. Art. 7:678 (2) (i) of the Bur-

90 Art. 2 of the EC Product-piracy Regulation.

91 Art. 23 Wetboek van Strafrecht [Criminal Code].

92 Art. 23 Wetboek van Strafrecht [Criminal Code].

93 The Burgerlijk Wetboek [Civil Code] of 20 February 1990 came into operation on 1 January 1992 and as most recently amended on 1 February 2006.

gerlijk Wetboek [Civil Code] indicates that a breach of such confidentiality obligations is grounds for dismissal. The scope of the confidentiality obligation depends upon the circumstances. For instance, it should be made sufficiently clear to the employee that the knowledge in question is considered secret and should be kept strictly confidential.[94] In view of the above, when drafting employment agreements involving employees with access to Know-How, it would be advisable for such agreements to contain sufficient confidentiality and non-compete provisions. If no confidentiality or non-compete clause was agreed upon between the company and the employee, the use of Know-How from a former employer in a new employment setting is not unlawful *per se*.

B. Know-How Piracy as Unfair Competition

See paragraph V A.

C. Know-How as a Trade Secret

Trade secrets are not a separate legal concept under Dutch law and are thus not specifically protected under Dutch law. The provisions above relating to Know-How also apply to trade secrets.

VI. Music, Film and Software Piracy

A. Legal Requirements of Copyright Protection According to the Dutch Copyright Act

In the Netherlands, music, film, and software are in principle protected under the AW [Copyright Act].[95] According to Art. 1 of the AW [Copyright Act] copyright is the exclusive right of the author of a literary, scientific or artistic work or his successors in title to communicate that work to the public and to reproduce it, subject to the limitations laid down by law. Art. 10 AW [Copyright Act] contains a non-exhaustive list of literary, scientific, and artistic works that may qualify for copyright protection and describes twelve categories. Art. 10 paragraphs 1 (5), (10) and (12) of the AW [Copyright Act] provide that music, film, and computer programs are considered works that fall within the scope of the AW [Copyright Act] and are therefore protected (to the extent that the general requirement for copyright protection is met). Copyright does not arise through registration or publication. To qualify for copyright protection under Dutch law, it is only required that the work has an individual and original character which bears the personal stamp of the originator.[96] This requirement is not included in the AW [Copyright Act] but was developed in case law. The requirement of originality is to be judged

94 *Huydecoper/Van Nispen*, Industriele eigendom, bescherming van technische innovatie, § V.2.3.

95 The AW [Copyright Act] of 1912 came into operation on 23 September 1912 and as most recently amended on 8 March 2007.

96 22 May 1987 Benelux Court of Justice [A 85/3], NJ 1987, 881 (Screenoprints).

ex tunc (i. e. on the basis of the situation when the work was first created). The work is not required to have artistic value. Copyright does not last in perpetuity. In the Netherlands as well as the rest of the EU, copyright protection ends 70 years after the death of the author.[97]

The AW [Copyright Act] contains separate chapters for copyright on film and computer programs. Chapter 5 contains particular provisions for cinematographic works (film) and chapter 6 contains particular provisions for computer programs.

As copyright law is partially harmonised with several European Directives, those provisions of the AW [Copyright Act] are interpreted taking into account the relevant Directives and decisions of the ECJ.[98]

In the Netherlands, there is also a complementary law that protects the rights of performing artists. These provisions are captured in the Wet de Naburige Rechten [Neighbouring Rights Act] (NL)[99] and are intended to protect actors, singers, musicians, and every other person who (i) performs, (ii) sings, (iii) recites or (iv) in any other way expresses a literary or artistic work (including artists that perform in circus acts and puppet shows). The performing artist has the exclusive right to grant permission for the following activities: (i) the recording of a performance, (ii) the reproduction of a performance recording, (iii) the sale, rental, lending, supply, or otherwise putting into circulation of a reproduction a performance recording, or to use the reproduction for the

---

97 Art. 37 of the AW [Copyright Act], amended pursuant to Council Directive 93/98/EC of 29 October 1993 harmonizing the term of protection of copyright and certain related rights, Official Journal of the European Communities 1993 No L 290/9.

98 For instance, Council Directive 91/250/EC of 14 May 1991 on the legal protection of computer programs, Official Journal of the European Communities 1991 No L 122/42; Council Directive 92/100/EEC of 19 November 1992 on rental right and lending right and on certain rights related to copyright in the field of intellectual property, Official Journal of the European Communities 1992 No L 346/61; Council Directive 93/83/EEC of 27 September 1993 on the coordination of certain rules concerning copyright and rights related to copyright applicable to satellite broadcasting and cable retransmission, Official Journal of the European Communities 1993 No L 248/15; Council Directive 93/98/EEC of 29 October 1993 harmonizing the term of protection of copyright and certain related rights, Official Journal of the European Communities 1993 No L 290/9; Directive 96/9/EC of the European Parliament and of the Council of 11 March 1996 on the legal protection of databases, Official Journal of the European Communities 1996 No L 77/20; Directive 2001/29/EC of the European Parliament and of the Council of 22 May 2001 on the harmonisation of certain aspects of copyright and related rights in the information society, Official Journal of the European Communities 2001 No L 167/10; Directive 2001/84/EC of the European Parliament and of the Council of 27 September 2001 on the resale right for the benefit of the author of an original work of art, Official Journal of the European Communities 2001 No L 272/32; Directive 2004/48/EC on the enforcement of intellectual property rights, Official Journal of the European Union 2004 No L 157/45 and Corrigendum to Directive 2004/48/EC, Official Journal of the European Union 2004 No L 195/16.

99 The Wet op de Naburige Rechten [Neighbouring Rights Act] of 1993 came into operation on 29 April 1993 and as most recently amended on 8 March 2007.

purpose of import, offer or supply, (iv) the broadcasting, rebroadcast, making it available to the public or any other method of disclosing the performance or its recording.

B. Particularities of Individual Products

1. Music

In the Netherlands, the registration of copyrights on music is arranged through a single organisation termed BUMA *(Bureau voor Muziekauteursrecht)*. Contractual arrangements must be made with BUMA for all public performances of musical works, including radio and television programs, unless the author is not registered with BUMA (which is rather exceptional). BUMA then distributes the collected monies for the performance of a musical work amongst its registered authors.

2. Movies

Art. 45 (a) of the AW [Copyright Act] defines cinematographic works as work consisting of a sequence of images, with or without sound, irrespective of the manner of fixation, if it is fixed. The natural persons who created the movie are considered the author(s).[100] However, pursuant to Art. 45 (d) of the AW [Copyright Act] unless otherwise agreed in writing between the author and the producer, the authors shall be deemed to have assigned to the producer the right to communicate the movie to the public and to reproduce the movie. Despite the foregoing the authors have the right to be mentioned as the author.

3. Software

Chapter 6 of the AW [Copyright Act] contains specific provisions regarding computer programs, which are included for the purpose of implementing the European Software Directive (Directive 91/250/EC of 14 May 1991 on the legal protection of computer programs)[101] of 1991. As a consequence, the provisions of this chapter are not consistent with the other provisions of the AW [Copyright Act].

The term "reproducing" which is one of the rights of the author of a copyright protected work, has been broadened regarding software. Art. 45 (i) of the AW [Copyright Act] provides that "reproducing" in the context of software includes loading, displaying, running, transmission, and storage, in so far as these acts are necessary for the reproduction of said work.

---

100 Art. 45 (a), Paragraph 2 and 3 of the AW [Copyright Act].

101 Council Directive 91/250/EC of 14 May 1991 on the legal protection of computer programs, Official Journal of the European Communities 1991 No L 122/42.

On the other hand, the AW [Copyright Act] specifies a number of activities regarding software which may fall under the broadened definition of reproduction, but which are explicitly excluded from infringement upon the copyright of the rights holder. For instance, the reproduction of a work by the lawful acquirer of a copy of said work, where this is necessary for the use of the work in its intended purpose, shall not be deemed an infringement of copyright.[102] Furthermore, the lawful user of software is allowed to make a back-up copy, where this is necessary for the use of the software for its intended purpose (Art. 45 (k) AW [Copyright Act]). Finally, the making of a copy of software and the translation of its code shall not be deemed an infringement of copyright if these acts are indispensable for obtaining the information necessary to achieve the interoperability of an independently created computer program with other programs.[103]

Art. 32 (a) of the AW [Copyright Act] provides that it is a crime for any person to intentionally offer for public distribution, possess for distribution, imports, exports, or keep for profit, any means designed exclusively to facilitate the removal or overriding, without the consent of the author of a technical device, of the protection of computer programs. This article is meant to address programs that are designed to hack protected computer programs. This crime can be punished with imprisonment of up to six months or a fine of up to EUR 18,500 for natural persons and EUR 74,000 for legal entities.[104]

4. Multimedia, Computer Games

There are no specific provisions in the AW [Copyright Act] relating to multimedia or computer games.

C. Infringement

Right to make copies for private use; Protective measures (Digital Rights Management); Liability of Users; Liability of online providers; Liability of makers of software facilitating copyright infringement; Liability for links

The author has the exclusive right to the publication and the reproduction of his work. The term "publishing" is interpreted broadly and applies to the extent that the work has been made available to the public in some form or another. New forms of communication such as the internet, cable, and video-on-demand fall within the definition of publishing.[105] The performance of activities that qualify as publishing or reproducing a work without the consent of the author constitutes copyright infringement (assuming that the work published or reproduced is derived from the copyright protected work).[106]

---

102 Article 45 (j) of the Auteurswet [AW] [Copyright Act].

103 Article 45 (m) of the Auteurswet [AW] [Copyright Act].

104 Art. 32a of the AW [Copyright Act] juncto Art. 23 Wetboek van Strafrecht [Criminal Code].

105 *Seignette*, Openbaarmaking en verveelvoudiging op het Internet: back to basics, AMI 1999, 69.

106 And to the extent no restrictions apply.

Art. 31 to 33 of the AW [Copyright Act] provide that piracy or intentional infringements on copyright law constitute criminal acts and are punishable with imprisonment of up to six months or a fine of up to EUR 18,500 for natural persons and EUR 74,000 for legal entities.[107] The penalty does not exclude the possibility of claims for damages in civil infringement actions.

Private use

The scope of the author's copyright is limited by a number of restrictions provided by the law.[108] These restrictions are more or less the same as the restrictions set in place by the Berne Convention[109] (BC) and the Universal Copyright Convention (UCC).[110] For instance, sections 16 (b) and 16 (c) of the AW [Copyright Act] provide that the copying a work for private use does not constitute copyright infringement. The right to make copies for private use is limited to a few copies only. Such copies may not be provided to others. To the extent that the publishing or reproduction of a copyright protected work exceeds the use that is allowed for private purposes, the user of such copyright protected works is liable for copyright infringement.

Protective measures

The new millennium has seen the spectacular rise, both in popularity and in performance, of peer-to-peer communication software that allow consumers to "share" vast amounts of largely illegally copyrighted content (music, video, software, images and even books). Concurrently, the roll-out of "legal" online content services, such as iTunes, and the rapid deployment of Digital Rights Management systems has created a real, rapidly growing and vibrant market place for digital content services in Europe and elsewhere.[111] Technical developments of the last decennia have gone very fast. Nowadays the average consumer has access to technical means that allow the copying of copyright protected works such as music CDs, movies, DVDs, and software programs.

Since Dutch copyright law acknowledges the right to copy for private use, copyright holders may not fight every reproduction of copyright protected material. Taking legal action against copyright infringement is costly and not always effective. Therefore, copyright holders tend to use other means to protect their copyright protected works,

---

107 Arts. 31-33 AW [Copyright Act] juncto Art. 23 Wetboek van Strafrecht [Criminal Code].

108 Restrictions apply for instance regarding the press, radio and television, education and science, personal use, church songs, art, libraries, museums, archives, disabled persons, portraits and compulsory licences.

109 The Berne Convention of 1871 for the protection of literary and artistic works, adopted on 9 September 1886 and as most recently amended on 28 September 1979.

110 The Universal Copyright Convention of 6 September 1952 and as most recently amended on 24 July 1971.

111 The Recasting of Copyright & Related Rights for the Knowledge Economy, Institute for Information Law.

such as Digital Rights Management or other access control technologies used by publishers and owners of copyright to prevent their unauthorised use.

Art. 29 (a) of the AW [Copyright Act] provides that knowingly circumventing purposive technical provisions is unlawful.[112] Those who provide services, make, import, distribute, sell, advertise, or possess equipment, products, or components that circumvent purposive technical provisions for commercial purposes will under circumstances be acting unlawfully.[113] In addition, Art. 29 (b) of the AW [Copyright Act] provides that those who intentionally, and without being entitled to do so remove or amend electronic information relating to the management of rights, will be acting unlawfully. Also those who distribute, import, or publish literary, scientific, or artistic works from which technological protection measures information has been removed or altered without permission, and who know that in doing so they are inciting infringement of the copyright or are enabling or facilitating copyright infringement act unlawfully.

Downloading of means to circumvent technological protection measures or the possession of such means also constitute an unlawful act. However, only when those means are in fact used to circumvent such measures are such acts unlawful pursuant to Art. 29 (a) of the AW [Copyright Act]. Unfortunately, it is very difficult for a right holder to investigate and find out where and when such means were in fact used to actually circumvent technological protection measures.[114]

Internet

Copyright infringement on the internet is a complex matter as it involves third parties, namely the internet providers or website owners who may not be participating in the copyright infringement themselves but may be providing access to the internet to the infringing parties.

In principle, making music available on the internet is considered publishing, which is one of the rights reserved for the copyright holder.[115] The technical manner of publishing is irrelevant. It could therefore concern materials published on a website that are

---

112 Art. 29 of the AW [Copyright Act] defines technical provisions as technology, equipment, or components whose normal use would include the prevention or limitation of actions in relation to works, which have not been permitted by the author or his right holders. Technical provisions will be deemed "purposive" if the use of a work protected by the author or his successors in title is managed through access control or by application of protective procedures such as encryption, encoding, or some other transformation of the work, or a copy protection that achieves the intended protection.

113 Those circumstances exist if such items are (a) offered, recommended or traded with the intention of circumventing the protected operation of purposive technical means, (b) of only limited commercial purpose or use apart from the circumvention of the protected operation of purposive technical means, or (c) primarily designed, manufactured or adapted with the purpose of circumventing the protected operation of purposive technical means.

114 *Nentjes*, Computerrecht 2007/2, 69.

115 *Spoor/Verkade/Visser*, Auteursrecht, § 4.39.

placed on the server of a hosting provider or materials which are available through peer-to-peer software on the hard disc of a personal computer. The provision of peer-to-peer software, which enables the exchange of files, is not considered reproduction or publishing.[116] As discussed in more detail below, this does not mean that the provision of such software or the hosting of bit torrent sites is lawful. Both downloading and uploading[117] are considered reproductions under the AW [Copyright Act]. However, according to the Dutch government,the downloading of materials for private use, whether or not such materials infringe upon copyright, is not unlawful pursuant to Arts. 16 (b) and 16 (c) of the AW [Copyright Act]. It is currently unclear if the Dutch courts share the opinion of the government in this respect. In recent preliminary proceedings, the District Court of The Hague ruled against this position of the government and found that downloading for private use of infringing materials was not covered by Art. 16 (c) of the AW [Copyright Act], and therefore an illegal action.[118] The downloading of software does not fall under the private use exemption and is therefore an infringement of copyright.[119] In addition, the uploading of copyright protected materials without the permission of the copyright holder is unlawful as such constitutes publishing pursuant to Art. 12 of the AW [Copyright Act], which is one of the rights reserved for the copyright holder.

Liability on the internet is further dealt with in the **E-Commerce Directive**,[120] which was implemented in the Burgerlijk Wetboek [Civil Code]. Art. 6:196 (c) of the Burgerlijk Wetboek [Civil Code] provides a number of exculpation grounds for intermediaries and indemnifies the hosting provider from liability under certain conditions (compare with Art. 13-15 of the E-Commerce Directive).[121] In simplified form this means that, the provider is not liable for the information transmitted, on condition that he (i) does not initiate the transmission, (ii) does not select the receiver of the transmission, and (iii) does not select or modify the information contained in the transmission.[122] Furthermore, the provider shall not be liable for stored information, on the condition that he does not have actual knowledge of any unlawful activity or information, or in the case of a claim for damages, should not reasonably have been aware of the unlawful activity or information, or upon obtaining such knowledge or awareness, acts expeditiously to remove or disable access to the information (the so-called notice and take down procedure). To the extent that the intermediaries act in accordance with Art. 6:196 (c) of the

116 28 March 2002 Amsterdam Court of Appeal [LJN: AE0805, Gerechtshof Amsterdam, 1370/01SKG], AMI 2002, nr. 13, p. 134 (KaZa/Buma, Stemra); 19 December 2003 Dutch Supreme Court [C02/186HR], AMI 2004, nr. 1 p. 6.

117 Uploading is also considered publishing to the extent files are uploaded to a website which is accessible by the public.

118 25 June 2008 District Court The Hague [HA-ZA 05-2233].

119 Art. 45k jo art. 16 jo art. 10 sub 12 of the AW [Copyright Act].

120 Directive 2000/31/EC of the European Parliament and of the Council of 8 June 2000 on certain legal aspects of information society services, in particular electronic commerce, in the Internal Market ('Directive on electronic commerce'), Official Journal of the European Communities 2000 No L 178/1.

121 *Seignette*, Auteursrechtinbreuk op internet, IER 2008/2, 49.

122 The e-Commerce Directive and Art. 6:196 (c) of Burgerlijk Wetboek [Civil Code] distinguish between hosting, caching and mere conduit activities with each a separate set of conditions.

Burgerlijk Wetboek [Civil Code] and their duty of care, they are not liable towards the IP rights holder. However, these exculpation grounds do not preclude the plaintiff from obtaining a judicial prohibition order.[123] If the intermediary does not act in accordance with Art. 6:196 (c) of the Burgerlijk Wetboek [Civil Code], he or she will be liable towards the copyright holder based on Art. 6:162 of the Burgerlijk Wetboek [Civil Code] (the general tort provision) for knowingly facilitating unlawful activities.

On the basis of the above provisions intermediaries such as internet providers could be liable towards the IP rights holder for damages suffered as a result of IP infringement and may be ordered to cease facilitating such unlawful acts (i. e. by removing unlawful materials from the relevant website(s) disabling access to such materials, or disabling the website altogether). The rules laid down in the Burgerlijk Wetboek [Civil Code] have been the subject of case law, since the E-Commerce Directive and Art. 6:196 (c) of the Burgerlijk Wetboek [Civil Code] do not cover the precise role of each player on the internet. For instance, the position on bit torrent sites, search engines, and auction sites is not clear.

The liability of bit torrent sites has been the subject of case law on numerous occasions. Bit torrent sites publish titles of movies and music, which can be downloaded. The downloading of materials that infringe upon copyright for private use is not considered unlawful by the Dutch government, but as mentioned above, it is currently unclear if the Dutch courts share this view.[124] The uploading of materials that infringe upon copyright is, however, unlawful. This means that persons who allow third parties to upload from their personal computer through the use of bit torrent sites act unlawfully, but third parties merely downloading through bit torrent sites do not act unlawfully. In most cases, the holders of the bit torrent sites work anonymously so that the copyright holder can only summon the hosting provider or the persons uploading materials. As the latter is rather inefficient, costly and time consuming, copyright holders or associations of copyright holders such as Brein mostly try to sue the holder of the website or the hosting provider for directly or indirectly facilitating copyright infringement.

In the years 2001-2003, the *Kazaa* cases were among the first cases in The Netherlands dealing with copyright infringement through bit torrent sites. These cases received quite some international attention. In preliminary proceedings, the District Court of Amsterdam held that the peer-to-peer website provider Kazaa was infringing upon the copyrights of composers represented by the collective rights organisation BUMA on a massive scale by providing its users with the opportunity to download music files.[125] The court further held that it was implausible that Kazaa could not take measures to prevent copyright infringement. The Court of Appeals of Amsterdam reversed the decision in first instance and held that in its view, Kazaa could not amend its website in such a way as to prevent copyright infringement, and as such, decided that the plaintiff's request that Kazaa should take measures to prevent copyright infringement could not be grant-

123 Art. 6:196 (c) (5) of the Burgerlijk Wetboek [Civil Code].

124 See above.

125 29 November 2001 District Court Amsterdam in preliminary proceedings [KG 01/2264 OdC], AMI 2002/1, 21 (BUMA/Kazaa).

ed.[126] The Dutch Supreme Court upheld the decision of the Court of Appeals since the Court of Appeals' decision was comprehenisve and was sufficiently motivated. It should be noted that the Dutch Supreme Court did not give a substantive answer to the question of whether the offering of file-sharing software was in fact unlawful or not. The Dutch Supreme Court was not in a position to answer that question in view of the formulation of the Court of Appeals' decision and the claims raised by BUMA. International reports claiming that the Dutch Supreme Court ruled that file sharing is legal are therefore incorrect.

In the more recent case of Brein v. KPN, Brein sued KPN because it provided the ADSL internet connection that allowed a bit torrent site to be online. The District Court in The Hague found in preliminary proceedings that the holder of the bit torrent site did not itself publish unlawful materials, as the site did not physically distribute the music and film materials. However, the site holder was acting unlawfully because he was structurally facilitating unlawful activities that he should have been aware of and generated income through those activities.[127] Under these circumstances the site holder was not permitted to await individual warnings from Brein regarding individual infringing titles. KPN was ordered to shut down the ADSL connection and to provide details regarding the identity of the bit torrent site holder. In a similar case between Brein and Leaseweb, the District Court of Amsterdam held in preliminary proceedings that the holder of a bit torrent site acted unlawfully by structurally and knowingly facilitating copyright infringement. The hosting provider Leaseweb was ordered to shut down the website and to provide details regarding the bit torrent site holder.[128] Courts in the Netherlands do not often deal with facilitating of structural infringement of copyright. The question of whether bit torrent site holders themselves publish materials remains to be answered.

The District Court in Amsterdam held that the search engine Google is not obliged to intervene, as long as it is not aware or should not reasonably have been aware, that

---

126 28 March 2002 Court of Appeal Amsterdam in preliminary proceedings [1370/01SKG], AMI 2002/4, 134 (BUMA/Kazaa).

127 5 January 2007 District Court of The Hague [276747/KG ZA 06-1417], AMI 2007/2, 55 (Brein/KPN).

128 Reference is made to a decision of the Dutch Supreme Court relating to the obligation of a hosting provider to provide name and address of a customer. In that case a natural person made serious accusations on its website concerning another person. As the website did not reveal the identity of the accuser the accused party tried to obtain the name and address of the accuser from the hosting provider. The Dutch Supreme Court held that even if is has not yet been established that the intermediary/provider acted manifestly unlawful or that the intermediary did not act unlawful itself, the intermediary could under circumstances still act unlawful by refusing to provide name and address of its customer to the party incurring damages as a result of statements of that customer. A minimum requirement is that there is no less radical means of obtaining the details and the statements of the customer concern serious accusations. The Dutch Minister of Justice has stated in a letter to Dutch Parliament dated 20 March 2008, parliamentary document 2007/2008 29838, nr. 7 that the Promusicae decision of the ECJ (29 January 2008 ECJ [C-275/06], GRUR 2008, 241 (Promusicae/Telefonica)) does not lead to a change of policy in this respect.

information on a website to which Google links is unlawful. This is the case because the links provided by Google are found using software and Google does not influence such links nor the content of the websites it links to.[129]

On the other hand, Marktplaats (a subsidiary of eBay based in the Netherlands), has influence over the content and availability of advertisements on its website. Nevertheless, District Court in Zwolle held that Marktplaats is not obliged to perform preventive screening of advertisements for unlawful content or IP infringements. Nor is Marktplaats obliged to collect details such as the name, address, and place of residence of its advertisers as a rule (in order to provide this information to the right holder in the event of infringing advertisements). The court came to this conclusion mainly because the requested measures are very costly and work intensive. The result of which was that Martkplaats' interests outweighed the interests of claimant Stokke.[130] An appeal has been filed against this decision.

Since the question of hosting provider liability is not only relevant in the Netherlands, but in other EU Member States as well, obtaining clarity from the ECJ in this respect would be beneficial.

D. Legal Consequences

Without prejudice to the plaintiffs right to damages, a copyright holder can request that the court in civil proceedings grant an injunction prohibiting the use of the infringing product or work. In addition, the copyright holder has a number of ancillary claims. The court can order a recall of the infringing goods and can order the infringer to provide information about the origin and distribution channels of the infringing goods.[131] In addition, the court can also order the destruction of the goods and/or of the materials or equipment that were used to infringe the copyright. The court can order the surrender of the infringing goods to the copyright holder, in which case, the court may stipulate that the surrender of goods take place only after payment of an amount by the copyright holder.[132]

Finally, the copyright holder can claim compensation for damages.[133] The copyright holder can claim the higher of either: (i) compensation for damages it incurred as a result of the infringement, or (ii) payment by the infringer of the profits it made as a result of the infringment.[134] In order to establish the amount of profits made, the in-

[129] 26 April 2007 District Court of Amsterdam [365193/KG ZA 07-480 OdC/SK], Mediaforum 2007/6, 205-208 (Jensen/Google).

[130] 3 May 2006 District Court Zwolle [zaaknummer/rolnummer: 106031/HA ZA 05-211], AMI 2006/5, 179 (Stokke/Marktplaats); 14 March 2007 District Court Zwolle [zaaknummer/rolnummer: 106031/HA ZA 05-211], IER 2007/73 (Stokke/Marktplaats).

[131] These ancillary claims have been developed in case law and are not laid down in the DCA.

[132] Art. 28 of the AW [Copyright Act].

[133] A licencee may independently claim damages to the extent the licencee explicitly agreed such competence with the copyright holder. Art. 27 (a) ¶ 2 of the AW [Copyright Act].

fringer will generally be ordered to report its profits after verification by a registered accountant.[135] As held by the Benelux Court of Justice, profit refers to net profit, which is calculated by deducting the purchase price of the products, taxes and costs from the sales price.[136] As an alternative to calculating the actual damages incurred by the copyright holder, the court can determine damages as a fixed amount based on elements such as the amount of royaltyies that the copyright holder would have received if the infringer had permission to use the copyright.[137]

E. Enforcement

Especially in the music, software, and movie industries, copyright infringement and piracy are an enormous problem. Music CDs, movie DVDs, and computer software can be copied easily and are distributed at low costs or free of charge. This causes huge damages for the industry. So far it has proven difficult to combat piracy effectively despite the existing legal tools including the Customs Regulation.

Once an author or copyright holder is aware of a possible infringement of its copyright, several civil actions are possible. The author can request the court to grant an injunction. Such requests can be made (i) as an ex-parte request to the court (if a delay would cause irreparable damage), (ii) in preliminary proceedings (where the plaintiff still needs to establish an urgent need to obtain preliminary relief), or (iii) in proceedings on the merits. For more details please refer to paragraph I A.

The author could seize the infringing goods before initiating court proceedings.[138] A seizure can be made either by asking the court for permission to seize the goods as provided for in the Wetboek on Burgerlijke Rechtsverdingen [Code of Civil Procedure] or by customs as provided for in the Customs Regulation. After the allegedly infringing goods are seized, the author will have to initiate either preliminary proceedings or proceedings on the merits.[139] Furthermore, the author could request the court to permit seizure of evidence or take measures relating to the collection and preservation of evidence.

---

134 The Supreme Court decided that the copyright holder can choose on the basis of the information to be provided by the infringer the most favourable of compensation of damages incurred by it or profits made by the infringer. The copyright holder cannot claim both compensation of damages and surrender of profit. 14 April 2000 Dutch Supreme Court [C98/270HR], NJ 2000/489, 134 (Danestyle/HBS). This was confirmed in 8 December 2006 Dutch Supreme Court [C05/215HR], IER 2007/21, 96 (De Vries/Laurus).

135 Art. 27a ¶ 1 of the AW [Copyright Act].

136 24 October 2005 Benelux Court of Justice, BIE 2006/28, 172 (Dior/Delhaize).

137 Art. 27 ¶ 2 of the AW [Copyright Act]. This paragraph was added as result of implementation of the Enforcement Directive.

138 Art. 28 ¶ 4 of the AW [Copyright Act].

139 Preliminary proceedings or proceedings on the merits are not required if the goods have been destroyed in accordance with the simplified destruction procedure as provided for in the Product-piracy Regulation.

Pursuant to Art. 3:305 (a) and 3:305 (b) of the Burgerlijk Wetboek [Civil Code], a foundation or association that represents the interests of copyright holders may also enforce copyrights. However, such organisations cannot make a claim for damages.

As set out in paragraphs VI C, infringement of copyright can constitute a crime under Dutch copyright law. Having said this, the enforcement of such criminal provisions is not a priority for the investigative authorities or the public prosecutor.

As set out in paragraph I A there are a number of organisations in the Netherlands combating counterfeiting and piracy. One of which is Foundation Brein (*Stichting Brein*), a joint anti-piracy program of the entertainment industry, including authors, artists and producers of music, film and interactive software. According to its website, Foundation Brein acts as a central contact for government, law enforcement, trade, and media in the Netherlands with respect to all issues concerning the unauthorised copying and distribution of entertainment products, both on and offline.[140] A large number of organisations participate in Foundation Brein.[141] Brein also works with the International Association of Music Producers (IFPI) to combat counterfeiting and maintains regular contact with the Business Software Alliance as well as the International Association of Interactive Distributors (IDSA).

As Foundation Brein indicates on its website, they are actively developing anti-piracy policies targeting both wide-spread piracy by individuals and large-scale piracy by criminal organisations. Foundation Brein focuses both on traditional offline trade in pirated products and the rampant online piracy on the internet. Foundation Brein investigates infringements, takes civil actions and supplies information and expertise for criminal, administrative, and fiscal actions. Foundation Brein cooperates with the criminal investigators of the FIOD-ECD anti-piracy team. Foundation Brein and FIOD-ECD also work closely with Dutch customs to intercept counterfeit products imported, or transported through the Netherlands. Foundation Brein has initiated quite a number of civil actions over the past several years.[142]

---

140 http://www.anti-piracy.nl/home/home.asp

141 Including the music, video and interactive departments of the Dutch association for producers and importers of image and sound carriers (NVPI); the Dutch Publishers Association (NUV), on behalf of the publishers of multimedia software; the Dutch association of phonogram retailers (NVGD); the international organisation of major motion picture producers, Motion Picture Association; the joint licensor of non-theatrical video performance rights, Videma; the Dutch association of film distributors (NVF); the Dutch music rights collecting society Buma/Stemra on behalf of composers, text writers and music publishers.

142 For example, the 15 June 2006 Court of Appeal of Amsterdam [rolnummer 1157/04], www.book9.nl (Brein/Techno Design); 24 August 2006 District Court Amsterdam [345291/KG 06-1112 AB], www.book9.nl (Brein/UPC); 5 January 2007 District Court of The Hague [276747/KG ZA 06-1417], AMI 2007/2, 55 (Brein/KPN); 21 June 2007 District Court Amsterdam [LJN BA7810, rolnummer: 369220/KG ZA 07-840 AB/MV], Computerrecht 2007/146 (Brein/Leaseweb); 24 January 2008 District Court Amsterdam, www.boek9.nl (Brein/Shareconnector).

Product Piracy in the United Kingdom

Alexandra Pygall/Daniel Royle

I. Overview of the Legal Framework in the United Kingdom

Protection and enforcement of the various forms of intellectual property has developed independently for the different areas of intellectual property, both through implementation of supranational regulations and domestic statutory law and jurisprudence.

This Chapter will discuss the general procedure and remedies for intellectual property enforcement in the UK. Thereafter, it will provide a brief overview of the principal IP rights in the UK, with a particular emphasis on where the law differs from European law.

II. Enforcement of IP rights in the United Kingdom

Intellectual property rights may be enforced through civil or, in relation to trademarks and copyright, criminal actions. There is no bar to bringing civil and criminal proceedings in relation to the same act(s) of infringement. Criminal proceedings are generally brought by the relevant governmental authority (Trading Standards or the Crown Prosecution Service) but it is also possible (although not common) for an individual to bring a private criminal prosecution. There are also public law remedies such as the power of Customs to seize infringing goods.

The procedures involved in the various methods of enforcement are discussed in more detail below.

A. Civil Action

1. Identity of Claimant

In many cases, actions to enforce intellectual property rights will be brought by the owner of the intellectual property right itself. In addition, exclusive licensees of intellectual property rights have a statutory right to bring proceedings in their own name.[1]

1 Patents Act 1977 § 67 (UK); Copyright, Designs and Patents Act 1988 § 101 (UK); Trade Marks Act 1994 § 31 (UK).

2. Procedural Steps

The procedural steps of any litigation in the UK are governed by the CPR (Civil Procedure Rules). The overriding objective of the rules is to deal with a case justly, by saving time, trouble and expense. By way of an example, both parties are obliged to make a reasonable search for and produce all relevant documents which either help or hurt their case.[2] The main exception to this rule is that legally privileged documents (for example, advice from lawyers or patent agents) may be kept private. The Court tends to take an active role in the conduct of the litigation and they will not allow it to drag on unnecessarily. Typically a Case Management Conference will be held at an early stage at which the Court will oversee the conduct of the proceedings and determine a timetable for the litigation.

Prior to issuing proceedings there is a general obligation on the parties to behave co-operatively towards each other. Care must also be taken as in some circumstances a threat to sue for infringement may be an actionable tort if the threat turns out to be unjustified. Further, a failure to attempt to settle disputes prior to trial (through, for example, mediation) may be taken into account when the Court decides who should pay the legal costs of the litigation.

Infringement proceedings are initiated by serving a claim form and the particulars of claim. These identify the parties and the intellectual property right(s) relied upon, set out the relief claimed and specify the acts which are alleged to infringe the intellectual property right(s). Detailed evidence is not generally pleaded at this stage.

Within 14 days of the service of the particulars of claim, the defendant must file an acknowledgment of service (a purely formal step).[3] Within 28 days (or 42 days in respect of patent or design cases) the defendant must file its defence (together with any counterclaim for revocation including the grounds of invalidity).

The claimant may then serve a reply and defence to counterclaim. This addresses any matters raised for the first time in the defence. In particular it is the claimant's opportunity to meet any allegations of invalidity.[4]

Prior to trial the parties must exchange written evidence from the witnesses which they propose to call at trial (including any expert witnesses). This evidence will not be read out at trial but a witness may be cross-examined on the evidence appearing in his or her witness statement.

---

2 Civil Procedure Rules Part 31 (UK).

3 Civil Procedure Rules Part 10 (UK).

4 Civil Procedure Rules Part 15 and 63.b (UK).

3. Interim Remedies

Prior to trial, the UK Courts have a broad power to grant a wide range of interim remedies in order to collect/preserve evidence or to prevent the acts complained of until trial. They may grant:

- a search order (formerly known as an Anton Piller order) requiring a party to admit another party to enter premises for the purpose of preserving evidence found at those premises;
- a freezing injunction (formerly known as a Mareva injunction);
- an interim injunction;
- an order for the detention, custody or preservation of relevant property;
- an order for the inspection of relevant property;
- an order for the taking of a sample of relevant property; and
- an order for the carrying out of an experiment on or with relevant property,

where 'relevant property' means property which is the subject of a claim or as to which any questions may arise on a claim.

Further detail about some of these interim measures follows.

a) Search Order

The stringent conditions for obtaining a search order, as well as the cost of complying with the onerous procedural rules make search orders a last resort for many IP rights-holders.

The conditions for the making of a search order are:

- there must be an extremely strong prima facie case;
- the damage, actual or potential, must be very serious for the applicant;
- there must be clear evidence that the defendants have in their possession incriminating documents or things; and
- there is a real possibility that the defendants may destroy such material before an application on notice is made.

As a result of this last requirement, search orders are rarely used in IP cases other than in relation to counterfeits. In addition, the harm likely to be caused to the respondent in his business affairs by the execution of the order must not be out of proportion to the legitimate object of the order.

Applications for search orders are made without notice to the other party. They are generally dealt with at a court hearing but in urgent cases can be dealt with by telephone. Applications can be made before the issue of proceedings if the matter is urgent or is otherwise necessary in the interests of justice. If a search order is granted before the issue of proceedings, the court will usually give directions requiring proceedings to be commenced.

The applicant has a duty to give full and frank disclosure of all facts relevant to the application to the court. Applications must also be supported by written evidence in the form of an affidavit. In addition, applications must be accompanied by an undertaking by the applicant to the court to pay any damages which the respondent sustains and which the court considers the applicant should pay.

There are a number of procedural safeguards against the potentially draconian nature of a search order which can sometimes be onerous. In particular search orders are executed by a Supervising Solicitor who is independent of the applicant's own solicitors, who will prepare a report regarding the execution of the search order (which further adds to the cost of the process). Strict rules apply to the conduct of the search and the materials that can be removed.

b) Freezing Injunction

A freezing injunction freezes access to assets such as money in a bank account and restrains a party from removing assets from the jurisdiction or dealing with such assets. The primary purpose of a freezing injunction is to ensure that the respondent does not seek to avoid any judgments made against it by disposing of assets. An application for a freezing order is made without notice to the party against whom it will be enforced. The applicant must prove the likelihood of the respondent moving his assets, which can be difficult.

c) Interim Injunction

In deciding whether to grant an interim injunction, the court will consider two issues. First, whether damages would be an adequate remedy (if they would then no injunction will be granted). Second, if damages would not be an adequate remedy, it will consider the 'balance of convenience' i. e. whether the grant of an interim injunction is likely to cause more injustice if the Claimants fail at trial than withholding it will cause if the Claimants succeed

4. Disclosure

UK courts have the power to order disclosure (formerly known as "discovery") both before and during proceedings.

a) Pre-action Disclosure

UK courts have the power to order disclosure before proceedings have started in certain circumstances. The conditions for making such an order are that:

- the respondent is likely to be a party to subsequent proceedings;
- the applicant is also likely to be a party to those proceedings;
- if proceedings had started, the respondent's duty by way of standard disclosure would extend to the documents or classes of documents of which the applicant seeks disclosure; and
- disclosure before proceedings have started is desirable in order to dispose fairly of the anticipated proceedings, to assist the dispute to be resolved without proceedings or to save costs.

As pre-action disclosure is often used by claimants in order to decide whether to bring proceedings, the court does not necessarily direct that a claim be commenced. The order for pre-action disclosure may require the respondent to indicate what has happened to any documents which are no longer in his control.

b) Disclosure during Proceedings – Standard Disclosure

Standard disclosure is usually ordered as one of the normal steps in the management of the case.

Under standard disclosure, each party must disclose to the other party:

- the documents on which it relies; and
- the documents which
  - adversely affect its own case;
  - adversely affect another party's case; or
  - support another party's case.

Documents that are privileged (for example, correspondence with solicitors) are not required to be disclosed. A party is not entitled to claim privilege for documents and information merely because they were supplied to him in confidence by a third party. Documents can be more than paper documents and include electronic documents and even physical samples. Any documents relating to the infringement would need to be disclosed.

As a general rule, disclosure in patent cases is more limited than cases involving other IP rights.

5. The Trial

The trial will typically be heard before a specialist intellectual property judge. The trial will be open to the public unless an application for it to be heard in confidence has been successful. A trial is generally no more than a few days in length (unless the matter is complex) and the judge will generally give judgment two to three weeks after the trial has finished.

There is an emphasis on greater expedition of proceedings, especially in patent actions, and it is not uncommon for a trial to be held less than 12 months after the initiation of proceedings. An application may also be made for a streamlined trial in which case it might be possible for the trial to be held as little as 6 months from the initiation of proceedings.

6. Appeals

Following judgment the unsuccessful party may apply to appeal to the Court of Appeal. Further appeal to the House of Lords is rare and may only occur with permission, which may only be given if there is a point of law of importance or public interest at stake.

7. Remedies

At trial, the remedies typically sought in claims for infringement include:

- damages or in the alternative an account of profits;
- an injunction;
- the delivery up of infringing items (or their destruction); and
- payment of legal costs.

Note that neither damages nor an account of profits will be assessed at the trial of the issues. Once the decision on infringement has been handed down, the parties will usually agree damages/account of profits. If there is no agreement then an assessment will be made at a separate hearing for which fresh pleadings and evidence needs to be prepared.

B. Criminal Action

IP crimes include counterfeiting (trademark infringement) and piracy (copyright infringement). There are no equivalent criminal offences for patent or design right infringement.

All criminal proceedings begin in the magistrates courts and most IP offences are triable "either way" which means they may be tried either by a lay magistrate or in the crown court before a judge and jury. Criminal proceedings are commenced by applying to the court for a summons.

The maximum penalties for copyright and trademark offences are (i) 6 months imprisonment and/or GBP 5,000 fine (on summary conviction) and (ii) 10 years imprisonment and/or an unlimited fine (on indictment). There are also provisions under the Proceeds of Crime Act 2002 which provide routes for funds from criminal activities to be recouped by the Assets Recovery Agency.

It is extremely unusual for a right holder to choose to bring a private criminal prosecution as opposed to a civil action. This is because the procedures involved in a civil action, such as pre-trial disclosure and general conduct of the action are more appropriate to the assertion of private rights amongst business people; the civil remedies such as interim injunctions and damages are more useful than punishment by the state; and, significantly, the burden of proof is higher in criminal matters which require proof beyond all reasonable doubt in contrast to proof on the balance of probabilities in civil matters.

C. Public Law

Customs officials can intervene at borders to arrest the movement of pirate and counterfeit goods. This is an area covered largely by EU Legislation[5] and due to the integration of the Member States the main impact is now at the external boundaries of the EU. Customs officials may seize goods and refuse to release them to the importer ("detaining" goods), however, the right holder owes the authority a duty to indemnify it against any liability or expense. The UK has implemented the 'simplified procedure' which enables counterfeit goods to be detained and destroyed on the basis of a written opinion from the rights holder that the goods are counterfeit (assuming the declarant/owner of the goods does not oppose). This procedure avoids the need for court proceedings.

Trading Standards authorities enforce measures of consumer protection, including in relation to safety and trade description issues. The Trade Descriptions Act 1968 places a positive duty to act on these authorities and they can seize goods and documents and make test purchases.

5 The principal legislation is Council Regulation (EC) No 1383/2003 concerning customs action against goods suspected of infringing certain intellectual property rights and the measures to be taken against goods found to have infringed such rights, Official Journal of the European Union 2003 No L 196/7 as amended by Council Regulation (EC) No 806/2003 of 14 April 2003 adapting to Decision 1999/468/EC the provisions relating to committees which assist the Commission in the exercise of its implementing powers laid down in Council instruments adopted in accordance with the consultation procedure (qualified majority), Official Journal of the European Union 2003 No L 122/1 as is implemented in the UK by The Goods Infringing Intellectual Property Rights (Customs) Regulations 2004 SI 2004/1473 (UK).

Ofcom (for broadcast media); the Office of Fair Trading (for non-broadcast media); and the Advertising Standards Authority (established by the advertising industry and to which the supervisory powers of Ofcom and the OFT have now largely been delegated) supervise the content of advertisements.

III. Trademarks

As a result of harmonisation, the substantive civil law of validity and infringement of trademarks in the UK[6] is very similar to the regime discussed above, *Diana Kaufmann*, Trademark Piracy.

The procedure for civil and/or criminal enforcement is as discussed above in section II.

Criminal offences under UK law include:[7]

A. applying to goods or their packaging a sign identical to, or likely to be mistaken for, a registered trademark;
B. selling or letting for hire, offering or exposing for sale or hire or distributing goods which bear, or the packaging of which bears, such a registered trademark;
C. having in one's possession, custody or control in the course of a business any such goods with a view to the doing of anything, by oneself or another, which would be an offence under the paragraph above;
D. applying a sign identical to, or likely to be mistaken for, a registered trademark to material intended to be used (i) for labelling or packaging goods, (ii) as a business paper in relation to goods, or (iii) for advertising goods;
E. using in the course of a business material bearing such a sign for labelling or packaging goods, as a business paper in relation to goods, or for advertising goods;
F. having in one's possession, custody or control in the course of a business any such material with a view to the doing of anything, by himself or another, which would be an offence under the paragraph above; and
G. making an article specifically designed or adapted for making copies of a sign identical to, or likely to be mistaken for, a registered trademark, or having such an article in one's possession, custody or control in the course of a business, knowing or having reason to believe that it has been, or is to be, used to produce goods, or material for labelling or packaging goods, as a business paper in relation to goods, or for advertising goods.

For there to be an offence the above acts must be committed with a view to gain to the person doing the act(s) or another or with intent to cause loss to another and without the consent of the rights holder.

---

6 Principally, in the Trademarks Act 1994 (UK).

7 Trademarks Act 1994 § 92 (UK).

It is a defence for a person charged with any of the above offences to show that he believed on reasonable grounds that the use of the sign in the manner in which it was used, or was to be used, was not an infringement of the registered trademark. The burden of proving such a defence is with the accused.

UK law also contains provisions[8] regarding treatment of infringing goods by the Commissioners of Customs and Excise. The provisions only apply to goods entered, or expected to be entered, for free circulation in respect of which the rights holder is entitled to lodge an application under Article 3(1) of Council Regulation 3842/86.[9] Further, they are of narrow scope as the rights holder must give notice of the time and place the infringing goods are expected to arrive in the United Kingdom (i) from outside the European Economic Area, or (ii) from within that Area but not having been entered for free circulation. When a notice is in force under this section the importation of the goods to which the notice relates, otherwise than by a person for his private and domestic use, is prohibited; but a person is not by reason of the prohibition liable to any penalty other than forfeiture of the goods.

IV. Passing Off

The tort of passing off protects the reputation and goodwill which one trader has built up in a mark or "get-up" against the misleading conduct of another trader which causes consumers to think there is a connection between the two traders resulting in damage to the first trader.

Passing off is a tort that can be considered the common law equivalent of trademark law. It can be used by brand owners to protect elements of their goodwill that are not (or cannot) be protected as registered trademarks – for example elements of trade dress or "get-up" that might be used to distinguish its products from others. These elements are sometimes referred to as "unregistered trademarks". In order to succeed in a claim in passing off, the claimant must:

A. establish that it has a goodwill or reputation attached to the relevant goods or services;
B. demonstrate a misrepresentation by the defendant to the public leading or likely to lead the public to believe that the goods and services offered by it are the goods or services of the claimant. In order to establish misrepresentation, it is not necessary for this misrepresentation to be deliberate; and
C. demonstrate that it has suffered or is likely to suffer damage by reason of the defendant's misrepresentation.

---

8 Trademarks Act 1994 § 89 (UK).

9 Council Regulation (EC) No 3842/86 of 1 December 1986 laying down measures to prohibit the release for free circulation of counterfeit goods, Official Journal of the European Communities 1986 No L 357/1.

Passing off is a civil action which is commenced in the courts in the ordinary way. In some ways passing off can be seen as the equivalent of an unfair competition action. However, passing off has a much narrower scope than unfair competition. In particular, establishing misrepresentation on behalf of the defendant is a high evidential burden. It is for this reason that registered trademarks are a great advantage when considering enforcement.

Remedies for Trademark Infringement and Passing Off

The full range of legal and equitable remedies is available in cases of infringement of trademark and/or passing off, including injunctions and damages as set out above (II. A. 7).

V. Unfair Competition

The Unfair Commercial Practices Directive (2005/29/EC) has been implemented in the UK by the Consumer Protection from Unfair Trading Regulations 2008. The Regulations are, however, of limited use as they may not be enforced by right holders. The Regulations can only be enforced by local authority Trading Standards and the Office of Fair Trading. Whilst these bodies have a duty to enforce the Regulations, this does not mean that enforcement action (civil or criminal) must be taken in respect of each and every infringement of which they are made aware. Instead, promotion of compliance by the most appropriate means, in line with their enforcement policies, priorities and consistent with available resources has been encouraged. The decision as to whether enforcement action will be taken is not within the control of the right holder.

VI. Design Rights

Design law protects the look, feel and shape of objects. The law of designs in the UK represents a combination of UK and EU law, and registered and unregistered rights. The various design rights applicable to the UK are as follows:

- UK Design Right
- Unregistered Community Design Right
- UK Registered Design
- Community Registered Design

A. UK Design Right

UK Design Rights protect any aspect of the shape or configuration (internal or external) of the whole or part of an article. Important exclusions to UK design rights are:

- a method or principle of construction;

- features of an article which enable it is be connected to another article ("must fit") or are dependent on the appearance of another article ("must match"); and
- surface decoration.

The UK Design Right is an unregistered right that arises automatically and expires 15 years after the end of the calendar year in which the design was created, or, if articles made to the design are first made available for sale/hire within 5 years from the end of that year, 10 years from the end of the calendar year in which that occurred.

In order for a UK Design Right to subsist, the design must be original – that is the design must not be commonplace in the field in question at the time of creation. Complex rules govern the nationality of designers that qualify for UK Design Rights, but for the purposes of the EU, if the designer was based in the EU, he or she qualifies for UK Design Rights.

In order to infringe a UK Design Right, the design must be copied by making articles exactly or substantially to the design or making a design document recording the design for enabling articles to be made.

B. UK Registered Design

It is also possible to obtain a national registered design right in the UK. As a result of harmonisation, the substantive law of validity and infringement with respect to UK Registered Designs is very similar to the Community Design regime discussed above (II. A. 7.).

C. Remedies for Design Infringement

The full range of legal and equitable remedies is available in cases of infringement of design right or registered designs, including injunctions and damages as set out above (II. A. 7.).

VII. Patents

A. Sources of Law

The principal piece of legislation governing patents in the UK is the Patents Act 1977 (the "UK Act"). This has been amended and supplemented by the Copyright, Designs and Patents Act 1988 and the Patents Act 2004.

There is also a significant body of UK and European case law. The UK is a precedent-based legal system and, therefore, case law is of great importance in interpreting the legislation.

B. What is patentable in the United Kingdom?

Section 1 of the UK Act contains a definition of patentable inventions. This closely parallels the definition in the EPC (European Patent Convention). To be patentable an invention must be new, involve an inventive step and be capable of industrial application. It must also not fall within one of the excluded categories in sec. 1(2), such as a mathematical method, aesthetic creation or program for a computer.

C. Agreements regarding Patents

Patents may be the subject of various types of agreements including assignments (agreements transferring ownership), licence agreements, co-ownership agreements, security agreements, and research and development agreements.

The UK Intellectual Property office maintains the register of UK patents. Changes in owner and details of registrable transactions may be entered on the register, which serves as constructive notice to third parties.

Where patents are co-owned, the UK Act provides that each owner is entitled to an equal undivided share in the patent. A co-owner may not assign, grant a licence of, or grant security over a co-owned patent without the consent of the other co-owner(s).

D. The Courts

Patent proceedings can be conducted before one of two courts: (i) the Patents Court (a part of the Chancery Division of the High Court of Justice), or (ii) the Patents County Court. The Patents County Court is best suited to shorter and less significant cases. It was set up as a less expensive forum for patent litigation.

E. Types of Proceedings

1. Infringement

The claims of a patent define the scope of the monopoly claimed in a patent. In construing claims the English courts adopt a "purposive" construction. This means that the court will consider how a skilled person would construe the claims of the patent with the inventor's purpose in mind. At least one expert witness is usually called to assist the court with this task. The witness is chosen by the parties (each party may have their own witness or they may appoint a single expert jointly) but the witness's duty is to the Court.

2. Validity/Revocation

Any infringement claim is likely to met with a counter-claim for invalidity. In this case both actions will be heard together by a single court. An application to revoke a patent may also be brought by any person (ie. it need not be in the context of an infringement claim).

A patent may be declared invalid on various grounds, the most common of which are lack of novelty, obviousness or insufficiency. The relevant date is the priority date of the patent. It is at this date that the state of the prior art is assessed. The state of the art includes publications made anywhere in the world (not just in the UK) as well as what was commonly known to the averagely skilled person in the relevant field at that time.

3. Amendment

An application to amend a patent may be made at any time. It is not uncommon for an application to amend a patent to be made during the course of revocation proceedings. An amendment may be necessary to overcome prior art which was not considered during the drafting or prosecution of the patent. An amendment may not 'add material' to the patent but may only narrow its claims.

F. Border Measures

The Customs Regulation (Council Regulation (EC) No. 1383/2003 concerning customs action against goods suspected of infringing certain intellectual property rights and the measures to be taken against goods found to have infringed such rights) applies to goods which infringe a patent under the law of the relevant Member State. Therefore, UK Customs have the power to detain goods which they suspect of infringing a UK patent. The simplified procedure does not apply in respect of patents so if the patent owner wishes to take action the matter must be referred to a UK patent court within 10 days of the patent owner being notified of the detention.

G. Criminal Sanctions

There are currently no criminal sanctions in the UK regarding patent infringement. The proposed EU Directive on Criminal Measures may introduce such sanctions but questions surrounding the competency of the Commission to harmonise criminal sanctions means that the progress of the directive is currently stalled.

VIII. Confidential Information

A. Nature of Confidential Information

Confidential information is a term that covers a wide variety of concepts including trade secrets, know-how, discoveries, customer lists, recipes and manufacturing methods. Confidential information is protected in the UK by the common law principles of the law of confidence, and not by statute. Confidential information is not a species of intellectual property, but the law of confidence can protect information that could not be protected under other categories of intellectual property – such as unpatentable inventions. An additional advantage of confidential information is that it does not require disclosure (unlike patents), so it can be protected indefinitely.

In some cases, the relevant parties will have entered into a confidentiality agreement in relation to the disclosure and use of the information. The enforcement of such contractual provisions is governed by the ordinary principles of contractual interpretation. However, the law of confidence protects confidential information even if there is no contract.

B. Breach of Confidence

The test in the UK for breach of confidence is that:

- The information itself must have the necessary quality of confidence about it. In particular, the information must not be something which is public property or public knowledge;
- The information must have been imparted in circumstances imparting an obligation of confidence. There is no requirement that the information be recorded (in contrast to copyright) – for example, it can be imparted orally. Whether an obligation of confidence arises will be subject to an objective test; and
- There must be an unauthorised use of that information to the detriment of the party communicating it.

  It is important to note that the law of confidence does not prevent a third party who does not have access to the confidential information from independently replicating (or "reverse engineering") the information or product.

C. Confidential Information in Employment Relationships

Issues relating to confidential information often arise in employer/employee relationships and in particular the right of the employee to use confidential information learnt during his employment after the period of his employment has come to an end. The law distinguishes between information acquired by the employee that becomes part of his own knowledge and skill, and information that consists of genuine trade secrets, the misuse of which would cause the employer significant harm. The former type of information can be used by the employer after he has left employment, but the latter type of information cannot. Into which category the confidential information falls will always depend on the facts of the case.

IX. Copyright

A. Copyright Works

Copyright subsists in "copyright works". A summary of the key works in which copyright subsists is shown in the table below:

Copyright Work	Comments	Duration[10]
Original literary, dramatic or musical works	Literary works can extend beyond conventional literary works (such as books, articles and business plans) to include tables, compilations, graphics, emails, website text and computer software.	70 years from the end of the calendar year in which the author dies.
Original Artistic works	For example, photographs, graphic art, sculpture, collage, works of artistic craftsmanship, diagrams and bitmaps.	70 years from the end of the calendar year in which the author dies.
Sound recordings	Recording of sounds or a recording of the whole of any part of a literary, dramatic or musical works.	50 years from the end of the calendar year in which the recording was made or (if published within that 50 years) published.
Films	"Films" includes the sound track.	70 years from the end of the calendar year in which the director, screenplay author, dialogue author or soundtrack composer dies (whichever is last).
Broadcasts	Defined as "electronic transmissions".	50 years from the end of the calendar year in which the broadcast is made.

For some products, copyright may be the core intellectual property right that protects the product from piracy, for example, software or CDs. However, copyright can also exist in the words and images contained on the packaging of any product. In this instance, a copyright claim may prove to be a useful adjunct to a trademark or passing off claim.

It is also important to appreciate that a single work might have a number of copyrights subsisting in it. For example, a song on a CD will have the copyright in the lyrics (a literary work), the music (a musical work) and the recording itself (a sound recording).

Copyright automatically subsists on creation of a relevant work: it is not possible to register a copyright work. Pursuant to various international treaties, copyright is automatically recognised in most countries in the world on creation.

10 Duration of copyright in English law is a notoriously complex area of law, and these periods should be treated as guidelines only. If a question arises as to whether copyright has expired in respect of any given work, specialist legal advice should be sought.

Copyright in a work is first owned by the author of the work, unless the work has been created in the course of employment, in which case the employer is the first owner of the copyright in the work subject to any agreement to the contrary. This is important to bear in mind in relation to works that have been commissioned – the author, not the commissioner, will own the copyright, and the commissioner will need to have the copyright expressly assigned to it.

B. Civil Infringement and Defences

The key right of the copyright owner is the exclusive right to copy the work. Therefore, a person who copies the work prima facie infringes the copyright. Note that the act of copying is an essential element of copyright infringement – copyright does not prevent the independent creation of a work.

There are a number of defences to a claim of copyright infringement. The most relevant defence to copyright infringement is "fair dealing". Fair dealing includes copying for the purposes of private study or non-commercial research, criticism or review or the reporting of current events. In order to be "fair", the dealing must usually be accompanied by a sufficient acknowledgement. Copyright in a work is not infringed by incidental inclusion in another work.

Persons can also be liable for secondary infringement if (among others) they import or deal with articles where they know, or have reason to believe that the article is an infringing copy of a work.

C. Remedies

The full range of remedies is available to the successful claimant in a copyright action, including damages or account of profits, injunctions and delivery up of infringing copies, as set out above (II. A. 7.).

A peculiarity of UK copyright law is that the court may award additional damages having regard to the flagrancy of the infringement and any benefit accruing to the defendant by reason of the infringement.

D. Criminal Infringement and Defences

Criminal offences under UK law include doing the following acts without sufficient consent in relation to a recording which is, and which the person committing the act knows or has reason to believe is, an illicit recording:[11] (a) making for sale or hire; (b) importing into the UK otherwise than for his private and domestic use; (c) possessing in the course of business with a view to committing another infringing act; and (d)

---

11 Section 198 Copyright, Design and Patents Act 1988.

in the course of business, selling or letting for hire, offering or exposing for sale or hire or distributing.

It is also a criminal offence to cause a recording of a performance made without sufficient consent to be shown or played in the public or communicated to the public if the person causing the recording to be shown knows or has reason to believe that the recording is an infringing recording.

Abbreviations

§	section
¶	paragraph
5e ch. corr.	5ème Chambre Correctionnelle (5th Criminal Chamber)
a. A.	andere Ansicht (different view)
ADSL	Asymmetric Digital Subscriber Line
AfP	AfP – Zeitschrift für Medien- und Kommunikationsrecht (name of a German law journal)
AG	Amtsgericht (local court in Germany)
AIC	Chinese Administrative for Industry and Commerce
AIPPI	Association Internationale pour la Protection de la Propriété Intellectuelle (International Association for the Protection of Industrial Property)
AktG	Aktiengesetz (German Stock Corporation Act)
ALJ	Administrative law judge
AMI	Tijdschrift voor Auteurs, Media en Inforrmatierecht (name of a Dutch law journal)
APM	Aktionskreis gegen Produkt- und Markenpiraterie (German Business Action Group against Product and Trademark Counterfeiting)
ArbNErfG	Gesetz über Arbeitnehmererfindungen (German Employee Inventions Act)
Art.	Article
BC	Berne Convention
BDSG	Bundesdatenschutzgesetz (German Data Protection Act)
BetrVG	Betriebsverfassungsgesetz (German Works Council Constitution Act)
BGB	Bürgerliches Gesetzbuch (German Civil Code)
BGH	Bundesgerichtshof (German Federal Supreme Court)
BGHZ	Entscheidungssammlung des Bundesgerichtshof in Zivilsachen (Law Reports from the German Federal Supreme Court)
BIE	Bijblad bij de Industriële Eigendom (name of a Dutch law journal)
BlPMZ	Blatt für Patent-, Muster- und Zeichenwesen (name of a German law journal)
BMI	Bundesministerium des Innern (German Federal Ministry of the Interior)
BMJ	Bundesministerium der Justiz (German Federal Ministry of Justice)
BOIP	Benelux-Bureau voor de Intellectuele Eigendom (Benelux Office for Intellectual Property)
BSA	Business Software Alliance
BT	Bundestag (German Federal Parliament)
BT-Drucks.	Bundestagsdrucksache (German Federal Parliament document)

BTIP	Benelux-Verdrag inzake de intellectuele eigendom (Benelux Treaty on Intellectual Property)
BUMA	Bureau voor Muziekauteursrecht, see Buma/Stemra
Buma/Stemra	Bureau voor Muziekauteursrecht an Stichting Stemra (Dutch music rights collecting society on behalf of composers, text writers and music publishers)
BVerfG	Bundesverfassungsgericht (German Federal Constitutional Court)
CA	Court of Appeal
CAFC	Court of Appeal for the Federal Court (USA)
Cass. com.	Chambre commerciale de la Cour de cassation française (Commercial Chamber of the French Court of Cassation)
CC	Criminal Code [refers to Spanish Criminal Code]
CD	Compact Disc
CDR	Community Design Regulation
CEE	Comunidad Económica Europea (EEC)
cf.	confer (compare)
C. F. R.	Code of Federal Regulations
COM	European Commission
CPI	Code de la propriété industrielle (French Intellectual Property Code)
CPR	Civil Procedure Rules (for England and Wales)
CR	Computer und Recht (name of a German law journal)
CTM	community trademark
CTR	Community Trademark Regulation
DB	Der Betrieb (name of a German law journal)
DCA	Dutch Copyright Act
DCC	Dutch Civil Code
DIHK	Deutscher Industrie- und Handelskammertag (German Chamber of Commerce and Industry)
DIN	Deutsche Industrie Norm (German Industry Standard)
DMCA	Digital Millemium Copyright Act
DNS	Domain Name System
DPA	Dutch Patent Act 1995
DRM	Digital Rights Management
DVD	Digital Versatile Disc
EC	European Community
ECJ	European Court of Justice
EEA	Economic Espionage Act of 1996
EEA	European Economic Area
EEC	European Economic Community
EEG	Elektornischer Geschäftsverkehr-Gesetz (German Draft Act regarding the legal framework for electronic commerce)
e. g.	exempli gratia (for example)
EGRL	Richtlinie der Europäischen Gemeinschaften (EC Directive)
ElGVG	Elektronischer-Geschäftsverkehr-Vereinheitlichungsgesetz (German Electronic Commerce Standardization Act)

EPC	European Patent Convention
EPLA	European Patent Litigation Agreement
EPO	European Patent Office
ES	España (Spain)
etc.	et cetera (and other things)
et seq	et sequens (and the following one)
ETSI	European Telecommunications Standards Institute
EU	European Union
EUR	Euro
Eurojust	the EU's Judicial Cooperation Unit
Europol	European Police Office
EWS	Europäisches Wirtschafts- und Steuerrecht (name of a German law journal)
Fasc.	Fascicule (Fascicle)
FDA	Unites States Food and Drug Administration
Federal Circuit	United States Court of Appeals for the Federal Circuit
FIOD-ECD	Fiscale inlichtingen – en opsporingsdienst en Economische controledienst (Dutch Fiscal Information and Investigation Service and Economic Investigation Service)
Fn.	Fußnote (footnote)
F. R.	French Republic
FRAND standard	Fair, Reasonable and Non Discriminatory terms
F. R. C. P.	Federal Rules of Civil Procedure
F. R. G.	Federal Republic of Germany
FSR	Fleet Street Reports
FTP	File Transfer Protocol
GebrMG	Gebrauchsmustergesetz (German Utility Model Act)
GEMA	Gesellschaft für musikalische Aufführungs- und mechanische Vervielfältigungsrechte (German royalty collection society for musical works)
GeschmMG	Geschmacksmustergesetz (German Design Act)
GG	Grundgesetz (German Basic Law)
GmbHG	Gesetz betreffend die Gesellschaften mit beschränkter Haftung (German Limited Liability Companies Act)
GMP	Good Manufacturing Practice
GPSG	Geräte- und Produktsicherheitsgesetz (German Product Safety Act)
GPTO	German Patent and Trademark Office
GRUR	Gewerblicher Rechtsschutz und Urheberrecht (name of a German law journal)
GRUR Int	Gewerblicher Rechtsschutz und Urheberrecht International (name of a German law journal)
GRUR-RR	Gewerblicher Rechtsschutz und Urheberrecht Rechtsprechungs-Report (name of a German law journal)
GSM	Global System for Mobile communications

GVL	Gesellschaft zur Verwertung von Leistungsschutzrechten (German society responsible for the exploitation in Germany of performers' rights, producers of sound storage mediums and of music video clips)
GWB	Gesetz gegen Wettbewerbsbeschränkungen (German Act Against Restraints on Competition)
HalblSchG	Halbleiterschutzgesetz (German Semiconductor Protection Act)
HansOLG	Hanseatisches Oberlandesgericht (Hamburg Higher Regional Court)
IDSA	international association of interactive distributors
i. e.	id est (that is)
IER	Intellectuele Eigendom & Reclamerecht (name of a Dutch law journal)
IFPI	International Federation of the Phonographic Industry
IMPACT	International Medical Products Anti-Counterfeiting Task Force
INPI	Institut national de la propriété industrielle (French Intellectual Property office)
InstGE	Entscheidungen der Instanzgerichte zum Recht des geistigen Eigentums (name of a German law journal)
IP	Intellectual Property
IP	Internet Protocol
IPR	Intellectual Property Rights
IR trademark	International trademark registration
ISP	Internet service provider
ITC	International Trade Commission
ITRB	Der IT-Rechts-Berater (name of a German law journal)
IuKDG	Gesetz zur Regelung der Rahmenbedingungen für Informations- und Kommunikationsdienste (German Act Regulating the Framework for Information and Communication Services)
IZS	1st Civil Division
J	Mr/Mrs Justice
JCP E	Jurisclasseur périodique édition "Entreprise" (name of a French law journal)
KG	Kammergericht (Higher Regional Court Berlin)
KG	Kort Geding (Dutch procedure for obtaining provisional and protective measures)
KPN	Koninklijke PTT Nederland (Royal Dutch Telecom)
K&R	Kommunikation & Recht (name of a German law journal)
LEC	Ley de Enjuiciamiento (Spanish Law on Civil Procedure)
LG	Landgericht (district court in Germany)
lit.	litera (letter)
LPI	Ley de Propiedad Intelectual (Spanish Copyright Act)
Ls.	Leitsatz (headnote)
LSSI	Ley de servicios de la sociedad de la información y de comercio electrónico (Spanish Information Society and Electronic Commerce Act)

MarkenG	Markengesetz (German Trademark Act)
MarkenR	Markenrecht (name of a German law journal)
MarkenVO	Markenverordnung (German Trademark Regulation)
MB	Megabyte
MD5	Message-Digest algorithm 5
MDStV	Staatsvertrag über Mediendienste (German Treaty on Media Services)
MittdPA	Mitteilungen der deutschen Patentanwälte (name of a German law journal)
MMA	Madrid Agreement Concerning the International Registration of Marks
MMR	Multimedia und Recht (name of a German law journal)
MP3	MPEG-1 Audio Layer 3
MPAA	Motion Picture Association of America
NJ	Nederlandse Jurisprudentie (name of a Dutch law journal)
NJW	Neue Juristische Wochenschrift (name of a German law journal)
NJWE-WettbR	NJW-Entscheidungsdienst Wettbewerbsrecht (name of a German law journal)
NJW-RR	NJW-Rechtsprechungs-Report Zivilrecht (name of a German law journal)
NJW-WettbR	NJW- Entscheidungsdienst Wettbewerbsrecht (name of a German law journal)
NL	Netherlands
no.	number
NStZ	Neue Zeitschrift für Strafrecht (name of a German law journal)
NUV	Nederlands Uitgeversverbond (Dutch Publishers Association)
NVF	Nederlandse Vereniging van Filmdistributeurs (Dutch association of film distributors)
NVGD	Nederlandse Vereniging van Grammofoonplaten Detailhandelaren (Dutch association of phonogram retailers)
NVPI	Nederlandse Vereniging van producenten en Importeurs van beeld- en geluidsdragers (Dutch association for producers and importers of image and sound carriers)
obs.	Observations
OCI	Office of Criminal Investigations
OECD	Organisation for Economic Co-operation and Development
Ofcom	Office of Communications (UK)
OHIM	Office of Harmonization for the Internal Market
OLAF	Organisation de la Lutte anti Fraude (European Anti-Fraud Office)
OLG	Oberlandesgericht (higher regional court in Germany)
OLGR	OLG-Report (Law reports from the German Higher Regional Courts)
OVG	Oberverwaltungsgericht (higher administrative court in Germany)
OVG	optically variable devices
OWiG	Ordnungswidrigkeitengesetz, (German Regulatory Offences Act)
para.	paragraph
PatG	Patentgesetz (German Patent Act)

PbEG	Publicatieblad van de Europese Gemeenschappen (Official Journal of the European Communities)
PC	Personal Computer
PCT	Patent Cooperation Treaty
PIBD	Propriété industrielle – Bulletin documentaire (name of a French law journal)
PR	Public Relations
PRC	People's Republic of China
ProdSG	Produktsicherheitsgesetz (German Product safety Act in force until 2004)
PrPG	Gesetz zur Stärkung des Schutzes des geistigen Eigentums und zur Bekämpfung der Produktpiraterie (German Act to Strengthen Protection of Intellectual Property and to Combat Product Piracy)
P. T. O.	United States Patent and Trademark Office
R&D	Research and Development
RBÜ	Revidierte Berner Übereinkunft (Berne Convention for the Protection of Literary and Artistic Works)
RD immatériel	Revue Lamy Droit de l'Immatériel (name of a French law journal)
RD propr. intell	Revue de Droit de la Propriété Intellectuelle (name of a French law journal)
RGZ	Entscheidungen des Reichsgerichts in Zivilsachen (decisions of the Court of the German Reich)
RIAA	Recording Industry Association of America
RiStBV	Richtlinien für das Straf- und Bußgeldverfahren (German Guidelines for Criminal and regulatory Proceedings)
RLD	Real Decreto Legislativo (Spanish Legislative Royal Decree)
RMB	Renminbi (currency of the PRC)
RTD com.	Revue Trimestrielle de Droit Commercial (name of a French law journal)
SCMGA	Stop Counterfeiting in Manufactured Goods Act of 2006
Schufa	Schutzgemeinschaft für allgemeine Kreditsicherung (German credit reference agency)
sec.	section
sent.	sentence
SNB-REACT	Dutch Anti Counterfeiting Group and part of the European Anti-Counterfeiting Network (formerly Stichting Namaakbestrijding)
SortenschutzG	Sortenschutzgesetz (German Plant Variety Protection Act)
SSOs	standard setting organisations
StGB	Strafgesetzbuch (German Penal Code)
StPO	Strafprozessordnung (German Code of Criminal Procedure)
STOP	Strategy Targeting Organized Piracy
TCA	Trademark Counterfeiting Act
TD	Trademark Directive
TDG	Teledienstgesetz (German Teleservices Act)
TGI	Tribunal de grande instance (French Court of First Instance)
TMG	Telemediengesetz (German Telemedia Act)

TRIPS	Agreement of Trade Related Aspects of Intellectual Property Rights
TRO	Temporary restraining order
TSB	Chinese Technical Services Bureau
UCC	Universal Copyright Convention
UK	United Kingdom of Great Britain and Northern Ireland
UMTS	Universal Mobile Telecommunications System
UNE	Una Norma Española (Spanish industry standard)
UrhG	Urheberrechtsgesetz (German Copyright Act)
UrhWG	Urheberrechtswahrnehmungsgesetz (German Copyright Administration Act)
URL	Uniform Resource Locator
U. S.	United States
USB	Universal Serial Bus
U. S. C.	United States Code
USD	US Dollar
UTSA	Uniform Trade Secrets Act
UWG	Gesetz gegen den unlauteren Wettbewerb (German Act Against Unfair Competition)
VeRO	Verified Rights Owners
VG	Verwaltungsgericht (administrative court in Germany)
VG Bild-Kunst	Verwertungsgesellschaft Bild-Kunst (German collecting society on behalf of fine-artists)
VGF	Verwertungsgesellschaft für Nutzungsrechte an Filmwerken mbH (German collecting society on behalf of cinematographic works)
VG Wort	Verwertungsgesellschaft Wort (German collecting society on behalf of authors and publishers)
VHS	Video Home System
Videma	(joint licensor of non-theatrical video performance rights in the Netherlands)
WCT	World Copyright Treaty
WHO	World Health Organisation
WIPO	World Intellectual Property Organization
WPPT	WIPO Performances and Phonograms Treaty
WRP	Wettbewerb in Recht und Praxis (name of a German law journal)
WTO	World Trade Organisation
ZEuP	Zeitschrift für Europäisches Privatrecht (name of a German law journal)
ZGR	Zentralstelle Gewerblicher Rechtsschutz (Intellectual Property Office)
ZPO	Zivilprozessordnung (German Civil procedure statute)
ZUM	Zeitschrift für Urheber- und Medienrecht (name of a German law journal)
ZUM-RD	Zeitschrift für Urheber- und Medienrecht Rechtsprechungsdienst (name of a German law journal)

Literature

Germany

Ann, Christoph — Know-how: Stiefkind des Geistigen Eigentums?, GRUR 2007, 39-43

Arnold, Bernhard/Timmann, Tobias — Ist die Verletzung des § 95a Abs. 3 UrhG durch den Vertrieb von Umgehungsmitteln keine Urheberrechtsverletzung?, MMR 2008, 286-291

Arnold, Bernhard — Rechtmäßige Anwendungsmöglichkeiten zur Umgehung von technischen Kopierschutzmaßnahmen?, MMR 2008, 144-148

Arriola, Maria Trinidad — Aktuelle Entwicklungen im Patentschutz von Computerprogrammen und mathematischen Algorithmen in den USA, GRUR Int 1996, 9-19

Bartenbach, Kurt/Söder, Antje — Lizenzvertragsrecht nach neuem GWB: Lizenzgebührenpflicht über den Inhalt des Schutzrechts hinaus und nach Schutzrechtsende, MittdPA 2007, 353-365

Bartenbach, Kurt/Volz, Franz-Eugen — Arbeitnehmererfindergesetz, Kommentar zum Gesetz über Arbeitnehmererfindungen, 4. Auflage, Köln 2002

Bartenbach, Kurt/Volz, Franz-Eugen — Erfindungen an Hochschulen – Zur Neufassung des § 42 ArbEG, GRUR 2002, 743-758

Basinski, Erwin/Beaumont, Michel de/Betten, Jürgen/Faria Correa, Jose Antonio/Freischem, Stephan/Laurie, Ronald S./Miyasaka, Mishihiro/Tani, Yoshikazu/Visscher, Fernand de — Patentschutz für computer-softwarebezogene Erfindungen, GRUR Int 2007, 44-51

Baudenbacher, Carl — Erschöpfung der Immaterialgüterrechte in der EFTA und die Rechtslage in der EU, GRUR Int 2000, 584-596

BECK, SIMON MARKUS/ KREISSIG, WOLFGANG — Tauschbörsen-Nutzer im Fadenkreuz der Strafverfolgungsbehörden, NStZ 2007, 304-310

BECKER, ROMAN A. — Kennzeichenschutz der Hörmarke, WRP 2000, 56-69

BECKERMAN-RODAU, ANDREW — The Choice Between Patent Protection and Trade Secret Protection: A Legal and Business Decision, 84.J. P. T. O.S. 371 (2002)

BERGER, CHRISTIAN — Die internationale Zuständigkeit bei Urheberrechtsverletzungen in Internet-Websites aufgrund des Gerichtsstands der unerlaubten Handlung nach Art. 5 Nr. 3 EuGVO, GRUR Int 2005, 465-469

BENKARD, GEORG — Patentgesetz, Gebrauchsmustergesetz, Kommentar, 10. Auflage, München 2006

BERLIT, WOLFGANG — Das neue Geschmacksmusterrecht, GRUR 2004, 635 -642

BERSCHEID, ERNST-DIETER/ KUNZ, JÜRGEN/ BRAND, JÜRGEN — Praxis des Arbeitsrechts, 2. Auflage, Recklinghausen 2003

BOEHRINGER, INGO — Die Novellierung des "Hochschullehrerprivilegs" (§ 42 ArbnErfG), NJW 2002, 952-954

BRINKEL, GUIDO — Haftung für Peer-to-Peer-Software, CR 2006, 306-308

BULLING, ALEXANDER/ LANGÖHRIG, ANGELIKA/ HELLWIG, TILLMANN — Gemeinschaftsgeschmacksmuster, Designschutz in Deutschland und Europa, 2. Auflage, München 2006

BULLING, ALEXANDER — Zur Wirkung international eingetragener Muster und zur Nichtigkeit/Löschungseinwilligung bei deutschen Geschmacksmustern, MittdPA 2007, 59-63

BUSSE, RUDOLF — Patentgesetz, Kommentar, 6. Auflage, Berlin 2003

CORDES, CHRISTOPH — Die Grenzbeschlagnahme in Patentsachen, GRUR 2007, 483-490

CZYCHOWSKI, CHRISTIAN — Auskunftsansprüche gegenüber Internetzugangsprovidern „vor" dem 2. Korb und „nach" der Enforcement-Richtlinie der EU, MMR 2004, 514

DIENERS, PETER — Zusammenarbeit der Pharmaindustrie mit Ärzten – Rechtliches Umfeld, Steuern und Compliance Governance, 2. Auflage, 2007

Doepner, Ulf — Anmerkungen zum wettbewerbsrechtlichen Geheimnisschutz im Zivilprozess, 105-119, in: Festschrift für Winfried Tilmann zum 65. Geburtstag, München 2003,

Döring, Reinhard — Die Haftung für eine Mitwirkung an Wettbewerbsverstößen nach der Entscheidung des BGH „Jugendgefährdende Medien bei eBay", WRP 2007, 1131-1141

Dreier, Thomas/ Schulze, Gernot — Urheberrechtsgesetz: UrhG, 2. Auflage, Kommentar, München 2006

Dreier, Thomas — Ausgleich, Abschreckung und andere Rechtsfolgen von Urheberrechtsverletzungen, GRUR Int 2004, 706-712

Drexl, Josef/Hilty, Reto/ Kur, Annette — Designschutz für Ersatzteile – Der Kommissionsvorschlag zur Einführung einer Reparaturklausel, GRUR Int 2005, 449-457

Deutsche Vereinigung für Gewerblichen Rechtsschutz und Urheberrecht — Denkschrift über den Rechtsschutz der Datenverarbeitungssoftware, GRUR 1979, 300-307

Eichmann, Helmut/ von Falckenstein, Roland Vogel — Geschmacksmustergesetz, Kommentar, 3. Auflage, München 2005

Eisenkolb, Julia — Die Enforcement-Richtlinie und ihre Wirkung – Ist die Enforcement-Richtlinie mit Ablauf der Umsetzungsfrist unmittelbar wirksam?, GRUR 2007, 387-393

Erdmann, Willi/Rojahn, Sabine/Sosnitza, Olaf) — Handbuch des Fachanwalts Gewerblicher Rechtsschutz, Köln 2008

Ensthaler, Jürgen — Produktpirateriegesetz, GRUR 1992, 273-282

Falck, Kurt von — Überlegungen zum „Formstein"-Einwand, GRUR 1998, 218-222

Fezer, Karl-Heinz — Lauterkeitsrecht: UWG, Kommentar zum Gesetz gegen den unlauteren Wettbewerb, München 2005

Fezer, Karl-Heinz — Markenrecht – Kommentar zum Markengesetz zur Pariser Verbandsübereinkunft und zum Madrider Markenabkommen, 3. Auflage, München 2001

Frey, Dieter/ Rudolph, Matthias — EU-Richtlinie zur Durchsetzung der Rechte des geistigen Eigentums, ZUM 2004, 522-529

Freytag, Stefan — Providerhaftung im Binnenmarkt – Verantwortlichkeit für rechtswidrige Inhalte nach der E-Commerce-Richtlinie, CR 2000, 601-609

Fuchs-Wissmann, Georg — Neuere Entwicklungen in der markenrechtlichen Rechtsprechung des Bundespatentgerichts und des Bundesgerichtshofs, MarkenR 2008, 1-7

Gollin, Michael — Biopiracy: The Legal Perspective, 2001, American Institute of Biological Sciences, abrufbar unter http://www.actionbioscience.org/biodiversity/gollin.html

Haedicke, Maximilian — Informationsbefugnisse des Schutzrechtsinhabers im Spiegel der EG-Richtlinie zur Durchsetzung der Rechte des geistigen Eigentums, S. 19-32, in: Festschrift für Gerhard Schricker zum 70. Geburtstag, Perspektiven des Geistigen Eigentums und Wettbewerbsrechts, München 2005

Harte-Bavendamm, Henning — Handbuch der Markenpiraterie in Europa, München 2000

Harte-Bavendamm, Henning/ Henning-Bodewig, Frauke — Gesetz gegen den unlauteren Wettbewerb (UWG) mit Preisangabenverordnung, Kommentar, München 2004

Hasselblatt, Gordian N. — Münchner Anwaltshandbuch Gewerblicher Rechtsschutz, 2. Auflage, München 2004

Heckmann, Jörn — Zum Erfordernis der Einwilligung in eine retrospektive Digitalisierung von Printwerken zu Werbezwecken – Dargestellt am Dienst „google book search“, AfP 2007, 314-319

Hefermehl, Wolfgang/ Köhler, Helmut/ Bornkamm, Joachim — Gesetz gegen den unlauteren Wettbewerb UWG mit PangV, UklaG, UGP-RL Anh. 1, Kommentar, 2. Auflage, München 2008

Hefermehl, Wolfgang/ Köhler, Helmut/ Bornkamm, Joachim — Wettbewerbsrecht – Gesetz gegen den unlauteren Wettbewerb, Preisangabenverordnung, Unterlassungsklagengesetz, Kommentar, 25. Auflage, München 2007

Heermann, Peter W./ Hirsch, Günter — Münchener Kommentar zum Lauterkeitsrecht, Band I, München 2006

Hoeren, Thomas/ Sieber, Ulrich — Handbuch Multimedia – Recht, Rechtsfragen des elektronischen Geschäftsverkehrs, Stand: März 2008, München 2008

Hümmerich, Klaus/ Boecken, Winfried/ Düwell, Franz Josef — Anwaltkommentar Arbeitsrecht, Bonn 2008

Ingerl, Reinhard/ Rohnke, Christian — Markengesetz, Gesetz über den Schutz von Marken und sonstigen Kennzeichen, Kommentar, 2. Auflage, München 2003

Jänich, Volker Michael — „Automobilplagiate" – Zum Schutz des Designs von Kraftfahrzeugen vor Nachahmung, GRUR 2008, 873-878

Jestaedt, Dirk — Der Schutzbereich des eingetragenen Geschmacksmusters nach dem neuen Geschmacksmustergesetz, GRUR 2008, 19-24

Kazemi, Robert — Rechtswirkungen von Registereintragungen im Marken- und Geschmacksmusterrecht – Fiktion oder gesetzliche Vermutung der Rechtsinhaberschaft?, MarkenR 2007, 149-154

Klawitter, Christian/ Zintler, Mathias — Neuer Mustervertrag für F & E-Kooperationen zwischen Wirtschaft (industriellen Auftraggebern) und Hochschulen, MittdPA 2006, 116-118

Knaak, Roland — Die EG-Richtlinie zur Durchsetzung der Rechte des geistigen Eigentums und ihr Umsetzungsbedarf im deutschen Recht, GRUR Int 2004, 745-750

Koch, Frank A. — Die „Enforcement"-Richtlinie: Vereinheitlichung der Durchsetzung der Rechte des geistigen Eigentums in der EU, ITRB 2006, 40-42

Köhler, Helmut — Das Verhältnis des Wettbewerbsrechts zum Recht des geistigen Eigentums – Zur Notwendigkeit einer Neubestimmung auf Grund der Richtlinie über unlautere Geschäftspraktiken, GRUR 2007, 548-554

Koschtial, Ulrike — Zur Notwendigkeit der Absenkung der Gestaltungshöhe für Werke der angewandten Kunst im deutschen Urheberrecht, GRUR 2004, 555-560

Köster, Oliver/ Jürgen, Uwe — Die Haftung von Suchmaschinen für Suchergebnislisten, K&R 2006, 108-112

Köster, Oliver/ Jürgen, Uwe — Haftung professioneller Informationsvermittler im Internet – Eine Bestandsaufnahme nach der Novellierung der Haftungsregelungen, MMR 2002, 420-425

Krasser, Rudolf — Grundlagen des zivilrechtlichen Schutzes von Geschäfts- und Betriebsgeheimnissen sowie Know-how, GRUR 1977, 177-196

Krasser, Rudolf	Der Schutz des Know-how nach deutschem Recht, GRUR 1970, 587-597
Kühnen, Thomas	Die Tenorierung des Warnhinweises in Fällen mittelbarer Patentverletzung, GRUR 2008, 218-220
Kur, Annette	Die Auswirkungen des neuen Geschmacksmusterrechts auf die Praxis, GRUR 2002, 661-670
Kur, Annette	Die notorisch bekannte Marke im Sinne von 6bis PVÜ und die „bekannte Marke" im Sinne der Markenrechtsrichtlinie, GRUR 1994, 330-340
Lang, Jon	The Protection of Commercial Trade Secrets [2003] E. I. P. R. Issue 10, 462
Lange, Paul	Marken- und Kennzeichenrecht, München 2006
Langhoff, Helge/ Oberndörfer, Pascal/ Jani, Ole	Der Zweite Korb der Urheberrechtsreform, ZUM 2007, 593-603
Leible, Stefan/Sosnitza, Olaf (editors)	Versteigerungen im Internet, Heidelberg 2004
Leible, Stefan/ Sosnitza, Olaf	„3 – 2 – 1 – meins!" und das TDG, WRP 2004, 592-599
Leitzen, Mario	Innergemeinschaftlicher Transit, Markenverletzung und Produktpiraterie – Zugleich eine Anmerkung zu BGH „Diesel" und EuGH „Class International/Colgate Palmolive", GRUR 2006, 89
Lewalter, Ivo	Akustische Marken – Anmerkung zu EuGH „Shield Mark/Kist" und HABM „Roar of a Lion" und „HEXAL", GRUR 2006, 546-548
Lubberger, Andreas	Schutzrechtsverletzungen bei eBay & Co. – Einordnung, Verantwortlichkeit, Abwehrstrategien, MarkenR 2006, 515-522
Lubberger, Andreas	Alter Wein in neuen Schläuchen – Gedankenspiele zum Nachahmungsschutz, WRP 2007, 873-880
Luckhaus, Ulrich	Haftung einer Handelplattform für „gebrauchte Domains" – Zugleich Anmerkung zu LG Düsseldorf, GRUR-RR, 122 – Domain-Parking, GRUR-RR 2008, 113-114

MEHLER, ULRICH — Die Verantwortlichkeit des Betreibers von Internetauktionen für Markenverletzungen in Deutschland und den USA, WRP 2006, 819-829

MEIBOM, WOLFGANG VON — Durchlassansprüche (Reach-Through-Ansprüche) bei Patenten für Reseach Tools, MittdPA 2006, 1-5

MEYER, OLAF — Haftung der Internet-Auktionshäuser für Bewertungsportale, NJW 2004, 3151-3154

MEYER, SEBASTIAN — Aktuelle Rechtsentwicklung bei Suchmaschinen 2007, K&R 2008, 201-208

MILBRADT, CLAUDIA — Urheberrechtsschutz von Datenbanken, CR 2002, 710-715

MILBRADT, CLAUDIA — Schutzfähigkeit von Software, K&R 2002, 522-526

MOSTERT, FREDERICK W. — Famous and Well-Known Marks, London 1997

NÄGELE, THOMAS/ NITSCHE, CHRISTINA — Gesetzentwurf der Bundesregierung zur Verbesserung der Durchsetzung von Rechten des geistigen Eigentums, WRP 2007, 1047-1058

NAUTA, WALTHER — Ausnahmen vom Erschöpfungsgrundsatz im Markenrecht, GRUR Int 2004, 994-1002

OHLY, ANSGAR — Designschutz im Spannungsfeld von Geschmacksmuster-, Kennzeichen- und Lauterkeitsrecht, GRUR 2007, 731-740

OHLY, ANSGAR — Die Europäisierung des Designrechts, ZEuP 2004, 269-318

OLDEKOP, AXEL — Das nicht eingetragene Gemeinschaftsgeschmacksmuster – Eine Chance für Designer?, WRP 2006, 801-810

OSTHAUS, WOLF — Fighting Piracy and Counterfeiting in the Light of the European Principles of eCommerce – The eBay Strategy and Experience, GRUR Int 2007, 644-648

OTT, STEPHAN — Die Google Buchsuche – Eine massive Urheberrechtsverletzung?, GRUR Int 2007, 562-569

OTT, STEPHAN — Die Entwicklung des Suchmaschinen- und Hyperlink-Rechts im Jahr 2007, WRP 2008, 393-414

OTT, STEPHAN — Haftung für Embedded Videos von YouToube und anderen Videoplattformen im Internet, ZUM 2008, 556-564

PETER, MARKUS — Die „Flucht in die Nebentätigkeit" – ein Schlupfloch aus der Neuregelung des § 42 ArbnErfG bei Erfindungen von Hochschullehrern?, MittdPA 2004, 396-401

PICKRAHN, GÜNTER — Die Bekämpfung von Parallelimporten nach dem neuen Markengesetz, GRUR 1996, 383-389

PIPER, HENNING/ OHLY, ANSGAR — Gesetz gegen den unlauteren Wettbewerb mit Preisangabenverordnung, Kommentar, 4. Auflage, München 2006

RAHLF, SILVIA/ GOTTSCHALK, ECKART — Neuland: Das nicht eingetragene Gemeinschaftsgeschmacksmuster, GRUR Int 2004, 821-827

REIMANN, THOMAS — Einige Überlegungen zur Offenkundigkeit im Rahmen von §§ 17 ff. UWG und von § 3 PatG, GRUR 1998, 298-302

RÖHL CHRISTOPH/ BOSCH, ANDREAS, — Musiktauschbörsen im Internet – Eine Analyse der aktuellen tatsächlichen und rechtlichen Entwicklungen, NJOZ 2008, 1197-1215

ROSSNAGEL, ALEXANDER — Recht der Multimedia-Dienste, Kommentar zum IuKDG und zum MDStV, 7. Auflage, Stand. April 2005, München 2005

RÜBEL, CLEMENS — Patent infringement by transit of goods through Germany, Patent World, November 2006, Download unter http://www.bardehle.com/fileadmin/bardehle/sonstiges/Publikationen/CRue_transit.pdf

RUHL, OLIVER — Gemeinschaftsgeschmacksmuster, Kommentar, München 2007

SACK, ROLF — Der Benutzungszwang im internationalen Markenrecht, in: Festschrift für Henning Piper zum 65. Geburtstag, München 1996, 603-626

SACK, ROLF — Export und Transit im Markenrecht, RIW 1995, 177-186

SCHACK, HEIMO — Urheber- und Urhebervertragsrecht, Kommentar, 4. Auflage, Tübingen 2007

SCHLÖTELBURG, MARTIN — Musterschutz an Zeichen, GRUR 2005, 123-127

SCHMITZ, FLORIAN/ LAUN, STEFAN — Die Haftung kommerzieller Meinungsportale im Internet, MMR 2005, 208-213

SCHMITZ, STEFAN D. — Zur grafischen Darstellbarkeit von Hörmarken: EuGH contra Freiheit des markenrechtlichen Schutzes?, GRUR 2007, 290-290

Schnabel, Christoph — Böse Zensur, guter Filter? – Urheberrechtliche Filterpflichten für Access-Provider, MMR 2008, 281-286

Schnabel, Christoph — Porn not found – Die Arcor-Sperre, K&R 2008, 26-31

Schöttle, Hendrik — Sperrungsverfügungen im Internet: Machbar und verhältnismäßig?, K&R 2007, 366-370

Schricker, Gerhard — Urheberrecht, Kommentar, 3. Auflage, München 2006

Schricker, Gerhard — Werbekonzeptionen und Fernsehformate – Eine Herausforderung für den urheberrechtlichen Werkbegriff?, GRUR Int 2004, 923-927

Schulz, Andreas — Einstweiliger Rechtsschutz gegen Markenanmeldungen – Begehungsgefahr – Unterlassungsanspruch – Dringlichkeit, WRP 2000, 258-264

Schwarz, Mathias/Brauneck, Anja — Verbesserung des Rechtsschutzes gegen Raubkopierer auf der Grundlage der EU-Enforcement-Richtlinie und deren Umsetzung in deutsches Recht, ZUM 2006, 701-713

Schultz, Detlef von — Markenrecht, Kommentar, 2. Auflage, Frankfurt 2007

Seichter, Dirk — Die Umsetzung der Richtlinie zur Durchsetzung der Rechte des geistigen Eigentums, WRP 2006, 391-400

Spindler, Gerald/Schmitz, Peter/Gleis, Ivo — TDG, Teledienstegesetz, Teledienstedatenschutzgesetz, Signaturgesetz, Kommentar, München 2004

Spindler, Gerald/Leistner, Matthias — Die Verantwortlichkeit für Urheberrechtsverletzungen im Internet – Neue Entwicklungen in Deutschland und in den USA, GRUR Int 2005, 773-796

Spindler, Gerald — Hyperlinks und ausländische Glücksspiele – Karlsruhe locuta causa finita?, GRUR 2004, 724-729

Spindler, Gerald/Weber, Marc Philipp — Die Umsetzung der Enforcement-Richtlinie nach dem Regierungsentwurf für ein Gesetz zur Verbesserung der Durchsetzung von Rechten des geistigen Eigentums, ZUM 2007, 257-266

Spindler, Gerald/Volkmann, Christian — Die zivilrechtliche Störerhaftung der Internet-Provider, WRP 2003, 1-15

STRAUS, JOSEPH — Ende des Geschmacksmusterschutzes für Ersatzteile in Europa? Vorgeschlagene Änderungen der EU-Richtlinie: Das Mandat der Kommission und seine zweifelhafte Ausführung, GRURInt 2005, 965-979

STRÖBELE, PAUL/ HACKER, FRANZ — Markengesetz: MarkenG, Kommentar, 8. Auflage, München 2006

TILMANN, WINFRIED — Beweissicherung nach Art. 7 der Richtlinie zur Durchsetzung der Rechte des geistigen Eigentums, GRUR 2005, 737-740

TEPLITZKY, Otto — Wettbewerbsrechtliche Ansprüche und Verfahren, 8. Auflage, Köln 2002

UHRICH, RALF/ ZECH, HERBERT — Patentierung von Nanomaschinen – Stoffschutz versus Vorrichtungsschutz, GRUR 2008, 768-771

VRIUS, OLIVIER/SCHNEIDER, MARIUS (EDITORS) — Enforcement of Intellectual Property Rights through Border Measures, New York, USA 2006

WANDTKE, ARTUR-AXEL/ BULLINGER, WINFRIED — Praxiskommentar zum Urheberrecht: UrhG, 2. Auflage, München 2006

WANDTKE, ARTUR-AXEL/ OHST, CLAUDIA; — Zur Reform des deutschen Geschmacksmustergesetzes, GRUR Int 2005, 91-102

WELSER, MARCUS VON/ GONZÁLEZ, ALEXANDER — Marken- und Produktpiraterie, Weinheim 2007

WELSER, MARCUS VON — Die neue europäische Produktpiraterieverordnung, EWS 2005, 202-208

WENZL, FRAUKE — Musiktauschbörsen im Internet, Baden Baden 2005

WESTERMANN, INGO — Handbuch Know-How-Schutz, München 2007

WILMER, THOMAS — Überspannte Prüfpflichten für Host-Provider? – Vorschlag für eine Haftungsmatrix, NJW 2008, 1845-1851

WIMMER-LEONHARDT, SUSANNE — Softwarepatente – eine „Never-Ending-Story", WRP 2007, 273-281

WINZER, WOLFGANG — Forschungs- und Entwicklungsverträge, Ein Vertragshandbuch, München 2006

Wolfram, Markus — „Reach-Through Claims“ und „Reach-Through Licensing“ – Wie weit kann Patentschutz auf biotechnologische Research Tools reichen?, MittdPA 2003, 57-64

Wolpert, Marga — Parallelimporte von Arzneimitteln, WRP 2008, 453-463

Wüterich, Christoph/ Breucker, Marius — Wettbewerbsrechtlicher Schutz von Werbe- und Kommunikationskonzepten, GRUR 2004, 389-392

Zentek, Sabine — Präsentationsschutz – Von der Vorlagenfreibefreiung bis zu Individualvereinbarungen wegen eigenmächtiger Verwertungen ungeschützter Entwürfe, WRP 2007, 507-519

France

Rojinsky, Cyril — *Sens interdit : la responsabilité du créateur de lien hypertexte du fait du contenu illicite du site cible;* Lamy, Cah. dr. informatique et réseaux (J) févr. 2003, n° 155, p. 7

Sardain, Frédéric — Liens hypertextes : J.-Cl. Communication, Fasc. 4730, p. 7, n° 23

Sardain, Frédéric — *La contrefaçon du fait des liens hypertextes*, Com. Com. Elct. 2005, n° 6, Etude 21

Netherlands

Brohm, Ronald — Namaakbestrijding: onvoldoende rechtsmiddelen?, March 2001

Gielen, Charles — Kort begrip van het intellectuele eigendomsrecht, 9 edition, Zwollle 2007

Huydecoper, J. L. R. A./ Van Nispen, Constant J. J. C. — Industriele eigendom, Part 1, bescherming van technische innovatie, Deventer 2002

M. Nentjes Michiel — Computerrecht 2007/2, 69 [141-148]

Schmutzer, Olov — 'Montex: is transitohandel ongrijpbaar geworden', IER 2007/5, 287

Seignette, Jacqueline — Openbaarmaking en verveelvoudiging op het Internet: back to basics AMI 1999, 69-73

Seignette, Jacquenline — Auteursrechtinbreuk op internet, IER2008/2, 49

Spoor, Jaap H./Verkade, D. W. F./Visser, Dirk J. G. — Auteursrecht, third edition, Deventer 2005

US

Fairbairn, Daryl/Shum, Audrey/Schönig, Wolfgang/Milbradt, Claudia — Intellectual property and the fight against counterfeit drugs, IAM supplement, February 2007, 19-22

Author

Dr. Claudia Milbradt has studied at the universities in Frankfurt and Hamburg and has worked in Cape Town, New York and Geneva before she started to work as an attorney-at law with the former law firm Pünder Volhard Weber & Axter, now Clifford Chance in 1999. Since 1999, Claudia Milbradt has concentrated on the field of intellectual property. In 2005, Claudia became a partner in the Dusseldorf office of Clifford Chance. Claudia Milbradt advises national and international clients in the field of intellectual property (including patents, German Employee Inventions Act, licensing law, technology transfer, trademarks and copyright). Clients are mainly from the pharmaceutical, medical devices and biotech as well as from the media industry. She is experienced in litigation, any form of product piracy as well as non-contentious matters, in particular on licence, cooperation and research and development agreements. Claudia Milbradt is a member of the Deutsche Anwaltsverein, the Gesellschaft für Gewerblichen Rechtschutz und Urheberrecht (GRUR) and of the International Trademark Association (INTA).

Tel: +49 (0) 211 43 55 59 62
Fax: +49 (0) 211 43 55 56 00
Email: claudia.milbradt@cliffordchance.com